Microsoft® SharePoint®
2010 Administration

Microsoft® SharePoint® 2010 Administration

Real-World Skills for MCITP Certification and Beyond

Tom Carpenter

James Pyles

Wiley Publishing, Inc.

Acquisitions Editor: Jeff Kellum
Development Editor: Kelly Talbot
Technical Editors: Sean Cantellay and Randy Mueller
Production Editor: Christine O'Connor
Copy Editor: Kathy Grider-Carlyle
Editorial Manager: Pete Gaughan
Production Manager: Tim Tate
Vice President and Executive Group Publisher: Richard Swadley
Vice President and Publisher: Neil Edde
Media Project Manager 1: Laura Moss-Hollister
Media Associate Producer: Marilyn Hummel
Media Quality Assurance: Josh Frank
Book Designers: Judy Fung and Bill Gibson
Proofreader: Rebecca Rider
Indexer: Nancy Guenther
Project Coordinator, Cover: Katherine Crocker
Cover Designer: Ryan Sneed

Dear Reader,

Thank you for choosing *Microsoft SharePoint 2010 Administration: Real-World Skills for MCITP Certification and Beyond*. This book is part of a family of premium-quality Sybex books, all of which are written by outstanding authors who combine practical experience with a gift for teaching.

Sybex was founded in 1976. More than 30 years later, we're still committed to producing consistently exceptional books. With each of our titles, we're working hard to set a new standard for the industry. From the paper we print on, to the authors we work with, our goal is to bring you the best books available.

I hope you see all that reflected in these pages. I'd be very interested to hear your comments and get your feedback on how we're doing. Feel free to let me know what you think about this or any other Sybex book by sending me an email at nedde@wiley.com. If you think you've found a technical error in this book, please visit http://sybex.custhelp .com. Customer feedback is critical to our efforts at Sybex.

Best regards,

Neil Edde
Vice President and Publisher
Sybex, an Imprint of Wiley

I dedicate this book to my family and God—the two most important relationships in my life. Thanks for all you do.
—Tom Carpenter

Acknowledgments

I would like to acknowledge my amazing family who continue to find the energy to support me during long writing projects. Tracy, I love you and appreciate the unending patience you've shown during the writing process. Faith, Rachel, Thomas and Sarah, you are the most amazing children any father could hope to lead. I would also like to thank Kelly Talbot, an excellent editor who greatly improved the quality of this book. Additionally, I'd like to thank Jeff Kellum for the opportunity to write a book on one of Microsoft's most interesting products—SharePoint. Of course, I must acknowledge all of my training attendees and consulting clients. They have provided me with the greater depth of knowledge required to write a book like this.

—Tom Carpenter

About the Authors

Tom Carpenter   is a consultant and trainer based out of Marysville, OH. He is the founder and current Senior Consultant for The Systems Education and Consulting Company (SysEdCo). SysEdCo provides training and educational services for Microsoft technologies, wireless networking, security, and IT professional development. SysEdCo also provides consulting services in the central Ohio area related to the same technologies.

Tom has delivered more than 600 training classes in the past 14 years on Windows Server administration, wireless network administration, information security, database administration, and SharePoint implementation and administration. He has developed courses on more than two dozen topics and has worked as a technical editor on more than three dozen projects. His company, SysEdCo, provides technical editing services for the technologies they teach and write about.

Tom is the author of several books on topics ranging from wireless network administration to SQL Server database administration and optimization. Tom holds several certifications including MCITP: SQL Server 2008 Database Administrator, SharePoint, CWNA, CWSP, Project+, and several additional Microsoft certifications. He spends every spare moment he can with his amazing wife and children.

James Pyles   is as a consultant, author, editor, and technical writer. He has been involved in numerous Ethernet rollout projects, software and hardware installations and upgrades, and Windows and Unix operating system upgrades. He has provided support services for a city government IT department and a wireless network vendor, has supported a usability lab for Hewlett-Packard (HP), and has served as the technical writer for EmergeCore Networks, Aquent Studios, and iAnywhere/Sybase and as a developmental editor for Global Support Content Operations at Hewlett-Packard (HP).

His most recent book is *MCTS: Microsoft SharePoint 2010 Configuration Study Guide* (Sybex, 2011). He also wrote *PC Technician Street Smarts, 2nd Edition* (Sybex, 2009), completely updated for the 2009 version of the A+ exams; *MCTS: Microsoft Office SharePoint Server 2007 Configuration Study Guide* (Sybex, 2008); *and SharePoint 2007: The Definitive Guide* (O'Reilly, 2007). Additionally, he was the technical editor for *SharePoint for Project Management* (O'Reilly, 2008) and *Essential SharePoint 2007* (O'Reilly, 2008). James has been a regular contributor to *Linux Pro Magazine* and has written for *Ubuntu User Magazine*. He has bachelor's degrees in psychology and computer network support and a master's degree in counseling. James currently works at Keynetics Inc. in Boise, Idaho.

Contents at a Glance

Contents

Table of Exercises

Introduction

SharePoint 2010 is a complex product, and a diverse skill set is required to administer it. You have to be part database administrator (DBA), part web developer, part network administrator, and part server administrator to fully wrap your mind around this product. This book was written to help you do just that.

This book was written from two perspectives. First, it provides coverage of the most important administrative tasks that SharePoint administrators in organizations of all sizes will need to perform. These are covered with a real-world focus on SharePoint 2010 administration. Second, it provides coverage of the MCITP PRO: SharePoint 2010, Administrator exam objectives (exam 70-668) through the written pages of the book and the videos and practice exam on the included DVD. Whether you're preparing for these exams or preparing for life as a SharePoint administrator, you'll find this book a useful reference.

As you read through the book, you will notice that SharePoint is not the only product covered. In addition, the products that actually make SharePoint possible must be addressed. These products include Windows Server, Internet Information Services (IIS), Domain Name System (DNS), Active Directory, and SQL Server. This book provides sufficient information on these supporting technologies to get SharePoint up and running from scratch, which is vitally important if you want to build a lab environment to prepare for your certification.

Who Should Read This Book

As you can probably tell by the title, *Microsoft SharePoint 2010 Administration: Real World Skills for MCITP Certification and Beyond*, this book is primarily aimed at two groups: those seeking real-world SQL Server database administration knowledge and those preparing for the MCITP SharePoint Administrator exam. Yet a third group may benefit from reading this book as well. Following are some descriptions of the three groups who will find this book useful:

- SharePoint 2010 administrators looking for a reference for common administrative tasks. Everything from planning the SharePoint deployment to backing up your SharePoint sites is covered in this book. You'll find coverage of SharePoint search, Business Intelligence (BI), and Microsoft Office 2010 integration.

- Exam candidates preparing to take the MCITP PRO: SharePoint 2010, Administrator exam number 70-668. You'll find that all of the objectives are covered when you use the complete training kit this book provides, which includes the book, the practice exam on the included DVD, and the video training. It's important to note that what you hold in your hands is more than just a book. The DVD includes video training, memory jogging flashcards, and a practice exam to help you master the objectives the MCITP exam.

- Programmers will also find value in this book. This book does not contain programming guidance or detailed explanations on the use of Visual Studio 2010 for SharePoint solution development; however, it does provide the programmer with a reference to the SharePoint 2010 functionality and how to install and manage the SharePoint servers that may be used to build a development environment.

As you can see, this book is useful to several groups. I have worked as a systems engineer creating applications that use SharePoint 2010 as the foundation, so I know the value of a good administration book sitting on my shelf, and I've strived to write this book with that in mind. I've also taken the 70-668 exam, so I understand the stresses related to preparing for these challenges and the inside information needed to pass them. And although I could have provided the exam information in a series of bulleted lists, I wrote this book from a practical perspective instead, as I feel that this approach makes the information easier to remember and it certainly makes it more valuable for your real life outside of the exam.

What You Will Learn

As you progress through this book, you will go from understanding what SharePoint 2010 has to offer to your organization to implementing it with all the bells and whistles it provides. You'll learn to select the appropriate hardware for your servers and then install SharePoint 2010 the right way the first time. This includes installing the right version. (Yes, there are many.) Then you'll move on to learn how to use the administration tools provided through the Central Administration web interface to get your administrative tasks done. Chapters 1 through 4 will get you up-to-speed on the planning and installation of a SharePoint 2010 deployment.

Next, you'll learn how to design and plan the various features of SharePoint. This begins with the very important topic of security. SharePoint will eventually house much of your organization's data and this data must be secured. This demands an understanding of authentication and permissions, which are covered in Chapter 5.

An important part of SharePoint administration is operations planning and management. Operations planning includes maintenance strategies, monitoring plans and provisioning methods. The SharePoint environment must be maintained in order to provide the quality of service demanded by your users. You must monitor the environment to ensure stability and performance. Provisioning is used to supply the sites and features required by your users. You can allow users to perform self-provisioning or you may choose to implement IT-only provisioning, which demands more time of the SharePoint administrators. Chapter 6 addresses these important issues.

Many organizations have service level agreements (SLAs) between the IT group and the serviced departments. To maintain these SLAs, high availability may be required, but backup and recovery procedures are certain to be required. Chapter 7 helps you understand your options for high availability and scaling a SharePoint installation. From scaling up (adding more processing capabilities to the existing servers) to scaling out (adding more servers to the SharePoint installation), it's all covered in Chapter 7. You will also learn about backup options and recovery procedures.

SharePoint 2010 can be customized in many ways. You can customize it by picking and choosing the services you wish to provide and you can customize it by developing custom features and solutions. Chapters 8 and 9 help you understand the service applications (SAs) available in SharePoint 2010 and how to plan, implement, and configure them. These chapters also provide coverage of web application creation and configuration and the planning of features, solutions, and site customizations.

Eventually, the SharePoint installation will include hundreds (maybe thousands) of pages and hundreds (maybe thousands) of documents. When you have a lot of information, it becomes unrealistic to expect users to always browse through the sites looking for the information they require. Instead, you'll have to provide a well-planned search solution. Chapter 10 provides the information you need to effectively plan and implement search in SharePoint 2010.

One of the major improvements in the SharePoint 2010 product line is the inclusion of more social computing features in the SharePoint Server 2010 editions. This includes tagging, notes, and indicating approval or disapproval of content. The search functions can even use the social features to change the relevancy of search results. Chapter 11 helps you understand these social computing features as well as other collaboration, content management, and Business Intelligence (BI) components.

If you have an existing SharePoint 2007 installation, you may want to start your journey in Chapter 12. This chapter provides information on upgrading or migrating to SharePoint 2010. Reading Chapter 12 first can help to set the stage for understanding how Chapters 1 through 4 may apply to your upgrade. If you are studying for the 70-668 exam, you should follow the book in its written order instead of reading Chapter 12 first.

This book was written to address the collection of tasks the SharePoint administrator will most often be required to perform in the real world, while also covering all exam topics so readers can pass their MCITP exams. Each section offers real-world exercises so you can learn with hands-on tasks. I have also provided videos of important planning tasks and administrative actions so that you can see exactly how the tasks are performed. These videos are on the accompanying disc that is available in the back of this book.

Yet it's also important that you remember what this book is not; this book is not a programming reference. My goal here is not to teach you everything about the development of SharePoint solutions and features. That would require a 600+ page volume itself and is well beyond the scope of this book. However, I have good news for you: If you are new to SharePoint 2010 and you will also be responsible for some development, on the disc I provide an overview video of the development tools and methods you can use. Additionally, you can visit www.TomCarpenter.net to find blog posts related to SharePoint 2010 and other technologies. In these posts, I often cover SharePoint best practices and optimization techniques.

What You Need

The exercises in this book assume that you are running Windows Server 2008 R2 as your operating system. If you are using Windows Server 2008, the exercises should work in most cases; however, they were only tested on Windows Server 2008 R2.

If you do not have a Windows Server 2008 R2 machine, you might want to create a virtual machine so that you can go through every exercise in the book. Here are your options:

- You can download VMware Player from `http://downloads.vmware.com/d/info/desktop_downloads/vmware_player/3_0` and use it to create a single 64-bit VM of Windows Server 2008 R2 on which all software for this book may be installed. VMware Player is recommended because it can run 64-bit operating systems. Microsoft's Virtual PC and Windows Virtual PC cannot run 64-bit operating systems; however, Hyper-V can, so you could install Windows Server 2008 R2 natively on a machine and then use Hyper-V. Any machine that has Windows 7 drivers can run Windows Server 2008 R2. Both operating systems use the same device drivers.

- You can also download a trial version of Windows Server 2008 R2 from `http://www.microsoft.com/windowsserver2008/en/us/trial-software.aspx` and install it as a virtual machine within VMware player. I recommend a machine with at least 6 GB of RAM to perform virtualization, though 8 GB of RAM would be better.

You will also need the SQL Server 2008 R2 media for installation. If you do not have a licensed copy of SQL Server 2008 R2, you have two choices.

- First, you can download a trial version from Microsoft's website at `http://www.microsoft.com/sqlserver/2008/en/us/R2Downloads.aspx`.

- Second, you can purchase the Developer Edition of SQL Server 2008 R2. It usually costs between $50 and $70 and is exactly the same as the Enterprise Edition except for the licensing. The Developer Edition license allows you to develop solutions but not deploy them. For example, you cannot implement a production database server for your users with the Developer Edition; however, you can work through every exercise in this book using it.

Finally, you will need the SharePoint 2010 installation media. Like the other products, you can acquire this as a trial edition.

- Download the trial edition of SharePoint Server 2010 from `http://technet.microsoft.com/en-us/evalcenter/ee388573`. You will be required to register for the download, and a product key will be provided during the registration process.

What Is Covered in This Book

Microsoft SharePoint 2010 Administration: Real World Skills for MCITP Certification and Beyond is organized to provide you with the information you need to effectively administer your SharePoint 2010 installation. The following list provides an overview of the topics covered in each chapter.

Chapter 1 — Planning the Logical Architecture: In this chapter, you will be introduced to the SharePoint product line and then you will begin the planning process for your SharePoint 2010 installation. This begins with an understanding of Information Architecture (also known as a logical taxonomy) and then moves on to the actual planning steps involved in designing the logical taxonomy.

Chapter 2 — Designing the Physical Architecture: With the logical architecture planned and documented, you are ready to design the physical architecture. This includes translating the logical to the physical, planning services, and planning for capacity. All of these important topics are covered in this chapter.

Chapter 3 — Integrating SharePoint with the Network Infrastructure: SharePoint exists on a network and this chapter explains the network components of greatest significance to SharePoint deployments. You will learn to plan farm communications, perimeter configurations, and integration with network services such as Active Directory and DNS.

Chapter 4 — Planning for Farm Deployment: Finally, after getting all of the parts and pieces in place in Chapters 1 through 3, you are ready to plan and deploy the SharePoint server farm itself. You will learn to plan for different deployment scenarios and installation methods. You will actually perform an installation of SharePoint 2010 in this chapter. Additionally, you will learn about sandbox solutions and how to plan for them in your deployment.

Chapter 5 — Planning the Security Architecture: Security is an important component of your SharePoint installation and planning tasks. The data stored in SharePoint will likely have great value to you and you must properly protect this important information. This chapter describes the authentication methods available and helps you plan secure sites. You will learn to design authorization techniques and plan for web application and code access security.

Chapter 6 — Designing an Operations Strategy: Once you've installed and secured your SharePoint deployment, you must maintain it. SharePoint provides several tools to assist you with this maintenance and this chapter introduces you to these tools. You will learn to design a maintenance strategy, plan and use monitoring tools, and implement provisioning strategies.

Chapter 7 — Designing a Strategy for Business Continuity: Business continuity is all about ensuring data is there when you need it. Stated differently, business operations can continue when business continuity is achieved. This chapter explains methods of business continuity in relation to SharePoint including high availability options, scaling strategies, and backup and recovery techniques.

Chapter 8 — Planning Service Applications: Service Applications are the brains behind the beauty of SharePoint 2010. They provide the functionality that makes SharePoint special, such as Excel Services, Business Connectivity Services, and other services. This chapter explains the SA architecture and the planning process for SA deployment.

Chapter 9 — Planning a SharePoint Component Strategy: SharePoint 2010 is not just one thing, but it is several things working together to provide a collaboration and content management system. This chapter helps you plan several of the things that are important to SharePoint functionality including web applications, features, solutions, and web parts.

Chapter 10 — Planning Search Solutions: As your SharePoint 2010 environment grows, search will become more and more important. Your users will need to find the right information at the right time to make the right decision. This is the core of Business Intelligence (making right decisions). Search will help your users find this information, and you will have to plan search effectively to make it happen. In this chapter, you'll learn to define search requirements, plan the search topology, design a search strategy, and ultimately plan enterprise-level search implementations.

Chapter 11 — Planning Business Management Strategies: One of the key features of SharePoint 2010 is collaboration. This chapter provides information on collaboration components, content management, social computing, and Business Intelligence (BI). You will also learn about the different topologies available for supporting your collaboration needs.

Chapter 12 — Planning an Upgrade and Migration Strategy: Existing SharePoint environments may be upgraded or migrated to SharePoint 2010. Choosing between an upgrade and a migration is an important decision and this chapter provides you with the information required to make this decision. You will learn to plan an upgrade strategy and to design a migration strategy.

Appendixes

Microsoft's Certification Program: This appendix discusses the details of the Microsoft certification program, as well as includes a discussion of how to become an MCITP: SharePoint 2010 Administrator. It also shows how this book maps to the exam objectives for Exam 70-688.

What's on the CD: The CD includes excellent live action videos of actions SharePoint administrators will have to perform. Most of these videos correspond to exercises in the book. Look for the following icon for exercises that have a corresponding video on the CD:

In addition, you'll find videos specifically aimed at introducing you to planning concepts for SharePoint 2010 deployments. But that's not all. You'll also receive a practice exam and flashcards.

The companion CD is home to all the demo files, samples, and bonus resources mentioned in the book. It also offers videos that step you through various exercises, flashcards, and a bonus exam to help you study for the exams. See Appendix A for more details on the contents and how to access them.

Glossary: The final element of the book is the Glossary. You'll find definitions of important terms related to SharePoint 2010 and the role of an administrator. If you're preparing for the exams, be sure to read the Glossary the morning of the exam. This action will ensure your understanding of the most important topics covered.

How to Contact the Author

If you have any questions on your certification or administration journey, please contact me. My email address is carpenter@sysedco.com, and I always respond when I receive an email from a reader. More than 15 years ago, I sent an email to a well-known technical industry author and he responded. I was shocked because I had never gotten a response from any other author I had attempted to contact. I told myself then that if I ever had the chance to write a book, I would respond to any and all email messages that I received. When I respond to your email, just remember that you have Mark Minasi to thank, since he was the author who responded to me. If you don't hear back within a few days, please email me again. You know how spam filters are! This is my tenth book and I still love hearing from my readers.

Finally, if you ever get the chance to attend one of my seminars on SharePoint 2010 or any other topic, please let me know you've read my book. I always enjoy speaking with my readers face-to-face, learning how the books have helped the reader, and hearing suggestions on how to improve the books as well. My speaking schedule is posted at www .SysEdCo.com, and I look forward to seeing you at a future event.

Chapter

1

Planning the Logical Architecture

TOPICS COVERED IN THIS CHAPTER

- ✓ SharePoint Editions and Features
- ✓ Understanding the SharePoint Logical Architecture
- ✓ Designing a Logical Taxonomy

Implementing a SharePoint Server 2010 solution begins with understanding the features and services offered by the product line and the way in which SharePoint structures information. In addition, you should understand how you can impact the structure of this information. In this chapter, your journey will begin with an explanation of these important topics.

First, you will explore the different editions of SharePoint 2010 and the features offered by these editions. You must understand them to ensure that you select the right one for your needs. A project is doomed to experience budget overruns if the wrong edition is selected from the start.

Next, you need to understand the SharePoint information architecture. You will look into the hierarchy of technologies and logical components used in a SharePoint information structure. From server farms to individual pages and list items, they are all defined in this chapter.

Finally, you should understand how to plan your logical hierarchy. This planning process is called "designing a logical taxonomy" in the Microsoft 70-668 objectives. If you are preparing for the 70-668 exam, this chapter will provide the information you need to understand the Design a Logical Taxonomy objective and subobjective set.

SharePoint Editions and Features

In this section, the SharePoint product line will be introduced. You will be provided with a definition of the SharePoint products and be given examples of the business uses of the software. Next, you will explore the different SharePoint editions and learn about licensing and acquisition. Finally, you will compare the different editions and the features they offer.

The terms used to describe Microsoft's SharePoint products can be rather confusing. For example, the term *SharePoint 2010* can be used to reference the entire product line; however, several different editions of SharePoint 2010 exist. SharePoint Foundation 2010 is comparable to WSS in previous SharePoint versions. SharePoint Server 2010 is comparable to MOSS in SharePoint 2007. This chapter will help you clarify the differences among the editions so you can make an educated decision during product selection.

SharePoint Defined

SharePoint 2010 is a collection of products that serve as a business collaboration platform for organizations. SharePoint is a multitier application that relies on several other Microsoft technologies. For example, SharePoint requires a database and uses SQL Server for that database. SharePoint requires a web server and uses Internet Information Services (IIS) for that web server.

SharePoint has often been called a content management system (CMS). A CMS is a system used to add, modify, approve, and delete content within websites. Although it is true that SharePoint is a CMS, it is much more than a simple CMS. SharePoint includes several features that take it far beyond the typical CMS. These features include:

- Access to external databases and data sources
- Built-in calendaring functions
- Discussion forum support capabilities
- File sharing through document libraries
- Advanced search functions and customization
- Microsoft Office application integration
- Customizations and feature additions through simple web parts
- Social tagging capabilities
- Business process automation through workflows

The preceding list does not include all the ways that SharePoint provides customization of the content delivery method through the use of blogs, wikis, user profiles, versioning, surveys, and task lists. The point is that SharePoint is more than just a simple CMS. It is an entire-enterprise-content-collaboration solution.

Businesses and organizations can use SharePoint for many purposes, including:

- **Standard intranet provisioning:** SharePoint can be used to provide the traditional web services of a corporate intranet, serving up web pages and documents for internal users.

- **Project management:** SharePoint is an excellent tool for centralization of project management information. Tasks can be managed from within SharePoint and calendars can be associated with these tasks. Project workers can be notified when their tasks should begin and when they are due for completion.

- **Document sharing:** Everything from Excel workbooks to Adobe PDF documents can be stored in SharePoint document libraries. In some cases, SharePoint understands the document format and can offer special functions, such as data analysis for Excel workbooks. In other cases, SharePoint simply provides the storage location for the documents.

- **Resource library management:** Resources such as images, media files, and other data resources can be managed using SharePoint resource libraries and external data lists.

- **Line-of-business integration:** SharePoint can pull data from line-of-business (LOB) applications, such as SAP and J.D. Edwards, into reports and lists in SharePoint sites.

- **Team collaboration:** The collaboration features of SharePoint include discussion forums, task lists, document libraries, and workflows. Each of these features adds to the collaboration capabilities of SharePoint and can be customized for the needs of the organization.

As you can see, SharePoint is a flexible application offering many different uses for the modern information-based organization. Exercise 1.1 will help you explore the SharePoint product capabilities further.

EXERCISE 1.1

Exploring the SharePoint Product Capabilities

In this exercise, you will use the Microsoft SharePoint product capabilities page to explore the features and uses of the SharePoint product line.

1. Open the Internet Explorer web browser.

2. Navigate to http://sharepoint.microsoft.com/en-us/product/capabilities/Pages/default.aspx.

3. You are presented with a graphical representation of the primary capabilities of SharePoint 2010.

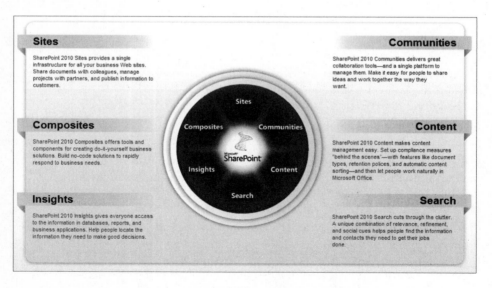

4. Click the Sites capability in the upper-left corner of the screen to learn more about sites.

5. Click the Back button in the Internet Explorer browser.

6. Click on the next capability to learn more about it.

7. Repeat steps 5 and 6 until all six capabilities have been explored.

SharePoint 2010 is not an entirely new product. SharePoint has existed as a product in previous versions, and the SharePoint 2010 release adds new features. One of the primary new features is a major interface overhaul. The result is a look-and-feel similar to Microsoft Office 2007 and 2010 with the use of the Ribbon. Exercise 1.2 will help you explore the new interface using Microsoft's website.

EXERCISE 1.2

Viewing the New SharePoint 2010 Interface

In this exercise, you will use the Microsoft website to access and view a video of the new SharePoint 2010 interface. You will learn how to install SharePoint 2010 in Chapter 4, "Planning for Farm Deployment." This video will allow you to experience the interface without installing the product.

1. Open the Internet Explorer web browser.

2. Navigate to http://www.microsoft.com.

3. In the Bing search field, enter the phrase **sharepoint 2010 feature details sharepoint ribbon** and click the Search Microsoft.com magnifying glass button.

4. Click the first link titled "Feature Details" to navigate to the page. (Instead of searching in steps 2 and 3, you can navigate directly to the following URL: http://sharepoint .microsoft.com/en-us/product/Pages/Feature-Details.aspx?Capability=Sites& FeatureID=16).

5. Click in the video window anywhere to begin playback. (Alternatively, you may download the video to your computer and then play it.)

SharePoint Editions

When planning a SharePoint implementation, you must understand the four different editions so that you can select the right one for your needs. The four editions are

- SharePoint Foundation 2010
- SharePoint Server 2010 Standard
- SharePoint Server 2010 Enterprise
- SharePoint Server 2010 for Internet Sites

In implementation, the SharePoint Server 2010 editions are really just different licenses. The only installation difference is in selecting the appropriate license you plan to implement. During installation and configuration, you are asked to provide the Client Access License (CAL) product key. If you enter a standard CAL, you will enable the Standard Edition feature set. If you enter an enterprise CAL, you will enable the Enterprise feature set.

SharePoint Foundation 2010 is a free download. The only license required to use the product is the Windows Server operating system license. SharePoint Foundation 2010 provides the basic SharePoint features, but it is missing such features as social tagging, My Content, My Profile, enterprise wikis, Secure Store Service, and web analytics.

SharePoint Server 2010 Standard Edition adds the features missing in SharePoint Foundation 2010 (social tagging, My Content, My Profile, enterprise wikis, Secure Store Service, and web analytics) and additional features. It is the entry-level licensed SharePoint product for businesses and organizations; however, SharePoint Server 2010 Standard Edition still lacks some features, such as Visio Services, InfoPath Forms Services, Excel Services, and Access Services.

To get the full feature set, the SharePoint Server 2010 Enterprise Edition must be purchased. The Enterprise Edition includes all the features of the SharePoint Server 2010 Standard Edition as well as the missing features referenced in the preceding paragraph.

SharePoint Server 2010 for Internet Sites can be purchased as either a Standard Edition or Enterprise Edition license. If you require the full feature set for an Internet-facing website, you will need the SharePoint Server 2010 for Internet Sites, Enterprise license. The SharePoint Server 2010 for Internet Sites license allows for deployment of SharePoint for Internet websites, but only for a single domain with subdomains. For each additional domain set, you will have to purchase an additional license. An unlimited number of clients may access a SharePoint site hosted using the for Internet Sites licenses.

For more information about licensing, visit the Licensing Q&A page at http://sharepoint.microsoft.com/en-us/buy/Pages/Licensing-Details.aspx. The questions answered on this page are among the licensing questions I am most frequently asked at SharePoint planning meetings.

Table 1.1 lists the three core editions of SharePoint and significant highlights related to each edition.

TABLE 1.1   SharePoint 2010 Core Editions and Important Facts

SharePoint 2010 Edition	Licensing	Important Facts
Foundation	Windows Server must be licensed; SQL Server Standard Edition is recommended (SQL Server Express Edition may be used for small-scale deployments); Foundation Edition license is free.	Provides a collaboration and content-management platform. Web-based applications may be built and customized atop this platform. Is useful for small businesses and departmental deployments.
Standard	Windows Server must be licensed; SQL Server Standard or Enterprise Edition is recommended; SharePoint Server 2010 must be licensed.	Provides all of the capabilities of the Foundation Edition. Supports search capabilities. Supports My Sites and user profiles. Supports social tagging. Is useful for medium to large businesses and smaller deployments demanding the features provided by this edition.
Enterprise	Windows Server must be licensed; SQL Server Enterprise Edition is recommended; SharePoint Server 2010 must be licensed.	Provides all of the capabilities of the Foundation and Standard Editions. Supports Business Intelligence components such as Access Services and Excel Services. Supports PerformancePoint services. Is useful for large businesses and smaller deployments demanding the features provided by this edition.

Features by Edition

One of the most important decisions you will make when implementing SharePoint 2010 is which edition to install. You cannot make this decision without considering the features offered by each edition, and this section provides the rather lengthy list of features offered by the SharePoint product line.

First, the SharePoint Foundation 2010 Edition features are included with every edition of SharePoint. The following list of SharePoint Foundation 2010 features shows just how powerful the product is

- Accessibility
- Blogs
- Browser-based Customizations
- Business Connectivity Services
- Business Data Connectivity Service
- Claims-Based Authentication
- Client Object Model (OM)
- Configuration Wizards
- Connections to Microsoft Office Clients
- Connections to Office Communication Server and Exchange
- Cross-Browser Support
- Developer Dashboard
- Discussions
- Event Receivers
- External Data Column
- External Lists
- High-Availability Architecture
- Improved Backup and Restore
- Improved Setup and Configuration
- Language Integrated Query (LINQ) for SharePoint
- Large List Scalability and Management
- Managed Accounts
- Mobile Connectivity
- Multilingual User Interface
- Multi-Tenancy
- Out-of-the-Box Web Parts
- Patch Management
- Permissions Management
- Photos and Presence
- Quota Templates
- Read-Only Database Support
- Remote Blob Storage (SQL Feature)
- REST and ATOM Data Feeds
- Ribbon and Dialog Framework

- Sandboxed Solutions
- SharePoint Designer
- SharePoint Health Analyzer
- SharePoint Lists
- SharePoint Ribbon
- SharePoint Service Architecture
- SharePoint Timer Jobs
- SharePoint Workspace
- Silverlight Web Part
- Site Search
- Solution Packages
- Streamlined Central Administration
- Support for Office Web Apps
- Unattached Content Database Recovery
- Usage Reporting and Logging
- Visual Studio 2010 SharePoint Developer Tools
- Visual Upgrade
- Web Parts
- Wikis
- Windows 7 Support
- Windows PowerShell Support
- Workflow
- Workflow Models

In addition to the preceding list of features, SharePoint Server 2010 Standard Edition adds the following features:

- Ask Me About
- Audience Targeting
- Basic Sorting
- Best Bets
- Business Connectivity Services Profile Page
- Click Through Relevancy
- Colleague Suggestions
- Colleagues Network
- Compliance Everywhere

- Content Organizer
- Document Sets
- Duplicate Detection
- Enterprise Scale Search
- Enterprise Wikis
- Federated Search
- Improved Governance
- Keyword Suggestions
- Managed Metadata Service
- Memberships
- Metadata-driven Navigation
- Metadata-driven Refinement
- Mobile Search Experience
- Multistage Disposition
- My Content
- My Newsfeed
- My Profile
- Note Board
- Organization Browser
- People and Expertise Search
- Phonetic and Nickname Search
- Query Suggestions, "Did You Mean?", and Related Queries
- Ratings
- Recent Activities
- Recently Authored Content
- Relevancy Tuning
- Rich Media Management
- Search Scopes
- Secure Store Service
- Shared Content Types
- SharePoint 2010 Search Connector Framework
- Status Updates
- Tag Clouds
- Tag Profiles

- Tags
- Tags and Notes Tool
- Unique Document IDs
- Web Analytics
- Windows 7 Search
- Word Automation Services
- Workflow Templates

Finally, SharePoint Server 2010 Enterprise Edition includes all of the features of Foundation and Standard, but adds the following features:

- Access Services
- Advanced Content Processing
- Advanced Sorting
- Business Data Integration with the Office Client
- Business Data Web Parts
- Business Intelligence Center
- Business Intelligence Indexing Connector
- Calculated KPIs
- Chart Web Parts
- Contextual Search
- Dashboards
- Data Connection Library
- Decomposition Tree
- Deep Refinement
- Excel Services
- Excel Services and PowerPivot for SharePoint
- Extensible Search Platform
- Extreme Scale Search
- InfoPath Forms Services
- PerformancePoint Services
- Rich Web Indexing
- Similar Results
- Thumbnails and Previews
- Tunable Relevance with Multiple Rank Profiles
- Visio Services
- Visual Best Bets

As a planning exercise, you can go through the preceding three lists and highlight or in some way mark the features you will need for your implementation. If no Enterprise Edition features are marked, the Standard Edition may suffice for your implementation. If no Standard Edition or Enterprise Edition features are marked, the SharePoint Foundation 2010 free license may suffice. Be sure to consider future plans when making this decision. If you will require Enterprise Edition features one or two years in the future, it is probably best to implement this edition from the start of the project.

For more information describing each feature, visit the Microsoft SharePoint Editions Comparison page at http://sharepoint.microsoft.com/en-us/buy/Pages/Editions-Comparison.aspx.

Of course, in addition to the features, you must consider the cost of the edition you choose. In smaller organizations, the cost of licensing may be prohibitive and features may be sacrificed in order stay within budget. In such cases, the features you want could potentially be implemented using custom development on top of the SharePoint Foundation 2010 installation; however, the time spent customizing the product to get a simple feature like Access Services (explained in more detail in the "Access Services Makes the Difference" Real World Scenario) can cost hundreds or even thousands of hours.

 Real World Scenario

Access Services Makes the Difference

I was involved in a SharePoint 2010 planning project for a small business in central Ohio. They were implementing SharePoint for the first time and had no existing SharePoint infrastructure. New implementations are always fun because you have full flexibility in how and what you implement—as long as the organization budgets for the required edition licenses.

In the beginning, the organization planned to use SharePoint Foundation 2010. At our first meeting I shared with them the differences between the SharePoint 2010 editions so that they could make an educated decision. I do not resell SharePoint licenses in my business. I simply assist organizations in the implementation of the Microsoft products that they license themselves, so I have no motive for encouraging organizations to implement the licensed versions of SharePoint 2010 over the free Foundation version. In fact, my company could make more money (charging by the hour) by customizing the free Foundation version to meet their needs; however, when the required features already exist in either the Standard Edition or Enterprise Edition, I want to what is in the best interest of my client.

As I was reviewing the list of features in the Enterprise Edition, I came to the Access Services feature. Immediately, the IT Director interrupted me and said, "Are you telling me that we can take our existing Access databases, upgrade them to Access 2010, and then publish them into the SharePoint site so that other users can access them and manage the data in them?" I asked him if he would like a demonstration and he said that he would. I booted up my SharePoint Server 2010 Enterprise Edition virtual machine, took a copy of one of their Access 2007 databases, and opened it in Access 2010. Next, I published the database into the SharePoint server and then accessed it within the web browser. Needless to say, this simple demonstration caused the organization to choose the Enterprise Edition of SharePoint Server 2010.

In this scenario, the organization estimated that they had more than 60 Access databases they wanted to import into the SharePoint sites. In fact, they had been considering converting all of their Access databases to SQL Server and creating custom web applications to access the data. With SharePoint Foundation 2010, this more complex and time-consuming process would have been the only option. With SharePoint Server 2010 Enterprise Edition, the process was simpler and took far less time. In fact, the organization had all of their databases up and running through SharePoint 2010 Access Services within three weeks of implementing the SharePoint product.

In larger organizations, converting the Access databases to a SQL Server database application may be preferred. The reason is simple: larger organizations tend to use larger databases. Smaller organizations, however, often work with several small Access databases, and the ability to easily centralize these databases through SharePoint is phenomenal.

Understanding the SharePoint Logical Architecture

SharePoint 2010 deployment planning involves the creation of a logical architecture, which is also called a logical taxonomy, and a physical architecture. The SharePoint administrator should be involved in the planning of these architectures and will hopefully be leading the project. Both architectures are designed very early on in the SharePoint deployment project, and the rest of the project (the actual development, testing, and installation of the production environment) will depend heavily on these architectures. The goal is to create a SharePoint 2010 production environment that meets the needs of your users and allows them to work as efficiently as possible. A production environment or production system, in Information Technology (IT) terms, is really just an installed system that users utilize for real business activity.

The logical architecture defines the structure of the SharePoint content. It is usually considered to be synonymous with the information architecture (IA). IA is usually referenced in the context of websites. SharePoint 2010 is used to implement such websites, so it is important to get the IA right and to get it right from the very beginning of your deployment project. Figure 1.1 shows the logical architecture.

FIGURE 1.1 The SharePoint 2010 logical architecture

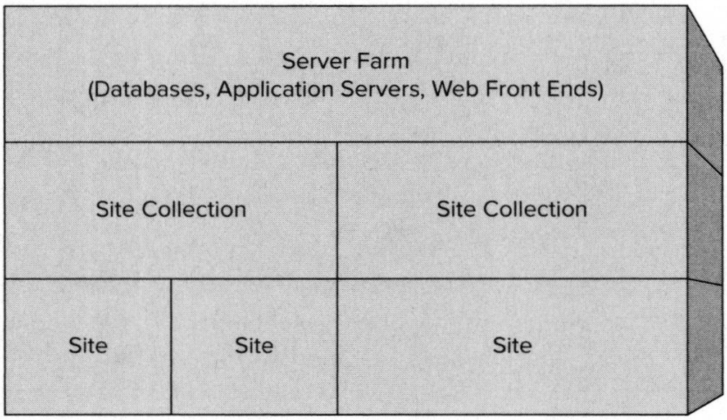

Server Farm
(Databases, Application Servers, Web Front Ends)

Site Collection	Site Collection
Site · Site	Site

The logical architecture includes three elements in a SharePoint 2010 deployment including:

- Server farms
- Sites
- Site collections

All three components are explained in the following sections.

The physical architecture is explained and developed in Chapter 2, "Designing the Physical Architecture." In that chapter, you will learn to plan for the various servers and services that allow the logical architecture to exist. For now, just remember that the logical architecture defines the way SharePoint appears to the users, and the physical architecture defines the actual hardware and software used to implement the logical architecture.

The Server Farm

The server farm is the top-level component in the SharePoint 2010 logical architecture. Figure 1.1 shows the logical architecture of SharePoint 2010. The architecture is considered a logical architecture because the server farm is not attached to a single physical device, although it is a single logical entity. The server farm may be spread across multiple servers, including database servers, application servers, and web frontend servers.

Many organizations will implement a single-server farm and require no further deployments. However, some scenarios require the use of more than one server farm, including these:

- Physically separate data centers or sites that are better optimized by having the entire SharePoint server farm localized
- Security policies that require the separation of data and application management according to strict rules that cannot be implemented in a single-server farm

- Extremely large organizations that demand better performance than can be achieved through single-server farms in such large-scale installations

It is important to understand that all three server types (database, application, and web frontend) can exist as a single physical server or as three or more separate servers. Additional complexity is added in that three or more servers can be used, through virtualization, on a single physical server. This is why the server farm is considered to be a logical concept, and the physical implementation of it (the three server types mentioned here) can vary greatly from organization to organization and from deployment to deployment within an organization. All three server types must run on Windows Server 2008 or Windows Server 2008 R2. The server types and Windows Server 2008 are further explained in the following sections.

The Database Server

The database server stores the databases for both configuration and content in the SharePoint server farm. The configuration database is smaller, usually less than 100 MB, but the Content databases can be several gigabytes in size. SharePoint 2010 supports only SQL Server database servers running SQL Server 2005 or later; however, SQL Server Express Edition may be used for small-scale deployments and testing environments.

SharePoint 2010 is a 64-bit-only product, meaning that a 32-bit version is not available. This is why the database server used by SharePoint 2010 must be running a 64-bit edition of SQL Server. I recommend using SQL Server 2008 Enterprise Edition to achieve the best in performance, scalability, and reliability.

When you're planning SharePoint 2010 databases, one of your key considerations is database size. Although exact sizes can't be known until the details are planned, you can determine relative size. For example, the SharePoint Configuration database for a server farm will be between 40 MB and 45 MB right after installation and creation of the first site collection and site. This is a small database compared to Content databases. The following databases and their relative sizes must be considered when planning a SharePoint Foundation 2010 deployment:

Configuration   The Configuration database contains information about the other SharePoint databases; the IIS websites and web applications; trusted solutions; Web Part packages; site templates; and web application and farm settings for SharePoint 2010 products, including default quotas and blocked file types. This database is relatively small compared to other SharePoint 2010 databases, and it must be stored on the same database server as the Central Administration Content database. One Configuration database is allowed per server farm, and significant growth is not likely to occur. This is a read-heavy database once production begins, but read operations are infrequent when compared to Content databases.

Central Administration Content   The Central Administration (CA) Content database contains the content for the CA site. One CA Content database is allowed in the server farm, and it must be stored on the same database server as the Configuration database. Significant growth is not likely to occur. This is a read-heavy database, but read operations are infrequent.

Content   The Content databases are among the most important databases in your SharePoint 2010 deployments. They contain all of the site content. This includes files and documents in document libraries, list data, properties of web parts, audit logs, usernames and rights, and sandboxed solutions. The complete data set for a single site is contained in a single Content database; however, more than one site can be contained in a single content database. If Office Web Applications is in use, the data for this service is also stored in the Content database.

Content databases can be hundreds of gigabytes in size; however, Microsoft recommends limiting the size of Content databases to 200 GB. If a single site is larger than 200 GB, the Content database must also be larger because the entire site is stored in a single Content database. In such scenarios, a database larger than 200 GB must be used, and the storage method must be carefully considered. For example, using SQL Server Enterprise Edition, table partitioning could be used so that part of the database is stored on one RAID array and another part is stored on another RAID array. Such configurations can allow for acceptable performance with very large databases (VLDBs).

Content databases will vary in read and write operations, depending on use. In some implementations, Content databases are write-heavy with extensive data entry operations in lists. In other implementations, the site content remains mostly static and for every change made, hundreds of view or read operations take place. You will have to analyze your environment and optimize the SQL Server database storage for the read-heavy, write-heavy, or balanced read/write operations taking place.

Usage   The Usage database is used by the Usage and Health Data Collection service application. It temporarily stores health monitoring and usage data, and it may also be used for reporting and diagnostics. The database is extra-large when compared to other SharePoint 2010 databases, but the size will vary depending on the data retention policy. It is a write-heavy database.

Business Data Connectivity   The Business Data Connectivity database is used by the service application of the same name. It stores external content types, which are created by the administrators, and their related objects and properties. It is a small database in relation to other SharePoint 2010 databases. It is a read-heavy database.

Application Registry   The Application Registry database is used by the service application of the same name. It stores data required for backward compatibility with the Business Data Connectivity API. This database is used only during an upgrade. Once the upgrade is complete, the database may be safely deleted. It is a small database when compared with other SharePoint 2010 databases, and it is a read-heavy database.

Subscription Settings   The Subscription Settings database is used by the Microsoft SharePoint Foundation Subscription Settings service, and it stores features and settings information for hosted customers. The database does not exist by default and must be created in SQL Server if you are deploying a multitenant SharePoint 2010 installation. The database is relatively small compared to other SharePoint 2010 databases, and it is a read-heavy database.

When deploying SharePoint Server 2010 Standard Edition, the SharePoint Foundation 2010 databases must all be considered, and several additional databases must be considered as well. The following databases are added when Standard Edition is used instead of Foundation:

Search Administration   The Search Administration database is used by the search service application. It stores the Search application configuration information as well as the access control list for the crawl component of SharePoint 2010. The database is medium-sized in relation to other SharePoint 2010 databases. The database is read-heavy, but read operations are infrequent.

Crawl   The Crawl database is used by the search service application, and it stores the state of the crawled data as well as the crawl history. The crawl history tracks when the content sources were last crawled for indexing. The database is extra-large in relation to other SharePoint 2010 databases, and it is read-heavy.

Property   The Property database is used by the search service application. It stores information associated with the crawled data, such as properties (also called metadata), crawl queues, and history data. The history data includes when the metadata was first discovered (by the crawler) and when it was last updated. The database is from large to extra-large in relation to other SharePoint 2010 databases, and it is a write-heavy database.

Web Analytics Reporting   The Web Analytics Reporting database is used by the Web Analytics service application, and it stores aggregated standard report tables; data aggregated by groups of sites, date, and asset metadata; and diagnostics information. The database can be from extra-large to enormous in relation to other SharePoint 2010 databases, and the size varies depending on data retention policies. If the database becomes too large, you may want to consider retaining data for shorter periods of time or archiving the data to a separate reporting server. This database tracks all of the use accesses so you can see what is being used on your SharePoint sites. Because the Web Analytics service application can take advantage of a SQL Server Enterprise Edition feature called table partitioning, the SQL Server Enterprise Edition should be used to store this database.

Web Analytics Staging   The Web Analytics Staging database is used by the Web Analytics service application for storage of unaggregated data, asset metadata, and queued batch data. The database is medium-sized in relation to other SharePoint 2010 databases.

State   The State database is used by the State, InfoPath Forms Services, and Visio Services service applications. It stores temporary state information for these service applications, as well as for the chart web part. The database size is medium to large in relation to other SharePoint 2010 databases. It is a slightly read-heavy database with moderate write operations.

Profile   The Profile database is used by the User Profile service application, and it stores and manages user information and data. The database is medium to large in relation to other SharePoint 2010 databases. It is a read-heavy database.

Synchronization   The Synchronization database is used by the User Profile service application. It stores configuration and staging data for use when profile information is synchronized with Active Directory Domain Services (AD DS). This is a medium to large database when compared to other SharePoint 2010 databases. The size of the database will depend on the number of users and groups and the ratio of users to groups. This is a balanced read/write database.

Social Tagging   The Social Tagging database is used by the User Profile and Metadata Management service applications. The database stores social tags and notes created by users along with the associated URLs. Depending on the number of tags, the database varies greatly in size. In an environment with heavy use of social tagging, the database can be extra large in relation to other SharePoint 2010 databases. This is a read-heavy database.

Managed Metadata Service   The Managed Metadata Service database is used by the service application of the same name. It stores managed metadata and syndicated content types for the server farm. The database is medium-sized relative to other SharePoint 2010 databases. It is a read-heavy database.

Secure Store   The Secure Store database is used by the Secure Store service application, and it stores credentials such as account names and passwords. It is a relatively small database. For security reasons, the Secure Store database should be placed on a separate database instance with limited access (allow only one administrator to access the database instance).

When SharePoint Server 2010 Enterprise Edition is used, all of the databases included in SharePoint Standard and Foundation Editions must be considered and two additional databases are used:

Word Automation Services   The Word Automation Services database is used by the Word Automation Services service application. It stores information about pending and completed document conversion processes. This database is relatively small compared to other SharePoint databases and significant growth is unlikely.

PerformancePoint   The PerformancePoint database stores temporary objects and permanent user comments and settings. The database is relatively small compared to other SharePoint databases. This is a read-heavy database, so it should be storage optimized for read operations.

Because of the large number of databases involved in an Enterprise Edition deployment, it is common to implement more than one SQL server. Chapter 2 provides more information about sizing and configuring SQL Server database servers and databases for SharePoint 2010 deployments.

The Application Server

The second server type at the server-farm level is the application server. The application server runs the service applications used by the SharePoint sites within the server farm. Multiple application servers are supported and may be used for performance improvements or for fault tolerance. Service applications and application servers are covered in more detail in Chapter 8, "Planning Service Applications."

The Web Frontend Server

The final server type used in the server farm is the Web Front End (WFE) server. The WFE server provides the actual websites that users see when using the SharePoint 2010 services.

The WFE servers run Internet Information Services (IIS) as the web server software. IIS serves up the ASP .NET web pages that comprise the SharePoint sites. It also drives the engine used for uploading and downloading documents to and from document libraries. In the end, IIS does most of the actual processing work that delivers content to users.

In Chapter 2, the WFE server is discussed more from a physical implementation standpoint. It is also discussed in Chapter 4 from the perspective of farm deployment planning.

Windows Server 2008 and Active Directory Domain Services

Of course, the database servers, application servers, and WFE servers have to run on an operating system and that operating system is Windows Server 2008 or Windows Server 2008 R2 for production environments. If you choose to use Windows Server 2008, you will need to apply service pack 2 (SP2) for compatibility with SharePoint 2010. Windows Server 2008 R2 may require hotfixes (small patches) to be compatible with SharePoint 2010 as well.

When installing the RTM release of SharePoint 2010 on Windows Server 2008 R2 RTM, you will need to apply the hotfixes referenced in knowledge base articles 160770 and 166231, which can be downloaded from http://go.microsoft.com/fwlink/?linkID=160770 and http://go.microsoft.com/fwlink/?linkID=166231, respectively.

The Windows server must be running as a 64-bit operating system. Windows Server 2008 comes in either a 32-bit or 64-bit installation, so you must choose the 64-bit version and install it on 64-bit hardware. Windows Server 2008 R2 is available only in 64-bit editions so this should cause no problems in deployment. However, it is important to make sure that your virtual environment supports 64-bit operating systems if you plan to deploy SharePoint through virtualization. Microsoft Hyper-V does support 64-bit operating systems, and VMware's ESX servers also support 64-bit operating systems when deployed on 64-bit hardware.

In addition to using Windows Server 2008 or R2 for your server operating system on your SharePoint servers, you must also be running Microsoft Active Directory Domain Services (AD DS). The AD DS will be running on one or more servers separate from the SharePoint server in most installations. The servers on which you plan to install SharePoint should be members of the AD DS domain for user account and group provisioning. The AD DS domain provides the users and groups that SharePoint uses for authentication and authorization.

Although you can install SharePoint 2010 on Windows Vista or Windows 7, this support is intended only for development and testing and should not be used for production deployments of the SharePoint infrastructure. SharePoint 2010 may be installed on Windows Vista running SP1 or later. For both Windows Vista and Windows 7, the Professional, Enterprise, or Ultimate Editions must be used.

Site Collections and Sites

As shown in Figure 1.1, the next layer under the server farm in the SharePoint logical architecture is the site collection. A single farm may provide more than one site collection. Site collections are really just administration boundaries that provide trickle down or inherited management for the sites contained within the site collection. For example, a site collection administrator is, by default, an administrator of all sites within the collection.

When a site collection is created, a top-level site is also created within that collection. Site collections provide the central location for permissions and rights management. The site collection permission may be overridden at the site and subsite levels, but the permissions start at the site collection and top-level site. Figure 1.2 shows a potential hierarchy from a site collection downward.

FIGURE 1.2   Potential site collection hierarchy

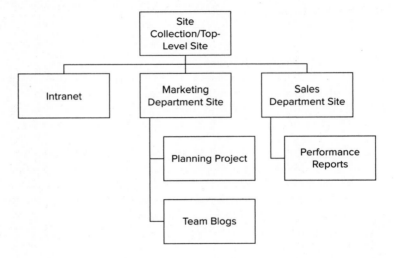

When you create multiple site collections in a server farm, it is important to keep several considerations in mind:

- Site collections are not connected. If you want users to be able to navigate from one site collection to another, you will have to manually create the navigation links.

- Search results come only from the current site collection in which the user is operating.

- When subsites are created in a site collection, they inherit the permissions of the top-level site. Permissions do not cross site collection boundaries and must be manually duplicated in each site collection if desired.

- Each site collection has up to two administrators. One is the primary site collection administrator, and the other is the secondary administrator.

Site collections may include several different kinds of sites, and within sites, subsites may also be used. Going further, within sites are pages, lists, libraries, folders, and documents. Each site and component is further described in the following sections.

Collaboration Sites

At the heart of SharePoint 2010 is the concept of collaboration. *Collaboration* is defined as the ability to share information and ideas and to make decisions as a team. Many of the SharePoint 2010 site templates are aimed at collaboration. Several features of SharePoint 2010 assist in the collaboration process:

- **Lists:** Lists allow you to share information with other users of the same site. This information can include contacts, product details, item details, sales statistics, and just about anything else you can imagine.

- **Document libraries:** Document libraries allow you to share documents such as Excel workbooks, Word documents, and more.

- **Pages:** SharePoint 2010 pages allow you to create custom pages like traditional website pages. These pages may or may not contain information from lists. They may be static or dynamic, depending on the data sources. Anything you can do on a traditional website can be done on a SharePoint 2010 page.

Figure 1.3 shows the different site templates that are available when creating a new site within SharePoint 2010. Notice all of the collaborative site types in this screenshot along with the other site types. The Team Site, Document Workspace, Basic Meeting Workspace, Decision Meeting Workspace, Social Meeting Workspace, Multipage Meeting Workspace, and Group Work Site are certainly in the collaboration category. However, even the Blog site template can be considered a collaboration template because it allows information to be shared with or about the department or organization.

FIGURE 1.3 A subset of the site templates available in SharePoint 2010

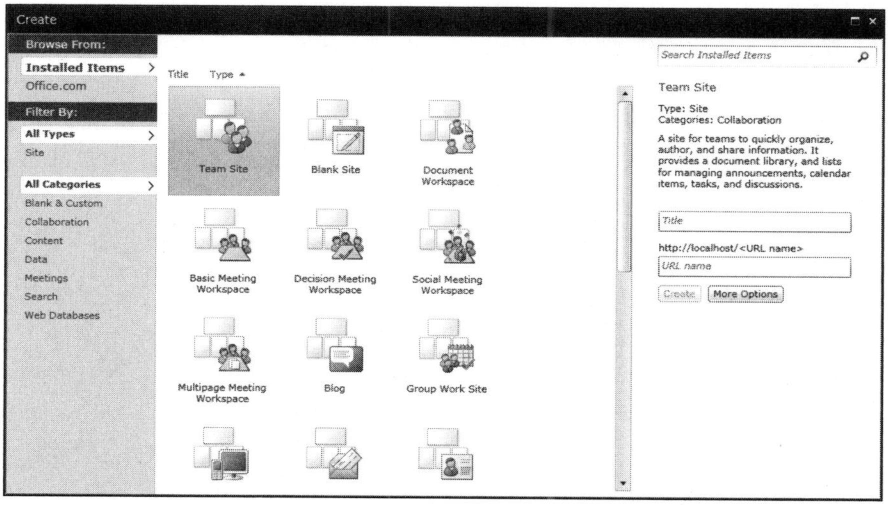

My Sites

My Sites provide a place each user can customize for himself or herself. A My Site allows you to list the colleagues with whom you work, your interests, and personal newsfeeds customized to your liking. Figure 1.4 shows the My Site page as it looks by default when first visited by a user.

FIGURE 1.4   The default My Site page in SharePoint 2010

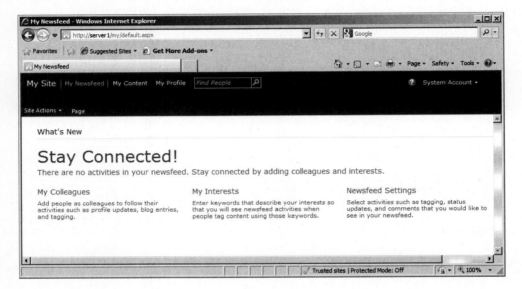

Users can customize the look-and-feel of their My Site, and they can track colleagues and other information. Colleagues may be added as long as they have a SharePoint profile as well. If an AD DS user exists, but does not have a SharePoint 2010 profile, the user may not be added as a colleague. Figure 1.5 shows the My Site page after some minor customization.

The My Site section of SharePoint also allows a user to configure his or her profile settings. Figure 1.6 shows a user editing his profile.

FIGURE 1.5   A customized My Site page in SharePoint 2010

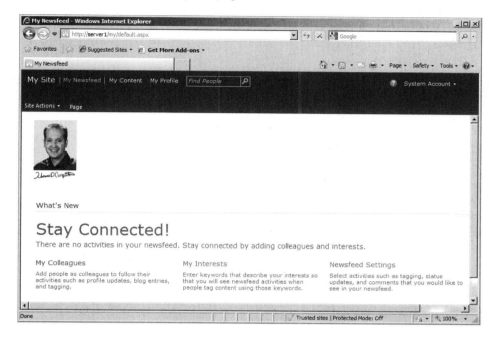

FIGURE 1.6   A user editing his profile within his My Site

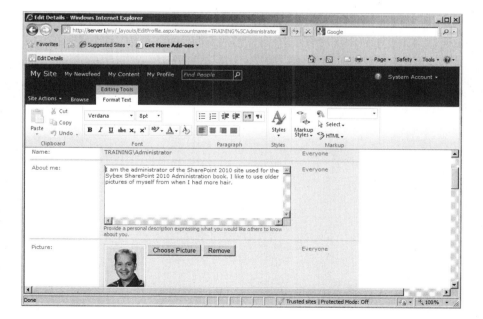

The most important thing to remember is that My Sites provide two primary information purposes: providing information about the users and providing customized information to the users. Each SharePoint user can search the profiles to get publicly available information about others users. Additionally, each SharePoint user may customize her My Site so that she sees information on the site that is most useful to her.

Sub-sites

Within a site, subsites may also be created. In fact, by default, all sites that you create are subsites of the top-level site within the site collection. To build a hierarchy like the one shown in Figure 1.3, you simply specify the folder hierarchy on the server during site creation. For example, the intranet site could be at `http://localhost/Intranet` and the Sales department site could be at `http://localhost/Sales`, while the sales performance reports are located at `http://localhost/Sales/PerformanceReports`. The PerformanceReports folder will contain the site for performance reports, but it will still be under the inheritance influence of the Sales folder and the top-level site.

Libraries, Folders, and Document Sets

Within each site you have libraries, folders, and document sets. You should understand and plan for each of these items.

Libraries   Libraries are used to store related items for collaboration purposes. As shown in Figure 1.7, multiple library types can be added to a SharePoint 2010 site, including Asset, Data Connection, Document, Form, Picture, Report, Slide, and Wiki Page libraries. The content from the libraries may be used in other areas of the site.

FIGURE 1.7   The new library creation screen showing the various library types in SharePoint 2010

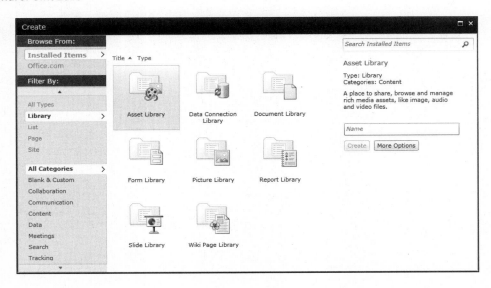

Folders   Within libraries, folders can be created for organizational purposes. For each library, you can choose whether folders should be enabled or not. Figure 1.8 shows a document library with folders used for organization. In addition to organizational benefits, much like folders within the operating system, library folders can be assigned permissions so that users who can access the library may not automatically be granted access to all folders within the library.

FIGURE 1.8   A document library that contains folders for organization purposes

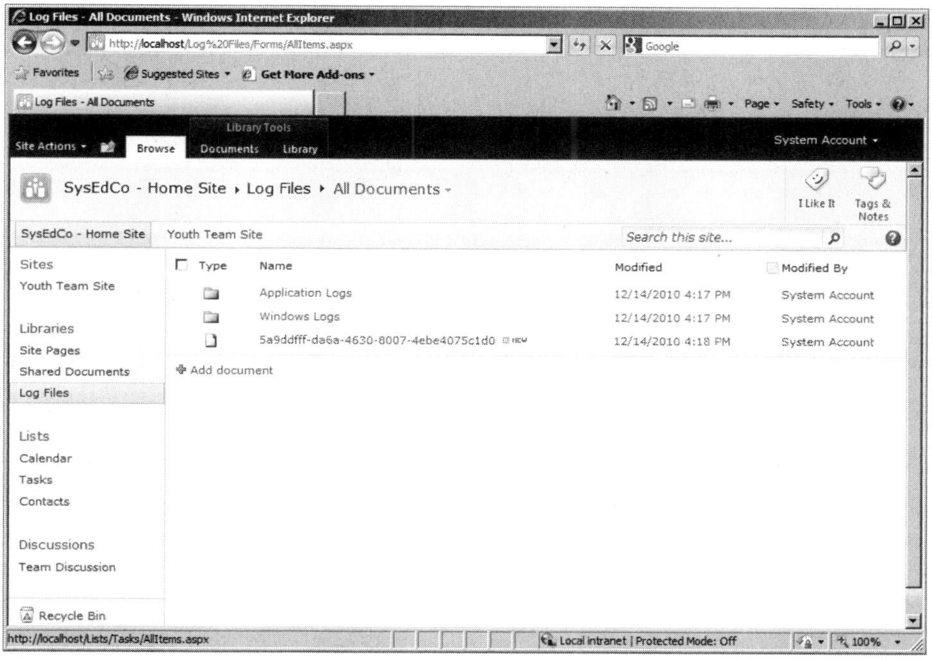

Document Sets   Document sets are new to SharePoint Server 2010 and exist only in the Standard and Enterprise Editions. They allow you to group multiple documents together for collaboration purposes. The documents may be stored in one or more document libraries. The document set includes a welcome page that displays the contents of the document set and its configuration properties. The document set may be restricted to include specific content types as well.

NOTE   Because document sets are new in SharePoint Server 2010, you probably will see questions related to this feature on the exam. If you are preparing for the exam, be sure to work through Exercise 1.3 on a default installation of SharePoint Server 2010 Standard or Enterprise Edition.

It is very important that you know how to enable document sets. Exercise 1.3 provides instructions for enabling document sets. After working through the exercise, you can spend more time working with the document set configurations if you like.

EXERCISE 1.3

Enabling Document Sets

In this exercise, you will enable document sets at the site-collection level. To perform this exercise, you should have a SharePoint Server 2010 Standard or Enterprise Edition server farm installed with the default options. You should also have a site collection and top-level site created.

1. Open the home page of the top-level site in Internet Explorer.

2. Click the Site Actions link and select Site Setting from the drop-down list.

3. Scroll down, if necessary, and click the Site Collection Features link in the Site Collection Administration category.

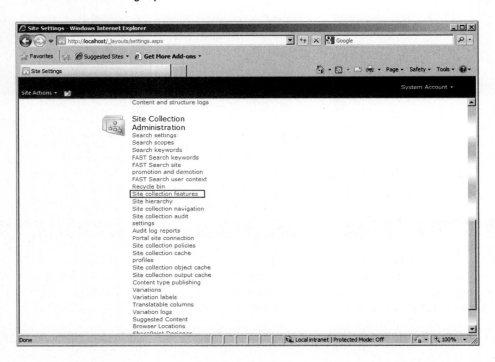

4. Scroll down, if necessary, and click the Activate button for the Document Sets feature.

5. When the process completes, the Site Collection Features page will reload and the status for the Document Sets feature will change to Active.

Once the document sets feature is enabled, you can create document sets in your SharePoint 2010 sites. Document sets are created from within the document library Documents tab view. You must enable content type management for the document library. Exercise 1.4 provides instructions for enabling content type management on a document library.

EXERCISE 1.4

Enabling Content Type Management

In this exercise, you will learn to enable content type management on a document library, which must be performed before you can work with document sets even with the Document Sets feature activated as in Exercise 1.3.

1. Open the home page of the top-level site in Internet Explorer.

2. From the list of Libraries on the left navigation bar, click the document library on which you want to enable content type management.

3. When the document library page loads, select the Library tab on the Ribbon.

4. In the Setting group on the Ribbon, click the Library Settings button.

EXERCISE 1.4 *(continued)*

5. In the General Settings category, click the Advanced Settings link.

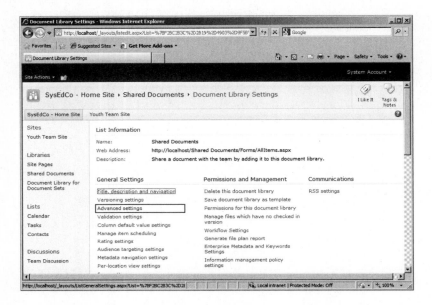

6. Choose Yes for the Content Types Allow Management Of Content Types option.

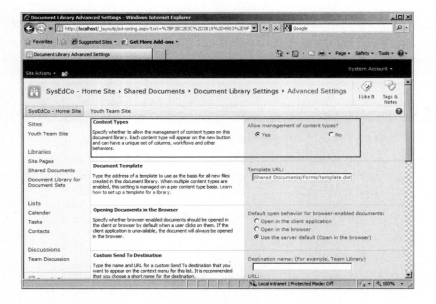

7. Scroll down and click the OK button to save your changes.

After completing Exercises 1.3 and 1.4, you will be ready to associate the Document Set content type with the document library. This action will enable the creation of document sets in the document library in question. Exercise 1.5 shows you how to add the Document Set content type to the document library.

EXERCISE 1.5

Adding the Document Set Content Type

In this exercise, you will add the Document Set content type to a document library so that document sets may finally be created.

1. Open the home page of the top-level site in Internet Explorer.

2. From the list of Libraries on the left navigation bar, click the document library on which you want to enable content type management.

3. When the document library page loads, select the Library tab on the Ribbon.

4. In the Setting group on the Ribbon, click the Library Settings button.

5. Scroll down on the Document Library Settings page until you see the Content Types section. To add a new content type, click the Add From Existing Site Content Types link.

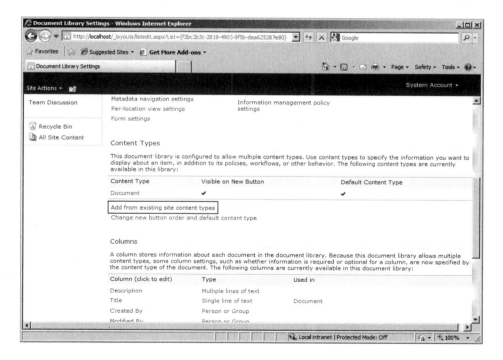

EXERCISE 1.5 *(continued)*

6. On the Add Content Types screen, click the Document Set content type and then click the Add button.

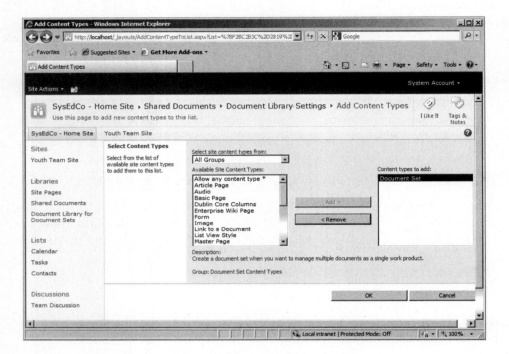

7. Click OK to add the content type to the document library.

You can also create new content types based on the Document Set content type. This allows you to customize the content type and limit the types of documents included in the document set.

Items and Pages

So far, you have explored the hierarchy of SharePoint 2010 from a container perspective. The server farm contains site collections. The site collections contain sites. The sites contain subsites, libraries, document sets, and lists. Now it's time to explore in the contents of the libraries, lists, and sites.

Items are stored in lists and libraries. A Word *document* is a document in a document library, but it is also an item. *Items* are database entries in the Content database for the site. For example, you may create a custom list to track the inventory of projectors used in conference rooms at your facility. This list will be stored in the Content database for the site. Exercise 1.6 provides instructions for creating such a list.

EXERCISE 1.6

Creating a Custom Tracking List

In this exercise, you will create a list for tracking projectors used in conference rooms in your facility. You will track the projector name, current location, and the person using the projector, if applicable.

1. Open the home page of the top-level site in Internet Explorer.

2. On the left navigation bar of the home page, click the Lists item.

3. On the All Site Content page that is displayed, click the Create button.

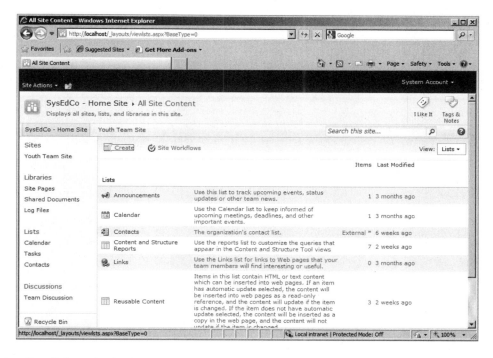

4. Scroll down in the list and select the Custom List item.

5. In the right sidebar, enter the name **Project Tracking** and click Create to create the custom list.

EXERCISE 1.6 *(continued)*

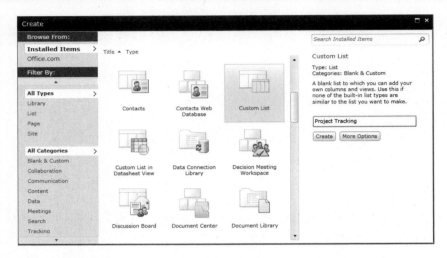

6. You will be taken to the Project Tracking - All Items page. When this page loads, click the List Settings button on the List tab in the Ribbon.

7. Scroll down the page until you see the Columns section. In this section, click the Title link to edit the column.

8. Change the Column Name value to **Projector ID** and click OK.

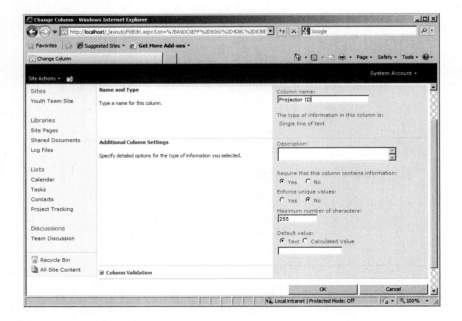

9. You will return to the List Settings page. Scroll down to the Columns section again and click the Create Column link to create a new column.

10. Enter **Current Location** for the Column Name, scroll down the page, select Yes for Require That This Column Contains Information, and then click OK.

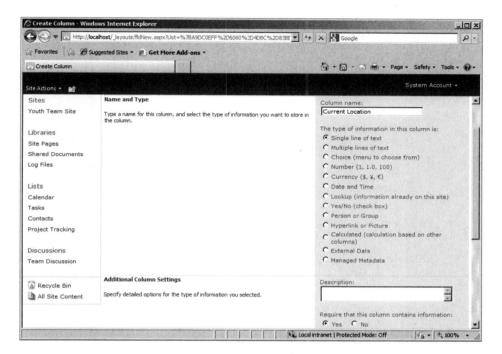

11. Repeat steps 9 and 10 to create a column named **Person Requesting**; however, do not select Yes for the Require That This Column contains Information item (because if the projector is in storage, no one is responsible for its use at this time).

12. When properly completed, the Columns section on the List Settings page will look like the following screen:

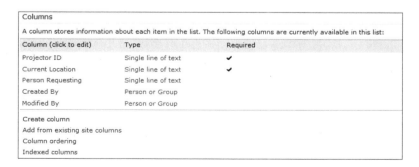

13. Within the Lists category in the left sidebar, click the Project Tracking link to view the custom list.

14. Click the Add New Item link to add an entry to the list.

15. In the Project Tracking - New Item screen, enter the following values for the item:

Projector ID: Sony 01

Current Location: Storage

Person Requesting: *{leave empty}*

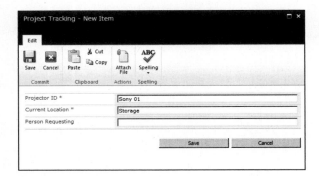

16. Click Save to save the new item into the list in the database.

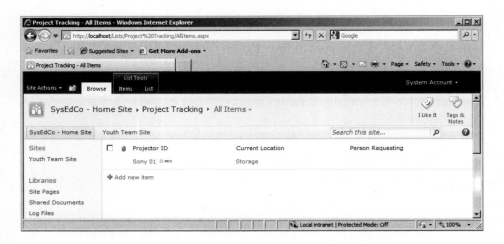

After creating the custom list in Exercise 1.6, you can add additional items to the list. These items are stored in the SQL Server database on the backend. Figure 1.9 shows a view of the SQL Server database in SQL Server Management Studio after several items have been added to the custom list created in Exercise 1.6.

FIGURE 1.9 Viewing the custom list within SQL Server Management Studio

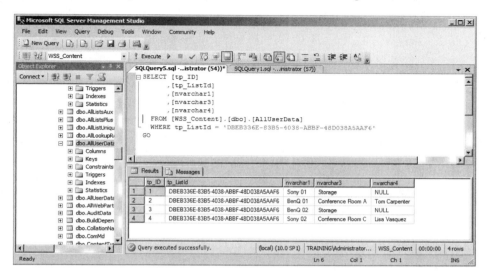

Typically, you would not use SQL Server Management Studio to directly access data in SharePoint lists; however, it is useful here to actually see the data in the backend database. Directly accessing data, particularly with INSERT, UPDATE, and DELETE T-SQL commands, can cause severe problems for your SharePoint sites and could result in the loss of support from Microsoft.

In addition to items stored in lists, you can create custom pages in the SharePoint sites. Custom pages are stored as items in lists within the Content database. You can then link to these custom pages from the home page of the site or from any other page. Custom pages are useful for delivering static content or custom collections of dynamic content within your SharePoint site.

SharePoint Zones

The final element in the logical hierarchy is the SharePoint zone. A *zone* represents a logical path used to gain access to the sites in the SharePoint web application. Stated as simply as possible, a zone is an IIS website used to access SharePoint web applications. The logical path could be an intranet path, such as SharePoint.company.local, or an Internet path, such as SharePoint.company.com. Up to five zones may be associated with the web application. All web applications start with the default zone, but the intranet, extranet, Internet, and custom zones may also be used.

Don't be confused by the zone names, such as intranet and extranet; the names are only there as a reference. For example, you could implement a zone using the Internet name that is never accessed from the Internet. That is not Microsoft's intention, but it could be done. The names are simply there to help you remember why you are using the zone. Therefore, you should use the appropriate name with the most logical source. You may use the extranet zone when you are building a zone to be accessed only by partnering organizations. You may use the Internet zone when building a zone used by public Internet access users who access the site anonymously. What users accessing the site from the Internet zone can see and do can then be further controlled through the Anonymous User Policy in SharePoint 2010. The custom zone is really just there for any use that doesn't fall into the other logical categories. It's not anything special when compared to the other zones, but it has a generic name so you can use it for any purpose.

In most cases, multiple zones are used only for the implementation of different authentication methods. If you use the new claims based authentication (CBA) in SharePoint 2010, multiple authentication methods can be used with a single zone. If classic mode authentication is used, each zone is limited to a single authentication method. Additional zones are added by extending the web application. Exercise 1.7 provides instructions for extending a web application for an additional custom zone.

EXERCISE 1.7

Extending a Web Application

In this exercise, you will extend the default SharePoint - 80 web application to exist in the custom zone as well. You will verify the extension by viewing the authentication providers.

1. Log on to the SharePoint 2010 server as an administrator.

2. Launch SharePoint 2010 Central Administration.

3. In the Application Management group, click Manage Web Applications.

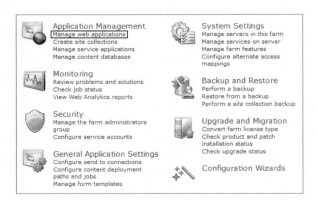

4. Click on the SharePoint - 80 web application to select it, and then click the Extend button on the Ribbon.

5.   In the Name field, change the name to **SharePoint - Custom Zone** so that you can easily identify the site at a later time.

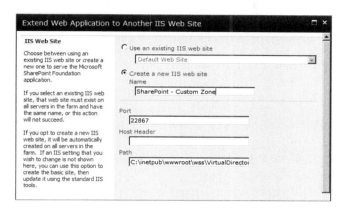

6.   Accept the default Port settings and scroll down the page to the Security Configuration section. In this section, change the Allow Anonymous setting to Yes.

7.   Scroll further down the page, change the Zone setting to Custom, and then click OK.

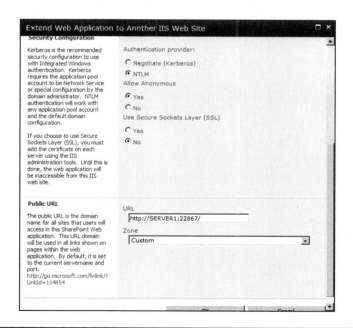

After you complete Exercise 1.7, the default site will be accessible to anonymous users and this authentication structure will be applied as the custom zone. In some scenarios, you might want to unextend a web application so that a particular zone is no longer supported. This action is accomplished in the Web Applications Management page of Central Administration using the Delete ➢ Remove SharePoint from IIS Web Site option. Be careful to delete only the extended web application. Figure 1.10 shows the Remove SharePoint from IIS Web Site dialog that would be used to remove the Custom Zone settings enabled in Exercise 1.7.

FIGURE 1.10   Removing a zone or unextending a web application

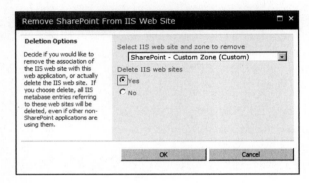

Designing a Logical Taxonomy

Now that you understand the logical architecture of SharePoint 2010 deployments, you can begin planning the structure and naming convention for it. Remember, this is also called a logical taxonomy and that is how Microsoft references it in the exam objectives for exam 70-668. Don't let the fancy word *taxonomy* confuse you if you're new to information management and information architectures. It means exactly the same thing it does in the field of biology. A taxonomy is a naming and classification structure, usually hierarchical in nature, used to conceptualize and organize complex systems. The logical taxonomy of your SharePoint deployment will simply be the logical architecture or structure you choose to implement. Stated differently, it is the structure of the server farms, site collections, and sites that you choose to deploy.

Site hierarchy planning is an important consideration early in your SharePoint deployment. If the hierarchy is too simple, it may not meet your later information needs. If it is too complex, it may be difficult for your users to navigate.

In most organizations, the following questions must be answered in order to properly design a logical taxonomy:

- Which departments will use the SharePoint server?
- What features of SharePoint will they utilize?
- What security policies may impact the administration or use of the SharePoint infrastructure?
- What, if any, custom development will be performed on the SharePoint servers?
- What is the budget for the project?

Sadly, that last item is often overlooked, but in the real world you cannot simply assume the budget is unlimited. The budget will often constrain your logical design. For example, one department may inform you that they want to use the SharePoint server; however, if they use the server, they will require completely separate administration and security boundaries to the extent that a separate server farm will be required. Because it exists in the real world, this department may simply have to put off using SharePoint, for now, if the budget does not allow for the second server farm. Hardware costs can often be reduced through virtualization, and virtualization may allow you to meet the needs of this department, but licensing costs will still be a factor and may simply make the endeavor too expensive for your organization at this time.

In the logical design process, you should be sure to include the following tasks:

- Build a business team that can work together to plan the SharePoint deployment effectively. This team must have or establish relationships with all departments in the organization so that no department is overlooked.

- Prepare a list of questions for the department heads or the department representatives. These questions should be in business terms and not in technical SharePoint terms that individuals will not understand.

- Focus on the business requirements at this stage to ensure that you build a solution that allows the organization to perform as needed.

- Include both functional and nonfunctional requirements. Functional requirements define actions that the SharePoint installation must be capable of supporting. Nonfunctional requirements define how the system must operate, including considerations such as performance, capacity, security, and so on.

- Determine the budget for the project. This budget should include licensing and hardware costs in every deployment. In some deployments, consulting fees and labor costs may also be required in the budget.

- Document everything. Documentation should begin even as you are building the business team and should continue through every phase of the logical design process. By the end of the process, you will want to more formally finalize the documentation.

To assist you in the planning process, Microsoft provides several planning worksheets at their TechNet website. The worksheets are available to individuals with or without a paid TechNet account at http://technet.microsoft.com/en-us/library/cc262451.aspx.

Building a Business Team

The first and most important step in planning a SharePoint 2010 logical design and deployment is the formation of a planning team. The team should include members from several areas of business. At a minimum, the following team members should be selected:

- Stakeholders
- SharePoint administrators
- SharePoint developers

Stakeholders will be most heavily involved during the requirements gathering process and the later testing processes. If they do not have input in the requirements gathering process, you are likely to overlook several important requirements. The stakeholders include business users, management, and IT support staff who do not directly interact with the SharePoint implementation. For example, while the network administrators may never perform actions directly against the SharePoint servers, they manage the network that must be used to access the servers. If the network administrators are not involved in the planning, you will be sure to overlook key factors in the network infrastructure.

The SharePoint administrators and developers should be included on the team for input from two very different perspectives. The first is the perspective of administration, which includes the operational portion of the SharePoint implementation. The administrators will be responsible for backups, security management, feature activation, search administration, external data connections, and any other responsibility that falls in the category of administration. This book is focused primarily on the job role of administration.

The second perspective is that of the developers. The developers are responsible for creating custom features, solutions, and pages. They may not activate these additions in the production environment, but they will be responsible for creating, troubleshooting, and updating them. In small environments, an individual may be responsible for both the development and administration tasks. In larger environments, these duties are typically separated for both efficiency and security reasons. It's more efficient because the individuals can focus their efforts on a smaller subset of knowledge. It's more secure because no one individual is responsible for both the development of new code and the implementation of that code. Separation of duties helps to increase security.

In addition to the key roles of shareholders, SharePoint administrators, and SharePoint developers who should be on the business team, you may consider other roles as well. The following team members may be considered in addition to the three core team member roles:

- **Solution architects:** In the largest organizations, an individual playing the role of solution architect will use the logical design to plan the physical implementation of SharePoint. In smaller organizations, this is the responsibility of the SharePoint administrator.

- **Database experts:** The SharePoint solution depends on a SQL Server database backend. A database expert may be included on the team to ensure that the databases perform as needed. If no such expert is available, this responsibility will fall back to the SharePoint administrator.

- **Active Directory administrators:** SharePoint uses the users and groups from Active Directory (AD) for authentication and authorization in most SharePoint installations.

In the smallest implementations, the SharePoint administrator is likely to be the AD administrator as well. In smaller companies, one or two IT professionals will perform the roles of several dozen professionals in larger companies.

 As you can see, the SharePoint administrator has more responsibilities in smaller organizations than in larger organizations. However, even the SharePoint administrator in larger organizations would benefit greatly from understanding all of the parts and pieces that make SharePoint work on the network. These parts include the network itself, DNS, AD, and SQL Server. All of these components are addressed in greater detail in Chapter 2, "Designing the Physical Architecture," and Chapter 3, "Integrating SharePoint with the Network Infrastructure."

Preparing Questions

Once you have the business team assembled, you can begin preparing questions that will help you clearly define business requirements. These questions can be of two types:

- Questions you must answer as a team
- Questions you must ask of the organization

The team questions can be reviewed in a brainstorming meeting format. The team questions should be reviewed and answered before asking questions of the organization. After the organization questions are answered, the team should reconvene to answer any new questions that came out of the organizational questions. Examples of team questions include:

- Why are we implementing SharePoint?
- From what features of SharePoint are we most likely to benefit?
- Which departments will need to use the SharePoint installation immediately?
- Which departments will be brought onto the SharePoint installation over time?
- What custom code do we foresee developing?
- Will we need to purchase any third-party add-ons for the installation?

As you read the preceding list of questions, if you thought that many of these questions should be asked of the organization or derived from discussions with the organization, you were correct. However, by reviewing the questions with the team first, you gain a greater understanding of the issues, and you can determine the best way to ask the questions so that the organization will understand the questions when asked of them.

For example, imagine sending out an email survey to discover how your employees might use the SharePoint servers and asking the question "How do you think you will use the web parts available in SharePoint 2010?" Clearly, the future users will not even know what web parts are much less how they would use them. A better question might be "Would you benefit from the ability to create custom pages and, if so, in what scenarios?" While the latter question might still require some explanation, the question is much easier to understand because the technical jargon of SharePoint has been removed.

During the team meeting, you will want to develop the survey for the organization's employees. This survey is a primary reason for having business users on the team. They can help you make sure the survey is understandable for the business users.

 Real World Scenario

Using Video for Simplification

While working with a company in central Ohio, my company came up with a very creative method for performing surveys like those discussed in this section. Instead of sending out simple one-sentence questions, we created a mandatory online video solution to ask the questions. The employees were given a five-dollar gift certificate to a popular local lunch place for watching the video and answering the questions.

Each question was developed into a 60 to 90 second video. In the video, the question was asked and explanations were given. When appropriate, quick demonstrations of features were even performed. After each video, the user was presented with a page of 1 to 3 questions they could answer. They were required to answer at least 50 percent of the questions to get the lunch certificate.

Yes, it was bribery and yes, there were likely those who really didn't give it much thought; however, that didn't matter to us because the questions could be answered in two ways. Each question had a yes, no, or maybe response, but each question also had an area for the users to type in their own answers. The vast majority of users typed in ideas that were both useful for gathering requirements and creative for improving the product we were installing.

The benefit of the video method was two-fold. First, it allowed us to better explain the system and the questions we were asking. Second, it whetted the users' appetites so that they really wanted the system. Breaking down resistance to change in technology is never an easy thing, and by showing them the system and gathering their input for it, we accomplished both tasks simultaneously.

Defining Business Requirements

When you have interviewed stakeholders, gathered survey results, and performed team brainstorming, you are ready to define the business requirements. The most important priority in your SharePoint planning should be meeting business requirements. A well-implemented technology that fails to meet the business demands is really nothing more than an expensive way to heat your facility. Let the heating system do its job and make sure the SharePoint servers do theirs by clearly defining business requirements.

Requirements analysis is a complex topic by itself, which could occupy hundreds of pages. For more information on requirements analysis, consider reading the book *How to Cheat at IT Project Management* by Susan Snedaker (Syngress Press, 2005).

Requirements analysis can be defined as the process of discovering a project's requirements. A *requirement* is anything, physical or logical, that must be provided by the product of the project in order for the project to be considered successful. Simply stated, requirements are the things you must achieve at the completion of the implementation of your SharePoint 2010 deployment. The *product of a project* is defined as the result or outcome of the project. It is what the project gives you. The requirements, then, are those things that the product must provide in order for the project to be deemed successful.

Business requirements come from two primary sources: internal business requirements and external business requirements. Internal requirements will be based on organizational objectives and policies such as security policies, employment policies, and so on. External requirements will be based on regulations from local regulatory bodies such as federal and local governments and their agencies.

Business requirements can be determined through several methods. The first is the user surveys discussed in the preceding section. Additional methods include:

- Interviews with the project sponsor
- Focus groups
- Business process analysis

Regardless of the method used to gather the information, it is the responsibility of the project manager and the team to ensure that the business requirements are well established.

Out of the business requirements will come the functional and nonfunctional requirements. Functional requirements define the capabilities that a system or its components must provide. For example, the following is a list of functional requirements:

- Users must be able to store documents in the SharePoint 2010 server farm.
- Users must be able to create custom My Sites.
- Users must be able to customize their starting portal page with information they want to see.
- Administrators must be able to schedule backups.

Nonfunctional requirements define how the system must behave. Nonfunctional planning items include:

- Security
- Performance
- Availability
- Manageability
- Capacity

- Scalability
- Interoperability
- Business continuity

 The major difference between functional and nonfunctional requirements is that functional requirements specify the "what" and nonfunctional requirements specify the "how." While some crossover may exist, this is the primary point of separation.

Defining the Budget

The budget will be based on hardware purchases, software licenses, and man hours. If you do not bring in any consultants for the implementation and your organization does not track the cost of employee time against project budget, you may disregard man hours. However, hardware and software costs should always be considered.

The budget can be developed in two ways. The first method is called bottom-up budgeting. With *bottom-up budgeting,* you determine what you want to do, how much it will cost, and then gain approval for the budget required. This is the preferred budgeting method, but it is not necessarily the most common.

Top-down budgeting indicates that you are given a budget and you must implement the technology within that budget. This is the more common method of deployment. In some organizations, a fixed IT budget is assigned and something like a SharePoint deployment will be taken out of that budget. In these scenarios, you often see a mixture of bottom up and top down. It's bottom up in the feasibility stage (you tell the IT director what it would cost to implement the SharePoint farm or farms you need), and then it becomes top-down in the implementation stage (the IT director tells you how much you actually have and it's usually less than the bottom-up method determined). Although it is important to be prepared for these politics, you shouldn't let them unduly frustrate you. It is just the way business is done, and there are many justifiable factors that result in this reality. If you are doing the administration and implementation, you get to discover creative ways to make it happen within the budget.

Regardless of the method used to determine the budget, it is the SharePoint administrator's responsibility to find a way to balance the constraints of the budget with the demands of the users. For example, if you determined the need for a three-server SharePoint farm but you can only implement a two-server farm, make sure the database server is well optimized so that you get the best performance possible.

Documenting Everything

The final action in the design of a logical taxonomy is the gathering and creation of documentation. As you go through the previously described processes, you should be creating documentation. If you are doing so, you will have a head start when you get to the end and are ready to finalize the documentation.

After designing the logical architecture for your SharePoint 2010 deployment, you should have at least three sets of documents:

- Logical architecture diagrams
- Business requirements
- A budget sheet

The logical architecture diagrams will visually describe your SharePoint implementation from a logical view. It should show the number of server farms, site collections, and sites that you will deploy.

The business requirements will document what the SharePoint implementation capabilities should be and how it should perform. You may want to create documents listing requirements categorized as functional, nonfunctional, departmental, and organization-wide. This documentation should be approved (signed-off) by the sponsor and key stakeholders.

The third item listed is the budget sheet. This can be created as a simple Excel workbook with the software, hardware, and man-hour costs listed where appropriate. This sheet can be used for budget tracking throughout the project as well.

Consider this suggestion: Implement a single-server SharePoint installation before your first business team meeting. Use this installation to view features and even to document your project. This method allows you to take care of two problems at once. First, you have a place to store your documents. Second, you have a test server to use during deployment planning.

Summary

In this chapter, you began your exploration of SharePoint 2010 by learning about the different editions and features in the product line. You learned that SharePoint 2010 is a 64-bit-only product and that it runs on 64-bit editions of Windows Server 2008 and Windows Server 2008 R2. You also learned about the features provided by the different SharePoint 2010 editions and which edition you need to get the features you require. Next, you learned about the SharePoint information architecture, which consists of server farms, site collections, and sites. You also learned about the different objects stored in sites such as lists, libraries, and pages. You explored the backend database in which these objects are placed. Finally, you looked at the logical taxonomy design process as an important part of your SharePoint deployment.

Exam Essentials

Knowing SharePoint editions and features.   Understand the different editions of SharePoint 2010 so that you can choose the right edition when given a scenario. Know the features that are not available in the SharePoint Foundation 2010 server.

Understanding the SharePoint logical architecture.   Know the logical hierarchy of a SharePoint deployment and the purpose of each level in the hierarchy. SharePoint starts with a server farm, then site collections, then sites, and then the objects within the sites, such as lists, libraries, and pages.

Designing a logical taxonomy.   Ensure that the logical design you create is able to expand to support the information it will contain and that it is simple enough for users to navigate easily.

Chapter 2

Designing the Physical Architecture

TOPICS COVERED IN THIS CHAPTER

When you have completed the logical design for your Share-Point deployment, you will be ready to move to the physical design phase. In this phase, you will define the physical servers and their configurations. This process includes identifying requirements, implementing supporting components, and planning capacity. All of these topics will be addressed in this chapter. You will learn how to translate the logical architecture of your deployment into a physical implementation.

If you are preparing for the 70-668 exam, this chapter will cover important objectives for you. Along with the major topic of designing the physical architecture, several minor objectives are addressed, including translating the information architecture (the logical structure) to a physical architecture, determining capacity requirements, and scaling the web farm and services infrastructure.

Translating the Logical to the Physical Architecture

The process of planning a physical design for the SharePoint 2010 implementation includes the consideration of several factors represented in Figure 2.1. First, you must ensure that the servers you plan to use meet the system requirements for the planned edition of SharePoint 2010. Next, you must ensure that the components required for the support of SharePoint 2010 exist in your environment. These components include things like Active Directory, DNS resolution, the IIS web server, and the SQL Server database server. Of course, you must always consider the business environment or context in which you are installing SharePoint. The security policies and administration practices that already exist can be used or modified in order to best manage the SharePoint implementation.

After considering all of these factors, you will be ready to map the logical design to a physical implementation that will work for your environment. This will include choosing the number of Web Front End (WFE) servers based on the number of web applications and implementing the appropriate number of SQL Server database servers based on the quantity of content. Additional logical to physical mapping should be considered as well.

FIGURE 2.1   The physical design-planning process

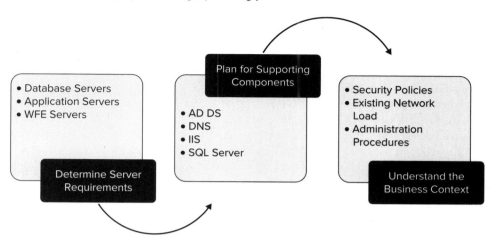

Your final step will be to document the physical implementation plan. This documented plan will be your guide as you perform the actual installation steps, which are discussed in detail in Chapter 4, "Planning for Farm Deployment."

Now that you have been exposed to the scope of the physical architecture planning process, let's begin exploring each part step-by-step.

Server Requirements

It is important that you implement servers that meet the SharePoint minimum requirements, but it is even more important that the servers meet your specific implementation requirements. Server requirements simply document the processing speed, memory, networking, and storage requirements for the server. Server requirements planning must address three SharePoint-specific servers:

- Database servers
- Application servers
- WFE servers

These three servers are the essential servers in any SharePoint implementation. They may be implemented in several ways. For example, you could choose to implement a single-server topology that includes all three roles on a single Windows server. This option works well for small environments, departmental deployments, and testing and development installations.

The second option is to have one or more WFE/application servers and one database server. The minimum number of required servers for this deployment option is two. With this entry-level distributed deployment topology, you have the efficiency provided by a dedicated database server, but you may not have redundancy. For example, if you install one WFE/application server (this server runs the WFE role and the service applications for the server farm) and one database server and either server fails, the entire server farm will be unavailable.

The next level of distributed deployment is that where four or more servers are used. For example, with two WFE/application servers and two database servers (implementing backend database mirroring), the server farm can survive in small-scale failure scenarios. If one WFE/application server fails, the other server and the applications it runs will continue to operate. If one of the database servers should fail, the other can continue serving up the databases.

Of course, you can scale out your deployment as much as required. With multiple WFE servers providing access to the same SharePoint sites, any one of the servers can fail and the sites will still be available. You can also use Windows Server Network Load Balancing (NLB) for the application servers to provide fault tolerance there. Chapter 7, "Designing a Strategy for Business Continuity," provides more information on the high-availability options for SharePoint 2010 deployments. In summary, you can use clustering or mirroring for the database servers and NLB for the WFE and application servers.

Microsoft defines the minimum requirements for SharePoint 2010 based on the different deployment models. The hardware requirements for a SharePoint 2010 WFE server, application servers, and single-server installations, which would include the database server, are listed in Table 2.1.

TABLE 2.1 Hardware Requirements for WFE Servers, Application Servers, and Single-Server Installations

Component	Minimum Requirements
Processor	64-bit with four cores.
RAM	4 GB for development and testing. 8 GB for production use.
Hard Disk	80 GB on the system drive and additional free space for day-to-day operations. Additionally, you should maintain twice as much free space as the total amount of RAM installed on the server.

In case you are installing a separate database server, Table 2.2 lists the minimum requirements for this server.

TABLE 2.2 Hardware Requirements for a Dedicated SharePoint Database Server

Component	Minimum Requirements
Processor	64-bit with four cores for small environments. 64-bit with eight cores or more for medium to large environments.
RAM	8 GB for small environments. 16 GB or more for medium to large environments.
Hard Disk	80 GB on the system drive and additional free space for day-to-day operations. Additionally, you should maintain twice as much free space as the total amount of RAM installed on the server.

In addition to the minimum requirements, you should add more hardware capabilities based on how you plan to use the SharePoint installation. The later section of this chapter titled "Capacity Planning" provides additional information on storage estimation and hardware requirements for real-world scenarios.

The minimum requirements should be considered the baseline onto which you always add more capabilities. The last thing you want to do is to implement a SharePoint installation that users refuse to use due to performance issues.

In addition to the hardware requirements, you must also consider the software requirement for these servers. The database server must run SQL Server, but it also must run the proper edition of SQL Server. WFE servers will have specific requirements as well. Even client computers will have a minimum set of requirements they must meet in order to have full SharePoint utilization capabilities.

In fact, Microsoft places browsers into one of three support modes: supported, supported with known issues, and not tested. Browsers that are supported will enable all the functionality that SharePoint provides. Browsers that are supported with known issues will work with SharePoint 2010, but an occasional feature may not work or may be disabled by design in the browser. Browsers that are not tested are just that: not tested. They may work completely. They may work in part. They may not work at all. If you want to use a browser that has not been tested, you will have to test it yourself. In most cases, you will use the Internet Explorer 7 or 8 browsers because they have full support for all features. Table 2.3 provides an overview of the popular browsers and their support modes.

TABLE 2.3 Browser Support Levels as SharePoint Clients

Browser	Supported	Supported with Limitations	Not Tested
Internet Explorer 8 (32-bit)	X		
Internet Explorer 7 (32-bit)	X		
Internet Explorer 8 (64-bit)		X	
Internet Explorer 7 (64-bit)		X	
Internet Explorer 6			X
Firefox 3.6 on Windows		X	
Firefox 3.6 on non-Windows		X	
Safari 4.04 on Windows		X	
Safari 4.40 on Mac			X

For more information on browser compatibility and the specific limitations in the 64-bit editions of Internet Explorer and in the Firefox browsers, visit the following website: http://technet.microsoft.com/en-us/library/cc263526.aspx.

In addition to the browser support, you should consider additional applications that you may require on the client computers. If you want the users to edit Excel workbooks, PowerPoint presentations, and Word documents that are stored in document libraries by using their local installation of Microsoft Office, you will need to have Microsoft Office 2010 installed on the client computers. Microsoft Office 2007 will work with documents downloaded from document libraries, but full support for SharePoint 2010 is actually included in the Microsoft Office 2010 suite.

The software requirements for the database server are different from the WFE and application servers; however, the WFE and application servers share the same requirements even though they may play different roles. When you plan the software requirements for a SharePoint solution, you are ensuring that all required modules are installed and configured on the server.

Database servers must run an installation of SQL Server. The version running must be a 64-bit edition; and SQL Server Express, Standard, and Enterprise editions are all supported. SQL Server Express Edition is only recommended for development and testing, but it may be used for small scale deployments. SQL Server 2005 or later may be used.

You must run a 64-bit edition of SQL Server or SharePoint 2010 will not work with it. If you have an existing 32-bit server, it may be possible to upgrade it to a 64-bit edition of SQL Server and then attach existing databases. Check with your database solution vendors or programming staff to find out more.

The following list summarizes the minimum requirements for a SharePoint database server (only one version of SQL Server is required among the optional versions listed):

- Windows Server 2008 or R2 in a 64-bit edition
- SQL Server 2005 with SP3 and cumulative updates in a 64-bit edition
- SQL Server 2008 with SP3 in a 64-bit edition
- SQL Server 2008 R2 in a 64-bit edition

The WFE and application servers both run web server technologies as well as additional SharePoint services and applications. To support these additional services and applications, certain software requirements must be met. SharePoint 2010 WFE and application servers require the following:

- Windows Server 2008 with SP2 in a 64-bit edition
- Windows Server 2008 R2 in a 64-bit edition
- Web Server (IIS) role
- Application server role
- Microsoft .NET Framework version 3.5 SP1
- Microsoft Sync Framework runtime v1.0 (x64)
- Microsoft Filter Pack 2.0
- Microsoft Chart Controls for the Microsoft .NET Framework 3.5
- Windows PowerShell 2.0
- SQL Server 2008 Native Client
- Microsoft SQL Server 2008 Analysis Services ADOMD.NET
- ADO.NET Data Services Update for .NET Framework 3.5 SP1
- Windows Identity Foundation (WIF)

The good news is that the SharePoint 2010 installation engine can add all of the previously listed components for you. It is usually best to install Windows Server 2008 R2, apply all updates to the operating system, and then install SharePoint 2010 with the listed prerequisites. Chapter 4 provides step-by-step instructions for these procedures.

🌐 Real World Scenario

Windows Server 2008 R2 May Be Better

I realize that new software technologies are often implemented on existing servers. I've worked on SharePoint deployment projects where we used existing file servers for the SharePoint installation. Of course, this plan can certainly work, but I want to argue for upgrading the servers and operating system during the SharePoint 2010 deployment.

I performed a lab installation of SharePoint 2010 from scratch during the writing of this book. In order to test the differences between installing on Windows Server 2008 and installing on Windows Server 2008 R2, I timed the installation on each while paying close attention to the installs and responding as soon as the process asked something of me.

During this process, I started with a clean virtual machine running on Hyper-V R2 for each installation. I installed the operating system, necessary drivers, and the required service packs and patches; and then I performed a single-machine installation of SharePoint Server 2010 Enterprise Edition. The end result was very revealing. It took about 73 minutes longer to do the install with Windows Server 2008 than it did with Windows Server 2008 R2.

If you plan to install several servers in your environment, this could have a significant impact on installation times. However, this is not the end of the story. Other reasons for using Windows Server 2008 R2 as the base installation are simply that it is the latest version of the operating system and it provides several enhanced features that may be useful on SharePoint 2010 servers.

- R2 is 64-bit only so there is no concern about selecting the right edition.

- R2 supports remote server management from within the Server Manager application.

- R2 is the newer version of the two operating systems and is likely to support running newer technologies longer.

In addition to these factors, it is likely that you will want new hardware to run SharePoint 2010. SharePoint 2010 is a processor-intensive, heavy storage access, memory-consuming beast (don't get me wrong, I love it!); and the more power you can throw at it, the better it performs. This is particularly true with single-server installations. Remember, that server is running the operating system, IIS, SQL Server, and all of the SharePoint services. For this reason, older servers may not be up to the task of running this newer product. Unless your server was purchased after 2007, it is not likely to meet the requirements for a single-server SharePoint installation. Of course, if you are installing to multiple servers, even the earliest 64-bit processors may be adequate.

In the end, due to the complexity of installation on Windows Server 2008 and the improved features in Windows Server 2008 R2, I recommend installing SharePoint on Windows Server 2008 R2 machines only. Simply make this your baseline for a SharePoint server, and make it clear to all departments that it is required for a SharePoint installation.

Supporting Components

SharePoint is not a product that works by itself; it must be installed in an environment that includes the required supporting components. Four key components must exist and will be explained in this section:

- DNS
- Active Directory Domain Services (AD DS)
- Internet Information Services (IIS)
- SQL Server

DNS

The Domain Name System (DNS) is an Internet standard for name resolution. SharePoint depends on DNS for Internet-style name resolution. These Internet-style names are often called URLs, but in fact the URL is the complete path to a location on a host. For example, `http://hostname.domain.name.com/site/default.aspx` is a URL. However, `hostname.domain.name.com` is a DNS name that is technically called a fully qualified domain name (FQDN). The domain name, in this case, is `domain.name.com` and the host name is hostname. When you put the domain name and the host name together, you have the FQDN. In SharePoint implementations, DNS is used to provide FQDN to IP address resolution for access to the SharePoint servers and sites.

In a Microsoft environment, the DNS service is installed on Windows servers and is maintained using the DNS Manager in the Administrative Tools Start Menu group. DNS is used by Active Directory as well. In this section, you will learn to install the DNS service, create domain names, and create host records for FQDN resolution.

DNS Installation

The first step to using DNS in a Microsoft environment is the installation of the service. In Windows Server 2008 and later versions, this means adding the DNS server role. Exercise 2.1 provides instructions for doing this.

 If you want to perform all of the activities in this book, you will need a Windows Server 2008 R2 installation on which you can perform the activities. If you want instructions for installing Windows Server 2008 R2, see Exercise 4.1 in Chapter 4. The book's exercises assume the SharePoint server computer name is SERVER1. A machine with two processor cores will work, but four cores are preferred. Additionally, the machine should have 6 GB of RAM or more.

EXERCISE 2.1

Installing the DNS Server Role in the Server Manager

In this exercise, you will install the DNS server role. This exercise requires a basic installation of Windows Server 2008 R2. No additional roles or features are required on the server to install the DNS server role. Although the following exercises may seem short, be sure to give yourself time for completion. In several cases, minutes pass between steps while you wait on system processing. This exercise should take approximately 10 minutes.

1. Log onto the Windows Server 2008 R2 machine as an administrator.

2. If the Server Manager does not start automatically, click Start ➢ Administrative Tools ➢ Server Manager. (Alternatively, you can click Start and then right-click Computer and select Manage to access the Server Manager.)

3. Click the Roles node in the left pane.

4. In the right pane, click the Add Roles link to add a new role to the server.

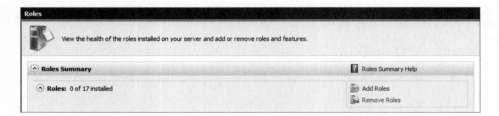

5. If the Before You Begin screen is displayed, click Next to continue.

6. On the Select Server Roles screen, check the DNS server role item and then click Next.

7. Read the information about the DNS Server and then click Next.

8. Click Install to add the DNS server role to the Windows Server installation.

9. When the installation process completes, click Finish to exit the Add Roles Wizard.

10. You are returned to the Server Manager. In the left pane, expand the Roles node and note that a new DNS Server node is available. In the screenshot, it is named SERVER1, but your server may have a different name.

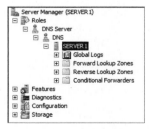

After completing Exercise 2.1, you will have a complete installation of the DNS server role, which is the Windows Server DNS service. You do not have a domain at this time, but the next section provides information on creating a DNS domain or zone.

Creating a Domain

To create host records, you must first create a domain. Domains can be created at the second level of the DNS hierarchy (like *company.*com) or at the third and deeper levels (like *marketing.*company.com or *outside.sales.*company.com). The top-level domains, such as .com, .net, .org, and .info, are managed by the Internet Corporation for Assigned Names and Numbers (ICANN). Your domain name will be managed by your DNS server or the DNS server of a service provider. It is not uncommon for organizations to have one domain name for internal use (such as *company.local*) and another for external use (such as *company.*com). You will have to make this decision for your organization or it may already have been made. For more information on planning DNS namespaces (domains and host names), visit http://support.microsoft.com/gp/gp_namespace_master.

In most Microsoft deployments, a DNS domain is synonymous to a zone; however, it is important to note that a zone is technically a portion of the total DNS namespace that is managed by a specific server or set of servers. For example, your DNS server that is responsible for the SharePoint.local zone may also be responsible for the training .SharePoint.local child domain within that zone. A zone is really just an authority boundary for a DNS service.

Do not confuse DNS zones with the zones in SharePoint 2010. DNS zones define the namespace for which a DNS server or group of DNS servers is responsible and authoritative. SharePoint zones simply refer to points of entry into the SharePoint site. For more information on SharePoint zones, see Chapter 1, "Planning the Logical Architecture."

Creating a domain is a simple process; however, you should take time to plan the domain before creation. The planning can take hours or days. The creation will take a few minutes. In Exercise 2.2, you will create a domain named SharePoint.local using the DNS server role installed in Exercise 2.1.

EXERCISE 2.2

Creating the *SharePoint.local* Domain

In this exercise, you will create a domain named SharePoint.local. Because Active Directory is not yet installed, you will store the domain in standard DNS text files on the hard drive. After Active directory is installed, you can integrate DNS into the AD DS database.

1. Log onto the Windows Server 2008 R2 installation as an administrator.

2. Click Start ➢ Administrative Tools ➢ DNS.

3. Expand the DNS server node. In the following screenshots, it is named SERVER1, but your server may have a different name.

4.   Right-click on the Forward Lookup Zones node and select New Zone.

5.   On the Welcome To The New Zone Wizard screen, click Next to begin.

6.   On the Zone Type screen, choose to create a Primary Zone. This is a zone that is
     managed directly by the currently accessed DNS server. Click Next.

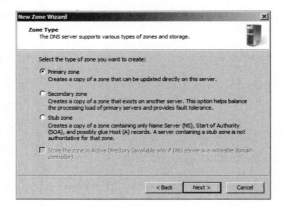

7.   On the Zone Name screen, enter the name **SharePoint.local** in the Zone Name field and
     click Next.

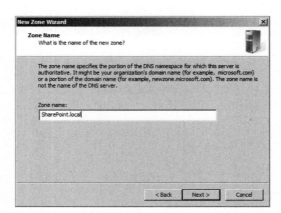

8. The Zone File screen allows you to specify an existing file or create a new file for storage of the DNS records (host names and so on). If you had a previous installation of DNS, you could use the file from that installation. In this case, select Create a New file with this File Name, accept the default value of **SharePoint.local.dns**, and click Next.

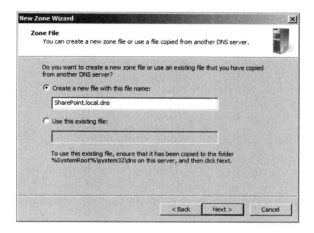

9. On the Dynamic Update screen, choose Allow Both Nonsecure And Secure Dynamic Updates. The preferred option, Allow Only Secure Dynamic Updates, is disabled at this time because Active Directory is not available. In a later exercise, after Active Directory is installed, you will change the DNS server to allow only secure updates. Click Next.

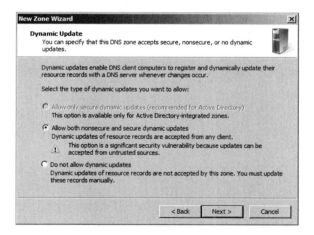

10. Click Finish on the Completing the New Zone Wizard screen to create the new zone and domain named SharePoint.local. You will be returned to the DNS Manager, and a new node named SharePoint.local will appear under Forward Lookup Zones.

After creating a forward lookup zone, you may want to create a matching reverse lookup zone. Reverse lookup zones are used to resolve IP addresses to host names, while forward lookup zones resolve host names to IP addresses. The Reverse Lookup Zones node is used to create the reverse lookup zones.

Creating Host Records

Now that you have a DNS domain, you can begin to create host records. Windows clients from Windows 2000 through to Windows 7 all support dynamic DNS registration. This means that they will automatically create their own host records in the DNS server. Windows 2000 Server through Windows Server 2008 R2 also support dynamic DNS registration. Even though the machines may dynamically register themselves, you may still want to create host records manually for several reasons:

- You want to use alternative FQDNs to reference the same machine within the DNS domain name. For example, corp.SharePoint.local and sales.SharePoint.local can both point to the same SharePoint server.

- You want different DNS domain names and host names to map to a single machine. For example, corp.SharePoint.local and portal.marketing.local can both point to the same SharePoint server.

- Your administrative policies require manual configuration of host names for all servers and infrastructure devices.

Exercise 2.3 provides instructions for creating host names in the DNS Manager. The steps described in the exercise can be repeated as many times as required to create as many host names as you need.

EXERCISE 2.3

Creating Host Records

In this exercise, you will create a host record in the SharePoint.local domain. The host record will be named **portal** and will point to the IP address of the DNS server itself. For this exercise, it is assumed that the DNS server's IP address is 192.168.10.99; however, your environment may be different.

1. Log onto the DNS server as an administrator.

2. Click Start ➢ Administrative Tools ➢ DNS.

3. Expand the DNS server node and then expand Forward Lookup Zones and click on the SharePoint.local zone.

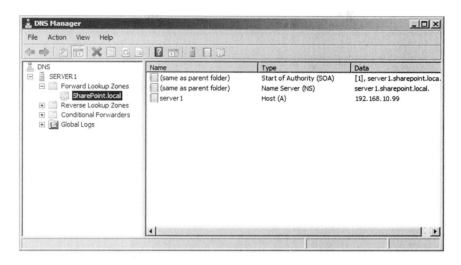

4. One or more host records may already be in the zone. Right-click on the SharePoint
    .local zone in the left pane and select New Host (A or AAAA).

5. In the New Host dialog, enter the value **portal** into the Name field and the value
    192.168.10.99 in the IP Address field. If you created a reverse lookup zone, check the
    Create Associated Pointer (PTR) Record check box. Click on the Add Host button.

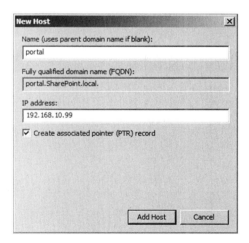

6. Click OK when informed that the host record was created.

7. In the New Host dialog, click Done to close the dialog.

8. Notice the new host record named portal in the list.

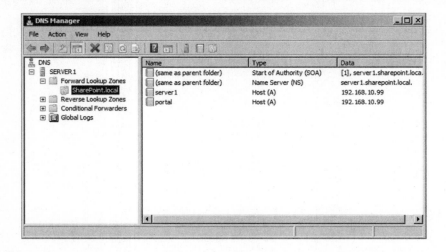

After creating the host record, you can use the **NSLOOKUP** command at the command prompt to verify that the DNS server is able to resolve the address. However, your DNS server must be configured properly in your IP address settings. Exercise 2.4 provides instructions for configuring the DNS server to point to itself as the DNS server and then to forward DNS queries to the Internet DNS servers.

EXERCISE 2.4

Configuring DNS IP Settings on the DNS Server

In this exercise, you will first configure the DNS server to use itself for DNS name resolution. Next, you will configure the DNS service to forward DNS queries it cannot resolve to an Internet DNS server.

1. Log onto the DNS server as an administrator.

2. Open a command prompt by clicking Start, typing **CMD**, and pressing Enter.

3. At the command prompt, execute the **ipconfig /all** command. Notice that the current DNS server settings point to a DNS server other than the local machine. Exit the command prompt by executing the **exit** command.

4. Click Start, right-click on Network, and select Properties to launch the Network and Sharing Center.

5. Click the Change Adapter Settings link in the left menu.

6. Right-click on the adapter you use to connect to the network and choose Properties.

7. Double-click on the Internet Protocol Version 4 entry.

8. Change the Preferred DNS Server value to read 127.0.0.1, which is the loopback address referencing the local machine, and click OK.

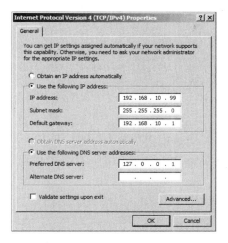

9. Click OK again to save the changes.

10. Close the Network Connections screen.

11. Launch the DNS Manager by clicking Start ➢ Administrative Tools ➢ DNS.

12. Right-click on the DNS service node, in this case SERVER1, and select Properties.

13. Select the Forwarders tab.

14. Click the Edit button to add new DNS forwarders.

15. Click where it reads Click Here To Add An IP Address Or DNS Name and enter the value 8.8.8.8.

16. Repeat step 15 adding the value 8.8.4.4. These two IP addresses point to Google's free DNS servers on the Internet for name resolution outside of your SharePoint.local zone.

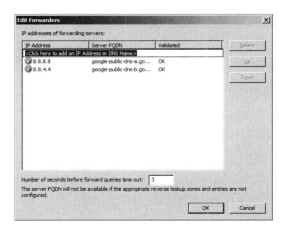

17. Click OK to save your changes.

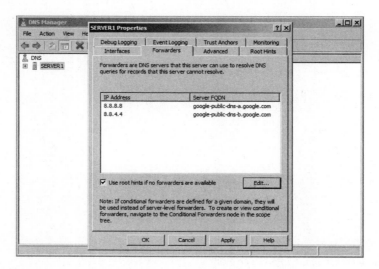

18. Click OK again in the SERVER1 Properties dialog to save your changes.

19. Close the DNS Manager tool.

Now that you have completed Exercise 2.4, your server is able to resolve DNS queries for the SharePoint.local zone and domain itself. It can also use the Internet DNS servers at 8.8.8.8 and 8.8.4.4 to resolve Internet domain names. These DNS servers are provided free to Internet users by Google. Several other free Internet DNS servers exist, and a list can usually be found by searching for **free Internet DNS servers** on your favorite search engine. Exercise 2.5 provides instructions for verification of proper DNS operation.

Verifying DNS Operation

In this exercise, verify proper DNS operations using the nslookup command.

1. Log onto the DNS server as an administrator.

2. Open a command prompt by clicking Start, typing **CMD**, and pressing Enter.

3. Execute the command **nslookup portal.SharePoint.local**. The command should resolve the FQDN of portal.SharePoint.local to 192.168.10.99 or the IP address you used for the host record.

4. Execute the command **nslookup www.TomCarpenter.net**. The command should resolve the IP address to an Internet address as opposed to an internal address.

5. If the DNS queries resolved correctly, you are ready to move on to the next phase of SharePoint server preparations, which is the Active Directory deployment. If they did not resolve correctly, rebooting will usually solve the problem; otherwise, go back through the steps in Exercises 2.1 through 2.4 and verify proper execution of the instructions.

AD DS

Active Directory Domain Services (AD DS) is Microsoft's network directory service. A network directory service contains the objects tracked and managed by the network. It includes objects such as users, groups, computers, servers, and printers. If you are already very familiar with AD DS, you can move on to the next section titled IIS; however, to perform the exercises throughout the book, an AD DS installation will be required and this section provides exercises for that installation. If you are not familiar with AD DS concepts, you should read through this section carefully. It explains the components that make up AD DS and the way in which SharePoint utilizes the AD DS components.

AD DS Architecture

There are a lot of important aspects to Active Directory Domain Services (AD DS or AD for short). Several objects are stored in the domain database and you need to understand these objects. Additionally, it's important to understand the domain structures, which include both a logical and a physical structure. Next, you should understand what the Global Catalog is and the role it plays in AD. Because an AD implementation can become large, you'll also need to understand the trust relationships that allow users in one domain to access resources in other domains. Finally, you should understand how DNS, which is also important to SharePoint implementations, is used to build the AD domain namespace. Let's examine each of these topics more closely.

AD is Microsoft's network directory service. A network directory service provides a centralized or distributed database of network objects, services, and configurations. This database is used for user logons, permission management, and tracking of events (auditing).

To understand AD, you will need to understand the different objects it contains and manages. These objects and services include:

- **Users:** The objects representing individual users on the network.

- **Groups:** The objects representing collections of users on the network.

- **Computers:** The devices used by the users for access to the network.

- **Domain controllers:** The servers that act as domain controllers, which provide authentication and authorization services to the AD domain.

- **Domain and forest roles:** Specialized roles played by domain controllers for better management of the AD objects and relationships between those objects.

- **Additional services:** Replication services allow data to be synchronized among all domain controllers. Group policies allow central control and administration of users and computers. User profiles may be stored on the servers and replicated. All of these are examples of the additional services AD offers.

Users and groups are discussed further in the later section titled "Creating Users and Groups." Before you can create these users and groups, you must have a basic understanding of AD terminology. These terms are used to describe AD and its operations:

Domains   A *domain* is defined as a group of computer systems (servers and clients) and network resources (printers, services, etc.) that share a like namespace. Windows 2000 through 2008 R2 domains use DNS namespaces. A domain acts as a security, replication, and administrative boundary.

Trees   A *tree* is a collection of domains that share the same root namespace. Domain trees share a single schema and Global Catalog. All domains in a tree automatically trust all other domains in the same tree through transitive trusts. (Trusts are discussed in more detail later in this section.)

Forests   A forest is one or more domain trees using the same Global Catalog but having different namespace roots. Even with one domain, both a forest and a tree exist in the thinking of Active Directory.

Sites   *Sites* are physical locations on your network, which are defined by IP subnets and site configuration objects in AD.

Domain Controllers   Domain controllers (DCs) are the servers that store the AD database and allow users to log onto the network. They also authorize users for access to other servers.

Like SharePoint itself, the AD includes a logical structure or architecture and a physical structure. You must be aware of these two basic domain structures. You should understand to what they refer and the impact they will have on your network.

The logical structure refers to the conceptual way an organization is divided into units and subunits. As an example, an organization may be separated into departments and divisions. These departments and divisions are reflected in AD with the use of groups and/or organizational units. Domains may also be used to implement a logical structure.

For example, you may have a domain named *corporate.local* and then departmental domains for each department such as *sales.corporate.local* and *hr.corporate.local*. When you use domains for the logical structure, instead of groups and organizational units, it is important to know that permission management will become more complicated. For example, when you want to give everyone on the network access to a resource, you will have to be sure and include the Domain Users group from each domain in your logical structure. If you can keep the domains to just one single domain, the single Domain Users group will always include all users.

The physical structure refers to the geographical structure of your network. It answers the question, where are your network resources located? This structure is reflected in AD with the use of sites. An AD network may consist of a single site or of multiple sites. A single domain may span multiple sites. A common mistake is to assume that you must have a separate AD domain for each site. In most cases, one or more domain controllers will be placed at each site, but a separate domain is not required.

 As you're probably beginning to understand, it is always best to limit the AD implementation to a single domain if possible. In some scenarios, such as very large organizations or distributed organizations with only slow WAN links, you may not be able to maintain a single domain; however, creating multiple domains should be a last resort and not a first impulse.

Another important AD concept is the Global Catalog (GC). The GC server replicates and stores AD information shared among all domains in the forest. The domain forest schema and the configuration data are included in this data subset. The GC provides for faster searches of the AD. It lists every object in a domain tree or forest; it only contains a partial list of the object attributes. Several important facts about the GC server should be considered during AD planning:

- It is both a domain controller and a GC server.
- The **first** domain controller in the forest is the GC server by default.
- If required, it can be moved to another server.
- A GC is not required at each physical location after Windows Server 2003 because of the group membership caching feature.
- By default, Active Directory clients cannot log on without a GC in a multidomain environment—though this can be changed with a registry modification on your domain controllers.

The next important component is the trust relationship. Trust relationships are important parts of your AD planning. By default, all Windows domains in a forest trust all other domains in the same forest, which means that users from any domain can be granted access to resources in any other domain in the forest. The trust is automatic and cannot be removed. The trusts that provide this default behavior are called transitive trusts. Transitive trusts pass trust through to the next level. For example, if research.sales.com trusts

`sales.com` and `sales.com` trusts `marketing.sales.com`, then `research.sales`
`.com` trusts `marketing.sales.com` through the `sales.com` domain. While that may sound a
bit confusing, it is really very simple. All domains in an AD domain tree trust the domain
above them and any domains below them. These trusts are transitive and, therefore, every
domain in the tree and forest ends up trusting every other domain in the tree and forest.

Don't be alarmed. The automatic trust relationships do not grant access to
resources in other domains automatically. But administrators may grant
access when required.

In very large forests, shortcut trusts between specific domains in the forest may be used.
Normally, authentication travels up one domain tree and down another, through the use
of transitive trusts, for a user to be granted access to a resource in a domain in a different
tree within the forest. The authentication process can be optimized by creating a shortcut
trust directly between the two domains. Creating a shortcut trust requires the same steps as
creating an explicit or direct trust—they are technically the same thing.

Figure 2.2 shows the benefit of a shortcut trust relationship. Notice that three levels of
authentication are required without the shortcut trust. With the shortcut trust, a single
direct authentication link is available.

FIGURE 2.2 Shortcut trust relationships demonstrated

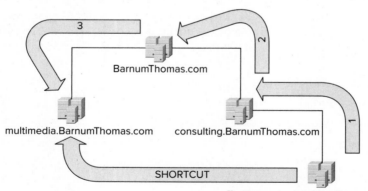

DNS, covered earlier in the "DNS" section of this chapter, is also important to AD.
When the IP networks were initially implemented, the HOSTS file was used to resolve
domain and host names. This file-based method became a problem as the number of clients
on the IP networks grew into the thousands and eventually millions. Every client required a
local or network-accessible copy of the HOSTS file. Because of this dilemma, the concept of
DNS was developed to provide a name resolution service for IP networks.

DNS, or the Domain Naming System (also called Domain Name Service), provides host name resolution from a central database that is queried by client computers on the network. Microsoft supports DNS through the DNS Server Role service and DNS is required by Active Directory. The Windows Server 2003 and later implementations of DNS meet the specifications of RFC 2136 for dynamic updates.

It is important that you understand how Active Directory utilizes the DNS service. The following list details the ways in which Active Directory clients depend on the DNS service:

- DNS provides the names of domain controllers (DC) to the client computers so they can locate a DC and log on.

- The services offered on the DC are provided through SRC records in DNS.

- The port to use for the service is provided, though port 389 is typically used for directory service queries.

Clearly, DNS is an important part of a Windows Active Directory environment. Windows domain hierarchies simply mirror the DNS domain hierarchy you configured through DNS in Exercise 2.2.

AD DS Installation

The first step required to install AD DS, once a DNS infrastructure is in place, is to add the AD DS role to a Windows Server machine. In Exercise 2.6, you will add the AD DS role to the server.

EXERCISE 2.6

Adding the AD DS Role

In this exercise, you will add the AD DS server role to the server on which you previously installed the DNS server role. By the end of Chapter 4, you will have a single server that runs DNS, AD DS, IIS, SQL Server, and SharePoint 2010, which is a perfect installation for lab testing and development procedures, and you will have learned about the SharePoint products.

1. Log onto the Windows server onto which you previously installed the DNS server role as an administrator.

2. Click Start ➢ Administrative Tools ➢ Server Manager.

3. Click the Add Roles link to add a new role to the server.

4. If the Before You Begin screen is displayed, click Next.

5. On the Select Server Roles screen, choose Active Directory Domain Services and click Next.

EXERCISE 2.6 *(continued)*

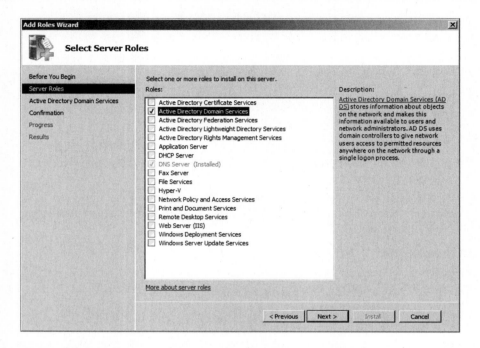

6. After reading the information on the Active Directory Domain Services screen, click Next.

7. Click Install to install the new role.

8. The installation process will complete in a few moments. When it completes, click Close to exit the Add Roles Wizard.

9. Close the Server Manager.

Now that the AD DS role is installed on the server, you can configure the AD DS domain. Exercise 2.7 provides the instructions for doing this.

EXERCISE 2.7

Creating the *SharePoint.local* Domain

In this exercise, you will run DCPROMO.EXE to create the SharePoint.local domain. You should have performed all previous exercises in this chapter in order for this exercise to work properly.

1. Log onto the server onto which you added the AD DS server role in Exercise 2.6 as an administrator.

2. Click Start and type **dcpromo** and press Enter to launch the Active Directory Domain Services Installation Wizard.

3. On the Welcome screen, click Next to begin the AD installation.

4. Read the information on the Operating System Compatibility screen and click Next.

5. On the Choose a Deployment Configuration screen, choose Create A New Domain In A New Forest and click Next.

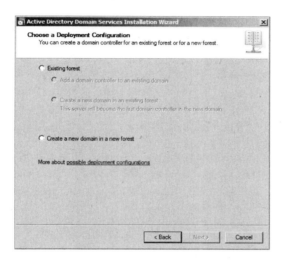

6. On the Name The Forest Root Domain screen, enter the value **SharePoint.local** into the FQDN Of The Forest Root Domain field and click Next.

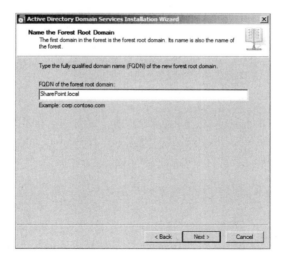

EXERCISE 2.7 *(continued)*

7. On the Set Forest Functional Level screen, because this is a lab deployment and you are not concerned about backward compatibility, choose Windows Server 2008 R2 for the Forest Functional Level value and click Next. Be patient. The Examining DNS Configuration process, which begins when you click Next, can take several minutes in some cases.

8. On the Additional Domain Controller Options screen, you should see that the DNS Server service is already installed. Click Next.

9. On the Create DNS Delegation screen, choose No, Do Not Create The DNS Delegation. This is the only DNS zone and AD domain in your lab and DNS delegation is not required. Click Next.

10. Accept the default settings on the Location For Database, Log Files And SYSVOL screen and click Next.

11. On the Directory Services Restore Mode Administrator Password screen, enter a password at least seven-characters long into the Password and Confirm Password fields. (The password must consist of at least one uppercase letter, one lowercase letter, and one digit.) Then click Next. (The password value of **Password1** is always a good choice for lab installations because it is easy to remember and security is not typically a huge concern.)

12. On the Summary screen, review the selections and then click Next to begin the AD domain installation.

13. When the Active Directory Domain Services Installation Wizard installation screen is displayed, check the Reboot On Completion check box so that the server will automatically reboot when installation is complete. (If you receive a message stating that the DNS zone could not be created, click OK. This message is normal because you created the DNS zone in an earlier exercise.)

After performing the steps in Exercise 2.7 and rebooting the server, you can log on as the SharePoint\Administrator user with the same password the Administrator account used before the AD domain installation. You can launch Server Manager to verify that the AD DS role is functioning correctly. In the Server Manager, you should see a new node under the Roles node that is named Active Directory Domain Services.

Now that the AD DS installation is complete, you can integrate DNS into the AD database. Integrated DNS is more secure than the file-based DNS, and it also allows for automatic backups of your DNS database when the AD database is backed up. Exercise 2.8 provides instructions for integrating DNS into the AD database and enabling secure-only updates.

EXERCISE 2.8

Integrating DNS with AD

In this exercise, you will integrate the DNS installation with AD. This will allow for more secure updates and simpler backups of the DNS database.

1. Log onto the server as a domain administrator.

2. Click Start ➤ Administrative Tools ➤ DNS.

3. Expand SERVER1 ➤ Forward Lookup Zones ➤ SharePoint.local in the left pane.

4. Right-click on the SharePoint.local node and select Properties.

5. On the General tab, click the Change button for the Type property, which is currently set to Primary.

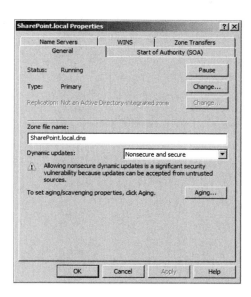

6. In the Change Zone Type dialog, check the box for Store The Zone In Active Directory and click OK. When asked if you want the zone to become Active Directory integrated, click Yes.

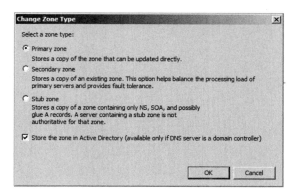

7. Click the Apply button in the SharePoint.local Properties dialog.

EXERCISE 2.8 *(continued)*

8. In the Dynamic Updates field of the SharePoint.local Properties dialog, choose the Secure Only option and click OK.

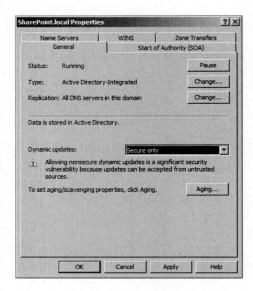

9. The configuration of the DNS zone is complete. You may exit the DNS Manager.

Creating Users and Groups

After completing the preceding exercises in this chapter, you will have a working AD DS implementation. DNS is up and running, which is an important component for SharePoint implementations. However, AD DS is currently empty for all intents and purposes. No custom users or groups have been created. You want to create the following users for your lab environment:

- Tom Carpenter
- Fred Peters
- Barney Stone
- Betty Stone
- Wilma Peters

In Exercise 2.9, you will create all five users. The exercise provides specific instructions for creating the Tom Carpenter account and then allows you to create the remaining four accounts based on the same process while simply changing the usernames. Because groups are used to identify different permissions and rights, the accounts will be created identically at this point.

EXERCISE 2.9

Creating User Accounts

In this exercise, you will create basic user accounts for Tom Carpenter, Fred Peters, Barney Stone, Betty Stone, and Wilma Peters. These are simply randomly chosen names (okay, maybe not so random) and have no significant meaning. In your real environment, you will create names based on actual users.

1. Log onto the AD DS server that you configured in the previous exercises in this chapter as an administrator.

2. Click Start ≻ Administrative Tools ≻ Active Directory Users And Computers.

3. In the left pane, expand SharePoint.local ≻ Users.

4. Right-click on Users and select New ≻ User.

5. In the New Object - User dialog, enter the following values:

   ■ First Name: **Tom**

   ■ Last Name: **Carpenter**

   ■ Full Name: **Tom Carpenter**

   ■ User Logon Name: **tom**

   ■ User Logon Name (pre-Windows 2000): **tom**

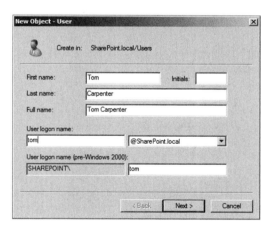

6. With the values entered, click Next.

7. On the Password Management screen, enter the Password and Confirm Password value of **Password1**. Deselect User Must Change Password At Next Logon and select Password Never Expires so that you will not have to worry about changing passwords as you use this lab installation. When the settings are configured, click Next.

8.   Click Finish to create the account for Tom Carpenter.

9.   Repeat steps 4 through 8 for the additional user accounts, changing the name values where appropriate. (You may use the same password for each account, because AD does not require that different users have different passwords.)

With the user accounts created, all that remains is the creation of groups. In a production environment, you should go through an extensive group planning process as documented at http://technet.microsoft.com/en-us/library/bb727067.aspx. Because this process is typically performed by network administrators and not specifically by SharePoint administrators, it will not be covered in detail within this book. However, if you are responsible for the group-planning process as well, the referenced link will be helpful.

When you are implementing a production environment, you will use better passwords than those used here. A lab setting is usually a less-secure setting because no critical data is located there. If you are using real data that is sensitive to theft in your lab environment, the security of the lab should be stronger.

For this deployment, you will create the following custom groups and group members used within SharePoint 2010 (the SharePoint 2010 installation will also create additional groups in the AD database):

- SharePoint Organizational Managers (Tom)
- SharePoint List Managers (Tom, Betty, and Wilma)

Exercise 2.10 provides the instructions for creating groups. You will create both groups referenced previously.

EXERCISE 2.10

Creating Groups

In this exercise, you will create two groups. The first group is the SharePoint Organizational Managers group. The second group is the SharePoint List Managers group.

1. Log onto the AD DS server that you configured in the previous exercises in this chapter as an administrator.

2. Click Start ➤ Administrative Tools ➤ Active Directory Users And Computers.

3. In the left pane, expand SharePoint.local ➤ Users.

4. Right-click on Users and select New ➤ Group.

5. Enter the Group Name value of **SharePoint Organizational Managers**. Accept the default Group Scope of Global and the Group Type of Security. Click OK to create the group.

6. Right-click on Users and select New ➤ Group.

7. Enter the Group Name value of **SharePoint List Managers**. Accept the default Group Scope of Global and the Group Type of Security. Click OK to create the group.

Now that the two groups exist, you can create the group memberships. Exercise 2.11 provides instructions for this process.

EXERCISE 2.11

Managing Group Memberships

In this exercise, you will add users to groups. Tom Carpenter will be added to the SharePoint Organizational Managers group through his account properties interface. Tom, Betty, and Wilma will be added to the SharePoint List Managers group through the group properties interface. This exercise provides two methods for creating group memberships: through the user accounts and through the group settings.

1. Log onto the AD DS server that you configured in the previous exercises in this chapter as an administrator.

2. Click Start ➤ Administrative Tools ➤ Active Directory Users and Computers.

3. In the left pane, expand SharePoint.local ➤ Users.

4. Double-click on the Tom Carpenter account object.

5. In the Tom Carpenter Properties dialog, select the Member Of tab.

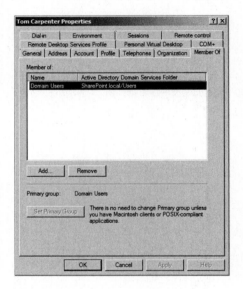

6. Click the Add button to add a new group membership.

7. In the Enter The Object Names To Select field, enter the value **SharePoint Organizational Managers** and click the Check Names button. The text you entered will become underlined to indicate that the group was located in AD. Click OK to add Tom Carpenter to the SharePoint Organizational Managers group.

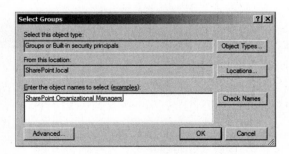

8. Click OK in the Tom Carpenter Properties dialog to exit the properties for the user account.

9. Double-click on the SharePoint List Managers group to add Tom, Betty, and Wilma to this group.

10. In the SharePoint List Managers Properties dialog, select the Members tab.

11. Click the Add button to add new members.

12. Type the values **Tom Carpenter; Betty Stone; Wilma Peters;** (including the semicolons) in the Enter The Object Names To Select field and click Check Names to look up the full names in AD, and then click OK to add the new members. (When you click Check Names, the full logon name values will be entered for you automatically.)

13. With the new members added to the group, click OK to exit the SharePoint List Managers Properties dialog.

The users and groups created in this chapter are for demonstration purposes only. You will not be required to create these exact users and groups in a production SharePoint implementation; but you will use the same processes to create the users and groups you need for your environment.

AD DS Groups and SharePoint Permissions

It's important to understand that SharePoint 2010 uses the user accounts and groups from AD for permission management within the SharePoint infrastructure. Security is discussed in greater detail in Chapter 5, "Planning the Security Architecture," but you should be aware of the AD interactions at this point.

AD provides two basic kinds of groups: security groups and distribution groups. Security groups may be assigned permissions and distribution groups may not. For this reason, only security groups may be added to SharePoint groups. SharePoint groups define the roles (collections of rights and permissions) within the SharePoint environment. AD security groups and users are added to the SharePoint groups to provide the AD users with permissions within SharePoint. This hierarchy is represented in Figure 2.3.

FIGURE 2.3 The AD group and SharePoint group hierarchy

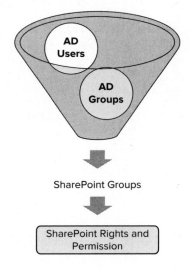

IIS

Internet Information Services (IIS) 7.0 or 7.5 is the web server component used by SharePoint 2010. Effectively, SharePoint is simply an application (albeit a complex one) that runs on the web server. Windows Server 2008 ships with IIS 7.0, and Windows Server 2008 R2 ships with IIS 7.5. From the perspective of a SharePoint administration role, you should understand how to add the IIS or web server role to a Windows server and how to perform basic administration tasks. Both topics are addressed in this section.

Adding the Web Server Role

Before you can run SharePoint or administer IIS, you will have to add the web server (IIS) role. The SharePoint installation processes can add this role for you or you can install it before you install SharePoint. Either way IIS must be on the servers that run the WFE and the application server roles for SharePoint.

Exercise 2.12 provides instructions for adding the IIS role on Windows Server 2008 R2. The process is the same for Windows Server 2008.

EXERCISE 2.12

Adding the IIS Server or Web Server Role

In this exercise, you will add the web server (IIS) role to a Windows Server 2008 R2 server.

1. Log onto the Windows server as an administrator.

2. Launch the Server Manager.

3. Click the Add Roles link to add a new role.

4. If the Before You Begin screen is displayed, click Next.

5. Choose the Application Server and Web Server (IIS) roles from the list of roles. If you are asked to add features required for the application server, click Add Required Features. Click Next.

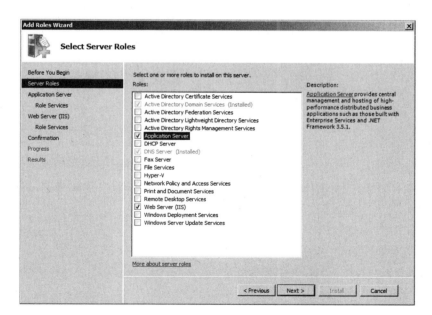

6. On the Introduction To Application Server screen, read as much information as desired and then click Next.

7. On the Select Role Services screen, ensure that the following services are selected (if any dialogs pop up asking to add roles and features required by the component, simply select Add Required Role Services or Add Required Features):

- .NET Framework 3.5.1

- Web Server (IIS) Support

- TCP Port Sharing

- HTTP Activation

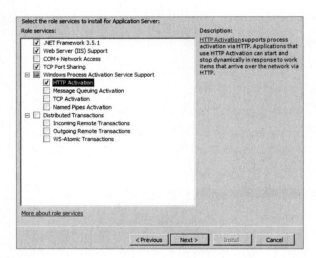

8. After all of the listed role services are selected, click Next.

9. On the Introduction To Web Server (IIS) screen, read as much information as desired and then click Next.

10. Accept the default selection of role services on the Select Role Services screen and click Next.

11. Review the Confirm Installation Selections screen and click Install. Processing will take several minutes.

12. When the processing is complete, click Close to complete the installation.

13. Close Server Manager.

14. Restart the server to refresh all services after this major installation. This task is not required, but it is recommended.

After performing the steps in Exercise 2.12, the IIS server will be up and running; however, no real websites exist. In fact, if you access the server, you will see a default screen that simply says welcome in several languages and has the IIS 7 name in the center. You have to create the sites and pages that will be served by the IIS web server. In fact, the primary function of SharePoint is to offer up web pages that provide access to backend content used for collaboration and information sharing.

Basic IIS Administration Tasks

Of course, the most common initial task required when working with IIS is the creation of websites. In IIS, websites run in application pools. Application pools are simply processes in which websites run. These processes include configuration settings for features such as .NET utilization and the account context in which the process will run. Exercise 2.13 provides instructions for creating a new website in a new application pool.

EXERCISE 2.13

Creating a Website and an Application Pool

In this exercise, you will create a new website in the IIS server and a new application pool for that website.

1. Log onto the server as an administrator.

2. Click Start ➤ Administrative Tools ➤ Internet Information Services (IIS) Manager.

3. Expand the SERVER1 node in the Connections pane and then expand the Sites child node.

4. Right-click on the Sites node and select New Site.

5. In the Add Web Site dialog, enter a Site Name of **Test** and accept the default matching Application Pool name.

6. For the Physical Path field, click the Build button (the button with the . . . on it), expand the C: drive in the Browse For Folder dialog, and click Make New Folder. Enter a folder named **test** and click OK.

7. In the Binding section of the Add Web Site dialog, change the Port field value to **8099** and then click OK.

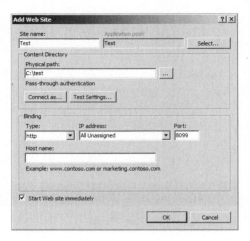

8. At this point, the Test website exists and the Test application pool exists; however, if you open it in your web browser (by navigating to http://localhost:8099), you will receive an HTTP Error 403.14, which means you are forbidden access. This is because no default document exists in the folder. (IIS supports several default documents without customizing the configuration, including the following: default.asp, index .htm, index.html, iisstart.htm, index.php, and default.aspx.)

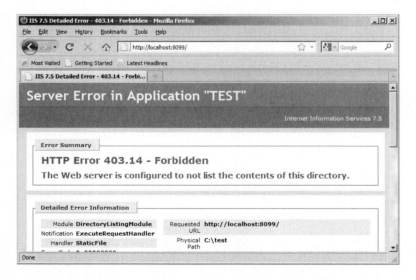

9. To create a basic default document, select and expand the Test node under the Sites node in the Connections pane.

10. In the right-side Actions pane, click Explore.

11. The root of the Test website is opened in Windows Explorer. Right-click in the empty folder area and select New ➢ Text Document.

12. Change the document name to index.htm. (If file extensions are not being displayed, click Organize ➢ Folder And Search Options, select the View tab, and deselect Hide Extensions For Known File Types.)

13. Right-click on the `index.htm` document and select Open With ➢ Notepad.

14. Enter the following code into the file to create a very basic test page:

```
<html>
<head>
<title>Test</test>
</head>
<body>
Test Page
</body></html>
```

15. Save the file by pressing Ctrl+S.

16. Exit Notepad.

17. Load the site `http://localhost:8099` in your browser again and notice that a valid page now loads.

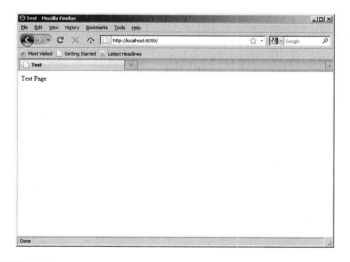

In Exercise 2.13, both the website and the application pool were created in a single process. You can alternatively create an application pool manually and then create the website and place it in that application pool.

For SharePoint administrators, one of the most important administration tasks to understand is application pool recycling. It is not uncommon for an administrator to have to restart the application pool that runs a SharePoint site because resources are consumed over time and can eventually reach a point that is too much for the server to handle. For example, if thousands of users use a SharePoint site, the caching of documents and web pages could eventually consume large amounts of memory. A quick recycle of the application pool or website can refresh the memory. Additionally, third-party add-ons could have memory leaks or other problems requiring a refresh. Exercise 2.14 provides instructions for this task.

EXERCISE 2.14

Recycling a Website or Application Pool

In this exercise, you will first learn how to recycle an application pool. Next, you will see how to restart a website in that application pool.

1. Log onto the server as an administrator.

2. Click Start ≻ Administrative Tools ≻ Internet Information Services (IIS) Manager.

3. Expand the SERVER1 node in the Connections pane.

4. Click on the Application Pools node.

5. In the center area, labeled Application Pools, click on the Test application pool.

6. Click the Recycle link in the Actions pane to stop and restart the Test application pool. The recycle process can happen very quickly for basic websites, so don't be alarmed if nothing appears to happen. If you want to be sure it is happening, click the Stop link and then the Start link to get the same results as the Recycle link.

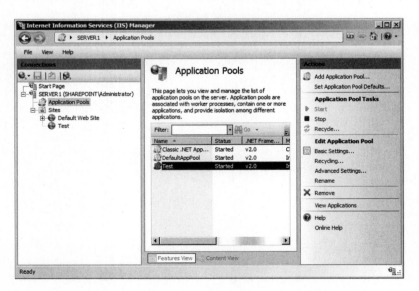

7. To perform recycling for a website within an application pool, you use a different link. First expand SERVER1 ➢ Sites ➢ Test in the Connections pane.

8. Click the Restart link in the Actions pane under the Manage Web Site section.

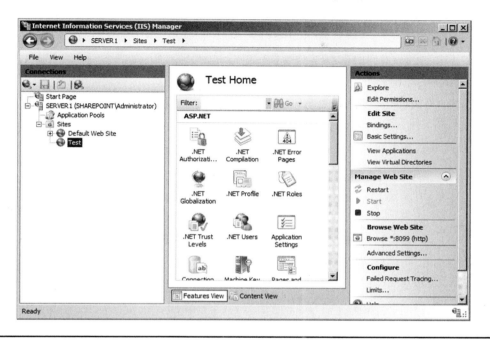

If you want to delete the Test website and application pool, you may do so at this time. They will not be used for any future exercises in this book and were created here only to provide experience in creating websites and application pools. To delete the website and application pool, simply right-click on each one and select Remove. You will also need to manually delete the C:\test folder after removing the website and application pool in the IIS Manager.

In many deployments, IIS is used to provide the SMTP (Simple Mail Transfer Protocol) service so that SharePoint 2010 can send email alerts and notifications. SMTP is the Internet standard for sending email from server to server. It is defined in RFC (request for comments) 5321. In Exercise 2.15, you will learn how to add the SMTP service to your IIS server installation.

EXERCISE 2.15

Adding the SMTP Service

In this exercise, you will add the SMTP service so that it can be utilized by SharePoint 2010 when it is installed. SMTP is a feature instead of a role, so you will use the Add Feature Wizard to add the SMTP server.

1. Log onto the server as an administrator.

2. Launch the Server Manager.

3. Double-click the Features node in the left pane to expand it.

4. Click the Add Features link to add a new feature.

5. Scroll down in the list and select SMTP Server. When you select the SMTP Server, you are asked to add additional required services. Simply click Add Required Role Services. Click Next to move to the next screen in the wizard.

6. On the Introduction To Web Server (IIS) screen, read as much information as you want and then click Next.

7. Accept the defaults on the Select Role Services screen and click Next.

8. Click Install on the Confirm Installation Selections screen.

9. On the Installation Results screen, click Close to complete the installation.

Although SMTP is no longer "tied" to IIS in Windows Server 2008 R2, you will still use the IIS (6.0) Manager console to manage it. Additionally, the SMTP service requires that the IIS 6.0 Compatibility service be on the server. Exercise 2.15 will result in these tools and services being installed for you.

Now that the SMTP service is installed, you can configure it for operations. You will need to configure the SMTP domain and the authentication used by the server. Exercise 2.16 provides instructions for configuring SMTP.

EXERCISE 2.16

Configuring the SMTP Service

In this exercise, you will configure the SMTP domain and authentication for the SMTP service installed in Exercise 2.15.

1. Log onto the server as an administrator.

2. Click Start ➢ Administrative Tools ➢ Internet Information Services (IIS) 6.0 Manager.

3. Expand the SERVER1 ➢ [SMTP Virtual Server #1] nodes.

4. By default the SMTP service is not started. Right-click on the [SMTP Virtual Server #1] node and select Start to start the service.

5. To modify the SMTP server properties, right-click on the [SMTP Virtual Server #1] node and select Properties.

6. On the General tab, determine the IP addresses on which the SMTP mail server will respond, choose whether to limit the number of concurrent connections, and set a connection time-out value. You may also choose to enable logging on this tab, which will keep a log of email attempts.

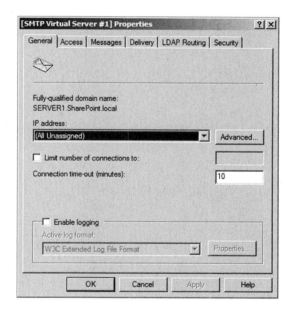

7. On the Access tab, you may define who can use the SMTP server by specifying an authentication method using the Authentication button. The default authentication information settings allow anonymous emails to be sent using the SMTP server, which could result in an attacker using the server as a mail relay server for sending SPAM. You can also control connections by IP addresses and domain names, and you can choose whether or not to allow relay of email through this SMTP server, which would even prevent authenticated users from using the server as a relay server. The following images show the Access tab and the dialog displayed when you click the Authentication button.

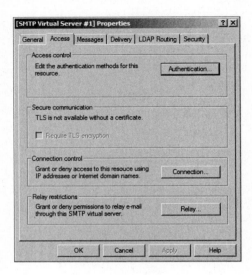

8. The Messages and Delivery tabs are used to constrain message size, message volume, and the number of delivery retries attempted, as displayed in the following images.

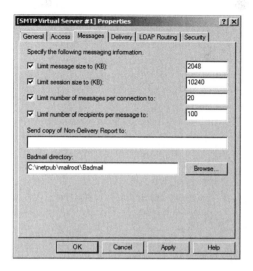

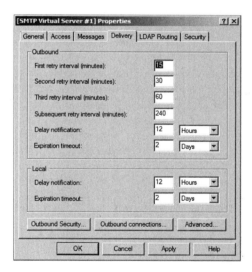

9. After configuring the SMTP server settings to your needs, click OK to save the changes and exit the dialog.

In small SharePoint 2010 deployments, the IIS SMTP service may be all you use for sending email notifications from the SharePoint sites to the users. In larger deployments, you will likely have an Exchange server or some other email server that can send the SMTP messages from the SharePoint server. Knowing about this SMTP service can really assist you during lab developments and training and programming implementations.

SQL Server

SQL Server is a database server. Simply put, a *database* is a place for your data. In the past, the word *database* was written as two words. The word *data* is defined as meaningful information, and it may include words, numbers, letters, and binary information such as an image. The word *base* means foundation or place. For example, a concrete slab is a base for building a home, and first base is the initial goal of any batter in baseball. It is the place they want to reach without being tagged. Putting these two definitions together provides the simple definition given to you in the beginning of this paragraph: a database is a place to put your data.

 A more technical definition of a database would be something like this: A computer *database* is (usually) a structured collection of information stored according to a defined model and accessible through standard or proprietary database communications languages. Now, do you see why I define it as a place to put your data?

It is important that you do not confuse the database itself with the database management system. The database management system is the software that manages the integrity of the databases and access to those databases. The database is separate from the database management system, and it can usually be transferred from one computer running the compatible database management system to another computer running the same database management system. For example, you can move a SharePoint content database from one SQL server to another SQL server (keeping in mind that you would have to redirect the SharePoint sites to the new location). SQL Server is the database management system, and the database is the storage location within that system for your data.

A SQL server is the most important component in a SharePoint deployment, although it is often overlooked. It is the primary storage location for all of your configuration and content data. For this reason, it will be covered in greater depth in this chapter than other components.

To understand SQL Server as it relates to SharePoint implementations, you should understand the following topics at a minimum:

- SQL Server core features
- Database system components
- Data read and write methods
- SQL Server deployment planning
- Installing SQL Server
- Understanding the SQL Server Management Studio
- Querying databases

SQL Server Core Features

Several core features have existed in the SQL Server product going all the way back to SQL Server 6.5 and earlier. These important features include:

- Support for concurrent users
- Transactional processing
- Large database support
- Advanced storage mechanisms
- Large object support
- Replication

Support for concurrent users is provided using worker threads and connections. Each connection receives its own process ID and can be managed individually (for example, a single connection can be killed). The number of concurrent users that can be supported will be determined by the resources available in the server, such as memory, processors, network cards, and hard drives. This concurrency allows multiple SharePoint application servers and WFE servers to work with the same SQL Server databases at the same time.

Transactional processing ensures that the database maintains consistency. For example, in a banking application, you would not want to allow a transfer from savings to checking to take place in such a way that the money is removed from savings but doesn't make it into checking. Transactional processing ensures that the entire transaction is successful or none of the transaction components are allowed. Transactions can be implicit or explicit, and all changes are treated as transactions. In SharePoint installations, this transaction processing ensures that two users cannot add identical items to the same list at the same time. This is just one example. The transactional nature of SQL Server also assists with everything from configuration databases to content databases.

SQL Server supports large databases. SQL Server 2000 allowed for database sizes as large as 1,048,516 terabytes, which is equivalent to 1 exabyte in size, which is very large. Of course, finding hardware that can handle a database that size is a different story. Interestingly, according to Microsoft's documentation, the maximum allowed database size was reduced in SQL Server 2005 and 2008 to 524,272 terabytes. This size constraint is still very large at 524 petabytes, so it will not likely be a problem anytime soon. Very few databases exceed 5 to 10 terabytes in size today, and few SharePoint databases will exceed 1 terabyte.

The storage mechanisms provided by SQL Server allow databases to be stored in single files or multiple files. The database can be spread across multiple files located on multiple storage volumes. By using filegroups, the database administrator (DBA) or SharePoint administrator can control on which file tables will be placed. These storage mechanisms are far more advanced than those available in a simple database system like Microsoft Access.

Large objects (LOBs), up to 2 GB, can be stored in SQL Server databases. Depending on the application, it may be better to store the large objects outside of the database and simply reference them in the database; however, internal storage is supported. You may store large amounts of text in the text data type—up to 2 GB of text. You may store any binary data in the image data type, which also allows for up to 2 GB of data to be stored in a single record.

Sometimes, you need to distribute your data to multiple locations. You may need to provide localized reporting servers at branch offices or you may need to aggregate new data from several remote offices into a central reporting server. Whatever the motivation behind data distribution, SQL Server offers replication as a solution. SQL Server 6.5 supported basic replication features. With each version since then, more capabilities were added. For example, SQL Server 2005 added support for replication over HTTP and SQL Server 2008 adds a new graphical tool for creating peer-to-peer replication maps and an enhanced version of the Replication Monitor tool.

These core features, and more, have been with SQL Server for well over ten years, and they continue to evolve and improve. They have a tremendous impact on the roles that SQL Server can play within your organization, and they can help you decide between it and other database systems—particularly single-user database systems. Of course, with SharePoint 2010, SQL Server is the only database system you can use as your primary SharePoint data storage location.

Database System Components

SQL Server is a complex system and entire volumes are written to help you understand its architecture and functionality. As a SharePoint 2010 administrator, you should understand the basic components used by a SQL Server. This section provides an overview of these components.

First, you should understand that a user accesses databases through the SQL Server Services and has no direct access to the physical database files. This is reflected in Figure 2.4 through the notation indicating that access to the MDF data file is denied, while access to the SQL Server Services is granted. All access to data within SQL Server databases occurs through the Database Engine services for standard application access.

Second, you should understand that a database application running on a client computer impersonates the user running that application. This means that the application can do whatever the user running the application can do. SharePoint 2010 works a little differently here. The SharePoint application is the client to the SQL Server content databases, but it uses a single managed account for access to the SQL server. This way, individual user permissions are managed by the SharePoint application, and the managed account with access to the content databases is unrestricted. SharePoint permission management and implementation is much simpler this way. Otherwise, every single SharePoint user would also have to exist as a user for every single SQL Server database.

With this general understanding of SQL Server, you can begin to review the components that make up a SQL Server data-access process (or application). In Figure 2.4 you see the basic components involved in a typical SQL Server 2008 or 2008 R2 application. As you can see, database access is more complex with a server-based system than the access provided by a single-user system, such as Microsoft Access. The following components must be understood:

- Database server
- SQL Server Services
- Logical databases
- Data files
- Transaction logs
- Buffer memory

FIGURE 2.4   SQL Server represented in a logical architecture

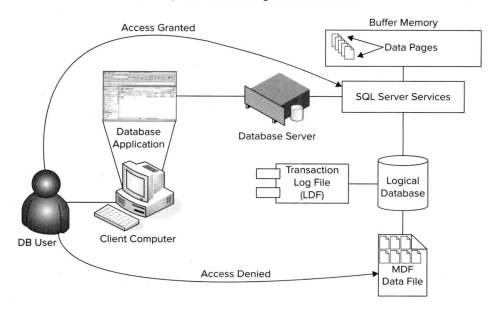

Database Server   The database server will run a compatible version of Windows Server. SQL Server 2008 supports several versions of Windows Server, and it does operate differently depending on the version used. Windows XP and later clients as well as Windows Server 2003 and later servers can all run SQL Server 2008. However, enhanced security features are available when you install SQL Server 2008 on a Windows Server 2008 or later server. If you choose to install the database management system on Windows Server 2003 or Windows XP, the operating systems must be running service pack 2 or higher. In addition, with SharePoint deployments, SQL Server must run on a 64-bit edition of Windows because the 64-bit edition of SQL Server must be used.

Along with selecting the proper operating system, you must ensure that the users requiring access to the SQL server have access to the Windows server. Think of this structure as a layered approach. Before the users can access a database, they must have access to the SQL Server Services. Before the users can access the SQL Server Services, they must have access to the server. Three layers protect your database and, when configured properly, can provide functionality that supports multiple databases used by different users on the same instance in the same server.

The most important thing to remember is that the users must have access to the database server first and then the database services on that server. Starting with Windows 2000

Server, Windows servers have supported a Group Policy right named *Access this computer from the network*. The policy is still in Windows Server 2008 R2, and the users who need access to the databases stored on a server must be granted this right. You can grant the right through Windows groups so that you are not required to add each individual user. For SharePoint 2010 deployments, the context (user account) in which the WFE and application server application pool runs must have access to the database server.

SQL Server Services   Several services are used to provide the various functions of SQL Server. The two most frequently used are the SQL Server service (also known as the Database Engine) and the SQL Server Agent service. The SQL Server service for the default instance is named MSSQLSERVER in SQL Server 2008 and is sometimes more completely called the SQL Server Database Services service. The service shows up as SQL Server (MSSQLSERVER) in the Services management tool, but the name MSSQLSERVER is assigned to the service by default and used with the NET STOP command at the command line. When you run multiple instances of SQL Server, each instance runs its own services. The SQL Server service is named MSSQL$Instance_Name for a named instance and shows up in the Services management tool as SQL Server (Instance_Name). Figure 2.5 shows these services running with a default instance and a named instance, which is named Marketing. The core functionality of SQL Server data storage and retrieval is performed by the SQL Server service.

FIGURE 2.5   SQL Server Services displayed in the Services management interface

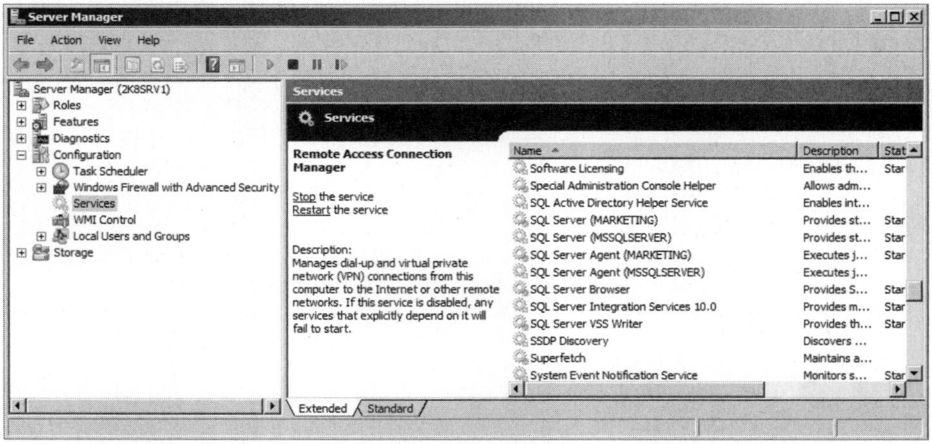

The SQL Server Agent service is used to monitor the databases and database server. It is also used to automate maintenance and administration tasks through the use of jobs. The SQL Server Agent service is named SQL Server Agent (MSSQLSERVER) for the default instance and SQL Server Agent (MARKETING) for the Marketing instance.

As depicted in Figure 2.4, all user database access occurs through the SQL Server service. Users do not have direct access to the physical data files that store the databases. These

MDF and NDF files are accessed by the SQL Server service on behalf of the users. Since the users do not have access to the physical data files, the system is more secure than a single-user database system that does require the user to have access to the database files.

Logical Databases   The database is referenced as a logical database in Figure 2.4. The reasons for this are twofold. First, a database may be stored as one physical file or as several files. To reduce confusion, the database that the users access is referred to as the logical database. The database appears to be a single entity and the users are unaware of the actual storage method used for the data. We can refer to this apparent single entity as a database or a logical database and both terms are acceptable. Modern databases are frequently built from several underlying files.

Second, users never access the actual database. They feel like they are accessing the database, but they are actually communicating with the SQL Server service, which is representing the database to the users based on the users' permissions and not based on what is literally in the database. For example, some users may only be able to read data through views that have been implemented by the DBA. To these users, the database "looks like" the representation provided by the views; however, a real physical database exists beneath this representation.

If you prefer to think of the database without this logical conceptualization, that is fine. Just remember to consider that different users may see the database very differently. Also, remember that users never access the database, but they interact with a representation of the database provided to them by the SQL Server service and the SQL Server service accesses the database on their behalf.

Data Files   The actual data stored in your database must be placed on a physical disk somewhere. SQL Server uses a default data file extension of MDF for the master data file and NDF for additional database files. Databases always use one MDF file and may use one or more NDF files. The MDF file contains the schema information or the structure for the database objects.

The data files are structured using pages and extents. A data page is 8 kilobytes (8,192 bytes) in size and provides up to 8,060 bytes for an individual record consisting of standard data types. When eight pages are grouped together, they form an extent. The result is a 64 kilobyte extent. SQL Server allocates space in data files on an extent-by-extent basis, but the actual data is stored and retrieved from the individual 8 kilobyte data pages. The extents may be uniform (the entire extent belongs to a single table or index) or mixed (the extent is shared among up to eight different tables or indexes).

SQL Server database data is never modified directly in the physical database files at processing time. You will understand this statement better after you learn about buffer memory in the next few pages, but it is very important that you understand this concept. Without this understanding, you'll never be able to grasp how SQL Server uses transaction logs for automatic recovery or how to best optimize a database. If you assume data modifications are made directly in the data file, you may focus solely on hard drive performance; however, when you know that data modifications happen in memory and understand how that buffer memory is used, you will know that memory optimization can often have a greater impact on database performance.

Transaction Logs   Transaction logs are used by every database attached to a SQL Server instance. If you've worked with SQL Server for awhile, you may have heard the rumor that Simple Recovery databases do not use a transaction log. This statement is not correct. Even databases in the Simple Recovery model use a transaction log. They simply wrap around to the beginning of the log and overwrite the oldest transactions instead of preserving them between backups. Why does a Simple Recovery database still use a transaction log? To grasp the answer to this question, you must understand the three primary benefits of a transaction log–based database system.

Database Atomicity   *Atomicity* is a database system term that means all tasks in a transaction are completed successfully or no task is performed. The transaction log assists with atomicity in that every step in the transaction is entered in the transaction log, but if a step fails all previous steps can be removed (rolled back). The transaction log is essential because many transactions may be too large to completely perform in memory.

Automatic Recovery   Automatic recovery occurs when the SQL Server service starts. During startup, the service looks in the transaction log for any transactions that are completely entered in the log but have not been committed. Data is committed to the physical MDF file only when a checkpoint occurs. The automatic recovery process uses checkpoints and transaction commits to determine which transactions should be executed again (rolled forward) and which should be ignored (rolled back).

Disaster Recovery   Disaster recovery is a manual process performed by an administrator. Assuming your data (MDF and NDF files) is on one physical drive and your transaction log (LDF file) is on another physical drive, you can restore to the point of failure. This restoration is accomplished by using the transactions in the current transaction log that were executed since the last backup.

Buffer Memory   The buffer memory or buffer pool is used to store data in RAM so that it can be read from and written to. A buffer is a storage location in RAM that can hold a single 8 kilobyte data or index page from a SQL Server database. When data is accessed and the data already exists in the buffer pool, access is much faster. When data is accessed and the data does not exist in the buffer pool, buffers must be requested in the buffer pool (this request may result in some buffers being flushed or emptied to free space for the requested data) and the pages must be loaded from the physical database data files into the assigned buffers.

If your SharePoint deployment seems to be slow in response times, check the BufferCacheHitRatio values in the Performance Monitor on the SQL server and ensure that it is 90 percent or higher. A reading lower than 90 percent on a SharePoint database server usually means you have insufficient RAM for the amount of data you are trying to serve. For more information on using the Performance Monitor, look in Chapter 6, "Designing an Operations Strategy."

Data Read and Write Methods

Now that you understand the major components in the SQL Server logical architecture, you can explore the way in which data is accessed. For this explanation, assume that a user executed the following SQL statement against a database located on a SQL Server 2008 or 2008 R2 server:

```
SELECT CustomerID, FirstName, LastName, eMail
FROM Sales.Customers
WHERE LastName = 'Smith';
```

Assume that 1,200 records match this query and are spread across 750 data pages. Furthermore, assume that none of the needed pages are in memory. SQL Server uses the following high-level steps to retrieve the data for the user:

1. Locate the pages containing the matching records and read the pages into buffers.

2. Read the records from the pages and return them to the user as a result set or record set.

Notice that the pages are not removed from memory after the data is transferred to the user. The pages are left in the buffers until the buffers are needed for other pages. This behavior allows future reads of the same pages without the need to load the pages from disk. For example, imagine the following SQL statement was executed immediately after the previous one:

```
SELECT CustomerID, FirstName, LastName, eMail, Phone
FROM Sales.Customers
WHERE LastName = 'Smith' and FirstName = 'John';
```

This statement would need data that is located in the same pages as the previous statement. While all pages would not be required, all required pages would already be in the buffers (assuming the buffers had not been required for an intermediate statement because the previous statement and this latter statement both process records where the LastName column is equal to Smith). Performing data access in this manner dramatically improves the performance of read operations and, as you can image, enhances read operations when SharePoint accesses similar data for different users of the sites in your environment.

Data write operations work much like data read operations—at least in the initial stages. For example, imagine the following SQL statement is executed against a database:

```
UPDATE Sales.Customers
SET Phone = '937-555-1029'
WHERE CustomerID = 63807;
```

Remember, data modifications are never performed directly against the physical data files at the time of processing. Therefore, the first step is reading the data into the buffers just like a data read operation. Once the appropriate pages are loaded into the buffers, the data changes are made in the buffer memory at the time of processing. Next, the transaction is recorded in the transaction log. Believe it or not, the data write is complete.

You may be wondering how the data gets back into the actual data files on disk. At this point, the data is in memory and the transaction is in the log, but the data file has not been updated. However, keep in mind that you have only modified a value in a specific column for a specific customer. Furthermore, remember that the page is retained in memory so that the data is available for future reads and writes. You have not created the demand for any new data pages at this point.

The key to understanding how the data is updated in the data files is found in SQL Server actions performed by checkpoints, lazy writers, and workers. Any page that has been modified is designated as a *dirty page*. When a checkpoint occurs, the SQL Server service processes the pages in the buffered memory buffers. Dirty pages are written back out to the data files during a checkpoint and are designated as not dirty pages. The buffers holding the dirty pages before the checkpoint are not cleared or freed for use at this time.

The lazy writer and workers are responsible for freeing buffers so that sufficient buffers are available as needed by applications. The *lazy writer* sleeps much of the time, but when it wakes, it evaluates the free buffers and, if they are not sufficient, writes dirty pages to disk so that the buffers can be freed. The lazy writer uses an algorithm that is dependent on the size of the buffer pool to determine sufficient free buffers. In addition, the *workers* (processes that work with data) are also responsible for writing dirty pages and freeing buffers. When a worker accesses the buffer pool, it is also assigned 64 buffers to analyze. Any buffered pages in those 64 buffers that are not worth keeping in memory are written to the disk or discarded depending on whether they were dirty pages or not. Dirty pages are always written to disk before they are discarded.

As you can see, it is quite a myth that dirty pages are written to disk only when a checkpoint occurs (though this is a frequent recurring theme in blog posts and discussion forums). Indeed, if the server has massively more memory than it requires for the attached databases, dirty pages may be written to disk only during checkpoints, but it is far more common that dirty pages are written to disk by all three processes: checkpoints, lazy writer actions, and worker actions. The primary purpose of checkpoints is to make sure that dirty pages are written to disk frequently enough so that the auto recovery process completes in a timely fashion should the SQL Server service require a restart for any reason.

Understanding these data read and write methods will help you better plan for storage with your SharePoint SQL Server installations. For example, if your SharePoint installation will be used frequently by a large number of users, you may need to store the SQL Server database files on RAID storage arrays with high performance.

SQL Server Deployment Planning

Several features and configuration options must be considered to effectively plan a SQL Server installation. These features and options include:

- SQL Server components
- Multiple instances
- TCP ports
- Installation options

When you install SQL Server, you have the option of installing several components. You will need to understand these components and what they offer in order to determine whether they are needed for your installation or not. The most important components include the database engine, Integration Services, administration tools, Analysis Services, Reporting Services, full-text search, and books online.

Database Engine   This is the core of SQL Server. Without the database engine, you can't really do much so you will install this with every instance. The database engine provides access to your databases. The database engine is the most heavily used service in a SharePoint deployment.

Integration Services   The Integration Services component is the extraction, transformation, and loading (ETL) tool set provided by SQL Server. With this service, you can move data from one server to another and massage the data (transform or modify it in some way) during the process. Additionally, database maintenance plans depend on Integration Services starting with the SQL Server 2005 version and higher. Integration Services could be used to extract data from the SharePoint content databases into reporting or analysis databases. Doing so would prevent the reporting processes or analysis processes from impacting the performance of the SharePoint sites. Of course, the Integration Services job would have an impact on the performance of the sites, but this would be an infrequent impact and it could be scheduled for off-peak hours.

Administration Tools   You may not want to install the administration tools, such as SQL Server Management Studio and Visual Studio for SQL Server, on the server itself. However, it is often convenient to have the tools installed on the server so that you can access them locally if need be. Installing the administration tools is usually a good idea, unless the policies within an organization disallow it.

Analysis Services   The Analysis Services (AS) component is one of those special components of SQL Server that warrants its own book. For now, it's enough to know that AS is used for business intelligence work and for data warehousing operations.

Reporting Services   Reporting Services provides a report generation service for your SQL Server and possibly other databases. Larger organizations usually choose to install dedicated reporting servers, but smaller organizations may opt to install Reporting Services on one or more servers used as standard database servers as well.

Full-Text Search   The full-text search feature allows searching for large- and small-text data types. Normal WHERE clause searches are limited to string-based patterns. Full-text searches perform word searches and understand language elements. For example, inflection forms (such as tooth and teeth) can be found when you specify search words (such as teeth). Additionally, searches can be performed for words close to one another and the results ranked based on how close together the words are.

Books Online   Books Online is the famous, and sometimes infamous, electronic help for SQL Server. The SQL Server 2008 Books Online is, of course, larger than its predecessor and according to Microsoft weighs in at 240 MB. If you've ever downloaded an eBook, you know that a 200 MB eBook is huge and SQL Server 2008 Books Online is just that—huge. However, it is searchable, and you can usually find what you need after several search attempts and several forward and backward clicks.

SQL Server 2008 supports multiple instances on the same machine. In fact, you can run SQL Server 2000, 2005, and 2008 all on the same server at the same time. In some upgrade and migration scenarios, this multiversion configuration may be desired. All instances share certain components, such as the Books Online, but each instance has its own set of executables. Several reasons exist for installing multiple instances. The following reasons represent the most common:

Service Pack Compatibility   You can install several instances of SQL Server 2008 on the same physical host and install different service packs. For example, one vendor may require service pack 1 (SP1) at a minimum, while another does not yet support SP1. You could install one instance with SP1 and the other without it and support both applications on the same server.

SQL Server Version Compatibility   Similar to the service packs, you may need to run multiple versions of SQL Server on the same physical host. If you have an internal application that does not work on SQL Server 2008, you can run it in a SQL Server 2000 or 2005 instance and run other applications in a SQL Server 2008 instance on the same server.

Policy Compliance   Many organizations have security policies that require limiting user access to database services. In fact, the policy could state something like, "A single database service shall provide access only to databases that share a common set of users." A policy such as this may force you to create separate instances to house different databases accessed by different users without requiring multiple physical servers.

Testing and Development   Building test and development labs can be expensive. With multiple instances, a single physical host can house several instances for various development projects. These instances can be used for testing different service packs, SQL Server versions, and code bases for the supported applications.

Global Settings   Finally, any time you must implement one global setting value for one application and a different value for the same setting for another application, you will be required to either implement separate instances or separate physical hosts. A global setting value is one that impacts the entire instance because it impacts the services in that instance. Of course, implementing separate instances would be cheaper. An example global setting is the authentication mode. You cannot have one database using Windows authentication and another database using Mixed authentication within the same instance.

Another flexible configuration option is the TCP port on which SQL Server listens for incoming connections to the databases. A default instance of SQL Server uses port 1433 by default, but this can be changed. Named instances use a dynamically assigned port, but it can be changed as well. You use the SQL Server Configuration Manager to configure the TCP ports for installed instances.

> **WARNING**   Be very thoughtful when changing the TCP port. If you are not also the network administrator, you should check with her or him to verify that the new port will function properly on the network. Many networks block communications using deep packet inspections and a port other than 1433 may not work properly or the administrator may need to adjust the network configuration.

Several options are available for the installation of each instance. You can choose the installation directory for the instance and the shared components. You can configure the service accounts for improved security, and you can choose to enable the new filestream support. The filestream feature allows for the storage of large external data sets so that the MDF and NDF files do not become unnecessarily large. In the past, DBAs stored videos, large drawings, and other binary large objects (BLOBs) outside of the database and simply stored a reference to the file location inside the database. This structure resulted in difficulty for management of the database and the application. With the filestream feature, both database management and application updates become easier.

Make sure to take the time to plan your SQL Server installation as it relates to SharePoint 2010. In addition to considering components, multiple instances, TCP ports, and other installation options, answer the following key questions:

- Will the SQL server be used for anything other than SharePoint? If the server will be used for other purposes, increased processing power, memory availability, and storage availability should be used.

- Will the SharePoint sites be used for Internet-facing websites? If the answer is yes, extra caution should be taken when developing custom code in order to avoid SQL injection attacks.

Installing SQL Server

The SQL Server installation process will vary depending on the version and edition you are installing. In this chapter, you will install the trial edition of SQL Server 2008 R2 Enterprise. In real-world lab and development environments, you may choose to use the SQL Server 2008 R2 Express Edition; however, it is good to gain exposure to the full SQL Server deployment with all the features so that you will know what you will have to work with in a production scenario.

> **NOTE**   You can download the SQL Server 2008 R2 trial edition from http://msdn .microsoft.com/en-us/evalcenter/ff459612. Registration is required, but the trial works for 180 days, which is plenty of time for the lab-based learning process. Be sure to download the 64-bit edition, as it is required by SharePoint 2010.

In Exercise 2.17, you will perform a basic installation of SQL Server 2008 R2 x64. The installation will be used in Chapter 4 to install SharePoint. It will also be used as the backend database server for the SharePoint 2010 installation.

EXERCISE 2.17

Installing SQL Server 2008 R2 x64 Trial Edition

In this exercise, you will install SQL Server 2008 R2 x64 with the required components to support a SharePoint deployment and additional SQL Server management tasks, such as data export through SQL Server Integration Services and database maintenance plans (which also require SQL Server Integration Services). You may alternatively install the full licensed version of SQL Server 2008 R2. If you do, you will use the DVD instead of the downloaded executable to start the installation.

1. Log onto the server as an administrator. This is the same server on which all exercises in this chapter have been performed.

2. Download the SQL Server 2008 R2 x64 trial from http://msdn.microsoft.com/en-us/ evalcenter/ff459612.

3. When the download completes, launch the SQLFULL_x64_END.EXE file that was downloaded.

4. Enter an extraction directory, such as C:\SQL_INST and click OK.

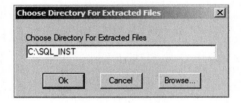

5. When the extraction is complete, click the OK button on the Extraction Complete notification dialog.

6. Browse to the extraction directory, in this case C:\SQL_INST, and launch the setup .exe file located there. Be patient, the setup initialization process can take a few moments.

7. In the SQL Server Installation Center screen that appears, click the Installation link on the left navigation pane.

8. Click the New Installation Or Add Features To An Existing Installation option.

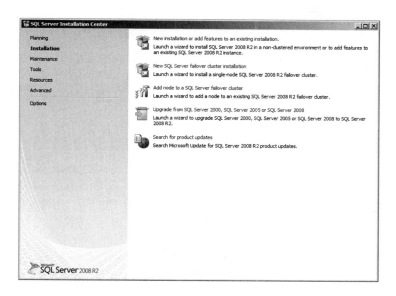

9. On the Setup Support Rules screen, click OK.

10. On the Product Key screen, accept the default setting of Evaluation and click Next. Notice that this screen also allows you to choose Express Edition from this installation source.

11. On the License Terms screen, read the license terms and check I Accept The License Terms and then click Next.

12. On the Setup Support Files screen, click Install to install the support files required by SQL Server setup.

13. On the Setup Support Rules screen, notice the warning about the Computer Domain Controller and the Windows Firewall. Microsoft does not recommend installing SQL Server on a Domain Controller in a production environment, and you may have to allow communications through the firewall (or simply disable it) for SQL Server network communications to work. Because this is a lab installation, you are not concerned about the domain controller issue. Click Next.

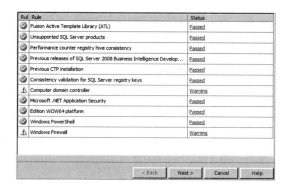

14. On the Setup Role screen, choose the option to perform a SQL Server Feature Installation and click Next.

15. On the Feature Selection screen, choose the following features:

- Database Engine Services

- Full-Text Search

- Business Intelligence Development Studio

- Client Tools Connectivity

- Integration Services

- SQL Server Books Online

- Management Tools (Basic and Complete)

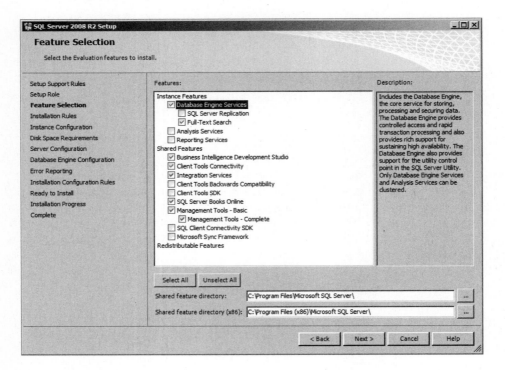

16. After selecting the identified features, accept the directory defaults and click Next.

17. On the Installation Rules screen, click Next to configure the SQL Server instance.

18. Install the SQL server role as a Default Instance, select the default values for the Instance ID and Instance root directory, and click Next.

19. On the Disk Space requirements screen, read the information and click Next.

20. On the Server Configuration screen, configure all services to use the same account by clicking the button that reads Use The Same Account For All SQL Server Services. In the dialog that appears, select the NT AUTHORITY\SYSTEM account and click OK. Also configure all services except the SQL Full-text Filter Daemon Launcher to have a Startup Type value of Automatic, as in the following image. Click Next.

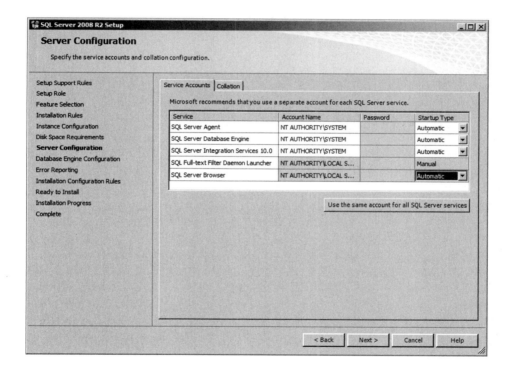

21. On the Database Engine Configuration screen, choose Windows Authentication Mode as the Authentication Mode setting. Click the Add Current User button to add the administrator account with which you are performing the installation as a SQL Server administrator. Click Next.

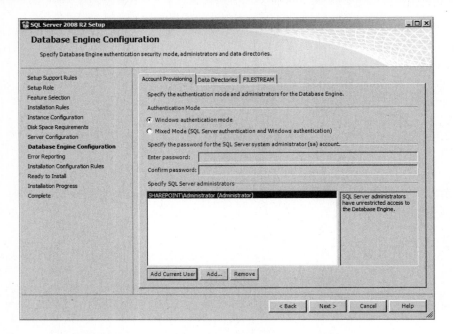

22. On the Error Reporting screen, accept the defaults and click Next.

23. On the Installation Configuration Rules screen, click Next.

24. On the Ready To Install screen, review the installation plan and click Install to begin the installation. The installation can take more than 20 minutes to complete.

25. When the installation completes, the Complete screen should appear. You should see a message reading, "Your SQL Server 2008 R2 installation completed successfully." Click Close.

Understanding SQL Server Management Studio

SQL Server 2005 introduced the new SQL Server Management Studio (SSMS). When compared with the Enterprise Manager, which was used in earlier versions of SQL Server, the SSMS interface provides many enhancements. Much like the Enterprise Manager, the vast majority of actions taken in SSMS are really just calls to the Database Engine using Transact-SQL (T-SQL) code. At least two benefits arise from this architecture. First, you can learn to automate administrative tasks by capturing the actions when a Script button is not available or by viewing the code directly when a Script button is available. Second, you can discover which settings are stored in the Registry (and some still are) and which settings are stored in the internal configuration tables (system tables). When settings are stored in the Registry, the SSMS application must call for Registry access instead of using the normal T-SQL code to access the system tables.

Figure 2.6 shows the SSMS interface. Like most Windows applications, you have a menu bar across the top as well as a toolbar area. The panes, such as the Object Explorer shown on the left, can be docked or undocked; and they can be located on the left, top, right, bottom, or middle of the screen.

FIGURE 2.6   The SSMS interface

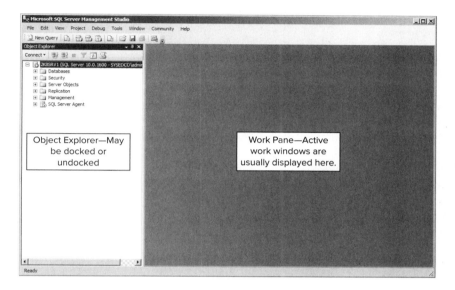

 When I teach SQL Server administration, I usually joke with the class about the need for a 30-inch widescreen LCD for all administrators; however, it's only a joke if your budget will not allow it. I use a 28-inch screen for most of my administrative tasks. The larger screen space (sometimes called screen real estate) allows more of what I need to be on the screen at the same time. You will need to have a minimum resolution of 1024×768 for many dialogs to function as designed in SSMS.

The SSMS tool is used for the vast majority of SQL Server 2008 administrative tasks. The major tasks include:

- Configuring Database Engine properties
- Creating, altering, securing and deleting databases, tables, views, and other database objects
- Creating and working with jobs, operators, and alerts
- Performing backups with the built-in backup toolset
- Reporting on server performance and operations
- Monitoring server activity and managing connections

As you can see, the list is long and quite complete. With SQL Server 2008, very few tasks require you to write administrative code as a DBA. However, the writing of such code is yet another capability within SSMS. In fact, it has been improved with a new error-tracking feature and better IntelliSense support.

The first thing you'll need to do in SSMS is configure it to your liking. This means adjusting fonts, determining default window layouts, and establishing other important global settings. To configure global settings, click the Tools menu and select Options. You'll be presented with a dialog like the one in Figure 2.7. As you can see, you have several configuration options including:

- **Environment:** Startup window layouts, tabbed interfaces versus multiple document interfaces (MDIs), fonts and text colors, keyboard shortcut schemes, and options for Help configuration.

- **Text Editor:** File extensions mapped to editor configurations, statement completion options, editor tab, and status bar configuration settings.

- **Query Execution:** Configure the batch separator keyword (that's right, you could use something instead of GO), stipulate the number or rows a query is allowed to return before the server cancels the query, and configure advanced execution settings such as deadlock priorities and transaction isolation levels.

- **Query Results:** Specify that query results are presented as a grid, text, or a file, and configure various parameters for the different kinds of result sets.

- **SQL Server Object Explorer:** Change the top number of records to a value greater or less than 1000, and configure options for automatic scripting of objects such as tables or entire databases.

- **Designers:** Configure settings for the table designer and the maintenance plan designer.

- **Source Control:** Configure settings for source control management.

FIGURE 2.7 The SSMS options

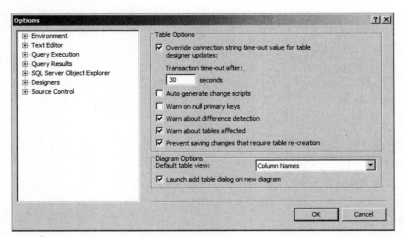

You will want to look through these various options and make sure the environment is configured so that it is optimized for the way you work. For example, you might want to start SSMS with the Environment set to open the Object Explorer and the Activity Monitor automatically on startup. This will make your SSMS screen look like Figure 2.8 on initial startup. You may not like this configuration, but that's the beauty of the tool: you can configure it the way you like it.

FIGURE 2.8   An optional SSMS startup screen

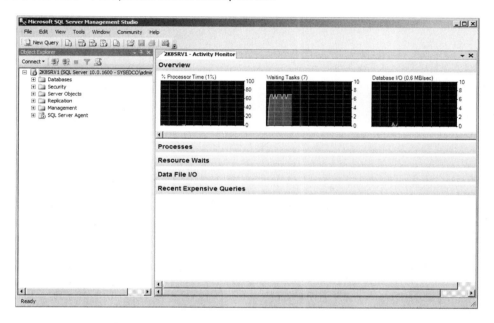

Exercise 2.18 will help you load SSMS and work with windows within the application.

EXERCISE 2.18

Working with SQL Server Management Studio

In this exercise, you will learn to configure the various windows in SSMS.

1.   Log onto the Windows server as an Administrator.

2.   Launch SQL Server Management Studio by selecting Start ➢ All Programs ➢ Microsoft SQL Server 2008 R2 ➢ SQL Server Management Studio.

3.   You will be presented with a connection dialog like the one in the following image. Select the appropriate server (the default instance in this case) and choose Windows Authentication to allow your administrative credentials to pass through. Click the Connect button when everything is configured appropriately in the Connect to Server dialog box.

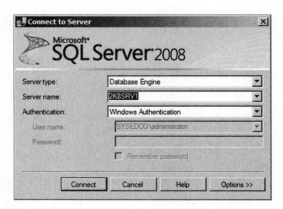

4. To modify the status of the Object Explorer window (also called a pane or panel), click the Windows Position button, which looks like an arrow pointing down, in the upper-right corner of the Object Explorer window.

5. Select Floating from the list and notice that the window is released from the rest of the SSMS interface, as in the following image.

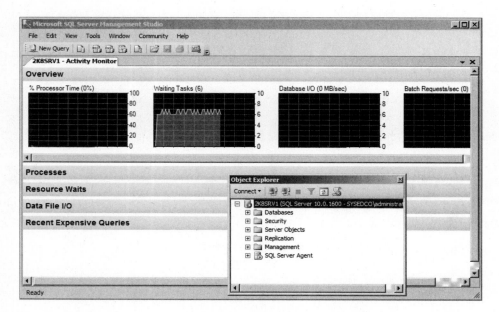

6. Right-click the title bar at the top of the now-floating Object Explorer window and select Dockable.

7. Left-click and drag the title bar of the Object Explorer window and notice that several docking indicators appear. Drag the Object Explore window until your mouse hovers over the left-docking indicator and a blue shaded area appears indicating that the windows will be docked there. Release the mouse button to dock the window.

You can add more windows to the SSMS interface from the View menu. For example, if you select View ➢ Other Windows ➢ Web Browser, you can open a web browser inside the SSMS interface.

In Exercise 2.19, you will learn to open a T-SQL query window and view the error list pane for debugging purposes.

EXERCISE 2.19

Opening a New Query Window

In this exercise, you will open a new query window and work with the error list pane.

1. Click the New Query button or press Ctrl+N to open a Query Editor window as seen in the following image.

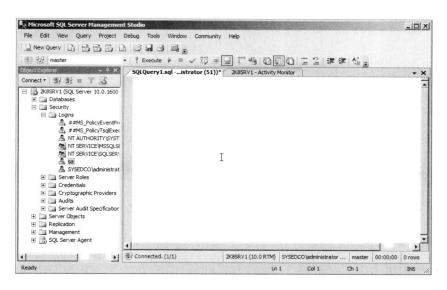

2. Enter the following code into the Query Editor window:

```
USE master;
CREATE Database test;
USE test;
```

EXERCISE 2.19 *(continued)*

3. Notice that the word *test* in the USE `test;` line of code is underlined in red, which indicates an error.

4. Click View ➤ Error List to view the cause of the error, as shown in the following image.

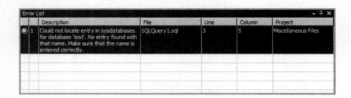

5. To close the Query Editor, click the X in the upper-right corner of the SQLQuery1.sql window and choose No when the Save Changes dialog appears.

6. Click the X in the upper-right corner of the Error List window to turn it off.

The Error List view is a new feature of the Query Editor in SQL Server 2008 and later versions, and it is very helpful in tracking down problems. To resolve the problem in the code snippet in Exercise 2.19, you would insert a GO directive between the CREATE Database statement and the USE `test` statement.

SSMS also comes with built-in reports. SQL Server 2005 first introduced integrated reports into the SSMS interface. SQL Server 2008 improved on these reports and increased the number of reports. However, the method for accessing the reports changed with the released of SQL Server 2008. Because most SharePoint installations will use SQL Server 2008 or later, Exercise 2.20 provides instructions for working with these reports in the newer versions.

EXERCISE 2.20

Viewing Reports

In this exercise, you will work with built-in reports in SSMS.

1. Expand the Databases node in the SSMS Object Explorer.

2. Right-click on the AdventureWorks database and select Reports ➤ Standard Reports ➤ Disk Usage.

3. View the report in the right panel, as shown here:

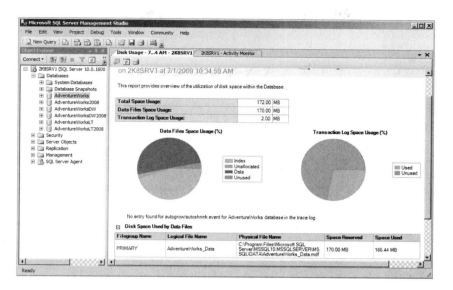

4.   Close the report by clicking the X in the upper-right corner of the report window.

You can view any report on any database by repeating the steps listed here and replacing AdventureWorks with the intended database and Disk Usage with the intended report. You can also view server level reports by right-clicking the root server node and selecting Reports.

You may want to spend some more time exploring SSMS. As long as you are on a test machine, you really can't do any damage, so go ahead and explore its many features.

Querying Databases

As a SharePoint 2010 administrator, you will rarely have to perform direct queries against the backend SQL Server databases. However, the data certainly is stored in SQL Server and you can create your own reports and jobs against this data. In case you are new to SQL Server, Exercise 2.21 provides a brief example of querying the SQL Server databases using the SSMS query editor.

EXERCISE 2.21

Querying the AdventureWorks Database

In this exercise, you will execute three different queries against the AdventureWorks database. The first query will simply return all information from the Production.Product table. The second query will return only a subset of the columns from the table and the third query will return only a subset of the columns and rows from the table.

1.   Launch SSMS and log onto the SQL server.

2.   In the Object Explorer, expand Databases and select the AdventureWorks database by clicking on it.

3. Click the New Query button on the toolbar.

4. Enter the following SELECT statement into the new query window:

   SELECT *
   FROM Production. Product;

5. Click the Execute button and notice the results.

6. Modify the SELECT statement to look like the following:

   SELECT ProductID, Name, ProductNumber, ListPrice
   FROM Production.Product;

7. Click the Execute button and notice that only the four selected columns are returned. The explicit column listings limit the columns returned by the query.

8. Modify the SELECT statement to look like the following:

   SELECT ProductID, Name, ProductNumber, ListPrice
   FROM Production.Product
   WHERE ListPrice > 0;

9. Click the Execute button and notice that now 200 fewer rows are returned. The WHERE clause limits the records returned based on filtered values in one or more columns.

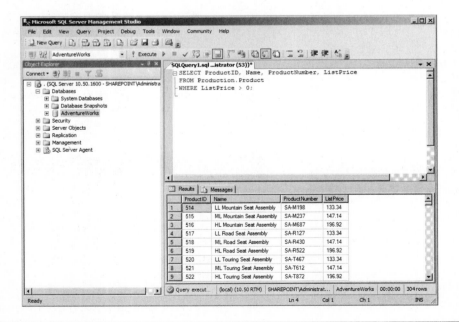

While the T-SQL query language used in SQL Server is much more powerful than the simple examples in Exercise 2.21 could possibly demonstrate, this exercise did expose you to the query editing tool within the SSMS. For more information on the T-SQL language, see the SQL Server 2008 R2 Books Online, which is the included help system with SQL Server.

Business Context

Understanding the business context is not about determining requirements. It is about determining the existing environment into which you will be implementing SharePoint 2010 and ensuring that your physical plan will allow SharePoint to work properly in that environment. Three areas must be considered:

- Security policies
- Existing network load
- Administration procedures

Each organization has or should have security policies. These policies will dictate how various technologies may be implemented, and they may bar some technologies from implementation within the organization. Be sure to review these policies as you develop your SharePoint physical architecture implementation plan. For example, existing policies may require that all SQL servers be installed using Windows authentication only. If this is the case, you must ensure that your plan complies with this policy.

The existing network load will also impact decisions you make during your implementation planning. If the network is already at 70 percent or greater utilization and you add a new technology such as SharePoint, which is typically a heavily used application, you are headed for trouble. Upgrade the network infrastructure first (more on this in Chapter 3, "Integrating SharePoint with the Network Infrastructure,") so that your SharePoint deployment will be successful from the start.

You can determine the network load on a single server or client computer by using the Windows Performance Monitor and tracking the Bytes Total/sec counter in the Network Interface counter group. However, you will need enterprise management software from your switch and router vendor or from a third-party to analyze the actual network infrastructure's load. Cisco provides software for such use with their routers and switches. Two third-party vendors that can provide such software are iTRACS and Avocent.

Finally, administration procedures dictate how technologies should be administered and by whom. For example, your IT staff may perform administration using Remote Desktop on Windows servers or they may be required to physically access the servers for administration. Whatever the requirements, be sure to configure your SharePoint servers for administration procedure compliance.

Mapping Logical Design to Physical Specifications

In the end, the most important thing you can do is make sure your physical implementation plans meet the requirements of your logical design. You may recall, from Chapter 1, that your logical design is driven by business requirements. The end result is that, if your physical plan does not meet the demands of the logical design, you will not meet the business requirements.

Table 2.4 provides an example of what the map from logical to physical may look like. This is intended only as an example, but the creation of a similar map can help to ensure that you do not miss any logical design requirements during your physical implementation.

TABLE 2.4   Mapping Logical Designs to Physical Implementations

Logical Design Specification	Physical Implementation Consideration
Number of web applications	Additional WFE servers may be required to distribute the web application load.
Use of Office web apps (editing Office documents within the browser)	Extra network bandwidth may be required as more bandwidth will be consumed.
Size of the content	Dedicate search servers may be required to quickly search large content farms.
Size of the content	Additional database servers may be required; enhanced storage systems may be required.
Access URLs for different access methods	Extra DNS host records may be required.
Use of streaming media (video and audio)	More bandwidth may be required.
Provision of external access	Certificates for SSL may be required from a trusted third-party.

Documenting the Design

The final step in the physical design process is the documentation of the design. Much of the work will be done already as you will likely create documentation along the way. The following items should be documented at a minimum:

- Server hardware configuration
- Server farm breakdown

- Description of each server in the farm falling into the categories of database server, application server, and WFE server
- Documentation of which logical components exist on the different physical servers
- Network diagrams
    - Number of servers and locations
    - Server types
    - Non-Sharepoint server requirements
    - Storage type and size

With these documents in hand, you are less likely to miss an important factor when performing the actual SharePoint installations. The documents can exist as Word documents, Visio diagrams, Excel workbooks, or some combination of these. Of course, you could also use non-Microsoft software to create the documentation, but, as you've chosen to install SharePoint, it is more likely that you are using the Microsoft Office suite in your organization.

Capacity Planning

An important part of the physical design process requires capacity planning and growth forecasting. For example, you cannot really determine the number of SQL Server database servers you will require until you have performed storage capacity analysis in order to determine the quantity of content storage required. Additionally, you must plan for the required network bandwidth to support the number of users accessing the SharePoint servers. While Chapter 3 provides details on network infrastructure technologies, you will learn about network bandwidth estimation in this section. Ultimately, you must ensure that you have sufficient storage space, sufficient network bandwidth, and enough processing power to meet your needs. All three will be discussed in this section, and the topic of processing power will also address the need for sufficient memory.

Storage

As you should certainly know by now, SQL Server is the storage solution for your SharePoint deployments. All of your website content ends up in a SQL Server database. These databases must be stored somewhere. In today's world of storage technology, you have many options to choose from, but for server-based systems you are most likely to use SCSI, SATA, and RAID technologies for internal storage. You can also use Storage Area Networks (SANs), which are accessed using IP networks or Fibre Channel networks, but they still use SCSI, SATA, and RAID for their internal storage.

Beyond the drives themselves, you also have to consider the way in which the data is stored in SQL Server. The SQL Server database recovery model determines how the transaction log is used with the database. Because the transaction log is the key to recovering to the point of failure, this setting is one of the most important settings for any database. SQL Server supports three different recovery models for the databases, and you should understand these models:

- Simple
- Bulk-logged
- Full

The first choice, the simple recovery model, means that the transaction log is used for data changes, but the transactions are lost at each checkpoint. As changes are made to the data, the changes take place in buffer memory. Once the change is made in buffer memory, the transaction is written to the transaction log. Every so often, a checkpoint occurs. When the checkpoint occurs, the dirty pages are written from buffer memory to the data file and the transaction log is truncated. The term *truncate* means that the data is removed from the log, but the log size is not reduced.

The striking thing in the preceding paragraph is the shattering of a common myth about SQL Server and the simple recovery model. It is commonly said that the simple recovery model does not use the transaction log, but this statement is false. The transaction log is still used (it helps to recover from a power failure or any other sudden system crash), but it is not retained for backups. You do not—and cannot—back up the transaction log for a database in the simple recovery model.

The simple recovery model is useful for test databases, lab environments, development databases, and even production databases that are read only (which are uncommon for SharePoint deployments). Additionally, if the only changes that are ever made to the database are done using bulk scripts once each day or once each week, you may consider using the simple recovery model on these databases. Since all of the changes are made using scripts, the imported data should still be available. In other words, you can restore the database from a backup and then rerun the scripts in sequence.

 The recommendation to use the simple recovery model for a production read-only database or a database that is updated only through bulk scripts assumes that the database is never updated by individual users. If the database is updated by individual users, you will not be able to resynchronize the data after a restore when using the simple recover model.

The bulk-logged recovery model is the in-between model. It's not as basic as the simple recovery model, and it doesn't provide the complete transaction logging of the full recovery model. Like the simple recovery model, some misunderstandings exist in relation to the functionality of the bulk-logged recovery model. The misinformation usually goes something like this, "If you use the bulk-logged recovery model, you cannot recover to a point-in-time anymore." That statement is not necessarily true. Let me explain.

When in the bulk-logged recovery model, the transaction log is still used; however, for certain types of actions—bulk actions—minimal logging is performed. These actions include several things as represented by the following list:

- SELECT INTO statements

- Some INSERT INTO statements that use a SELECT statement to provide the data values

- When the OPENROWSET(BULK. . .) function is used

- When data totaling more than an extent (64 K) is inserted and the TABLOCK hint is used

- BULK INSERT operations

- Write actions performed by the BCP command-line program

- When using the .WRITE clause with an UPDATE statement

- INDEX creation (CREATE INDEX), modification (ALTER INDEX), or deletion (DROP INDEX)

When a bulk action occurs, the action is logged to the transaction log. It is noted that it occurred. In the database, for each extent that was modified by the bulk action, the Bulk Changed Page (BCP) bit for that extent is set to 1. All extents have a bit value of 0 on the BCP if a bulk action has not modified their data.

Here's where the interesting part comes in. When you back up the transaction log for a database that is in the bulk-logged recovery model, the transaction log is not backed up alone. Instead, every extent with a BCP bit of 1 is also backed up with the log. By performing this extra action, an administrator can use the SQL Server backup tools to restore the database—including the bulk transactions.

What about the point-in-time recoveries? If the database is in the bulk-logged recovery model and no bulk actions have occurred since the last full backup, the database can be restored to a point-in-time. If, however, a bulk action has occurred, it can only be fully restored.

The final option in the recovery model is the full recovery model. The full recovery model logs every single transaction to the log. A transaction is a change. Any time a change occurs on a database in the full recovery model, an entry is added to the transaction log. If a read operation occurs, nothing is entered in the transaction log because no change has occurred. The vast majority of production databases operate in the full recovery model during normal operations.

 You've probably sensed that I work with SQL Server quite a lot. To learn much more about SQL Server, you can read my book titled *SQL Server 2008 Administration: Real World Skills for MCITP Certification and Beyond (Exams 70-432 and 70-450)* also published by Sybex.

Exercise 2.22 provides instructions for setting the recovery model on the AdventureWorks sample database. In order to perform Exercise 2.22 you will need to download and install the AdventureWorks sample database on your SQL Server database server. The AdventureWorks sample database can be downloaded from http://msftdbprodsamples.codeplex.com/releases/view/37109.

EXERCISE 2.22

Setting the Recovery Model for a Database

In this exercise, you will set the recovery model for a database in SQL Server Management Studio. You will also explore the T-SQL code used to accomplish this task.

1. In the Object Explorer's Databases node, right-click on the AdventureWorks database and select Properties.

2. Select the Options page in the Database Properties - AdventureWorks dialog.

3. Change the Recovery model value to Full as in the following image.

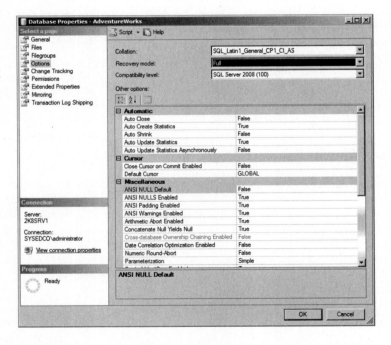

4. Do not click OK. Instead, click the Script button and you may see some brief screen flashing behind the Database Properties - AdventureWorks dialog. This behavior is normal.

5. Click Cancel to close the dialog.

6. You should now see a query editor window with code similar to the following:

```
USE [master]
GO
ALTER Database [AdventureWorks] SET RECOVERY FULL WITH NO_WAIT
GO
```

7. Execute the code by clicking the Execute button or by pressing F5 on the keyboard.

At this point, the AdventureWorks database is running in the Full recovery model and you've learned how to generate a script from within an administrative GUI dialog.

In addition to planning for the recover model, you should estimate the expected size of the SharePoint databases. Microsoft provides the following formula for estimating capacity requirements for content databases:

$$\text{Database size} = ((D \times V) \times S) + (10\ \text{KB} \times (L + (V \times D)))$$

The formula is used based on the following process:

1. Calculate number of documents (D).

2. Estimate average document size (S).

3. Estimate number of list items (L).

4. Determine approximate number of versions (V).

For example, assume that 125 documents of an average size of 43 KB are stored in a single document library. Further, assume that 4,300 list items are in the content database and that three versions of documents are maintained. The formula would look like the following:

```
Database size = ((125 × 3) × 43 KB) + (10 KB × (4300 + (3 × 125)))
Database size = 62875 KB
Database size = 61.4 MB
```

Using this formula, you can estimate the database size for each database in your environment. In a real environment, things will become quite a bit more complex. For example, you may have more than 100 document libraries. Some libraries may have 10 documents in them and others have more than 1,000 documents in them. Some libraries may average 25 KB per document and others may average over 1 MB per document. Additionally, you may have more than 500,000 list items. You are probably beginning to see the picture. Here's a good recommendation: create an Excel workbook to track all of these. The formula provided in this section can easily be converted into an Excel formula and then it's simply a matter of filling in the blanks. Keep in mind that every list item consumes 10 KB, and this is true for document library items as well. Figure 2.9 shows such an Excel workbook.

FIGURE 2.9   Calculating database sizes in Excel

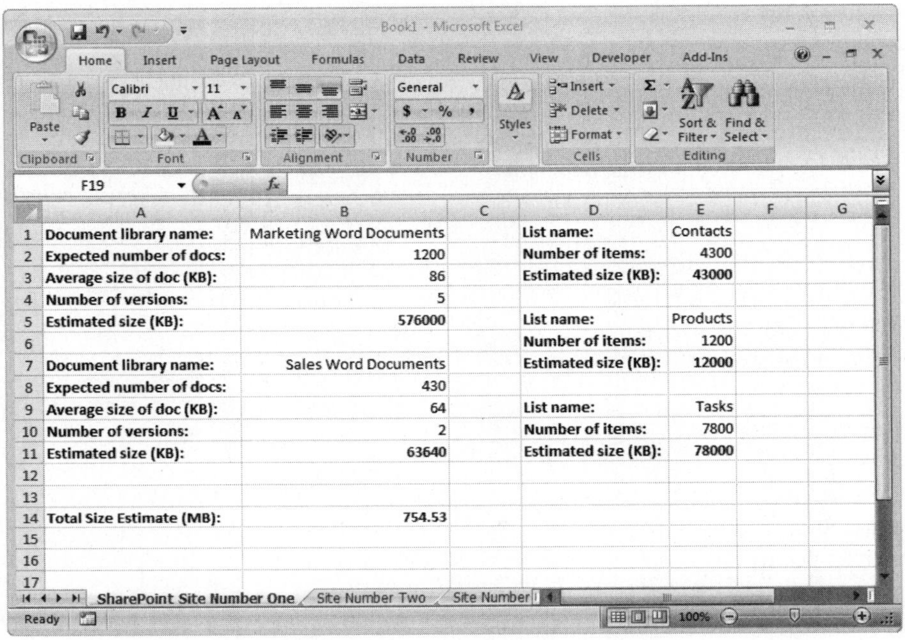

	A	B	C	D	E	F	G
1	Document library name:	Marketing Word Documents		List name:	Contacts		
2	Expected number of docs:	1200		Number of items:	4300		
3	Average size of doc (KB):	86		Estimated size (KB):	43000		
4	Number of versions:	5					
5	Estimated size (KB):	576000		List name:	Products		
6				Number of items:	1200		
7	Document library name:	Sales Word Documents		Estimated size (KB):	12000		
8	Expected number of docs:	430					
9	Average size of doc (KB):	64		List name:	Tasks		
10	Number of versions:	2		Number of items:	7800		
11	Estimated size (KB):	63640		Estimated size (KB):	78000		
12							
13							
14	Total Size Estimate (MB):	754.53					
15							
16							
17							

Cell reference: F19. Sheet tabs: SharePoint Site Number One, Site Number Two, Site Number. Status: Ready. Zoom: 100%.

Bandwidth

Network bandwidth is another important item to plan for your physical network implementation. Chapter 3 covers the network infrastructure, the impact that SharePoint will have on it, and the demands SharePoint will place on it. For now, it is enough to know that you must ensure that you have sufficient network bandwidth for your SharePoint installation. Areas of consideration include:

- **DNS server queries:** Users accessing the SharePoint servers will now be performing queries against your internal DNS servers to locate them. Be sure the network paths to the DNS servers have sufficient bandwidth.

- **Active Directory lookups:** Because users are provisioned for SharePoint 2010 through AD, you will have to accommodate for more AD queries than may have occurred in the past.

- **SQL Server access:** Ensure that the network path between the WFE servers and application servers and the SQL servers is free of unnecessary communications that would consume the bandwidth. It's not a bad idea to implement a separate network for these backend communications.

Processing

After you have made sure that your storage and network bandwidth is sufficient for the SharePoint implementation, you have to further analyze the individual servers that will run the SharePoint products. Microsoft recommends analysis of the following components within the servers:

- **Processor:** Ensure that the processor can meet the demands that will be placed on it. In a production environment, this typically means using a quad core processor or two dual-core processors at a minimum.

- **Disk I/O:** Make sure you are using a disk subsystem that performs well. This is particularly true for the SQL Server servers.

- **Memory:** The more memory you have, the happier SQL Server is—at least it seems to be this way. Make sure all of your servers have sufficient memory, but go beyond what you expect your SQL servers will need.

- **Network I/O:** Make sure you are using the newest network adapter drivers for your server installation. Improved drivers can significantly enhance the performance of network operations.

Because SharePoint servers do very little in the way of video rendering, the video subsystem is not usually very important. In fact, very basic video capabilities will usually suffice. If you plan to use the Performance Monitor to analyze the SharePoint servers' performance, Microsoft recommends monitoring the following counters:

- **Processor - % Processor Time:** A value below 40 percent is desired and a value about 70 percent is critical.

- **Memory - Available Mbytes:** While no specific value is recommended, the more free memory you have, the more your server can adjust to sudden spikes in demand.

- **Physical Disk - Current Disk Queue Length:** A value below 2 or 3 is best, because it indicates that the waiting line for access to the hard drives is not very long.

- **Network Interface - Output Queue Length:** Anything more than two packets in the queue indicates a potential bottleneck. Either the NIC is not fast enough (you are using a 100 Mbps NIC and should be using a 1 Gbps NIC) or the drivers are subpar.

Forecasting Deployment Architecture Growth

When you are planning a physical implementation, it is good to have some sort of guidelines for when you may need to move up to the next level. For example, when do you need to move from a single-server farm to a two-tier farm (a single database server and a single WFE/application server)? When do you need to move from a simple two-tier farm to a three-tier farm (one or more database servers, one or more application servers, and one or more WFE servers)? Microsoft makes the following recommendations:

- A single-server farm should be used for evaluation or for up to 100 users.

- A simple two-tier farm can be used for up to 10,000 users with just two servers in production (of course, this provides no fault tolerance).

- A two-tier distributed farm (one database server and two WFE/application servers) could handle up to 20,000 users.

- With more than 20,000 users, Microsoft recommends moving to a three-tier farm and the scaling out of that farm will depend on the number of list items and documents in libraries and custom applications.

To learn more about Microsoft's recommendations for deployment architectures, download the Topologies for SharePoint Server 2010 poster at http://www.microsoft.com/downloads/en/details.aspx?FamilyID=fd686cbb-8401-4f25-b65e-3ce7aa7dbeab&displaylang=en.

Summary

In this chapter, you learned the details of what it takes to plan and implement the physical servers required for SharePoint 2010 deployments. You learned about hardware requirements and software requirements. You also learned how to install DNS, AD, and IIS with SMTP. Finally, you learned how to install SQL Server. You finished the chapter by learning about capacity analysis for SharePoint 2010 physical architecture deployments. In the next chapter, you will explore the impact of SharePoint 2010 on your network infrastructure and the demands it will place on that infrastructure.

Exam Essentials

Translating the logical to the physical architecture.   Know how to define requirements for SharePoint servers including WFE servers, application servers, SQL servers, and single-server installations. Understand how to plan for and implement DNS, AD, IIS, SMTP, and SQL Server.

Capacity planning.   Remember that capacity planning addresses storage, network bandwidth, and internal server processing. Know that Microsoft recommends using only a single-server deployment of SharePoint 2010 for up to 100 users.

Chapter

3

Integrating SharePoint with the Network Infrastructure

TOPICS COVERED IN THIS CHAPTER

- ✓ Planning Farm Communications
- ✓ Networking Protocols: A Summary
- ✓ Network Services

If the preceding two chapters did not make it clear that SharePoint 2010 will have a significant footprint on your network environment, this chapter will certainly provide that clarity. SharePoint 2010 is an exceptionally powerful collaboration and content management suite, and along with that power come major requirements. In this chapter, you will delve deeper into the requirements and impact that SharePoint will place on your network infrastructure.

To appreciate the impact SharePoint will have on your infrastructure and the demands it will make of your infrastructure, you must begin by understanding how to plan for farm communications. Next, you will need to understand the fundamentals of network protocols at the lower layers of network communications. Finally, you will have to grasp the functions performed by important network and infrastructure services.

If you are preparing for the 70-668 exam, this chapter covers the important objective titled Design SharePoint Integration with Network Infrastructure. This component is often overlooked in the SharePoint planning process, and it was a very good thing that Microsoft added it to the 70-668 exam. This objective requires that you understand how to plan for farm communications, that you understand networking fundamentals, and that you understand the roles played by Active Directory, DNS, SQL Server IIS, and other infrastructure services.

It is important that you consider the road to becoming an MCITP: SharePoint 2010 Administrator. It passes through the 70-667 exam and then ends after the 70-668 exam. The point is that you can acquire the MCITP-level certification in SharePoint 2010 without really touching on the Windows Server or Network Fundamentals certifications. For this reason, Microsoft has included this information about the network infrastructure as part of the 70-668 exam. It simply would not do to have a large number of SharePoint admins out there who weren't aware of the impact their SharePoint installations are having on the network infrastructures on which they run. Preventing this scenario is what this chapter is all about.

Planning Farm Communications

A SharePoint 2010 server farm consists of three core roles: the database server, the application server, and the Web Front End (WFE) server. When all three servers are installed on a single Windows server installation, the communications within the farm are internal. No network traffic is required for farm communications within a single-server installation. When the farm scales out to support multiple servers playing different roles within the farm, farm communications must be considered with more planning and detail.

Farm communications can be categorized as internal or external. Both communication types are addressed in this section. An important content synchronization method, called a content deployment path, is also covered within this section. This section is a quick overview of the considerations that you must make when planning farm communications. To make the best decisions during farm communications planning, you will need to understand the details presented in the later sections named "Network Protocols: A Summary" and "Network Services."

Internal Farm Communications

Internal farm communications are the communications that take place between the SharePoint servers and services within a single farm. These SharePoint servers include the database server, the application server, and the WFE server. The communications will differ depending on whether you implement a single-server farm or a multiserver farm.

When using a single-server farm, all communications within the farm take place within that single server. The SharePoint applications communicate with the SQL server using the Shared Memory protocol, which means that no network communications are required. The Shared Memory protocol is intelligent enough to realize that the application accessing the SQL server is on the same machine as the SQL server, and it allows the communications to occur without the use of the network interface controller (NIC). Of course, this is much faster than networked communications.

When you use a multiserver farm, TCP/IP is used for communications between the SharePoint applications on the IIS server or servers and the SQL Server database server. All of the knowledge provided in this chapter's later "Network Protocols: A Summary" section is required to fully optimize the communications within a multiserver farm; however, the following guidelines will be helpful:

- Install all of the servers in the farm on the same network segment whenever possible. This configuration removes the requirement for a router and speeds up internal farm communications.

- Disable any unused protocols on the servers. For example, if you are not yet using IPv6 in your environment, IPv6 should be disabled on all of the SharePoint 2010 servers.

- Use fast and reliable switches. Do not go cheap on the switches. Consumer-grade switches simply do not perform at the level of enterprise-grade switches.

External Farm Communications

When your SharePoint 2010 farm requires communication with another farm or simply another web server, you must plan for these communications. As an example, RSS feeds are very popular today and SharePoint servers can display the contents of an RSS feed using a web part. The server must be able to communicate with the hosting server in order to display this information. The most common issue that prevents such external communications from working is the limitations imposed by a network firewall or the

Windows Firewall running on the server itself. Exercise 3.1 provides instructions for disabling the built-in Windows Firewall on Windows Server 2008 R2.

EXERCISE 3.1

Disabling the Windows Firewall on Windows Server 2008 R2

In this exercise, you will disable the Windows Firewall on the server. This exercise assumes that you are running a firewall at the network perimeter. You can alternatively open ports in the Windows Firewall, but this exercise will simply disable it and allow communications on all ports.

1. Log onto the server as an administrator.

2. Click Start and enter **Windows Firewall** in the search field, and then click the link that reads Windows Firewall (not the link that reads Windows Firewall With Advanced Security) in the results.

3. In the Windows Firewall window, click the link on the left panel that says Turn Windows Firewall On Or Off.

4. Choose the Turn Off Windows Firewall (Not Recommended) option for the Domain Network, Home Or Work Network, and the Public Network Location Settings, and then click OK.

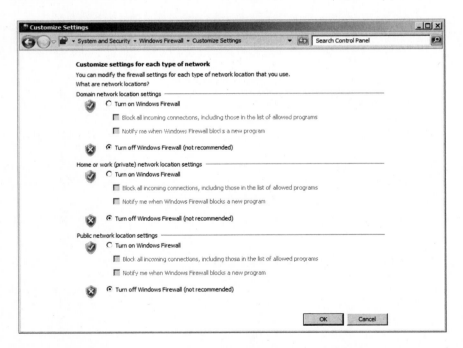

5. Click the X in the upper-right corner to close the Windows Firewall window.

If you prefer to enable or disable ports individually within the Windows Firewall feature of Windows Server, it is typically easier to do that from the Windows Firewall with the Advanced Security interface. The most common port used to access remote web servers, including RSS feeds, is port 80. As long as your server can communicate with that port and the perimeter firewall allows the same port through, you should be able to access remote servers. If communications fail, check with the server administrator to find out what ports are used. Alternatively, you could use a low-level protocol analyzer, such as WireShark, to capture the attempted communications originating from your server. This capture would reveal the protocols and ports used.

Content Deployment Paths

Content deployment paths are used to create connections between site collections. One site collection acts as the source, and the other as the destination. The SharePoint content deployment engine uses the connection to publish content from the source site collection or farm into the destination site collection or farm. The great thing about these content deployment paths is that they can be created between farms so that you can deploy content once and have it automatically distributed to every farm where it is needed.

This benefit is most clearly seen in very large deployments. With an organization including thousands of employees who use the SharePoint sites, you may choose to deploy several farms. Now consider how you would deploy content to all of those farms. If you wanted to have the same content in all of the farms and content deployment paths did not exist, you would have to either manually enter the content in each farm or you would have to build your own content distribution engine.

A content deployment job is used to schedule the content moves using the content deployment paths. This is a one-way job, meaning that content is always changed at one location and it is pushed out to one or more receiving locations. In fact, if you create new content in the destination site, it can cause the content deployment job to fail. You could potentially prevent modifications of the content in the destination site through the use of permissions. Simply set the permissions to read-only for everyone in that site, and you will not have to worry about local modifications.

Content deployment paths and jobs are created from Central Administration (CA). In the General Application Settings section, you will see a link titled Configure Content Deployment Paths and Jobs. When you click this link, you will be taken to the Manage Content Deployment Paths and Jobs screen shown in Figure 3.1. From there, you can create either a new path or a new job. You cannot create a job until a path is defined.

FIGURE 3.1 The Manage Content Deployment Paths And Jobs screen

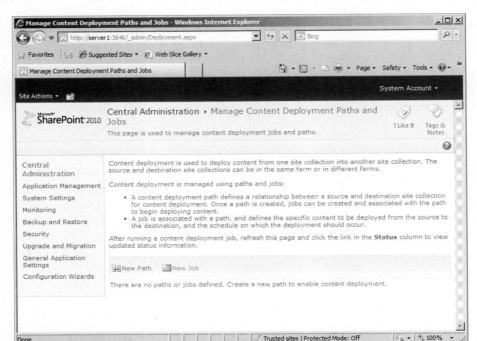

When you create a new path, you will be asked to define the following information:

- Name of the path
- Source web application
- Source site collection in that web application
- Destination Central Administration server
- Authentication type and credentials
- Destination web application and site collection

Be sure to collect this information before creating the new path. Additionally, you must be able to connect to the destination during the creation of the content deployment path. Therefore, the destination server, web application, and site collection must already exist.

Network Protocols: A Summary

Entire books are written on the topic of network protocols. In fact, entire books are written on individual protocols. As a SharePoint 2010 administrator, you need understand the basics of network protocols and how they will impact your SharePoint deployments. The basics include:

- The OSI model
- Networking hardware
- Physical layer protocols
- Communications protocols

The OSI Model

It is usually easier to understand how a complex system works by comparing it to an abstract model. That's exactly what the Open System Interconnection (OSI) model is. It is an abstract model of networking, and it is important for you to know that no actual working OSI-based network is used in organizations today. While this model is not directly implemented in the TCP/IP networks that are most common in organizations, it is still a valuable conceptual model that helps you relate different technologies to one another and implement the right technology in the best way. It is common to find references to the OSI model throughout vendor literature from Microsoft, so it is important for you to understand what these references mean.

According to document ISO/IEC 7498-1, which is the OSI Basic Reference Model standard document, the OSI model provides a "common basis for the coordination of standards development for the purpose of systems interconnection, while allowing existing standards to be placed into perspective within the overall reference model." The model is useful both for new standards as they are developed and for thinking about existing standards, such as the TCP/IP model. In fact, one common way of using the OSI model is to relate the TCP/IP suite to the layers of the OSI model. Even though TCP/IP was developed before the OSI model, the TCP/IP suite can be placed in perspective in relation to the OSI model.

The OSI Basic Reference Model document may be downloaded from the ECMA website located at http://www.ecma-international.org/activities/Communications/TG11/s020269e.pdf.

The OSI model allows you to think about your network in sections or layers. You can focus on tuning each layer, securing each layer, and troubleshooting each layer. Through this method you can take a very complex communications process (computer networking) apart and evaluate its components (those that work at each layer). To better understand why these benefits are realized, you will need to know that the OSI model is broken into seven layers. The seven layers are

- Application
- Presentation
- Session
- Transport
- Network
- Data Link
- Physical

Each layer is said to provide services to and receive services from the layers above and below it. For instance, the Data Link layer provides a service to the Physical layer and receives a service from the Physical layer. The Data Link layer converts packets into frames for the Physical layer, and the Physical layer transmits these frames as bits on the medium (wired or wireless). The Physical layer reads bits off the medium and converts them into frames for the Data Link layer.

The layered model provides for abstraction. The higher layers do not have to know the actions and reactions of the lower layers. In addition, the lower layers do not have to know what the upper layers are doing with the results of the lower layers' labors. The abstraction of activity means that you have the ability to use the same web browser and HTTP to communicate on the Internet regardless of whether the lower-layer connection is a dial-up 300 baud modem, a 20 Mbps high-speed Internet connection, or somewhere in between. The resulting speed or performance will certainly vary, but the functionality will remain the same thanks to the abstraction.

Figure 3.2 illustrates the layered structure of the OSI model. Data passes down through the layers, across the chosen medium, and then back up through the layers on the receiving end. Most networking standards allow for the substitution of nearly any Data Link and Physical layer.

FIGURE 3.2   A basic depiction of the OSI model

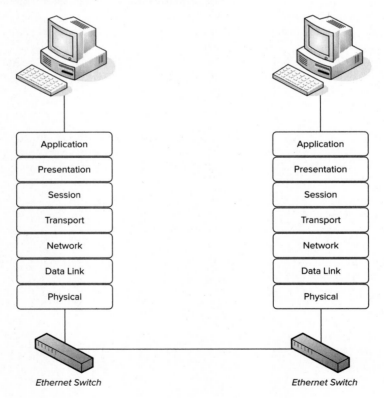

| Application |
| Presentation |
| Session |
| Transport |
| Network |
| Data Link |
| Physical |

Ethernet Switch   *Ethernet Switch*

While Figure 3.2 shows a wired Ethernet connection between the two machines, the OSI model can also depict a wireless connection using the IEEE 802.11 standard for the descriptions of the Data Link and Physical layers. This example uses the IEEE 802.3 Ethernet standard for the lower layers. The most popular upper-layer protocol suite, TCP/IP, can work across most lower-layer standards such as 802.3 (Ethernet), 802.5 (Token Ring), 802.11 (Wireless LANs), and 802.16 (WiMAX).

In order to fully understand the OSI model and be able to relate to it throughout the rest of your career in technology, it is important that you evaluate each layer. You will need to understand the basic description of each layer and the services that the layer provides to the networking process. Each layer is defined in the following list:

Application Layer   The seven layers of the OSI model are described in Clause 7 of the document ISO/IEC 7498-1. The Application layer is described in Subclause 7.1 as the highest layer in the reference model. It acts as the sole means of access to the OSIE (Open System Interconnection Environment). Stated differently, the Application layer is the layer that provides access to the other OSI layers for applications and to applications for the other OSI layers. Examples of Application layer protocols and functions include HTTP, FTP, and SMTP. The Hypertext Transfer Protocol (HTTP) is used to transfer HTML, ASP, PHP, and other types of documents from one machine to another. The File Transfer Protocol (FTP) is used to transfer binary and ASCII files between a server and a client. The Simple Mail Transport Protocol (SMTP) is used to move e-mail messages from one server to another and typically works in conjunction with other protocols for mail storage.

According to the OSI model standard, the processes operating in the Application layer are known as application-entities. An application-entity is an active element that embodies a set of capabilities pertinent to OSI and that is defined for the Application layer. Application-entities are the services that run in Layer 7 and communicate with lower layers while exposing entry points to the OSI model for applications running on the local computing device. SMTP is an application-entity, as are HTTP and other Layer 7 protocols.

Presentation Layer   The Presentation layer as described in Subclause 7.2 of the standard is the sixth layer of the OSI model. It provides services to the Application layer above it and the Session layer below it. The Presentation layer provides for the representation of the information communicated by or referenced by application-entities. The Presentation layer provides for syntax management and conversion as well as encryption services. Syntax management refers to the process of ensuring that the sending and receiving hosts communicate with a shared syntax or language. Examples of Presentation layer protocols and functions include any number of data representation and encryption protocols. For example, if you choose to use HTTPS instead of HTTP, you are indicating that you want to use Secure Sockets Layer (SSL) encryption. SSL encryption is related to the Presentation layer, or Layer 6 of the OSI model.

The processes running at Layer 6 are known as presentation-entities in the OSI model documentation. Therefore, an application-entity is said to depend on the services of a presentation-entity, and the presentation-entity is said to serve the application-entity.

Session Layer   The Session layer is described in Subclause 7.3 of the standard as providing the means necessary for cooperating presentation-entities to organize and synchronize their dialogue and to manage their data exchange. This exchange is accomplished by establishing a connection between two communicating presentation-entities. The result is simple mechanisms for orderly data exchange and session termination. Examples of Session layer protocols and functions include the iSCSI protocol, RPC, and NFS. The iSCSI protocol provides access to SCSI devices on remote computers or servers. The Remote Procedure Call (RPC) protocol allows subroutines to be executed on remote computers. A programmer can develop an application that calls the subroutine in the same way as a local subroutine. RPC abstracts the Network layer and allows the application running above Layer 7 to execute the subroutine without knowledge of the fact that it is running on a remote computer. The Network File System (NFS) protocol is used to provide access to files on remote computers as if they were on the local computer.

The services and processes running in Layer 5 are known as session-entities. Therefore, RPC and NFS would be session-entities. These session-entities will be served by the Transport layer.

Transport Layer   Layer 4, the Transport layer, is described as providing transparent transfer of data between session-entities and relieving them of any concern with the detailed way in which the reliable and cost effective transfer of data is achieved. This simply means that the Transport layer is the layer where the data is segmented for effective transfer. Examples of Transport layer protocols and functions include TCP and UDP. The Transmission Control Protocol (TCP) is the primary protocol used for the transmission of connection-oriented data in the TCP/IP suite. HTTP, SMTP, FTP, and other important Layer 7 protocols depend on TCP for reliable delivery and receipt of data. The User Datagram Protocol (UDP) is used for connectionless data communications. For example, when speed of communications is more important than reliability, UDP is frequently used.

TCP and UDP are examples of transport-entities at Layer 4. These transport-entities will be served by the Network layer. At the Transport layer, the data is broken into segments if necessary. If the data will fit in one segment, then the data becomes a single segment. Otherwise, the data is divided into multiple segments for transmission.

Network Layer   The Network layer is described as providing "the functional and procedural means for connectionless-mode (UDP) or connection-mode (TCP) transmission among transport-entities and, therefore, provides to the transport-entities independence of routing and relay considerations." The Network layer says to the Transport layer, "You just give me the segments you want to be transferred and tell me where you want them to go and I'll take care of the rest." This segregation of communication is why routers do not have to expand data beyond Layer 3 to route the data properly. For example, an IP router does not care if it's routing a packet from SharePoint servers to a client or a voice conversation. It only needs to know the IP address for which the packet is destined and any relevant QoS parameters in order to move the packet along. Examples of Network layer protocols and functions include IP and ICMP. The Internet Protocol (IP) is used to address and route data packets so they can reach their destination. That destination can be on the local network or a remote network. The local machine is never concerned with this, with the exception of the required knowledge of an exit point, or default gateway, from the local machine's network. The Internet Control Message Protocol (ICMP) is used for testing the TCP/IP communications and for error-message handling within Layer 3.

The services and processes operating in the Network layer are known as network-entities. These network-entities depend on the services provided by the Data Link layer. At the Network layer, Transport layer segments become packets. These packets will be processed by the Data Link layer.

Data Link Layer   The Data Link layer is described as providing communications between connectionless-mode or connection-mode network-entities. This method may include the establishment, maintenance, and release of connections for connection-mode network-entities. The Data Link layer is also responsible for detecting errors that may occur in the Physical layer. Therefore, the Data Link layer provides services to Layer 3 and Layer 1.

Examples of Data Link layer protocols and functions include Ethernet, PPP, and HDLC. Ethernet is the most widely used protocol for local area networks (LANs) and will be the type of LAN you deal with when using most modern LAN technologies. The Point to Point Protocol (PPP) is commonly used for wide area network (WAN) links across analog lines and other tunneling purposes across digital lines. The High-Level Data Link Control (HDLC) protocol is a solution created by the ISO for bit-oriented synchronous communications. It is a very popular protocol used for WAN links.

The IEEE has divided the Data Link layer into two sublayers: the Logical Link Control (LLC) sublayer and the Medium Access Control (MAC) sublayer. The LLC sublayer is not actually used by many transport protocols, such as TCP. The varied IEEE standards identify the behavior of the MAC sublayer within the Data Link layer and the PHY layer as well.

Physical Layer   The Physical layer, sometimes called the PHY, is responsible for providing the mechanical, electrical, functional, or procedural means for establishing physical connections between data-link-entities. The connections between all other layers are really logical connections, as the only real physical connection that results in true transfer of data is at Layer 1—the Physical layer. For example, we say that Layer 7 HTTP on a client creates a connection with Layer 7 HTTP on a web server when a user browses an Internet website; however, the reality is that this connection is logical and the real connections happen at the Physical layer.

Layer 1 is responsible for taking the data frames from Layer 2 and transmitting them on the communications medium as binary bits (ones and zeros). This medium may be wired or wireless. It may use electrical signals or light pulses (both actually being electromagnetic in nature). Whatever you've chosen to use at Layer 1, the upper layers can communicate across it as long as the hardware and drivers abstract that layer so that it provides the services demanded of the upper-layer protocols.

Examples of Physical layer protocols and functions include Ethernet and Wi-Fi. You probably noticed that Ethernet was mentioned as an example of a Data Link layer protocol. This is because Ethernet defines both the functionality within Layer 2 and the PHY for Layer 1. Wi-Fi technologies (IEEE 802.11) are similar in that both the Data Link layer and Physical layer functions and procedures are specified in the standard. The Data Link and Physical layers are often discussed in standards together. You could say that Layer 2 acts as an intermediary between Layers 3 through 7 so that you can run IPX/SPX (though hardly anyone uses this protocol today) or TCP/IP across a multitude of network types (network types being understood as different Data Link and Physical specifications such as 802.3 and 802.11).

Why Is the OSI Model Important?

The OSI model should be considered as more than a set of facts that you memorize for certification exams. It has become the most common method for referencing all things related to networking. Many resources assume that you understand this model and reference it without explanation. You may read statements like the following:

"The domain controller, member server, and the client computer should be on an isolated network and should be connected through a common hub or Layer 2 switch."

This statement is quoted from an article at Microsoft's website. The article does not explain what is meant by Layer 2. It simply assumes that you know what this means. The OSI model, therefore, has become required foundational knowledge for anyone working in the computer or data networking industry—and this includes SharePoint administrators. Many certification exams will not test you on the OSI model directly but will phrase questions so that you must understand the OSI model—as well as other facts—in order to answer the questions correctly.

For example, it is not uncommon to see questions like this: "You are a SharePoint 2010 administrator working for a product development company. You want to enable secure communications with the SharePoint servers at Layer 2 or Layer 3 of the OSI model. What technologies can you use to implement this security?"

The possible answers will, of course, be a list of protocols and other security technologies that operate at these layers. You'll have to know which of these protocols both provide security and operate at Layer 2 (Data Link) or Layer 3 (Network) of the OSI model.

Although the information provided here will not be directly addressed on the 70-668 examination, you will benefit greatly by learning the OSI model for both your certification examination and everyday workload—and you'll actually be able to understand all those articles, whitepapers, and books that refer to the various layers of the OSI model.

Now that you have reviewed the layers of the OSI model, it is important for you to understand the communications process used within the model. Each layer communicates with a peer layer on another system. For example, the Application layer on one device communicates with the Application layer on the other device. In the same way, all seven layers communicate with the matching peer layer on remote devices. The virtual communication between peer layers is accomplished through segmentation and encapsulation.

Segmentation is the process of segmenting or separating the data into constrained sizes for transfer. As an example, the standard Ethernet frame can include a payload (the actual data to be transferred) of no more than 1,500 octets. An octet is 8 bits and is usually called a byte. Data that is larger than 1,500 bytes must be broken into chunks that are 1,500 bytes or smaller, and this process is called *segmentation*. The segmentation begins at Layer 4, where TCP segments are created and may continue at Layer 3, where IP fragmentation can occur in order to reduce packet sizes so that they can be processed by Layer 2 as Ethernet frames.

Encapsulation is used to envelope information within headers so that it can be passed across different networks. For example, IP packets (also called datagrams) are encapsulated inside of Ethernet frames to be passed on an Ethernet network. The encapsulation means that the IP packet is surrounded by header and possibly footer information that allows the data to be transmitted. Ethernet frames consist of a header that includes the destination and source addresses. Ethernet frames also have a footer that consists of a frame check sequence (FCS) used for error correction.

The most important thing to remember about all of this is that the Application layer on one device never links directly to the Application layer on another device, even though they are said to be communicating peers. Instead, the communications travel through many intermediaries (OSI layers) on the way to the final destination. You might think of it like a letter sent through the letter carrier service of your choice. You provide the letter to the service provider in a sealed envelope. The service provider carries it to the destination. The recipient opens the letter, but he or she was not involved in the transport of the communication. The letter carrier service was responsible for all of the links in the chain that allowed the letter to move from the originating location to the destination. The enveloping and opening of the letter is like the Application layer, and all of the rest of the transport is like Layers 1 through 6 of the OSI model.

This layered effect is really no different than human communications. Behind all human communications is an initial thought that needs to be transferred from one human to another. This thought may or may not already be in a language that both humans share. If not, the thought must be translated to a shared language, such as English. After the thought is translated into English, the brain must send signals to the vocal chords and mouth to transmit the signals of sound that result in English enunciation. Now the signals (sound waves) travel through the environment in which they are spoken until they reach the recipient's ears. The eardrums receive these signals and send the received information to the brain. Here the information is interpreted and may or may not have been received correctly. The recipient can send back a signal (verbal or visual) to communicate her understanding of the information so that the sender can be sure the recipient received the communication properly.

Do you see the similarities? The goal here is to provide peer communications from the "thought area" of the brain to another person's "thought area." Much as the Session layer represents data in a way that the remote machine can understand it, the sender's brain had to translate the original thought into a shared language. Much as the Physical layer has to transmit electrical signals on a wired network, the vocal cords and mouth had to transmit signals as sound waves to the recipient's ears. The point is that you can break human communications into layers that are similar to the ones described in the OSI model.

It is important for you to remember that the OSI model is a reference and not an actual implementation. It is used to better understand and plan networking technologies.

Networking Hardware

The hardware that is used to build your network is clearly an important part of your SharePoint infrastructure. Switches will provide access to the network. Routers will build the segmentation structures. Network adapters allow devices to function on the network. Wireless networks introduce significant differences when compared to wired networks. This section introduces you to these important topics.

In order to fully understand the following sections, you should understand the OSI model, which explains concepts such as layers, MAC, and segmentation. This information is covered in the section "The OSI Model" earlier in this chapter.

Switches

Switches are used to provide communication among devices on the same subnet or network. The term *switching* refers to the actions carried out by a switch. A *switch* is a device that performs packet forwarding for packet-switched networks. A switch can forward packets from an incoming port to the necessary outgoing port or ports in order to enable the packet to reach its destination. It is inside of these switches—as well as the routers you will learn about next—that much of the data processing is performed. The switch can extract a frame and determine if it is destined for a device connected to the same switch and, if it is, quickly forward it on without requiring a router. When the destination is on a different network segment, the switch must send the frame out through a port that is connected to a router that can reach the remote network segment.

In order to help you understand the benefit an Ethernet switch brings to your network, let's explore the method used to access the medium in Ethernet networks. Ethernet uses CSMA/CD, or Carrier Sense Multiple Access with Collision Detection. Just as there are rules of etiquette for human discussions (though they are sometimes assumed and not really taught), Ethernet networks have rules for communicating on the network.

Every Ethernet device complies with the rules of CSMA/CD. These devices need to be able to detect activity on the wire before they attempt to use it for their own transmission. This method is like being in a meeting and using your ears to listen for other conversations before you speak. In addition, the Ethernet device needs to have a method for detecting a collision when it does transmit. It is possible for two Ethernet devices connected to the same medium to begin communicating at exactly or nearly the same moment. This situation will result in a collision. When a collision happens, a jam signal is sent on the medium letting all the devices know that a collision has occurred and that they should all begin the backoff operation before attempting to communicate again. Relating again to the business meeting, this event is like you beginning to speak at the same moment as one of the other attendees. You both sense this "collision," and according to many possible parameters, one of you will back off and let the other speak.

Here's the question: If there are 200 people in a room, is it more or less likely that two people will begin talking at the same moment? The answer is clearly that it is more likely. The same is true on your Ethernet network. When more nodes (network communicating devices) are connected to the same wire or hub (a network device that sends incoming communications out all connected ports), collisions are more likely on the network. The goal is to reduce the number of nodes on the wire or local network segment. This task can be done by using routers to implement smaller collision domains, but there is also another way.

What if you could implement a network where there were never any collisions? You can, and that network is a switched network. For this reason, hubs have been all but removed from enterprise-class networks and switches have been implemented in their place. A switch filters, forwards, or floods Ethernet frames based on the destination MAC address of each frame. A MAC address is an address for the physical adapter on the network. In Exercise 3.2, you will see how to view the MAC address of a network adapter in Windows Server 2008 R2. Knowing a computer's MAC address is not a requirement for implementing or building networks, but it is helpful when troubleshooting switching problems. For example, you could use the Windows command-line ARP command to verify that the MAC address or a remote machine is properly stored in your computer's cache. If the wrong MAC address is stored in the cache, you could use the ARP command to empty the cache and force a new IP address to MAC address-resolution process.

EXERCISE 3.2

Viewing the MAC Address

In this exercise, you will use the graphical interface of Windows Server 2008 R2 and the command-line interface to view the MAC address of the network adapter.

1. Log onto the server as an administrator.

2. Click Start, type `cmd` into the search field, and press Enter.

3. Execute the command `ipconfig /all` at the command prompt.

4. Note the Physical Address for the Ethernet adapter. This is your adapter's MAC address.

```
Administrator: Command Prompt                                            _|□|x|
   Primary Dns Suffix  . . . . . . . : SharePoint.local
   Node Type . . . . . . . . . . . : Hybrid
   IP Routing Enabled. . . . . . . : No
   WINS Proxy Enabled. . . . . . . : No
   DNS Suffix Search List. . . . . : SharePoint.local

Ethernet adapter Local Area Connection:

   Connection-specific DNS Suffix  . :
   Description . . . . . . . . . . : Intel(R) PRO/1000 MT Network Connection
   Physical Address. . . . . . . . : 00-0C-29-D8-97-68
   DHCP Enabled. . . . . . . . . . : No
   Autoconfiguration Enabled . . . : Yes
   Link-local IPv6 Address . . . . : fe80::196c:b3da:a400:a9e3%11(Preferred)
   IPv4 Address. . . . . . . . . . : 192.168.10.99(Preferred)
   Subnet Mask . . . . . . . . . . : 255.255.255.0
   Default Gateway . . . . . . . . : 192.168.10.1
   DHCPv6 IAID . . . . . . . . . . : 234884137
   DHCPv6 Client DUID. . . . . . . : 00-01-00-01-14-A3-C0-7B-00-0C-29-D8-97-68

   DNS Servers . . . . . . . . . . : ::1
                                     127.0.0.1
   NetBIOS over Tcpip. . . . . . . : Enabled

Tunnel adapter isatap.{6E91AC18-AE7F-4AC2-87FF-DC748FCD8297}:
```

5.   Execute the command **exit** to end the command prompt session.

___

To best understand switches, you should understand the differences between unicast, multicast, and broadcast traffic.

- *Unicast traffic* is traffic that moves from one point (the source) to another point (the destination). The traffic or frame is intended for a single endpoint.

- *Multicast traffic* is traffic that moves from one point to multiple specified points. The traffic or frame is intended for multiple endpoints that are defined or listed.

- *Broadcast traffic* is traffic that moves from one point to all other points in a broadcast domain. The traffic or frame is intended for all endpoints rather than a list of endpoints or a single defined endpoint.

It is essential that you understand these three types of traffic, because they are all processed by switches. Switches can handle broadcast and multicast traffic, but their great power is in how they handle unicast traffic. A hub, now an outdated device, receives frames on each port and floods those frames out all other ports. A switch receives frames on each port and then analyzes the frame to see if it is a unicast, multicast, or broadcast frame.

It is important that you understand this guideline: a switch implements a number of segments (at the Data Link layer) equal to the number of ports it provides, and these segments experience no collisions. This guideline assumes that you are using full-duplex communications. This assumption is because full-duplex communications use one pair of wires to send data to the switch and another pair of wires to receive data from the switch. Because this configuration is a pair of one-way streets, there will be no collisions and CSMA/CD is not used. A full-duplex design greatly improves actual data throughput and reduces management overhead. It also allows you to grow routed network segments much larger. Many enterprise networks have segments with as many as 500 nodes on the segment. Growing segments larger than that is not recommended.

Routers

Routing is the process of moving data packets from one network to another or from one segment on your network to another. When a data packet is transmitted from a computing device, it may move directly to another device on the same network, or it may require a router to forward it to another network. This is the primary job of a router: to connect otherwise disconnected networks.

Here's a good way to remember the difference between a switch and a router: if you connect multiple switches together, you are just creating a bigger physical network segment. The same is not true with routers. In fact, you should not really think of routers as being connected together. Instead, routers have two or more interfaces. As shown in Figure 3.3, one interface will be connected to one network and the other interface will be connected to another. This separation allows the router to be used as a packet routing device when a device in Network A wants to send a packet to a device in Network B.

FIGURE 3.3　Routing illustrated

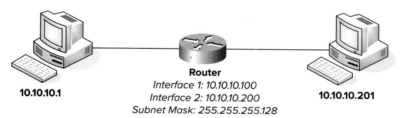

Router
Interface 1: 10.10.10.100
Interface 2: 10.10.10.200
Subnet Mask: 255.255.255.128

10.10.10.1

10.10.10.201

A *router* is a computing device that is capable of moving data from one network to another network using different algorithms, which differ based on the network protocols the network uses. Most networks today use an IP router. Additionally, routers are used as connections to WAN service providers so that they have an interface connected to the LAN and another interface connected to the WAN. When data needs to travel to the remote network, it will pass in through the LAN interface and out through the WAN interface. From the WAN network, the data will pass in through the WAN interface and out through the LAN interface. When the communications are reversed, so is the interface utilization.

Routers are key to networking performance, and networking performance is key to SharePoint performance. Compared to routers, switches are pretty basic devices. Certainly, you want to select a fast switch, which would be 100 Mbps or 1,000 Mbps for switches through which computers access the network; however, the routers will have to process all of the traffic that moves from one segment to another on your network.

The impact of this reality is made clear in Figure 3.4. Notice that three different network segments are connecting into the central data center. SharePoint servers are installed in the data center. Each network segment has more than 100 nodes or computers connected. While the switches in each network segment may perform switching for between 20 and 50 devices each, the routers have to forward packets from all 100 nodes in each segment into the data center. In addition, the routers have to forward packets from one segment to the other. In the end, routers are more frequently the cause of network bottlenecks than switches.

FIGURE 3.4   A routed network infrastructure

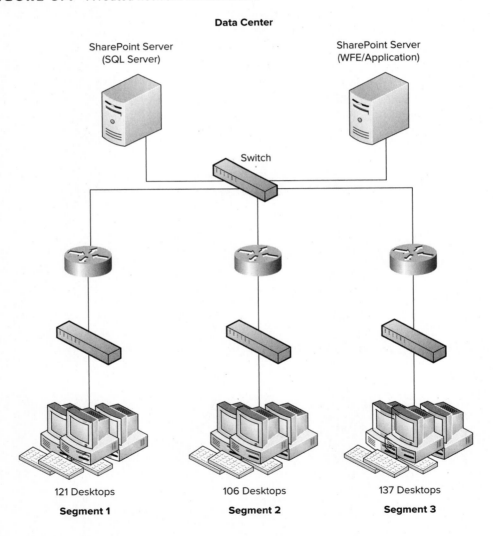

In order to help you better understand routers so that you can avoid bottlenecking as much as possible, the following sections will discuss them from five perspectives:

- Functionality
- Common features
- Physical installation options
- Configuration process
- IP routing basics

Functionality

To help you understand what a router really is and what it does, consider that a router is nothing more than a computer. You could install two network adapters in a single computer and then connect one adapter to one network and the other adapter to another network. After this configuration is in place, your computer could be configured to route between the two networks. The Windows operating system has had routing capabilities in it since the Windows NT days back in the 1990s, and Linux systems have this capability as well. In fact, a few routers on the market actually run a scaled-down version of the Linux operating system embedded into the ROM of the device.

Where most computers have hard drives, memory chips (RAM), and a processor, most routers have nonvolatile random access memory (NVRAM) for permanent storage during the powered-off state, memory chips (RAM) for temporary storage during the powered-on state, and a processor or set of special processors. Computers use the hard drive to store permanent information that needs to be retained between boots, and routers use the NVRAM for this purpose. This difference allows the routers to boot quickly and reboot quickly. It also reduces moving parts and therefore common points of failure, which extends the life of most routers.

Many routers function for well over a decade. In comparison to computers, network routers very rarely fail. Even a consumer-grade router, such as one from Linksys, will usually work for well over ten years; however, most computers do well if they make it four or five years without needing a hard drive replaced. Notice what it is that is most likely to fail—the hard drive. This problem is why the NVRAM is so beneficial.

Things do seem to be changing somewhat. Hard drives seem to be outlasting processors and memory these days. I'm not sure if it's just an illusion of my experience or if it's true, but it seems that the great heat in the average computer case is causing failures in areas less frequently seen in the past.

Don't Use a Computer as a Router!

You can use a computer to perform the functions of a router. This is possible for one simple reason: all routers are computers. If you take a router apart, you will see a processor, memory, and sometimes even a hard drive (for example, a hard drive used for voicemail storage).

A computer may be running Windows Server, and routing may be enabled across two networks by using two network cards. When the computer with the IP address of, say, 10.10.1.5 needs to communicate with the computer at, say, 10.10.2.7, it must communicate through the computer. The Windows server receives the communication on the adapter at 10.10.1.1 and sends it out of the adapter at 10.10.2.1 so that it can reach the destination of 10.10.2.7. As this routing process is taking place on a computer running Windows Server, the routing may be slower because the server is not likely to be a dedicated router. This server may be providing DHCP services, DNS services, domain services, or any other service supported by the Windows server. This additional overhead is why dedicated devices are usually used as routers.

A dedicated device has at least two major benefits. First, the processing will most likely be faster, because it is dedicated to the process of routing. Second, the up time will most likely be greater, because you will have to perform fewer upgrades and you will experience fewer hardware failures (remember, nonmoving parts). On the first point, the processing will not only be faster because the entire device is dedicated to routing, but also because the software is optimized for that purpose. With a regular PC running an operating system that supports routing, the operating system is most likely doing many things not related to routing.

Routers, in most cases, route IP traffic. Where does the IP operate in the OSI mode? It operates at Layer 3 or the Network layer. This tells you that a router is a Layer 3 device. Routers are most commonly used to connect switches, which are Layer 2 devices in most implementations (some vendors do make specialized switches that work at Layer 2 as well as upper OSI layers), together to form larger networks than could be otherwise created. It is important to know that some routers can perform switching with added components and some switches can perform routing. However, for simplified explanations, they are treated as completely separate devices, and the customized modern routers and switches offered by today's vendors will be ignored.

 Concepts such as layers and segmentation are covered in more detail in the section "The OSI Model" earlier in this chapter.

Common Features

Regardless of the vendor, routers share a common set of features, which include

- CPU
- Memory
- NVRAM
- ROM or BIOS
- Operating system
- Interfaces
- Management considerations

CPU   Processor speeds vary in routers from less than 100 MHz to greater than 1 GHz. Keep in mind that the router is dedicated to routing, so a speed of, say, 200 MHz is not as slow as it sounds by today's standards for desktop computers and servers. Enterprise-class routers, such as those from Cisco, HP, and Nortel, will have both faster processors and more memory than consumer-grade routers in most cases. Additionally, many consumer-grade routers are hard-coded to disallow data from the Internet that is not based on a previous internal request and this firewalling feature simply cannot be disabled. Such a feature is unacceptable in enterprise networks.

Memory   Modern routers support 1 gigabyte or more of RAM for massive processing capabilities with special features like built-in firewalls, intrusion-prevention systems, and VoIP management. Again, keep in mind that these dedicated devices do not have the 100 to 500 megabytes being consumed by the operating system as a desktop computer does. Most of this RAM is being utilized for the work of routing. Older and consumer-grade routers may have only a few megabytes of memory. Routers with less than one megabyte of memory are of little use today.

NVRAM   The NVRAM in routers and other network devices is usually used to store the configuration settings for the device. In addition to storing the configuration in NVRAM, you can usually upload the configuration to an FTP or TFTP server or you can save the configuration to a local PC when connected via the console port on the router or an HTTP web-based configuration interface.

ROM or BIOS   The ROM or BIOS in a router contains the bootstrap program used to get the device up and running. This may include initial system checks known as the Power On Self Test (POST), and it may include features related to customizable components in the router. The ROM or BIOS is often updated using a flash mechanism and downloaded modules from the router vendor's website.

Operating System   Again, like a PC, a router has an operating system. The famous Cisco Internetwork Operating System (IOS) is used on nearly all newer Cisco routers and is probably the most well-known router OS in the world. However, each vendor typically uses its own proprietary OS, because that gives the vendor a competitive advantage. Even consumer-grade routers have an OS; it's usually just much less powerful than those in the enterprise-class routers. In fact, sometimes the only difference between a consumer device and an enterprise device is the software it's running.

Interfaces   Routers typically come with one or more built-in interfaces and the ability to add more interfaces through add-on modules. Each vendor refers to these add-on modules with differing terminology, but you can think of them like PCI cards for a desktop computer. Just as you can add a PCI wireless network card to a computer and—poof—the computer now has wireless capabilities, you can add a new card to a router and provide additional capabilities. Cisco typically refers to the modules as network modules or interface cards, but other vendors may use different terminology.

Management Methods   When it comes to managing routers, the options are nearly endless. You can manage most enterprise routers in any of the following ways:

- **Console:** This connection uses a serial interface and a terminal emulation program allowing command-line management of the router.

- **Telnet:** This application gives you the same options as the console (as long as Telnet is enabled), only you manage your router across the network.

- **Web-based:** Using a web browser, you can connect to the router and configure it using a graphical management interface.

- **Custom applications:** Some vendors provide custom applications that run on Windows, Linux, or the Mac OS and can be used to configure the router. Third-party companies also sometimes provide such applications.

- **SNMP:** The Simple Network Management Protocol may be able to be used with some routers to configure them on a large scale.

These are just the most common configuration and management options. You may also be able to use SSH, SFTP, and other methods with the routers that you implement. The key is to know the most secure and efficient methods. If you implement an insecure management solution, such as Telnet across an unencrypted channel, the administrative account will be exposed and attackers can easily find their way into your network.

Physical Installation Considerations

Most enterprise-class routers are designed to fit into rack mounts, since rack mounts are commonly used in data centers and wiring closets. Consumer-class routers may simply be shelf devices, meaning that they rest on a shelf, but even these devices usually come with mounting hardware (or the hardware can be purchased separately) to mount them to the wall or even in a rack. The big items to consider when installing routers are

- The distance from the router to the switches or Internet connections or other routers. You must ensure that you can run a cable without incurring signal loss because of increased length.

- The power source. There must be a source of power where the router is installed. Some devices may accept Power over Ethernet (PoE), but most routers will not, because they are core infrastructure devices.
- Ease of access. If you need to test a port, change a cable, or replace an interface, you will want to be able to access the router easily.

The Configuration Process

The complete details for configuring a router are beyond the scope of this book. However, there is a basic process that should be followed when installing and configuring any infrastructure device, including a router. The general rule is to configure it offline and then connect it to the network. Here's the basic flow:

1. Unpack the router and place it on a stable surface for initial configuration.
2. Connect the router to a power source.
3. Connect to the router using the appropriate mechanism (console, Ethernet, etc.).
4. Power on the router.
5. Update the router's software if necessary.
6. Perform the basic configuration of the interfaces so that they will function appropriately on your network.
7. Perform any security configuration steps required.
8. Save the configuration.
9. Power off the router.
10. Install the router in the production location and power it on.

At this point, you have configured and installed the router, and it should be performing as configured for your network. You'll want to test the network and ensure that this is correct. Can you reach the network on the other side of the router from each side? Can only the nodes that should be able to pass through the router indeed do so?

IP Routing Basics

As stated previously, routers perform their most important tasks at Layer 3. This layer is where IP operates, and IP routing is the primary function of a Layer 3 router in TCP/IP networks. It is very useful for you to understand how a router works its magic. It all begins at Layer 1 and it ends at Layer 1 as well. To understand this concept, consider Figure 3.5.

FIGURE 3.5   The router functioning as a basic three-step process

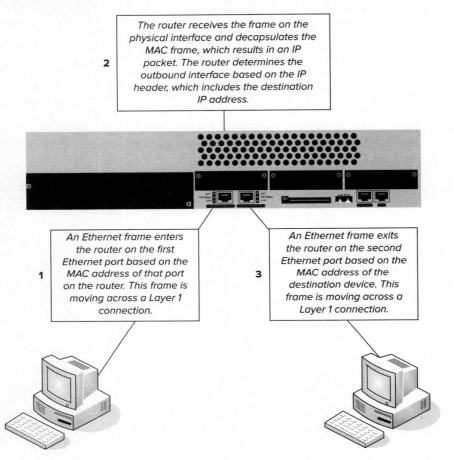

The work of a router can be summarized as follows:

1. Receive incoming frames on each interface.

2. Extract the IP packet from the incoming frame.

3. Evaluate the IP header in order to determine the destination of the packet.

4. Look in the routing table to determine the best route to the destination.

5. Encapsulate the IP packet inside a new frame and transmit it on the interface that connects to the next step in the route.

6. Process the next received frame.

As you can see, the process is really quite simple. The router must remove the preamble and MAC frame header and the Frame Check Sequence (FCS) from the Ethernet frame, which results in the original IP packet. This original IP packet will remain the same as it moves from source to destination as long as no dynamic tagging is used. The header of the IP packet contains the destination address as well as the source address. The router can use the destination address to determine the best way to reach the network on which that destination address exists. To do this task, it will use its routing table.

The router's routing table is a listing of known networks and the routes to those networks. Each entry will contain an IP address and a subnet mask. These two values are used to determine a destination network. The same IP address can be listed multiple times with different subnet masks and would result in different networks based on the subnet masks. The final important entry in the routing table represents the "way to the destination" network or host. This final element is the IP address of the device that knows how to get to the destination.

These routing tables can be built manually or automatically. If they are built manually, they are said to be static routes; if they are built automatically, they are said to be dynamic routes. Static routes are entered by an administrator who understands the structure of the network. The benefit of static routes is that they give you, the administrator, full control over the routing process. The problem with static routes is that they must be manually modified any time the network changes. This task can become time-consuming and burdensome.

Automatic building of routing tables is the point where routing protocols come into the picture. Don't get confused about the phrase *routing protocol*. A routing protocol is a protocol that discovers the neighbor networks around a router and dynamically builds the routing table for IP to utilize in routing decisions. The key is to remember that a routing protocol does not perform routing. IP is in charge of the actual routing, but the routing protocol provides the information to IP so that it can make the best decisions.

Network Adapters

The network adapter is the interface to the network. Each server and client computing device on your network must have a network adapter. The network adapter is also known as a network interface card (NIC). The NIC has several important characteristics that you must define for your networking needs:

- **Speed:** Today, most new computers come with 1 Gbps NICs, but some do still ship with 100 Mbps adapters. Be sure to select the speed you require. Your speed requirements will be based on the capacity analysis you perform during implementation planning in Chapter 2, "Designing the Physical Architecture."

- **Form factor:** NICs come as PCI, PCI Express, CardBus, and USB adapters. You will need to select the form factor required by your connecting device. Most motherboards also include a built-in network adapter.

- **Operating system support:** Some adapters come with only Windows drivers. If you want to use another operating system, be sure to stay away from such adapters.

Wireless Networks

Wireless networks based on the IEEE 802.11 standard can become quite complicated in enterprise deployments. Because of this complexity, they will not be covered in great depth here; however, it is important that you understand a few factors about 802.11 networks that could impact your SharePoint 2010 users:

Wireless Roaming   Wireless networks allow for roaming, but all roaming solutions are not created equally. Roaming occurs when a wireless client moves from one access point (AP) to another AP on the same enterprise network. When it is seamless, the users will not lose connections. When it is not seamless, connections will be lost. Be sure to test your wireless networks to determine the roaming behavior supported and then educate your users. Users will be very frustrated if they think they can start uploading a large document to a SharePoint 2010 document library and then walk with their laptop down the hall only to lose the connection during the transfer.

Wireless Performance   Most newly implemented wireless networks use 802.11g at the least and possibly even 802.11n. Both of these technologies will provide sufficient bandwidth for accessing and fully utilizing a SharePoint 2010 site as long as the wireless network is not overly congested. However, older standards such as 802.11 (original) and 802.11b may not be sufficient for using SharePoint document libraries with large documents. Even 802.11b can be used with acceptable performance for web-page-only SharePoint sites (sites without large document libraries).

Wireless Security   Wireless security concerns are often exaggerated. Certainly, you should secure your wireless network, but it is much easier than the fear that is generated about wireless computing would indicate that it is. As long as you implement the newer wireless security standards, such as WPA and WPA2, with sufficiently strong passphrases, you have nothing to worry about from a data theft or passive sniffing perspective. Fortunately, these security standards are easy to implement. For more information on this, see Tom Carpenter's book on wireless networking and security, called *CWNA Certified Wireless Network Administrator & CWSP Certified Wireless Security Professional All-in-One Exam Guide (PW0-104 & PW0-204)* (McGraw-Hill Osborne Media, 2010).

Physical Layer Protocols

The Physical layer protocols used in most business networks today are Ethernet (802.3) and Wi-Fi (802.11). Both of these IEEE standards receive updates regularly. For example, the 802.11 standard has received four new Physical layer (PHY) specifications since it was originally released in 1997. The original standard included two PHYs that worked at 2 Mbps and were implemented in many devices. An additional infrared PHY was also specified but never implemented. In 1999, two new PHYs were specified. The first running at 11 Mbps (802.11b), and the second at 54 Mbps (802.11a). In 2003 another new PHY was introduced at 54 Mbps (802.11g). Finally, in 2009, a PHY with maximum speeds of up to 600 Mbps was released (802.11n). Of course, new PHYs will be released in the future, taking the speeds even higher.

The Ethernet standard has also been updated over the years. In fact, it has received many more updates than 802.11, in part, because it has been around longer. Today, the Ethernet standards allow for data rates of 10 Mbps, 100 Mbps, 1000 Mbps, 10 Gbps, and 100 Gbps.

The most important thing you can do in relation to Physical layer protocols is select the right match of speed and cost for your environment. For example, you could implement 10 Gbps to each node on your network, but the cost would be unbelievably high. Instead, it's more practical to implement 100 Mbps or 1 Gbps to the clients and use 1 Gbps or 10 Gbps on the infrastructure. This solution is an excellent balance of cost and performance.

Communications Protocols

The primary communications protocol used on networks today is the TCP/IP suite. You should understand the functionality of this suite in a sufficient level of detail to support the SharePoint servers and the infrastructure on which they operate. HTTP, which is used for Application layer communications, should also be understood. Both protocols are explained in the following sections.

TCP/IP

Unlike the seven layers of the OSI model, the TCP/IP model contains just four layers. These four layers are named:

- Application layer
- Transport layer
- Internet layer
- Link layer

The Application layer of the TCP/IP model can be said to encompass the Application and Presentation layers of the OSI model. Layer 4 of the TCP/IP model performs the services required of Layer 5 through Layer 7 of the OSI model. RFC 1122, which defines the TCP/IP model and is available at http://tools.ietf.org/html/rfc1122, specifies two categories of Application layer protocols: user protocols and support protocols. User protocols include common protocols like FTP, SMTP, and HTTP. These protocols are all used to provide a direct service to the user. FTP allows the user to transfer a file between two machines. SMTP allows the user to send an email message. HTTP allows the user to view web pages from a website. Support protocols include common protocols like DNS,

DHCP, and BOOTP. DNS provides name resolution for user requests. For example, if a user requests to browse the homepage at www.TomCarpenter.net, the DNS support service resolves the website's domain name to an IP address for actual communication. Because this is an indirect service for the user, it is considered a support service as opposed to a user service. DHCP and BOOTP are both used to configure IP—and possibly other TCP/IP parameters—without user intervention.

The TCP/IP Transport layer provides host-to-host or end-to-end communications. Transport layer protocols may provide reliable or nonguaranteed data delivery. TCP is an example of a Transport layer protocol that provides reliable delivery of data (usually called segments), and UDP is an example of a protocol that provides nonguaranteed delivery of data (usually called datagrams). TCP does not provide guaranteed delivery of data. No network protocol can provide guaranteed delivery of data; however, *reliable* protocols do provide notice of undelivered data, and UDP does not provide such a notice.

The next layer is the TCP/IP Internet layer. The Internet layer is where host identification is utilized to route TCP segments and UDP datagrams to the appropriate end device. The protocol that all Application and Transport layer protocols use within the TCP/IP model is IP. IP provides the routing functionality that enables the implementation of very large LANs and communications across the Internet. You'll learn much more about this protocol in the IP section coming up next. In addition to IP, the Internet Control Message Protocol (ICMP) is considered an integral part of IP even though it actually uses IP for communications just as TCP and UDP do. So ICMP is considered an Internet layer protocol because of its integral use in IP-based communications.

The final or bottom layer of the TCP/IP model is the Link layer. This is where the upper layer of the TCP/IP suite interfaces with the lower layer physical-transmission medium.

Some say that the Link layer is equivalent to the Data Link layer of the OSI model, and of the TCP/IP layers, this is probably the most accurate linkage of all. It is also interesting to note that protocols such as ARP and RARP that actually service IP are not actually Link layer protocols themselves. Instead, they seem to exist in some magical land between the Link layer and the Internet layer. I would suggest that they are simply part of the Internet layer and that you could represent the Internet layer as having an upper-management layer (ICMP, IGMP, etc.), a routing layer (IP), and a routing-service layer (ARP and RARP); however, this is only my thinking and not really part of the standard TCP/IP model.

Figure 3.6 shows a common mapping of the TCP/IP model to the OSI model. Again, keep in mind that this mapping is for educational purposes only and that the TCP/IP suite of protocols makes no attempt or claim to mapping in this way. It is simply a helpful way of thinking about the functionality of the suite.

FIGURE 3.6 The TCP/IP model compared to the OSI model

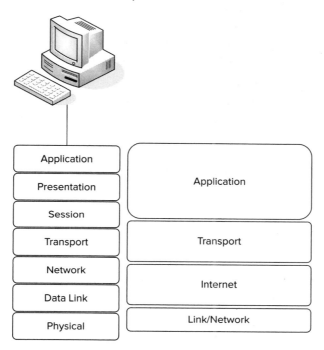

In order to fully understand how TCP/IP works, investigating the core protocols is essential. The following sections will explain the basic functionality of IP, TCP, and other important TCP/IP protocols.

Network Congestion, Segmentation, and Routing

On Ethernet networks, addresses are used to identify each node on the Ethernet. These addresses are called MAC addresses. Another address that each node possesses on a modern network is a Layer 3 address known as an IP address. MAC addresses are Layer 2 addresses, and IP addresses are Layer 3 addresses. The significance of this will become very clear in a moment.

The Internet Protocol (IP) is the Network layer (OSI) or Internet layer (TCP/IP) solution to node identification. This protocol is responsible for addressing, data routing, and servicing the upper layers in the TCP/IP suite. The question is this: Why do you need a Layer 3 address in addition to a Layer 2 address?

To understand the answer to this question, you must understand the concepts of network congestion, network segmentation, and network routing. Network congestion occurs when the bandwidth on the network is insufficient to meet the demands placed on the network. In other words, you can have too many nodes on a single network. This congestion can be detrimental to network communications, causing failed file transfers or simply frustrated users through network delays.

Consider a network with only three computers connected to a 100 Mbps switch. These computers will be able to communicate with each other very rapidly. Now, imagine that you add three more computers to double the size of the network. Each computer will now have an average of half the throughput available to it as was available when there were only three computers on the network. The guideline is that for every doubling of communicating nodes on the network segment, you halve the average throughput for each node. If you doubled the network four more times, you would have 96 nodes on the network. Each node would have an average of about 1 Mbps of throughput available, assuming all nodes were trying to communicate at the same time. This may or may not be enough, and it could indeed lead to network congestion problems because it is now more likely that a number of nodes will use more than their "fair share" of network bandwidth.

> The reality is a bit more complicated. At any given time, only 10 to 20 percent of the nodes on a network are typically trying to communicate. This would mean that a total of 100 Mbps of bandwidth would provide from 5 to 10 Mbps of bandwidth to each communicating device.

So what can you do when you have too many nodes on a network segment? Create more segments. *Network segmentation* is the act of separating the network into reasonably sized broadcast domains. A *broadcast domain* is a shared medium where all devices can communicate with each other without the need for a routing or bridging device. The most commonly implemented network segmentation protocol is IP. IP can be used, in conjunction with routers, to split any network into infinitely smaller and smaller segments—even down to a single node on each segment, which would not be practical or beneficial.

If you are implementing network segmentation, you must implement network routing. IP is responsible for the routing of the data. A router may be a computer with multiple network interface cards (NICs) acting as a router or it may be a dedicated routing device.

> Remember that routers often introduce delay into the communications process. While vendors may claim line speed switching or routing, the truth is that you cannot "do extra steps" without introducing delay. The processor has to take at least a few milliseconds to process the incoming frames and forward them to the next hop along the way. On really small networks of 10 to 20 users, it is usually better to have all of the clients on a single segment for this reason.

IP Addresses: Notation, Bits, and Bytes

The IP address itself is a 32-bit address divided into four octets or four groups of 8 bits. For example, the following bits represent a valid IP address:

00001010.00001010.00001010.00000001

This is sometimes called binary notation, but it is the actual form that an IP address takes. To understand this notation, you'll need to understand how to convert binary bits to decimal. You are probably used to seeing the previous IP address shown as 10.10.10.1. These dotted decimal notation IP addresses are comprised of four octets and can contain decimal values from 0 to 255. Let's look at how you would convert an 8-bit binary number into the decimal version that you're used to seeing.

The smallest element that can be transmitted on any network is a bit. A bit is a single value equal to 1 or 0. When you group these bits together, they form bytes. An 8-bit byte is the most commonly referenced byte and is the base of most networking measurements. It is specifically called an *octet* in most standards, even though the vendors and networking professionals have leaned more toward the term *byte*. For example, one kilobyte is 1,024 bytes and one megabyte is 1,048,576 bytes. You will often see these numbers rounded to say that 1,000 bytes is a kilobyte or 1,000,000 bytes is a megabyte. The term octet could also be used in these statements; for example, one kilobyte is 1,024 octets.

You might be wondering how a simple bit, or even a byte, can represent anything. This is an important concept to understand, otherwise, you may have difficulty truly understanding how a network works. Let's consider just an 8-bit byte. If you have one bit, it can represent any two pieces of information. The 1 can represent one piece of information and the 0 can represent another. When you have two bits, you can represent four pieces of information. You have the values 00, 01, 10, and 11 available to use as representative elements. When you have three bits, you can represent eight pieces of information; and for every bit you add, you effectively double the amount of information that can be represented. This means that an 8-bit byte can represent 128 pieces of information or 256 elements. You have now received a hint about why the numbers 0 through 255 are all that can be used in an IP address octet. (Remember, IP addresses are four octets or four 8-bit bytes grouped together.)

There are standard mapping systems that map a numeric value to a piece of information. For example, the ASCII system maps numbers to characters. Because you can represent up to 256 elements with an 8-bit byte, you can represent 256 ASCII codes as well. A quick Internet search for ASCII codes will reveal a number of sites that provide tables of ASCII codes. For example, the ASCII codes for the six characters in "802.11" (one of the author's absolute favorite IEEE standards) are 56, 48, 50, 46, 49, and 49 in decimal form. Since you can represent any number from 0 to 255 with an 8-bit byte, you can represent these numbers as well. Table 3.1 shows a mapping of characters to ASCII decimal codes to 8-bit bytes.

TABLE 3.1   ASCII Codes and Binary Values for the Characters 802.11

Character	ASCII Decimal Codes	8-Bit Byte
8	56	00111000
0	48	00110000
2	50	00110010
.	46	00101110
1	49	00110001
1	49	00110001

In order for all this to work, both the sender and the receiver of the bytes must agree on how the bytes will be translated. In other words, for information to be meaningful, both parties must agree to the meaning. This is the same in human languages. If you speak a language that has meaning to you, but the person to whom you are speaking does not understand that language, it is meaningless to them and communication has not occurred. When a computer receives information that it cannot interpret to be anything meaningful, it either sees it as noise or corrupted data.

To understand how the binary bits, in an octet, translate to the ASCII decimal codes, consider Table 3.2. Here you can see that the first bit (the right-most bit in the table) represents the number 1, the second bit represents the number 2, and the third bit represents the number 4 and so on. The example, in the table, is 00110001. Where there is a 0, the bit is off. Where there is a 1, the bit is on. You add up the total values in the translated row, based on the represented number for each bit, and find the result of 49 because you only count the values where the bit is equal to 1. This is how the binary octet of 00110001 represents the ASCII decimal code of 49, which represents the number 1 in the ASCII tables.

The point is that each column in the binary number represents a value. When the binary position or column is equal to 1, the bit is said to be on, and when it is equal to 0, the bit is said to be off. All you have to do is sum the total for the representative values for each position or column where the binary bit is equal to 1. In Table 3.2, positions 1, 5, and 6 are set to 1 and their values are 1, 16, and 32 respectively. Adding up the translated decimal values, you come to the total of 49. Therefore, the 8-bit binary number 00110001 is equal to the decimal number 49.

TABLE 3.2 Converting Binary Numbers to Decimal Values

Bit Position	8	7	6	5	4	3	2	1
Represented decimal value	128	64	32	16	8	4	2	1
Example binary number	0	0	1	1	0	0	0	1
Translated	0	0	32	16	0	0	0	1

So how does all this apply to IP addressing? IP version 4 addresses are comprised of four 8-bit bytes or four octets. Now, you could memorize and work with IP addresses like 00001010.00001010.00001010.00000001, or you could work with addresses like 10.10.10.1. The latter representation certainly seems easier to work with; however, the former is not only easier for your computer to work with, it is the only way your computer thinks. Therefore, IP addresses can be represented in dotted decimal notation to make it easier for humans to work with. The dotted decimal notation looks like this: 10.10.10.1.

IP version 4 (which is the current widely used implementation) addresses cannot just have any number in each octet. Remember that there are only 8 bits available so the number in each octet must be an 8-bit number. This means it will be a decimal value from 0 to 255 for a total of 256 valid numbers. There is no IP address that starts with 0. In other words, you'll never see an address like 0.0.0.1 assigned to a device. In fact, the address 0.0.0.0 is reserved to indicate the default network and/or the default device. In this context, the term default should be understood according to context. For example, the IP address of 0.0.0.23 would refer to host identification 23 in the current (default) network because the zeros indicate the default network and only the 23 represents a unique value. If we place the zero in the host position, the IP address of 192.168.12.0 refers to the entire network as a collective because the zero represents all hosts and the 192.168.12 value specifies an exact network. Similarly, 255.255.255.255 (11111111.11111111.11111111 .11111111 in binary) is reserved to indicate all nodes or hosts. Of course, on the Internet, 255.255.255.255 would actually refer to every one of the millions of connected devices and it is never used for any practical purpose.

Another special address that is important for you to know about is the loopback address. This is IP address 127.0.0.1. For example, if you use the PING command to communicate with 127.0.0.1, you are actually communicating with your own TCP/IP network stack or protocol implementation. This is sometimes called *pinging yourself* and is used to troubleshoot the local TCP/IP implementation and ensure that it is working properly. Additionally, if you ping the localhost name, it will also ping this 127.0.0.1 loopback address. Exercise 3.3 provides instructions for using the PING command.

EXERCISE 3.3

Pinging the Loopback Address

In this exercise, you will use the PING command to ping the loopback address directly and through the localhost name.

1. Log onto the server as an administrator.

2. Click Start, type cmd into the search field, and press Enter.

3. Execute the command ping localhost and view the output. Notice that an odd address is listed in the "Reply from" response messaged. This is an IPv6 loopback address, and it is being used because IPv6 is both enabled and preferred by default in Windows Server 2008 R2.

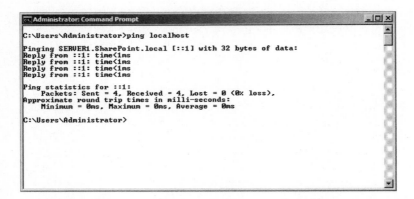

4. Execute the command ping 127.0.0.1 and view the output. Notice that the reply is coming from the specific IPv4 address of 127.0.0.1 now.

```
Administrator: Command Prompt                                    _ □ ×
Pinging SERVER1.SharePoint.local [::1] with 32 bytes of data:
Reply from ::1: time<1ms
Reply from ::1: time<1ms
Reply from ::1: time<1ms
Reply from ::1: time<1ms

Ping statistics for ::1:
    Packets: Sent = 4, Received = 4, Lost = 0 (0% loss),
Approximate round trip times in milli-seconds:
    Minimum = 0ms, Maximum = 0ms, Average = 0ms

C:\Users\Administrator>ping 127.0.0.1

Pinging 127.0.0.1 with 32 bytes of data:
Reply from 127.0.0.1: bytes=32 time<1ms TTL=128
Reply from 127.0.0.1: bytes=32 time<1ms TTL=128
Reply from 127.0.0.1: bytes=32 time<1ms TTL=128
Reply from 127.0.0.1: bytes=32 time<1ms TTL=128

Ping statistics for 127.0.0.1:
    Packets: Sent = 4, Received = 4, Lost = 0 (0% loss),
Approximate round trip times in milli-seconds:
    Minimum = 0ms, Maximum = 0ms, Average = 0ms

C:\Users\Administrator>_
```

IP Addresses: Classes and Subnetting

Private IP addresses are used within organizations and are not routed on the Internet. These private IP addresses fall into three different ranges that were originally set aside according to the A, B, and C classes. These address ranges are

- 10.*x.x.x*
- 172.16.*x.x* – 172.31.*x.x*
- 192.168.*x.x*

The class A private address range from 10.0.0.1 to 10.255.255.254 provides about 16.7 million IP addresses and can be divided into thousands of networks using classless subnetting. The class B private address range from 172.16.0.0 to 172.31.255.254 provides about one million IP addresses and can be divided into hundreds of networks. Finally, the class C private address range from 192.168.0.1 to 192.168.0.254 provides 65,556 addresses and can be divided into hundreds of networks as well.

The class B private address range is the only one that provides more than one starting set of decimal values. For example, all of the class A private addresses start with 10 and all of the class C private addresses start with 192.168. The class B private address range can start with any numbers from 172.16 to 172.31.

There is a big difference between a globally assigned IP address and a private IP address. Globally assigned addresses are assigned by the Internet Assigned Numbers Authority (IANA) or one of the agencies serving the IANA. Private addresses can be assigned by an organization in any way they want, as long as they have implemented a network infrastructure that can support them. The benefit of private addresses is that they are set aside by the IANA and are guaranteed to never be the destination of an actual "on-the-Internet" host. This means that you'll be able to use the same IP addresses on your network as those being used on someone else's and you'll still be able to communicate with each other across the Internet as long as you both implement a network address translation (NAT) solution and possibly port forwarding depending on the scenario.

As you can imagine, a private network that uses the *ten space* (a phrase for referencing the private IP addresses that are in the 10.*x.x.x* range) can be rather large. In order to reduce network traffic on single segments, you can subnet your network and increase performance. To do this, you will need to implement the appropriate subnetting scheme with subnet masks.

A subnet mask is a binary-level concept that is used to divide the IP address into a network ID and a host ID. The network ID identifies the network on which the host resides and the host ID identifies the unique device within that network. There are two basic kinds of subnetting: classfull and classless.

Classfull (also written classful) subnetting simply acknowledges the class of the IP address and uses a subnet mask that matches that class. For example, a class A IP address would use the first 8 bits for the network ID and therefore the subnet mask would be

```
11111111.00000000.00000000.00000000
```

Notice that the portion of the IP address that is the network ID is all 1s and the portion that is the host ID is all 0s. For example, if the IP address were 10.12.89.75 and you were using classfull subnetting, the subnet mask would be 11111111.00000000.00000000 .00000000, which is represented as 255.0.0.0 in dotted decimal notation. As one more example, consider a class C IP address of 192.168.14.57. What would the classfull subnet mask be? Correct. It would be 11111111.11111111.11111111.00000000. This is because a class C IP address uses the first 24 bits to define the network ID and the last 8 bits to define the host ID. This would be represented as 255.255.255.0 in dotted decimal notation. Keep in mind that the subnet mask defines the portion of the IP address that is the network ID and the host ID. So the 255.255.255.0 subnet mask indicates that the network ID for 192.168.14.57 is 192.168.14 and the host ID is 57.

Most configuration interfaces allow you to enter the IP address in dotted decimal notation and also the subnet mask. This allowance makes configuration much easier; however, if you want to perform classless subnetting, you will need to understand the binary level where we now reside in the discussion.

Classless Inter-Domain Routing (CIDR) is the standard replacement for classfull addressing and subnetting. Classless subnetting allows you to split the network ID and the host ID at the binary level and, therefore, right in the middle of an octet. For example, you can say that 10.10.10.1 is on one network and 10.10.10.201 is on another. How would you do this? Let's look at the binary level. Here are the two IP addresses in binary:

00001010.00001010.00001010.00000001 (10.10.10.1)

00001010.00001010.00001010.11001001 (10.10.10.201)

In order to use CIDR and indicate that the final octet should be split in two so that everything from 1 to 127 is in one network and everything from 128 to 254 is in another, you would use the following subnet mask:

11111111.11111111.11111111.10000000

Because of the fact that CIDR subnetting allows subnet masks that mask part of an octet, you will see subnet masks like 255.255.255.128. Instead of representing the subnet mask in decimal notation, it is often simply appended to the end of the IP address. For example, the IP address and subnet mask combination of 10.10.10.1 and 255.255.255.128 could be represented as 10.10.10.1/25. This representation that is sometimes called Variable Length Subnet Mask (VLSM) representation or CIDR representation is becoming more and more common. It indicates that the IP address is 10.10.10.1 and the network ID (sometimes called the subnet or subnetwork) is the first 25 bits of the IP address. This leaves the final 7 bits of the fourth octet to be used for the host ID.

At this point you're probably beginning to wonder why all this subnetting really matters and whether you need to master this knowledge. Other than the fact that it can be used to reduce the size of a network segment, which may or may not be a benefit depending on the infrastructure type you've implemented, it allows IP routing to function. To simplify the process down to the level that you really need to know in order to work with modern networks, the local TCP/IP implementation on a device needs a method for determining if it can send the data directly to the end IP address or if it needs to send it through a router.

Going back to the example where you used classless subnetting to split the network ID and the host ID at the binary level, imagine that IP address 10.10.10.1 is attempting to send a packet to IP address 10.10.10.201. How does the machine at 10.10.10.1 know if it needs the router (also called the default gateway) or not? The answer is that it determines the network ID of its own address and looks at the destination address to see if it has the same network ID. If the network IDs match, the Address Resolution Protocol (ARP) can be used to discover the MAC address of the destination IP address because they are on the same network. If the network IDs do not match, ARP is used to discover the MAC address of the router and the IP packet is sent to the router. The local device assumes that the router knows how to get to any IP address in the world.

The router must find the best path to the destination IP. Once this is determined, the router discovers the MAC address of the nearest router in that path and forwards on the IP packet. This process continues until the target end node is reached. However, it all started when that first device evaluated the IP address against the subnet mask and determined that it needed the help of the local router or default gateway.

TCP Ports

While IP is used to move data around on internetworks until that data reaches its intended target, the Transmission Control Protocol (TCP) is used to both provide reliability in those deliveries and determine the application that should process the data on the receiving device. The reliability is provided by segmenting, transmitting, retransmitting, and aggregating upper-layer data. The application determination is accomplished through the use of TCP ports.

TCP takes data from the upper layers and segments that data into smaller units that can be transferred and managed. Because IP sometimes drops IP packets due to congestion and because packets can travel different routes to the destination, some TCP segments (which are sent across IP) may arrive at the destination out of order or not arrive at all. For this reason, TCP provides resequencing when data arrives out of order and resends data that doesn't make it to the destination. This provides reliable delivery of data and makes TCP very useful for such solutions as file transfers, email, and NNTP (Network News Transfer Protocol). Each of these applications needs reliable delivery, and this means TCP is a prime candidate.

In addition to reliable delivery, TCP uses ports to determine the upper level applications that should receive the arriving data. Some port numbers are well-known, others are registered, and still some are unassigned or private. Common ports include 21 for FTP, 80 for HTTP, and 25 for SMTP. Knowing which port a service uses has become very important in modern networks due to the heavy implementation of firewalls. Firewalls often block all Internetwork traffic except certain ports. If you don't know the port number the service is attempting to utilize, you won't know what exception to create in your firewall. You can find commonly used port numbers at http://www.iana.org/assignments/port-numbers. You can use a network scanner, like Angry IP Scanner or NMap, to discover active TCP ports as well.

Why Is TCP/IP Important?

TCP/IP is the foundational protocol of the Internet. Modern private networks primarily use this protocol as well. If you do not know the basics of IP, TCP, and other protocols in this suite, you will not be able to administer a modern network.

The success of TCP/IP has been largely due to its utilization on the Internet. If you wanted to browse web pages, download from FTP sites, or read text at gopher sites, you had to be running TCP/IP. Many early networks ran TCP/IP as well as some other protocol like IPX/SPX or Banyan Vines. First, network vendors began by supporting TCP/IP alongside their proprietary protocols and eventually they moved their systems to not only support the TCP/IP suite, but to rely on it. Today, Novell, Microsoft, Unix, Linux, and Apple computers all use TCP/IP as the primary communication protocol.

At this moment, a very gradual transition is happening in relation to IP. IPv6 has been available for a number of years and operating systems have slowly incorporated it into their available protocols. Windows Vista has very integral support of IPv6 as does Windows Server 2008. Unix and Linux machines have supported it for some time and Apple's Mac OS X also supports it. Once IPv6 support is available on the vast majority of computers, you'll likely see it used more and more on networks; however, the SharePoint exams will not test your knowledge of this protocol. For the SharePoint exams, you will need to know the basics of IP version 4 addressing and the way TCP uses ports for connection establishment.

Exercise 3.4 provides instructions for viewing TCP statistics. The netstat command is a useful command to understand for network analysis. It will show you the amount of data transmitted and received from and to your server. This can be useful for analyzing network loads. For example, you could use this command to monitor network activity while users access the SharePoint server. It could be helpful in tuning the server and in troubleshooting network congestion issues.

EXERCISE 3.4

Viewing TCP Statistics

In this exercise, you will use the netstat command to view statistics for TCP on your server.

1.   Log onto the server as an administrator.

2.   Click Start, type **cmd** in the search field, and press Enter.

3.   Execute the command **netstat -s -p tcp** at the command prompt and view the results. You will see the number of segments sent and received and the number of retransmissions.

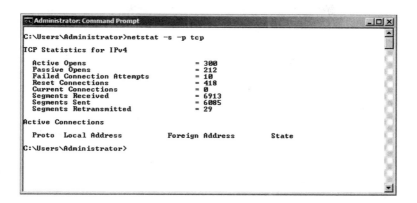

HTTP

The final protocol you must understand is the Hypertext Transfer Protocol (HTTP). HTTP is the primary protocol used for communications with SharePoint servers at the Application layer. HTTP provides some useful services:

- Data requests
- Status updates

Data requests are used to get data from the server and send data to the server. The HTTP GET command is used to retrieve data. The HTTP PUT and POST commands are used to send data. HTTP supports the following commands or methods:

- **GET:** Used to download data from the server
- **PUT:** Used to send data to the server
- **POST:** Used to send data to the server in the body of the request message
- **DELETE:** Used to remove a resource on the server
- **TRACE:** Used to echo back the received request so that the client can verify it was not changed by an intermediate server
- **OPTIONS:** Used to retrieve the HTTP methods supported by the server

It is not uncommon for a single web page to require more than 100 GET commands just to load the page. Each graphic requires an individual GET command. Each external file, such as a CSS or JavaScript file, requires an individual GET command. This is where the difference between hits and page views comes into play in most web analytics engines. A hit is effectively a GET request in most engines. A page view is a single request for a page that may include more than 100 hits.

The status updates are sent as status codes. What some people refer to as HTTP error messages are actually just status codes that indicate an error. The following are several important status codes:

- **200:** Used to indicate an OK response, which suggests success
- **202:** Used to indicate an Accepted response, which means the server is processing the request
- **301:** Used to indicate a Mode response, which means that the requested item has been moved permanently to a new location where all future requests should be made
- **400:** Used to indicate a bad request, which means that the syntax of the request is incorrect
- **401 and 403:** Used to indicate an authorization failure
- **404:** Used to indicate that the requested item was not found on the server
- **500:** Used to indicate an internal server error, which is a generic message that can apply to anything from .NET being improperly configured to a service being turned off that is required for the request

You can see all of the HTTP status codes by reading the HTTP standards document at http://www.w3.org/Protocols/rfc2616/rfc2616.html. The same document provides detailed information about the requests and methods supported by HTTP.

Network Services

Several network services impact the functionality of your SharePoint environment. These services include IP addressing services such as DHCP, DNS, Active Directory Domain Services, Internet Information Services, and SQL Server. The following sections explain the way these services relate to SharePoint in your network infrastructure.

IP Addressing

IP addressing was discussed earlier in the "TCP/IP" section of this chapter. Here, you need to understand that these addresses can be assigned in two ways and you need to understand the pros and cons of each method. The two methods are dynamic host configuration using DHCP or static IP addressing using manual configuration.

The Dynamic Host Configuration Protocol (DHCP) is used to dynamically configure the host's protocol. This is a better description than saying that DHCP provides automatic IP addressing because DHCP provides far more than just IP addresses. DHCP completely configures IP including:

- IP address
- Subnet mask
- Default gateway (router)
- DNS server
- Time server
- WINS server

In early TCP/IP networks, many administrators avoided DHCP, thinking that it was not the best way to configure IP; however, very few networks today run without it. DHCP has become the primary way to configure most devices on the network. Exceptions do exist, and many people argue that they should, including Microsoft and the authors of this book.

The key exceptions that should not be configured with DHCP are

- Servers
- Printers
- Infrastructure devices

By using a static IP address for these devices, you ensure that the address never changes and bring greater consistency to your environment. This is very important for servers accessed with DNS names. If the IP address changes for a server, it can take hours for it to properly propagate to all of the clients and overwrite the DNS cache in those clients. This delay can cause clients to receive errors when attempting to connect to the SharePoint servers.

Static addresses are configured using either the GUI interface or the command prompt, with the NETSH command. Because you are likely to have to configure static IP addresses on a Windows Server 2008 R2 machine, Exercise 3.5 provides instructions for doing this in both the GUI and the command-line interfaces.

EXERCISE 3.5

Setting a Static IP Address

In this exercise, you will learn to configure static IP addresses in the GUI and at the command prompt.

1. Log onto the server as an administrator.

2. To configure static IP setting in the GUI, click Start and then right-click on Network and select Properties.

3. In the Network and Sharing Center, click the link in the left panel that says Change Adapter Settings.

4. Right-click on the Local Area Connection and select Properties.

5. Double-click on the Internet Protocol Version 4 (TCP/IPv4) item in the list.

6. Configure the static IP settings here as required.

7. Click OK in the two dialogs to close them. Close the Network Connections window.

8. To configure static IP settings at the command prompt, click Start and then type cmd in the search field and press Enter.

9. Execute the command `netsh interface ipv4 set address "Local Area Connection" static address=10.10.10.10 mask=255.255.255.0 gateway=10.10.10.1` or you can leave the address, mask, and gateway keywords and simply type the parameters in the order specified. Of course, you should change the addresses to the correct ones for your configuration.

DNS

DNS was covered in Chapter 2 from the perspective of installation and configuration. In addition to that information, you should understand how to query a DNS server from a Windows client, how to view the DNS cache, and how to empty the DNS cache. Exercise 3.6 provides instructions for doing all three activities at the Windows Server command prompt.

EXERCISE 3.6

Working with DNS Name Resolution

In this exercise, you will use the Windows Server command prompt to query a DNS server, view the DNS cache, and clear the DNS cache.

1. Log onto the server as an administrator.

2. Click Start and then type **cmd** and press Enter.

3. To query the DNS server, execute the **nslookup** command with the hostname as the parameter. For example, to query for the IP address of www.SysEdCo.com, you would execute **nslookup www.sysedco.com**.

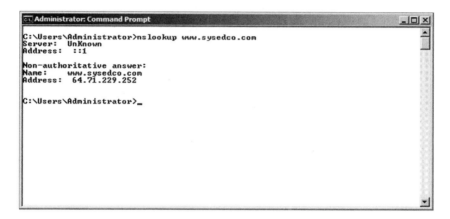

4. To view the DNS cache, use the ipconfig /displaydns command.

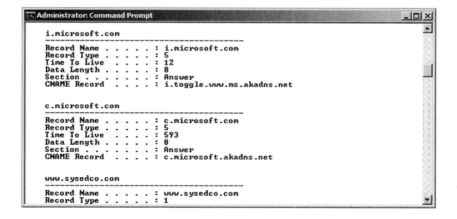

EXERCISE 3.6 *(continued)*

5. To empty the DNS cache, use the `ipconfig /flushdns` command. This is sometimes required when the cache contains old resolution values that are no longer accurate.

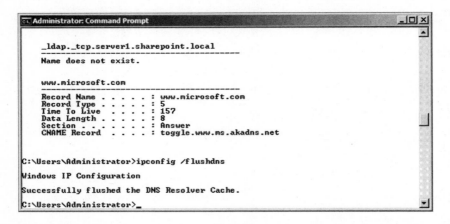

Active Directory Domain Services (AD DS)

Like DNS, the AD DS was explained in detail in Chapter 2. Here, it is important that you understand how AD DS uses the network infrastructure and how you should plan for SharePoint interactions with AD DS.

AD DS depends on DNS for name resolution. This works both from the clients to the domain controllers and from the domain controllers to other devices. The most important direction is from the clients to the domain controllers. Windows clients use DNS to locate domain controllers and services in the domain.

Clients use the domain database to locate network objects and properties related to those network objects. SharePoint 2010 is actually a client of the AD domain. It uses the user accounts and groups from the domain for authorization within the SharePoint infrastructure. This is why AD DS is required for a fully functioning SharePoint environment. It is important that the communications between the domain controllers and the SharePoint servers be maintained so that users can log on and access appropriate resources. As a best practice, as least two domain controllers should be implemented to provide fault tolerance.

Internet Information Services (IIS)

IIS, as you learned in Chapter 2, is the web server that SharePoint 2010 uses. SharePoint 2010 cannot run on any other web server. IIS has several important features that allow you to troubleshoot problems when clients receive errors. For example, it is not uncommon for the client to receive a 500 Internal Server error without any useful information to troubleshoot the error. IIS allows you to enable detailed error reporting to both local and remote browsers. To do this, you will have to edit the IIS_Schema.xml file that is located in C:\Windows\System32\inetsrv\config\schema. You will change the systm.webServer/httpErrors/errorMode value to Detailed instead of the default of DetailedLocalOnly. Figure 3.7 shows this file and the setting that should be changed. After making the change, a restart of the web server is required for it to work.

FIGURE 3.7   Modifying the IIS_Schema.xml file

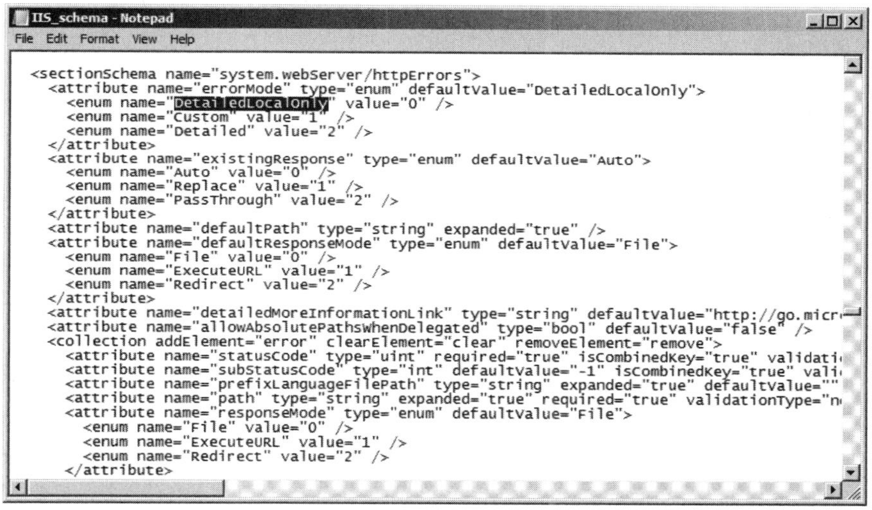

SQL Server

You learned about the SQL Server service in Chapter 2. This is an important network service for any SharePoint 2010 deployment. In the same way that IIS is the only web server SharePoint can use, a SQL server is the only database server SharePoint can use directly. You can access other database servers through external data connectors, but the core content and configuration databases for SharePoint are managed and provided by SQL Server.

Summary

In this chapter, you learned about the importance of the network infrastructure and services as they relate to SharePoint 2010. Farm communications include both internal and external communications and you must plan for each type. As a SharePoint 2010 administrator, it is useful to understand the basics of networking technologies. These basics include networking hardware and protocols. It is also important to understand the services that run on modern networks and allow them to function the way you have come to expect them to function.

Exam Essentials

Planning farm communications.   Know the difference between internal and external farm communications. Internal farm communications include communications between the three core SharePoint 2010 server roles: database, WFE, and application servers. External farm communications take place between the farm servers and servers in other farms or on the Internet. Understand what content deployment paths are and when they are used.

Network protocols: a summary.   Understand the basics of the TCP/IP suite including IP addressing and name resolution. Know the different network hardware devices and how they are used to form a network infrastructure.

Network services.   Be able to explain the network services commonly used on modern networks, which include DNS, DHCP, and directory services. Additionally, understand the roles played by IIS and SQL Server to provide infrastructure services to SharePoint 2010.

Chapter

4

Planning for Farm Deployment

TOPICS COVERED IN THIS CHAPTER

✓ Planning Farm Deployment

✓ Installing a Single-Server Farm

✓ Planning for Sandbox Solutions

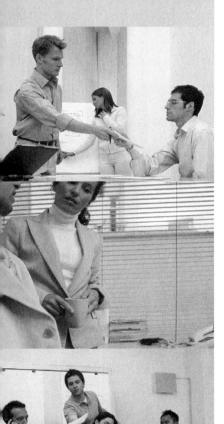

In Chapters 1 through 3, you learned how to plan the SharePoint architecture and prepare your environment for the SharePoint installation. In this chapter, you will consider the final steps in planning for farm deployment based on the logical and physical architectures you have designed. You will begin by learning about the different deployment types in more detail. These deployment types include sequential, standalone, single-server farm, and multiserver farm deployments. You will also learn about the important decisions related to virtual server-based deployments.

Next, you will learn to perform a single-server farm installation. You will start by installing the Windows Server 2008 R2 operating system and then add the required components on top of this installation. Sandbox solutions are briefly introduced so that you will understand your role as a SharePoint administrator as it relates to sandbox solution deployment.

If you are preparing for the 70-668 exam, several important objectives that are covered in this chapter will be especially helpful. The major objective titled Plan for Farm Deployment is certainly covered here. Additionally, the major objective of Planning for Sandbox Solutions is also considered.

Planning Farm Deployment

SharePoint 2010 farms may be deployed in several ways. In this section, you will learn about each deployment method and the items to consider when deploying to virtual servers. The topics covered in this section include:

- **Sequential Deployments:** Installing SharePoint 2010 in the right sequence
- **Standalone Deployments:** Installing SharePoint 2010 and all required components, including AD, on one server
- **Single-Server Farm Deployments:** Installing SharePoint's three roles on a single server
- **Multiserver Farm Deployments:** Installing SharePoint's three roles on two or more servers
- **Virtual Environment Design:** Using virtualization to provision the servers for SharePoint

Sequential Deployments

Microsoft SharePoint 2010 should be installed in a planned sequence. Microsoft has specific recommendations for this installation sequence; however, they also recommend a plan for the entire deployment project. The SharePoint 2010 deployment project phases are shown in Figure 4.1.

FIGURE 4.1 SharePoint deployment project phases

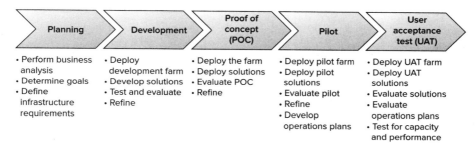

The important thing to keep in mind about the five phases in Figure 4.1 is that they represent the planning of SharePoint and not a final production installation. If you look at Figure 4.1 closely, you will see that Microsoft recommends four installations (from the development through UAT phases) of your SharePoint 2010 server farm in order to reach production-ready status. One more installation, for a total of five, is required to reach production, and this is assuming that your earlier installations were basically sound and the refinements did not require a complete reinstallation.

Are you always required to do five installations to reach a production installation? No, you are not required to do so. You can simply install SharePoint 2010 and begin using it. However, going through all of the Microsoft recommended phases—or even some of them—can certainly increase the stability of your environment. It will also help you better understand how you are using SharePoint in the production implementation. The pilot and user acceptance test (UAT) phases are very important for meeting the users' needs. If you do not involve the users in your testing process, their needs are unlikely to be met by the production system.

The following information describes each of the six phases (including the Production phase not listed in Figure 4.1) in the Microsoft recommended sequential deployment:

Planning The planning phase is what Chapters 1 through 3 were all about. In this phase, you are performing business analysis to better understand the needs and the uses of SharePoint 2010. You then define goals and objectives based on the business analysis. Finally, you will clearly define the infrastructure requirements. The end result of this phase is a set of documents outlining the SharePoint solution plan (here, *solution* simply means "the way in which you use the product") and the topology and resource requirements lists.

Development   The development phase is used to develop applications and customizations for the SharePoint 2010 deployment. You will deploy a farm (a single-server farm is often used in this phase), develop the solution (which may include multiple customizations), test and evaluate the solution, and then make changes as necessary. The end result of this phase is a SharePoint 2010 solution that can be further tested.

Proof of Concept (POC)   The POC phase is about testing the solution developed in the previous phase to ensure business requirements are met. This is also the phase where the infrastructure requirements are verified. A farm is deployed that is very similar to the final farm that will be in production. Benchmark data is collected and the POC is evaluated. Goals and infrastructure requirements are refined as needed. The end result of this phase is an updated solution plan and potentially updated topology and resource requirements.

Pilot   The pilot phase is about testing the solution on a small scale. The number of test users will vary depending on the scale of the production SharePoint installation. For example, with an end-user base of 1,000 users in production, you may choose to pilot with between 25 and 50 users. With an end-user base of 100 users, you may pilot with only 8 to 15 users. The end result of the pilot phase is an updated solution plan, an update of the topology and resource requirements, and an operations plan.

User Acceptance Test (UAT)   The UAT phase is about deploying a preproduction environment that can be used for testing against production data. Additionally, this phase is used to validate operational procedures, which includes your backup methods. The end result of this phase is an updated operations plan.

Production   The production phase is where the final installation of SharePoint 2010 is performed. Depending on how you installed SharePoint during the UAT phase, you may be able to continue using that installation. However, at this point, the entire farm must be deployed as needed for production. This will be the largest deployment so far if your UAT deployment was not installed to scale for production. The end result of this phase is a final working SharePoint 2010 installation.

Another view of the phrase "sequential deployment" is related to the order in which SharePoint components are installed. From no infrastructure through to a final working SharePoint 2010 deployment, the following order should be used:

1. Install the network infrastructure (switches, routers, cabling, etc.).

2. Install the Windows Server OS on a server that will be configured as a domain controller.

3. Install Domain Name System (DNS) on the Windows server or on another separate server, if desired.

4. Configure DNS.

5. Install Active Directory (AD) on the domain controller.

6. Install another Windows Server OS and install SQL Server on this new server.

7. Install SharePoint 2010 on one or more servers, depending on the topology deployed.

The most important thing to remember about the process of building an environment from scratch to support SharePoint 2010 is that it will depend on Active Directory for all user account objects.

Standalone Deployments

A standalone deployment is a complete all-in-one installation of SharePoint 2010 and the infrastructure components in a single server. This installation should be used only for testing and development; however, it is an excellent option for the individual learning about SharePoint 2010 as well as trainers and developers. You will need to install the following components on the single server:

- Windows Server 2008 or later
- DNS
- Active Directory
- SQL Server 2005 or later
- SharePoint 2010

 For trainers and individuals learning the SharePoint product, all five components can be installed in a virtual machine. For more information on this process, read the later section of this chapter titled "Designing a Virtual Environment."

Single-Server Farm Deployments

A single-server farm is not the same as a standalone installation. A single-server farm is simply a SharePoint 2010 installation that includes all SharePoint-specific components (SQL Server database, WFE, and an application server) on a single server. The AD domain and DNS are provided by separate servers and typically already exist in the environment in which SharePoint is to be installed. The result is that you will have a single server for your SharePoint-specific components and one or more other services for your AD DS and DNS services. This differs from a multiserver deployment where the SharePoint-specific components are distributed among multiple servers.

A single-server farm can be used for up to 500 users if the load is light enough, but Microsoft recommends an upper limit of 100 users for a single-server farm.

When installing a single-server farm, the following components must already exist on the network:

- AD domain
- DNS server
- IP infrastructure

The following components will be installed on the single SharePoint 2010 server:

- IIS
- SQL Server
- SharePoint 2010

If you are preparing for the 70-668 exam, remember that Microsoft recommends that a single-server farm should be used only for up to 100 users. Although you may be able to support more users in some production scenarios, for the exam, 100 users is the limit.

Multiserver Farm Deployments

A multiserver farm is an N-tier deployment of SharePoint 2010. The "N" in N-tier specifies how many tiers or layers are in the application. When an application is designed to be an N-tier application, it means that it can be implemented in two or more tiers. SharePoint can be implemented in two or three tiers and can include dozens of servers with several in each tier.

Multiserver farms can be deployed in small topologies and large topologies. A small topology may be as few as two servers, and a large topology may include as many as fifteen or more servers. Technically, there is no limit on the upper number of servers allowed in a multiserver deployment. Realistically, few organizations would ever need more than eight to ten servers, which could easily handle many thousands of users. Of course, the largest multinational organizations require dozens of servers, but they comprise the smallest number of actual organizations that are implementing SharePoint. The vast majority of implementations qualify as medium to large deployments.

When you are installing a multiserver farm, you need to make several additional considerations:

- Where will each server be deployed?
- How many users will access each WFE server?
- Which applications should run on each application server?
- Will you use one database server or multiple servers?

If you've planned your logical and physical architectures well, these questions are easy to answer. Reflect back on the documents you created during the planning phases and you will know exactly how many servers you will need. You will also know where each server should be physically located. WFE servers should be as close to the accessing users as possible, meaning that as few switches and routers should be placed between the users and the servers as possible. For large remote sites, a replicated copy of the SQL Server content database may be beneficial.

Microsoft suggests five different farm deployment models for multiserver farms:

- **Small farm:** This deployment consists of one database server and at least one WFE and application combination server. It may include one or two additional WFE servers.

- **Medium farm:** This deployment consists of one database server and an application server tier and a WFE server tier.

- **Extended medium farm:** This deployment is the same as the medium farm, but it includes a second database server.

- **Large farm:** This deployment model includes at least two database servers and several WFE servers. It uses application server proxy groups to provide fault tolerance for service applications. Proxy groups are similar to network load balancing (NLB) in that they group together application servers providing the same services and route requests to them from WFE servers.

- **Extended large farm:** This deployment is the same as the large farm, but it includes dedicated application and WFE servers for things like search and business intelligence.

To help you plan your multiserver deployments, keep the following concepts in mind:

Service Applications   Service applications are the services that are used by the SharePoint sites within the farm. These services include Search, Access, and Excel Services. The service applications may be shared across multiple farms in some scenarios. The service applications are deployed on the application servers in the application server tier of a multitier deployment.

Server Groups   Microsoft uses the phrase *server groups* to refer to multiple servers running the same services in a network load balancing configuration. It is recommended that you group services and databases together that have similar characteristics. For example, you may group all of the Office-type services (Excel, Access, and Visio) into a server group.

Three-Tier Model   SharePoint 2010 supports a three-tier model through the use of database servers, application servers, and WFE servers. You can use one server in each tier or dozens of servers in each tier. You may have all of the WFE servers providing access to the same sites using NLB, or you may have each WFE providing access to different sites with the same or different back end content databases. This is where multiserver farm planning comes into play. You can implement SharePoint in a way that works well for your organization.

As you plan multiserver deployments, you are also likely to find yourself planning multifarm deployments. A multiserver deployment is a single farm that is installed through distributed components on more than one server. A multifarm deployment may include two or more farms installed on single-server or multiserver topologies. As you plan multifarm deployments, keep the following list of cross-farm services in mind (all of these services may be shared across SharePoint farms):

- User Profile
- Managed Metadata

- Secure Store Service
- Web Analytics
- Business Data Connectivity
- Search

Services that are single-farm and cannot be shared across farms are

- Excel Calculation Services
- Visio Graphics Services
- Access Services
- Word Services
- Usage and Health Data Collection
- Performance Point
- State Service
- Microsoft SharePoint Foundation Subscription Settings

As you plan a multiserver or multifarm deployment, it is best to create network diagrams depicting the servers, their proper site installation locations, the services they should run, and the hardware requirements for those servers. Such documents will help you avoid problems during the actual installation process.

 Real World Scenario

A Case of the Redos

Several years ago—and before SharePoint even existed as a product—I was involved in a project that permanently embedded an important lesson in my brain. We were deploying Active Directory for the first time in an organization. They had a few thousand users and desktops, so it was a large-scale deployment. The project manager thought it would be a good idea to install a domain controller and just start working with the tools provided in Windows 2000 Server (that was the first version to support Active Directory).

As you can imagine, that domain became nothing short of a disaster. In the end, we had to reinstall everything and start all over again. Sadly, the project manager still didn't want to do the proper planning. Even though the new domain was being built based on lessons learned, it was not being built based on shared lessons learned. In other words, we all learned lessons, but we didn't get together and share those lessons. Because of this, several of us made mistakes that others had made first time around.

You can probably guess what happened next: We had to start all over again. However, this time the project manager had learned his lesson (even though all of us administrators had been asking him to spend more time planning all along), and we developed a full set of implementation plans over the period of about two weeks. The next installation went very well. Oh, we still had some problems, but nothing that forced us to start over again.

The important lesson for SharePoint 2010—or any other complex implementation—is to plan twice and work once. You'll be much more likely to achieve success the first time around.

Designing a Virtual Environment

Virtualization has become a popular topic at IT conferences, training events, and in the industry magazines and journals. It is popular for a good reason. Virtualization allows you to reduce costs and more fully utilize the resources in your servers. In the past, you might have set up a single server for one or two tasks that consumed less than 50 percent of the server's capabilities. With virtualization, you can run multiple virtual servers on a single physical machine. The end result is better utilization of resources and reduced hardware costs.

In addition to reduced hardware costs, software license costs may also be reduced in some scenarios. When you license Windows Server 2008 R2 Enterprise Edition, you are granted four virtual machine licenses. This means that you can run the physical machine as a Hyper-V host server and then run four virtual Windows Server 2008 R2 installations on that physical machine. Because of this licensing option, costs may be reduced.

To perform more specific calculations, visit http://www.microsoft.com/windowsserver2008/en/us/hyperv-calculators.aspx to use the Hyper-V planning calculators that Microsoft provides for free.

Microsoft has two primary virtualization products at this time. The first is the Hyper-V server-based product and the second is Windows Virtual PC, which is a client-based product and runs on Windows 7. Virtual PC 2007 and Virtual Server 2003 R2 can still be used for virtualization of other servers, but they do not support 64-bit hosts and cannot be used for SharePoint 2010 virtualization.

VMware Workstation 7, running on Windows 7, is an excellent choice for running Windows Server 2008 R2 in a virtual machine for SharePoint 2010 testing and development. If you are preparing for the 70-668 examination, using VMware Workstation as a virtualization platform can save you quite a bit compared to purchasing physical servers for your learning labs.

In order to use VMware Workstation to run a test or development implementation of SharePoint 2010, you should run the following physical hardware (or greater) in your Windows 7 machine:

- Quad core processor
- 8 GB RAM (12 GB will provide more flexibility)
- 200 GB free hard disk space

If you plan to use Windows Server 2008 or 2008 R2 with Hyper-V, similar specifications should work for virtual deployments. In fact, these specifications should work even for a production deployment. So you can see an example of a fully planned virtual environment, assume that you need to implement the following SharePoint component servers:

- One database server
- One application server
- Two WFE servers

In this scenario, the following guidelines for the VM deployments should work well:

- Place the database server on a VM host with plenty of resources. For example, at least 8 GB free RAM and less than 30 percent disk utilization.
- Place the application server and one of the WFE servers on the same VM host in two separate VMs. Give each VM 6 to 8 GB of RAM.
- Place the final WFE server on another VM host with 6 to 8 GB of RAM as well.

The deployment scenario described in the preceding list will provide for distribution of the VMs across multiple physical hosts, which can help with overall server farm performance. Additionally, because the servers are actually VMs, they can be moved to other VM hosts if the need arises. For example, after three months of production operations, you may determine that the application server and WFE server need to be on separate VM hosts. With Hyper-V R2, this is not a problem. Simply move the VM from one host to another, and the users can continue accessing it with no apparent interruptions.

When planning virtual implementations, the biggest priority should be on providing the VMs with sufficient resources. These resources include memory, processing cycles, network bandwidth, and hard disk storage.

Installing a Single-Server Farm

Now that you understand the different server farm deployment types, it's time to learn to perform the actual installation of a single-server farm. Remember, the single-server farm is a SharePoint 2010 deployment where everything SharePoint requires is installed on a single server, with the possible exception of infrastructure services such as DNS and AD. To complete this single-server farm installation, several steps will be required:

- Installing Windows Server
- Applying updates
- Installing SQL Server 2008 R2
- Installing Microsoft Office 2010
- Installing SharePoint Server 2010 Enterprise
- Configuring SharePoint Server 2010

This section assumes that you have AD running on a separate server. If you do not and you want a single server to act as the entire SharePoint 2010 infrastructure, perform Exercise 4.1 in this chapter and then go back to Chapter 2 and perform Exercises 2.1 through 2.10.

Installing Windows Server

Before you can get SharePoint 2010 up and running, you must first get a Windows Server up and running. In this section, you will install Windows Server 2008 R2. If you do not have a licensed version to install, you can install the trial edition, which is a free download from Microsoft.

In Exercise 4.1, you will install Windows Server 2008 R2 Enterprise Edition. The exercise assumes you are using the free trial edition of the product available for download from Microsoft.com.

EXERCISE 4.1

Installing the Windows Server 2008 R2 Enterprise Edition Trial Version

In this exercise, you will install the trial edition of Windows Server 2008 R2 Enterprise Edition. This can be downloaded from http://www.microsoft.com/windowsserver2008/en/us/trial-software.aspx. You can install this in a virtual machine (using Hyper-V Server, Windows Virtual PC, or the VMware Player—all are free) or on a physical computer. You will perform a basic installation and ensure that all drivers are loaded properly. This installation will be used for exercises throughout the book.

1. Insert the Windows Server 2008 R2 DVD and power on the machine. You will see a screen that says "Starting Windows" for a few moments. Eventually, you will be taken to the Language Selection screen.

2. For this installation, choose English for the Language To Install. Choose English (United States) for the Time And Currency Format and choose US for the Keyboard Or Input Method. If you choose options other than those specified here, future screens may look different than those displayed in this book.

3. Click Next to continue the installation.

4. Click Install Now. You will see a message that reads "Setup is starting. . . ." Be patient because this screen may be displayed for one minute or more.

5. On the Select The Operating System You Want To Install screen, choose the Windows Server 2008 R2 Enterprise (Full Installation) x64 option and click Next.

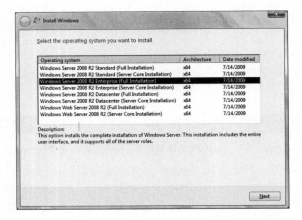

6. Read and accept the license agreement on the Please Read The License Terms screen and click Next.

7. Choose the Custom (Advanced) option on the Which Type Of Installation Do You Want screen.

8. On the Where Do You Want To Install Windows screen, simply click Next to use all of the available drive space for the operating system installation.

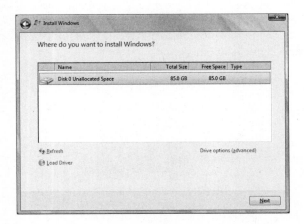

9. The Installing Windows screen will appear. Processing may take up to 30 minutes. The system may also reboot multiple times. Wait patiently as the installation processes run.

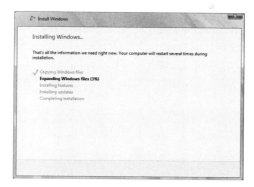

10. The next screen on which you will need to take action is the password reset screen. You will receive a prompt that reads, "The user's password must be changed before logging on the first time." Click OK and then change the password (by default, Windows Server 2008 R2 requires a password with uppercase letters, lowercase letters, and digits).

11. When you receive the message that reads, "Your password has been changed," click OK. You will be taken to the Windows Server 2008 R2 desktop, and shortly after you will see the Initial Configuration Tasks screen.

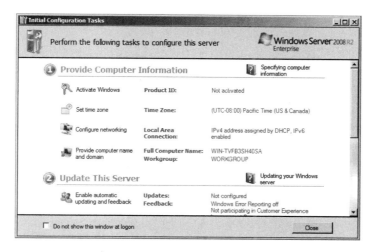

12. In the Initial Configuration Tasks screen, if you have installed a licensed version of Windows Server 2008 R2, click Activate Windows. If you are using the trial edition, you will have to rearm the activation system every 10 days because Microsoft no longer provides a trial product key for newer versions of Windows. The slmgr.vbs -rearm command can be executed at the command prompt to rearm the trial installation and the rearm command can be used five times.

13. Click the Set Time Zone link and configure the time zone for your area.

14. Click the Configure Networking link and configure networking as appropriate for your environment.

15. Click the Provide Computer Name And Domain link to configure the computer name.

16. In the System Properties dialog, click the Change button on the Computer Name tab.

17. Change the Computer Name field value to read **SERVER1**.

18. Click the More button and change the Primary DNS Suffix value to **SharePoint.local**. Click OK.

19. Click OK again in the Computer Name/Domain Changes dialog to save the changes.

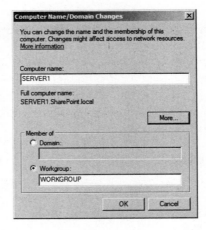

20. Click OK when prompted that you must restart your computer, and then click Close in the System Properties dialog.

21. Click Restart Now to finish the installation of Windows Server 2008 R2.

As an alternative to installing Windows Server 2008 R2, you can download evaluation virtual hard drive (VHD) images from http://www.microsoft .com/downloads/en/details.aspx?FamilyId=9040a4be-c3cf-44a5-9052-a70314452305&displaylang=en. These images can be used with Hyper-V to build a test, development, or learning lab.

Now that the server is installed, you should add it to your existing domain. If you plan for this server to run AD as well as SharePoint 2010, be sure to perform the Chapter 2 Exercises 2.1 through 2.10 on the server that you just installed in Exercise 4.1 before continuing on with this chapter.

Applying Updates

Before you begin installing too many additional components on your newly installed Windows Server 2008 R2 machine, you should make sure that it is updated. These updates may fix stability issues, but more often than not they repair security problems that are very important for a SharePoint deployment. Think of it like this: If the foundation of your system is not secure, none of the system will be secure. The operating system is the foundation of your SharePoint system. SharePoint does not know how to talk to the network; the operating system does. SharePoint also does not know how to talk to your hard drives; the operating system does. These comparisons could continue, but it is important for you to understand that the SharePoint deployment can be no more secure (or stable) than the underlying operating system.

In Exercise 4.2, you will perform an update check and install any important updates that are available.

EXERCISE 4.2

Installing Updates for the Operating System

In this exercise, you will check for and install important updates for the Windows Server 2008 R2 operating system. You should either check for updates periodically or enable automatic updates for your servers so that they maintain their security.

1. Log onto the server as an administrator.

2. Click Start ➢ All Programs ➢ Windows Update.

3. Click the Check for Updates link in the left panel.

4. When the update check completes, you will be presented with a count of the total updates available.

5. Regardless of the number of updates, click the Install Updates button. This will install only the important updates by default.

6. If you are asked to agree to a license at any point during the update, accept the license and click Finish or Install.

7. When the update is complete, reboot your server.

You should either check for updates periodically—at least weekly—or configure your servers for automatic updates. The updates not only maintain the security of your servers, but they also help with stability issues and often introduce wanted features.

Installing SQL Server 2008 R2

In Chapter 2, "Designing the Physical Architecture," you learned the steps required to install SQL Server 2008 R2. Because you are installing a single-server deployment of SharePoint 2010 in this section, you will have to install SQL Server 2008 R2 on your Windows Server 2008 R2 machine. If you performed Exercise 4.1 and then worked through Chapter 2, you can skip Exercise 4.3 in this chapter and move on to Exercise 4.4, "Installing Microsoft Office 2010"; otherwise, Exercise 4.3 should be performed in order to have a completely working version of SharePoint 2010.

EXERCISE 4.3

Installing the SQL Server 2008 R2 x64 Trial Version

In this exercise, you will install SQL Server 2008 R2 x64 with the required components to support a SharePoint deployment and additional SQL Server management tasks, such as data export through SQL Server Integration Services and database maintenance plans (which require SQL Server Integration Services). You may alternatively install the full, licensed version of SQL Server 2008 R2. If you do, you will use the DVD instead of the downloaded executable to start the installation.

1. Log onto the server as an administrator. This is the same server on which all exercises in this chapter have been performed.

2. Download the SQL Server 2008 R2 x64 trial file from http://msdn.microsoft.com/en-us/evalcenter/ff459612.

3. When the download completes, launch the SQLFULL_x64_END.EXE file that was downloaded.

4. Enter an extraction directory, such as C:\SQL_INST, and click OK.

5. When the extraction is complete, click the OK button on the Extraction Complete notification dialog.

6. Browse to the extraction directory, in this case C:\SQL_INST, and launch the setup.exe file located there. Be patient, the setup initialization process can take a few moments.

7. In the SQL Server Installation Center screen that appears, click the Installation link on the left navigation pane.

8. Click the New Installation Or Add Features To An Existing Installation option.

9. On the Setup Support Rules screen, click OK.

10. On the Product Key screen, accept the default setting of Evaluation and click Next. Notice that this screen does allow you to choose Express Edition from this installation source.

11. On the License Terms screen, read the license terms and check I Accept The License Terms and then click Next.

12. On the Setup Support Files screen, click Install to install the support files required by SQL Server setup.

13. On the Setup Support Rules screen, notice the warning about the computer domain controller and the Windows Firewall. Microsoft does not recommend installing SQL Server on a domain controller in a production environment, and you may have to allow communications through the firewall (or simply disable it) for SQL Server network communications to work. Because this is a lab installation, you are not concerned about the domain controller issue. Click Next.

14. On the Setup Role screen, choose the option to perform a SQL Server Feature Installation and click Next.

15. On the Feature Selection screen, choose the following features:

    - Database Engine Services
    - Full-Text Search
    - Business Intelligence Development Studio
    - Client Tools Connectivity
    - Integration Services
    - SQL Server Books Online
    - Management Tools (Basic and Complete)

16. After selecting the identified features, accept the directory defaults and click Next.

17. On the Installation Rules screen, click Next to configure the SQL Server instance.

18. Install the SQL Server role as a Default Instance and select the default values for the Instance ID and Instance Root Directory and click Next.

19. On the Disk Space Requirements screen, read the information and click Next.

20. On the Server Configuration screen, configure all services to use the same account by clicking the button that reads Use The Same Account For All SQL Server Services. In the dialog that appears, select the NT AUTHORITY\SYSTEM account and click OK. Also configure all services except the SQL Full-text Filter Daemon Launcher to have a Startup Type value of Automatic. Click Next.

21. On the Database Engine Configuration screen, choose Windows Authentication Mode as the Authentication Mode setting. Click the Add Current User button to add the administrator account with which you are performing the installation as a SQL Server administrator. Click Next.

22. On the Error Reporting screen, accept the defaults and click Next.

23. On the Installation Configuration Rules screen, click Next.

24. On the Ready To Install screen, review the installation plan and click Install to begin the installation. The installation can take more than 20 minutes to complete.

25. When the installation completes, the Complete screen should appear. You should see a message reading, "Your SQL Server 2008 R2 installation completed successfully." Click Close.

Installing Microsoft Office 2010

SharePoint 2010 and Office 2010 work very well together. Office 2010 has several features that are tied to SharePoint 2010. For example, you can publish an Access database directly to the SharePoint server for others to access. In order to use these features, you will need Office 2010 and not Office 2007 or earlier. Exercise 4.4 provides instructions for installing the trial version of Office 2010.

EXERCISE 4.4

Installing Microsoft Office 2010

In this exercise, you will install Microsoft Office 2010. A free trial edition is available at http://office.microsoft.com/en-us/try. Download the Office Professional 2010 trial edition from there and proceed with the exercise.

1. Execute the downloaded EXE file that contains Office 2010.

2. The files for the installation will be extracted, and you will be taken directly to the Installation Wizard. Enter the trial product key that was provided during the download and click the Continue button.

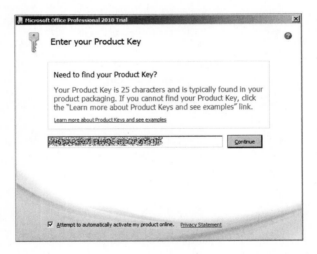

3. Read and accept the terms of agreement and click Continue.

4. Click the Customize button to allow the complete installation of the Office 2010 suite.

5. On the Installation Options tab, click the button to the left of Microsoft Office and select Run All From My Computer and click Install Now.

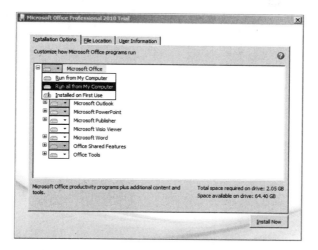

6. On the Complete Your Office Experience screen, simply click Close.

With Office 2010 installed on the same server as SharePoint 2010, you can learn about all of the features of SharePoint including the Office 2010 integration.

Installing SharePoint Server 2010 Enterprise

Installing SharePoint Server 2010 is practically a nonevent after all of the efforts required to get to this point. To recap, you have installed and configured the following components (or they already existed in your environment):

- Windows Server 2008 R2
- SQL Server 2008 R2
- DNS
- Active Directory
- Microsoft Office 2010

Now it's time to perform the installation of SharePoint Server 2010 Enterprise Edition itself. Exercise 4.5 provides instructions for this installation process.

EXERCISE 4.5

Installing the SharePoint Server 2010 Enterprise Trial Version

In this exercise, you will install SharePoint Server 2010 Enterprise Edition. If you do not have a license for SharePoint 2010, you can download the trial version from http://technet .microsoft.com/en-us/evalcenter/ee388573.

1. After downloading the trial executable, launch it from the directory into which you downloaded it.

2. The installation routine will extract the files much like the Office 2010 trial installation, and you will be taken directly into the Installation Wizard. Before you can actually install SharePoint Server, you must install the prerequisites, so click on the link that reads Install Software Prerequisites.

3. A list of components that need to be installed will appear. After reviewing this list, click Next.

4. Check the box that reads I Accept The Terms Of The License Agreement(s) and click Next.

5. The process will take anywhere from 5 to 30 minutes, depending on the speed of your server. When it is completed, click Finish and wait for the server to restart.

6. After the server restarts, log onto the machine as an administrator. The installation of the prerequisites will continue. When the Installation Complete screen is displayed, click Finish.

7. Once again, launch the SharePoint trial executable that you downloaded.

8. When the files finish extracting and the Setup Wizard begins, click Install SharePoint Server.

9. You will be asked for a product key, which is available at http://www.microsoft.com/ downloads/en/details.aspx?FamilyID=43162af5-5b7b-40e0-b879-a77dac8f58bc&displ aylang=en. Make sure to select the Enterprise Client Access License features key. Once you have entered the key, click Continue.

10. Check the option that reads I Accept The Terms Of This Agreement and click Continue.

11. On the Choose A File Location screen, accept the installation defaults and click Install Now. The Installation Progress screen will appear, updating you on the status of the installation.

12. When the Run Configuration Wizard screen appears, deselect Run The SharePoint Products Configuration Wizard Now and click Close. You will run the Configuration Wizard in Exercise. 4.6.

Configuring SharePoint Server 2010

Interestingly, the installation of SharePoint Server 2010 does not result in a SharePoint site. It doesn't even provide a properly functioning Central Administration interface. You must also run the SharePoint Products Configuration Wizard. Exercise 4.6 provides the instructions for doing this.

EXERCISE 4.6

Running the SharePoint Products Configuration Wizard

In this exercise, you will take the final steps required to get a SharePoint server farm up and running. To do that, you will run the SharePoint Products Configuration Wizard.

1. Log onto the server on which you have installed SharePoint Server 2010 as an administrator.

2. Click Start ➢ All Programs ➢ Microsoft SharePoint 2010 Products ➢ SharePoint 2010 Products Configuration Wizard.

3. You will be presented with a Welcome screen. Read the provided information and click Next.

4. When you receive the warning about services having to be started or reset, click Yes to accept this.

5. On the Connect To A Server Farm screen, select Create A New Server Farm. You only select Connect To An Existing Server Farm when adding additional SharePoint servers to the existing farm. Click Next after choosing to Create A New Server Farm.

6. On the Specify Configuration Database Settings screen, enter **localhost** for the Database Server or your server's hostname, such as **server1.sharepoint.local**, and use the Username of **SharePoint\Administrator** and the Password you configured for that same account. (In a production environment, you would create a dedicated account for this purpose.) Click Next.

7. On the Specify Farm Security Settings screen, enter a passphrase to secure the configuration data. Confirm the passphrase and then click Next.

8. On the Configure SharePoint Central Administration Web Application screen, accept the defaults, but review the settings and then click Next.

9. On the Completing The SharePoint Products Configuration Wizard screen, review the settings. If they are acceptable, click Next to perform the configuration.

10. When the configuration processes complete, you will see a Configuration Successful screen. Click Finish.

After installing and configuring SharePoint, the Configuration Wizard automatically launches Central Administration to perform the initial farm configuration. You will see a screen similar to the one in Figure 4.2. Go through the prompt screens, answering the questions for your organization's needs.

FIGURE 4.2 Running Central Administration for the first time

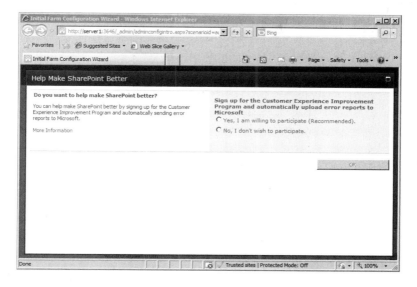

After all of the configuration and initialization wizards are complete, you will see a Central Administration screen like the one in Figure 4.3. From there, you can manage the entire server farm.

FIGURE 4.3 Central Administration after installation and configuration is complete

Planning for Sandbox Solutions

Sandboxed solutions provide a special way to deploy solutions within SharePoint Server 2010. When a solution is sandboxed, it is restricted in access to network and other local resources (CPU and memory) and provides greater security and stability. Security is increased because sandboxed solutions are more limited and run in a separate process from other solutions. Stability is increased for the same reason and because sandboxed solutions only run for a maximum of 60 seconds by default. This execution time limit prevents the solution from bringing down the server through high CPU utilization.

Microsoft recommends using sandbox solutions in the following situations:

- When you want to load balance solutions between multiple SharePoint servers
- When you need to run code that has not been fully reviewed and tested
- When a hosting provider wants to allow customers to run code on shared SharePoint servers

 By default, sandbox solutions are not turned on in SharePoint Server 2010. You must activate the SharePoint 2010 User Code host service on each server where the sandbox solutions will be deployed.

Several capabilities are intentionally removed from solutions that run in a sandbox so that they are more secure. These capabilities are

- Connecting to resources on different servers
- Writing to disk
- Accessing a database
- Accessing resources in a different site collection
- Calling unmanaged code
- Changing the threading model

These limits are very important because sandboxed solutions can be deployed by authorized users. These users may not be fully aware of the impact their code may have on the servers or network. When deployed as a sandboxed solution, this lack of knowledge on the part of the users cannot damage your SharePoint server farm.

Interestingly, sandboxed solutions can come back to haunt you if not carefully planned. Too many sandboxed solutions can cause tremendous overhead because each solution runs in its own worker process. The management of these processes and containment of the solution can cause performance to degrade. For this reason, Microsoft suggests not using sandboxed solutions on externally facing sites and high-performance sites.

Part of sandboxed solution planning is the governance of the solutions. Questions that must be answered include:

- At what point should a sandboxed solution become a fully trusted solution and be taken out of the sandbox?

- Who can deploy sandboxed solutions?
- How will solutions be approved (unblocked) or rejected (blocked)?
- Should a dedicated server be used for sandboxed solutions?

The answer to the first question will vary, but the ultimate goal should be to convert the sandboxed solution to a trusted solution so that the performance of the server will not degrade as one sandboxed solution after another is added. You should also limit who can actually deploy sandboxed solutions so that fewer "accidents" happen.

An important part of governance is approval. You must consider how the sandboxed solutions will be approved. In some scenarios, the administrator may want to block all sandboxed solutions by default and allow only those to run that are specifically unblocked by an administrator. In other scenarios, the administrator may want to allow new sandboxed solutions to run automatically. It really comes down to how much you trust the users who can deploy the solutions.

In an ideal world, sandboxed solutions would always run on their own server. In reality, your budget will likely determine whether this is possible or not. If it is in the budget, dedicate a server to sandboxed solutions in any larger SharePoint 2010 deployment. In smaller deployments, you will simply determine the application server (or potentially a WFE server in some cases) with the most available resources and place the sandboxed solutions there.

Chapter 9, "Planning a SharePoint Component Strategy," provides more information about solutions in general. If you want to learn more about solutions right now, flip over to Chapter 9 and read the section titled "Designing Features and Solutions."

Summary

In this chapter, you stepped through the process of planning a server farm installation. You started by defining the type of installation and then performed a single-server installation from start to finish. You also explored the topic of sandboxed solutions. You learned what they are and why they should be used. You also learned about the importance of governing sandbox solutions.

Exam Essentials

Planning farm deployment. Know the different topologies, including single-server, standalone server, and N-tier deployments (multiserver). Know when to use the different deployment models.

Installing a single-server farm. Know how to install a single-server farm because the same steps are taken to install a multiserver farm. The difference between the two is that you install some components on some servers and other components on other servers in multiserver farm deployments.

Planning for sandbox solutions. Understand what a sandbox solution is and the benefits they provide. Know the actions or capabilities that sandboxed solutions cannot perform.

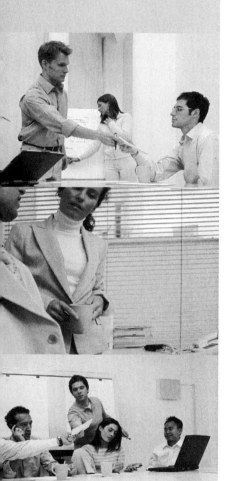

Chapter
5

Planning the Security Architecture

TOPICS COVERED IN THIS CHAPTER

- ✓ Planning Authentication Methods
- ✓ Planning for Secure Sites
- ✓ Designing Authorization
- ✓ Planning Web Application Security
- ✓ Planning Code Access Security

The simplest way to deploy SharePoint Server 2010, or any other content-management and collaboration system, would be to give all users access to all information. However, in the real world of modern organizations, such a security plan is simply not sufficient. To securely implement SharePoint Server 2010, you must understand the authentication and authorization capabilities of the system.

In this chapter, you will learn about the authentication methods available for access to SharePoint Server 2010 sites and the process used to plan for secure sites. You will then learn about the authorization design for the SharePoint organization and, finally, you will explore the steps required to plan web application and code access security. Security is a key factor in any SharePoint deployment, and this chapter will provide you with the information you need to properly plan the security for your organization.

If you are preparing for the Microsoft Certified IT Professional (MCITP) exam number 70-668, you will find important information related to security objectives in this chapter. The exam covers designing a security architecture and planning and deploying authentication methods. Both objectives are covered in this chapter.

Planning Authentication Methods

SharePoint Server 2010 is ultimately an Internet Information Services (IIS) web application; therefore, authentication is typically provided through the IIS server using Integrated Windows authentication. Most users accessing the SharePoint sites will be Windows domain users, and their credentials will simply pass through to the SharePoint Server 2010 server. While Windows Integrated authentication is the most common authentication method, additional methods are also supported. The SharePoint Server 2010 authentication methods include:

- Windows Integrated authentication
- Claims-based authentication

In addition to these various authentication methods, SharePoint Server 2010 introduces the Secure Store Service, which is similar to the single sign-on (SSO) feature in Microsoft Office SharePoint Server 2007. The authentication methods and the Secure Store Service are covered in this section. First, the basic concept of authentication will be explored to ensure your understanding of this important security component in a SharePoint Server 2010 deployment.

Authentication Explored

One of the most important components of a SharePoint Server 2010 security strategy is an identity management system (IMS). An IMS provides a storage location for identity objects, typically called user accounts, and one or more methods for connecting to that storage location and proving identity ownership—a process known as authentication. For SharePoint Server 2010 deployments, the IMS is most often provided by the Microsoft Active Directory Domain Services (AD DS). AD DS provides user accounts, which are objects that identify users and are owned by users and are called security principals. The user accounts provide properties or attributes for use by authentication systems and network operating systems. In addition to user accounts, certificates, biometrics, tokens, and other credentials may also be used for authentication or identity management.

Without a clear understanding of authentication and identity management, you will have difficulty planning and deploying a secure SharePoint Server 2010 solution. Both basic and advanced authentication systems exist and many systems include the ability to support both. Basic authentication methods are identified by weak to moderate credentials and weak to moderate authentication algorithms. Advanced authentication systems are more secure because the credentials are either stronger or multifactored and the authentication algorithm is stronger as well. Windows Server systems allow for advanced authentication mechanisms through special servers such as RADIUS (Remote Authentication Dial-In User Service) servers and basic authentication using simple passwords against the AD DS database. Both basic and advanced authentication systems serve a valid purpose and are best for certain scenarios. When you determine the method that is right for your scenario, you have taken the first step to secure authentication.

Advanced authentication is more secure than basic authentication because advanced mechanisms are used to protect the user's credentials. This usually means protecting a username and password pair, but it can also include protecting a user/certificate combination, a user/machine combination, or any other user/object combination used to identify a specific user.

Once you've selected the appropriate advanced or basic authentication method, you must determine whom to authenticate. Will you authenticate only known or identified users or will you allow some level of anonymous access? For internal SharePoint sites, you may allow only identified users. If you use SharePoint as the engine behind a public website, you may allow anonymous users to access the site.

Authentication should not be confused with authorization. *Authentication* can be defined as proving a person or object is who or what he or it claims to be. *Authorization* is defined as granting access to a resource by a person or object. Authorization assumes the identity has been authenticated. If authentication can be spoofed or impersonated, authorization schemes fail. From this, you can see why authentication is such an integral and important part of network and information security. When an attacker breaks your authentication system so that he is seen as an authenticated user, the authorization becomes irrelevant. Authentication must be strong if authorization is to serve its purpose.

You use authentication every day of your life. When you are at a seminar or training event and the speaker says he is an expert on the topic of his speech, you use authentication mechanisms to verify this information. You listen to the information he delivers and use it to determine if he is truly an expert. In addition, suppose someone walks up to you and says, "Hi, my name is Susan and I am tall." You would look at her and compare her height with a height you consider to be tall and authenticate whether she is truly tall or not. If she is not tall, by your standards, she will lose credibility with you.

Remember the word *credentials*? Consider a couple of other important "cred" words: credit and credibility. Do you see how they are related? They all have to do with having proof of something. When you have good credit, you have proof of your trustworthiness to pay debts. When you have credibility, you have proof that you are authentic, persuasive, and dynamic. When you have credentials, you have an object or the experience that proves your skill or identity. Authentication results in the verification of credentials.

The root of these many "cred" words is the Latin word *credo,* which means "I believe." This original meaning is why the word *incredulous* means you are unwilling to believe. In summary, authentication uses credentials, and credentials are used to prove identity so that the system can "believe" you are who you say you are.

Credentials

Many different credential solutions are available for securing your networks. It's important that you select the right solution for your needs. In this process, you will consider the primary features of a credential solution and whether you need a multifactor authentication system. In addition, you should be aware of the various credential types available to you.

A credential solution should provide a means of user or computer identification that is proportional to your security needs. You do not want to select a credential solution that places unnecessary burdens on the users and results in greater costs (of both time and money) than the value of the information assets you are protecting. You should evaluate whether the selected authentication solution provides for redundancy and integration with other systems such as AD DS. The system should also support the needed credential types such as smart cards and/or biometrics. In addition, consider the following factors when selecting a credential solution:

- The method used to protect the credentials
- The storage location of the credentials
- The access method of the credential store

If an authentication system sends the credentials as cleartext, any protection method is effectively nonexistent. Advanced authentication systems will protect user credentials by encrypting them or avoiding the transmission of the actual credentials in the first place. Instead of transmitting the actual credentials, many systems use a hashing process to encode at least the password. *Hashing* the passwords means that the password is passed through a one-way algorithm resulting in a fixed-length number. This number is known as the *hash* of the password or the message digest. The hash is stored in the authentication database and can be used as an encryption key for the challenge text in a challenge/response authentication system.

The credentials, both username and password (or hash) or certificates, must be stored in some location. This storage location should be both secure and responsive. It must be secure to protect against brute force attacks, and it must be responsive to service authentication requests in a timely fashion. Certificates are usually stored in a centralized certificate store (known as a certificate server or certificate authority) as well as on the client using the certificate for authentication. Both locations must be secure, or the benefit of using certificates is diminished. In addition to the standard certificate store, users may choose to back up their certificates to disk. These backups are usually password protected, but brute force attacks against the media store may reveal the certificate given enough time. For this reason, users should be well educated in this area and understand the vulnerability presented by the existence of such backups.

Access methods vary by authentication system and storage method, but there are standards that define credential access methods. One example is LDAP (Lightweight Directory Access Protocol). LDAP is a standard method for accessing directory service information. This information can include many objects, but it is usually inclusive of authentication credentials. LDAP is used by Microsoft's AD DS among other network operating systems.

Sometimes, one type of authentication alone is not sufficient. In these cases, multifactor authentication can be used. *Multifactor authentication* is a form of authentication that uses more than one set of credentials. An example of a multifactor authentication process would be the use of both passwords and thumb scanners. Usually, the user would place his thumb on the thumb scanner and then be prompted for a password or PIN (personal identification number) code. The password may be used for network authentication or it may only be used for localized authentication before the thumb data is used for network authentication. However, in most cases the password and thumb data are used to authenticate to the local machine and then the network or just to the network alone. A common example of multifactor authentication would be your ATM card. You have the card and you know the pin (something you have and something you know).

Common Authentication Methods

Many common credential types and, therefore, authentication types exist. They include:

- Username and password
- Certificates
- Biometrics

Username and password pairs are the most popular type of credentials. They are used by most network operating systems including Novell NetWare, Linux, Unix, and Windows. Of course, SharePoint Server 2010 supports password-based authentication—either indirectly through Windows logins or directly through basic authentication in the IIS website (though basic authentication is not recommended unless SSL is also used to secure the authentication process). Due to the human factor involved in the selection of passwords, they often introduce a false sense of security. This is because the chosen password is usually too weak to withstand dictionary attacks and, depending on the length of the password, certainly brute force attacks. In addition, passwords are often written down or stored in plaintext files on the system and then changed infrequently resulting in a longer attack opportunity window.

It is not uncommon to see passwords written down on notes and then attached to the display monitor of a user's computer. To prevent this, implement password use policies and educate users on the problems caused by such actions. Additionally, teach users to create passwords that are easy to remember. See the sidebar in this chapter titled, "Creating Strong Passwords" for more information.

An alternative to username and password pairs is certificates. In order to use certificates throughout an organization, a certificate authority must exist. This certificate authority can be operated by the organization or an independent third party. In either case, the costs are often too prohibitive for widespread use due to the need for an extra server or even a hierarchy of servers. Small and medium-sized organizations usually opt for server-only certificates or no certificates at all because of the cost of implementation. A full PKI (Public Key Infrastructure) would usually consist of more than one certificate authority. Each certificate authority would be a single server or cluster of servers. The PKI is the mechanism used for generation, renewal, distribution, verification, and destruction of user and machine certificates.

Yet another authentication credential is you. Biometrics-based authentication takes advantage of the uniqueness of every human and uses this for authentication purposes. For example, your thumb can be used as a unique identifier, as can your retina. The balancing of cost and security is important with biometric credentials. While hair analysis could potentially be used to authenticate a user, the cost and time involved is still too high for practical use. Today, both thumb scanners and retina scanners are becoming more popular.

Creating Strong Passwords

If you've been reading closely up to this point, you know that passwords can be a point of weakness in your SharePoint Server 2010 security. For that matter, they can be a point of weakness in the security of any system. If you must use passwords (and most of us must), you'll need to do three things to make them as secure as possible.

First, you should write password policies. *Password policies* describe an acceptable password from the perspective of length and complexity and length of life. Here's an example statement: A strong password is a complex password (including uppercase letters, lowercase letters, and digits or special characters) that is at least eight characters long and is changed every 30 days. This is just one example. For a more detailed example, see the Password Protection Policy template at http://www.sans.org/security-resources/policies/.

Second, you should enforce the password policies where possible. AD DS allows you to force users to create strong passwords. If you use the Windows Integrated authentication mode, you can force these policies on the users for SharePoint Server 2010 as well, because the authentication passes through based on the user's existing domain authentication.

Third, you should teach users to create passwords that are easy to remember. By doing this, you will reduce the number of sticky notes on monitors throughout your environment (you know, those sticky notes with passwords on them). Here's an example of a password that is easy to remember: 9apec18C.

Now, you're probably wondering how 9apec18C is a password that is easy to remember. Let me help you out. It's my (Tom Carpenter) last name. Well, it's my last name passed through an algorithm. The algorithm is as follows. Start with a word that is at least six characters in length. Count the number of vowels in the word and multiply the number by three. This is the first part of the password and, when using carpenter as the input, is equal to 9. Next, take the second, fourth, fifth and first characters in the word for the second, third, fourth, and fifth positions of the password, which is equal to apec, in this case. The next step is to count the total number of letters in the word and multiply by two, which is equal to 18 for the word *carpenter*. Finally, we take the first letter of the word and capitalize it for the final character of the password. The end result is 9apec18C.

You're probably thinking that this is very time-consuming. Instead, it's actually very liberating. Here's why. You can write down the word that you use as the source of your password and never have to worry about it causing a security problem. Why? Because you're not going to use the exact algorithm mentioned here. You may count the vowels and multiply by four. Or you may count the vowels and divide by two and then multiply by three and then round down. Get the point? Just this one part of the algorithm could be altered in hundreds of ways. Literally trillions of possible algorithms exist.

In summary, teach users to create their own algorithms for password generation. Then, in the best scenario, they pick a word each month that they don't have to write down and pass it through the algorithm to reset their password. For the first week after changing the password, they may have to think for 30 to 45 seconds to regenerate the password—depending on the complexity of their algorithm, but they will have it memorized after that first week and will simply be able to log in. It's a simple method but very powerful and it's why I (Tom) haven't forgotten a password in the last ten years—I haven't memorized one. I simply have a few algorithms that I apply to the appropriate systems.

Regulatory Compliance

When implementing authentication, as well as other components of SharePoint Server 2010 security, you must consider applicable regulations. Governing bodies define and enforce regulations related to many different information domains. Information has evolved to become an extremely valuable resource in modern economies. With this fact in mind, many regulatory agencies have defined regulations related to information management. For example, in the United States, the government has passed health information management policies as the HIPPA guidelines. As a SharePoint administration professional, you must understand the basics of these regulations in order to implement solutions that comply with them. Similarly, Payment Card Industry (PCI) Data Security Standard (DSS). guidelines are the standard for the payment card industry. These regulations and guidelines are discussed in the following sections and are examples of guidelines you must consider when planning authentication and security for SharePoint sites.

An additional regulation that applies to the financial management of an organization is the Sarbanes-Oxley (SOX) act, also known as the Public Company Accounting Reform and Investor Protection Act. This act requires specified steps for the management and retention of financial information. If SOX applies to your organization, you should learn more about it and be prepared to comply with it in your SharePoint Server and database implementations. The SOX act applies to publicly traded companies and not to privately run organizations. Because the SOX act applies to less than 20 percent of all existing companies, it will not be covered here. You can view the text of the act at `http://thomas.loc.gov/cgi-bin/bdquery/z?d107:S2673:` if you want to learn more.

PCI Compliance

Payment Card Industry (PCI) compliance is a statement of conformity to the PCI Data Security Standard (DSS). PCI DSS is a set of standards that help to ensure that companies processing payment cards (credit cards, debit cards, etc.) do so in a secure manner. The standards encompass payment card processing, storage, and information transfer. SharePoint may not be the most common place to store payment processing information for many companies; however, it is entirely possible that this payment information data may find its way into the SharePoint databases. For this reason, a retail organization must consider how they can ensure PCI DSS compliance in the SQL Server databases where the SharePoint content is stored.

The PCI DSS document is a 73-page document (version 1.2) that outlines the process of implementing a secure payment card processing environment. The document covers the following topics:

- Building and maintaining a secure network
- Protecting card holder data
- Maintaining vulnerability management programs
- Implementing strong access control measures
- Regularly monitoring and testing networks
- Maintaining an information security policy

If you've been a student of information security, you'll immediately recognize most of these topics as standard security best practices. Indeed, the only unique topic is that of protecting card holder data, and even that can be classified under the normal heading of protecting valuable data. In the end, there is nothing new in the PCI DSS document; however, more and more states and credit card companies are requiring compliance with it in order to process payment cards. At this point, the U.S. government does not require compliance with PCI DSS, but it is a likely future development. The good news is this: if you implement security best practices, you'll have very little to change in order to comply with PCI DSS.

The PCI DSS lists both recommended practices and required practices. The standard lists the following requirements for secure data storage:

- Keep cardholder data storage to a minimum. Develop a data retention and disposal policy. Limit storage amount and retention time to that which is required for business, legal, and/or regulatory purposes, as documented in the data retention policy.

- Do not store sensitive authentication data after authorization (even if encrypted).

- Do not store the full contents of any track from the magnetic stripe (located on the back of a card, contained in a chip, or elsewhere).

- Do not store the card-verification code or value (three-digit or four-digit number printed on the front or back of a payment card) used to verify card-not-present transactions.

- Do not store the personal identification number (PIN) or the encrypted PIN block.

- Render primary account number (PAN), at minimum, unreadable anywhere it is stored (including on portable digital media backup media, in logs) by using any of the following approaches: one-way hashes based on strong cryptography, truncation, index tokens, and pads (pads must be securely stored), or strong cryptography with associated key-management processes and procedures.

- If disk encryption is used (rather than file- or column-level database encryption), logical access must be managed independently of native operating system access control mechanisms (for example, by not using local user account databases). Decryption keys must not be tied to user accounts.

- Protect cryptographic keys used for encryption of cardholder data against both disclosure and misuse. Restrict access to cryptographic keys to the fewest number of custodians necessary. Store cryptographic keys securely in the fewest possible locations and forms.

- Fully document and implement all key-management processes and procedures for cryptographic keys used for encryption of cardholder data.

In summary, to comply with PCI DSS, a database system that stores payment card processing data must store as little information as possible about the payment card. The stored information should be encrypted, and the encryption should be based on a centralized network authentication system, such as AD DS. The key management processes should be documented in a policy and the policy should be followed and audited.

HIPPA Compliance

The HIPPA regulations require that healthcare organizations (including hospitals, doctors, and any other organization that handles health information) implement policies and procedures to ensure that only authorized individuals may access patient health information. HIPPA stands for Health Insurance Portability and Accountability Act, and it was enacted within the United States in 2006. Organizations covered by the act and, therefore, required to comply include:

- Health plan providers
- Health care clearinghouses
- Any healthcare provider who transmits health information in electronic form

The health information protected by HIPAA includes all individually identifiable health information. This information is identified as information that is unique to an individual and related to the health of that individual. Examples include:

- Past, present, or future mental or physical health condition
- Healthcare that has been provided to the individual
- Healthcare payment information

Information classified as *de-identified* does not require compliance with HIPAA regulations. De-identified information is information that neither identifies nor provides a foundational knowledge base on which a patient may be identified.

The HIPAA regulations are nonspecific, allowing organizations of differing sizes to implement appropriate security measures that result in the protection of health information. The general requirements include:

- Privacy policies and procedures must be documented.
- A privacy official must be designated to oversee the HIPAA regulation implementation and maintenance.
- All workforce members must be trained to understand and comply with the privacy policies.
- Mitigation efforts must be taken when privacy policies are breached.
- Effective data safeguards must be implemented.
- Complaint processing procedures must be implemented.
- Patients must not be asked to waive privacy rights, and retaliation against complaints is not allowed.
- Privacy policies and incident documentation must be maintained for six years.

With an understanding of the HIPAA regulations, the only remaining question is this: How do these regulations apply to a SharePoint Server 2010 solution? The answer is simple. They apply to SharePoint Server 2010 in the same way they apply to any database-driven system. Regardless of the database-driven system used, the following five security solutions should be used in order to effectively comply with HIPAA regulations:

- Authentication
- Authorization
- Confidentiality
- Integrity
- Nonrepudiation

All of these requirements can be met with SharePoint Server 2010 and SQL Server, which is the backend database for SharePoint Server 2010. Authentication is best provided through AD DS. Authorization is achieved through the use of permissions, and the permissions may be applied directly to users or indirectly through groups. Confidentiality is accomplished through the use of SSL for access to the SharePoint sites. Integrity is accomplished through consistency checks within the database. *Nonrepudiation,* which is the inability to deny an action, can be achieved with a combination of strong authentication and database auditing.

 You will not be required to know the details of PCI DSS or HIPPA for any SharePoint Server 2010 exam. The information is provided here to help you understand why the security features addressed in this chapter are so important.

Integrated Windows Authentication

Integrated Windows authentication is also known as the classic mode authentication (CMA) in SharePoint Server 2010. This authentication model is the same model as that provided in SharePoint Server 2007 and in Internet Information Services (IIS) as a web server. CMA allows the following authentication methods:

- Anonymous
- Basic
- Digest
- Certificate
- NTLM
- Kerberos

Anonymous authentication is used when the SharePoint site is a public access site. For example, the site may be available on the Internet or on a guest intranet. In such scenarios, you will have no method for establishing credentials with the guests browsing the SharePoint site and anonymous access must be allowed.

Basic authentication uses usernames and passwords and should be used only when an SSL connection (HTTPS) is established with the SharePoint site. If SSL is used, the basic authentication process is encrypted in the SSL secured connection. If SSL is not used, the credentials are transferred in a manner that allows easy interception by an attacker. The credentials are sent in Base64 encoding, which is easily decoded without the need for an encryption key. Once the credentials are sniffed from the network and decoded, the attacker can use them to log on as the valid user. It is for this reason that basic authentication should never be used without an SSL connection.

> Additional authentication types have been introduced in SharePoint Server 2010, such as claims authentication (covered in the later section titled "Claims-Based Authentication"), which can provide alternatives to basic authentication for Internet-facing sites.

Digest authentication is based on RFCs 2617 and 2831. A Request for Comment (RFC) is a document used to develop Internet standards. Digest authentication is based on secret keys. While basic authentication sends the password across the network in an easily decodable form, digest authentication depends on the secret keys and passwords are not sent across the network in any form. An example of digest authentication is the default installation of Exchange Server 2010 Outlook Web Application (OWA), which depends on Windows domain accounts by default. Digest authentication should be used when the full encryption of HTTP communications are not required. SSL is preferred when full encryption is required.

Certificate authentication requires that a certificate be installed on the client computer used to access the website. Certificate authentication can become quite expensive because a PKI is required to implement it. Don't confuse certificate authentication with the use of certificates for SSL. SSL requires only a server-side certificate and a PKI is not required to implement this. The server-side certificate can be issued by a trusted third party, self-signed, or issued by an internal PKI. The point is that a PKI is not required to implement SSL, while it will be required to authenticate hundreds or thousands of client computers. Microsoft states the certificate authentication is not supported for access to SharePoint 2010 sites. It can be implemented, because Internet Information Server (IIS) supports it, but it is not supported. Do not confuse the certificates used for SSL encryption (HTTPS) with certificate authentication. Certificate authentication requires that a certificate be installed on each endpoint or client. SSL requires only a single server certificate to encrypt the communications.

NT LAN Manager (NTLM) authentication is required by older client systems that are not fully Active Directory–aware. Such systems include NT 4.0 and Windows 98 computers and even newer operating systems when they are not members of the domain. Because SharePoint relies on the IIS server for authentication behind the scenes, the IIS authentication process applies when connecting to a SharePoint site. The authentication process dictates that the authentication protocols be used in the order from most secure to least secure. For this reason, you can enable both NTLM and Kerberos for your SharePoint installations. Kerberos will be used when it is available and NTLM can be used when Kerberos is not available.

NTLM is not as secure as Kerberos. You will want to use Kerberos as much as possible. When NTLM must be used, ensure that strong passwords are chosen. Such passwords are 7 or 14 characters long and include multiple character types. Due to an odd anomaly in the NTLM authentication process, passwords of between 8 and 13 characters are less secure than passwords of 7 or 14 characters.

Many browsers do not support NTLM or Kerberos authentication and will require the use of basic authentication. If you must support such browsers for your SharePoint sites, ensure that SSL is used.

Kerberos authentication is the best method for internal SharePoint installations accessed only by domain clients. The clients must have access to the Key Distribution Center (KDC), which is the domain controller in an Active Directory environment. The KDC provides a ticket-granting ticket (TGT) at initial logon to the domain. The TGT is used to acquire session tickets (STs) for access to individual servers, such as SharePoint 2010 servers. Microsoft refers to the session ticket as a *service ticket* and the ticket granting ticket as a *user ticket*. This different terminology is found in the Group Policy settings used to configure Kerberos policies.

Windows Server domains allow the administrator to configure five specific policies in relation to Kerberos authentication. The following information describes these policies:

Enforce User Logon Restrictions   When this policy is enabled, the domain controller validates each request against the user rights policy. If the user does not have the right to access the target server from the network, the domain controller (remember, this is the Key Distribution Center) will not grant a session or service ticket for access to the target server. This policy can be enabled to allow for simplified control of access to all servers including the IIS servers providing access to SharePoint sites.

Maximum Lifetime for Service Ticket   This policy determines the lifetime for a service or session ticket. The service ticket is used to access a resource within the domain. If the service ticket is expired, the server returns an error message to the client and the client must request a new service ticket from the domain controller in order to access the server again. The default setting for this policy is 600 minutes or ten hours.

Maximum Lifetime for User Ticket   This policy determines the lifetime for the ticket-granting ticket or the user ticket. The user ticket is acquired at initial logon to the domain and may be renewed up to the *Maximum lifetime for user ticket renewal* (addressed next). The default is ten hours, but the default for renewal is seven days. Therefore, a user ticket may be maintained for a seven-day period without requiring a new logon when the default Kerberos policy settings are used.

Maximum Lifetime for User Ticket Renewal   This policy determines how long a user ticket may be maintained through renewals without requiring a complete logon process. The default is seven days. If this default time period is extended, it can produce interesting problems. For example, group memberships are processed at logon. If the user ticket is simply renewed for a long period of time, any new group memberships will not be processed. By forcing a new logon each week (every seven days by default), you are forcing users to log off and log on again to continue network use.

Maximum Tolerance for Computer Clock Synchronization   To avoid replay attacks against the network, the time is encrypted in the authentication exchange with the domain controller. If this time varies by more than five minutes (this is the default policy setting), the authentication will be rejected. For this reason, a centralized time server should be used to synchronize the clocks on all servers and clients. This policy setting is rarely changed.

Clients must have access to the KDC (the domain controller) to use Kerberos; therefore, Internet-facing SharePoint sites will not use Kerberos. In most cases, such sites will use basic authentication with SSL for security; however, additional authentication types have been introduced in SharePoint Server 2010—for example, claims authentication (covered in the later section titled "Claims-Based Authentication"), which can provide alternatives to basic authentication for Internet-facing sites.

 Real World Scenario

NTLM Is Still Out There

Recently, I (Tom) was working with a company on a SharePoint Server 2010 deployment plan. The company wanted to provide access to the SharePoint server for several interesting scenarios. These scenarios included older computers running Windows 2000. The computers were in a manufacturing environment and, if you've ever worked in such an environment, you know that such computers can be used for many years beyond vendor support timeframes.

The good news is that the Firefox browser supports Windows 2000 machines and SharePoint 2010 can work with Firefox browsers. Additionally, you can configure the Firefox browser (using the secret about:config URL) to automatically perform NTLM authentication. Why was this important in our scenario? The answer is simple. Microsoft is no longer updating the web browsers that run on Windows 2000 machines. Internet Explorer 8.0 and later will not support Windows 2000 client machines. Firefox still supports Windows 2000 (at least as of Firefox 3.6.10) and so it was a perfect solution for this client's needs. We added Firefox to the implementation plan for these clients and ensured that the plans included NTLM authentication support on the SharePoint servers. More good news comes from the fact that SharePoint Server 2010 automatically supports both Kerberos and NTLM if you choose Negotiate (Kerberos) as the authentication method during the Initial Configuration Wizard.

This is just one example of a scenario where NTLM is still being used. Remember, it will be used when a nondomain client connects to the SharePoint server and you do not want to use basic authentication. It may also be used from mobile devices browsing the SharePoint site, assuming they run a Windows pocket OS that supports NTLM authentication.

CMA is discussed further in the section "Windows Integrated Authentication" later in this chapter.

Claims-Based Authentication

When you create a web application in SharePoint Server 2010, you can choose between classic mode authentication or claims-based authentication (CBA), as shown in Figure 5.1. CBA is the new authentication method introduced in SharePoint Server 2010 that allows non-Windows authentication systems to be utilized. CBA actually supports three different authentication providers with a default install of SharePoint Server 2010:

- Windows authentication
- Forms-based authentication (FBA)
- Security Assertion Markup Language (SAML) token-based authentication

Windows authentication will use the same authentication methods provided with classic mode authentication. Basic authentication, digest, NTLM, and Kerberos can all be used. These authentication types were covered in the preceding section.

FBA uses ASP.NET connections to databases and other authentication credential sources for the authentication process. FBA is available only in web applications configured for CBA. If you choose to use FBA, you must enable CBA for the site in which they will operate.

SAML token-based authentication depends on Active Directory Federation Services (ADFS) in most cases, but it can also work with Windows Live ID or third-party authentication systems.

FIGURE 5.1   The Authentication selection screen in SharePoint Server 2010

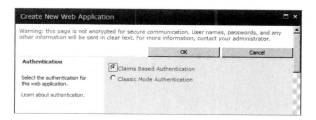

The core concept in CBA is identity and access management. CBA works with identities and uses open protocols that can communicate with most identity management systems (IMSs). Active Directory is an example of an IMS, but CBA could work with Novell Directory Services, RADIUS servers, and any number of other identity providers.

SharePoint Server 2010's CBA provides several benefits over the CMA provided in SharePoint Server 2007, including:

- Multiple authentication providers can be used with a single SharePoint site URL. This required two zones or two URLs for two authentication providers in SharePoint Server 2007.

- The claims-based model removes SharePoint from a tight connection with authentication providers and allows the authentication to truly be "outside" of SharePoint.

- CBA provides federation between organizations so that one organization's SharePoint Server 2010 installation can authenticate another organization's users.

CBA utilizes three different potential technologies on the Windows Server platform:

- **Windows Identity Foundation (WIF):** This set of APIs is used to develop claims-based applications.

- **ADFS 2.0:** ADFS 2.0 provides the identity federation and single sign-on (SSO) capabilities.

- **Windows CardSpace 2.0:** An identity selection solution that acts as an alternative to usernames and password pairs. Digital user identities are stored and presented in Information Cards.

If you are new to authentication systems, you may want to delve deeper into this Microsoft technology. You can learn more at http://technet .microsoft.com/en-us/library/cc262350.aspx#section1.

Several terms should be understood in relation to CBA. Table 5.1 lists these terms and their meanings.

TABLE 5.1   CBA Terms and Definitions

CBA Term	Definition
Identity	The security principal used to configure the security policy and in authentication.
Claim	An identity attribute such as the login name, group memberships, and so forth.
Issuer	The trusted party that creates the claims for the identities.
Security Token	A set of claims in a digitally signed package created by the issuing authority.

CBA Term	Definition
Issuing Authority	The source of the security tokens that is aware of claims needed by the target application (such as SharePoint Server 2010).
Security Token Service (STS)	The actual service that creates, signs, and distributes the security tokens.
Relying Party	The application that performs authorization actions based on claims provided by an issuing authority.

In order to utilize an issuing authority other than the local Active Directory installation, you will need to create a farm trust. The farm trust can be created in the Security section of SharePoint Central Administration. The Manage Trust hyperlink from the General Security section is used to access the farm trusts. When you create a new farm trust, you will see a screen similar to the one in Figure 5.2.

FIGURE 5.2   Creating a new farm trust in SharePoint Central Administration

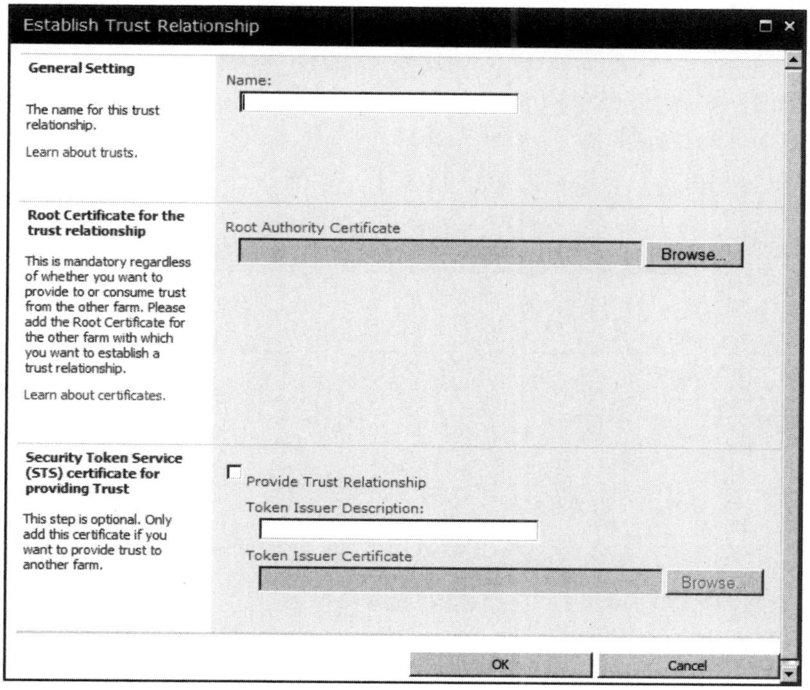

As you can see in Figure 5.2, three configuration options are available when setting up the farm trust. The first is the Name for this trust, which is found in the General Setting section. The name should be something meaningful so that you will recognize the trust within the configuration interface. The second is the Root Certificate for the trust relationship. This certificate is used to establish the trust with the remote issuing authority and then any tokens that are provided by the issuing authority and signed with this certificate will be trusted. The third setting is the Provide Trust Relationship option in the Security Token Service (STS) certificate for providing Trust section. If you want to provide trust to the other farm so that it can authenticate against your database, you can use this option.

In Exercise 5.1, you will configure the authentication method for a WebApp as it is created in Central Administration. You will configure the new WebApp to use CBA.

EXERCISE 5.1

Creating a New WebApp and Configuring CBA

In this exercise, you will configure a new WebApp to use CBA for authentication. You will create a WebApp from Central Administration and configure the CBA during the creation of the WebApp.

1. Launch Central Administration.

2. Select the Application Management section from the left menu.

3. In the Web Applications collection, select Manage Web Applications.

4. On the Web Applications tab of the Ribbon, select New.

5. In the New Web Application screen, select Claims Based Authentication.

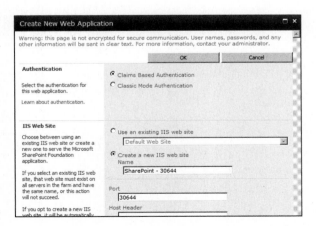

6. Accept all other defaults and click OK. Be patient. The process of creating a new WebApp can take several minutes.

7. The Application Created screen will be displayed. Read the provided information and click OK.

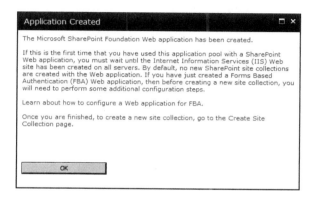

It is important to know that you cannot switch from CBA to CMA. Through a complicated PowerShell script, it is possible to convert from CMA to CBA, but it is a one-way street. Once you convert to CBA, you cannot go back to CMA. The following TechNet article explains the CMA to CBA conversion process: `http://technet` `.microsoft.com/en-us/library/gg251985.aspx`.

CBA is discussed further in the section "Windows Integrated Authentication" later in this chapter.

Secure Store Service

The Secure Store Service (SSS) replaces the single sign-on feature in SharePoint Server 2007. SSS is claims-aware and includes a secured credential storage database for credentials associated with applications. When SharePoint Server 2010 needs access to external data sources, SSS can store the credentials (users and passwords) for access to these data sources.

Microsoft recommends the following guidelines when deploying SSS:

- Use a separate application pool for the SSS.
- Use a separate application server when possible.
- Do not use the same SQL Server installation used for SharePoint content for the SSS secure storage.

- The SSS database is encrypted so you should back up the encryption key when it is created and anytime it is replaced.

- Store the backup media for the encryption key in a different location from the secure credential database.

Three components of SSS should be understood to properly plan for its implementation. These components are application IDs, SSS mappings, and claims authentication integration.

Application IDs are used to retrieve credentials from the secure store database. Permissions may be applied to application IDs, limiting the users or groups who can access the credentials the application IDs reference. The SharePoint Server 2010 web applications will access the credentials on behalf of users based on the application IDs.

The SSS mappings are used to connect a user or group to a credential set using the application IDs. A user may be mapped to a credential set via the application ID, and this is called an *individual* mapping. Individual mappings allow for logging information about user access to resources. A group may also be mapped to a credential set. The group option makes management easier, and Microsoft indicates that it may also improve performance.

The Secure Store Service may also work with CBA. When used with CBA, the SSS receives an encrypted token from the SharePoint Server 2010 Security Token Service and then decrypts the token in order to perform an application ID lookup. Once the application ID is located, the credentials are used for secure access to resources. CBA integration is really no different from user and group mappings with the exception that the application ID is provided as a claim in the token.

Planning for Secure Sites

Authentication and authorization must be considered when planning for secure sites. Authentication was covered in detail in the preceding section and will be explored here from a planning perspective. Authorization is covered in detail in the next section, but this section will address the planning steps required to ensure your environment can support the needed authorization processes. To best address both pieces of the security puzzle this section will be broken into two subsections:

- Planning Secure Authentication
- Planning a Secure Authorization Environment

Planning Secure Authentication

When planning for secure authentication, you must first determine the supported authentication methods for the technology in question. For SharePoint Server 2010, any of the following authentication methods may be utilized:

- NTLM
- Kerberos

- Anonymous

- Basic

- Digest

- Forms-based (LDAP)

- Forms-based (SQL database)

- Forms-based (customer or third-party providers)

- SAML token-based authentication

Depending on the authentication method chosen, you will also have to plan for the authentication mode. The options are either classic mode or claims-based authentication. All of the previously listed authentication methods will work with CBA; however, CMA does not support forms-based authentication or SAML token-based authentication. For these latter two methods, CBA must be used.

 Earlier in this chapter, CMA was discussed in some detail in the section "Windows Integrated Authentication." CBA was introduced in the section "Claims-Based Authentication."

Microsoft suggests the following guidelines for choosing the authentication mode:

- Use CBA for all new implementations of SharePoint Server 2010. This guideline assumes you are not incorporating any existing custom code that depends on CMA.

- When upgrading from an earlier SharePoint version that is implemented with only Windows accounts, use CMA. This allows the existing zones and URLs to function properly in SharePoint Server 2010.

- When upgrading from an earlier SharePoint version that uses forms-based authentication, you must use CBA. Forms-based authentication is only supported by CBA.

When you upgrade from previous versions of SharePoint to SharePoint Server 2010 and choose to use CBA, several issues must be considered. First, you should know that custom code often requires updates to work properly with CBA. If Windows identities are used by the web parts or custom code in question, the code will have to be updated. Second, search alerts are not supported with CBA. If you require search alerts, you will have to use CMA. Also, the migration of hundreds or thousands of users to claims identities can take quite a lot of time. Windows PowerShell must be used to convert the identities, so make sure you allow for the time to complete this process. Finally, if you convert from CMA to CBA, you cannot switch from CBA back to CMA.

Table 5.2 provides recommendations for the best authentication method to use in a given scenario. Use this table both to help with decisions related to implementation and to better answer exam questions if you take the SharePoint certification exam.

TABLE 5.2 Authentication Scenarios and Recommended Modes

Authentication Scenario	Recommended Authentication Mode
Upgrading from WSS 3.0 to SharePoint Server 2010 with custom code included in the existing installation	Use CMA in the beginning and transition over to CBA as the custom code is updated.
Upgrading from WSS 3.0 to SharePoint Server 2010 with no custom code or web parts using Windows identities	Use CBA from the beginning of the SharePoint Server 2010 installation.
Installing a new SharePoint Server 2010 installation in an environment that has never used SharePoint in the past	Use CBA from the beginning as it supports all authentication methods supported by CMA.
Installing a new SharePoint Server 2010 installation and restoring applications from earlier versions of SharePoint	If Windows identities were used in the applications, use CMA for authentication.

In addition to planning for the authentication mode, you must also select the best authentication method. For internal users, you will likely use either NTLM or Kerberos. Remember that Kerberos is more secure and should be used whenever possible; however, nondomain computers and devices that cannot join the domain may require the use of NTLM.

For external users, when anonymous access is not sufficient, SSL should be used any time basic authentication is allowed. In order to use SSL, the following actions must be taken:

- A certificate must be installed on the IIS server for use by SSL.
- SSL must be enabled for the website in IIS.
- The Alternate Access mapping should be changed to reference https:// instead of http://.

You can also enable SSL during the creation of the web application.

To see example plans for both CMA and CBA, visit the TechNet website at http://technet.microsoft.com/en-us/library/cc263199.aspx.

Planning a Secure Authorization Environment

In order to provide a secure authorization environment, users and groups must be properly created in Active Directory. Exhaustive coverage of this process is not required here because it is typically an action performed by the domain administrators and not the SharePoint administrators. However, some important guidelines may be useful:

- When working with groups, prefer Active Directory groups over SharePoint groups as much as possible. SharePoint groups are limited to the site collection in which they are created. Therefore, groups will have to be re-created for each SharePoint site collection if Active Directory groups are not used.

- SharePoint groups do not support nesting. You can place Active Directory groups within SharePoint groups, but you cannot place SharePoint groups within other SharePoint groups.

- Users can submit requests to join a SharePoint group. No such feature is provided for Active Directory groups.

- Active Directory distribution groups (as opposed to security groups) cannot be added to SharePoint groups. You can expand the users in the distribution group into the SharePoint group, but you will have to synchronize the future changes to the distribution group manually.

- Prefer security groups over distribution groups for easier additions to SharePoint groups and because they can be assigned permissions.

Whether you choose to use SharePoint groups or Active Directory groups, it is important that you understand the benefits of using groups instead of individual users for permission management. If you have only five users, individual user-based permission management will not be a problem; however, few organizations of this small size would implement SharePoint Server 2010. In larger organizations, managing direct user permissions will become complicated and cumbersome very quickly. Using groups allows for simpler management.

To understand the simpler management provided through the use of groups, consider the following scenario. You have 30 lists in a SharePoint site collection and you want to manage direct permissions on these lists. Each list has a select set of users who need access to the list; however, a unique set of 60 users requires access to 18 of the lists and another unique set of 27 users requires access to the remaining 12 lists. If the permissions were set based on individual users, you would have to perform 60 actions on 18 lists and 27 actions on 12 lists for a total of 1,404 actions.

Now, consider the same scenario references in the preceding paragraph when using groups. One group could be created with the 60 users and another group with the 27 users. These two steps will require a total of 89 actions (2 actions to create the groups and 87 actions to add the users to the groups). Next, you will assign permissions to the lists, which will require another 30 actions. In the end, you've reduced the work from 1,404 actions to 117 actions. Clearly, group-based management is more efficient than direct user-based management.

In the next section, you'll learn about the specific hierarchies of security in SharePoint Server 2010 and the default SharePoint groups available within the system. In Exercise 5.2, you will create an Active Directory group using the Active Directory Users and Computers administration console.

EXERCISE 5.2

Creating Groups in Active Directory

In this exercise, you will create an Active Directory group. This group may be used for permissions within SharePoint Server 2010. You will create the group in Active Directory Users and Computers.

1. Click Start ➢ Administrative Tools ➢ Active Directory Users and Computers.

2. Select the container in which you want to place the group, such as the Users container.

3. Click Create A New Group in the current container icon on the toolbar. (You can also right-click the container in which you want to create a group.)

4. In the New Object - Group dialog, enter the group name of **SharePoint Site Managers**. Select the Group Scope of Global and the Group Type of Security.

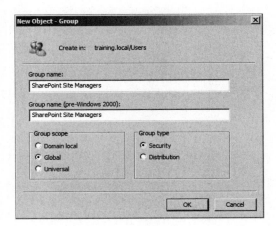

5. Click OK to create the group.

You can create as many groups as you need for SharePoint management. In order to create such groups in a production environment, you will have to have Domain Admins group membership for your account. Otherwise, you may have to ask another administrator to create the groups for you.

You can add as many users as you require to the groups. For example, the SharePoint Site Managers group created in Exercise 5.2 may serve the purpose of granting granular management capabilities to a collection of users. The built-in SharePoint groups may grant more capabilities than you want. An Active Directory group provides an easy means for custom permission management.

Designing Authorization

When designing authorization for SharePoint Server 2010, you must consider several factors:

- Security levels
- Taxonomy of SharePoint groups
- Permission levels

Each factor is addressed in the following sections.

Security Levels

SharePoint Server 2010 provides multiple levels of security. This concept can be considered in two ways. First, there is the concept of the SharePoint Server 2010 architecture, which allows different permissions at different levels in the architecture. Second, there is the concept of permission levels within the SharePoint Server 2010 permission management model. Permission levels are covered in the later subsection titled "Permission Levels."

Figure 5.3 illustrates the hierarchy of the SharePoint Server 2010 architecture. Permissions and administrative capabilities may be delegated at each level in this hierarchy. For example, you can assign a farm administrator and you can create site collection administrators. You can also give an individual user the ability to manage permissions (perform administration) for other users right down to the individual documents in libraries or list items in lists.

FIGURE 5.3   The SharePoint Server 2010 hierarchy

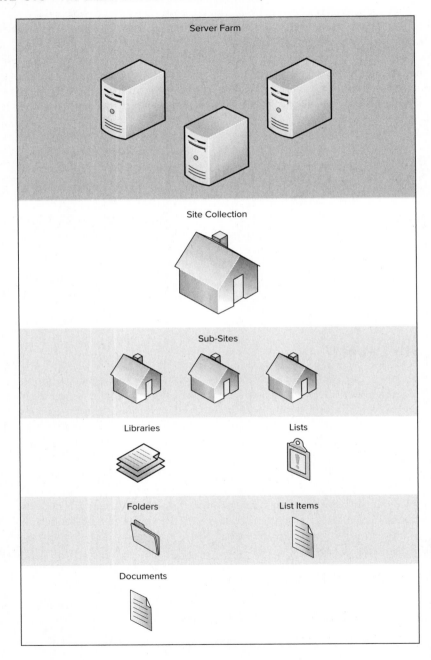

It's also important that you understand the concept of inheritance. Each level, by default, inherits permissions from the level above it. For example, if you make a user the site collection administrator, you are effectively granting full control to that user at the site collection level. Through inheritance, that user will also have full control of all sites, libraries, lists, folders, list items, and documents within the site collection. To break this inheritance chain, you must choose the option to Stop Inheriting Permissions at the level where you want the inheritance to break, as shown in Figure 5.4.

FIGURE 5.4   The Stop Inheriting Permission button at the document level

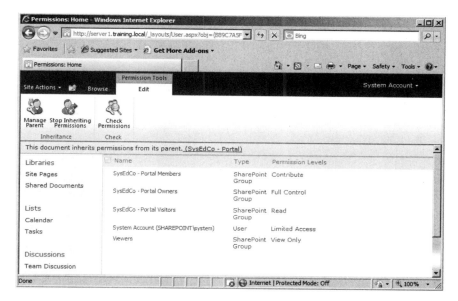

Exercise 5.3 provides instructions for blocking permission inheritance on the default SharePoint site objects created during a typical installation. The same basic steps can be used to block permission inheritance for any site object you have created.

EXERCISE 5.3

Blocking Permission Inheritance

In this exercise, you will perform the steps required to block permission inheritance on the default site object that builds the Tasks list for the site.

1. Log on as an administrator of the SharePoint default site.

2. Open your web browser and navigate to the default site. For example, if your default site is on Server1, navigate to http://server1.

EXERCISE 5.3 *(continued)*

3. Select Site Permissions from the Site Actions menu.

4. Click the Tasks link in the Lists section of the left navigation bar.

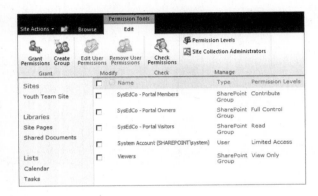

5. Select the List tab in the List Tools section of the Ribbon.

6. Select the Setting button and choose List Permission from the callout menu.

7. Click the Stop Inheriting Permission button on the Ribbon.

8. You will be prompted with a warning that says, "You are about to create unique permissions for the list. Changes made to the parent site permissions will no longer affect this list." Click OK to accept this message and block permission inheritance.

9. Notice that the old permissions, which were inherited, are copied to the list. You did not lose the older permissions; however, new permissions created at a higher level will no longer apply to this list.

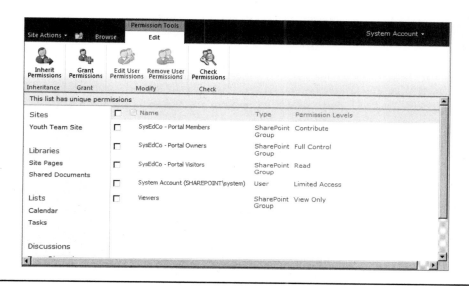

If you ever disable permission inheritance and then want to enable the inheritance again, you can click the Inherit Permissions button in order to revert to the default permission inheritance setting.

Taxonomy of SharePoint Groups

If you have read the exam objectives for Microsoft exam 70-668, you have probably noticed the use of the word *taxonomy*. In case you've forgotten your biology classes, taxonomy, in the world of biology, is a classification of organisms into groups that are usually hierarchical in nature. The taxonomy of the SharePoint security groups is the defined hierarchy of special groups used within SharePoint to assign permissions.

To help you understand the security groups within SharePoint Server 2010, Table 5.3 provides a listing of the default SharePoint groups and the permission levels they have within a Team Site. Keep in mind that different site templates may provide additional default security groups. Permission levels are detailed in the later subsection titled "Permission Levels."

TABLE 5.3   Default Security Groups within Team Sites

Security Group	Permission Levels
Approvers	Have Approve permission level for the site
Designers	Have Design permission level for the site
Hierarchy Managers	Have Manage Hierarchy permission level for the site
Members	Have Contribute permission level for the site
Owners	Have Full Control permission level for the site
Quick Deploy Users	Have custom permissions that allow members to contribute to the Quick Deploy Items library within the site
Restricted Readers	Have restricted Read permission level for the site
Style Resource Readers	Have custom permissions that allow members to read the Master Page Gallery and Style Library for the site
Visitors	Have both Read and View Permission levels for the site

SharePoint also provides several special powerful groups. The following special groups should be understood:

Site Collection Administrators   Site collection administrators can access any and all features and permissions within a site and on every object in the site. Site collection administrators are set up as the contact for the site collection. They can also audit site content, enable or disable features within the site collection, and monitor search usage within the sites.

Farm Administrators   The Farm Administrators group is managed from Central Administration and not from within a site or site collection. This group can manage settings for the server farm; however, no access is provided to site content by default. Farm administrators can take ownership of site content in order to gain access to the content.

Administrators   Administrators have the capabilities of farm administrators plus the ability to install new applications, distribute web parts throughout the farm and start SharePoint services. Like the farm administrators, no access is granted to site content by default.

SharePoint permissions differ from the Windows Server permissions to which you may be accustomed. SharePoint permissions are inclusive while Windows Server permissions may be exclusive. This simply means that with SharePoint permissions you can define activities users can do, but you cannot define activities users cannot do.

Permission Levels

SharePoint Server 2010 provides several default permission levels. Think of these permission levels as collections of capabilities for users and groups. Rather than specifying each individual capability, you can select a permission level that encompasses the needed capabilities. Table 5.4 describes the different permission levels within SharePoint Server 2010 and the capabilities provided by each permission level. In Table 5.4, notice that some permission levels are available only in the publishing template.

TABLE 5.4   Permission Levels in SharePoint Server 2010

Permission Level	Site Template	Description of Capabilities
Limited Access	Team or Publishing Template	Specific lists, document libraries, list items, folders, or documents may be viewed; but access to all elements of the site are not granted. Limited Access is designed to be used with fine-grained permissions.
Read	Team or Publishing Template	Items can be viewed on the site pages.
Contribute	Team or Publishing Template	Users can add or change items on the site pages or in existing lists or document libraries.
Design	Team or Publishing Template	Page layout can be modified by members in the browser or from within SharePoint Designer 2010. Design permissions also allow for the creation of lists and document libraries.
Full Control	Team or Publishing Template	All capabilities are provided including permission management.
View Only	Publishing Template	Users may view pages, list items, and documents.
Approve	Publishing Template	Users may approve pages, list items, or documents submitted by others.

TABLE 5.4 Permission Levels in SharePoint Server 2010 *(continued)*

Permission Level	Site Template	Description of Capabilities
Manage Hierarchy	Publishing Template	Users may edit pages, list items, and documents. Manage Hierarchy permissions also allow the users to create sites.
Restricted Read	Publishing Template	Users may view pages and documents; however, historical versions are not available.

In SharePoint Server 2010, you can easily check the permission assigned to a user or group from within Site Settings. Access Site Setting from the root of the site collection and then open Users and Permissions ≻ People and Groups. From there you can select Settings ≻ View Group Permissions to see the applicable permissions for the currently selected group as shown in Figure 5.5. Exercise 5.4 provides instructions for viewing group permissions on a list.

FIGURE 5.5 Viewing permissions assigned to a group

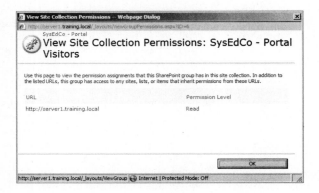

EXERCISE 5.4

Viewing Permissions for a Group on a List

In this exercise, you will view the permissions assigned to a group on the Tasks list in the default SharePoint site. This exercise assumes that the default SharePoint site was created during installation.

1. Access the SharePoint site as an administrator.

2. Open the list on which you want to check permissions.

3.   Select the List tab in the List Tools section of the Ribbon.

4.   Click the List Permissions button.

5.   Click the Check Permissions button.

6.   Enter the group name you want to check and click Check Now.

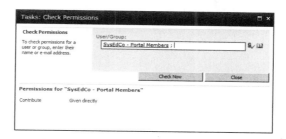

Planning Web Application Security

Managing web application security is accomplished in two ways. First, you must manage the actual security of the WebApp site collection. This can be accomplished through Central Administration or the IIS Manager. Second, you must manage the security of the services that actually operate the SharePoint environment. This can be accomplished through the use of managed accounts. These topics are addressed in the following sections.

WebApp Site Collection Security

From within Central Administration, you can manage the following WebApp security settings:

Authentication Providers   This interface allows for configuration of membership and role providers for each web application zone. For example, Windows may be used as an authentication provider indicating that Active Directory and local system accounts may be authenticated to the WebApp.

Self-Service Site Creation   You can choose whether to allow self-service site creation or not. Self-service site creation allows users to create sites within the site collection. The feature can be in either an on or off state, and a secondary contact may be required if desired. When a secondary contact is required, it simply means that each site must have two contact names associated with it instead of only one.

Blocked File Types   This setting allows you to determine the file types that may not be added to document libraries. Some file types pose a security risk, such as scripts, documents with macros, and so on.

User Permissions The User Permission button is used to indicate the permission that will be allowed within the WebApp. You can choose from the common permissions and several not-so-common permissions such as Use Remote Interfaces and Use Client Integration Features (for more details on the full list of available WebApp permissions, see Table 5.5).

Web Part Security Web Part Security allows the configuration of web part connections, the online web part gallery, and scriptable web parts. You can allow or disallow data values to pass from one web part to another. You can determine whether users are allowed access to the Online Web Part Gallery or not. Finally, you can choose whether contributors can edit scriptable web parts.

User Policy The User Policy button allows you to access the users configured for the WebApp and to manage the permissions for those users.

Anonymous Policy The Anonymous Policy is used to determine whether anonymous users have access to the WebApp or not. Additionally, you can decide to grant permissions with deny write so that anonymous users can access the sites, but they cannot modify site content.

Permission Policy The Permission Policy dictates the permission levels available within the WebApp. From here, you can also create custom permission levels using the 33 different permissions references in Table 5.5.

User permissions, referenced in the preceding list should be considered in more detail. More than 30 user permissions exist in three categories and they are documented in Table 5.5.

TABLE 5.5 User Permissions for WebApp Security

Permission	Category	Description
Manage Lists	List Permissions	Create and delete lists, add or remove columns in a list, and add or remove public views of a list.
Override Check Out	List Permissions	Discard or check in a document that is checked out to another user.
Add Items	List Permissions	Add items to lists and add documents to document libraries.
Edit Items	List Permissions	Edit items in lists, edit documents in document libraries, and customize Web Part Pages in document libraries.
Delete Items	List Permissions	Delete items from a list and documents from a document library.

Permission	Category	Description
View Items	List Permissions	View items in lists and documents in document libraries.
Approve Items	List Permissions	Approve a minor version of a list item or document.
Open Items	List Permissions	View the source of documents with server-side file handlers.
View Versions	List Permissions	View past versions of a list item or document.
Delete Versions	List Permissions	Delete past versions of a list item or document.
Create Alerts	List Permissions	Create alerts for the list item.
View Application Pages	List Permissions	View forms, views, and application pages. Enumerate lists.
Manage Permissions	Site Permissions	Create and change permission levels on the website and assign permissions to users and groups.
View Web Analytics Data	Site Permissions	View reports on website usage.
Create Subsites	Site Permissions	Create subsites such as team sites, Meeting Workspace sites, and Document Workspace sites.
Manage Web Site	Site Permissions	Perform all administration tasks for the website as well as manage content.
Add and Customize Pages	Site Permissions	Add, change, or delete HTML pages or Web Part Pages, and edit the website using a Microsoft SharePoint Foundation–compatible editor.
Apply Themes and Borders	Site Permissions	Apply a theme or borders to the entire website.
Apply Style Sheets	Site Permissions	Apply a style sheet (.CSS file) to the website.

TABLE 5.5   User Permissions for WebApp Security *(continued)*

Permission	Category	Description
Create Groups	Site Permissions	Create a group of users that can be used anywhere within the site collection.
Browser Directories	Site Permissions	Enumerate files and folders in a website using SharePoint Designer and Web DAV interfaces.
Use Self-Service Site Creation	Site Permissions	Create a website using Self-Service Site Creation.
View Pages	Site Permissions	View pages in a website.
Enumerate Permissions	Site Permissions	Enumerate permissions on the website, list, folder, document, or list item.
Browse User Information	Site Permissions	View information about users of the website.
Manage Alerts	Site Permissions	Manage alerts for all users of the Web site.
Use Remote Interfaces	Site Permissions	Use SOAP, Web DAV, the Client Object Model, or SharePoint Designer interfaces to access the website.
Use Client Integration Features	Site Permissions	Use features that launch client applications. Without this permission, users will have to work on documents locally and upload their changes.
Open	Site Permissions	Allows users to open a website, list, or folder in order to access items inside that container.
Edit Personal User Information	Site Permissions	Allows a user to change his or her own user information, such as adding a picture.
Manage Personal Views	Personal Permissions	Create, change, and delete personal views of lists.
Add/Remove Personal Web Parts	Personal Permissions	Add or remove personal Web Parts on a Web Part Page.
Update Personal Web Parts	Personal Permissions	Update Web Parts to display personalized information.

In Exercise 5.5, you will create a custom permission level. Permission levels allow you to specify the exact permissions you want.

EXERCISE 5.5

Creating a Custom Permission Level

In this exercise, you will create a custom permission level named User Support. The custom permission level will allow user information to be viewed for the site and groups to be created by users granted the permission level.

1. Log on as a SharePoint administrator.

2. Open the site on which you want to create the customer permission level in the web browser.

3. Select Site Actions ➤ Site Permissions from the upper-left menu.

4. Choose the Permission Levels button in the Manage section of the Ribbon.

5. Click the Add A Permission Level link.

6. Enter the value of **User Support** in the Name field within the Name and Description section.

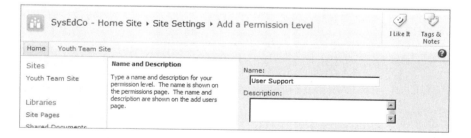

7. In the Permissions section, check the Create Groups permission and the Browser User Information permission.

8. Scroll to the bottom of the page and click Create.

After you have created a custom permission level, you can create a SharePoint group and assign the permission level to that group. Then, you can add users to the group so that they can receive the permissions provided by the custom permission level. Exercise 5.6 provides instructions for creating a SharePoint group that uses the User Support permission level created in Exercise 5.5.

EXERCISE 5.6

Creating a SharePoint Group

In this exercise, you will create a SharePoint group named User Support Staff. This group will be assigned the User Support permission level. The steps in this exercise depend on the previous completion of Exercise 5.5.

1. Log on as a SharePoint administrator.

2. Open the site on which you want to create the customer permission level in the web browser.

3. Select Site Actions ➤ Site Permissions from the upper-left menu.

4. Click the Create Group button in the Grant section of the Ribbon.

5. Enter the value **User Support Staff** in the Name field within the Name and About Me Description section. Enter a description if desired.

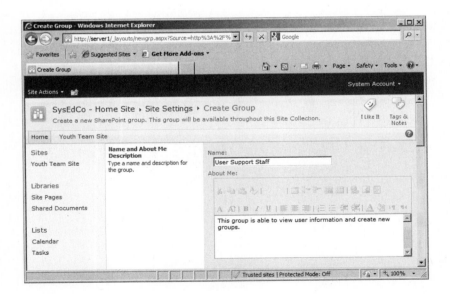

6. Scroll down the page to the Owner section and note that the default group owner is the System Account.

7. In the Group Settings section, define who can manage the membership of the group and who can modify the membership of the group.

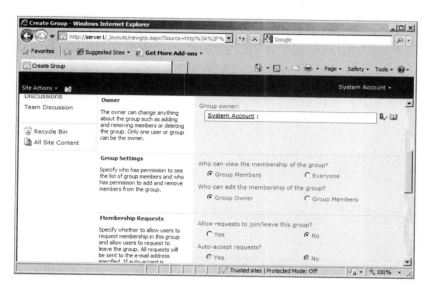

8. Scroll down the page and in the Membership Requests section determine whether requests to join or leave the group will be allowed and whether requests will be auto-accepted or not. If membership requests are to be accepted, identify an email address to be notified as requests come into the SharePoint site.

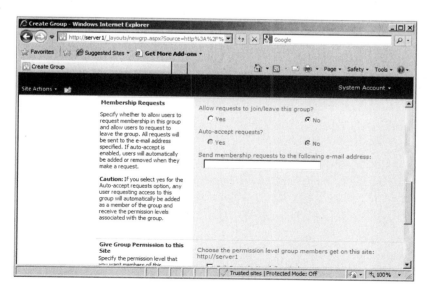

9. Scroll down the page and in the Give Group Permission to this Site section, choose the User Support custom permission level, and click Create to create the SharePoint group.

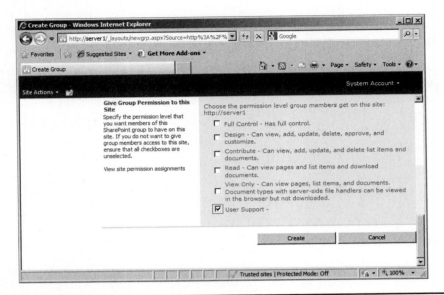

After creating the SharePoint group, you will be taken to the group management page for that group. Here, you can add new users to the group, send emails or messages to the group members, and configure the group settings.

The WebApp security can also be managed to some extent from within the IIS Manager; however, you should be very careful about making direct changes to the Application Pool and sites within the IIS Manager. You can easily break a SharePoint installation by changing settings within IIS Manager.

One example of a WebApp security task you must perform from within the IIS Manager is the enabling of SSL. You cannot enable SSL within SharePoint. It must be enabled in the IIS Manager. The basic process for enabling SSL in IIS is as follows:

1. Open the IIS Manager.

2. With the target server selected, open Server Certificates.

3. From the Actions pane, select Create Certificate Request and generate a certificate request in the displayed wizard.

4. Access the certificate authority and use the request to generate a certificate.

5. Return to the IIS Manager and use the Complete Certificate Request action to import the certificate provided by the certificate authority.

6. Bind the certificate to the SharePoint site in the IIS Manager.

7. In Central Administration, modify the Alternate Access mapping to allow for HTTPS://.

As you can see, some actions require changes in both IIS Manager and the Central Administration interface. In general, if you can do it in Central Administration instead of the IIS Manager, you should.

Managed Accounts

In previous versions of SharePoint, the service accounts had to be managed in the Services snap-in within the MMC (Microsoft Management Console). The SharePoint Central Administration interface provided no simple method for management of the service accounts. SharePoint Server 2010 provides a feature called *managed accounts* that allows for the management of these service accounts.

Managed accounts are Active Directory or local system accounts managed by the SharePoint application. The most important features of managed accounts are automatic password management (see Figure 5.6) and the simple linking of a managed account to a SharePoint service.

FIGURE 5.6   The Automatic Password Change interface for managed accounts

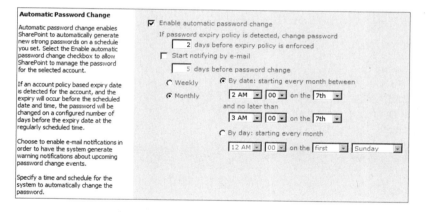

SharePoint can automatically change the password for the service account when password expiration policies are set. Figure 5.6 shows the interface used to configure this password management. Once automatic password changing is enabled, you can indicate the following parameters:

- How long before password expiration the password should be changed
- When and if to notify the administrator of upcoming password changes
- A schedule for password changes rather than relying on the expiration policy alone

Of course, with automatic password changes, the administrator will not know the password for the managed account; however, the password can be manually changed within Active Directory or local user management interfaces and then the new manually set password can be entered in SharePoint Central Administration, as shown in Figure 5.7.

FIGURE 5.7   Manually configuring the managed account password

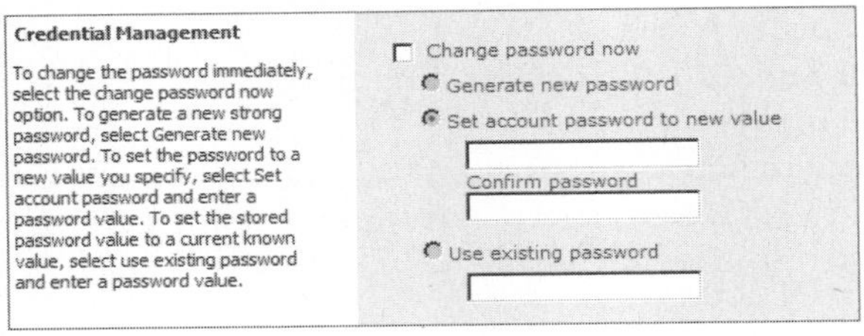

Credential Management

To change the password immediately, select the change password now option. To generate a new strong password, select Generate new password. To set the password to a new value you specify, select Set account password and enter a password value. To set the stored password value to a current known value, select use existing password and enter a password value.

☐ Change password now
   ○ Generate new password
   ◉ Set account password to new value

   Confirm password

   ○ Use existing password

The second benefit of managed accounts is the simple linking of a managed account to a SharePoint service or component. Figure 5.8 shows the interface used to select the managed account for a specific SharePoint component.

FIGURE 5.8   Assigning a managed account to a SharePoint component

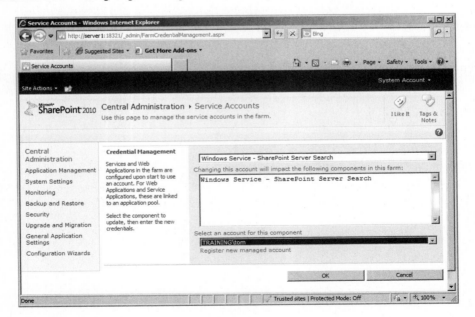

Planning Code Access Security

Code access security is used to trust code to varying degrees depending on the source of the code and other information related to the programming code properties. The following functionality is provided by code access security in SharePoint Server 2010:

- Allows code to require specific permissions of the calling application or user
- Allows code to require a digital signature for the calling application or user
- Allows administrators to use associating sets of permissions to configure security policy
- Describes the permission sets that provide the rights to access system resources
- Restricts code at runtime based on permissions provided by the caller
- Allows code to request the permissions it requires as well as permission that would be useful

When planning security, you should ensure that you have the minimum set of permissions required for your WebApp. Code access security helps you accomplish this. You can also set the <trust> element in the Web.config file for each WebApp to WSS_ Minimal, which will reduce the power of the SharePoint applications running within the context of the WebApp.

For additional information on security best practices for SharePoint WebApps and Code Access Security, see: http://technet.microsoft .com/en-us/library/cc288143.aspx.

Summary

In this chapter, you learned about the importance of authentication and authorization in SharePoint Server 2010 installations. You learned about the hierarchies of security from the server farm through to the individual list items and documents. You also explored the permission levels available and the specific list, site, and personal permissions. You learned the different features available for securing WebApps and the foundational knowledge required to plan security for your SharePoint deployments.

Exam Essentials

Planning authentication methods.   You should be able to differentiate between classic-mode authentication (CMA) and claims-based authentication (CBA). Be sure to know which authentication methods will work with the two modes of authentication.

Planning for secure sites.   Understand the difference between Active Directory groups and SharePoint groups as they relate to security of sites and permission management. Understand how to choose the best authentication method and mode.

Designing authorization.   Be sure to understand the inheritance feature within SharePoint authorization models. Also, remember that SharePoint Server 2010 uses an inclusive permission model in that you grant, but do not deny, access.

Planning web application security.   Know the permissions available in the list, site, and personal categories. Know the dangers of reconfiguring WebApp settings directly within the IIS Manager, but that SSL must be configured from the IIS Manager first and then the alternative mapping URL must be properly configured within Central Administration.

Planning code access security.   Determine the minimum permissions required by your application and ensure that only those minimum requirements are met. This starts with the use of the `<trust>` parameter in the `Web.config` file.

Chapter 6

Designing an Operations Strategy

TOPICS COVERED IN THIS CHAPTER

✓ Designing a Maintenance Strategy

✓ Planning a Monitoring Strategy

✓ Developing Provisioning Strategies

Once you've installed and secured your SharePoint Server 2010 deployment, you must enter operations mode. Operations will include maintenance, monitoring, provisioning, and backups. SharePoint backups will be covered in Chapter 7, "Designing a Strategy for Business Continuity." In this chapter, you will learn about the other three important components of a SharePoint Server 2010 operations strategy.

You will begin by exploring maintenance strategies. SharePoint maintenance involves patching the SharePoint components and maintaining the installation through daily tasks such as permission management and configuration management. Additionally, you must understand how to work with SQL Server databases for index management. The configuration and content for SharePoint Server 2010 is stored in the SQL Server database. Search maintenance is also an important operations task that can be automated to some extent, but it will require administrative interaction from time to time as well.

Next, you will learn about the monitoring tools available for SharePoint Server 2010. These tools include internal tools that are part of the SharePoint installation and external tools that are part of the operating system. You will learn to determine the monitoring point for different performance problems and how to use the various tools to pin down the cause of the problem. In many cases, performance can be increased dramatically with seemingly small changes to the system configuration or database indexing.

Finally, you must decide how you will provision the SharePoint sites. Ultimately, you have two options. The first option is manual provisioning (also called IT provisioning), which requires that the IT administrators create every site and manage the permissions and site configuration themselves. The second option is self-service site creation, which allows users to create their own sites as needed. Both methods will be discussed in this chapter.

If you are preparing for the 70-668 MCITP exam, you should find the coverage of important objectives in this chapter helpful. Specifically, designing a maintenance strategy and establishing an enterprise monitoring plan are addressed here. Along the way, you will learn information for the exam as well as real-world applications of the knowledge. The sections titled "Designing a Maintenance Strategy" and "Planning a Monitoring Strategy" are the most important ones for exam preparation.

Designing a Maintenance Strategy

Maintenance includes the actions you perform to keep the SharePoint Server 2010 implementation running smoothly and securely. SharePoint Server 2010 maintenance can be divided into two categories:

- Patch Management
- Ongoing Maintenance Tasks

Both categories are covered in the following sections.

Patch Management

Patch management is the process used to maintain the security and stability of a system through updates that repair vulnerabilities and bugs. New security vulnerabilities are discovered daily in the thousands of applications available today. Even so, SharePoint has a very good track record for being secure. For example, if you search the National Vulnerability Database (NVD) for all security issues with the keyword of SharePoint, fewer than 20 vulnerabilities were listed as of the Fall of 2010. Many of these vulnerabilities date back to 2005 and have long since been repaired. However, even with this solid track record, one major security flaw can cause severe problems in your environment. Therefore, patch management is essential to maintaining security.

In fact, during the first six months of the year 2010, three vulnerabilities were discovered in SharePoint Server. All three vulnerabilities applied to SharePoint Server 2007 and earlier versions. No serious security vulnerabilities were discovered and reported in SharePoint Server 2010 through the Fall of 2010. Of course, multiple vulnerabilities could be discovered and reported in a single day, but SharePoint's overall track record is particularly strong. In comparison, while the Open Source Vulnerability Database (OSVDB) reported fewer than 20 vulnerabilities in SharePoint Server (remember, these vulnerabilities were all in pre-2010 editions of the product) from 2005 through the Fall of 2010, Joomla—an open source alternative to SharePoint Server—had more than 20 vulnerabilities in July 2010 alone due to the many plug-ins used within within the product. You could, of course, deploy Joomla without any plug-ins, but then the features—in comparison to SharePoint Server 2010—would be far fewer than those available in the Microsoft product. The point is simple: when you compare SharePoint to a competitor, such as Joomla with the necessary plug-ins to make it comparable to SharePoint, SharePoint has actually performed quite well in the area of security.

All of this information about vulnerabilities is provided to encourage you in two areas. First, if you've chosen SharePoint Server 2010 as your portal and content management system, you've chosen a system with a security track record as good as or better than any other product on the market. Second, regardless of the track record, you must keep up with the most recent discoveries and ensure that your deployment is secure.

The National Vulnerability Database is managed by the National Institute of Standards and Technology (NIST) and can be found at http://nvd .nist.gov/home.cfm. An alternative vulnerability database is the Open Source Vulnerability Database (OSVDB) located at http://osvdb.org.

Security is not the only factor that demands patch management. A system as large and complicated as SharePoint Server 2010 includes thousands of lines of software code. It is common for errors to exist in this code, and the system must be updated to resolve these errors.

With a product like SharePoint Server 2010 (or any other portal and content management system that runs on an operating system), you have even more complexity than the SharePoint product itself introduces. You must deal with the many components that make up the totality of the SharePoint system. These components include the following items:

- Windows Server
- SQL Server
- Internet Information Services
- SharePoint Server 2010

Each item or component of the SharePoint Server 2010 system is addressed in the following sections.

Windows Server

The Windows server must be patched and maintained because it is the foundation of the SharePoint deployment. Whether you are managing a single server deployment with SQL Server, Internet Information Services (IIS), and SharePoint Server 2010 all running on the same machine, or a distributed environment, each server in the SharePoint deployment must be maintained.

 In addition to the fact that each server in the SharePoint deployment must be maintained, you should ensure that the patches are as close to the same as possible in all of the servers. For example, you would not want one frontend server to have a patch that another frontend server (within the same farm) does not have.

Windows Server can be updated through individual patches and through service packs. A *patch* fixes a single problem or a small number of problems. A *service pack* includes all patches up to the time of the service pack and may include additional patches and features.

As you plan your patch management for Windows servers, which may ultimately include SQL Server, IIS, and SharePoint patches, you have three basic options for the patch management.

Manual Patches Manual patches may be applied to the Windows Server system or to the other SharePoint components (IIS, SQL Server, and SharePoint itself). This method may be useful if you do not use Windows Software Update Services and you need to apply a single patch to resolve a security or stability problem. In a small environment, manual patches may be an option. In large-scale deployments with dozens of servers, it is simply not feasible to perform manual patches, which require administrative interaction, considering all the other tasks you must perform to maintain the deployment.

Windows Update The next step up from manual patches is the use of Windows Update. Through Windows Update, you can manually check for patches, but the patches will be installed automatically once selected. This is a feasible process for medium-sized deployments, but it will not likely serve large-scale deployments well. Windows Update defaults to receiving updates only for the Windows server. In Exercise 6.1, you will see how to run Windows Update and enable updates for additional Microsoft products.

Windows Server Update Services Windows Server Update Services (WSUS) is used to centrally manage updates and choose those that you want to deploy to client computers. WSUS supports clients ranging from Windows 2000 Professional to Windows Server 2008 R2. You may install all updates or choose only those you want to be installed. Figure 6.1 show the deployment architecture for WSUS. Exercise 6.3 provides instructions for enabling WSUS on a Windows Server 2008 R2 server machine. WSUS is an excellent solution for large-scale deployments and may even be used in small deployments with just a few servers and clients.

For more information on the deployment of WSUS, see the Microsoft Windows Server Update Services Deployment Guide available at http://www.microsoft.com/downloads/en/details.aspx?FamilyID=113D4D0C-5649-4343-8244-E09E102F9706.

Figure 6.1 shows the deployment model for a typical WSUS deployment. The WSUS server sits between the internal servers and clients and acts as the update server to those internal clients. The WSUS server becomes a client of the Microsoft Update servers. All updates are downloaded to the WSUS server and the clients and other servers download and apply the updates from the WSUS server. Because the WSUS server acts as an intermediary, you have the opportunity to choose the updates you want to deploy before they are applied.

FIGURE 6.1 The WSUS implementation model

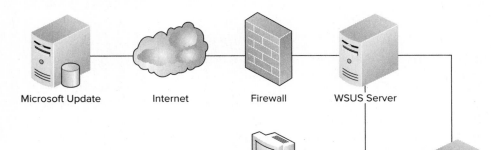

The benefits of WSUS over manual patches or direct use of Windows Update are twofold. First, you have the power to choose the updates globally. You will not have to select from a list of updates again and again on dozens or hundreds of computers. Second, your Internet bandwidth is more efficiently used. The updates are downloaded once to the internal server. All internal machines then download the updates from that internal server, which reduces the required Internet bandwidth. You can even schedule the WSUS server to do all of the update downloads in the middle of the night when fewer employees are accessing the Internet in most organizations.

Exercise 6.1 first steps you through the use of Windows Update so you can see the automatic method used to perform updates on individual machines.

EXERCISE 6.1

Using Windows Update Automatically

In this exercise, you will use Windows Update to check for updates on a Windows Server 2008 R2 machine. You will enable the download of updates for additional components beyond the Windows operating system.

1. Open the Start menu and select All Programs ➢ Windows Update.

2. In the Windows Update screen, click the Find Out More link in the text pane that reads Get Updates For Other Microsoft Products. A web browser window appears.

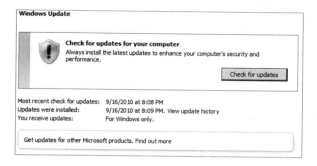

3. On the right side of the Microsoft Update web browser window, click the link that reads More Supported to see the supported products.

4. In the new browser window, read through the list of products that receive updates from Windows Update and then close the new browser window to return to the Microsoft Update window.

5. In the Microsoft Update window, check the I Agree To The Terms Of Use For Microsoft Update check box and click Next.

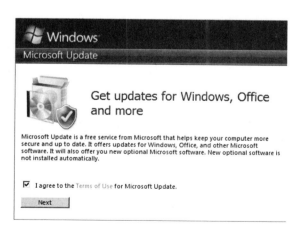

6. Select Use Recommended Settings and click Install. If a screen appears asking you to allow the program to make changes to the computer, click Yes.

7. The Windows Update screen will reappear, and the check for updates will begin automatically. You may close all windows at this time as Windows Update is now configured to download updates automatically.

In some cases, you will want to disable automatic updates and configure Windows Update so that it never checks for updates. You would do this if you want to check for updates manually. For example, some organizations assign this responsibility to an administrator. The administrator is required to check for updates at a specific time each week and apply whichever ones are important. This is often performed in environments that require high levels of uptime but where you do not want to implement WSUS. Exercise 6.2 steps you through this process.

Using Windows Update Manually

In this exercise, you will configure Windows Update to never check for updates. You will then perform a manual update check.

1. Click Start and select All Programs ➢ Windows Update.

2. From the options list on the left, select the option that reads Change Settings.

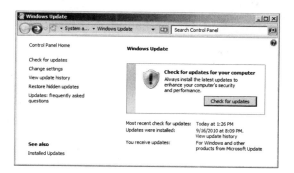

3. From the Important Updates drop-down selection box, choose Never Check For Updates (not recommended) and click OK.

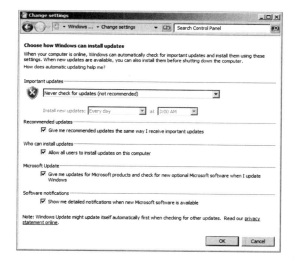

4. Click the Check For Updates button and wait patiently while the system looks for available updates.

5. On the results screen, click the important updates link. For example, in the following image, you would click the link that reads 3 Important Updates Are Available.

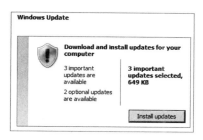

EXERCISE 6.2 *(continued)*

6. From the listed updates, choose the updates you want to install and then click OK.

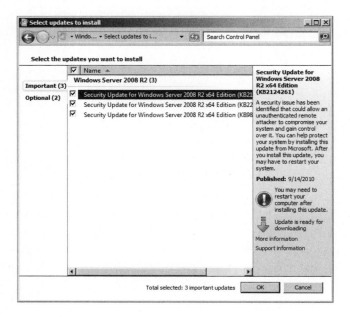

7. Click Install Updates to install the selected updates.

Exercise 6.3 provides the steps required to install WSUS on a Windows Server 2008 R2 machine.

EXERCISE 6.3

Installing Windows Server Update Services

In this exercise, you will install Windows Server Updates Services on a Windows Server 2008 R2 machine.

1. Open the Start menu and select Administrative Tools ➢ Server Manager.

2. In the left page, expand the Roles node and then right-click on Roles and select Add Roles.

3. If the Before You Begin screen appears, click Next.

4. Select the Windows Server Update Services role and click Next.

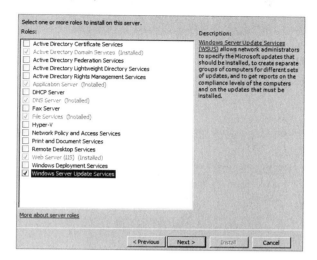

5. On the Introduction to Windows Server Update Services screen, read the information and then click Next.

6. On the Confirm Installation Selections screen, click Install. If a newer version is available online, the process will download that version and then install it on your Windows Server 2008 R2 machine.

7. The WSUS installation screen appears. Click Next.

8. Accept the terms of the License agreement and click Next.

9. If any missing component notifications appear, document the component names so you can download them and install them later and then click Next.

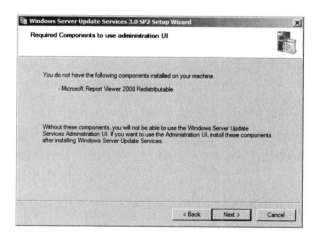

10. Specify the location for local update storage and click Next.

11. Accept the defaults on the Database Options screen, which indicates the use of the Windows Internal Database, and click Next.

12. On the Web Site Selection screen, choose Create A Windows Server Update Services 3.0 SP2 Web Site and click Next.

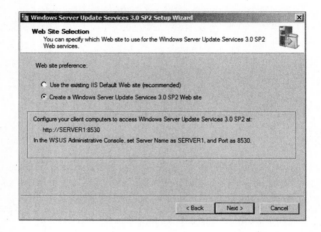

13. On the Ready to Install screen, click Next. The installation will begin.

After performing the steps in Exercise 6.3, you will need to configure the WSUS service according to your needs. Complete configuration is beyond the scope of this book; however, you will need to use the WSUS Configuration Wizard to configure the following items:

- Participation in the Microsoft Update Improvement Program.

- The upstream server, which indicates whether updates are received from Microsoft Update or another internal WSUS server. (A layered hierarchy of WSUS servers is often used in large organizations to better control update management and optimize the delivery of updates to various network segments and locations.)

- Whether a proxy server is required for Internet access.

- The languages for which you want to download updates (you can greatly reduce downloads by only selecting needed languages).

- The products for which you want to receive updates.

- The types of updates to receive, such as Security, Tools, Critical, etc.

- The synchronization schedule, which determines when the WSUS server will acquire updates from the Microsoft Update server on the Web.

Figure 6.2 shows the Choose Products screen of the Windows Server Update Services Configuration Wizard with the Office and SQL Server selections in view.

FIGURE 6.2   The WSUS Configuration Wizard Product Selection screen

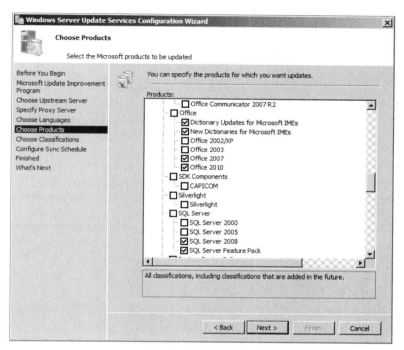

While WSUS and the other update methods discussed in this section may be used for Windows Server, SQL Server, IIS, and SharePoint, special considerations must be made for each product beyond that which was not discussed in this section. The following sections provide specific guidelines for patch management with these individual components that run on top of the Windows Server operating system.

SQL Server

The database behind SharePoint Server 2010 is SQL Server. SQL Server is a relational database management system (RDBMS) that includes features such as indexes, multiple user access, permission management, and high availability. SQL Server is an application or set of applications that run on Windows-based servers. These applications may have bugs and vulnerabilities and need to be updated on a frequent basis.

Like Windows Server, SQL Server may be patched with individual patches or with service packs. Because so many applications use SQL Server, it is more common to wait for service packs to update the product. The reasoning behind this decision is simple. If you apply a patch to the SQL Server every week or two, you will have to test all applications that use the SQL Server after every patch. This process could become very time consuming. Instead, applying service packs every 6 to 12 months is ideal.

Two exceptions to this recommendation exist. The first is related to security vulnerabilities. When a security vulnerability is discovered in the SQL Server, the patch that fixes the vulnerability should be applied as quickly as possible. In many organizations, a two-week security patch cycle is used. This simply means that security patches are applied every two weeks if new patches exist. Patches may be uninstalled if the server experiences problems after the patch.

 As a best practice, consider building a virtual lab that mirrors your production environment. Apply all patches in the lab first in order to test for compatibility with your implementation.

The second exception is related to specific problems you may encounter. For example, you may experience a problem with your SharePoint deployment that is related to the SQL Server. Microsoft may inform you of a patch that fixes the problem. Such patches should be applied according to your patch management procedures.

In addition to SQL Server service packs, Microsoft releases cumulative update packages. For example, the cumulative update package 4 for SQL Server 2008 was released in 2009 and it included 32 hotfixes (another Microsoft name for a patch). The SQL Server team at Microsoft uses an Incremental Servicing Model (ISM) for hotfix releases. The delivery mechanisms used in the ISM model include:

- **Critical On-Demand (COD):** A COD hotfix is defined as critical because security is impacted or a severe stability or functionality problem is detected.

- **On-Demand (OD):** An OD is released per customer request for specific problem scenarios to that customer. OD hotfixes may or may not be released to the general public.

- **Cumulative Update (CU):** A CU is released every two months by the support team. All previous COD hotfixes are included. OD hotfixes may be included if they meet hotfix acceptance criteria such as workaround availability, customer effect, reproducibility, and so on.

- **General Distribution Release (GDR):** GDR hotfixes address issues that have a broad customer impact, have security implications, or have both. A GDR is released through the download center.

As a Microsoft customer, you may contact the Microsoft support services in order to request assistance with a SQL Server problem (this is also true for the other components in a SharePoint deployment). If the support team determines that a new problem has been discovered, a new hotfix may be released. Otherwise, an existing solution may be recommended. These solutions include configuration changes and the application of existing hotfixes.

> ### Real World Scenario
>
> #### A Small Business Chooses an Update Solution
>
> I (Tom) recently worked with a small business that was implementing SharePoint Server 2010. I was involved in the project as the SQL Server consultant. They did not have a SQL Server in their environment and so the SharePoint Server 2010 project demanded more than simply installing a web server application (which is what SharePoint Server itself actually is). The project demanded full planning of the SQL Server deployment, the IIS server deployment, and the SharePoint services deployment.
>
> During the planning process, it was revealed that the company was currently performing all updates manually. For a small business, this was not a huge problem; however, we were about to install three additional servers. Two servers would run both SharePoint and IIS on each server, and the third server would be a dedicated SQL Server for the backend database. The business already had four other servers and they also had more than 40 client computers. Clearly, it was time to move beyond manual updates.
>
> The good news for this client was that WSUS is not processor or memory intensive. With some analysis, it became clear that one of the servers running SharePoint and IIS would be underutilized. We installed WSUS on this server and scheduled it to download updates between 1 and 5 a.m. This small business did not have a second or third shift, so the heaviest Internet downloads could happen in the middle of the night when no other users needed Internet access.
>
> In the end, the client was able to implement an automated update solution with absolutely no extra cost to the project. The internal administrator set up the WSUS service on the server so no consulting fees were required. This scenario illustrates the fact that even small businesses can benefit from and easily implement WSUS in their environments.

Internet Information Services

IIS is updated through the Windows Update or WSUS services. No additional information needs to be considered for the update process. However, it is important to consider the impact of an update to IIS. While Microsoft attempts to release updates that will not break ASP .NET code, it is still possible that an update could change the functionality of code functions and APIs. The update administrator should carefully read the information provided with the update to ensure that code will continue to operate as expected.

In most cases, assuming you have not modified the code that ships with SharePoint Server 2010 and all changes are made in custom code alone, updates should apply without introducing problems. However, if your custom code calls a SharePoint API or function, it is possible that problems could occur. For this reason, like all other updates, IIS updates should be first tested in a lab environment that includes your custom code before being deployed to the production environment.

SharePoint Server 2010

SharePoint Server 2010 can be updated in a pseudo-automated manner. Sadly, full automation is not really available. You can receive updates through the WSUS service for SharePoint Server, but the update must be manually installed through Central Administration. The automated update procedure will simply download the binaries from the WSUS server to the SharePoint server, and then the administrator must apply the updates.

The SharePoint Server 2010 update process is divided into two phases. The first phase is the patching phase (also known as updating), and the second phase is the upgrading phase. Figure 6.3 shows this process.

During the first phase (patching or updating), the binary files are copied to the Central Administration server, but no files are patched at this point. Any services requiring patches are stopped so that reboots will not be required in many update scenarios. The next task during the first phase is the deployment of support files to the appropriate folders on the server running SharePoint. These files are used to ensure that all WebApps run the appropriate binary files for proper operations after the update.

During the second phase (upgrading), the upgrade process is started and the patching takes place. Once all files are patched, the services are restarted. If a reboot is required, you will be notified of this requirement. You may also be required to run the SharePoint Configuration Wizard again in order to update all databases to the new version of the patch. If this is required, you will be notified during the patching process or in the documentation provided with the patch.

FIGURE 6.3   The SharePoint update process

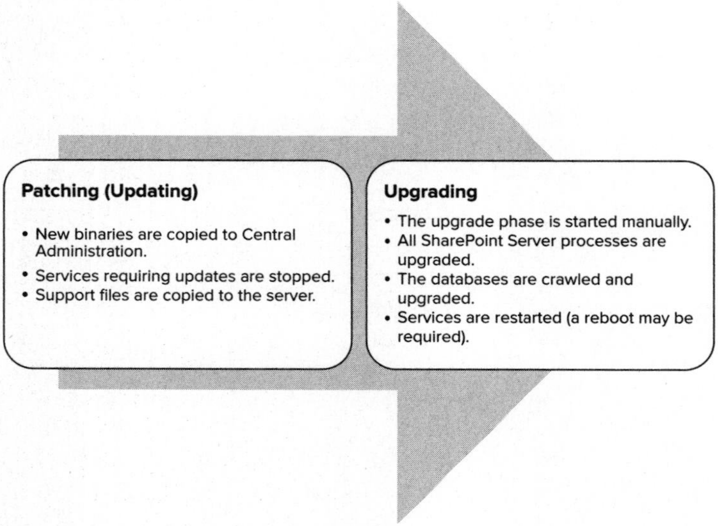

Patching (Updating)

- New binaries are copied to Central Administration.
- Services requiring updates are stopped.
- Support files are copied to the server.

Upgrading

- The upgrade phase is started manually.
- All SharePoint Server processes are upgraded.
- The databases are crawled and upgraded.
- Services are restarted (a reboot may be required).

As you plan your SharePoint software update deployments, consider Microsoft's recommended deployment lifecycle, which is illustrated in Figure 6.4. Each phase is defined in the following list:

Learn   In this phase, you will discover the requirements and prerequisites for an update or set of updates. You will also choose an update strategy. You can do an in-place update or a database attach. These are the same strategies used when upgrading from an earlier version of SharePoint Server, such as SharePoint Server 2007. You should plan for downtime reduction by ensuring that all update dependencies are in place before the upgrade begins. You may use read-only content databases and perform parallel upgrades to reduce downtime.

Prepare   During the prepare phase, you will document the environment including the farm topology and site hierarchy, the language packs and filter packs that are installed, and any customizations that could be affected by the update. This information may already be documented. You will also want to manage the customizations in place in your SharePoint deployment. Using a test environment to install the update can help locate the customizations that may be impacted.

In addition, you must plan the update strategy during this phase of update deployment. This includes determining hardware, storage, and software requirements; however, it may also include the update sequence for the farm servers, the order of operations, the downtime limits with which you must comply, and a rollback process in case severe problems occur. You should also include a communications plan and an update schedule in your update strategy plan.

Test   In this phase, you will test the update or updates in a lab environment. Microsoft recommends that you build a test farm that mirrors your production environment. We suggest that you use a copy of your production database in this test farm so that it mirrors the production environment exactly. Virtual machines can be used to easily deploy a test farm without heavy licensing costs.

In this test farm, you will perform your update strategy developed in the preceding phase. This allows you to ensure that your strategy is accurate and that severe problems will be unlikely during the production implementation.

Implement   The implement phase involves performing the update on your production environment. The update strategy that was developed during the prepare phase and tested during the test phase will now be used to implement the update.

Validate   During the validate phase, you will monitor the SharePoint farm closely to ensure proper operations. Watch the logs closely and look for complaints coming into the help desk or support line in your organization. Many times problems are missed during the testing phase because you do not always know how the users use the SharePoint sites and you may not have fully tested the functionality. Be prepared to respond to any new issues that disrupt business operations.

FIGURE 6.4 The Microsoft recommended SharePoint software update deployment lifecycle

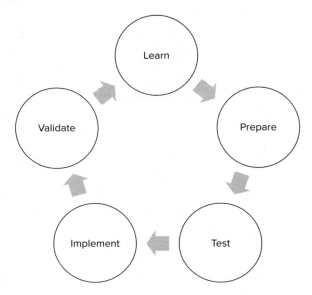

You can check for updates from within the SharePoint Server 2010 Central Administration console. Exercise 6.4 provides the steps required to perform this update check.

EXERCISE 6.4

Checking for Updates from SharePoint Central Administration

In this exercise, you will check for updates to your SharePoint Server 2010 installation using Central Administration.

1. Launch Central Administration.

2. Select the Upgrade and Migration group.

3. Select Check Product And Patch Installation Status.

4. Select the option that reads "Click here for the latest information on available updates for SharePoint 2010 products."

5. A new browser window will appear. Scroll down to the section titled Latest Updates, and download any updates you want to apply to your SharePoint Server 2010 installation.

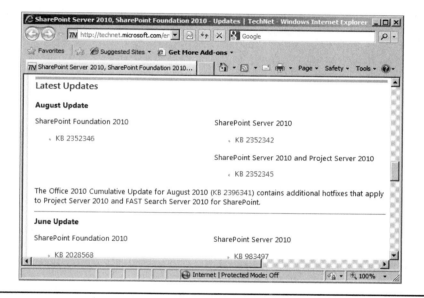

Ongoing Maintenance Tasks

In addition to patch management, several tasks should be performed for ongoing maintenance of the SharePoint Server 2010 installation. These tasks include using the SharePoint Maintenance Manager, working with SQL Server indexes, and performing search maintenance.

Using the SharePoint Maintenance Manager

The SharePoint Maintenance Manager (SMM) is an automated process that runs on your SharePoint servers for health analysis and monitoring. It is included with Foundation and the full SharePoint Server product as well. SMM automatically checks for potential configuration, performance, and usage problems. You can view any detected problems in the logs and potentially the Event Viewer, depending on the problem detected. Log viewing is covered in more detail later in this chapter in the section titled "Logging."

Working with SQL Server Indexes

SQL Server indexes are used to improve the performance of data access in SQL Server databases. As a SharePoint Server 2010 administrator, you will not have to master indexes, but it is important to understand their basic functionality and to know how to rebuild the indexes periodically for performance consistency.

Understanding Indexes

A database index is like the tabs on a file folder in your filing cabinet. A database index is like the clothing size indicators on the clothing racks in departments stores. A database index is like the table of contents in a book or the index at the back of a book. A database index is like the structure of a dictionary or a phone book. A database index is like all of these things and, yet, it's also different.

Database indexes share one common feature with all of the items listed in the preceding paragraph: they help you find the actual thing you are looking for, though the index itself is not usually the thing you intend to retrieve. You do not need the tab on the file folder; you need the file, which the tab indicates is located therein. You do not need the clothing size indicator; you need the clothing of the size indicated. You do not need the table of contents or index at the back of the book; you need the information to which they point. You do not need the structure of the dictionary or phone book; you need the definition or phone number to which the structure points.

These analogies can help you understand the concept of an index. Too many DBAs define an index as something that improves the performance of a database. This definition is not necessarily accurate. Creating an index where one is not needed actually results in decreased performance of a database. Consider the file folders in the filing cabinet. If every single file was placed in a separate folder with its own tab, the benefit of the tabs would be diminished. The point of the tabs is to help you locate a subset of the files more quickly so that you can then locate a specific file in that subset. Database indexes are similar. For this reason, you must understand the way indexes are used by the database management system in question.

 NOTE   You probably will not need to create additional indexes in the default tables used by SharePoint Server; however, you may indeed need to create indexes for custom applications that may be used in unexpected ways in order to improve performance.

Most SQL Server database indexes are either clustered or non-clustered, and creating them is very simple. Choosing the proper columns to index is not always so simple. You must understand what an index is and how indexes are used so that you can make good choices about index creation.

A typical non-clustered index is, effectively, a separately stored copy of a database table with a limited number of table columns included. You will not read this definition in Microsoft's documentation, but it is an accurate description nonetheless. The object is technically called an index, but it can contain multiple columns just like a table and it is stored on data pages just like a table. The only real difference is that you cannot specify an index as the direct target of a FROM clause in a SELECT statement.

The term *clustered* describes the way in which the table is stored. Stated differently, when you create a clustered index on a table, you are changing the way in which the table itself is stored; you are not creating an object stored separately from the table. Microsoft acknowledges this concept in the following statement: "A table is contained in one or more partitions and each partition contains data rows in either a heap or a clustered index structure." This quote comes from the SQL Server 2008 Books Online (July 2009) article titled "Table and Index Organization." It clearly states that a table contains either a heap or a clustered index structure.

The table concept or object, therefore, can be stored as either a heap or a clustered index. For this reason, it is perfectly accurate to say that an index is a table. By stating it this way, you may more quickly understand the concept of the index and the benefits it brings. However, it is also important to keep in mind that the index is based on a separate table in all cases other than the clustered index.

At this point you may be wondering, what is a heap? A *heap* is a table without a clustered index. Think of it like a pile of unsorted clothes in the laundry room. Heaps are stored without any assigned structure for the rows.

 Where I (Tom) grew up in West Virginia, you might hear someone say, "Look at that heap o' clothes in there!" The term *heap*, in this context, means a disorganized pile, and that's what a table is without a clustered index.

In addition to the facts that a table may be stored as an index and a non-clustered index is really like a separate table with a subset of the columns represented in the base table, indexes are stored differently than heaps. Heaps use two primary page types: IAM pages and data pages. Index Allocation Map (IAM) pages indicate which data pages are used by the heap. The data is then stored in those data pages. Indexes use a completely different structure. They use a balanced tree or B-tree structure. This structure is basically a pyramid structure that allows the database system to quickly locate resources.

Clustered indexes are the most important type of index for most tables. A clustered index can reduce the decisions required to locate a specific record by a factor of many thousands. A clustered index is like a dictionary or a phone book. It is stored with the data and is the structure in which the data is stored.

The only tables that should not have a clustered index are very small tables (those with fewer than a few hundred records). If all of the records will fit in one data page, there is certainly no use in having a clustered index on that table. However, most production tables grow to hundreds if not millions of rows, and the clustered index will greatly improve the performance of these larger tables.

When you create a clustered index on a table, the index column is used to structure or sort the table. The table will be ordered based on the clustered index. In the vast majority of tables, the clustered index column will be a single column and that column will usually be the record ID. For example, a customer ID or a product ID makes a great clustered index candidate.

Non-clustered indexes are very different from clustered indexes. A *non-clustered index* is a separately stored index of a table. The indexed table may be a heap or a clustered index. If the indexed table is a heap, the non-clustered index uses the row identifier (RID) as the reference to the table. If the indexed table is a clustered index, the non-clustered index uses the clustered index key (the Primary Key value) as the reference to the table. You can create as many as 249 non-clustered indexes on a single table, but in most cases you'll create fewer than 20 to 40 percent of *n*, where *n* is the total number of columns in the table.

Non-clustered indexes are like the index at the back of a book. For example, if you are reading a book on the topic of wireless LAN administration and you want to read about management frames, you would turn to the index and locate frames and then management or you might just locate management frames. Either way, you will be given a page or collection of pages that reference management frames. Next you will turn to the provided page or pages and scan the page to locate the information about management frames. Non-clustered indexes work in a very similar manner.

In the end, you typically use a clustered index in order to improve search results when retrieving a record from a table when the record ID is known. For example, when the CustomerID is known for a Customers table, the clustered index will be used to optimize this query. Additionally, the clustered index will be used to retrieve a record or set of records once the unique IDs are known based on a non-clustered index query. The non-clustered index is used when you want to optimize searches based on columns other than the unique ID column. For example, you may create a non-clustered index on the LastName column in a Customers table. Now, when you perform a query that filters on the LastName column, all matching record unique IDs will be retrieved from the non-clustered index and then the unique IDs will be used to retrieve the records through the clustered index. This basic operation applies to both SharePoint databases and any other database you create in SQL Server.

Managing Indexes

Indexes must be managed. You cannot simply create them and then forget them. You must rebuild or reorganize them periodically. The good news is that you can configure maintenance plans to perform this index management automatically.

You must be aware of one final fact about indexes: they can become fragmented over time. When the files on your hard drive become fragmented, they can cause poor performance; a fragmented index can cause performance to suffer as well. You can check the fragmentation level on an index by right-clicking the index in question in the SQL Server Management Studio (which ships with the SQL Server product) and selecting

Properties. From there, click the Fragmentation page and not the Total Fragmentation page. Figure 6.5 shows the fragmentation level for an index in the WSS_Content database. Exercise 6.5 provides the steps required to check index fragmentation.

FIGURE 6.5 Viewing the fragmentation level of an index in the WSS_Content database

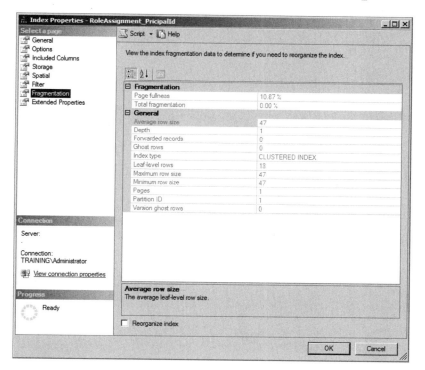

EXERCISE 6.5

Checking Index Fragmentation

In this exercise, you will check the fragmentation level of an index in SQL Server Management Studio.

1. Click Start and select All Programs ➤ Microsoft SQL Server 2008 ➤ SQL Server Management Studio.

2. Select the appropriate database server in the Connect to Server dialog and click Connect.

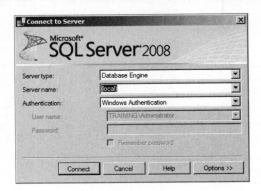

3. Expand the Databases node in the Object Explorer.

4. Expand the database in which the table resides that includes an index you want to check for fragmentation.

5. Expand the Tables container within the database.

6. Expand the table that includes the index you want to check for fragmentation.

7. Expand the Indexes container within the table.

8. Right-click on the target index and select Properties.

9. In the Index Properties dialog, select the Fragmentation page in the Select A Page section.

10. View the fragmentation level.

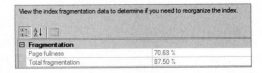

You can defragment an index in one of three ways:

- **Drop and re-create the index.** Because the index is being re-created from scratch, it will remove excess fragmentation.

- **Rebuild the index.** The ALTER INDEX. . . REBUILD statement actually drops and re-creates the index for you, and it can be executed from a New Query window in SQL Server Management Studio (SSMS).

- **Reorganize the index.** The ALTER INDEX. . . REORGANIZE statement attempts to do an online reorganization and lower fragmentation through this effort and can be executed from a New Query window in SSMS.

Which of these options should you use? When the decision is between dropping and re-creating the index or rebuilding the index, you can decide based on your personal preference because the end result is the same. When you're choosing between rebuilding or reorganizing, Microsoft recommends that you reorganize when fragmentation is between 5 and 30 percent. Any index fragmented above 30 percent should be rebuilt.

To rebuild or reorganize an index, right-click the index in SSMS and select Rebuild or Reorganize. You can also right-click on the Indexes node in a given table and choose Reorganize All or Rebuild All to massively defragment all indexes.

In most cases, you'll want to automate index maintenance. SQL Server jobs can be used to automate the reorganizing or rebuilding of indexes. The complete process of creating jobs is beyond the scope of this book, but it is covered in detail in the Tom Carpenter's book *SQL Server 2008 Administration: Real-World Skills for MCITP Certification and Beyond* (Sybex, 2010).

Index fragmentation can sneak up on you. You can use a database for years and notice no real change in performance. Then, in a period of a few weeks, performance can be degraded drastically. This is usually caused by massive changes to the data that happen only after years of use (creating archives, imports, exports, etc.). If you do not have automatic index maintenance in place, be sure to periodically check the fragmentation levels of the indexes.

Performing Search Maintenance

One of SharePoint Server 2010's major strengths is in the integrated search capabilities it provides. You can perform full-text searches without requiring the full-text search feature that is included in SQL Server. However, you must perform maintenance on the search services in order to ensure continued efficient operations. SharePoint Server 2010 performs two search services:

- Indexing
- Search

The indexing service is the process that crawls through all of your content and builds indexes for fast searches. The search service seeks within the indexes for content and then provides links to the pages containing the desired content.

Several tasks may need to be performed in order to optimize the search services within SharePoint Server 2010. These tasks include configuring the crawler or indexer schedule and analyzing search reports. Both tasks are addressed in the exercises in this section.

In Exercise 6.6, you will learn how to configure the indexer crawl schedules in a default installation of SharePoint Server 2010.

EXERCISE 6.6

Configuring Crawl Schedules for SharePoint Search

In this exercise, you will configure the crawl schedule for local SharePoint sites from within Central Administration. The result will be the proper indexing of the default SharePoint site created during the installation.

1.   Open SharePoint 2010 Central Administration.

2.   Select the General Application Settings group.

3.   In the Search category, select Farm Search Administration.

4.   On the Farm Search Administration page, click the Search Service Application link.

5.   In the left pane, select Content Sources.

6.   Click the Local SharePoint sites link in the Name column of the resulting page.

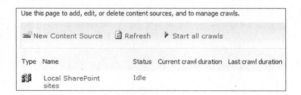

7. Verify that the proper settings are in place for the Start Addresses section. For example, if you have added an SSL certificate and are using HTTPS, make sure that HTTPS://*servername* is included in the list, where *servername* is the name of your SharePoint content server.

8. Scroll down to the Crawl Schedules section and create a Full Crawl and Incremental Crawl schedule.

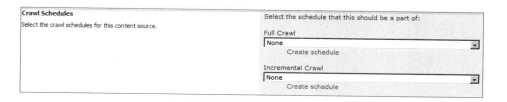

9. In the Start Full Crawl section, check the option to Start Full Crawl Of This Content Source and then click OK. You will be returned to the previous screen and should see the Status for Local SharePoint Sites as Starting.

10. Click the Refresh link above the Status column, and you should see that the Status changes to Crawling Full.

11. Allow the crawling to process and click Refresh every 2 to 3 minutes until the Status changes to read Idle. At this point, the crawl is complete and the SharePoint server will now index the Local SharePoint sites based on the crawl schedules you configured in step 8 of this exercise.

Once the crawl schedules are configured, you can update or change them anytime you like by accessing the same page and changing the full and incremental crawl schedules.

In addition to this task, you may also want to view search reports. The search reports are available in the same area of Central Administration. Exercise 6.7 provides the steps required to access the desired search report.

EXERCISE 6.7

Viewing Search Reports

In this exercise, you will view the Query Latency report in Central Administration.

1. Open SharePoint 2010 Central Administration.

2. Select the General Application Settings group.

3. In the Search category, select Farm Search Administration.

4. Select the Search Service Application link.

5. Scroll down, if necessary, and select Administration Reports from the Reports section in the left-side menus.

6. Click on Search Administration Reports in the resulting page.

7. Click the QueryLatency report to view the latency for search queries on your server.

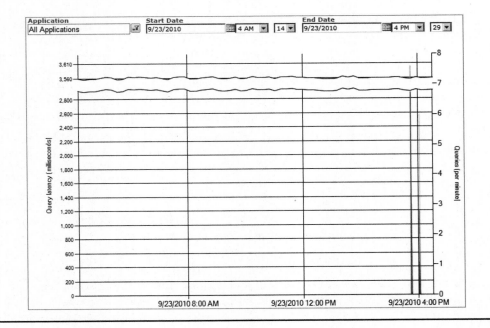

You should take some time to look through these reports if you plan to take the SharePoint certification exams. If you are not planning to take the exams, these reports are still very helpful as you can use them to gauge the performance of the search engine in your SharePoint Server 2010 deployment. The Search Administration Reports are defined as follows:

- **CrawlRatePerContentSource:** Shows recent crawl activity by content source. The report may be filtered by search service application, time, and content source.

- **CrawlRatePerType:** Shows recent crawl activity sorted by items or actions for a specific URL. Items and actions may include modified items, deleted items, errors, and retries. The report may be filtered by search service application and time.

- **QueryLatency:** Shows recent search activity and the latency from the different segments in the query pipeline (for example, the search service application as opposed to the database system). The report may be filtered by search service application and time.

- **QueryLatencyTrend:** Shows the current crawl rate in milliseconds and the query latency by percentile. The report may be filtered by search service application and time.

- **SharePointBackendQueryLatency:** Shows the recent search activity with latency details for the SharePoint backend, which includes the search components and the SQL Server databases. The number of average queries per minute is shown. The report may be filtered by search service application and time.

In addition to the Administrative Reports (also called search reports), you can view Web Analytics reports. In order to view them, you must provision a new WebApp for Web Analytics. This is accomplished in Central Administration by accessing the Manage Service Applications option under Application Management. From there, you can select New ➤ Web Analytics Service Application to provision the Web Analytics reporting engine.

If you are using your SharePoint 2010 site as an Internet-based website, the Web Analytics reports will be very important to you. You can view website traffic reports in the Web Analytics reports. For example, you can view any of the following statistics:

- Number of page views
- Top Referrers, such as search engines
- Top visitors
- Daily unique visitors
- Top pages
- Top browsers

In addition to website traffic, you can view search reports. These reports will show common search terms on your site and the response times for searches. This information can be useful in tuning and optimizing your pages. Also, if you notice that searches are being performed against the phrase "Internet usage rules" and you have a page on your Intranet titled "Internet Usage Policies," you could add the phrase "Internet usage rules" to the page so that it is returned as a search result. Using Web Analytics can certainly help you fine-tune your pages and sites.

> One important search report element is the number of queries with high failure rates. When a query fails, it means that no pages match the desired content. If hundreds of searches are being made for content that does not exist, it is important to make that content available.

Custom Web Analytics reports are created in Excel 2010. When you click the Customize Report button, which is on the Analyze tab in Web Analytics, the data you are currently viewing is exported to Excel. From Excel, you can filter the data, create custom charts, perform calculations against the data, or do anything else you know how to do in Excel. This flexibility in customization means that you can generate the reports you need without the clutter often included in generic reports.

More in-depth information on search planning and design is available in Chapter 10, "Planning Search Solutions."

Planning a Monitoring Strategy

Now that you've learned the basics of SharePoint maintenance processes and tasks, it's time to consider the task of monitoring. Monitoring a SharePoint environment is very important because it allows for availability and security. To best understand the components involved in a monitoring strategy, the following topics are explored in this section:

- Monitoring the SharePoint Installation
- Performance Monitoring
- Logging
- SharePoint Health Analyzer

Monitoring the SharePoint Installation

Monitoring a SharePoint installation can be somewhat confusing at first. This confusion comes from the fact that several servers are usually involved in a SharePoint deployment. At a minimum, you will have a SharePoint server running the Central Administration site, deployed SharePoint sites in IIS, and a database server in most deployments, although single server deployments are common in small businesses and lab environments. For this reason, it is important to begin planning your monitoring strategy by developing monitoring points for performance and availability.

You should also ensure that your SharePoint Server 2010 farm is designed to allow for your performance requirements. Both topics are addressed in the following two subsections.

Developing Monitoring Points

Developing or determining monitoring points is all about defining where you should do performance analysis in order to resolve performance problems. For example, if searches are slow, what server should be analyzed to improve the performance of the search engine? If typical page views are slow, what server should be analyzed to improve the performance of standard page views? To answer these questions, you'll need to answer the following questions:

- What database server is used for the SharePoint site in question?

- What server acts as the search server for the SharePoint site in question?

- What server manages the SharePoint site in question?

The database server must be known because many performance problems that occur in SharePoint farms originate in the backend database. If the database is slow, nearly everything about the SharePoint farm will be slow. To see this, use the SQL Server Profiler and monitor the requests made of the SQL Server during active use of the SharePoint site. You'll see that nearly every click requires one or more database reads.

The search server is also important. This is the server running the Search Service and crawling the sites. In many case, a single server will be configured to crawl content sources spanning multiple servers. If the performance is not sufficient, you may need to distribute the search functions across multiple servers.

Of course, the server managing or hosting the problematic SharePoint site (meaning the IIS server running the application and site) could be the performance bottleneck. In such a scenario, you should establish the site server as the monitoring point.

Ultimately, selecting the monitoring point is a simple task. Determine which server most directly impacts the performance or stability of the issue in question and then monitor that server. To do this, you must understand the farm topology.

Validating Farm Topology for Performance Requirements

In some cases, the performance of a SharePoint server farm is less than desired simply because of poor farm topology design. In Chapter 1, "Planning the Logical Architecture," and Chapter 2, "Designing the Physical Architecture," you learned about the development of the logical and physical architectures. In Chapter 4, "Planning for Farm Deployment," you learned about farm deployment. In these chapters, the important topics were addressed that allow you to implement a well-performing SharePoint server farm. The following guidelines are reviewed from a performance perspective:

- Determine the number of users who will access the farm and select a topology that can perform well with this number of users.

- Determine the usage patterns of these users to determine the bandwidth requirements.

- Select the best topology you can afford.

The last bullet item is a reality check. We would all implement a three-tier deployment model with a frontend web server, a middle-tier application server, and a backend database server if we could afford it. But budgets often limit our capabilities. In such scenarios, you should choose the best topology that your budget allows.

Performance Monitoring

Once you've identified the server on which performance analysis should be performed, you can use the Windows Server Performance Monitor tool to locate the source of the performance problem. Before you explore the tools used for performance monitoring on Windows Server, you should be aware of some common performance tuning myths. In addition to the performance tuning myths, you should understand tools that may be used for performance analysis alongside or in place of the Performance Monitor. Then you will explore the Performance Monitor, which is used to gather performance statistics related to SharePoint, IIS, SQL Server, or the Windows Server itself.

Performance Tuning

Before you investigate the specific tools used for performance monitoring and analysis, it's important that you understand the realities of performance testing and achieving a well-performing database implementation. To do this, you need to avoid falling into some of the myths that surround performance analysis and improvement. The following myths, with their truth counterparts, seem to continually propagate through the systems administration and DBA world:

- **MYTH:** If processor utilization is high, a faster processor is needed.
- **TRUTH:** One thing is seldom the culprit.
- **MYTH:** Eighty percent of the performance is determined by the application code.
- **TRUTH:** Better code is better, but better design is best.
- **MYTH:** An optimized server is the only key to database performance.
- **TRUTH:** It still has to travel the network.

The reasons for the myths and why the truths are more often the realities are covered in the following sections. These truths represent common realities, and rare scenarios will certainly exist where the myths are actually true. Such scenarios are, however, the exception and not the rule.

One Thing Is Seldom the Culprit

When Microsoft introduced Windows 2000 Server, they made an adjustment to the System Monitor (which was called the Performance Monitor in Windows NT) so that it started with three default counters (% Processor Utilization, Avg. Disk Queue Length, and Pages/sec). This change has been a tremendous help in overcoming the myth of the faster processor, but it does still lurk in the shadows. Sadly, Windows 7 and Windows Server 2008 R2 have gone back to showing only the % Processor Utilization counter; hopefully, most administrators now know that they must monitor more than this one counter.
It's no question that scenarios exist where a faster processor is needed. However, it's also no question that a faster processor is usually not the thing that will provide the greatest performance gain. In fact, the culprit is seldom one thing but is usually two or more things that need to be addressed.

Assume you have monitored the CPU utilization on your SharePoint server, the virtual memory pages per second, and the length of the hard drive queue. Additionally, assume that CPU utilization is at an average of 82 percent. This reading would be rather high as an average, though not necessarily high as a single reading. You could double the processor speed and only reduce utilization to 80 percent. How could this happen? It could happen if the pages per second were really high. A high pages per second reading would indicate that you do not have sufficient physical memory in the server. In a scenario like this, you may be able to cut CPU utilization as much as 20 to 40 percent by simply doubling the memory. If pages per second are very high, memory is the likely culprit. If the hard drive queue length is high, then you could also explore getting faster hard drives or using a RAID 0 array to store the virtual memory file. This configuration change would allow for faster reads and writes to virtual memory and may also reduce CPU utilization.

As this example shows, if you look at one counter and make your performance judgment based on that single counter alone, you may well make an errant decision. It is usually best to monitor multiple counters and then consider them as an integrated whole to make your performance improvement decisions.

Better Code Is Better, but Better Design Is Best

It is very true that poorly written custom code modules can reduce the performance of any SharePoint Server 2010 deployment. However, the common thinking that 80 percent of a system's performance comes from the code, which accesses the backend database, is frequently untrue. You can have the best written code in history and still have a poorly performing database if the physical and logical design are poorly implemented or created.

By improving the physical design of the database, you can often double or triple the performance of a SharePoint system that already has perfectly coded modules and queries. For example, placing the physical data files on a stripe set RAID array can improve physical writes and reads. Database tables can be partitioned onto separate filegroups to control which data ends up on the different drives in your server. The point is that many things can be done in the physical design of a database system to improve its performance, which will in turn improve the performance of the application, SharePoint Server 2010.

Additionally, the logical design—table structures, views, index choices, and data types—can greatly impact performance. As an example, consider a table used by custom SharePoint code where you've used the char(70) data type for a column that has variable length data ranging from 10 characters to 70 characters. This choice may unnecessarily increase the database size and, therefore, reduce query performance regardless of how well the queries are writing. Using the varchar(75) data type may improve performance in this scenario. As you can see, there are many factors, other than the coding, that impact the performance of a SharePoint solution, and they usually add up to an equal—if not greater—amount of impact as the code.

It Still Has to Travel the Network

Finally, you can do everything to optimize the server, code, and design and still have a poorly performing SharePoint solution if the network between the server and the clients is overloaded. Performance is both a measurable fact and a perceptive reality. Stated differently, you can measure the server's potential and ensure that it is fast enough, but still receive communications from users who feel that the "server is slow" because the network cannot handle the bandwidth demanded. With a well-performing server, the data still has to travel across the network. Therefore, you will need to ensure that the network bandwidth is sufficient for your purposes. If you do not have control of the physical network, be sure to check with your infrastructure network administrators before you implement a SharePoint solution that is bandwidth intensive (and, if you provide document sharing and have several hundred users, it will be bandwidth intensive).

Using Performance Monitoring Tools

Several tools are available for performance analysis and troubleshooting. Some of these tools are Windows tools, meaning that they are part of the Windows operating system. Others are SQL Server tools and come with the SQL Server product. The following key tools should be considered for performance analysis in your SharePoint Server 2010 server farms:

Performance Monitor   The Performance Monitor is often the first tool administrators think of when it comes to performance monitoring. Of course, its name can be blamed for this impulse. The Performance Monitor is the most powerful monitoring tool in Windows servers for performance analysis and is covered in detail later in this section. The Performance Monitor is a Windows Server tool.

Activity Monitor   The Activity Monitor is a SQL Server tool accessed from within the SQL Server Management Studio. With the Activity Monitor, you can view the processes used for connections to the SQL Server. Blocking can be monitored and locks can be viewed. The wait time can also be seen. The most common administrative task performed in the Activity Monitor is the killing of a connection that will not release resources.

Task Manager   The Task Manager is a process manager that ships with Windows operating systems. You can kill processes, set temporary process priorities, view performance information, and, on newer Windows systems, launch the Resource Monitor for enhanced process and activity analysis. The Task Manager is a Windows Server tool.

System Monitor   The System Monitor, which is a Windows Server component, is known by many names based on the interfaces through which it is provided. It is technically an ActiveX control that can be loaded into any MMC console, but it is loaded by default in the Performance console, the Performance Monitor, or the Reliability and Performance monitor depending on the version of Windows utilized.

SQL Server Profiler   The SQL Server Profiler is like a network protocol analyzer for SQL Server. It allows you to capture the events and requests related to SQL Server. You can use it to capture the actual SQL code executed against a database or to monitor for deadlocks and other negative events.

Database Engine Tuning Advisor   The Database Engine Tuning Advisor (DTA) is a tool used to analyze the physical implementation of a database and recommend changes for performance improvement. A workload file is passed to the DTA tool in order to locate potential changes that will create a performance advantage. The DTA is a SQL Server tool available from within the SQL Server Management Studio from the menus or from a direct shortcut in the Microsoft SQL Server program group on the Start menu.

Event Logs   Finally, the event logs provide a useful source of information when analyzing both performance and functional problems. The event logs are found in the Event Viewer application, which is part of the Windows operating system. If a SharePoint Server system experiences sporadic problems, check the Event Viewer logs to locate the problem.

The preceding list of tools includes those commonly used for performance analysis in Windows Server environments. While many pages could be included to address each tool, the most important tool for exam day and for your day-to-day operations is the Performance Monitor. For this reason, the remainder of this section will focus on the Performance Monitor.

The Performance Monitor is addressed in detail throughout the next few pages of this section. With this tool, you can view live performance data, create a Data Collector Set (DCS) for the logging of performance data, and view reports based on the DCS.

Viewing Live Performance Data

You can view live performance data in the Performance Monitor on Windows Server 2008 R2 machines. The live data shows the values of monitored counters moment-by-moment. Live monitoring is useful when you know something is about to happen and you want to see the values of various counters as it happens. For example, if searches are slow, you may want to watch live counter values while searches are performed. This can help you locate potential sources of the search performance problem. Exercise 6.8 provides instructions for viewing live performance counters related to SharePoint Server 2010.

EXERCISE 6.8

Viewing Live Performance Counters

In this exercise, you will view live performance counters on a Windows Server 2008 R2 machine running SharePoint Server 2010.

1. Select Start ➢ Administrative Tools ➢ Performance Monitor.

2. Expand Monitoring Tools ➢ Performance Monitor.

3. To add a counter, click the green plus sign icon.

4. In the Add Counters dialog, scroll down through the Available counters list and click the plus sign beside the SharePoint Foundation entry to expand the list of counters in the SharePoint Foundation collection.

5. Choose the Executing Sql Queries counter, ensure that _Total is selected in Instances Of Selected Object, and then click the Add button.

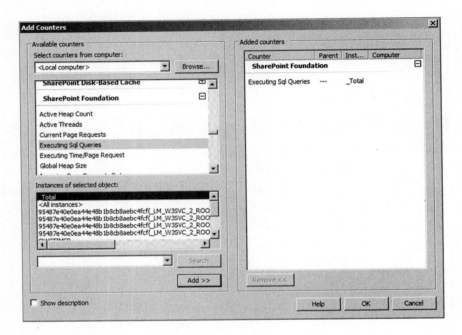

6. Click OK to close the Add Counters dialog.

7. Monitor the values for the counter by clicking on the counter in the list at the bottom of the Performance Monitor screen.

Creating a Data Collector Set

In addition to monitoring live performance data, you can log the performance statistics by creating a Data Collector Set (DCS). A DCS is a collection of performance counter values and possible trace values from lower-level operating system actions. The Performance

Monitor always includes two DCSs out-of-the-box and may include more depending on the components installed on the server. For example, an AD domain controller will include a DCS named Active Directory Diagnostics.

The two built-in DCSs that are always there are the System Diagnostics and System Performance DCSs. You cannot alter either DCS, but you can run them in order to generate reports.

You can also create a custom DCS to log the performance data of interest to you. For example, when you want to log SharePoint statistics over time, you will need to create a custom DCS. Exercise 6.9 provides instructions for creating a custom DCS to monitor SharePoint statistics.

EXERCISE 6.9

Creating a Custom SharePoint DCS

In this exercise, you will create a custom DCS for monitoring SharePoint performance counters.

1. Launch the Performance Monitor as in Exercise 6.8.

2. Expand Data Collector Sets ➢ User Defined.

3. Right-click on the User Defined node and select New ➢ Data Collector Set.

4. On the Create New Data Collector Set screen, name the DCS SharePoint, select Create From A Template, and click Next.

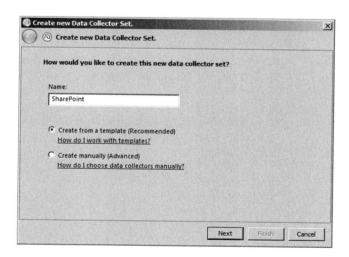

5. Choose the System Performance template and click Next.

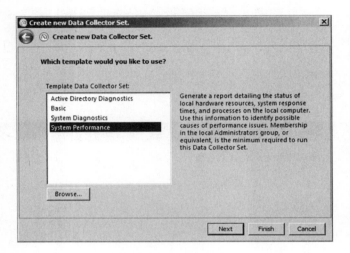

6. Accept the default data root directory and click Next.

7. Accept the default Run As option and click Finish.

After completing Exercise 6.9, you will have a custom DCS; however, this custom DCS will be identical to the built-in System Performance DCS and will not provide useful information specific to SharePoint Server 2010. Exercise 6.10 provides instructions for customizing the DCS.

EXERCISE 6.10

Customizing the SharePoint DCS

In this exercise, you will customize the SharePoint DCS created in Exercise 6.9.

1. If necessary, open the Performance Monitor and expand Data Collector Sets ➢ User Defined ➢ SharePoint.

2. Double-click on the Performance Counter object in the SharePoint DCS to open the Performance Counter Properties dialog.

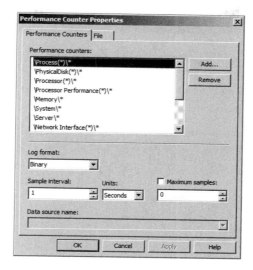

3. Click the Add button to add new SharePoint-specific performance counters.

4. To the list of available counters, add the counters SharePoint Foundation (Executing Sql Queries), SharePoint Foundation (Current Page Requests), SharePoint Foundation (Sql Query Executing time), and Web Service (Bytes Sent/sec) so that your dialog looks similar to the following and then click OK.

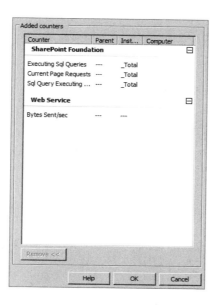

5. In the Performance Counter Properties dialog, change the Log format to Comma Separated. This change will allow many different applications, such as Excel or Crystal Reports, to parse and process the log data. Click OK.

6. Right-click on the SharePoint DCS node and select Properties.

7. In the SharePoint Properties dialog, select the Stop Condition tab and change the Overall Duration value to 60 minutes and click OK. This will allow the DCS to run for one hour.

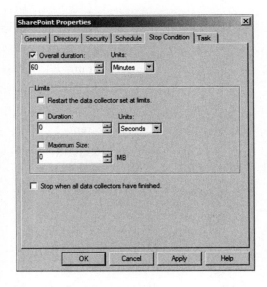

8. Right-click on the SharePoint DCS node and select Start.

After performing the steps in Exercise 6.10, you will need to wait for one hour before the report for the DCS will be available. After one hour, you can view the reports as described in the next section in Exercise 6.11.

Viewing Reports

The Performance Monitor is also the tool used to view the reports. In addition to the graphical view of reports, you can open the performance counter log in tools like Microsoft Excel in order to generate graphs and analyze the data in detail. Exercise 6.11 provides instructions for viewing of reports based on a custom DCS.

EXERCISE 6.11

Viewing Reports Based on the SharePoint DCS

In this exercise, you will view the report that results from performing the steps in Exercise 6.10. You must wait 60 minutes after performing Exercise 6.10 before performing the steps in this exercise.

1. If necessary, open the Performance Monitor and expand Reports ➢ User Defined ➢ SharePoint.

2. Select the report with the newest data by double-clicking on it.

3. View the graphical report that is displayed.

The three simple steps outlined in Exercise 6.11 allow you to view the custom DCS report. Figure 6.6 shows an example of how the report may appear. The report displayed in Figure 6.6 is based on a DCS that ran for 181 seconds instead of 60 minutes.

FIGURE 6.6   Viewing the custom SharePoint DCS report

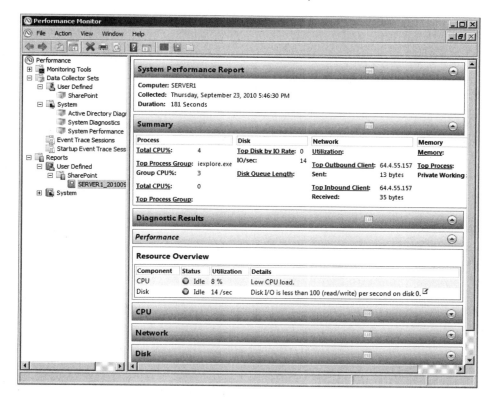

Logging

SharePoint Server 2010 supports diagnostic logging so that you can analyze problems that may occur in the SharePoint server farm. Additionally, usage logging is supported. Both topics are addressed in this section.

Diagnostic Logging

Diagnostic logging is used to determine what information is written to event logs and trace logs from the SharePoint server farm. You can configure three primary settings related to diagnostic logging:

Event Throttling   Event throttling is used to adjust the severity of events captured to the Windows event log or the trace logs. Severity levels include None, Critical, Error, Warning, Information, and Verbose; this list ranges from zero events logged (None) to all events logged that can be logged (Verbose). In most cases, the Warning level is the maximum logging level you would desire. The increased activity from the Information or Verbose levels could cause performance problems on the server.

Event Log Flood Protection   If you enable Event Log Flood Protection, events that are repeated will eventually stop being fully logged until you resolve the problem. For example, if a service is reporting an error, it may report this error every few seconds or even milliseconds. To prevent the log from flooding, SharePoint's diagnostic logging detects the repeated entries and simply suppresses the logging while including only a periodic summary entry. By default, Event Log Flood Protection works on a two-minute interval. If the same event fires multiple times in a two-minute window and Event Log Flood Protection is enabled; only one summary event is added to the Event Viewer event log. This default behavior can be changed in PowerShell using the `Set-SPDiagnosticConfig` command. The switches used to configure Event Log Flood Protection with this command include `EventLogFloodProtectionThreshold`, `EventLogFloodProtectionTriggerPeriod`, `EventLogFloodProtectionNotifyInterval` and `EventLogFloodProtectionQuietPeriod`.

Trace Log   You can specify the location to trace logs when tracing is enabled. You can also specify the number of days to store the trace log and the maximum storage space to use for the trace log.

Exercise 6.12 provides instructions for configuring diagnostic logging.

EXERCISE 6.12

Configuring Diagnostic Logging

In this exercise, you will learn how to access the configuration settings for diagnostic logging in SharePoint Server 2010.

1. Launch SharePoint 2010 Central Administration.

2. Click on the Monitoring page in the left Central Administration navigation menu.

3. In the Reporting group, select Configure Diagnostic Logging.

4. Configure Event Throttling by selecting the event categories you want to configure and then choosing the least critical event to report for both the event log and the trace log.

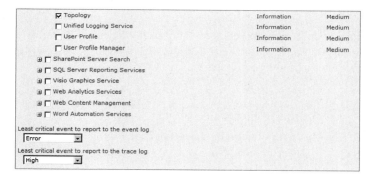

5. Scroll down and choose whether or not Event Log Flood Protection should be enabled.

6. Scroll down further and configure the Trace Log path and storage parameters as desired, and click OK to save your configuration changes.

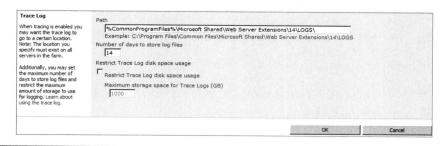

Usage Logging

Usage logging is configured separately from diagnostic logging. While diagnostic logging tracks errors that occur, usage logging is used for regulatory compliance and for tracking user actions for performance improvement, troubleshooting, and future planning. Regulatory compliance efforts are implemented in order to abide by rules or guidelines put forth by such regulations as Sarbanes-Oxley (SOX), Health Insurance Portability and Accountability Act (HIPAA), and the Payment Card Industry Data Security Standard (PCI-DSS). Information on these regulations and how to comply with them is included in Chapter 5, "Planning the Security Architecture."

In addition to regulatory compliance, usage logging provides information about how your users are using the SharePoint sites. This information can be used to troubleshoot problem scenarios and to plan for future upgrades. For example, if you see that a specific SharePoint site is being utilized three times as much as any other site that is hosted on the same server in the farm, you may begin planning to move that site to a dedicated server in the future.

Usage logging is configured on the Monitoring page of Central Administration by selecting the Configure Usage And Health Data Collection option. From there you can configure several items as shown in Figure 6.7.

FIGURE 6.7   Configuring usage logging settings

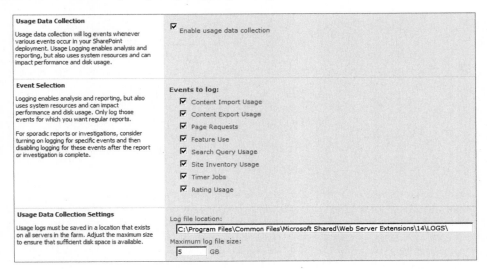

 Usage data is stored in log files on the hard disk and not in the Event Viewer logs.

SharePoint Health Analyzer

The SharePoint Health Analyzer (SHA) is used to monitor the configuration of the SharePoint server farm and alert the administrator when configuration problems are detected. SHA can be configured through rules, and the rules can be configured for evaluation hourly, daily, weekly, monthly, or on demand only. In addition, you can configure the rule to alert you so that you will receive an email or SMS text message notification if the rule evaluates to failure. Figure 6.8 shows the configuration screen for a rule alert.

FIGURE 6.8   Configuring a rule alert for SHA

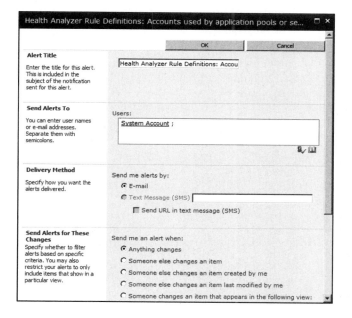

You can access the SHA rules in Central Administration by opening the Monitoring page and selecting Review Rule Definitions in the Health Analyzer section. Figure 6.9 shows the rules listing page. Additionally, the SHA will display red and yellow categories on the Central Administration main page so that you are notified when problems are detected.

FIGURE 6.9   Viewing the rule definitions for SHA

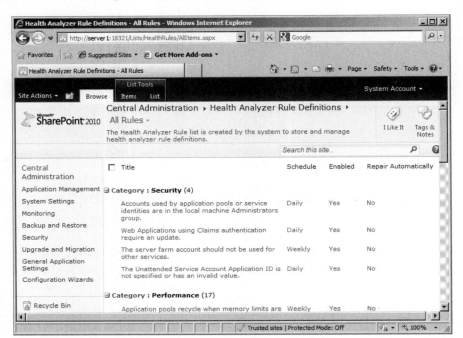

SHA rules are available in the following categories:

- **Security:** This category includes rules that monitor group memberships that may pose a security problem, improper service account configurations, and any updates that may be required.

- **Performance:** This category includes 17 rules by default, and they check such issues as fragmented database indexes, improperly configured virtual memory files within the operating system, issues with the Visio Graphics Service, issues with the Search service, and issues with Web Analytics.

- **Configuration:** This category includes 30 rules by default. The rules focus on configuration issues such as inconsistent Automatic Update configuration settings across the farm, missing configurations for email, and other configuration inconsistencies within the SharePoint server farm.

- **Availability:** This final category includes 13 rules by default. The rules include monitoring such items as available drive space, orphaned items in databases, databases that have grown too large, and nonresponsive servers.

Each rule can be enabled or disabled. A rule can be evaluated immediately by clicking on the rule and selecting the Run Now option, as shown in Figure 6.10.

FIGURE 6.10   Viewing a rule definition and using the Run Now option

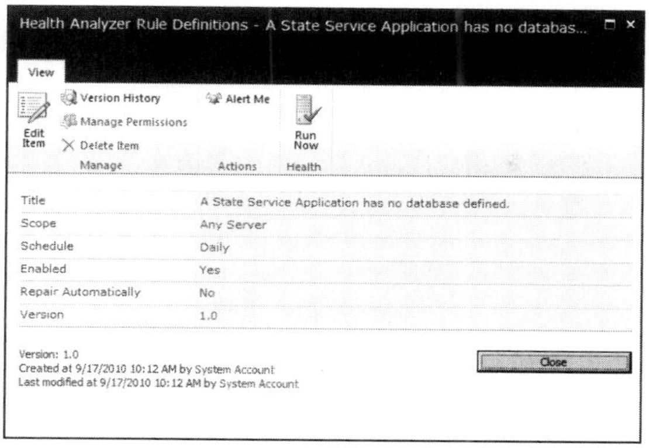

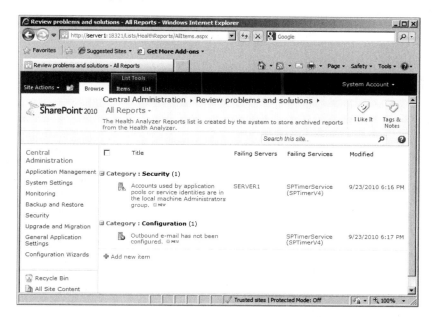

Finally, you can review problems and solutions from Central Administration by selecting the Monitoring page and clicking Review Problems And Solutions in the Health Analyzer grouping. You will see a screen similar to the one in Figure 6.11. Figure 6.12 shows an example problem and solution detail page that is accessed by clicking on a specific problem that was detected by the SHA.

FIGURE 6.11   Viewing problems and solutions in the SHA

FIGURE 6.12   Viewing the details of a problem and solution

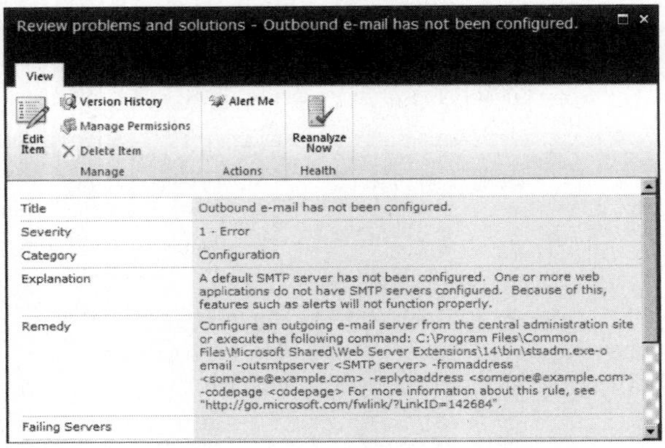

Developing Provisioning Strategies

Site provisioning is an important consideration related to SharePoint Server 2010 operations. Depending on the method you select, you can increase or decrease the workload of the IT support group. Additionally, although you can decrease the workload of the IT support group with self-service provisioning, as you'll learn in this section, doing so can also decrease the security of your SharePoint deployment.

Two primary provisioning methods exist. IT provisioning is the first, and it indicates that an IT administrator will create all sites. Site collections, sites within collections, and even personal sites are created by the IT administrators. The benefit of this provisioning model is that you have increased security. The negative aspect of the IT provisioning model is that you increase the workload for the IT administrators.

IT provisioning improves security because only administrators can create the sites or site collections. When users cannot create sites, they cannot implement a solution that allows the uploading of pirated files or the downloading of sensitive corporate data. The workload of the IT administrators will be increased, but this is usually worth the cost. In most cases, IT provisioning will be used for corporate SharePoint implementations. The exception to this would be when self-service provisioning is used to assign administrators. Stated differently, you could use self-service provisioning, but allow only IT professionals to perform the self-service provisioning. This would provide a hierarchy of administrative capabilities. Some administrators would be able to manage everything about SharePoint, while others could only create new sites or site collections without full administrative capabilities in the farm.

IT provisioning for site collections is performed in Central Administration. The Create Site Collections option within Application Management is used to create a site collection. If the IT administrator needs to provision a new site within an existing site collection, she can simply connect to the existing site and select Site Actions ➤ New Site to provision the needed site.

Alternatively, you may choose to use self-service provisioning. The configuration of self-service site provisioning was covered in Chapter 5, which introduces security concerns. If a user can create sites, then he can create sites that could cause problems for your SharePoint deployment. This is specifically true if the user can create Internet-facing sites that allow file uploads and downloads. Be very careful when creating such sites because they can be easily used to create pirate software and pirate media sites online that can quickly utilize all of your valuable Internet traffic.

Even with the inherent problems of self-service site creation in mind, certain scenarios exist where it might be useful. For example, some organizations implement an internal blogging farm so that users can share information with their peers. In such cases, a department manager may be allowed to create new blog sites for each employee as they come into the organization. The benefit to the organization is that the users are blogging about business-related issues and the organization is capturing information that would normally be only in the brains of the employees. Self-service provisioning means that each department head (or, more likely, an assigned person in the department) can perform the task of site creation so that the burden is removed from the IT staff. Whenever self-service provisioning is used, clear policies should be created so that users understand what is and is not allowed on these custom SharePoint sites.

Summary

In this chapter, you learned the importance of planning SharePoint Server 2010 operations. You began by learning to design a maintenance strategy, which includes patch and update management. You learned about the SharePoint Maintenance Manager, managing SQL indexes, and performing search maintenance. Then you explored the planning process for a monitoring strategy. You learned the important information related to determining the monitoring points and how to use the Performance Monitor to monitor SharePoint-related performance counters. You also learned how to configure and use both diagnostic logging and usage logging. Finally, you reviewed important considerations related to site provisioning.

Exam Essentials

Designing a maintenance strategy.   Understand the important of a patch management plan. Know how to perform updates to the SharePoint server farm. Know how to work with Windows Server Update Services.

Planning a monitoring strategy. As you plan your monitoring strategy, be sure to understand how to select the monitoring points based on the performance problems you're experiencing. Know how to use the Performance Monitor to select SharePoint performance counters. Understand how to configure and use both diagnostic logging and usage logging.

Developing provisioning strategies. Remember that self-service provisioning reduces administrative workloads, but decreases security. IT-only provisioning increases the administrative workloads, but it also increases security.

Chapter

7

Designing a Strategy for Business Continuity

TOPICS COVERED IN THIS CHAPTER

- ✓ Designing Availability
- ✓ Planning a Scaling Strategy
- ✓ Designing Recovery Strategies

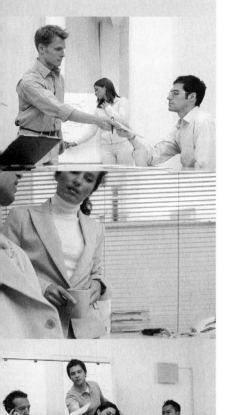

SharePoint Server 2010 will be used to house some of the most important data in your organization. Much of the data that was stored in databases and accessed with custom client-based applications in the past is being moved into SharePoint WebApps today. This information is often the most valuable asset possessed by modern organizations. For this reason, three factors are essential to a SharePoint Server 2010 deployment: availability, scalability, and disaster recovery. All three factors fall into the operational category of business continuity, and they are the focus of this chapter.

You will begin by exploring availability, which should not be confused with performance. Performance and availability are two different things. The section titled "Designing Availability" will make this clear and will also introduce you to recovery strategies for reduced downtime when the SharePoint farm fails.

Next, you will learn about scalability in the section titled "Planning a Scaling Strategy." Scalability is about increasing the ability of the SharePoint farm to handle more users or more activity from users. You can scale up or scale out, and both methods are addressed in this chapter.

Finally, in the section titled "Designing Recovery Strategies," you will learn about the actual steps required to perform backups and recoveries. You will also explore interesting SharePoint Server 2010 features such as exporting lists and sites and performing backups at the database level as opposed to the backups within SharePoint Central Administration.

If you are preparing for the SharePoint 2010, Administrator exam (exam 70-668), the coverage of important objectives in this chapter should be helpful. First, the section titled "Designing Availability" covers much of the information required for the objectives titled "Plan for availability" and "Plan SharePoint backup and restore." In this section, you will learn about Windows failover clustering for SQL Server and the creation of backup and recovery plans. Second, the section titled "Planning a Scaling Strategy" covers the remaining information required for the objective titled "Plan for availability." In this section, you will learn about scalability options for SharePoint server farm deployments. Finally, in the section titled "Designing Recovery Strategies," you will explore the remaining knowledge base required by the objective titled "Plan SharePoint backup and restore." In this section, you will learn about backup plans at a more granular level as you explore the different SharePoint components that can be backed up. You will also discover the various recovery options available to you.

Designing Availability

Availability should not be confused with performance. Performance is important, but in many cases availability is more important. Availability simply means that the resource is there when you need it. Preferably, it is there and performance is at the level of expectations or greater; however, achieving both high availability and high performance can be much more expensive than achieving availability alone. Because budgets are limited, you may have to choose between the two or set the balance of your implementation to lean more toward availability and less toward performance.

The first step to establishing availability is to implement redundancy servers, which can be accomplished with clustering and/or network load balancing. You must consider how you will make resources available again should they be lost completely due to storage failure or physical hardware failures. This means developing a recovery strategy. Once you have a recovery strategy, you should develop implementation plans. Both topics are covered in the following sections.

Redundancy Servers

Part of availability is the implementation of redundancy servers through features like Windows failover clustering and network load balancing. Both features are supported by Windows servers and the technologies on which SharePoint Server 2010 is built (these technologies are SQL Server and Internet Information Services). These two features offer two very different components for availability (and one of the two features can also enhance performance):

Windows Failover Clustering   Windows failover clustering is used to provide high availability. Failover clustering allows services normally running on one server to failover to another server so that they continue to operate on the network. SQL Server can be installed to a Windows failover cluster. Failover clustering provides high availability, but it does not provide increased performance in most implementations. Windows failover clustering is discussed in more detail in Chapter 12, "Planning an Upgrade and Migration Strategy."

Network Load Balancing (NLB)   The NLB feature of Windows Server operating systems allows workloads to be distributed among multiple Windows servers. The clients perceive only one server on the network, but the NLB service actually uses multiple servers to provide the requested services to the clients. NLB is most often utilized in SharePoint Server 2010 deployments for the web frontends and the application servers. If one of the web frontend servers in an NLB group fails, the other servers can continue to provide services, resulting in availability. NLB can also provide improved performance as long as all servers in the group remain online.

From these explanations of clustering and NLB, you can see that availability can certainly be provided to SharePoint deployments. In addition to clustering, high-availability mirroring may be used to make SQL Server databases highly available.

The most important thing to take away from the information provided up to this point is that increasing availability nearly always means increasing costs. While not directly stated before now, it is important to realize that clustering requires two separate machines. NLB also requires two separate machines. When implementing either availability solution, the cost of implementation is nearly doubled. It may not be quite doubled because you can implement NLB using two servers that are less powerful than you might have selected if you implemented the same solution with one server. Costs can also be reduced by implementing virtual machines (VMs) for the NLB server nodes. As long as both servers stay online, performance will be superior to that of the more powerful single server. If one of the servers fails, performance will suffer, but availability will be achieved.

Windows NLB uses multiple IP addresses to allow more than one machine to be reached using a single IP address. The first IP address is called the *dedicated IP* (DIP) and is the actual IP address of the NIC in the NLB node. The second IP address is the *virtual IP* (VIP), which Microsoft references as the cluster IP (CIP). The CIP is used to access the NLB applications and services. Each node in the NLB cluster will have one or more DIPs, and one CIP will be used to reference the entire cluster.

The Windows NLB feature requires advanced capabilities that may not be available in all network adapters. Be sure to verify that your network adapters support NLB before jumping into an implementation project. The adapters must support the appropriate Network Driver Interface Specification (NDIS) drivers.

Windows Server 2008 made several improvements to the NLB service that ships with the Windows Server operating system, including:

- IPv6 support
- NDIS 6.0 support
- WMI enhancements
- Multiple DIPs per node

NLB is a feature of Windows Server 2008 and later operating systems, and it must be installed like any other feature. You can install it from either the Server Manager tool or from the command prompt. At the command prompt, you will use the ServerManagerCMD .exe command as follows:

```
ServerManagerCMD.exe -install nlb
```

After installing the NLB feature, you can perform administrative tasks related to NLB. These tasks include:

Creating a New NLB Cluster   You will need several important items to create a new NLB cluster. First, you will need the host parameters, which includes the DIP for each host. Second, you will need the cluster parameters, which include the list of hosts and the CIP to use for the

NLB cluster. Third, you will need to configure port rules. The new NLB cluster can be created using the Network Load Balancing Manager found in Administrative Tools on the Start Menu.

Managing the NLB Cluster   Once the cluster is created, you can begin managing its use. The first step should be to test the cluster by connecting to it from a remote machine. You can manage the cluster from any host in the cluster. You may also want to configure NLB log settings. By default, administrative actions taken in the management tools are not logged; however, you can enable logging in the Log Settings option on the Options menu of the Network Load Balancing Manager.

Additional management tasks include adding and removing hosts from a cluster and deleting a cluster. Over time, you may need to increase the capabilities of a cluster by adding nodes to the cluster. Additionally, you may choose to add a more powerful node to the cluster and then remove an existing less powerful host. You may choose to delete a cluster when the services provided by the cluster are no longer needed. All of these administrative tasks can be performed within the Network Load Balancing Manager.

Troubleshooting NLB Clusters   Like any technology, you may experience problems with an NLB cluster. Microsoft provides an excellent troubleshooting guide for NLB clusters at `http://technet.microsoft.com/en-us/library/cc732592(WS.10).aspx`. Common problems are listed with possible solutions. In most cases, NLB failures are the result of improper configurations or hardware failures.

Recovery Strategies

Recovery strategies define the process used to back up data and restore that data in the event of system failure. The recovery strategy will include both backup procedures and recovery procedures. In this section, backup and recovery will be covered from a planning perspective. In the section titled "Designing Recovery Strategies" later in this chapter, you will learn specific steps for performing different backup and recovery types.

Server Backup and Recovery

The first thing you have to consider is server backups. Server backups are used to restore an entire server should the system be lost for any reason. Several disaster scenarios can result in complete server loss:

- Operating system drive loss
- System board or another critical component failure without available replacement parts
- Data corruption
- Viruses and other malware attacks
- Intentional or accidental destruction of data

Microsoft provides several tools in Windows Server 2008 R2 for performing backups. These tools include:

- **Windows Server Backup:** A graphical user interface tool used to create backups of the entire server or selected data on the server. Windows Server Backup is not installed by default and must be added through the Add Features Wizard of Server Manager.

- **Wbadmin:** A command-line interface to Windows Server Backup.

- **Windows PowerShell:** Windows Server 2008 R2 introduced PowerShell cmdlets for backing up Windows servers for the PowerShell command line or scripts.

- **Windows Recovery Environment:** A recovery environment accessed through the Windows Server 2008 R2 boot disc or by pressing F8 during system boot and selecting Repair Your Computer from the list of boot-time options. Windows Recovery Environment can be used to perform a bare metal restore (a complete restoration beginning with operating system reinstallation) if a Windows Server Backup full system backup is available.

 While you can back up Windows servers from the GUI interface with Windows Server Backup, the same tool cannot be used to perform a complete restore of the operating system. To do this, you must use the Windows Recovery Environment.

In addition to the Windows tools, SharePoint Server 2010 includes the ability to back up the farm from within Central Administration (see Figure 7.1). Using the backup features in the Backup and Restore section and the Farm Backup and Restore group, you can back up the entire farm or selected components of the farm. Two backup types are available:

- **Full:** A full backup will back up everything in the farm regardless of whether it has ever been backed up before.

- **Differential:** A differential backup will back up everything in the farm that has changed since the last full backup. Differential backups take less time than full backups.

FIGURE 7.1   The SharePoint 2010 Backup and Restore section in Central Administration

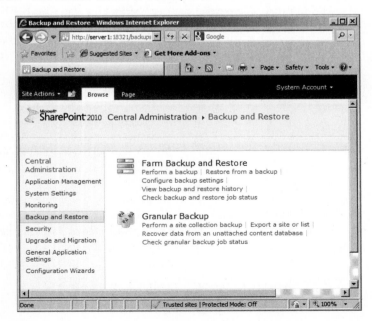

When choosing the backup type and building a plan for backup and recovery, remember that differential backups take less time because they back up only changed data. If you have used data backup software for several years, you may be familiar with a concept known as an incremental backup. Differential backups should not be confused with incremental backups. An *incremental backup* will back up the changes made since the last backup regardless of the last backup type. This means that you will have to restore the most recent full backup and then all incremental backups made in sequence since that full backup when recovery procedures are initiated. With differential backups, the recovery procedure is much simpler. The differential backup always backs up everything that has changed since the last full backup. The result is that you have to restore only the most recent full backup and then the most recent differential backup, which reduces the recovery window required. Incremental backups are not available in SharePoint Server 2010 with the built-in backup solutions. The reference to incremental backups is included here to help you better understand differential backups and the value they bring.

Granular Backup and Recovery

Granular backup and recovery occurs in SharePoint deployments using the built-in Central Administration backup features. In the Backup and Restore section of Central Administration, an entire subsection is dedicated to granular backups. From here, you can back up a site collection or export a single site or list. From a recovery perspective, you can recover data from an unattached content database.

In addition to the granular backup features within Central Administration, you can perform granular backups using SQL Server's backup features as well. SQL Server includes the internal ability to back up databases on a schedule or on demand. SQL Server backups can include full, differential, and transaction log backups, providing you with extensive flexibility in backup schedules. Full and differential backups in SQL Server work in the same way as described in the preceding section. Transaction log backups are used to back up the actions taken against the database that result in a change of the data. For example, transaction log backups will back up an action that results in data adds, removes, or changes; however, transaction log backups will not back up an action that results only in a data read.

Testing Recovery Processes

Whether you do full server backups or granular backups of each individual list, you should always test the recovery process. Testing the recovery process assists you in two ways. First, it ensures that the steps you plan to take for recovery will actually work. Second, it ensures that the data is being backed up correctly without corruption or missing data.

Don't just test the recovery process. Document it as well. If you document the tested recovery process in rigorous detail, you are less likely to make mistakes in a real disaster recovery scenario. In most disaster recovery situations, stress levels are very high. You are more likely to make a mistake when stress levels are high, so having detailed instructions to follow can help you avoid those mistakes.

I (Tom) keep a laminated sheet with recovery instructions near the location where I would have to perform recoveries in a disaster scenario. This practice has saved me from making disastrous mistakes on several occasions.

Implementation Plans

As you've seen in the preceding section, backup and recovery plans are very important. For this reason, you will need to create a backup and recovery implementation plan. Thankfully, this is not an arduous task. The implementation plan should answer the following questions:

- **Who is responsible for performing or scheduling backups?** An individual or a group should be the answer to this question, and they should be aware of the fact that they are the answer to this question.

- **What backup schedule or rotation should be used?** Many subquestions provide the answer to this question, including: Will you perform full backups nightly or only once each week? Will you perform differential backups between the full backups, and, if so, how often? Will you perform transaction log backups on the databases?

- **Who should be contacted when recovery procedures are required?** This contact can be the same as the backup group, but it could be a different group or individual.

- **How will recovery procedures be tested?** This should include performing an actual recovery in a lab environment and ensuring that the document recovery steps work and the data is indeed backed up appropriately.

If you answer these questions in your backup and recovery plan, you will be well on your way to establishing the ability to provide recovery in disaster scenarios. This plan should be distributed to and understood by all those involved in the backup and recovery process. Each individual must understand her responsibilities in relation to the backups and recoveries. Additionally, some system should be implemented that allows you to verify this knowledge distribution and understanding. Interestingly, a SharePoint site can be a perfect way to distribute this plan and view those who have accessed the plan documents.

To help you with the backup and recovery planning, Microsoft provides an excellent planning workbook for Microsoft Excel. Figure 7.2 shows the workbook loaded in Excel 2007. The workbook can be downloaded from `http://www.microsoft .com/downloads/en/details.aspx?FamilyID=a4e1a142-0797-4675-922d-6cc5cdb623f1& displaylang=en`.

FIGURE 7.2 The SharePoint 2010 Products backup and recovery planning workbook

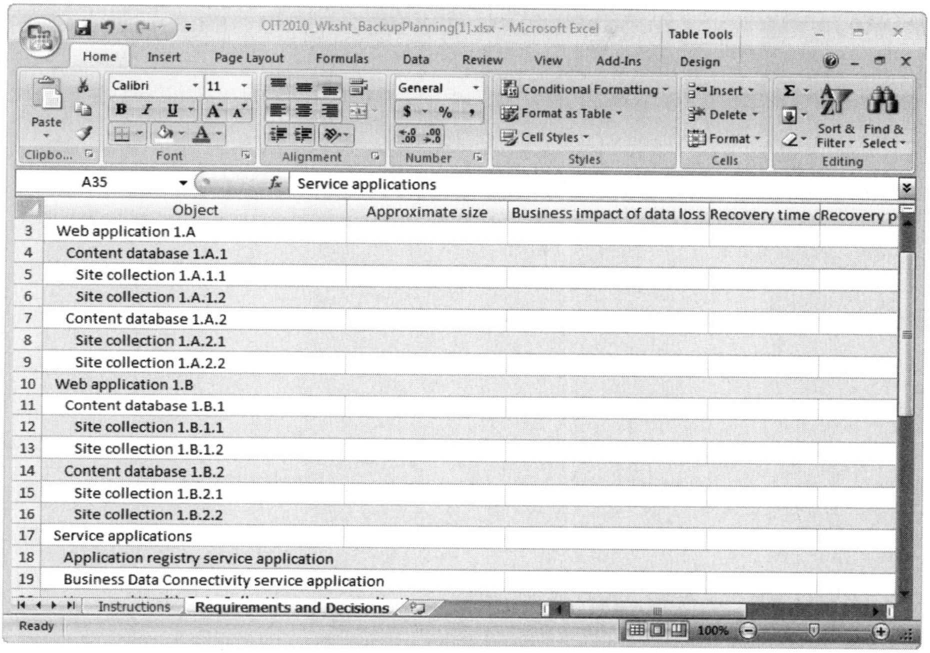

Planning a Scaling Strategy

When new technologies are first installed, it is not uncommon for the workload to be light. Users are learning the new system, and they are often hesitant to adopt it into their daily routines. However, as the weeks and months pass, more and more users not only adopt the system but use it heavily. This increased utilization leads to increased demands on the server or servers involved in the system. In a SharePoint Server 2010 environment, these servers include database servers, application servers, and web frontends.

As the use of your SharePoint farm grows, you may have to scale the farm so that more users and more activity can be supported. You can scale a farm in two ways: scale up or scale out. If you are using virtualization, the scaling of the SharePoint farm will be easier as provisioning new resources is as simple as changing virtual machine settings or adding new VMs to the farm. For example, you can add memory to a VM or add more processors to the VM, assuming the host has sufficient resources available. It is a common practice in modern virtual infrastructures to underutilize a host so that individual VMs can be scaled up when needed. The following subsections address scaling up, scaling out, and using virtualization for your SharePoint Server 2010 deployments.

Scaling Up

Scaling up is the simpler of the two scaling models. When you scale up, you simply add resources to the existing server or servers. For example, imagine you have a server that meets the specifications in Table 7.1. With this system, you could increase the ability to handle more users by adding memory, increasing processor speed, or increasing hard drive speed. Any of these actions would be considered scaling up.

TABLE 7.1 Server Specification Example

Resource	Current Value	Maximum Value
CPU	Dual-core 2.0 GHz	Dual-core 2.8 GHz
RAM	4 GB	8 GB
Hard drive	Single drive	Five drives RAID 5 or RAID 0
Network	1,000 Mbit NIC (1 Gbit)	Two 1000 Mbit NICs

You must remember that, even with a server like the one represented in Table 7.1, you cannot always solve a problem by scaling up. For example, imagine that you have the same server as the one represented in Table 7.1, but it has two 1,000 MBit NICs already installed and each NIC is at 80 percent utilization. At this point, you can increase the processing power or the RAM all you want and you will not likely improve the server's ability to handle more users. This constraint is because the network adapters are already used at a level close to maximum. The network adapters are the bottleneck and not the internal resources such as the CPU, RAM, or hard drive.

In a situation like that described in the preceding paragraph, you must consider either complete server replacement for scaling up or using the alternative solution of scaling out. A complete server replacement, however, also falls into the category of scaling up and is a common solution. For example, you could replace the server specified in Table 7.1 with the server specified in Table 7.2.

TABLE 7.2 A server used to replace the one specified in Table 7.1

Resource	Shipped Value	Maximum Value
CPU	Two processors running at dual-core 2.8 GHz	Four processors running at dual-core 2.8 GHz
RAM	12 GB	32 GB
Hard drive	Four 500 GB drive in RAID 5 array	Eight drives in mixtures of RAID 0, 1, and 5
Network	Four 1 Gbit NICs	Four 1 Gbit NICs

Clearly, the server in Table 7.2 is more powerful as it ships from the vendor than the server in Table 7.1. If your SharePoint installation is a single-server install on the server in Table 7.1, and it is working but performance is less than desired, replacing the server with the one in Table 7.2 will most likely solve the problem. In addition, you have the ability to double the processing power and more than double the RAM in the future. This would be an example of scaling up through replacement while also having the ability to scale up through upgrades in the future. Many scaling scenarios can be addressed through scaling up; for those that cannot, scaling out is the next option.

In this text, a *scaling scenario* is defined as a situation demanding improved performance or availability that cannot be achieved through tweaks and optimizations in your SharePoint Server 2010 deployment.

Scaling Out

Scaling out is defined as deploying multiple servers to meet your needs. If you begin with a single-server deployment (meaning that all three components of a SharePoint farm are installed on a single server), you can scale out in two ways:

- Install more single-server SharePoint server farms and spread applications and sites among them.
- Distribute the components of the server farm.

If you install more single-server SharePoint server farms, you are simply creating multiple SharePoint installations. Each installation may use the same Active Directory database for permissions and user access, but the installations are not aware of each other; Central Administration is not centralized as a separate Central Administration would be used for management of each server. This scaling out method may be acceptable for up to three servers. Beyond this three server limit, management becomes cumbersome and time-consuming, and the distribution of components in a single-server farm is preferred.

When you distribute the components of the server farm but maintain a single-server farm, centralized management is simpler because one Central Administration console is used to manage the entire farm. This is true even though you may have multiple application servers, database servers, and web frontends. Scaling out through distribution of components is the preferred method in all installations, but it is particularly preferred when more than three servers are involved.

> While it is beyond the scope of this chapter or this book to discuss in depth, you should be aware that SharePoint Server 2010 can be managed through System Center Operations Manager (SCOM). This was true for MOSS 2007, and it is still true for SharePoint Server 2010. Using SCOM, you can centrally manage all of your SharePoint servers and even your entire SharePoint farm to a certain extent. For example, you can implement central policies to check and verify configurations including which services are running and which services are not running. When you scale out to multiple servers, having a centralized management tool can provide a benefit in more efficient management.

You can consider scaling out as a process that occurs over time as your SharePoint deployment grows or is more heavily utilized. Each scaling scenario can be thought of as a phase or scaling event. The first phase or scaling event would be the first time you scale beyond the initial deployment. The second phase or scaling event would be the second time and so on. The following guidelines may be helpful, assuming you start with a single-server installation:

- **First phase:** Separate the SQL server from the application and web frontend. In this phase, the only SharePoint component running on a separate server is the database server.

- **Second phase:** Separate the application server from the web frontend. In this phase, three servers are involved in the deployment. The database server, application server, and web frontend server make up the three servers.

- **Third phase:** Distribute databases and applications across multiple application and web frontend servers. In this phase, you are still maintaining a single-server farm with a single Central Administration point, but you will distribute databases, applications, and web frontends as needed.

- **Fourth phase:** Create more SharePoint server farms. In this phase, you are implementing multiple, separated server farms for distributed administration. This phase is most often used in large organizations that span multiple physical locations. A separate server farm may be desired at each location or it may be required for regulation or policy compliance.

If you begin your SharePoint Server 2010 with a distributed server farm deployment, you can begin scaling at the third phase in the preceding list. You may add more application servers or more frontend servers as a first step. A single, dedicated SQL server can support dozens of applications without performance problems. In addition, before scaling out to multiple SQL servers, you might consider implementing SQL Server clustering for improved availability and performance. SQL Server clustering is discussed in more detail in Chapter 12.

> ### Real World Scenario
>
> #### A Small Organization Finds Big Uses for SharePoint
>
> Within a month of the release of SharePoint Server 2010, I (Tom) found myself involved in an implementation on a very small scale—or so I thought. I was installing SharePoint Server 2010 for a church with about 140 members and one paid staff member, the pastor of the church. All other staff members, due to the size of the congregation, were volunteers.
>
> We installed SharePoint Server 2010 on a single server with dual 3.4 GHz Xeon processors and 4 GB of RAM. A single 1 Gbit network adapter was installed in the server, and a single 500 GB hard drive was also included. The initial intended use was twofold. First, the music department needed a central location for song storage in both MP3 format and Microsoft Word documents. The second use was for the youth leadership team, who would use a SharePoint team site for collaboration.
>
> Within a few weeks of implementation, it became clear that other departments could use the SharePoint server. Eventually, the Sunday School department created a team site and began collaborating through the SharePoint server. The church administrator created a SharePoint site for reporting purposes on all financial and administrative functions. When the initial install provided access only on the local network, the music and youth departments asked for access from home.
>
> Because of this rapid acceptance of the SharePoint solution, I had to evaluate the situation and scale the solution to meet current and future needs. Thankfully, even with all of this activity, we were able to install a second inexpensive server for the SQL Server database and use the existing server as both the application server and the web frontend. We acquired a static IP address for the Internet-facing NIC and placed the server on the Internet as well. Security became more important, but thanks to the security features of SharePoint, the implementation of improved security was simple.
>
> In the end, we scaled out to handle the new demands, but the scaling out had an extra benefit. As the upgrade transpired, we realized that the SQL server would be about 40 percent utilized. For this reason, we were able to use the server as a file server as well, which allowed for simple file access for those documents that did not require storage in SharePoint Server 2010.

Choosing to Scale Up or Out

When considering whether to scale up, scale out, or do both, keep the following guidelines in mind:

- When you start with a single server for your SharePoint server farm, the typical best solution for the first scaling scenario is to scale out by moving the database server to a separate machine.

- When working with a multiserver farm, scaling up the individual servers is usually the best practice for the first scaling scenario.

- When working with a multiserver farm that is experiencing rapid growth, scaling out further and also scaling up is usually required.

The last guideline may require more information. In many scaling scenarios, you've reached a point of utilization saturation where the SharePoint server farm is working at such high levels of consumption that simple scaling solutions will not work. In scenarios like this, you may have to spread the SharePoint applications across multiple web frontend servers and application servers and you may have to install multiple SQL Server database servers. At the same time, you will likely upgrade existing server hardware. The result is both scaling out and scaling up at the same time.

Using Virtualization

Virtualization has become a common solution for SharePoint server deployments. *Virtualization* is the process of running multiple operating systems on a single physical host through the use of virtual hardware. Virtualization vendors include Microsoft, VMware, Sun, and Citrix. Although VMware has the stronger market share, Microsoft has a sizable following in small and medium businesses with their Hyper-V product. While this section will focus on implementing SharePoint Server 2010 using Hyper-V on Windows Server 2008 R2, keep in mind that VMware can be used for all of the functions and features discussed. Hyper-V is demonstrated here for one simple reason: Hyper-V is far simpler to implement for someone new to virtualization. This book is about SharePoint Server 2010 and not specifically about virtualization, so this section is simple and easy to follow.

Hyper-V is a hypervisor-based virtualization solution. This simply means that the Hyper-V solution works by implementing a layer between the hardware and the operating system to provide virtualization. This layer is called the hypervisor, and it runs directly on the hardware. This architecture provides improved performance over host-based virtualization. Virtual Server 2005 was host-based virtualization in that the virtualization engine ran on top of the Windows operating system (OS). Hyper-V is different. When installed, it adds a new boot process that loads the hypervisor before loading the host Windows Server OS. This newer architecture performs far better than the older host-based architecture of Virtual Server 2005.

Once Hyper-V is added to a Windows Server machine (using steps similar to those in Exercise 7.1), you can create virtual machines (VMs) that run on the host server. The processors will be shared among the different VMs. The number of virtual machines you can create is theoretically unlimited; however, the number of virtual machines you can run at the same time is constrained by hardware resources. Drive space and RAM are the two constraining factors that determine the maximum number of VMs you can run at a time. For example, if you have 8 GB of RAM, you can run only as many VMs as will fit in that amount of RAM. In addition, if processing power is insufficient, even though you can run multiple VMs, you would not want to run them for performance reasons.

Virtualization is a hot topic and will continue to grow in the future. It is one of the key enabling technologies for green IT. It has also been shown to significantly reduce the cost of IT implementations.

Exercise 7.1 provides the steps required to install Hyper-V on a Windows Server 2008 R2 machine. SharePoint Server 2010 could also be installed in a VMware ESX environment or even a VMware Workstation environment—although the VMware Workstation deployment would likely only be for testing and development. Hyper-V can also be installed on Windows Server 2008.

EXERCISE 7.1

Installing Hyper-V in Windows Server 2008 R2

In this exercise, you will install Hyper-V on a Windows Server 2008 R2 machine. To install Hyper-V, the operating system must be installed on a 64-bit machine supporting Intel VT or AMD-V. Check with your vendor to ensure compatibility.

1. Click Start ➢ Administrative Tools ➢ Server Manager.

2. Expand the Roles node and click the Add Role link in the right sidebar.

3. If required, click Next on the Before You Begin screen.

4. On the Select Server Roles screen, choose the Hyper-V role and click Next.

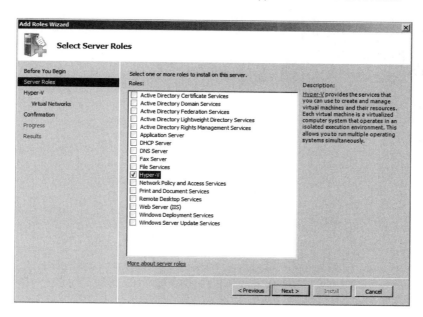

5. Review the information on the Introduction to Hyper-V screen and click Next.

6. Select the network adapter you want to use for Hyper-V's network communications and click Next.

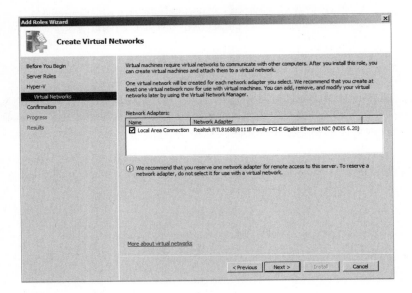

7. On the Confirm Installation Selection screen, click Install.

8. On the Installation Results screen, click Close.

9. When prompted, click Yes to reboot the system immediately.

After performing the steps in Exercise 7.1 and allowing the reboot, Hyper-V will be installed on the machine and you can begin using it to create VMs.

Exercise 7.2 provides the steps required to set up a single virtual machine to run all components of SharePoint Server 2010. A powerful virtual host (the native machine running Hyper-V) is required to run such a VM. A powerful virtual host, in this scenario, would have 8 GB or more of RAM and at least four processing cores.

EXERCISE 7.2

Creating a SharePoint VM for Single Machine Installs

In this exercise, you will create a Hyper-V VM for the installation of a single machine install of SharePoint Server 2010.

1. Click Start ➢ Administrative Tools ➢ Hyper-V Manager.

2. In the left pane, select the local Hyper-V server.

3. In the Actions pane, select New ➤ Virtual Machine.

4. On the Before You Begin screen, click Next to begin creating the VM.

5. On the Specify Name and Location screen, enter a name for the VM (such as **SharePoint Server**), specify the storage location to be used, and click Next.

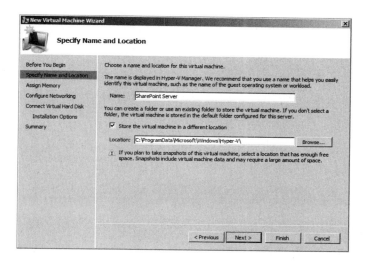

6. On the Assign Memory screen, enter a minimum of 3,072 MB of RAM or higher if your server has the available resources and click Next.

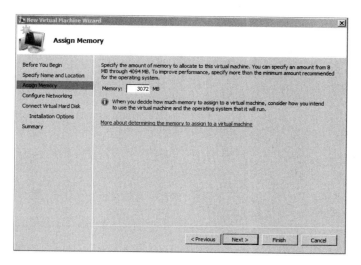

7. On the Configure Networking screen, choose the network you configured during Hyper-V installation and click Next.

8. On the Configure Virtual Hard Disk screen, choose the option to Create A Virtual Hard Disk and accept the default name and storage location. Enter the size of **120** GB and click Next.

EXERCISE 7.2 *(continued)*

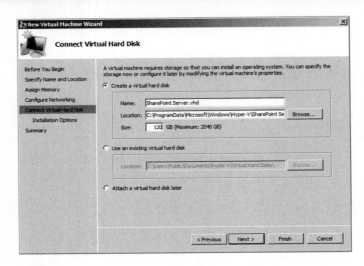

9.   On the Installation Options screen, choose Install An Operating System Later and click Next.

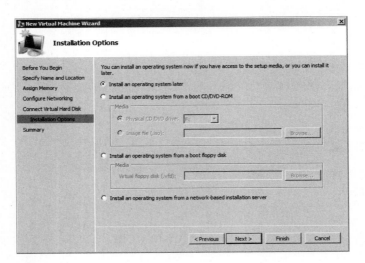

10. On the Completing the New Virtual Machine Wizard screen, click Finish.

After completing Exercise 7.2, you will have a VM capable of running Windows Server 2008 R2, with IIS, SQL Server, and SharePoint installed on a single VM. If you use the minimum of 3 GB RAM specified in the exercise, the machine may be acceptable for lab testing. (Microsoft recommends 4 GB of RAM for a developer or evaluation install, but you will find 3 GB works sufficiently if you are pressed for resources.) You should use 8 GB or greater for production single-machine installations of SharePoint Server 2010.

You will have to install Windows Server 2008 R2 itself on the VM. While this task is beyond the scope of this chapter, the process is quite easy as the operating system is fully detected and configured appropriately during the installation. After installing the operating system, you will need to perform the SharePoint installation within the VM.

Exercise 7.3 provides the steps required to set up a multiserver farm for a distributed SharePoint Server 2010 deployment. All three VMs may be created on a single virtual machine host. The host would have to be very powerful with 8 GB of RAM or more and at least four processing cores. The benefit of multiple VMs is that you can move a VM to a different host in order to scale up the VM. For example, if you begin your SharePoint Server 2010 deployment by installing three VMs on a single host, you can later scale up the VMs by distributing them across three different physical hosts (the host is the physical server that runs the VM). Once the VMs are distributed among multiple hosts, scaling up is as simple as increasing memory or processors as explained in Exercises 7.4 and 7.5.

EXERCISE 7.3

Creating a SharePoint Multiserver Farm

In this exercise, you will review the steps required to set up a multiserver farm completely within the Hyper-V virtualization environment.

1. Create the VM that will run SQL Server using the steps provided in Exercise 7.2. Use the following specifications:

    ■   Name: SQL Server

    ■   RAM: 2 GB

    ■   Hard Disk: 100 GB

2. Create the VM that will run SharePoint application services and Central Administration using the steps provided in Exercise 7.2. Use the following specifications:

    ■   Name: SP Central Admin

    ■   RAM: 2 GB

    ■   Hard Disk: 60 GB

3. Create the VM that will run SharePoint web frontends using the steps provided in Exercise 7.2. Use the following specifications:

    ■   Name: SP Web Sites

    ■   RAM: 2 GB

    ■   Hard Disk: 200 GB

As you create the SharePoint multiserver farm in Hyper-V, keep the following recommendations in mind:

■   Run the SP Central Admin VM and the SP Web Sites VM on two separate Hyper-V hosts if they are available.

- Run each VM on a separate Hyper-V host for the greatest availability. If one host fails, the VM can be moved to another host for recoverability.

- Assign twice the memory (if it is available) to each VM for improved performance. For example, provide 4 GB instead of 2 GB to each VM.

Exercise 7.4 explains how to increase the memory available to a Hyper-V VM. The steps may be performed only if sufficient physical memory is available on the virtual machine host.

EXERCISE 7.4

Increasing Memory for a Hyper-V VM

In this exercise, you will learn to modify memory settings for a VM running in Hyper-V on Windows Server 2008 R2.

1. Click Start ➤ Administrative Tools ➤ Hyper-V Manager.

2. In the left pane, select the Hyper-V host on which the target VM is installed.

3. In the Virtual Machines host on the target host, right-click the target VM and select Settings.

4. Select the Memory page.

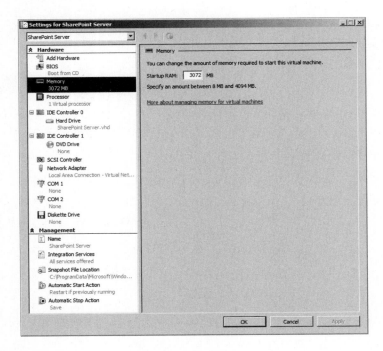

5. Enter the new desired value in Startup RAM and click OK.

Exercise 7.5 provides instructions for increasing CPU resources for a Hyper-V VM. The action can be performed only if sufficient CPU resources are available on the physical virtual machine host.

EXERCISE 7.5

Increasing CPU Resources for a Hyper-V VM

In this exercise, you will learn to adjust processor settings for a VM running on Hyper-V on Windows Server 2008 R2.

1. Click Start ➢ Administrative Tools ➢ Hyper-V Manager.

2. In the left pane, select the Hyper-V host on which the target VM is installed.

3. In the Virtual Machines host on the target host, right-click the target VM and select Settings.

4. Select the Processor page.

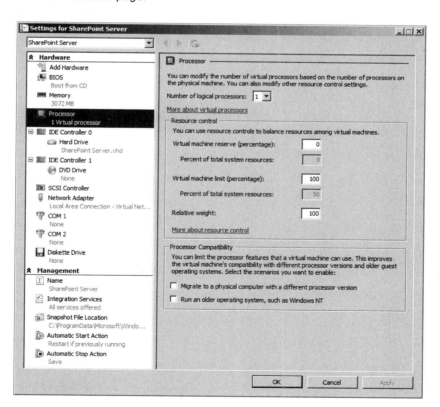

5. Increase the number of CPUs available to the VM. (Additional CPUs may not be available, depending on the physical hardware in the host system.)

6. Optionally, adjust the resource-balancing options to give more or less weight to the current VM and click OK.

Several other settings can be configured for each VM in the Settings dialog of the VMs in Hyper-V Manager. Explore these settings to learn about all of the options available to you. Effectively, you have the same settings you would choose when purchasing hardware. The difference, in this case, is that the settings are virtual instead of physical.

Virtualization is one way to provide increased scalability for your SharePoint Server 2010 deployments. With virtualization, you can easily move VMs from one host to another and change the available resources for a specific VM without requiring hardware installations.

Designing Recovery Strategies

In this final section of the chapter, you will explore the many different backup options that are available to you. You will begin by looking at the different types of backups that you can include in your backup plans. SharePoint Server 2010 is a complex system, and the many components of the system may be backed up individually or as a collective through farm backups.

Next, you will learn about the specific procedures used to back up servers, databases, and individual folders and files. You will perform exercises using the SQL Server management tools, Windows Server Backup, and the built-in SharePoint backup tools.

Backup Plans

Backup plans for SharePoint Server 2010 can include many considerations. This section will cover each of these considerations from a planning perspective. In a few cases, exercises will be provided to ensure you understand the basic steps required to perform the backups as well. The most important backup types will be covered as step-by-step procedures in the later section titled "Performing Backups."

Farms

The SharePoint server farm can be backed up from Central Administration. Use the Backup and Restore section to access the Farm Backup and Restore tasks. A farm backup can be used to restore the farm configuration settings as well as the web applications within the farm.

When you perform full farm backups, keep the following factors in mind:

- The farm backup will not back up any certificate used for trust relationships. These certificates must be backed up separately.

- Manual changes to the Web.config file are not backed up. If manual changes have been made to the file, ensure it is backed up separately.

- If Transparent Data Encryption (TDE) is used to secure the SQL Server databases, you must back up the TDE encryption keys separately.

Farm Configuration

At times, you will want to back up the farm configuration without performing a backup of the entire farm and its contents. Exercise 7.6 provides the steps required to back up the farm configuration without the content.

EXERCISE 7.6

Backing Up the SharePoint Server Farm Configuration

In this exercise, you will back up the server farm configuration using the backup features in Central Administration.

1. Launch SharePoint 2010 Central Administration.

2. Select the Backup and Restore section.

3. In the Farm Backup and Restore task group, select Perform A Backup.

4. Click on the check box to the left of Farm in the component list, and note that all subcomponents are automatically selected.

5. Scroll to the bottom of the page and click Next.

6. Ensure that Backup Type is set to Full and Back Up Only Configuration Settings is set to Back Up Only Configuration Settings.

7. Enter the proper path for backup storage and click Start Backup.

EXERCISE 7.6 *(continued)*

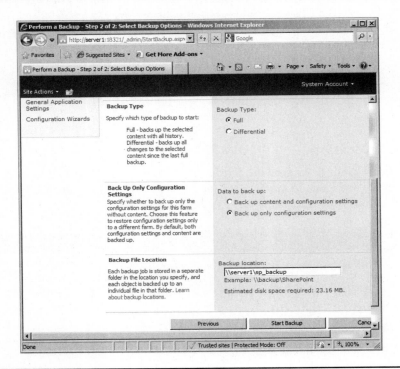

Site Collections

In many scenarios, the farm itself may not change for weeks or even months. However, the site collections are likely to change on a daily or even hourly basis. For this reason, site collections should be backed up on a daily or at least weekly basis. The interval between backups will depend on your tolerance for data loss. Generally speaking, due to the smaller sizes of the organizations, smaller businesses will back up less often than larger businesses. You must evaluate your situation and plan appropriately.

Web Applications

When you back up the entire farm, all web applications are also backed up. If you back up a single web application, you can back up only one web application at a time. A web application backup backs up the entire collection of IIS settings and all content databases associated with that web application. An example of a web application backup would be backing up the SharePoint - 80 default site installed with SharePoint Server 2010.

Secure Store Service

The Secure Store Service, discussed in Chapter 5, "Planning the Security Architecture," is used to provide single sign-on capabilities for SharePoint Server 2010. The Secure Store Service should be backed up when it is initially configured and every time you make configuration changes to the service or when you re-encrypt the credential information stored in it.

The Secure Store Service can be backed up from the Windows PowerShell using the `Backup-SPFarm` cmdlet or from Central Administration using the Backup and Restore section. The following is an example of a `Backup-SPFarm` command that will back up the Secure Store Service (the entire command should be entered on a single line in a PowerShell console with administrator rights):

```
Backup-SPFarm -Directory \\Server1\sp_backup -BackupMethod Full
-Item <Secure Store Service>
```

Snapshots

SQL Server, which is the backend database for SharePoint Server 2010, supports database snapshots. Database snapshots provide point-in-time data recovery and analysis. Snapshots do not provide for standby database access because the original database must be available to build the previous data state from the snapshot files and the original database files together. Database snapshots are useful for recovering from data entry or data processing errors, and they are also beneficial for data reporting.

Database snapshots are created almost instantaneously. This is because the snapshot of the original database contains no data at its initial creation. Instead, SQL Server takes advantage of a technology known as sparse files. Sparse files are files stored on NTFS partitions that allow unallocated space to be provided very quickly. These files are empty when the snapshot is first created and contain real data only when modifications are made to the original database. Before a data page is modified in the original database, that page is copied into the sparse files used by the snapshot. The interesting thing is that future changes to the page require no actions in the snapshot because the original page is already preserved. This makes for a very efficient and well-performing system.

When the snapshot is queried, SQL Server uses a list of pages known as the *catalog of changed pages* to determine if the data being requested is in the snapshot sparse files or in the original database. All pages that have not been changed since the snapshot was created will still be in the original database. All pages that have been changed will now be in the snapshot. From these two data sources, the result set is generated for query response.

Snapshots are read only, and the structure of the source (original) database cannot be changed as long as the snapshot exists. This means you cannot add new filegroups to the original database without first dropping the snapshot or snapshots based on it. In addition, the following restrictions apply:

- You cannot create full-text indexes against a snapshot.

- Backups, restores, and detachments of the original database are not supported as long as the snapshot exists.

- System databases do not support snapshots.

- Snapshots prevent the dropping of the original database.

- Snapshots must exist within the same instance of SQL Server as the original database.

- The maximum size of the snapshot will be the size of the original database at the time the snapshot was created so you will need to ensure that you have at least that much space on the drive where you create the snapshot.

There are many possible uses of database snapshots. They can be used to protect against user or administrative errors. They can be used to offload reporting to mirror servers in a mirroring partnership. They can be used to maintain historical data for reporting purposes, and they can be used to implement a test database. With SharePoint Server 2010, they can provide for nearly instant reversion to a previous state of the content or configuration databases.

Snapshot backups cannot be performed within Central Administration directly. However, snapshots can be completely managed using Transact-SQL (T-SQL) code, which is the SQL Server variant of the ANSI SQL language. Because of this feature, you can create jobs in SQL Server to schedule snapshot creation on a regular basis for your SharePoint server farms.

 For more information on creating snapshots for SharePoint Server 2010 server farms, see http://technet.microsoft.com/en-us/library/ ee748594.aspx.

Content Databases

You can back up content databases directly. If you have made no changes to a site collection configuration, simply backing up the content database can be a faster solution. The content database can be backed up from one of three locations easily:

- Central Administration

- Windows PowerShell

- SQL Server Management Studio

To back up the content database from Central Administration, simply access the backup section and select only the Content Database component within a Web Application for the backup. To perform the backup from Windows PowerShell, you will use the Backup-SPFarm command and you must know the content database name. The Backup-SPFarm command uses the following syntax:

```
Backup-SPFarm -Directory <Backup folder> -BackupMethod {Full | Differential}
-Item <Content database name> [-Verbose]
```

To back up from the SQL Server Management Studio, you will need to know the content database name and you will back up the database using procedures explained later in Exercise 7.12. To determine the name of the content database, open Central Administration, click on Application Management, choose View All Site Collections, and then click on the URL for the site collection in question. The Database Name field will display the content database as shown in the lower-right corner of Figure 7.3.

FIGURE 7.3   Viewing the content database name in Central Administration

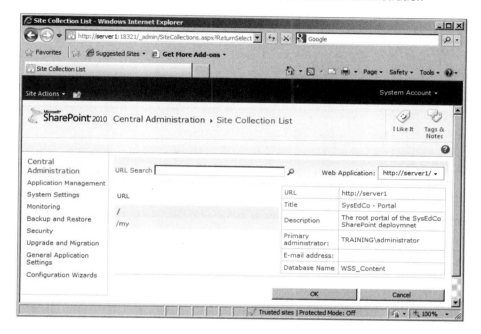

In the same way that you back up a content database, you can back up a configuration database. Use Windows PowerShell, Central Administration, or the SQL Server Management Studio tool. Whatever method you use, you are still backing up a SQL Server database in the end.

Services

Like databases, individual service applications can be backed up from Windows PowerShell or from Central Administration. Microsoft recommends that backups be performed only at the farm level and that the entire farm be backed up regularly; however, your business continuity plan may require component-level backups. This is often required because the recovery of a single failed component is much faster than the recovery of the entire farm. A farm recovery can take hours. A single database or service recovery can take minutes.

Sites, Lists, and Document Libraries

By this point, it has probably become clear that you can back up at increasingly smaller component levels. This includes the ability to back up a site, list, or document library through export procedures. You can export all these components through Central Administration or Windows PowerShell. The PowerShell syntax is as follows:

```
Export-SPWeb -Identity <Site URL> -Path <Path and file name>
[-ItemUrl <url of site, list, or library>] [-IncludeUserSecurity]
[-IncludeVersions] [-NoFileCompression] [-GradualDelete] [-Verbose]
```

Exercise 7.7 provides instructions for exporting a site using Central Administration.

EXERCISE 7.7

Exporting a Site Using Central Administration

In this exercise, you will learn to export a site using Central Administration. You will export the site to a UNC path on your network and a file in that path with the .CMP extension.

1. Launch Central Administration.

2. Select Backup and Restore from the left Central Administration menu.

3. Choose Export A Site Or List from the Granular Backup task group.

4. Click the combo box for the Site field and select Change Site.

5. In the Select Site dialog, click on the site you want to export and click OK.

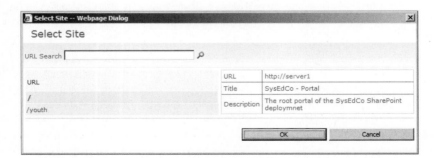

6. If you wanted to export a list and not the entire site, you could select a list in the List field. We are exporting the entire site in this exercise, so you will enter the full path and filename for the export in the File location section.

7. Choose whether or not all security settings should be exported in the Export Full Security section.

8. Choose to export All Versions in the Export Versions section and then click on Start Export.

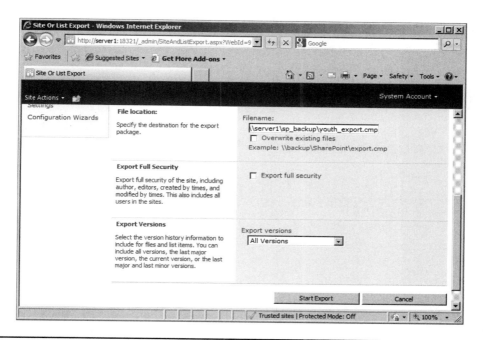

The same steps as those covered in Exercise 7.7 can be used to export lists and sites. A document library shows up as a list when exporting a site or a list. Do not be confused by the fact that the phrase "document library" does not show up in the backup process screens.

Recycle Bins

Recycle Bins are provided in SharePoint Server 2010 to allow for quick recovery from accidental deletions. For example, if a user deletes an item, it is not permanently removed immediately. Instead, it is placed in the first-stage Recycle Bin. When the item is deleted from the first-stage Recycle Bin, it is placed in the second-stage Recycle Bin. Only an administrator can restore items once they reach the second-stage Recycle Bin. Recycle Bins are managed at the web application level. Exercise 7.8 provides instructions for configuring Recycle Bin settings for the default web application in SharePoint Server 2010.

EXERCISE 7.8

Configuring SharePoint Recycle Bins

In this exercise, you will configure the Recycle Bin for the SharePoint - 80 web application that is installed by default with SharePoint Server 2010. The same basic steps can be used to configure the Recycle Bin for any other web application.

1. Launch Central Administration.

2. Select Application Management.

3. Choose Manage Web Applications.

4. Click on the web application named SharePoint - 80.

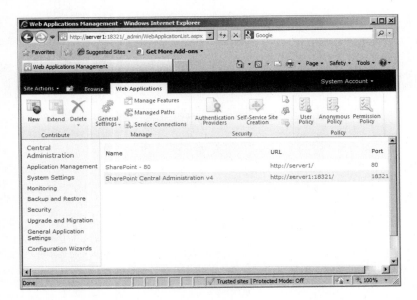

5. From the Ribbon, select General Settings ➢ General Settings.

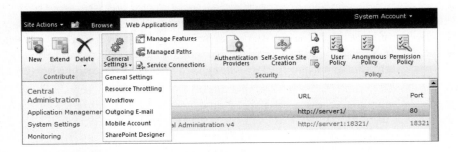

6. Scroll down to the Recycle Bin section and configure the settings according to your requirements. Then scroll to the bottom of the page and click OK (the OK button is not shown in the following image).

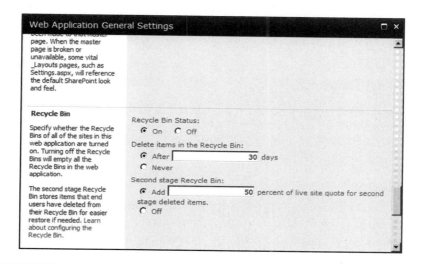

Custom Features

SharePoint sites can be customized in several ways. Those customizations on your sites can impact your backup decisions. The following customization categories exist:

- **Solutions:** Microsoft defines solutions as items containing developed site elements, which include web parts, workflows, site and list definitions, document converters, event receivers, timer jobs, and assemblies. Solutions can be backed up using the normal backup procedures in Central Administration.

- **Authored site elements:** These items are typically created by web designers and do not include compiled code. Authored site elements include master pages, cascading style sheets, forms, and layout pages. To back up the authored site elements, you must back up the farm, web application, or content database that includes the authored site elements.

- **Web.config changes:** The Web.config file contains the configuration settings for an ASP .NET web application. It is an XML document and may be modified directly. Direct changes made to the `Web.config` file (for example, changes are made outside of Central Administration) can be backed up only through file system backup procedures.

- **Browser-based design edits:** These edits occur when users make changes through the normal SharePoint access interface. When changes are made to lists, Microsoft recommends using the SharePoint Designer 2010 to save the new list as a template. The same action should be taken when changes are made to sites. Site collection changes can be backed up through site collection backups in Central Administration.

Customizations can be developed without deploying them through solution packages; however, this makes backups and recoveries much more complicated. Avoid this by only implementing customizations through solutions. For more information, see `http://technet.microsoft.com/en-us/library/ff607658.aspx`.

Performing Backups

In the preceding section, you learned about the different levels at which backups can be performed in SharePoint Server 2010. In this section, you will learn the specific steps required to perform backups at several important levels including servers, databases, folders, and files. You will also explore key information about backup scheduling.

Server Backups

Server backups can be considered at two levels: the entire server and the SharePoint server farm. In this section, you will learn to perform both backup types.

In order to back up the Windows server without purchasing third-party backup software, you must first install the Windows Server Backup component. In Exercise 7.9, you will perform the steps required to install Windows Server Backup on a Windows Server 2008 R2 machine.

EXERCISE 7.9

Installing the Windows Server Backup Component

In this exercise, you will install Windows Server Backup using Server Manager on Windows Server 2008 R2.

1. Click Start ➤ Administrative Tools ➤ Server Manager.

2. Expand Features in the left navigation pane.

3. Click the Add Features link to launch the Add Features Wizard.

4. On the Select Features screen, scroll down in the features list until you see Windows Server Backup Features. Expand the Windows Server Backup Features so that you see both options. Select both the Windows Server Backup and Command-Line Tools items and click Next.

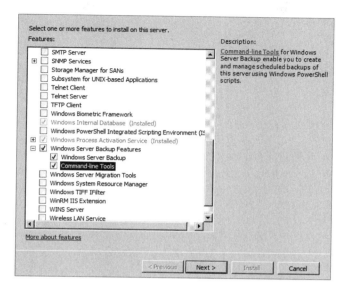

5. Click Install on the Confirm Installation Selections screen to begin the installation.

6. When the installation completes, click Close to complete the installation.

After performing the steps in Exercise 7.9, Windows Server Backup will be installed on the server. At this point you can perform a complete server backup, which can be used to restore configuration settings after a normal server installation or to perform a bare metal restoration using the Windows Recovery Environment. Exercise 7.10 provides instructions for performing a full server backup using Windows Server Backup.

EXERCISE 7.10

Performing a Full Server Backup Using Windows Server Backup

In this exercise, you will back up the entire Windows server using Windows Server Backup on a Windows Server 2008 R2 machine. This exercise assumes that Exercise 7.9 has been previously performed.

1. Click Start ➢ Administrative Tools ➢ Windows Server Backup.

2. Select Action ➢ Backup Once from the application's main menus.

3. Accept the default setting on the Backup Options screen of the Backup Once Wizard and click Next.

4. On the Select Backup Configuration screen, choose Full Server (recommended) and click Next.

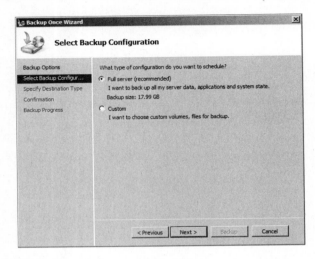

5. On the Specify a Destination Type screen, choose a storage location and click Next.

6. On the next screen, specify the exact location for the backup, accept the defaults for Access control, and click Next.

7. On the Confirmation screen, verify that the settings are according to your needs and click Backup to perform the backup of the entire server.

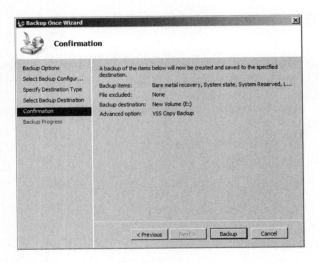

8. Observe the Backup Progress as shown in the following image.

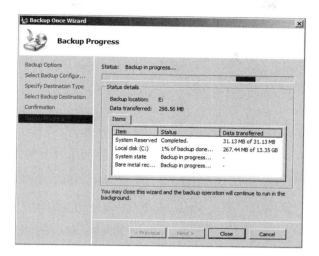

9. When the backup Status field is equal to Completed, click Close. The backup will now be listed in the Windows Server Backup screen and can be used for restoration in the future.

A complete server backup is useful any time you make changes to the server itself. Once the server is in a stable state, you will probably back up only the SharePoint server farm. This action can be performed from Central Administration.

Exercise 7.11 provides the steps required to perform a complete server farm backup. Before performing a server farm backup, you must create the share to which you want to perform the backup (or ask a file server administrator to perform the action for you if it is not within your area of responsibility). This share is used in step 7 of Exercise 7.11.

EXERCISE 7.11

Performing a Backup of the SharePoint Server Farm

In this exercise, you will back up the server farm using the backup features in Central Administration.

1. Launch SharePoint 2010 Central Administration.

2. Select the Backup and Restore section.

3. In the Farm Backup and Restore task group, select Perform A Backup.

EXERCISE 7.11 *(continued)*

4. Click on the check box to the left of Farm in the component list and note that all subcomponents are selected automatically.

5. Scroll to the bottom of the page and click Next.

6. Ensure that Backup type is set to Full and that all other defaults are accepted.

7. Enter the proper path for backup storage and click Start Backup.

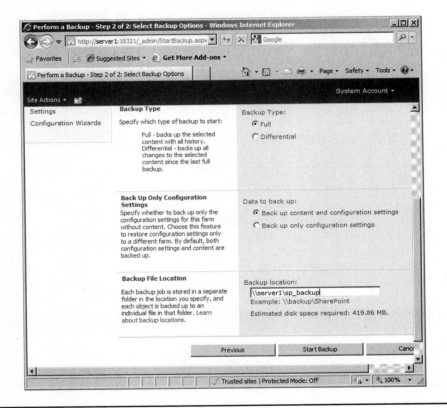

After the steps in Exercise 7.11 are performed, the backup process will begin. You can click Refresh to periodically check the status of the backup. As long as the backup phase status is equal to "In process," the backup is still running. When the phase status changes to "Completed," the backup is done. During the "In process" phase, you can also see the current item being backed up and the total items to be backed up as shown in Figure 7.4.

FIGURE 7.4   Viewing the backup status for a complete server farm backup

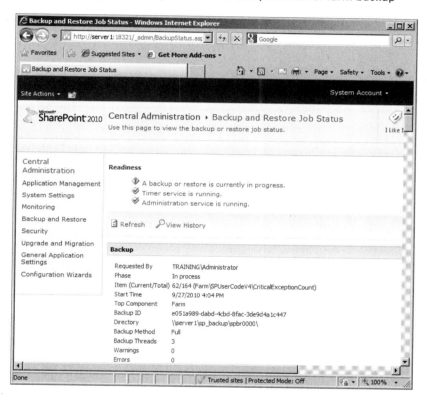

Using the same interface in Central Administration, you can back up only a site collection if you desire. For example, you may have a site collection with information that rarely changes. This is common for such data as security policies, corporate policies, and so on. Such a site collection may be backed up only once each week. However, more dynamic site collections will require more frequent backups. Figure 7.5 shows the screen used when only a single site collection is backed up in the Central Administration backup interface. This screen is accessed by clicking on Perform A Site Collection Backup in the Backup and Restore section of Central Administration.

FIGURE 7.5 Performing a site collection backup in Central Administration

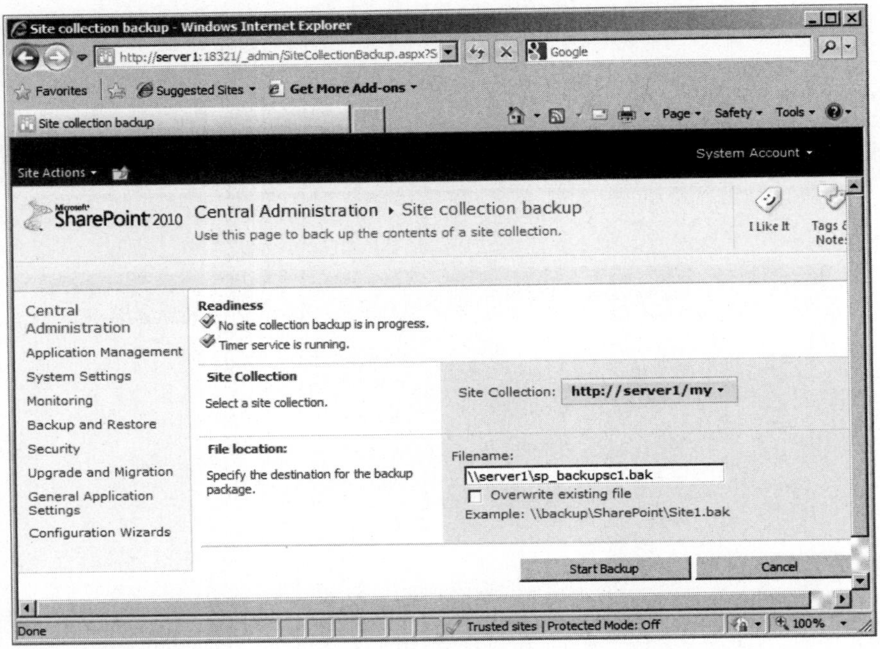

Folder and File Backups

In some cases, you may choose to go to the folder and file level to perform backups. This action can be performed in the Windows Server Backup application. Keep in mind that many SharePoint files are static and never change. Instead, when modified through Central Administration, the changes made are stored in the database. If you manually edit these static files, however, you will need to back them up manually as well. By default, the SharePoint site files are located in the following folder:

```
{install drive}:\Program Files\Common Files\Microsoft Shared\
Web Server Extensions\14
```

Any files changes within this folder hierarchy should be backed up using Windows Server Backup or another file system-based backup tool. Figure 7.6 shows the Backup Once Wizard of Windows Server Backup with only the SharePoint file folder selected for backup.

FIGURE 7.6   Backing up the SharePoint static files folder

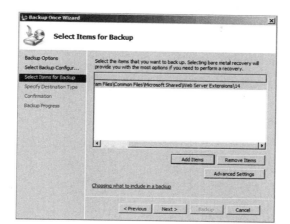

Database Backups

SQL Server supports three basic types of database backups:

- **Full:** The entire database is backed up with this type of backup.
- **Differential:** All changed data pages are backed up with this type of backup. The data page is the smallest storage object used within a SQL Server database file or set of files.
- **Transaction log:** The transactions in the log are backed up. This allows for recovery to any point in time in the past.

Exercise 7.12 provides the instructions for performing a full backup of the SQL Server WSS_CONTENT database, which is the default content database for a SharePoint Server 2010 installation.

EXERCISE 7.12

Creating a Full Backup of a Database

In this exercise, you will perform a full backup of the WSS_CONTENT database. You will back up the database to the default directory for backups, and you will back up to a file. Before you perform the backup, you will ensure that the recovery model for the WSS_CONTENT database is set to Full.

1. Launch SQL Server Management Studio.

2. Connect to the instance of SQL Server that houses your SharePoint databases.

3. Expand the Databases container in Object Explorer.

4. Right-click the WSS_CONTENT database and select Properties.

5. On the Options page, change the Recovery Model from Simple, as shown in the following image, to Full.

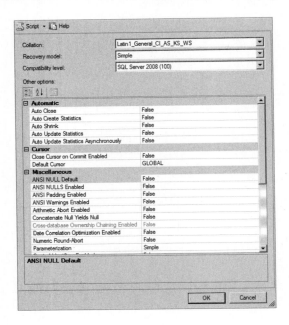

6. Click OK to save this change.

7. Right-click the WSS_CONENT database and select Tasks and then Backup.

8. In the Backup Database dialog, ensure that the Backup Type is set to Full and accept the default name of WSS_Content-Full Database Backup.

9. Under Destination, specify that the database should be backed up to Disk and click Add to add a location.

10. In the Select Backup Destination dialog, add **WSS_Content.bak** to the end of the existing path string as in the following image and click OK.

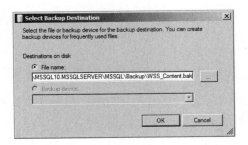

11. When your settings look similar to the settings in the following image, select the Options page.

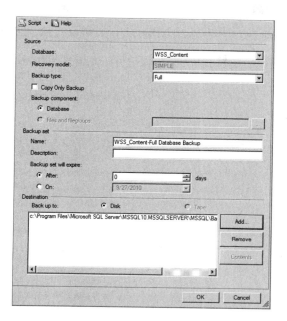

12. Browse the optional parameters available on the Options page. Note that you can verify the backup after it completes. This is a good idea for production backup jobs.

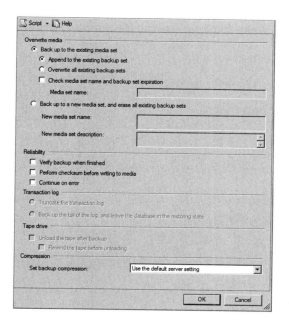

13. Without making any other changes, click the OK button to perform the Full backup.

Scheduling Considerations

Some SharePoint databases may require only a full backup once a week, while others will demand full backups nightly. In addition to full backups, you may determine that you need to implement differential backups in between the full backups and you may even decide to implement transaction log backups between the differential backups. Again, the solution will be determined by your acceptable recovery costs and acceptable transaction losses.

When the recovery cost tolerance is low (meaning you must recover as fast as possible), you will need more frequent backups. You do not, necessarily, have to perform a full backup on some frequent interval, but you will need to perform at least a transaction log backup with some frequency.

The issue of recovery cost is the major reason behind SQL Server's lack of support for incremental backups. An incremental backup only backs up the data that has changed since the last incremental backup. If you had a full backup from a week ago and five incremental backups since that time, you would have to restore the full backup and then each of the incremental backups in sequence in order to restore that database. Differential backups are different (no pun intended). A differential backup, as was explained in detail earlier in this chapter, backs up everything that has changed since that last full backup. Therefore, recovery is achieved by restoring the most recent full backup and then the most recent differential backup. Only two restoration processes are required regardless of how many differential backups have been taken since the most recent full backup.

SharePoint Server 2010 provides no real scheduling system for any of the backup types that can be performed from within Central Administration. Microsoft encourages the use of Windows PowerShell scripts for scheduling backups through the Windows Scheduling service.

Performing Recoveries

The ultimate purpose for a backup is to have a recovery option when disaster strikes. However, you should not wait until disaster strikes to perform your recovery for the first time. Always test the recovery procedures in a lab setting to verify that the data is being properly backed up and that you understand the recovery process properly. This section will provide recommendations for recovering a farm or a site collection, recovering a single list or library, or recovering from an offline database.

Recovering the Farm or Site Collection

Several important items should be considered when recovering a farm. The following list will help you plan farm recovery:

- Choose a recovery method. You can recover using Central Administration or using the `Restore-SPFarm` Windows PowerShell command.

- A single-server farm can only be restored to a single-server farm. A multiple-server farm can only be restored to a multiple-server farm.

- Backups and restores must take place within the same version of SharePoint Foundation.

- The restore process will not necessarily start all needed service applications automatically. You may have to manually start the applications using Central Administration.

Exercise 7.13 provides the basic steps required to restore a server farm using SharePoint Central Administration.

EXERCISE 7.13

Restoring a Server Farm

In this exercise, you will restore a server farm using SharePoint 2010 Central Administration.

1. Launch Central Administration.

2. Select the Backup and Restore section.

3. Click Restore From A Backup.

4. On the Restore From Backup - Step 1 Of 3 page, select the backup job that contains the farm you want to restore.

5. On the Restore From Backup - Step 2 Of 3 page, select the check box that is next to the farm and click Next.

6. On the Restore From Backup - Step 3 Of 3 page, in the Restore Component section, verify that Farm appears in the Restore the Following Component list and ensure that Restore Content And Configuration Settings is selected in the Restore Only Configuration Settings section.

7. Click Start Restore.

A site collection can be recovered using the same steps as those defined in Exercise 7.13. To recover either a farm or site collection, of course, you must have previously created a backup.

Recovering a Single List or Library

If you have exported a site, list, or library, as explained in Exercise 7.7, you can import that object again at a later time. Imports are performed using the Windows PowerShell interface. The following command syntax is used:

```
Import-SPWeb -Identity <Site URL> -Path <Export file name>
[-Force] [-NoFileCompression] [-Verbose]
```

You can access the SharePoint customized Windows PowerShell interface by clicking on Start ➢ All Programs ➢ Microsoft SharePoint 2010 Products ➢ SharePoint 2010 Management Shell.

Recovering from an Offline Database

You can recover data from an offline database, or an unattached content database as it is called in Central Administration. If you come from a SQL Server background the terminology here might be confusing. In SharePoint terminology an *unattached database* is a database that is attached to a SQL server, but it not connected to a SharePoint server farm. In SQL Server terminology, a *detached database* is one that is not attached to the SQL server at all. This similar terminology has caused some confusion among new SharePoint administrators coming from a SQL Server background. Just remember that the Unattached Content Recovery feature of SharePoint Server 2010 is used to recover lists and libraries from content databases that are attached to SQL Server but not to a SharePoint server farm.

Figure 7.7 shows the interface used to connect to an unattached content database in Central Administration. This interface is accessed by selecting Recover Data From An Unattached Content Database in the Backup and Restore section of Central Administration.

FIGURE 7.7   Connecting to an unattached content database within Central Administration

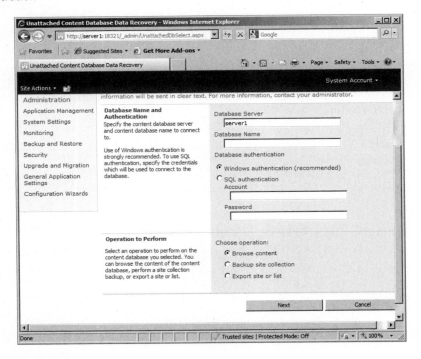

As shown in Figure 7.7, you must provide the database server name, the database name, and the credentials used to access the database. Once this information is entered, you can choose among three operations:

- **Browse content:** This operation allows you to navigate through the content in the database and select the information you need.

- **Backup site collection:** This operation can be confusing because of its name. You will not back up a site collection from your active site, but you will back up the site collection from within the unattached content database so that you may restore it to your active site.

- **Export site or list:** This operation can also be confusing. You will export the site or list from the unattached content database so that you can import it to your active content database.

Summary

In this chapter, you learned the importance of planning for disaster recovery and for scalability. You began by exploring availability options and the role that backups play in providing availability. Next, you investigated the different options available for providing scalability in your SharePoint deployments. These options included both scaling out and scaling up. Finally, you learned the specifics of performing different backup types and planning for disaster recovery.

Exam Essentials

Designing availability.   Know that availability can be provided through clustering for database servers and Network Load Balancing for application and web frontend servers. Understand that recovery of lost data is also key to providing availability.

Planning a scaling strategy.   Know that SharePoint Server 2010 installations can be scaled up or scaled out. When you scale up, you are adding resources to the existing physical installation. When you scale out, you are adding new servers to your SharePoint topology. Know that virtualization can be used as an easy way to provide for future growth.

Designing recovery strategies.   Know that a recovery strategy should include backup plans for servers, farms, site collections, sites and lists, and libraries. Know how to back up the farm and the site collections from within SharePoint 2010 Central Administration. Know how to perform database backups from within SQL Server Management Studio.

Chapter

8

Planning Service Applications

TOPICS COVERED IN THIS CHAPTER

✓ **Determining Service Application Server Roles**

✓ **Planning a Business Connectivity Services Strategy**

✓ **Planning an Excel Services Strategy**

✓ **Designing a Forms Strategy**

If you have worked with earlier versions of SharePoint, such as MOSS 2007, you know that Search Services, Excel Services, and other such functions were provided in a monolithic architecture. The Shared Service Provider was exactly what its name sounds like. It was a single service provider that was shared by all of the services, including Search Services and Excel Services, and each website could consume services from only one Shared Service Provider. This architecture caused many problems with scaling and performance in earlier SharePoint deployments.

SharePoint Server 2010 introduces a new, distributed service application (SA) architecture that allows for greater scalability and performance. In this chapter, you will learn about service applications and the roles they play in your SharePoint Server 2010 deployment. You will also learn to plan specific services such as Business Connectivity Services, Excel Services, and InfoPath Forms Services.

If you are preparing for the 70-668 exam, this chapter contains important information for you as well. The exam requires that you formulate a Business Connectivity Services strategy, plan a Microsoft Excel Services strategy, implement a Business Intelligence solution, plan service application server roles, and plan a forms strategy. All of these service application–related topics are addressed in this chapter.

Determining Service Application Server Roles

If you really want to understand the benefits of service applications in SharePoint Server 2010, you need to first understand the problems with its predecessor in Microsoft Office SharePoint Server (MOSS) 2007. This section begins with a discussion of Shared Service Providers (SSPs) in MOSS 2007 and then moves on to the service application architecture in SharePoint Server 2007. Next, you will explore the service application roles that are available or, more specifically, the individual service applications. The last topic in this section is an introduction to the Service Application security model, which includes an important discussion on planning the implementation of a Business Intelligence solution. This section provides the foundation you'll need to explore Business Connectivity Services, Excel Services, and strategies for web server forms and InfoPath forms later in this chapter.

The Way It Was

Before the release of SharePoint Server 2010, SharePoint deployments used a Shared Service Provider (SSP) architecture. All of the shared services were embedded within one provider. If you wanted one SharePoint site to use a different SSP than another SharePoint site, you had to implement another web application and another instance of the SSP. This second instance had all of the services of the first instance, even if you wanted only one or two of the services. The point is that SSPs were all or nothing. You could not implement an SSP with only Excel Services and all other services disabled.

This architecture meant that you could not implement a distributed services environment for the functions provided within the SSPs without implementing the entire collection of services at each distribution point (in each web application and SSP instance). Regulatory compliance, particularly related to security, may have demanded that only the Accounting Department employees could search the Accounting Department SharePoint sites and only the Human Resources employees could search the Human Resources sites. With such demands, you would typically implement a separate SSP for each site collection to ensure that the search was completely separated. The end result was often more hardware than you would have to implement if the services were distributed or componentized. This is exactly what SharePoint Server 2010 offers with the service applications architecture.

Before you explore the service application architecture, consider the services handled by the SSPs in SharePoint Server 2007 (specifically, MOSS 2007):

- Profiles
- Audiences
- My Sites
- Search
- Excel Services
- Business Data Catalog (BDC)

Each time you implemented an instance of the SSP, assuming you had the Enterprise client access license for MOSS 2007, you implemented this entire collection of services. Each web application that hosted site collections in MOSS 2007 consumed services from one and only one SSP. You created a web application and then created an SSP in that web application. Next, you created another web application and created a site collection in that web application and indicated that it should use the SSP previously created. All sites in the hierarchy of that site collection would use the same SSP.

Because a site collection was locked to only one SSP and because each SSP had all services available in it, it was typically recommended that you have only one SSP for your entire organization. However, several scenarios would demand a separate SSP, including:

- Separating the intranet from the Internet
- Providing separate search providers
- Providing separate BDC providers
- Providing separate Excel Services providers

In such scenarios, you could easily end up with four or five SSPs in larger organizations. With each SSP in its own web application, more memory and processing power were demanded of the server or servers that hosted the SSP, which in turn meant that you often needed more servers. As you will see in the next topic of discussion, service applications rid you of these woes by allowing you to implement each function, which was formerly bundled into the SSP, as an effectively independent service.

 Real World Scenario

One SharePoint Network; Two Companies

I was involved in a very interesting project recently. Two brothers ran two separate small businesses; however, to reduce costs they shared a common network. Both businesses were located in the same building with a barrier wall right down the middle. In the back of the building was a "server room," which was really more like a quickly partitioned area with very thin walls. This room housed the servers and Internet connections for both companies.

They were implementing SharePoint 2010 when I was called into the project to help optimize their SQL Server database server. The goal was to support a single SharePoint Server farm with the SQL Server database server that I was fine-tuning for performance. I suggested that they might want to create a separate service application (SA) instance for each company so that all data items were more easily separated. For example, search results for one company would never "accidentally" include pages from the other company.

In the end, they took the recommendation. Each company had its own SharePoint web application for its site collection and its own web application for its SAs. This provided better separation and clearer distinctions between the two companies' data sets.

The Service Application Architecture

Service applications (SA) provide background services for SharePoint sites, and each SA can serve one site or multiple sites. SAs replace the previously discussed SSPs and provide for more flexible farm deployments and configuration. The SA architecture is based on the Windows Communication Foundation (WCF), which means it is based on claims. A *claim* is a collection of properties provided to the authentication provider to be evaluated. If the authentication process returns true, the claims are trusted and the accessing party may perform any claimed rights or capabilities.

 The WCF solution is based on the .NET Framework and is beyond the scope or responsibilities of the typical SharePoint administrator. However, if you would like to learn more about it, visit the Getting Started Tutorial for WCF, which is located at http://msdn.microsoft.com/en-us/library/ms734712.aspx.

Figure 8.1 illustrates the basic architecture of the SA model used in SharePoint Server 2010. The communications start with the web application, pass through the service proxy, and communicate with the service application in order to access an instance of a service provided by the service application.

FIGURE 8.1   The SA architecture

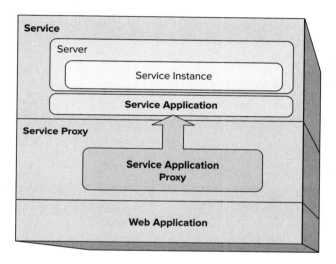

By default, all SAs run within one Internet Information Services (IIS) website. Each web application can have only one service proxy, but one service proxy can provide access for multiple web applications. When the farm is first installed, a default group of SAs is created for the farm. If your farm never scales beyond the need of a single server providing all SAs, you can scale this single SA provider out to support several SharePoint web frontends with several site collections and sites. However, you can also distribute the SAs by installing multiple instances of the SAs on different servers.

One of the benefits of the new SA architecture is that you can implement the services in a more granular fashion. You can choose to deploy only the SAs needed in your farm. You can also control which SAs are used by each web application. Multiple instances of the same SA can be deployed in a farm, and each instance can be assigned a different name. Finally, you can share the SAs across multiple web applications within the same farm to reduce memory and processor requirements.

SharePoint Server 2010 also allows you to use groups to define the SAs that should be available for a web application. The default group, which is created during the farm installation, includes all SAs. You can create a custom group for a specific web application so that only the needed services are available. For example, you may want to provide a limited set of services to some SharePoint sites while providing the full set of services to others. For the sites requiring the limited group of services, the server providing the SAs can service more frontend servers than the server providing the full default group of SAs. The flexibility of creating custom SA groups means that you can get more work out of a given SA server by limiting the services it offers. Exercise 8.1 provides the instructions for creating a custom group for service applications.

EXERCISE 8.1

Creating a Custom Group for Service Applications

In this exercise, you will use Central Administration to create a custom group for service applications. You will not save the custom group but will access the interface for its creation. You will do this for the default SharePoint - 80 site.

1. Launch Central Administration.

2. Select the Application Management page from the left navigation list.

3. In the Web Application group, click the Manage Web Applications link.

4. Click on the SharePoint - 80 site to select it.

5. From the Ribbon, select Service Connections.

6. In the resulting Configure Service Application Associations screen, you could select Custom from the Edit The Following Group Of Connections combo box and then select the specific services you want to use, as in the following image.

7. However, because you do not want to change the default settings for this particular web application, scroll down and click the Cancel button to avoid making changes.

In addition to being able to modify an existing web application, you can also specify the SAs to be consumed by a web application during its creation. The interface is very similar to the one presented in Exercise 8.1; however, it is a single screen that scrolls for several pages through all of the settings in the web application. The screen is accessed by simply clicking the New button in the Web Applications Management section of Central Administration, as shown in Figure 8.2.

FIGURE 8.2   Assigning SAs during the creation of a new web application

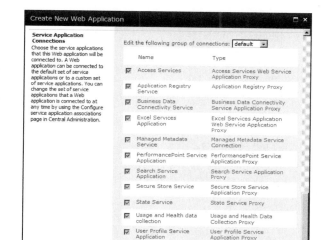

Service Application Roles

The service applications (also known as shared services) that are available in a given installation will depend on the SharePoint product installed. For example, SharePoint Server 2010 includes more SAs than SharePoint Foundation Server 2010. Each SA can be considered a role, and you can provide the roles on a single server or distribute them across multiple servers.

The terminology related to service applications can be confusing. To help you understand the relationship between *service applications* and *shared services*, remember that, technically, a service application is an instance of a shared service.

SharePoint Server will provide different SA roles or services depending on the version you implement. Table 8.1 lists the available services and the versions of SharePoint with which they ship.

TABLE 8.1 SharePoint SAs Available with Different Versions

Service Application	Description	Foundation 2010	Server 2010 Standard	Server 2010 Enterprise
Access Services	Views, edits, and interacts with Access 2010 databases within a web browser			X
Business Data Connectivity Service	Provides access to line-of-business data systems; typically, external data	X	X	X
Excel Services Application	Allows for live interaction with Excel 2010 files within a web browser			X
Managed Metadata Service	Manages the taxonomy, hierarchies, keywords, and social tagging infrastructure for the sites		X	X
PerformancePoint Service Application	Provides the PerformancePoint services to the SharePoint server farm			X
Search Service Application	Crawls the SharePoint sites and content, indexes the data, and services search queries		X	X
Secure Store Service	Allows for single sign-on for access to multiple applications and services		X	X
State Service	Provides temporary storage of user session data for various SharePoint components		X	X
Usage and Health Data Collection	Gathers usage and health data from the farm and provides views via reports	X	X	X

Service Application	Description	Foundation 2010	Server 2010 Standard	Server 2010 Enterprise
User Profile Service Application	Allows for My Site websites, user profile pages, social tagging, and additional social computing features		X	X
Visio Graphics Service	Views and refreshes published Visio 2010 diagrams within a web browser			X
Web Analytics Service Application	Provides web service interfaces with web analytic data		X	X
Word Automation Services	Converts bulk document conversion		X	X
Microsoft SharePoint Foundation Subscription Settings Service	Allows for multitenant functionality	X	X	X

As you build your SA architecture, it is important that you understand the basic purpose and functionality of each SA provided with SharePoint Server 2010. The following explanations should help you understand when you would use each of the products.

Access Services   The Access Services SA is used to allow users to access Microsoft Access 2010 databases through the SharePoint interface. Access Services is installed and activated automatically during the installation of SharePoint Server 2010. You do not have to configure the service, although you may want to change some default settings such as the maximum columns per query, the maximum rows per query, and the maximum records per table. Creating an Access database-driven site can be as easy as enabling one of the provided Access templates or simply creating a new template in Access 2010 and publishing it to Access Services.

Business Data Connectivity (BDC) service   Business Data Connectivity service is the primary service that drives Microsoft Business Connectivity Services. It allows you to connect your SharePoint site to external data sources such as databases, .NET assemblies, and custom data sources. The BDC service is initialized by default when you install SharePoint Server 2010; however, in some instances, you may have to configure the Secure

Store Service before you can access the external data sources. This is particularly true when the external data source is not part of the same Windows domain as the SharePoint site.

Excel Services Application   The Excel Services Application service allows users to view and share Excel workbooks with other SharePoint users. The workbooks can be updated and refreshed from other data sources and edited from within the SharePoint web browser.

Managed Metadata Service   The Managed Metadata Service allows you to configure a hierarchical collection of managed terms (a taxonomy) that can be used throughout your SharePoint sites. This service provides for consistency throughout the organization.

PerformancePoint Service Application   The PerformancePoint Service is a performance management service used to monitor your organization or analyze the data within your organization. PerformancePoint provides dashboard capabilities, scorecards, and key performance indicators (KPIs). PerformancePoint Server 2007 was previously a standalone server, but now it is integrated into SharePoint Server 2010.

Search Service Application   The Search Service Application service provides crawling, indexing, and querying services. This is the service that allows you to determine which parts of your sites or farms should be crawled, and it services the search requests made by your users.

Secure Store Service   The Secure Store service is the replacement for the Single Sign-on Service that was in SharePoint Server 2007. The Secure Store Service is a credential storage solution that maps credentials to application IDs for user access. The end result is the ability to access SharePoint sites and other applications with a single logon.

State Service   The State Service is used to maintain state for users. This allows features such as InfoPath forms and the Chart Web part to work properly when accessing backend SQL Server data sources.

Usage and Health Data Collection   Because it is incorporated into SharePoint Foundation 2010, this service application is available in all editions of SharePoint 2010. It collects usage and health data from the entire farm and provides reports on this information. The monitoring of usage and health data is accomplished using timer jobs that collect the information. The data collected may include performance counter data, event log entries, timer service data, search usage data, and other data elements from the web servers in your farm.

User Profile Service Application   The User Profile Service application implements a central storage location for user information. This information includes user profiles, organization profiles, My Sites, social tags and notes, and audiences.

Visio Graphics Service   Visio Services, or the Visio Graphics Service, is an SA that allows users to view and share Visio drawings. Visio is not required on the client computer browsing the Visio drawing in the web browser. As the administrator, you can limit the size of the Visio drawings, determine the users who can access them, and control many other settings through Central Administration. As a user, you can publish Visio drawings to Visio Services from within the Visio 2010 application.

Web Analytics Service Application   This service compiles web statistics related to SharePoint sites, such as search terms, page hits, and client browser information. This data can be used by the administrator to determine usage patterns and to better optimize the site and page content.

Word Automation Services   The Word Automation Services service is new to SharePoint Server 2010, and it allows documents to be converted into formats supported by Microsoft Word. The service can save documents in several formats including RTF, DOC, DOT, DOCX, DOTX, MHT, XML, and PDF.

Microsoft SharePoint Foundation Subscription Settings Service   This service application is included in SharePoint Foundation 2010 and is, therefore, included in SharePoint Server 2010 Standard and Enterprise editions. The Subscription Settings Service allows for multitenant usage of the service applications. Subscription IDs and settings for the services are managed within this service. The Subscription Settings Service is deployed using PowerShell and cannot be deployed using Central Administration.

In addition to a basic understanding of what the services offer, you should understand the CPU and memory load imposed by the services. According to Microsoft, the following services have a low CPU load:

- User Profile Service application
- Word Automation Services
- Visio Graphics Service
- Access Services
- Managed Metadata Service
- Web Analytics Service application

The following services have a medium CPU load:

- Excel Services Application
- Business Data Connectivity service
- PerformancePoint Service application

The following services have a high CPU load:

- SharePoint Foundation Subscription Settings Service

When Microsoft suggests that a service has a medium CPU load, this load is three times greater than the low CPU load services. High CPU loads are five times greater than low CPU loads. This information should be considered when placing SAs in a distributed environment. To discover the low CPU loads, for a baseline analysis, you would need to install SharePoint on the given server and measure the load with simulations. The simulations could be as few as three or four machines accessing the site's services and then extrapolating the findings out for the total number of users you will support. Once the low CPU load is established, you will know what the medium and high CPU loads will look like on that same server hardware.

The Service Application Security Model

In most cases, a single instance of a service application can be initiated for the entire SharePoint organization. However, if you have regulatory constraints that require strict separation of data for crawled sites or other such restrictions, you may be forced to implement multiple SA instances. This possible complexity demands thoughtful consideration during Business Intelligence (BI) planning. For this reason, this section addresses installing multiple SA instances and BI planning.

Installing Multiple Service Application Instances

You install multiple instances of the SAs by creating multiple SAs that run in multiple application pools. When the services run in separate pools, they can be configured with different permission levels and more granular control of access is provided. Exercise 8.2 provides instructions for creating a new SA instance in a new application pool, as well as creating a new SA instance in an existing application pool.

EXERCISE 8.2

Creating a New Application Pool and SA Collection

In this exercise, you will perform the steps required to create a new instance of the Excel Services Application service and the Search Service Application service. You will first create a new instance of the Excel Services Application service and create the new application pool at this time. Next, you will create a new instance of the Search Service Application service and place it into the pool created when the Excel Services Application instance was created. The new application pool will be named Temp, and the service instances will use their names with the word *Temp* as a prefix.

1. Launch Central Administration.

2. Select Application Management from the left navigation bar.

3. From the Service Applications group, select Manage Service Applications.

4. On the Manage Service Applications page, select New ➢ Excel Services Application.

5. In the Create New Excel Services Application screen, enter the Name **Temp Excel Services Application**. Select Create New Application Pool, and enter the name **Temp** as the Application Pool Name. Accept all other defaults and click OK.

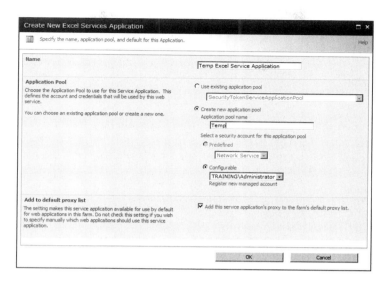

6. When the web browser returns to the Manage Service Applications page, click New ➤ Search Service Application.

7. In the Create New Search Service Application screen, enter the service application name **Temp Search Service Application**, select Use Existing Application Pool, and choose the **Temp** pool from the drop-down list for both the Application Pool For Search Admin Web Service and the Application Pool For Search Query And Site Settings Web Service. Accept all other defaults and click OK.

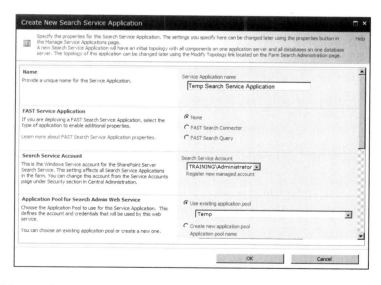

8. On the Manage Search Topology screen, you will receive a notification of the successful creation. Click OK.

Planning the Implementation of a Business Intelligence Solution

If you ask 100 different database administrators or business analysts to define BI, you will likely get 80 to 100 different answers. BI is a complex concept and is defined differently by different people. Much of the difference comes from the work responsibilities and experiences of the definer, which contribute to the different perspectives on Business Intelligence.

What most definitions agree on is the fact that BI should help businesses make good decisions at the right time. This quality means that you must be able to receive notifications of business changes and you must have the right data available to make a good decision when those changes occur. SharePoint Server 2010 helps with BI deployment through the following features:

Reports   Reports are provided in SharePoint Server 2010 through two primary sources: a report document library and integration with SQL Server Reporting Services. The report document library is used to store reports, and users can be notified when reports are added or updated. SQL Server Reporting Services is a complete reporting solution that allows for customized report creation. These reports can be viewed through Web Parts on the SharePoint sites.

Dashboards   Dashboards are created using the features of PerformancePoint. Managers can track sales, customer service, manufacturing, references to their organization on the Web, and many other things. The dashboards become a one-stop location for the most important information they need to see within their organization. Using PerformancePoint Services is a large enough topic to fill an entire book by itself.

Scorecards   Scorecards are also created using the features of PerformancePoint. These scorecards may include KPIs and other health measurements for the organization. The most important feature is that they provide a graphical quick summary but can allow for drilldown into the details of the data.

Charts   Charts are provided through a spreadsheet document in a document library, through Excel Services, and possibly through third-party charting tools installed as add-ons to SharePoint Server 2010.

Key Performance Indicators (KPIs)   KPIs are those numbers that indicate success or failure in an instance. They are easy to understand and respond to. For example, are sales up or down from the same period last year? This may be a KPI. These indicators can be provided through custom reports, simple Web Part entries on the homepage, and several other access points in SharePoint Server 2010.

When planning a BI implementation, consider the tools available to you and use the best tool to present the information simply and clearly. Remember, the key to successful BI implementations is having the right information at the right time. If the information is provided too early, you cannot yet act and may fail to act when you need to in the future. If the information is provided too late, there is no time left to act. This means that KPIs should be sent to decision makers as alerts at the right time so that the appropriate actions can be taken.

Planning a Business Connectivity Services Strategy

Business Connectivity Services (BCS) is the new implementation of SharePoint 2007's Business Data Connectivity (BDC) in SharePoint Server 2010. In fact, the primary supporting service is still called the Business Data Connectivity Service. BCS allows you to connect to external data providers and both read from and write to these data providers. Data providers include line-of-business (LOB) applications, web services databases, and even cloud services. LOB applications include SAP, JD Edwards EnterpriseOne, and many other business management and business processing solutions. The most common use of BDC in SharePoint 2007 was for accessing external data in LOB databases for SharePoint sites.

The BCS is built on the BDC service, external content types (ECTs), and external lists. The BDC service provides the storage repository for ECTs. The ECTs define the external content that should be accessed and the permissions used to access it. The external lists are used within SharePoint to provide views of the data provided through the ECTs. Figure 8.3 illustrates this architecture.

FIGURE 8.3   The BCS architecture

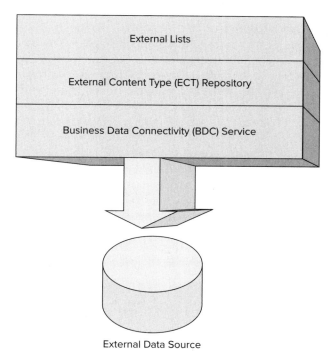

Microsoft provides two primary tools for working with BCS data in addition to Central Administration and the integrated lists management features of SharePoint itself. These tools are the SharePoint Designer 2010 tool and the Visual Studio 2010 development software. SharePoint Designer is used to create the ECTs without having to directly modify the XML definition files. Visual Studio 2010 can also create the ECTs. Once you have created the ECTs, you can access the data within SharePoint's standard web-based user interface via the new external list component.

Once the ECTs are created, they can be used within any of the following SharePoint components or external applications:

- External List (SharePoint component)
- Search (SharePoint component)
- Outlook
- Word
- SharePoint Workspace
- InfoPath
- Access
- Excel and third-party applications via code

Because the data is accessed through SharePoint via BCS, the user does not have to know the actual location of the data. BCS becomes a data aggregator of sorts, as it allows users to access the data from one centralized location even though it may reside in several distributed LOBs or data sources.

An additional benefit of BCS is its ability to link a single backend data source to multiple data access and modification methods. For example, you can create an ECT that gives access to your central Customers table in your customer management system. This table can then be viewed and modified from a SharePoint external list, from Outlook, or even from Access. Users can import the list into Outlook 2010 as a contact list. Once imported, users can modify a contact, and it will send the modification all the way back to the original backend data source. The changes will be reflected in all access methods because the data really only exists in the backend Customers table.

BCS supports three connectors for accessing external data out-of-the-box. These connectors are available in the SharePoint Designer when creating ECTs. The first connector is the database (DB) connector, which provides access to SQL Server databases. The second is the WCF connector, which provides access to other database types such as Oracle or MySQL. The final type is the .NET assembly connector, which is used to connect to .NET assemblies created by your developers.

NOTE   In order to perform the exercises in this section, which include Exercise 8.3 through Exercise 8.5, you will need to download and install the AdventureWorks sample database on your SharePoint SQL Server database server. These exercises assume that SQL Server 2008 is installed as the database server and that SharePoint 2010 and the SharePoint Designer 2010 are installed on the same server. The AdventureWorks sample database can be downloaded from http://msftdbprodsamples.codeplex.com/releases/view/37109. Be sure to download the AdventureWorks2008_SR4.exe file and not the SQL2008 .AdventureWorksLT2008_Only_database.zip file. The latter file contains a very different database than the one used in these exercises. During the installation, the only required database is the AdventureWorks OLTP database, which is the traditional AdventureWorks sample database Microsoft has provided for several years now.

In Exercise 8.3, you will create an ECT that connects to a table within the Microsoft AdventureWorks sample database. These exercises will help you understand the basic processes used to connect to external data. In real-world scenarios, of course, you will not be required to install a sample database as you will be using your production databases. The AdventureWorks sample database must be installed on your SQL server in order to perform this exercise.

EXERCISE 8.3

Creating an ECT in SharePoint Designer

In this exercise, you will create an ECT that connects to the Person.Contact table within AdventureWorks. You will allow all operations against the table, including reads and writes. SharePoint Designer 2010 must be installed on the server, and the AdventureWorks sample database must be installed on the SQL server. This exercise should not be performed on a production server.

1.   Launch your default SharePoint Site - 80 site by navigating to http://localhost in the web browser on the lab server.

2.   Select Site Actions ➤ Edit in SharePoint Designer.

3.   In the left Navigation pane, select External Content Types.

4. In the Ribbon, click the External Content Type button.

5. On the New External Content Type tab, click the blue text that reads New External Content Type, which is located next to the Name field. In the edit field that appears, enter the value **Contacts** and press the Tab key to exit the edit field.

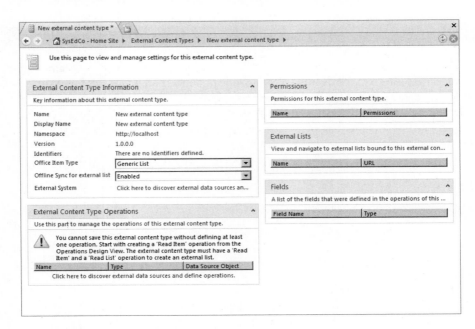

6. Click the blue text that reads Click Here To Discover External Data Sources, which is located next to the External System field.

7.   Click the Add Connection button.

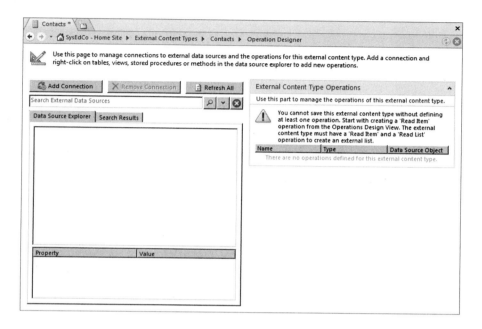

8.   In the External Data Source Type Selection dialog, select the Data Source Type of SQL Server and click OK.

9.   In the SQL Server Connection dialog, enter the Database Server value **localhost** and the Database Name value **AdventureWorks**. Accept the default value Connect With User's Identity and then click OK.

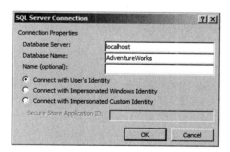

10.   In the Data Source Explorer, expand AdventureWorks ➢ Tables.

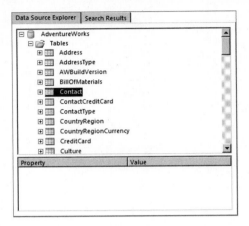

11. Right-click on the Contact table and select Create All Operations.

12. In the All Operations Wizard, click Next.

13. Review and accept the default on the Parameters Configuration page and click Next.

14. On the Filter Parameters Configuration page, select Add Filter Parameter to limit the return of the ECT to only 2,000 rows.

15. Click on the link that reads Click To Add, which is located next to the Filter field name in the Properties section.

16. In the Filter Configuration dialog, accept the default filter name, which is Filter, but change the Filter Type to Limit and click OK.

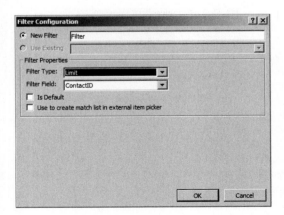

17. Set the Default Value for the filter to 2000 in the Properties section, and then click Finish to create the operation set.

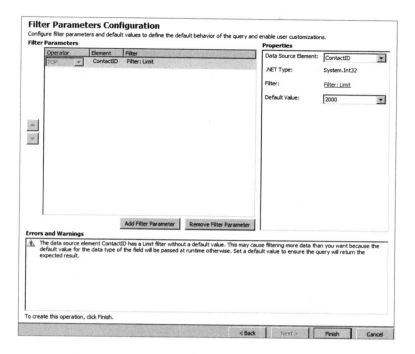

18. Click the Save button (the blue 3.5-inch diskette icon) to save the ECT to the BDC Metadata Store.

19. Close SharePoint Designer 2010.

In Exercise 8.3, you created all the operations in steps 12 through 17 as you worked through the wizard. This exercise enables the reading and writing of data. You can also create individual operations to only allow reading the data if you like.

By default, SharePoint limits the size of the external data source to fewer than 2,001 rows. For this reason, Exercise 8.3 applied a filter limiting the results to the first 2,000 rows. However, you can extend this limit using the throttling feature of BCS, which must be managed through PowerShell. For more information, see http://blogs.msdn.com/b/bcs/archive/2010/02/16/bcs-powershell-introduction-and-throttle-management.aspx.

It is important that you understand the default limitations of the BCS external list fetch engine. Table 8.2 lists these default limitations.

TABLE 8.2   BCS External List Fetching Limits

Data Source	Limit Description	Limit
Database	Rows per fetch	2,000
Database	Timeout	3 minutes
Web Service or WCF	Size of fetch	30 Megabytes
Web Service or WCF	Timeout	3 minutes

In Exercise 8.4, you will create an external list in the SharePoint site that displays the data from within the AdventureWorks database and allows for the editing of this data.

EXERCISE 8.4

Creating an External List in SharePoint 2010

In this exercise, you will create an external list that connects to the ECT created in Exercise 8.3.

1. Launch your default SharePoint Site - 80 site by navigating to `http://localhost` in the web browser on the lab server.

2. Select Site Actions ➢ More Options.

3. In the left pane of the Create window that appears, choose List in the Filter By section.

4. In the center selection area of the Create window, click External List and then click the Create button in the right pane to create the external list.

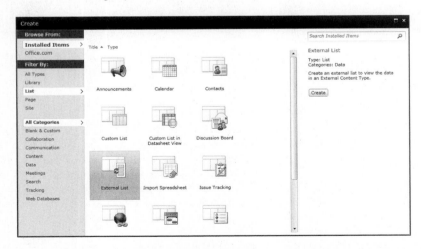

5. On the New List Creation page, enter the name **Contacts** and the description value **The organization's contact list**. Accept the default of displaying the list on the Quick Launch menu.

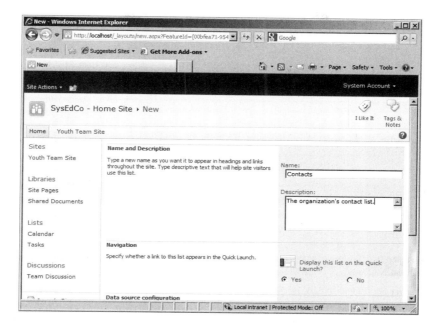

6. Scroll down the page, if necessary, enter the External Content Type value **Contacts**, and click the Check button to allow SharePoint to automatically enter the full ECT name for you.

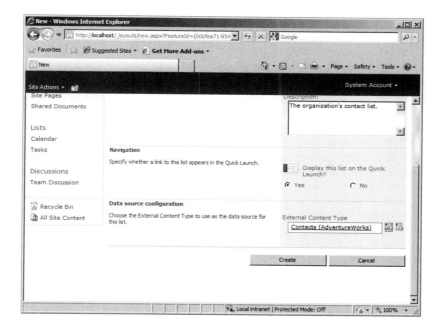

7. Click Create to create the external list object.

After completing the steps in Exercise 8.4, you will have an external list that can be viewed from within your web browser. Figure 8.4 shows what this list looks like by default. The list may contain columns you do not want to display, and it defaults to only 30 items per page. Exercise 8.5 provides the steps required to customize this list.

FIGURE 8.4   The default look of the Contacts external list in SharePoint

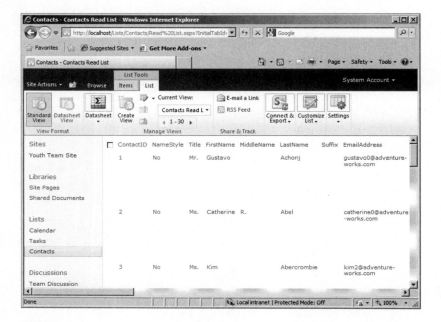

Customizing an External List

In this exercise, you will customize the external list created in Exercise 8.4. You will remove several columns from the display and allow up to 100 items to be displayed per screen.

1. Launch your default SharePoint Site - 80 site by navigating to http://localhost in the web browser on the lab server.

2. Click the Contacts link in the Lists group on the Quick Launch left-hand navigation bar.

3. On the Ribbon, choose the List tab.

4. On the List tab, in the Manage Views group, click the Modify View button.

5. Scroll down the page until you see the Columns section and then deselect the following columns so that they are not displayed:

- NameStyle

- MiddleName

- Suffix

- EmailPromotion

- PasswordHash

- PasswordSalt

- AdditionalContactInfo

- ModifiedDate

6. Scroll further down the page until you see the Sort section and change the First Sort By The Column value to equal **LastName**.

7. Scroll further down the page until you see the Item Limit section. Expand the Item Limit section and change the value for Number Of Items To Display to **100**.

8. Click OK to save your changes.

After completing Exercise 8.5, you will see a simpler list of contacts like the one shown in Figure 8.5.

FIGURE 8.5   The simpler external list displayed in SharePoint

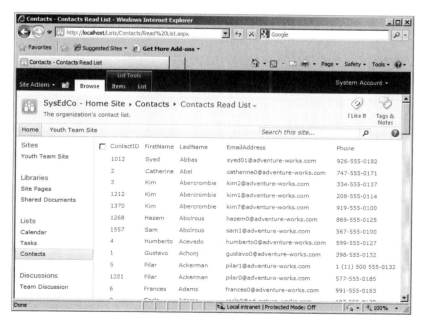

Now that you have the list formatted as you like, you can edit items. Exercise 8.6 provides steps for editing an item and then querying the SQL Server database directly to verify that the item changed in the database and not only in the SharePoint list display.

EXERCISE 8.6

Editing Items in External Lists

In this exercise, you will edit an item in the external list and then verify that the modification was made within the SQL Server database itself. You will modify the record with the ContactID of 3 and the LastName of Abercrombie. This exercise depends on Exercise 8.4 and will be much easier to perform if you have also performed Exercise 8.5.

1. Launch your default SharePoint Site - 80 site by navigating to http://localhost in the web browser on the lab server.

2. Click the Contacts link in the Lists group on the Quick Launch left-hand navigation bar.

3. If necessary, scroll until you see the row in view with a ContactID of 3 and a LastName value of Abercrombie.

4. Hover over the row referenced in step 3, click the down arrow next to the ContactID of 3, and select Edit Item.

5. Notice that the Contacts - Edit Item screen, which is displayed, shows all of the fields and not only those displayed in the view that was created in Exercise 8.5.

6. Change the LastName value to Abercrombie-Stephens and click Save.

7. Notice that the change is reflected immediately in the list within SharePoint.

8. Launch the SQL Server Management Studio by selecting Start ➢ All Programs ➢ Microsoft SQL Server 2008 ➢ SQL Server Management Studio.

9. Connect to the (local) server using Windows Authentication.

10. In Object Explorer, expand Databases AdventureWorks.

11. Click the New Query button.

12. Enter the following T-SQL query into the Query Editor window:

```
SELECT *
FROM Person.Contact
WHERE ContactID=3;
```

13. Click the Execute button or press F5 to run the query.

14. In the Results tab, notice that the LastName is equal to Abercrombie-Stephens, indicating that the change made in SharePoint was actually made in the backend database.

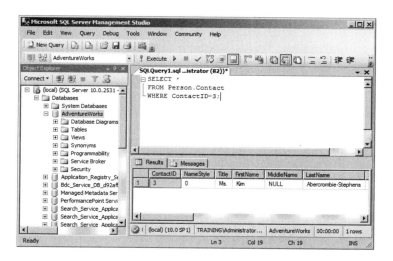

Planning an Excel Services Strategy

Excel Services is one of the most commonly used services in SharePoint Server 2010. It allows you to publish Excel 2010 workbooks on the SharePoint server so that users can access the workbooks from any location where a web browser is available. Excel Services includes three primary components:

- **Excel Calculation Services (ECS):** ECS is the Excel Services component that loads the workbook and calculates spreadsheets; it also loads external data and maintains state for users.

- **Excel Web Access (EWA):** EWA provides a web interface for delivering the Excel workbooks in a browser.

- **Excel Web Services (EWS):** EWS allows developers to build custom applications that draw data from the Excel workbooks.

The Excel Services components can reside on the WFE or on the backend application server. The Excel Services provide access to external data for Excel workbooks. The external data sources may be SQL Server databases or LOB application databases in other formats.

Because Excel workbooks used by Excel Services often access external data, authentication procedures must be considered. If you are implementing SharePoint Server 2010 in a Windows domain and all external data sources are on domain member servers, you can use Integrated Windows authentication and no further configuration will be required. If you are accessing external data sources outside of the domain, Microsoft recommends using the Secure Store Service to provide credentials for the authentication process.

The Excel Services SA has five configuration groups accessible from within Central Administration. These groups are shown in Figure 8.6.

FIGURE 8.6   The Excel Services configuration page

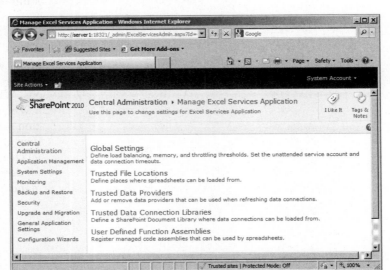

In the Global Settings group, you can configure basic settings such as load balancing, memory management, and throttling thresholds. The throttling thresholds are used to determine how long a connection to external data should remain active and how long items should remain in the cache.

The Trusted File Locations, Trusted Data Providers, and Trusted Data Connection Libraries allow you to control where Excel spreadsheets may be stored, the external data that can be used, and the document library used to store data connection information.

The final group, User Defined Function Assemblies, is used to register code with Excel Services that can be used within the spreadsheets. This code is custom developed and can be used to provide advanced analytical functions not included in the Excel Calculation Services.

Excel Services is up and running by default when you install SharePoint Server 2010. By default, Excel workbooks can be stored anywhere within your SharePoint organization. While this provides simplicity, you may consider changing the default settings to allow Excel workbooks to be stored only in defined sites or document libraries.

As you are planning your Excel Services strategy, consider the following important factors:

- Who will be accessing the services and working with Excel data?
- How many concurrent users will be accessing this data?
- How large will the Excel data sets be?

Asking "who" allows you to ensure that the right people have access to the data within SharePoint 2010. You may need to create special SharePoint groups for permission management or you may choose to use existing groups. Your decision will depend on whether the Excel Services users also have access to other information within the SharePoint sites.

The number of concurrent users becomes important because it impacts the performance of the server. Any process that involves number crunching is an intensive CPU and memory action, and Excel Services is all about number crunching. Make sure you plan for sufficient processor and memory resources based on the number of users who will access the server.

The final question is layered onto the answers to the previous two questions. When you know who needs access, you can ensure proper permissions are in place. When you know how many users will access the service, you know half of the information needed to effectively plan for resource availability. The other half is related to how they use the service. If large portions of Excel data must be processed or provided to Excel client applications, the server will require more resources than it would if only small data sets were accessed. Be sure to plan carefully so that the server can handle the demands placed on it.

Designing a Forms Strategy

SharePoint Server 2010 can provide dynamic forms for data modification. For example, when you create an external list and select to edit an item that is displayed in that list, the default form is a dynamic form. If these forms are sufficient for your needs, you will need to look no further; however, if you want to customize and brand the forms, you will need to use the InfoPath forms supported in the SharePoint product. The InfoPath Forms Services service provides the implementation of InfoPath browser-based forms in SharePoint Server 2010. The forms are created in InfoPath and published to the SharePoint Server.

InfoPath forms provide several advantages over the dynamic forms in SharePoint Server 2010. The advantages include custom data validation, a customized layout, and data connection flexibility.

Custom Data Validation   The dynamic form allows users to add any data values that will be accepted by the backend database. If you want to add an extra layer of protection or perhaps validations that are not included in the backend database, you can do it in the InfoPath form.

Customized Layout   The dynamic form is boring and bland like most dynamic forms. You can customize the layout with themes from InfoPath 2010 or by adding graphics such as logos and background images.

Data Connection Flexibility   The form can display important data related to the data that is included in the list. For example, you may want to display a read-only list of the three most recent orders on a customer's form page—even though the order data cannot be modified.

InfoPath Forms Services, configured in the General Application Settings section of Central Administration, allows users to access InfoPath forms through the web browser without installing InfoPath on their local machines.

InfoPath forms can be created through three basic processes:

- **SharePoint Designer 2010:** Generate the InfoPath form in the SharePoint Designer and then launch InfoPath to edit the form from within SharePoint Designer. This is a seamless solution for editing forms used by external lists based on ECTs.

- **InfoPath 2010:** Create new form templates in InfoPath 2010 and then upload them to a forms library. Users with InfoPath can access and use the forms from the library. This method works well for creating highly customized forms that take advantage of Data Connection Flexibility.

- **Direct Editing:** You can access a list within SharePoint 2010 and select to edit the forms in InfoPath. InfoPath will be launched, and the forms can be edited from here. This method works well for customizing the default forms in SharePoint.

Do not confuse InfoPath forms with forms-based authentication. *Forms-based authentication* is simply an authentication method that requires users to enter credentials rather than have the credentials pass through automatically. InfoPath forms provide a highly flexible method for developing and implementing forms for application and workflow processing.

Summary

In this chapter, you learned about an important new SharePoint concept: the service applications. You learned about the architecture of SAs and the different services available. You also learned more detailed information about Business Connectivity Services and performed exercises that allowed you to connect to and display external data. Next, you explored Excel Services and the considerations made during the planning of Excel Services deployment. Finally, you considered the features provided by InfoPath Services and the forms that can be provisioned through this service.

Exam Essentials

Determining service application server roles.   Be sure to understand the differences between the older Shared Services Provider and the new service applications. Understand the basic functionality of each SA and when it would be used.

Planning a Business Connectivity Services (BCS) strategy.   Make sure you know what the Business Connectivity Services is used for and that the Business Data Connectivity service is the engine that drives it. Know how to create an ECT and how to map an external list to it.

Planning an Excel Services strategy.   Understand the features offered by Excel Services and the three primary components that support it. Know the configuration options provided for Excel Services in Central Administration.

Designing a forms strategy.   Understand the difference between forms-based authentication of InfoPath Forms Services and dynamic forms. Know the different ways that you can create and edit InfoPath forms. Know the extra benefits InfoPath forms provide over the dynamic forms that are built into SharePoint Server 2010.

Chapter

9

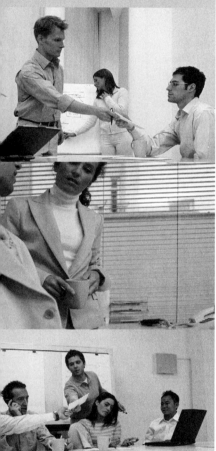

Planning a SharePoint Component Strategy

TOPICS COVERED IN THIS CHAPTER

✓ Designing Web Applications

✓ Designing Features and Solutions

✓ Understanding Parts

✓ Planning for Site Customizations

SharePoint Server 2010 is a complex product that can be customized and enhanced to accomplish many business-related tasks. For example, you can create new components through features and solutions so that SharePoint can perform completely new actions. You can also create custom web parts so that users can easily display important information on pages they create. Whether you are implementing custom features or simply tuning the web applications in which your SharePoint sites run, you must understand how to effectively plan for customizations so that your changes are both functional and manageable. They must be functional in that they perform the desired action. They must be manageable so that they can be easily maintained through modifications and upgrades to newer versions of SharePoint in the future. This chapter provides you with the information you need to plan and implement SharePoint components.

If you are preparing for the Microsoft MCITP 70-668 exam, you will learn about important exam topics in this chapter. Provisioning strategies for web applications are presented and the SharePoint component strategies are provided for proper component design and deployment planning.

Designing Web Applications

Designing and implementing web applications includes several concepts. First, you have to understand application pools, which are a feature of Internet Information Services (IIS), and the role they play in SharePoint web application management and configuration. Second, you have to understand the options available for web application implementation within the application pools. Third, you should understand web application policies from two perspectives: applied policies for security provisioning and logical policies for web application provisioning guidelines. Finally, you will need to understand the configurable features that may be used by sites within web applications, such as Microsoft .NET Frameworks and Microsoft Silverlight.

Understanding Application Pools

SharePoint Server 2010 uses IIS as the web server that provides access to the SharePoint sites. An IIS website runs in an IIS application pool. An application pool is really just a process or set of processes in which the website may run. Technically, Microsoft calls these processes *worker processes*. Stated as a whole, an application pool is a group of websites or URLs that are serviced by a set of worker processes. In IIS, a web directory or virtual directory may be linked to an application pool. Multiple web directories or virtual directories may be linked to a single application pool.

Application pools may be created in IIS Manager or within SharePoint Central Administration. If you create an application pool in the IIS Manager for use with SharePoint, you must assign an identity to use for logon. If you create the application pool from within SharePoint Central Administration, the identity is configured automatically. Exercise 9.1 provides instructions for creating an application pool in the IIS Manager and configuring the logon identity.

EXERCISE 9.1

Creating a New Application Pool

In this exercise, you will create a new application pool named IT-Site using the ISS Manager. You will configure the IT-Site application pool to use a valid username and password for the logon identity.

1. Click Start ➢ Administrative Tools ➢ Internet Information Services (IIS) Manager to launch the IIS Manager on your web server.

2. In the Connections panel, expand the node for the server on which you want to create the new application pool.

3. Click the Application Pools node on the expanded server.

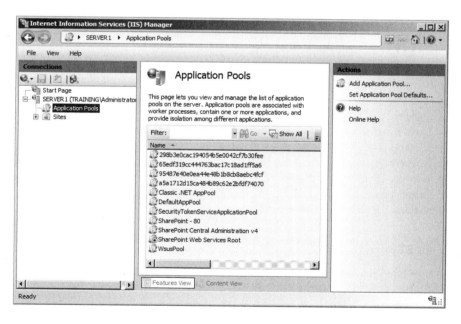

4. Click the Add Application Pool link in the Actions panel.

5. In the Add Application Pool dialog, enter the value **IT-Site** in the Name field, accept all other default settings, and click OK to create the new application pool.

6. Click on the new IT-Site application pool in the Application Pools list and then click the Advanced Settings link in the Actions panel.

7. In the Process Model section, click in the Identity field and then click the button to the right of the field to define the identity to use for logon.

8. Select the Custom Account option and then click the Set button.

9. Enter a valid username (typically an administrative user) and password. Confirm the password and then click OK.

As you performed Exercise 9.1, you probably noticed that you can configure only three settings, in addition to the application pool name, during the creation of an application pool. The first of the three additional settings is the .NET Framework version. If you have multiple versions installed on the server, you can choose from those available versions of the .NET Framework. If you are using third-party SharePoint code, check the literature from your application vendor to ensure that you are enabling support for the appropriate .NET Framework version.

The second setting is the managed pipeline mode, which can either be set to Integrated or Classic. When set to Integrated, the newer and more efficient request-processing pipeline is used. When set to Classic, requests for managed content are processed with the separate IIS and ASP.NET request-processing pipelines. Integrated pipeline mode is more efficient because one process handles standard web requests for HTML documents, images, and so on, as well as the ASP.NET requests. Classic pipeline mode requires two different processes to perform the same function and is, therefore, less efficient.

The third and final setting is the startup mode, which reads "Start application pool immediately" in the configuration dialog box. If this option is enabled, the application pool and the websites that it provides will be started automatically when the server boots. If it is disabled, you will be required to manually start the application pool or start it with some other scheduled task or trigger.

After creating an application pool, you can adjust several settings in addition to the four settings configured during creation. The settings configured during pool creation, such as the .NET Framework version and the managed pipeline mode, can be modified in the Basic

Settings of the application pool. Additional settings can be configured in the Advanced Settings of the application pool by selecting the pool and then clicking the Advanced Settings link in the Actions panel. Table 9.1 lists important configuration settings available in the Advanced Settings for application pools and their descriptions.

TABLE 9.1   Application Pool Advanced Settings in IIS Manager

Advanced Setting Name	Description
.NET Framework Version	This setting specifies the version of the .NET Framework used by the site. If set to No Managed code, ASP .NET requests will fail.
Enable 32-Bit Applications	If set to true, this setting requires that the application pool's worker processes run in WOW64 for 32-bit virtualization. This setting may be required for older system components that were not designed for 64-bit operating systems; however, it should be used with caution as stability problems may occur.
Queue Length	This defines the number of allowed HTTP requests to be queued by HTTP.sys before error 503 "Service Unavailable" responses will be generated. When considering this setting, remember that a single page can potentially require dozens of HTTP requests to be downloaded. A value of 1000 or greater is recommended.
CPU Limit Settings	The application pool can be throttled through the configuration of CPU limit settings. These settings are more powerful than the Resource Throttling settings within SharePoint Central Administration as they allow you to control the CPU cycles consumed by the application pool.
Processor Affinity Enabled	This setting allows you to assign the application pool to a specified CPU or CPU core.
Rapid-Fail Protection Settings	These settings are configured to allow the application pool to be reset if a specified number of worker process crashes or failures (Maximum Failures) occur within a given time period (Failure Interval).
Recycling: Regular Time Interval (minutes)	This setting allows the application pool to be reset at a regular time interval specified in minutes.
Recycling: Private Memory Limit (KB)	This setting allows the application pool to be reset when the memory consumed by the worker processes is equal to the Private Memory Limit setting.
Recycling: Request Limit	This setting allows the application pool to be reset when the pool has serviced a specified number of requests.
Recycling: Specific Times	This setting allows the application pool to be reset at specified times during the day.

Real World Scenario

If All Else Fails, Reboot

You may have heard the old saying, "If something stops working, try rebooting." The truth is that this action often does solve the problem. Many applications are problematic and a reboot can fix the problem. However, it's simply not reasonable to reboot your servers every day. In many organizations, servers need to be operational 24/7. This demand means that another solution is needed. I had to solve this problem for a client recently.

A client was running an IIS website (in this case, it was not a SharePoint site), and the website would stop working after about three days of operation. On a good week, it might last four days, but it would eventually have to be restarted. The problem seemed to be a memory leak that continued to consume more and more memory over time.

The website administrator was manually restarting the IIS service each time the website failed. Because the IIS server ran multiple websites, the administrator's action caused all websites to be unavailable until the IIS service had completely restarted. A better solution would have been to restart only the application pool that ran the troublesome website. The only problem was that all of the websites were in a single application pool.

We simply created a new application pool and pointed the troublesome website to this new pool. We then configured the application pool to recycle every day at 1:00 AM. This was a good time because the website was used only by internal employees and the company was a single-shift company—meaning that no employees worked during the night.

Would it have been better to fix the stability problem? Absolutely. However, the website was running a custom-built ASP.NET application that was outside of the organization's control. They had no access to source code and no knowledge of how to locate and fix the problem even if they had the code. Creating a separate application pool and then configuring an automatic recycle was an excellent solution in this case.

You may find similar situations where the IIS application pool recycle feature can benefit you. Remember, you can recycle an application pool automatically on a time schedule, at a time interval, after a specified number of requests, or when a specified amount of memory is consumed. These options provide you with exceptional flexibility when configuring application pool recycling.

Application pools run in the w3wp.exe process. If you open the Windows Task Manager (press Ctrl+Shift+Esc as a shortcut) and select the Processes tab, you will see the w3wp.exe process, as shown in Figure 9.1.

FIGURE 9.1   Viewing w3wp.exe processes in Windows Task Manager

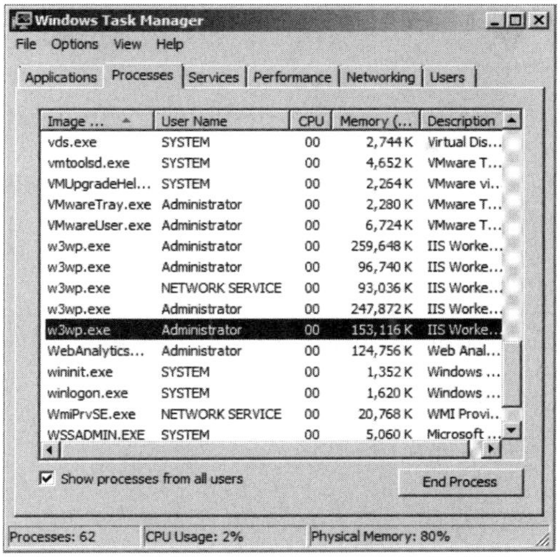

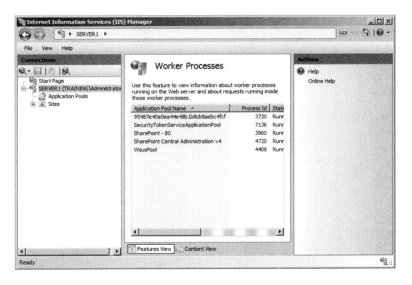

The Windows Task Manager does not link the w3wp.exe processes to the application pools in IIS. If you need to determine the application pool associated with a specific instance of w3wp.exe, you will need to use the IIS Manager and the Windows Task Manager together. Within the IIS Manager, in the Connections panel, click on the root server node. In the center panel, double-click on Worker Processes. You will see a screen similar to the one in Figure 9.2.

FIGURE 9.2   Viewing worker processes mapped to process IDs in IIS Manager

To see the CPU utilization and memory consumption of the associated w3wp.exe process, simply note the process ID in the IIS Manager Worker Processes view (as shown in Figure 9.2)

and then open the Windows Task Manager again. Select the Processes tab and then choose the View menu and the Select columns option. Add the PID (Process Identifier) column by checking the box next to it and click OK. You will see results similar to those in Figure 9.3.

FIGURE 9.3 Viewing the w3wp.exe processes with the PIDs displayed in Windows Task Manager

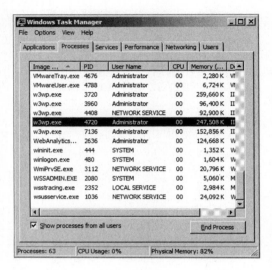

 When creating application pools manually, instead of within the Central Administration interface, you must specify an identity for the application pool as demonstrated in steps 6 through 9 of Exercise 9.1. If you do not do this, you will receive a "missing SID" error when you attempt to create a web application in the existing application pool.

Working with Web Applications

SharePoint references application pools as web applications, or web apps for short. From within SharePoint Central Administration, you can configure application pool settings that are specific to SharePoint Server 2010 and the way it uses the application pools. Because these settings are often unique to SharePoint, Microsoft uses the phrase *web application* to reference both the application pool and the settings configured for SharePoint. Simply defined, a web app is a collection of settings for SharePoint applications and the application pool to which these settings apply.

Web applications are created and managed from SharePoint 2010 Central Administration. The Application Management section provides access to the Web Applications group. In this group, two subsections may be accessed. The first is Manage Web Applications, and it is used to create new web applications and manage the settings for existing web applications. The second subsection is named Configure Alternate Access

Mappings, and it is used to configure the paths into the web application. For example, a web application can be configured for the internal URL of http://server1:24959, and it can be configured for the Internet URL of http://server1.company.com.

In Exercise 9.2, you will create a new web application that utilizes the application pool created in Exercise 9.1. The web application will be named IT-Site.

EXERCISE 9.2

Creating a New Web Application

In Exercise 9.1, you created a new application pool named IT-Site. In this exercise, you will use SharePoint Central Administration to create a new web application within this application pool.

1. Launch Central Administration.

2. Click the Application Management link in the Central Administration navigation panel on the left side of the Central Administration home page.

3. In the Web Application group, click the Manage Web Applications link.

4. On the Web Applications tab of the Ribbon, click the New button to create a new web application.

5. In the IIS Web Site settings section, enter the value **IT-Site** instead of using the default SharePoint port number for the Create A New IIS Web Site Name field.

6. The main point of this exercise is to see how you can configure a web application to use an existing application pool, such as the one created in Exercise 9.1. For this reason, scroll down on the Create New Web Application screen until you see the Application Pool section.

7. In the Application Pool section, choose the option that reads Use Existing Application Pool. From the drop-down list, select the IT-Site() application pool.

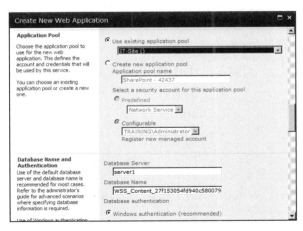

8. Scroll down on the Create New Web Application screen until you see the OK and Cancel buttons, and then click the OK button to create the new web application.

In addition to application pool assignment, you can configure several options for a web application during or after creation. These options include:

Authentication Mode   The authentication mode can be configured to either Classic Mode Authentication (CMA) or Claims Based Authentication (CBA). CBA is the newer authentication model and is preferred for new SharePoint sites; however, CMA is still commonly used for the migration of existing SharePoint sites or the installation of third-party SharePoint add-ons that are not compatible with CBA.

IIS Web Site Settings   The IIS Web Site Settings section allows you to define the name for the website, configure the TCP port used, specify the host header, and configure the storage path for the site. The name for the website should not be confused with the public URL. The public URL is that which is used to access the sites within the web application through a web browser. The name for the website is displayed in the IIS Manager.

The TCP port defines the port used to access the web application sites. The default port for HTTP is 80; however, only one service can respond to that port on a given IP address. By allowing multiple ports, a single server can host several SharePoint web applications and, therefore, websites.

The host header setting allows you to take advantage of a special feature of IIS. With this feature, for example, you can configure IIS to automatically service up the website at `http://10.10.10.85:30456` when a user navigates to `http://marketing.comany.local`. The value `marketing.company.local` would be entered in the host header setting for the web application. This configuration means that users are not required to remember the long IP/TCP port combination address of `10.10.10.85:30456`. In addition to configuring this setting, you must add a DNS entry for `marketing.company.local` to point to the `10.10.10.85` address. IIS will work its magic and understands that it should serve up the site at port 30456.

The path is simply the location where the web application sites will be stored. You may accept the default location or direct the files to be stored at an alternative drive or folder.

Security Configuration Settings   In the Security Configuration Settings section, you can define the authentication provider and determine if anonymous access will be allowed or not. If anonymous access is allowed, you should configure the Anonymous Policy after the web application is created. You can also specify that SSL is required for access to the site. This would demand that users access the site using the `https://` prefix instead of the `http://` prefix.

Public URL   The public URL provides a mapping used by visitors for access to the SharePoint web application. This URL will be the root or beginning of the sites within the site collection and web application.

In addition to the URL, you can select the zone to use for the URL. The zone maps an authentication scheme to the URL used to access the SharePoint 2010 web application.

Multiple zones can be created later by using the Extend button on the Ribbon for a given web application. From there, you can choose to use the Intranet, Internet, Custom, or Extranet zones. When creating a new web application, you can use the only default zone.

Database Name and Authentication   These settings allow you to define the database server and database used for content storage. You can also specify either Windows authentication or SQL Login-based authentication for access to the database. Windows authentication is recommended because it is more secure.

Failover Server   If you are using SQL Server database mirroring, you can configure the web application to failover to the mirror instance of the database in the primary database server or the database fails.

Service Application Connections   These settings allow you to choose the default group of service applications or create a custom group for your needs. When creating a custom group, you can choose only the service applications required of the site collections and sites that will function within the web application.

Web Application Policies

Two types of web application policies must be considered. The first type is built-in policy provisioning through web application policies. These policies allow you to configure permissions for authenticated and anonymous users. They also allow you to create custom permission levels. The second type is the organizational policies that control how content may be provisioned within SharePoint. These policies are logical and, hopefully, written down, but they are not directly enforced within SharePoint itself. Organizational policies are enforced through management procedures.

In this section, both web application policies will be addressed. First, you will learn about built-in policy provisioning with web application policies. Then you will learn about the organizational policies that impact your web application provisioning.

Security Provisioning Through Web Application Policies

Three web application policies are available in Central Administration. The first is the User Policy, which provides permissions for authenticated users. The second is the Anonymous Policy, which determines permissions for anonymous users accessing the sites within the web application. The third is the Permission Policy, which can be used to create custom permission levels.

In Exercise 9.3, you will create a User Policy for the IT-Site web application. The policy will define permissions for a user named Tom throughout the entire site collection hierarchy but will default in the web application. You can substitute the user named Tom with any other user for whom you want to create a User Policy.

EXERCISE 9.3

Creating a User Policy

In this exercise, you will create a new User Policy for the IT-Site Web application created in Exercise 9.2. To complete this exercise, you must have already completed Exercise 9.1 and Exercise 9.2.

1. Launch Central Administration.

2. Click the Application Management link in the Central Administration navigation panel.

3. In the Web Applications group, click the Manage Web Applications link.

4. Click on the IT-Site web application to select it.

5. In the Ribbon, click the User Policy button within the Policy group.

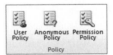

6. In the Policy for Web Application screen, click the Add Users link to add a new user to the list.

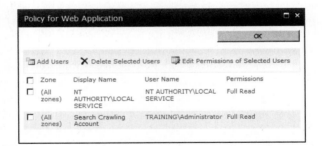

7. If you want to limit or configure the permissions for this user in a specific zone and the web application has been extended to multiple zones, choose the zone in the Select the Zone screen. Otherwise, accept the default of All Zones and click Next.

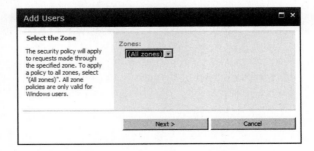

8. On the Add Users screen in the Choose Users section, enter the usernames for the users to whom you want this policy to apply. In this example, the name Tom Carpenter is added and the Check Names button is used to validate the user.

9. In the Choose Permissions section, select the permission level to apply to this user. In this example, Tom is being granted Full Control.

10. If you want this user account to be able to act as the operating system (i.e., perform actions in the context of the system account), choose this option in the Choose System Settings section. In this example, the Account Operates As System option will be disabled.

11. Click Finish to create the User Policy.

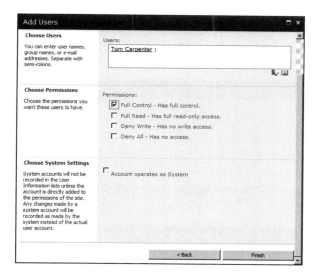

12. Click OK to close the Policy for Web Application screen.

The next Web Application Policy requiring your attention is the Anonymous Policy. If you did not enable anonymous access during the creation of the web application, you will have to first enable anonymous access before creating the policy. In Exercise 9.4, you will enable anonymous access for the IT-Site web application and then configure an Anonymous Policy.

EXERCISE 9.4

Configuring the Anonymous Policy

In this exercise, you will configure the Anonymous Policy for the IT-Site web application. To complete this exercise, you must have first completed Exercise 9.1 and Exercise 9.2.

1. Launch Central Administration.

2. Click the Application Management link in the Central Administration navigation panel.

EXERCISE 9.4 *(continued)*

3. In the Web Applications group, click the Manage Web Applications link.

4. Click on the IT-Site web application to select it.

5. To enable anonymous access to the web application, on the Ribbon, click the Authentication Providers button in the Security group.

6. In the Authentication Providers screen, click the zone for which you want to enable anonymous access. In this example, the Default zone should be clicked.

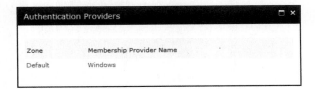

7. In the Anonymous Access section, check the Enable Anonymous Access option to enable it.

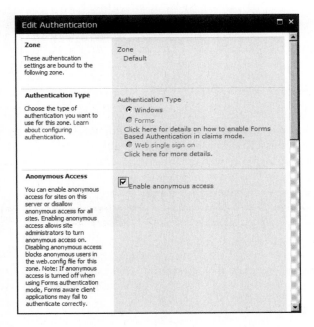

8. If necessary, scroll down in the Edit Authentication screen until you see the Save and Cancel buttons. Click Save to save your changes and enable anonymous access. Be patient, the changes can take a few moments to process.

9. Close the Authentication Providers screen by clicking the X in the upper-right corner.

10. With the IT-Site web application still selected in the Web Applications list, on the Ribbon, click the Anonymous Policy button in the Policy group.

11. In the Anonymous Access Restrictions screen, in the Select the Zone section, choose either All Zones or the specific zone you want to configure. In this example, All Zones will be configured.

12. In the Permissions section, choose the level of anonymous access to allow. In this example, Deny Write will be used. This will allow anonymous access to the site, but changes cannot be made by anonymous users.

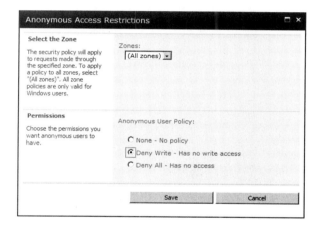

13. Click Save to create and save the policy.

This remaining web application policy is the Permission Policy. It is used to create custom permission levels for user policies and for permission assignments throughout the hierarchy of the SharePoint web application sites. In Exercise 9.5, you will create a new permission level policy in the IT-Site web application.

EXERCISE 9.5

Creating a New Permission Policy Level

In this exercise, you will create a new Permission Policy level for the IT-Site web application. To complete this exercise, you must have first completed Exercise 9.1 and Exercise 9.2.

1. Launch Central Administration.

EXERCISE 9.5 *(continued)*

2. Click the Application Management link in the Central Administration navigation panel.

3. In the Web Applications group, click the Manage Web Applications link.

4. Click on the IT-Site web application to select it.

5. On the Ribbon, in the Policy group, click the Permission Policy button.

6. In the Manage Permission Policy Levels screen, notice that the existing policies match those that were available when you created a User Policy in Exercise 9.3.

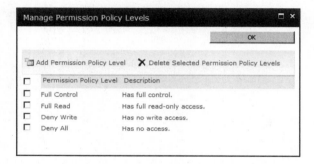

7. Click the Add Permission Policy Level link to create a new policy.

8. On the Add Permission Policy Level screen, enter **List Administrators** in the Name And Description section for the Name field.

9. In the Site Collection Permissions section, select the Site Collection Administrator so that you can grant permissions to lists in the Permissions section. Because you cannot grant Full Control without granting Full Read permissions, Site Collection Auditor is also selected automatically.

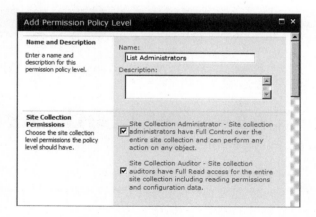

10. Scroll down to the Permissions section. In the list of permissions, select the Grant column check box for each of the List Permissions, but do not select any permissions for the Site Permissions or the Personal Permissions. In this case, if users are granted access within these latter two subcategories, it will be through other Permission Policy levels.

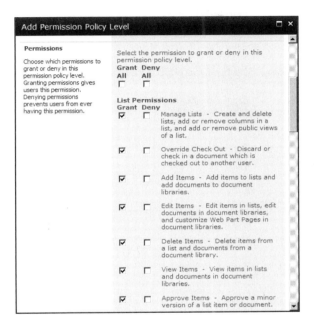

11. Scroll down to the bottom of the page and click Save to create the new permission-level policy.

12. The new policy will appear in the list on the Manage Permission Policy Levels screen.

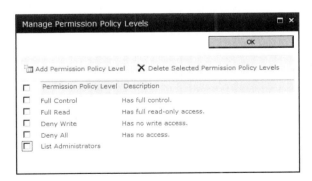

Now that you have created a new Permission Policy level, you can use it when creating user policies for the web application. When you click the User Policy button in Web Application Management and then click the username, you will see your new custom Permission Policy level, as shown in Figure 9.4. The List Administrators permission has a hyphen after it, but no explanation. This is because a description was not added when the permission was created.

FIGURE 9.4   Creating a new User Policy after creating a custom Permission Policy level

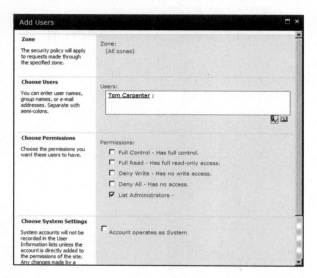

Organizational Policies for Provisioning Web Applications

Organizational policies, also known as guideline policies, are used to document and control how web applications and websites are provisioned within your environment. When a new web application is created, a logical entity is created on the network that can be accessed and manipulated through the network. This entity can introduce security, performance, and manageability concerns. This is why it is important to have organizational policies that dictate who can create web applications, how they should be created, and what security controls that should be enforced.

The first question you must answer is, Who can create web applications? You want to ensure that web applications are created in compliance with your organization's security policies. Because of such demands, most organizations will limit web application creation activities to a small group of core SharePoint and IIS server administrators. Such limitations will provide accountability and improved probability of compliance with application creation procedures.

Next, you must decide how the web applications should be created. You really have two options here. The first option is to create the application pool in the IIS Manager and then create the web application in SharePoint 2010 Central Administration. The second option is to do both from within SharePoint 2010.

The only real reason to use the first option is because you have separation of duties between the IIS web server managers and the SharePoint application managers. If the SharePoint administrators do not have the proper permissions to create application pools within IIS, you will have to separate the process into two phases. In the first phase, the IIS administrators will create the application pool with the proper identity for logon. In the second phase, the SharePoint administrators will create the SharePoint web application that connects to the IIS application pool.

In production environments, it is rare to implement security restrictions that prohibit a SharePoint administrator from creating and working with IIS application pools. For this reason, the second option of creating the web application and the application pool at the same time is the most common procedure.

Finally, you must determine the security controls that should be enforced. Consider that an application pool and a SharePoint web application using that pool act as a service running on the network. Any time you run an additional service on the network, you increase the size of the attack surface of that network. Stated differently, you introduce a new attack point that must be monitored, maintained, and secured. The web application must be created with security in mind so that the security of your entire system is not compromised.

 Remember that web applications do not equal websites. The website runs in the web application. Because of this hierarchy, you can allow only administrators to create web applications, while users can be given the option of self-provisioning for collaboration sites that run within the web application.

SharePoint Features Used by Websites and Web Applications

The term *features* can get confusing very quickly in relation to SharePoint 2010. A *feature* of SharePoint is a capability that the product offers. However, you can also create a *feature* that manipulates the SharePoint installation in some way. (Such features are discussed in the next section titled "Designing Features and Solutions.") In this section, you will learn about .NET and Microsoft Silverlight, two important features of SharePoint that are often used by websites and web applications.

SharePoint Server 2010 requires .NET version 3.5 with SP1 to be installed on the Windows server that runs the SharePoint application. If you are running Windows Server

2008, you will have to download the .NET update to install it on the server. If you are running Windows Server 2008 R2, it can be added in the Server Manager using the Add Features option.

In addition to ensuring that the proper version of .NET is installed on the server, you can optionally configure various .NET settings. When configuring an application pool in the IIS Manager, you can optionally set the application pool to use No Managed Code. If you set the SharePoint application pools to this No Managed Code setting, you will receive an error when attempting to access the site. The error will be a simple 403 "Forbidden" error, but the cause is the fact that .NET is not enabled and the server, therefore, does not know how to process the SharePoint code within the files included on the site. Simply change the application pool back to using .NET again and the site should work properly.

If you disable .NET in an application pool, the disabling will happen immediately. If you later enable .NET in that application pool, you will have to recycle the application pool for the change to take effect. Simply right-click on the application pool and select Recycle to resolve this issue.

Other than enabling and disabling .NET for your application pools, which you really shouldn't do on production SharePoint servers, the only other .NET action an administrator is required to perform is updating the runtime environment. From time to time security vulnerabilities and other problems may be detected in the .NET environment, and you should update your servers as needed. Always be sure to test .NET updates in a lab environment first, as changes to the .NET runtime could potentially cause problems for custom SharePoint applications.

The group that will use the .NET runtime environment the most is the developer group. If your organization plans to customize SharePoint extensively, it is very likely that some development work will be performed in Visual Studio 2010. But that work is for the programmers, and it is not something an administrator should have to perform very often.

Another important feature used by SharePoint sites is the Microsoft Silverlight component. Microsoft Silverlight is Microsoft's competing product to the Adobe Flash animation and application development interface. In SharePoint Server 2010, the Microsoft Silverlight component provides a rich interface when working with websites and even Central Administration.

Figure 9.5 shows the screen used to create a new site within a site collection when Silverlight is enabled. Compare this to Figure 9.6, which shows the same screen when Silverlight is disabled. If you are familiar with SharePoint Server 2007, you will recognize the screen in Figure 9.6 as similar to the one available in that version. The new Silverlight screens in SharePoint Server 2010 are richer and more intuitive, and Silverlight should be enabled to take advantage of this improved interface.

FIGURE 9.5   Adding a new site with Silverlight enabled

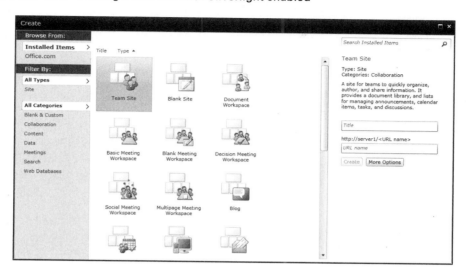

FIGURE 9.6   Adding a new site with Silverlight disabled

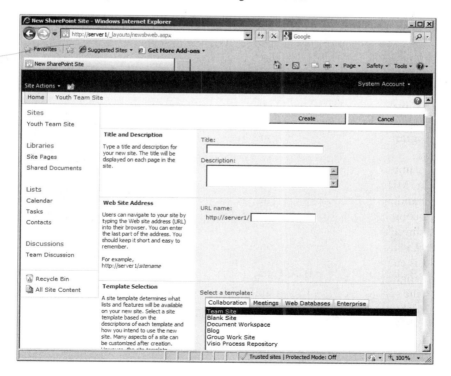

If you skip around in books as you read them, you should know that Chapter 1, "Planning the Logical Architecture," contains a more exhaustive list of features in the SharePoint 2010 product lines.

Designing Features and Solutions

SharePoint features and solutions are important to the SharePoint administrator. The administrator's role involves the installation of the features and solutions, as well as the activation and deactivation of these items. In this section, you will explore features, which are a type of solution in SharePoint Server 2010. You will then explore the options developers have for solution creation.

Features are really a subset of the object type known as a solution. A *feature* is a specific type of solution that is used to modify the SharePoint installation in some way. For example, you may use a feature to enable or disable a function in SharePoint. By bundling the action of enabling or disabling the function into a feature, you make it easier for beginning administrators to accomplish a task. Instead of going through several screens to enable and configure a function within SharePoint 2010, the beginning administrator can simply activate a feature that you have created, and it will take care of enabling the function and configuring it the way that you have specified in the feature.

After the discussion of features, this section will move on to the more general topic of *solutions*. SharePoint solutions can be features, but not all solutions are features. Many solutions are completely customized applications that work within the SharePoint architecture. For example, you can develop a web-based application that interacts with SharePoint lists and libraries but also adds functionality that is not included in SharePoint 2010. This would be an example of a SharePoint solution.

 Do not confuse the features discussed in this section with the concept of capabilities within the SharePoint product line. The features discussed here are used to enable and configure the capabilities of SharePoint. For more information on the capabilities of SharePoint including .NET and Silverlight, see the preceding section as well as Chapter 1.

Understanding Features

Features are SharePoint solutions or components that are used to manipulate the SharePoint installation. Features can be used to add functionality to farms, web applications, site collections, and individual sites. You can think of a feature as a deployment unit for SharePoint. The feature is used to deploy changes to the SharePoint environment.

Features are based on XML. Simple features will be implemented using XML code alone; more complex features may also require triggered .NET code execution at the time of installation, activation, deactivation, or uninstallation. The addition of triggered .NET code allows for increased flexibility and nearly limitless capabilities through the use of features.

Features are used for many configuration options, including:

- Modifying the user interface in SharePoint Server 2010

- Installing files onto the SharePoint server through libraries

- Defining and customizing site elements, such as columns, content types, and lists

- Creating and defining workflows

- Applying properties to various components

Features are installed in the SharePoint folder `{web extensions folder}\14\Template\Features`, where `{web extensions folder}` is equal to the Microsoft Shared folder location. This location defaults to `C:\Program Files\Common Files\Microsoft Shared\Web Server Extensions`. Within the Features subfolder are several additional folders. The feature name is derived from the folder name. For example, Figure 9.7 shows the folder displayed with the feature named Navigation highlighted.

FIGURE 9.7   Viewing the Features folder in a SharePoint 2010 server

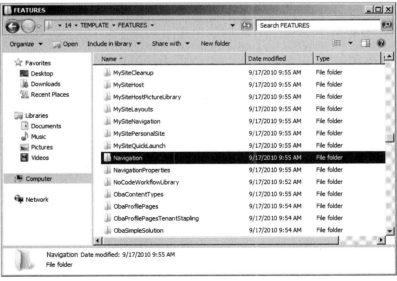

Figure 9.8 shows the Navigation folder expanded. Two files are displayed: `Feature.xml` and `NavigationSiteSettings.xml`. More complex features may include more files and even additional subfolders.

FIGURE 9.8   Viewing the contents of the Navigation feature

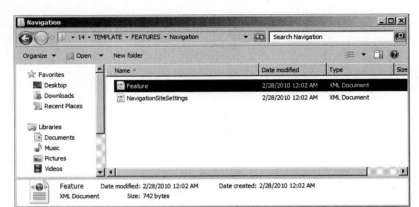

The Feature.xml file is required for all features. It specifies the globally unique identifier (GUID) for the feature, the display description, the version, and the name of the manifest file or files that actually do the work of the feature. Figure 9.9 shows the Feature.xml file for the Navigation feature displayed in Notepad. The Feature.xml file is a very simple file, but you will need to be aware of one important fact: the GUID must be unique for each feature. You cannot simply make up a GUID; you will need to generate one from the Visual Studio 2010 toolset. In Figure 9.9, the ID value represents the GUID for this feature.

FIGURE 9.9   Viewing the Feature.xml file contents in Notepad

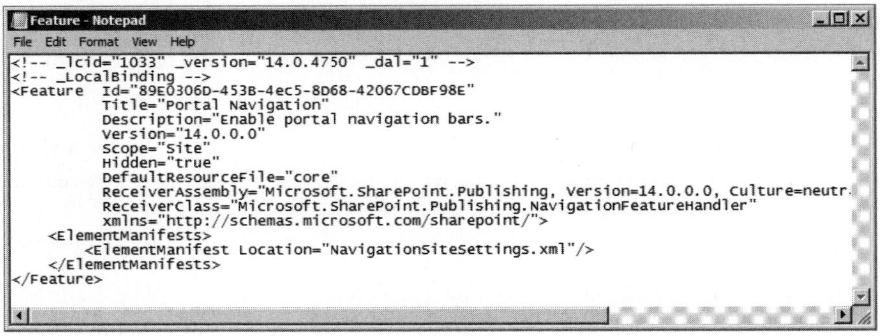

```
<!-- _lcid="1033" _version="14.0.4750" _dal="1" -->
<!-- _LocalBinding -->
<Feature   Id="89E0306D-453B-4ec5-8D68-42067CDBF98E"
           Title="Portal Navigation"
           Description="Enable portal navigation bars."
           version="14.0.0.0"
           Scope="Site"
           Hidden="true"
           DefaultResourceFile="core"
           ReceiverAssembly="Microsoft.SharePoint.Publishing, Version=14.0.0.0, Culture=neutr.
           ReceiverClass="Microsoft.SharePoint.Publishing.NavigationFeatureHandler"
           xmlns="http://schemas.microsoft.com/sharepoint/">
    <ElementManifests>
        <ElementManifest Location="NavigationSiteSettings.xml"/>
    </ElementManifests>
</Feature>
```

As an administrator, you may never have to create a feature. However, if you do software development as well as administration, you may be required to do so. The simplest way to create features is with the Visual Studio 2010 development tools. Visual Studio 2010 includes support for syntactical highlighting and code completion for feature development. This means you do not have to remember all of the elements required in the XML files. Visual Studio 2010 will help you during the development.

From a purely administrative perspective, you will need to know the basic process used to add a feature to a SharePoint installation. You might think that you would install a feature by placing it in the Features folder on the SharePoint server; however, the process is not quite so simple. You have to inform SharePoint of the feature's existence. The basic process is as follows:

1. Install the feature by doing one of the following.
   - Use a web solution package (WSP) generated in Visual Studio.
   - Use the `stsadm` tool from the command line.
   - Use the SharePoint Management Shell Install-SPFeature cmdlet.
2. Activate the feature by doing one of the following.
   - Use the site settings in a browser.
   - Use the `stsadm` tool from the command line.
   - Use the SharePoint Management Shell Enable-SPFeature cmdlet.

If you choose to use the `stsadm` tool for these tasks, you will need to either add it to the system path or navigate to the folder that contains the tool. It is located, by default, in the `C:\Program Files\Common Files\Microsoft Shared\Web Server Extensions\14\BIN` folder. The `stsadm` tool is used with the -o switch to install and activate features. The `InstallFeature` and `ActivateFeature` subcommands are used.

The preferred method is to use the new SharePoint Management Shell, which is a PowerShell command-line environment. The Install-SPFeature cmdlet is very easy to use. For example, if you have a feature in the Features folder with a subfolder named MyCustomColumn, you would execute the following command to install the feature:

```
Install-SPFeature MyCustomColumn
```

Once the feature is installed, you would execute the following command to enable the feature for a site located at `http://server1/site/mycustomsite`:

```
Enable-SPFeature MyCustomColumn -Url http://server1/site/mycustomsite
```

Features can be scoped to the farm, a web application, a site collection, or a site within the site collection. Farm features impact the entire farm, and web application features apply to all site collections within the application scope.

Developing SharePoint Solutions

Solutions based on SharePoint Server 2010 can be developed faster and with more flexibility than for any previous version of SharePoint Server. Visual Studio can be used to build, package, and deploy SharePoint 2010 solutions. The powerful APIs in SharePoint allow you to easily create rich Internet applications that interact with SharePoint lists and libraries. The Language Integrated Query (LINQ) language is also supported for intuitive interactions with SharePoint components.

Covering Visual Studio, SharePoint APIs, and LINQ in substantial detail is outside the scope of this book. For more detailed information on programming and SharePoint, see *Professional SharePoint 2010 Development* (Wrox, 2010).

Visual Studio 2010 has complete integration with SharePoint. When a developer creates a new project in Visual Studio 2010, she can select from a large number of project types based on the Visual C# language or other languages. As a SharePoint Server 2010 administrator, you will not be required to build custom SharePoint solutions; however, you should be aware of what they are and the tools developers use to create them. The following list provides a reference to the different SharePoint-related project types available to the developer:

- Empty SharePoint Project
- Visual Web Part
- Sequential Workflow
- State Machine Workflow
- Business Data Connectivity Model
- Event Receiver
- List Definition
- Content Type
- Module
- Site Definition
- Import Reusable Workflow
- Import SharePoint Solution Package

In addition to the support for varied SharePoint project types, Visual Studio provides the tools required to build SharePoint features, as discussed in the preceding section. These features include the GUID generator and support for syntactical highlighting based on the XML Schema for SharePoint features.

If you wear multiple hats and also work as a SharePoint developer, you should know that Visual Studio will list C# as the language for all SharePoint project templates even though many of them are based primarily on XML, such as features.

After the developer is finished creating a solution, Visual Studio can automatically package and deploy the solution to your SharePoint farm. The developer may select to package the solution, which will create a web solution package (WSP) file. This file can then be imported into SharePoint. If the developer selects to deploy the solution, it will be packaged and imported into SharePoint automatically.

The WSP file is really a CAB file. You may be familiar with the CAB file that has been used in Microsoft technologies dating back to Windows 95 in the mid-90s. The CAB file is an archive file format that allows for the storage of multiple files within one archive file for simpler distribution. The WSP extension is used with solutions to clearly distinguish them from other non-SharePoint CAB files.

Solutions are stored in the solution store. The solution store is a centralized collection of SharePoint solutions used by the entire server farm. Solutions can be added to the solution store using the SharePoint Management Shell. The Central Administration interface can be used to remove a solution, but it cannot be used to add a solution.

Understanding Web Parts

SharePoint Server 2010 continues the tradition of using web parts from previous versions of the product. Web parts allow you to quickly add capabilities and contents to a web page created within a SharePoint site. Custom web parts can be developed by programmers, but the built-in web parts meet the needs of many organizations.

SharePoint Server 2010 comes with several web parts out of the box. The most common web parts used are those in the Lists and Libraries category. Following are the common web parts in the Lists and Libraries category and their capabilities:

- **Announcements:** Used to track events, status updates, and team news
- **Calendar:** Used to provide calendar views of events and schedules
- **Contacts:** Used to track contact information
- **Customized Reports:** Used to create Web Analytics custom reports
- **Form Templates:** Used to create forms from form templates activated for the site collection
- **Links:** Used to add hyperlinks to web pages or locations within your SharePoint sites
- **Shared Documents:** Used to create a document library reference for document sharing
- **Site Assets:** Used to create a library for storage of images, media, and other files that may be used on other pages within the site
- **Site Pages:** Used to create a library for storage of site pages
- **Tasks:** Used to track work that the team needs to complete
- **Team Discussion:** Used to create a discussion forum for the team

In addition to the Lists and Libraries web parts, SharePoint Server 2010 includes web parts in nine other categories, which are

- Business Data
- Content Rollup

- Filters
- Forms
- Media and Content
- Outlook Web App
- Search
- Social Collaboration
- SQL Server Reporting

In addition to the built-in web parts, you can add new web parts through web solution packages. Web parts can be added in several ways. You can upload a web part during the editing of a page. You can also create web parts in the Visual Studio 2010 environment, and package and deploy them into the SharePoint server. By default, custom web parts will be displayed in the Miscellaneous category. The Miscellaneous category will not exist until a custom web part has been added to the site collection.

 Creating custom web parts is beyond the scope of this administration book; however, understanding the basic steps involved in web-part creation will be helpful so that you can work with developers. Microsoft provides an excellent training program free at http://msdn.microsoft.com/en-us/sharepoint/ee513147.aspx.

The best way to understand web parts is to work with them. Exercise 9.6 provides step-by-step instructions for creating a new page, adding an RSS feed web part, and pointing the RSS feed to a site on the Internet.

EXERCISE 9.6

Creating a Web Part Page with an RSS Feed Web Part

In this exercise, you will create a new web part page. You will then place the RSS feed web part on the page and configure the RSS feed to pull data from http://www.tomcarpenter.net/feed. You can also pull information from any other feed by entering an alternative URL in step 10.

1. Log on to the SharePoint server as an administrator.

2. Open the default SharePoint site by navigating to http://localhost in Internet Explorer.

3. Click the Site Actions menu and select New Page.

4. In the New Page dialog, enter the New Page Name value of **Tom Carpenter's Blog**.

5. When the new empty page loads, click the Insert tab on the Ribbon.

6. On the Insert tab, click the Web Part icon in the Web Parts group.

7. Choose the Content Rollup category and the RSS Viewer web part, and then click the Add button.

8. The RSS Viewer web part is now displayed on the page. Click the drop-down arrow to the right of the RSS Viewer title and select Edit Web Part to modify the settings for the RSS Viewer web part.

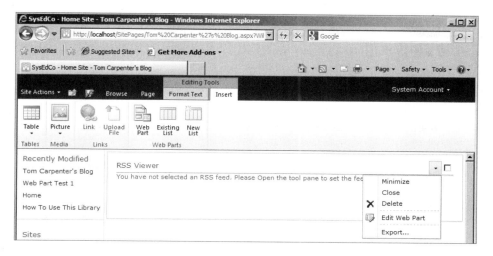

9. Expand the Appearance node and change the Title value to read **Tom Carpenter's Blog**.

10. Scroll down to the RSS Properties node and enter the RSS Feed URL value of **http://www.tomcarpenter.net/feed**.

11. Scroll down and click OK to save the changes.

12. On the Ribbon, click the Save Page icon (the one that looks like a 3.5-inch diskette with a blue arrow on it).

13. The page will be displayed with the blog feed content.

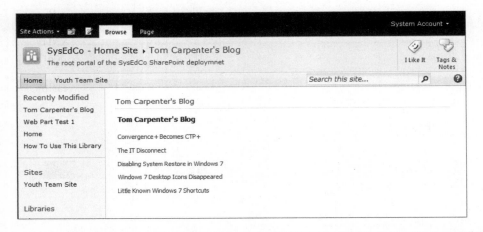

Regardless of the web part you are adding, you will have the option to edit the web part as shown in step 8 of Exercise 9.6. The options available for configuration will differ depending on the web part.

 Web parts are very useful for nontechnical users. They allow them to add technical capabilities to a site without requiring programming knowledge. Users simply add the web parts, configure the settings, and are done.

Planning for Site Customizations

The preceding sections of this chapter addressed web applications, features and solutions, and web parts. These three areas represent the core of SharePoint Server 2010 customizations and configurations. However, some additional components should be considered when planning for site customizations. They include:

■ Site templates and definitions

- Multilingual deployment
- Master pages

These components are addressed in the following sections.

Site Templates and Definitions

Site templates are the same as site definitions. In fact, Microsoft states, "A site definition is a template that determines, for example, the lists, files, Web Parts, Features, or settings with which to provision a new SharePoint site." (See source: `http://technet.microsoft .com/en-us/library/ff607735.aspx`.) Site definitions are built from multiple XML and ASPX files that are stored in the `%ProgramFiles%\Common Files\Microsoft Shared\web server extensions\14\TEMPLATE\SiteTemplates` folder.

SharePoint comes with several site definitions available as templates for creating a new site. Figure 9.10 shows the site templates list in the SharePoint interface.

FIGURE 9.10   Creating a new site and viewing the site templates list

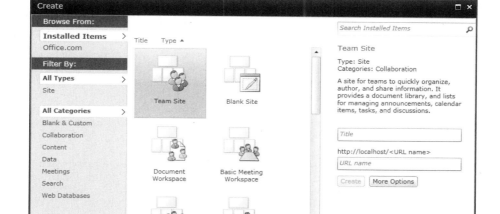

Table 9.2 lists the installed site templates commonly used with SharePoint Server 2010 and their descriptions.

TABLE 9.2 Common SharePoint Server 2010 Default Site Templates

Template Name	Description
Team Site	Creates a site for teams to quickly organize, author, and share information. It provides a document library and lists for managing announcements, calendar items, tasks, and discussions.
Blank Site	Creates a blank site for you to customize based on your requirements.
Document Workspace	Creates a site for colleagues to work together on a document. It provides a document library for storing the primary document and supporting files, a tasks list for assigning to-do items, and a links list for resources related to the document.
Basic Meeting Workspace	Creates a site to plan, organize, and capture the results of a meeting. It provides lists for managing the agenda, attendees, and documents.
Blank Meeting Workspace	Creates a blank meeting site for you to customize based on your requirements.
Decision Meeting Workspace	Creates a site for meetings that track status or make decisions. It provides lists for creating tasks, storing documents, and recording decisions.
Social Meeting Workspace	Creates a site to plan social occasions. It provides lists for tracking attendees, providing directions, and storing pictures of the event.
Multipage Meeting Workspace	Creates a site to plan, organize, and capture the results of a meeting. It provides lists for managing the agenda and meeting attendees. It includes two blank pages for you to customize based on your requirements.
Blog	Creates a site for a person or team to post ideas, observations, and expertise about which site visitors can comment.
Group Work Site	Creates a site that provides a groupware solution to enable teams to create, organize, and share information quickly and easily. It includes Group Calendar, Circulation, Phone-Call Memo, the Document Library, and the other basic lists.
Assets Web Database	Creates an assets database to keep track of assets, including asset details and owners.

Template Name	Description
Charitable Contributions Web	Creates a database to track information about fundraising campaigns, including donations made by contributors, campaign-related events, and pending tasks.
Contacts Web Database	Create a contacts database to manage information about people (such as customers and partners) with whom your team works.
Issues Web Database	Create an issues database to manage a set of issues or problems. You can assign, prioritize, and follow the progress of issues from start to finish.
Projects Web Database	Creates a project tracking database to track multiple projects, and assign tasks to different people.
Document Center	Creates a site to centrally manage documents in your enterprise.
Records Center	Creates a site designed for records management. Records managers can configure the routing table to direct incoming files to specific locations. The site also lets you manage whether records can be deleted or modified after they are added to the repository.
Personalization Site	A site for delivering personalized views, data, and navigation from this site collection into My Site. It includes personalization specific Web Parts and navigation that is optimized for My Site sites.
Enterprise Search Center	A site for delivering the search experience. The welcome page includes a search box with two tabs: one for general searches, and another for searches for information about people. You can add and customize tabs to focus on other search scopes or result types.
Basic Search Center	A site for delivering the search experience. The site includes pages for search results and advanced searches.
FAST Search Center	A site for delivering the FAST search experience. The Welcome page includes a search box with two tabs: one for general searches and another for searches for information about people. You can add and customize tabs to focus on other search scopes or result types.
Visio Process Repository	A site for teams to quickly view, share, and store Visio process diagrams. It provides a versioned document library for storing process diagrams, and lists for managing announcements, tasks, and review discussions.

You may want to disable several of these templates for the server farm so that users cannot use them to create site collections and subsites. To do this, you will have to edit XML files located in `%Program Files%\ Common Files\Microsoft Shared\Web Server Extensions\14\TEMPLATE\1033\XML`. The XML files are named:

- `webtemp.xml`
- `webtempoffile.xml`
- `webtempsrch.xml`
- `webtempvispr.xml`
- `webtempsps.xml`
- `webtemppppsma.xml`

In these files, you will find elements named Template Name with a property named Hidden that is equal to FALSE. Change this property value to TRUE, and the template will be hidden from use. For example, in Figure 9.11, the Blank Meeting Workspace template has been hidden so that users cannot use this template to create sites.

FIGURE 9.11   Disabling a site template from view

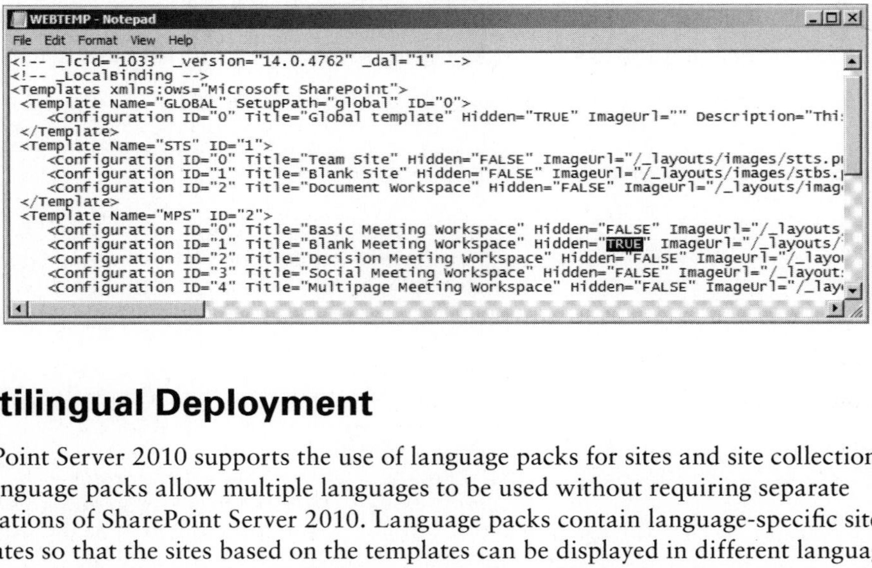

Multilingual Deployment

SharePoint Server 2010 supports the use of language packs for sites and site collections. The language packs allow multiple languages to be used without requiring separate installations of SharePoint Server 2010. Language packs contain language-specific site templates so that the sites based on the templates can be displayed in different languages.

SharePoint Server 2010 is installed as a language-specific version. For example, you may install the English version or the Spanish version or another language-specific version. By default, all sites are created using the language with which SharePoint Server 2010 was installed. If you install additional language packs, you will be able to specify the language to use for any new sites that are created. A language ID is associated with each site, and the pages are created with that same language ID by default. The language ID is a simple way to reference the language with a numeric value. For example, the English language uses language ID 1033 and the Hindi language uses language ID 1081.

 You may have noticed a directory on Microsoft operating systems with the name 1033. Now you know that the directory name is based on English being installed on the machine. This applies to Microsoft technologies across the board and not just to SharePoint Server language packs.

Microsoft supports dozens of languages. The language packs can be downloaded from http://www.microsoft.com/downloads/en/details.aspx?displaylang=en&FamilyID= 046f16a9-4bce-4149-8679-223755560d54. Microsoft adds new language packs frequently. For example, in the year 2010 alone Microsoft added 19 languages.

To add language packs, you must download them and then install them on the web servers running SharePoint Server 2010. After they are installed on the web servers, you must rerun the SharePoint 2010 Products Configuration Wizard. The wizard will automatically add the new language packs to the SharePoint server farm installation.

 If you ever have to uninstall SharePoint Server 2010 and you have installed language packs, you must uninstall the language packs before you can uninstall SharePoint Server 2010.

Master Pages

Master pages are used to define the layout of content in SharePoint pages separately from the content itself. This architecture allows you to have a consistent look in your SharePoint sites while varying the content. Several master pages exist, and four are very important:

- v4.master
- minimal.master
- simple.master
- default.master

The v4.master page defines the standard layout for the new SharePoint 2010 interface. This layout includes the Ribbon. Most of your look-and-feel customizations can be done in the v4.master file. The minimal.master page defines the layout for the search pages. It is a clean and simple layout to display search results quickly. The simple.master page is used for login screens and for error pages. Finally, the default.master page is used only if you install SharePoint Server 2010 with the traditional SharePoint 2007 interface. The v4.master page will still be there, but you can use the default.master page until your users are comfortable with the new interface and are ready to move to the Ribbon-based environment.

Master pages can be edited using SharePoint Designer. You can add custom logos to the page, content you want to display on each page, and more. Exercise 9.7 provides instructions for customizing the v4.master page.

EXERCISE 9.7

Customizing Master Pages

In this exercise, you will learn how to open the v4.master page in SharePoint Designer for editing. SharePoint Designer 2010, which is a free download from Microsoft.com, must be installed on the SharePoint server for these steps to work properly.

1. Log on to the SharePoint server as an administrator.

2. Open the Internet Explorer browser and navigate to http://localhost to access the default SharePoint site.

3. Click Site Actions and select Edit in SharePoint Designer.

4. After the site loads on the SharePoint Designer, select the Master Pages option in the Site Objects panel.

5. In the center panel, click on the v4.master page.

6. In the v4.master tab that is displayed, click the Edit File link in the Customization section.

7. Make any necessary changes. Be sure to make a copy of the master page before you start making changes. You always want to have an easy way to recover if accidental damage occurs.

Exercise 9.7 provided one set of instructions for editing a master page. You can also access the master pages for editing from within the SharePoint interface. Simply open the site that contains the target master pages and then view the site settings. In the Galleries group, select Master Pages and edit the target master page from here.

Summary

In this chapter, you learned about the ways in which you can customize SharePoint sites and farms. You learned about web applications in more detail than previously provided in this book. You learned how to work with features and solutions and how to use web parts for page development. Finally, you explored the considerations related to site customization details ranging from site templates to customizing master pages.

Exam Essentials

Designing web applications.   Understand the difference between an application pool and a SharePoint web application, which includes the SharePoint-specific settings not typically linked to an application pool. Know how to create and manage new Web applications.

Designing features and solutions.   Understand that a feature is a type of solution and that a solution may include anything from a simple page deployed on the SharePoint server to a complete custom SharePoint-based application. Features are based on XML.

Understanding web parts.   Know that web parts allow users to add complex logic to SharePoint pages without requiring them to learn complex programming languages. Understand the common web parts available and how to add a web part to a page and configure it for use.

Planning for site customizations.   Understand the different customization options available for SharePoint sites, which will include site templates and definitions, multilingual deployments, and master pages.

Chapter 10

Planning Search Solutions

TOPICS COVERED IN THIS CHAPTER

- ✓ Designing the search requirements
- ✓ Planning the search topology
- ✓ Designing the search strategy
- ✓ Planning Enterprise Search

SharePoint 2010 Search contains many exciting new features and capacities. Some of these new features include a dramatic increase in scale limits and the use of stateless crawlers that no longer have to contain the entire *index*. The index itself can now be partitioned into smaller units to increase manageability, and these units can be distributed across multiple server computers. More than one server computer can be allocated to crawl content. From an administrator's point of view, the entire search system is more transparent, allowing you access to more information about what's happening in search.

One of the new admin features is an improved administrative interface that provides a centralized location for performing administrative tasks for both farm administrators and search administrators. Also the Farm Configuration Wizard runs automatically once the server farm is installed, allowing to you create a fully functional search system on that particular server so search is available from the very start. In addition, the administration of search services is now separate and independent of all other shared services in SharePoint.

Scalability has been improved for increased crawling capacity, throughput, and reduced latency. You can adjust the current search topology while regular farm operations are still running, allowing search functionality to remain available to users during management activities.

In this chapter, we discuss how to design search requirements in SharePoint 2010. Search requirements can include designing for specific data types, distribution types such as intranet or extranet, index size and file location, *content sources,* search scopes, and search taxonomy.

This chapter will also cover designing a search strategy, which involves search topology planning, index partitioning, managing separate crawler servers, and property database management.

Finally, we look at the Enterprise Search strategy, which involves planning for metadata and search, people search, search reporting, and planning Enterprise Search technology.

The Microsoft SharePoint 2010 Administrator (Exam 70-668) exam tests the skills of candidates to design and deploy SharePoint Server 2010 platforms in a production environment on scales including the enterprise infrastructure. One of the significant content areas is Search and Enterprise Search planning. These tasks range from defining search requirements to planning a server topology optimized for different search requirements and planning an Enterprise Search strategy. This chapter closely follows the exam domains related to planning and configuring Search in SharePoint. To master these skills, you should focus not only on the chapter's content but practice the included exercises. Practice exercises are not meant to mimic actual Microsoft certification questions, but rather to assist you in honing your skills.

Designing the Search Requirements

In general, search requirements are the collection of search categories that define what content needs to be found in response to a query, what environments are to be searched to locate content, how search results are to be prioritized, and any other aspects of search that need to be specified in response to user and business requirements.

Defining Search Requirements

In its simplest terms, content is any specific information item you want to have crawled and indexed so that it will be available through search. Content resides in a content source, which is some form of information repository. SharePoint Search crawls items in multiple content sources so that the information in these repositories becomes available to end users who are using search to access data.

A content source can be almost any container of information including websites, file shares, public folders in Exchange, or any customized content repository. Items within a specific content source can be any type of file, including document types such as Word docs, PDFs, spreadsheets, and PowerPoint slides. Items can also be other data types such as text or links on a web page, database records, or items specific to a SharePoint site (for example, discussions, issues, or tasks).

Using a publicly accessible search engine such as Bing or Google will let you access content sources that are available on the Internet, including any items that are locatable within those sources, but the type and organization of that data may not be precisely what you require. In a business environment, using the SharePoint interface, your data needs can be quite different, necessitating a different configuration design for search. You likely will not want the ability to access irrelevant data types and sources, but you will want to access content and content repositories that are business requirements and data not generally accessible outside your infrastructure.

Planning Content Sources

Before adding content sources to SharePoint, you will first need to plan your search configuration based on your organization's needs. What content sources contain the required data items for your business? You may not require a content source outside of SharePoint and, when search is configured during the initial SharePoint installation, SharePoint is the default content source.

Follow the steps in Exercise 10.1 to view the currently configured content sources for search in SharePoint.

EXERCISE 10.1

Viewing Content Sources in SharePoint Search

In this exercise, you will learn how to view content sources with the search service application.

1. Open SharePoint Central Administration.

2. Under Application Management, click Manage Service Applications.

3. In the list that appears, click Search Service Application.

4. In the Quick Launch section on the Search Service Application page, under Crawling, click Content Sources.

If any content sources have been configured for SharePoint Search, they should be visible. The only content source likely to be available is Local SharePoint Sites, as shown in Figure 10.1.

FIGURE 10.1 Viewing available content sources

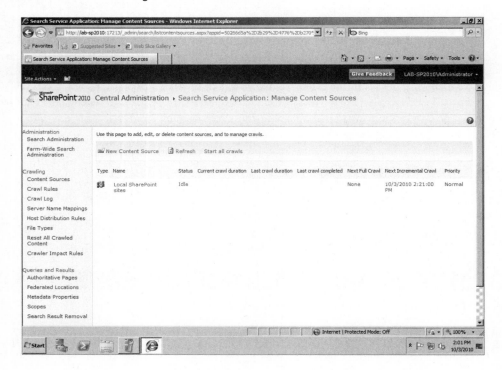

As previously mentioned, you can add other content sources to search, such as the following.

- SharePoint sites
- Websites
- File shares
- Exchange public folders
- Line-of-business data
- Custom repositories defined by custom connectors

Content sources are added by their URLs, UNCs, and so forth, so when planning your content source requirements, you will want to organize repositories using the previously referenced bullet list and collect the specific locations for each source, such as indicated in Table 10.1.

TABLE 10.1 Organizing Content Sources

Content Source	Content Source Type	Content Source Start Address
Local SharePoint Site	SharePoint site	`http://local.sharepoint.com`
Internet Website	Website	`http://www.publicwebsite.com`
Network File Share	File share	`//filesrv01/share/folder`
Exchange Public Folder	Exchange public folder	`\\servername\public_folder`

It is possible to have one content source with numerous start addresses; however, you will have a more flexible design if you plan for a separate content source for each of your major starting addresses. Specifying a content source for each start address lets you create a separate crawl schedule for each of the start addresses so you can start and stop crawls on a single address without interrupting other crawls. This also gives you more ability to distinguish specific content within search scopes.

In the desired search service application, you can create a content source and set the crawl schedule. Exercise 10.2 will show you how.

EXERCISE 10.2

Creating Content Sources in SharePoint Search

In this exercise, you will learn how to create a search content source and how to set the crawl schedule for the content source.

1. In Central Administration, click Application Management and then click Manage Service Applications.

2. On the Manage Service Applications page, select the desired search service application.

3. In the left menu under Crawling, click Content Sources and on the Manage Content Sources page, select New Content Source.

4. On the next page, under Name, give the content source a name in the available field.

5. Under Content Source Type, select the desired content type from the available radio buttons.

    - SharePoint Sites

    - Websites

    - File Shares

    - Exchange Public Folders

    - Line of Business Data

    - Custom Repository

6. In the Type Start Addresses Below (One Per Line) field, under Start Addresses, enter the names of the URLs from which search should begin the crawl.

7. Under Crawl Settings, select either Crawl Everything Under The Hostname For Each Start Address or Only Crawl The Site Collection Of Each Start Address.

8. Under Crawl Schedules, use the Full Crawl menu to select None or the default value; or click Create Schedule and in the Manage Schedules box, select the days and times when you want to start for Full Crawls.

9. Use the Incremental Crawl menu to select None or the default value, or click Create Schedule and in the Manage Schedules box, select the days and times when you want to start for Incremental Crawls.

10. Under Content Source Priority, either accept Normal as the default crawl priority or select High Priority.

11. To start a crawl immediately, select Start Full Crawl of the content source.

12. When you are finished, click OK.

Planning Data Types

Within each content course lies a wide variety of information contained within different types of data items. When creating a plan for your search requirements, consider the types of data items you want to gather, in what document types they are contained, and in what content repository types the document types are contained. A data type planning outline may look like the following:

- SharePoint sites
  - File shares
    - Network shares
    - Remote servers
  - Documents
    - PDF
    - Excel
    - PowerPoint
    - Word
  - SharePoint lists
    - Items
    - Issues
    - Tasks
  - Web content
    - Links
    - Text
  - Structured business database
    - Database records
    - Transactions

Planning for specific data and document types allows you to make sure that any required data items are included in your data crawling and indexing while also ensuring that irrelevant items that would waste time in a crawl and that would not be helpful if they appeared in a search result are eliminated.

To view, add, or remove specific file types for SharePoint Search, follow the steps in Exercise 10.3.

EXERCISE 10.3

Managing File Types in Search

In this exercise, you will learn how to view, add, and remove file types for the search service application.

1. Open Central Administration.

2. Under Application Management, click Manage Service Applications.

3. In the list that appears, click Search Service Application.

EXERCISE 10.3 *(continued)*

4. In Quick Launch, under Crawling, click File Types. The Manage File Types page appears.

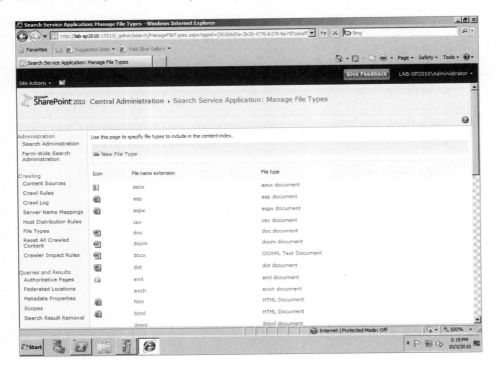

5. To add a new file type, click New File Type, enter a file type extension in the File Extension field, and then click OK.

6. To remove an existing file type, click to the right of a file extension to open the menu, click Delete, and when prompted click OK.

You may have to install third-party iFilters and custom file icons, such as PDF or Python files, if you are adding file types not found in SharePoint by default.

Planning Indexing

Once content sources have been configured, SharePoint must perform a full crawl of the sources to create an index. The search index has the same function as the index in the back of the book, allowing you to create a repository of all crawled content that can be accessed and retrieved when required.

Search Index Location

The default location of the index directory is

```
C:\Program Files\Microsoft Office Servers\14.0\Data\Applications\GUID
```

where GUID is the globally unique identifier that specifically references the index directory. The GUID is expressed as a hexadecimal value.

The directory contains subdirectories, each of which contain files that store the unique keywords representing all of the data items that have been crawled. You can also find gather logs, noise word files, and thesaurus files located in the subdirectories, as well as other pointer data.

> While the search index files are stored on the SharePoint server file system, the Metadata Property Store, which contains the property information used for search scopes and filters, is located in a SQL Server database.

Data File Size and Indexing

SharePoint Search will not index files larger than 16 MB due to matters related to pulling large files across the network and similar issues; however, the metadata for these large files is indexed, so you can search for such files as long as your search query is by the document's name or author. You cannot search by keywords in the document, however.

> The workaround for this 16 MB indexing issue is to add a Registry key called MaxDownloadSize and then put a numerical value between 17 and 64 in the key. This value will tell the search engine to ignore the 16 MB limitation and index files up to 64 MB in size. While this will enable indexing of very large files, SharePoint still will not download files larger than 16 MB.

Index Size

SharePoint 2010 uses index partitions, which are logical portions of the full index. To make sure that all index partitions stay at about the same size and grow at the same rate, search indexing adds data items in round-robin fashion across each of the components for each partition. User search queries span across all of the partitions that make up the full index.

Search index partitions use query components, which are modules that are required to respond to a search query. A component can have one or more mirrors, which are redundant copies of the components to satisfy throughput and availability needs.

If you anticipate a relatively large index, especially if it will contain large files such as image files, the way to decrease search latency is to keep index partitions small and to add multiple partitions. The maximum number of data items per partition, including documents, list items, people, web content, and so on, should be no more than 10 million items. Also, 33 percent of the active partitions on any given machine should be able to fit into the server machine's available memory.

Partition components can be active or passive. An active mirror provides improved throughput because end-user search queries are sent to one of the active partitions in a round-robin manner. A passive mirror provides improved availability because it services search queries only when no other active components are available in a specific partition.

Planning Federated Location Requirements

By default, SharePoint Search provides searches for only local SharePoint content; however, you can add third-party or remote SharePoint Search environments in the search service application to expand the reach of search from the SharePoint platform you administer. Search federation lets users access content from the local search index on the server as well as from database systems, search engines on the Internet, and from specific scopes on the local SharePoint server. Federated locations can be added manually or imported from a Federated Location Definition file (.FLD).

A practical example of the use of federated locations is where SharePoint users issue search queries and get search results back—not only from the search index for local SharePoint sites, but from external sources such as Bing and Google. Planning for federation is associated with planning for content sources outside the default selections that are available when adding SharePoint content sources. Exercise 10.4 illustrates how you can import federated locations search connectors.

EXERCISE 10.4

Importing Federated Locations Search Connectors

In this exercise, you will learn how to import and configure a federated search connector.

1. On the Search Administration page of the default search service application, under Queries and Results at the left of the page, click Federated Locations.

2. On the Manage Federated Locations page, click Online Gallery to find a new location for downloading and importing.

3. When the Enterprise Search from Microsoft page opens up in a separate browser tab or window, in the left-hand menu, click Federated Search Connectors.

4. In the Download Sample Connectors menu on the right of the page, expand the category of your choice and click the desired connector.

5. When the File Download dialog box appears, click Save, navigate to the location on the server where you want to save the file, and click Save, closing the dialog after the file is downloaded, if necessary.

6. Unless you plan to download more FLD files, close the Enterprise Search From Microsoft web page.

7. On the Manage Federated Locations page, click Import Location.

8. On the Import Federated Location page, under Location Definition File, click Browse and navigate to the location where you saved the FLD file.

9. In the Choose File To Upload dialog, select the FLD file and then click Open.

10. When the path to the FLD file populates the FLD file, click OK.

11. On the Success page, you can either click Edit Location to modify the settings for the location or you can click Done if you're finished. (If you click Done, the file import will be finished. You only need to edit the location if you want to change the default configuration.)

12. If you click Edit location, on the Edit Federated Location page, you can choose to modify items such as the Display Name, Description, the Trigger that determines how the user's query matches the location, Location information, and so on. When you're done here, click OK to complete the import and return to the Manage Federated Locations page.

Planning Search Scopes

A *search scope* lets you filter end-user search queries so that user queries address only a subset of the entire search index. You can create multiple search scopes, and an individual scope is made up of scope settings and scope rules. Scope settings define the name and description of the scope and the specific search results page used by the scope.

A scope rule is used to define the term or terms users will employ when searching within the scope. A scope rule is made up of a scope rule type (such as a web address or property query, like Author = James Pyles), the details for the scope rule type (such as a specific host name, folder location, or property restriction), and the behavior of the rule (such as including, requiring, or excluding items matching the rule).

Once one or more scopes are created, users can apply filters to their original search results to better refine their searches and acquire more specific results from a filtered or advanced query. For instance, you can set up a scope with rules that apply only to a specific website so that search results using the scope will offer the user results that are specifically tailored to the user's requirements. When you plan for search scopes, you must know the details of the content within the index most likely required by users in an advanced search.

Two basic tasks are related to scopes. The first task is to add or edit a scope, and the second is to add or edit rules within the scope. Exercise 10.5 teaches you how to add or edit a scope.

EXERCISE 10.5

Adding a Search Scope

In this exercise, you will learn how to add a basic search scope.

1. On the Search Administration page of the default search service application, under Queries And Results at the left of the page, click Scopes.

2. On the View Scopes page, click New Scope.

3. On the Create Scope page, give the scope a name in the Title field and enter a description in the Description field.

4. On the Target Results page, select Use The Default Search Results Page or select Specify A Different Page For Searching This Scope, and then enter the desired URL (for example, `testing.aspx`) in the Target Results page.

5. When finished, click OK.

You can also edit an existing scope on the View Scopes page by clicking to the right of the scope name to open the menu, selecting Edit Properties And Rules, and then clicking Change Scope Settings.

In addition to creating a scope from scratch, you can open the menu to the right of an existing rule and select the Copy option. Once you've created a copy of the scope, you can give it a different name and edit the properties and rules for the scope as you desire.

Once a scope has been created, you can add one or more rules to the scope to define its behavior. Exercise 10.6 shows you how this is done.

EXERCISE 10.6

Adding a Search Scope Rule

In this exercise, you will learn how to add a rule to a search scope.

1. On the Search Administration page of the default search service application, under Queries And Results at the left of the page, click Scopes.

2. On the View Scopes page, click to the right of the name of the scope you created in the previous exercise, and in the list that appears, click Edit Properties And Rules.

3. On the Scope Properties And Rules page, under Rules, click New Rule.

4. On the Add Scope Rule page, under Scope Rule Type, select the type of rule you want to define (such as Web Addresses, Property Query, Content Source, or All Content).

5. Depending on which option you selected in the previous step, you will have to add different information types (for example, selecting Web Address and adding either the URL or path to the resource, or selecting Property Query and then adding an Add Property Restriction using the available menu and field, such as Author = James Pyles).

6. Under Behavior, select Include, Require, Or Exclude to determine which action is applied to the web address, property, or content source rule.

7. When you are finished, click OK.

Planning Search Results by Prioritizing Locations

Another specified area of content source planning and configuration entails promoting or demoting specific websites and web pages. To promote and demote effectively, you need to have a good understanding of the business requirements of your users. You can manually rank and promote websites, marking them as most authoritative and second- and third-level pages. You can also demote sites you have determined to be less authoritative or nonauthoritative among the sites that are crawled and indexed.

If sites are not specified in terms of authority, all top-level pages for SharePoint web applications are treated as most authoritative by default. By manually promoting or demoting sites, you are in essence "stacking the deck" relative to how search results are ranked.

The Authoritative Pages page (Central Administration ➢ Search Service Application ➢ Quick Launch ➢ Queries and Results) lets you prioritize web pages by four levels of importance:

- Most authoritative pages
- Second-level authoritative pages
- Third-level authoritative pages
- Sites to demote

Consider all of the sites that are content repositories in relation to how users rank them in their importance as data sources, collect them into four separate containers listed by that ranking, and then use the Specify Authoritative Pages page in Central Administration to apply the prioritization.

Real World Scenario

Manually Prioritizing Indexed Web Pages

You are a SharePoint administrator for your company, and you are in a planning meeting with the company's management team. The current topic is "Improving the Relevancy of the Search Results for the Company's SharePoint Users." Right now, a large number of web pages with lesser or minor relevancy are being returned along with the desired web pages, particularly when SharePoint users search for information about the company's top three lines of merchandise.

At the end of the meeting, you and the management team create a priority list of the different web pages available by searching. Currently, all web pages are being indexed as most authoritative, and you have been tasked with manually setting the priority levels of the available web pages so that pages containing data about the company's top product are marked as most authoritative. Pages containing information about other products will be prioritized as second- or third-level authoritative pages, depending on product popularity. You have also been asked to specifically set web pages containing content about products being phased out of production as demoted.

Planning the Search Topology

After a SharePoint installation or upgrade, the Farm Configuration Wizard automates a variety of deployment functions, including creating the fully functional search system on the server, creating the search topology that supports an index for up to 100 million crawled documents, and creating a Search Center that users can access to issue queries.

However, this search topology is "off the rack" so to speak, and most likely won't fit the specific business requirements of your company. Enterprise Search in SharePoint Server 2010 is made up of a number of topological components that provide the different elements required for Search to operate correctly. The following information and task lists illustrate how search indexing, crawling, and other functions are configured.

Administering an Index Partition and Query Components

In the world of SharePoint Server 2010 Search, *index partitions* are groups of query components. Each index partition is used to contain a subset of the full-text index and returns search results to the submitter of the search query. Each of these index partitions is associated with a specific property database that contains the metadata associated with a specific set of crawled content. You can construct the topology for Search by creating query components on selected servers in your server farm.

You can add an index partition to a search service application and place query components on different farm servers to distribute the load of query services. The following task takes you through the steps. The first query component is created automatically when a new index partition is created.

Exercise 10.7 will show you the process of adding an index partition to a search service application.

EXERCISE 10.7

Adding an Index Partition to a Search Service Application

In this exercise, you will learn how to add an index partition to a search service application.

1. In Central Administration under Application Management, click Manage service applications.

2. On the Service Applications page, click the link for the search service application on which you want to add an index partition.

3. On the Search Administration page, under Search Application Topology, click the Modify button.

4. Click the drop-down on the new button and then select the Index Partition And Query Component.

5. When the Add Query Component dialog box appears, in the Server list, click the farm server on which you want to add the first query component for the new index partition.

6. In the Associated Property Database list, click the name of the property database for which you want to associate the new index partition.

7. In the Location of Index field, enter an optional location on the server for the storage of the index files after they're received from the crawl components, or accept the default location.

8. Under Failover-Only Query Component, make sure the Set This Query Component As Failover-Only check box is unchecked. (You are creating a new index partition.)

9. When you are done, click OK.

10. On the Manage Search Topology page, click Apply Topology Changes to start the SharePoint timer jobs that will add the new index partition and the first query component to the server you selected.

Not only can you add an index partition, but you can remove it as well. Exercise 10.8 will walk you through the process of removing an index partition from a search service application.

EXERCISE 10.8

Removing an Index Partition to a Search Service Application

In this exercise, you will learn how to remove an index partition to a search service application.

1. In Central Administration under Application Management, click Manage Service Applications.

2. On the Service Applications page, click the link for the search service application on which you want to remove an index partition.

3. On the Search Administration page, under Search Application Topology, click the Modify button.

4. On the Manage Search Topology page, click the query component in the index partition you want to remove and then click Delete.

5. In the dialog box that appears, click OK to confirm your decision.

6. On the Manage Search Topology page, click Apply Topology Changes to start the SharePoint timer jobs that will remove the index partition and the query components from the server.

If you choose to delete all of the query components from an index partition, you will also remove the index partition from the farm. All the data from the partition will automatically be copied and distributed to the remaining partitions. If there is only one index partition for a search service application, you will be unable to remove it.

As you learned earlier, a query component is a container for a particular subset of the full-text index and is used to return search results to the query submitter. A query component is part of an index partition and is also associated with a specific property database containing the metadata associated with a set of crawled content. Just as you can add or remove an index partition to a search service application, you can also add and remove a query component to an index partition. Exercise 10.9 will show you how.

EXERCISE 10.9

Adding a Query Component to an Index Partition

In this exercise, you will learn how to add a query component to an index partition.

1. In Central Administration under Application Management, click Manage Service Applications.

2. On the Service Applications page, click the link for the search service application on which you want to add a query component for an index partition.

3. On the Search Administration page, under Search Application Topology, click the Modify button.

4. On the Manage Search Topology page, click a query component in the index partition you want to modify and then click Add Mirror.

5. In the Location of Index field, you can add an optional location on the server to use for storage of index files after receiving them from crawl components, or you can use the default location.

6. Under Failover-Only Query Component, select the Set This Query Component As Failover-Only check box only if you want the query component to receive queries in the event of the primary query component failing in this index partition. Otherwise, do not select the check box.

7. Click OK when you are finished.

8. On the Manage Search Topology page, click Apply Topology Changes to start the SharePoint timer job that will add the new mirror query component for the index partition you selected.

Removing a query component from an index partition is very much like removing an index partition to a search service application, except that after you click the Modify button in step 3, on the Manage Search Topology page, you need to click the query component you want to remove and then click Delete. After that, click OK on the Manage Search Topology page, and then click Apply Topology Changes.

Remember, if you remove all of the query components from an index partition, you remove the index partition and all of the data will be copied to other partitions. You cannot remove the last index partition.

Administering Crawl Databases and Components

Crawl databases are used by a specific search service application to store information about the location of content sources as well as crawl schedules and other crawl-operation-related data. As you previously read, you can distribute the database load by adding crawl databases on different servers running SQL Server. Crawl databases are associated with crawl components, and you can dedicate a component to a specific host by creating host distribution rules.

Exercise 10.10 will show you how to add or remove a crawl database to a search service application. You will be unable to perform this task on a SharePoint single server with built-in database deployment.

EXERCISE 10.10

Adding and Removing a Crawl Database

In this exercise, you will learn how to add and remove a crawl database to a search service application.

1. In Central Administration under Application Management, click Manage Service Applications.

2. On the Service Applications page, click the link for the relevant search service application.

3. On the Search Administration page, under Search Application Topology, click the Modify button.

4. On the Manage Search Topology page, click New and then click Crawl Database.

5. When the Add Crawl Database dialog box appears, under Add Crawl Database, accept the default values or point to the database server on which you want to add the crawl database by entering the database name and the database authentication credentials.

6. If you like, enter the information for a failover database server in the Failover Database Server field, but you must have SQL Server database mirroring enabled to select this option.

7. Under Dedicated Database, if you like, select the Dedicate This Crawl Store to hosts as specified in Host Distribution Rules check box.

8. Once you have finished, click OK.

9. On the Manage Search Topology page, click Apply Topology Changes to start the SharePoint timer job that will add the new crawl database to the SQL Server computer.

10. To delete the crawl database, follow steps 1 through 3. Then click the Modify button on the Manage Search Topology page, click the desired crawl database, and then click Delete.

11. When the verification box appears, click OK.

12. On the Manage Search Topology page, click Apply Topology Changes to start the SharePoint timer job that will delete the new crawl database from the SQL Server computer.

Before you can delete a crawl database, you must disconnect any associations between the crawl components and the crawl database, either by assigning the components to a different crawl database or by removing the crawl components. If you do not do so, the Delete button will not appear as expected in step 10 of Exercise 10.10.

A crawl component is the portion of a crawl database that processes the crawls of content sources, and then it propagates the resulting index files to query components and adds the data about the location and crawl schedule to the associated crawl database.

As you learned in Exercise 10.10, you can add or remove a crawl component from a crawl database associated with a search service application. Exercise 10.11 outlines how to do so. As with all other search topology tasks, you will not be able to complete these steps if you are using a SharePoint single server with built-in database deployment.

EXERCISE 10.11

Adding and Removing a Crawl Component to a Crawl Database

In this exercise, you will learn how to add and remove a crawl component to a crawl database.

1. In Central Administration under Application Management, click Manage Service Applications.

2. On the Service Applications page, click the link for the relevant search service application.

3. On the Search Administration page, under Search Application Topology, click the Modify button.

4. On the Manage Search Topology page, click New and then click Crawl Component.

5. When the Add Crawl Component dialog box appears, use the Server list to select the farm server on which you want to add the crawl component.

6. Use the Associated Crawl Database list to select the crawl database you want to associate with the new crawl component.

7. If you like, you can use the Temporary Location of Index field to enter the location of the server you want to use for creating index files before propagating them to the query components, or you can accept the default location.

8. When you are finished, click OK.

9. On the Manage Search Topology page, click Apply Topology Changes to start the SharePoint timer job that will add the new crawl component to the specified server.

10. To remove the component, follow steps 1 through 3 in this Exercise (10.11). Then click the Modify button on the Manage Search Topology page, select the crawl component you want to remove, and then click Delete.

11. When the confirmation box appears, click OK to add the crawl component to the removal job queue.

12. On the Manage Search Topology page, click Apply Topology Changes to start the SharePoint timer job that will delete the crawl component from the server.

Administering Property Databases and Host Distribution Rules

In addition to crawl databases, SharePoint Search also uses property databases, which contain metadata associated with crawled content. These property databases can be added to and removed from SQL database servers in the server farm in much the same way as crawl databases. Because this is a search topology task, it cannot be performed on a SharePoint single server with built-in database deployment.

Adding and Removing a Property Database

The steps for adding the property database are almost identical to the steps for adding and removing a crawl database. Follow steps 1 through 3 for Exercise 10.11. Click the Modify button on the Manage Search Topology page, click New, and then click Property Database. Then, when the Add Property Database dialog box appears, either accept the defaults or add your own information for the database server name, database name, and authentication credentials. You can also specify a failover database server if you like, but you must have SQL Server database mirroring enabled to do so. After that, follow the final steps of clicking OK and then Apply Topology Changes to start the SharePoint timer job.

The process of removing the property database is identical to that of removing a crawl database, including the requirement that any associations with query components must be removed before the property database can be successfully deleted.

Adding and Removing a Host Distribution Rule

The final task in managing search topologies is adding and removing a host distribution rule. Host distribution rules are used to associate a server computer with a specific crawl database. The default distribution rule is to load balance hosts across crawl databases based on the availability of space; however, you can override this behavior and connect a host to a specific crawl database. This is sometimes done based on availability and performance requirements. More than one crawl database must be available in the search service application to add a host distribution rule.

See how the process works in Exercise 10.12.

EXERCISE 10.12

Adding and Removing a Host Distribution Rule

In this exercise, you will learn how to add and remove a host distribution rule to a search service application.

1. In Central Administration under Application Management, click Manage Service Applications.

2. On the Service Applications page, click the search service application on which you want to add the host distribution rule.

3. On the Search Administration page, in Quick Launch, click Host Distribution Rules.

4. On the Host Distribution Rules page, click Add Distribution Rule.

5. On the Add Host Rule page, enter the name of the desired host in the Hostname field.

6. Use the Distribution Configuration list to select the crawl database you want to use in the crawling action on the selected host.

7. Click OK to add the new job to the queue.

8. On the Host Distribution Rules page, click Apply Changes.

9. Click OK to apply the rule.

10. To remove a rule, follow steps 1 through 3 and on the Host Distribution Rules page, hover your cursor over the host distribution rule you want to remove, click the down arrow that becomes available, and then click Delete.

11. In the Confirmation box, click OK to add the job to the queue.

12. Click Apply Changes and then click OK.

Managing Crawler Server Specifics

The crawl component in SharePoint Server 2010 typically lives on the server that contains the crawler server role and each crawl component is associated with a crawl database. In server farms with more than one crawl database, each crawl database has two crawler components associated with a single crawl database. Typically, two crawler components will be installed on two separate crawler servers: so for every crawl database, you will have two crawler servers, each containing a crawler component associated with that database.

The crawler server role can cohabitate on the same server with other SharePoint services or live on a dedicated server machine. If you plan to crawl a large volume of content, need to crawl content across a wide variety of content sources, or require crawling to occur while queries are being performed, consider deploying at least one or more dedicated crawl servers.

You can have as many crawler components on a given crawler server up to the limit of the server machine's physical resources, but two components per server is recommended. If you have a variety of content sources, you can add crawlers and crawl databases and dedicate them to specific sources. Each crawler component on a specific crawler server should be associated with a separate crawl database.

Multiple crawler servers can be used for redundancy and to help ensure that crawl speed is fast enough to maintain freshness of the content. A crawler component is added to each of the crawler servers to accommodate multiple content locations, and a new crawl database is added on its own database server to service the new crawlers.

The Search Administration component also resides on the crawler server role and is responsible for managing the Shared Service Providers instance of SharePoint Enterprise Search. If you are maintaining multiple crawler servers in your infrastructure, the administration component will reside on only one crawler server.

The administration component can be moved from one server to another if the original server has suffered a failure or you are expanding your search infrastructure in order to reduce bottlenecks and to improve search performance as content sources and SharePoint users are added. Moving the administration component can only be done using Windows PowerShell. The following is an example of the code you would run at the PowerShell prompt as an administrator. The names of the servers and components are fictitious for the sake of the example.

```
# Retrieve the search server that will host the administration component
$searchInstance = Get-SPEnterpriseSearchServiceInstance <searchsrv01>
# Assign the administration component to the new server
$searchApp | get-SPEnterpriseSearchAdministrationComponent | set-
SPEnterpriseSearchAdministrationComponent -SearchServiceInstance $searchInstance
$admin = ($searchApp | get-SPEnterpriseSearchAdministrationComponent)
# Wait for the administration component to be initialized
do {write-host -NoNewline .;Start-Sleep 10;} while (-not $admin.Initialized)
```

You can also provision the SharePoint Server search administration website by moving it to another server in the GUI. You can also move the administration component to any server that you anticipate may need to host SharePoint Server search administration.

Planning Enterprise Search

Microsoft Search Server is an enterprise-wide search product designed to provide the search capacity for the SharePoint environment. SharePoint Search can scale to multiple servers for redundancy or to increase capacity and performance, scaling up to approximately 100 million items.

As you discovered in the previous section, planning for a search topology involves multiple elements, including index partitioning, query and crawler components, property databases, and crawler servers. In this section, you will take a look at the logical and physical aspects of planning for Enterprise Search.

Search Topology Introduction

When planning a search environment, you will often find it helpful to create and consult logical and physical diagrams of your Enterprise Search environment in order to conceptualize your needs.

Figure 10.2 illustrates a small search-server topology capable of serving up to approximately 10 million items. This topology possesses a single index partition that contains a primary copy of the query component and the mirror component, with the primary copy on the first server and the mirror copy on the second server for redundancy.

There is one crawler server containing the administration component and one crawler component. The crawler component is associated with the single crawl database present.

The database server contains the search admin database, the property database, and the crawl database.

FIGURE 10.2   A small search-server topology

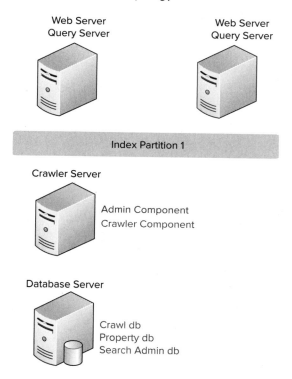

An example of a medium-sized search topology capable of supporting up to 20 million items would continue to place the web server and query server roles on the same server hardware, but there would be two index partitions present, each containing a primary query component and a mirror copy. (See Figure 10.3.) As in the previous example, the first server would contain the primary query component for each partition, and the second server would contain the redundant mirror copy for each partition.

In the current topology, there are two crawler server roles present, inhabiting one dedicated server machine each. The admin component is installed on the first server, and a crawler component is installed on each crawler server. Both crawler components are associated with the crawl database, but if there were more than one crawl database present, each of the crawl databases would have two associated crawler components each on a separate crawler server.

There are two database servers present. The first contains the search administration database, the crawl database, and the property database. The second database server contains all of the other SharePoint databases.

FIGURE 10.3 A medium-sized search topology

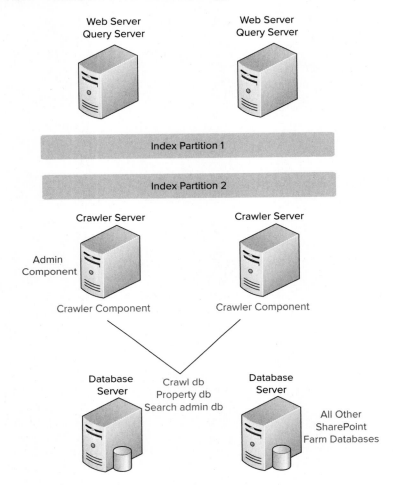

Designing the SharePoint Search Topology

A number of planning stages are required to develop a search infrastructure for a SharePoint Server 2010 server farm. As with many development processes, the first stage begins at an elementary level and successive stages provide the refinements required for your specific business model. The process includes stages for the following:

- Planning items and metrics
- Adjusting the topology for metrics
- Mapping logical and physical topologies
- Testing the design

Planning Items and Metrics

In the context of a SharePoint Search architecture, an item is any element in SharePoint that plays a role in determining your search requirements. Items can be SharePoint elements such as lists, items in document libraries, and SharePoint sites. The number of items you intend to include will determine the scale of your search architecture. Previously, you saw that 1 to 10 million items can be serviced by a small farm topology while 10 to 20 million items require a medium shared-farm topology. The following list provides a more comprehensive picture:

- Up to 1 million items require only a limited deployment.
- Up to 10 million items require a small farm topology.
- Up to 20 million items require a medium shared-farm topology.
- Up to 40 million items require a medium dedicated-farm topology.
- Up to 100 million items require a large dedicated-farm topology.

Shared versus dedicated-farm server environments are fairly easy to understand. For example, a shared server environment, such as you saw in the previous figures, describes a server infrastructure where two or more server roles are run on individual server hardware. As you can see in Figure 10.2, both the web server role and query server role are running on the same server machines. By contrast, a dedicated server is a machine that runs only a single role or performs only a specific, dedicated service in the server farm environment.

Expanding on this concept, a shared-farm topology contains more than one service or role provided to the SharePoint environment. Often only a single SharePoint server farm will provide all of the resources for your entire SharePoint system. A dedicated search farm topology is a server farm constructed exclusively to provide search services for SharePoint. Figure 10.3 illustrates a medium shared-farm topology.

In addition to the number of items involved, there are a number of metrics that factor into this initial stage of your design. While there are a plethora of metrics to consider, only a few make up what you could think of as the "big picture" of a SharePoint Search architecture.

Each metric is affected by several key factors involved in search performance:

- Availability of crawling and indexing operations
  - Hardware availability
- Availability of query functionality
  - Hardware availability
- Full crawl time and result freshness
  - Data source response time
  - Network bandwidth
  - Number of data sources
  - Query load during crawling
  - Size and type of files crawled
- Time to produce search results
  - Number of applications using Search
  - Number of concurrent user queries

The metrics and relevant factors driving the metrics are determined by the service level agreement or SLA, which defines the level of service to be provided in terms of delivery time and performance. For instance, an environment containing up to 20 million items and requiring a fast crawl speed, concurrent crawls on different content sources, and low query latency can be met by a medium shared-search topology, as previously shown in Figure 10.3.

A SharePoint environment with similar requirements but containing up to 40 million items requires a medium dedicated-search architecture. (See Figure 10.4.)

FIGURE 10.4   A medium dedicated-search architecture

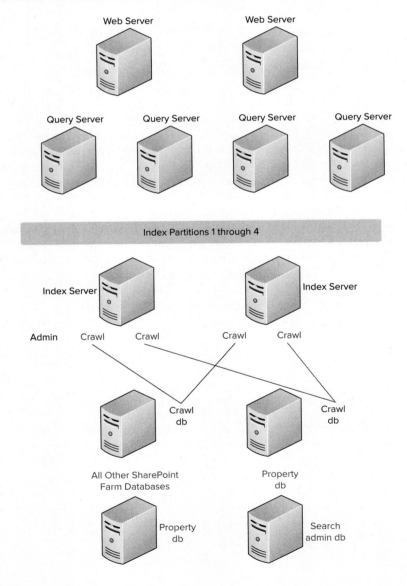

Remember, each index partition contains two query components, typically called Query component 1 and Query component 1m. In Figure 10.4, each of the four partitions contains two query components, and all four partitions and eight components are distributed across the four query servers in the dedicated architecture. In fact, each query server contains portions of two index partitions. For instance, the first query server may contain part of index partitions 1 and 4, while the second contains parts of partitions 2 and 1, and so forth.

While all your SharePoint web servers do not need to be hosted on your dedicated search farm, a server farm serving the SharePoint environment must include the presence of web servers. As previously noted, only one index server needs to contain the search admin component, but each index server can contain two search crawler components. As in previously presented topologies, each crawler component is associated with a crawl database and each crawl database is associated with two different crawler components.

In a dedicated architecture, each crawl database is installed on its own SQL Server computer. There are two additional SQL Server computers: one containing all other SharePoint databases as well as a property database and the other containing a second property database as well as the search admin database.

A large dedicated Search Server farm capable of supporting 100 million items may have a topological design that is substantially similar to a medium, dedicated server farm with the exception of the number of query servers, which are increased substantially to meet the needs of users accessing that many more items across a larger environment. You may have 10 query servers, instead of four, containing 10 index partitions. The environment will contain double the number of index and database servers. Each index server will still have two crawler components, with the first index server also hosting the admin component. Two SQL servers will contain two crawl databases each, with a third containing two Property databases as well as all other SharePoint databases and the fourth containing two Property databases and the Search admin database.

Index partitions and index components are distributed across the Index servers for both load balancing and redundancy so that each index server hosts parts of two index partitions.

 Real World Scenario

Constructing a Test Search Server Environment

You are currently setting up a testing server infrastructure to explore the configuration requirements for SharePoint Search. In your test environment, you are starting with a group of 10 million items that need to be indexed, which is minimal compared to an Enterprise Search infrastructure. For this environment, you will only need to use a single index partition, but you decide to use two physical servers, each running a web server and query server role. You configure the index partition to include both a primary copy and mirrored copy of the query component for redundancy, so each web/query server possesses one query component.

Next, you configure a single hardware server to act as the crawl server and set up both one administration component and one crawler component on this server.

Finally, you install and configure a single SQL database server and install a single crawl database and a single property database, as well as the search admin database. You also allow this hardware server to provide all other SharePoint database services.

Once you are finished testing the base functioning of this environment, you intend to expand the setup to support 20 million indexed items. For that scenario, you'll add a second index partition, with the primary and mirrored query components running on different servers. You'll also need to add a second hardware crawl server and install a crawler component on the server. Finally, you'll install a second SQL Server and move all of the SharePoint farm databases to that server, while leaving the crawl, property, and search admin databases on the first SQL Server.

Adjusting the Topology for Metrics

In the previous section, you saw how different metrics are affected by a number of different factors in the SharePoint server environment. Depending on which metric has the higher priority in your business plan, you can adjust the topology of your search environment accordingly.

Hardware availability is the primary factor in the availability of content crawling and indexing functionality. If this metric is a priority, increase the number of crawl servers in order to increase the number of crawler components. Also increase the number of SQL database servers to increase the number of crawl databases associated with crawler components. This will improve both availability and load distribution in the server farm.

Increasing the availability of query functionality is also a matter of hardware availability. Increase the number of index servers to increase index partitions and query components. Also, increase the number of database servers hosting crawl and property databases.

If reducing the time for a full crawl and improving search result freshness is a priority, you can add crawl servers, crawler components, and crawl databases to the topology. Each crawl database can contain content from separate and independent content sources. The more crawl components associated with crawl databases, the more search crawls you can schedule to occur concurrently, which reduces the overall time required for a full crawl operation. Performing faster and more frequent crawls improves the freshness of the search results in the environment.

If reducing the amount of time required for search results to be returned is a priority, you should deploy more query servers and make more query components available by increasing the number of index partitions. Moving the Property databases to dedicated servers will speed up search results by reducing the load per database. You might want to add more property databases as the number of items you support increases or if you are managing a large volume of metadata.

Mapping Logical and Physical Topologies

There's a difference between a query server role and a dedicated query hardware server. The query server role, like many other server roles, can coexist on the same server hardware with other server roles, also sharing the hardware resources. A dedicated query hardware server dedicates 100 percent of its physical resources to the query server role. The logical server topology is a map of the server roles relative to search regardless of the type or amount of server computer hardware involved. A physical topology illustrates the specific hardware components involved in providing search services and indicates which roles are occupying which specific hardware servers.

There are three basic server types that service a number of different roles and components: query server, crawl server, and database server.

Query Server

The query server hosts query server roles. The number of roles and, therefore, the number of physical servers are determined by the number of items the search architecture is expected to support. Any number of items less than 10 million can be managed by one or two query server roles. The query server role can run on a hardware server hosting any other SharePoint service; however, as the number of items increases, as well as the need to support a large amount of traffic and provide quick search result times, you will need to move the query server roles to dedicated hardware servers.

A general rule of thumb is to use one dedicated query server for each 10 million items supported. This would mean using two query servers for 20 million items, four query servers for 40 million items, and so forth.

Each index partition can support up to 10 million items, and each index partition can be mirrored using query components for the sake of redundancy. Each query server should be deployed for every two index partitions required in your environment. For every 10 million items to be supported, you will need two query components. This means, for example, if you are supporting 40 million items, you should have eight query components and if you're supporting 100 million items, you should have 20 query components. Remember, you will have two query components for each index partition.

Crawl Server

As with the query server role, the crawl server role can run on any physical server along with any other SharePoint service; however, if you expect to crawl a large amount of content across a wide variety of content sources, consider using dedicated crawl servers. You should need only one dedicated server for every 25 million items or so; therefore, for 100 million items, you may require only four physical crawl servers. Of course, each crawl server will host two crawler components; so for up to 100 million items, you will have eight crawler components. As you already know, two crawler components will be associated with each content database.

Database Server

Dedicated database servers host the crawl database, the property database, and the search admin database. If, for instance, you are supporting up to 100 million items requiring eight crawl components, you will need four crawl databases, which can be hosted on two to four database hardware servers. You will need the same number of property databases to contain the metadata for all of the crawled content, but you will need only a single search admin database for your environment.

Testing the Design

Once you've determined the search requirements for your organization and have created the appropriate design, the final step is to construct a testing environment and see how your topology performs under operational conditions. If you notice any performance inconsistencies, you can go back and adjust your design to accommodate the issues and redeploy your test environment.

Once the testing phase is complete, you can deploy the dedicated search architecture into actual production—but in a real sense, the process of design and testing is never over. A company's search requirements are as dynamic as the company itself. As you monitor the functionality of search, note performance changes so you can go back to your base design and make adjustments to manage more search items, additional content sources, and more users accessing search.

This phase offers a good opportunity to evaluate the search solution requirements for your company and to create a diagram of the necessary server logical and physical topology for your organization's SharePoint infrastructure.

Planning for People Search

In general, the use of Search is the attempt to locate appropriate resources to address issues, problems, or projects. The use of People Search is the attempt to locate people in the SharePoint environment who are resources for issues, problems, or projects. When People Search in SharePoint is properly configured, search results will return links to the public profiles of users, providing specific information about them as well as links allowing you to contact them via email or instant messaging.

Planning and configuring People Search is largely a matter of planning and configuring the User Profile Service and developing search service applications that take advantage of people as resources by developing search scopes and People Search tabs to illuminate specific groups of people. This process can be carried down to the site collection level and site collection administrators can create site-level search scopes for the people who are members of specific site collections.

Planning the User Profile Service

In order to plan the People Search, you must start with planning the User Profiles. The User Profile Service administers user profiles in the SharePoint environment, which means, the User Profile Service manages information about users and the administration of data connections used to synchronize information about users across the profile store, directory services, and LDAP.

A high-level planning scenario for the User Profile Service involves:

- Planning connections between User Profile Services, Directory Services, and line-of-business applications such as SAP.

- Planning the required User Profile Properties and Organization Profile Properties.

- Planning policies affecting the changing and displaying of user profiles.
- Planning how user profiles are to be used by other personalization features.

Service applications in SharePoint 2010 provide a central location from which to manage all of the different features and actions associated with the service. The User Profile Service application offers you a central place from which to specifically manage personalization settings. Among those settings are

- Audiences
- My Site settings
- Organization browsing and management settings
- Profile synchronization settings
- User profile properties

These sections of this chapter teach you the process of creating and configuring the User Profile Service application. Before you can continue with this part of the chapter, you must meet the following requirements:

- The version of SharePoint Server 2010 you are using must be either Standard or Enterprise.
- You must have configured at least one site collection that uses the My Site Host template.
- You must have an application pool that can be used by My Sites.
- You must be running an instance of the Managed Metadata Services.
- At least one managed path must exist.

The User Profile Service application comes with a default set of user profile properties. In addition to the defaults, you can add, edit, and delete customized user profile properties in the service application. This allows you to track specific data by associating specific properties of users with important business processes.

In addition to managing user profiles, you can also administer organizational profiles including components such as organization profile properties and organization subtypes.

So far we've been exploring user and organizational profiles that are specific to SharePoint; in fact, profile information can be stored in more than one location. User and group profiles stored in SharePoint's store profile can be synchronized with profile data stored in both directory services and business systems throughout the enterprise. To perform the following tasks related to profile synchronization, you must be a member of the User Profile Service administrator group. You must also possess at least Replicate Directory Changes permissions on Active Directory Domain Services (AD DS) if this is the directory service to be used.

One or more directory services must be available on the same network where you are running SharePoint Server 2010 in order for you to perform profile synchronization tasks. Directory services that can be synchronized with SharePoint include:

- Active Directory Domain Services (AD DS)
- Business Data Connectivity Services

- Novell eDirectory version 8.7.3 (LDAP)
- SunOne version 5.2 (LDAP)
- IBM Trivoli 6.2 (LDAP)

Profile synchronization can be set to occur when profile data has changed either in SharePoint or in the directory service. You determine how and when the import and export processes occur when you configure profile synchronization. By default, no user profile property is set to export.

Some user profile properties in SharePoint, including first name and last name, are automatically mapped to their counterparts in the external directory service by default. If you set synchronization to occur on a recurring schedule, the synchronization is incremental. This means the only information that is synchronized is data that has changed since the last scheduled synchronization. You can also use either a nonrecurring full synchronization or a nonrecurring incremental synchronization.

Configuring the User Profile Service for People Search

User Profile Service and the User Profile Synchronization Service must both be started. You will want the Forefront Identity Manager Service and Forefront Identity Manager Synchronization services to be started as well. To verify that these services are started, on the computer containing Central Administration and the User Profile Synchronization service, click Start ➢ Control Panel ➢ Administrative Tools ➢ Services. Either start the required services or verify that they are running. Once you have confirmed that these services are running, set up a profile synchronization connection specifying an account on the domain you want to use. This will provide the user profiles; however, right now, they still cannot be searched. Exercise 10.13 will take you through the setup process.

EXERCISE 10.13

Setting Up User Profile Synchronization

In this exercise, you will learn how to set up User Profile Synchronization.

1. In Central Administration under Application Management, click Manage Service Applications.

2. On the Service Applications page, click User Profile Synchronization Service.

3. On the User Profile Synchronization Service page, use the drop-down menu to select the desired User Profile Service application, and then click OK.

4. In Central Administration, click Monitoring, and under Timer Jobs, click Review Job Definitions.

5. In Quick Start, click Running Jobs, and on the Running Jobs page, verify that ProfileSynchronizationSetupJob is running.

6. Once the job is finished, go to Job History and verify that the job finished with a status of Successful. (Forefront Services will now be started and running under the administrator account.)

7. In Central Administration, click on Manage Service Applications and then select User Profile Service Application.

8. On the User Profile Service Application page, under Synchronization, click Configure Service Connections.

9. On the Synchronization Connections page, click Create New Connection.

10. On the Add New Synchronization Connection page, give the connection a name and select a connection type, such as Active Directory.

11. Under Connection Settings, if you chose Active Directory, enter a name in the Forest Name field and click Auto Discover Domain Controller.

12. Select an authentication provider, enter an account name, configure a password for the account, and enter a port number.

13. Under Containers, click the Populate Containers button to expand the tree, select the Users OU tree node, and then click OK.

14. Once the connection has been created, return to the User Profile Service Application page and under Synchronization, click Start Profile Synchronization.

15. On the Start Profile Synchronization page, select Start Full Synchronization and then click OK.

16. Once the job is finished, in Central Administration, go to the Manage User Profiles page to verify the user profiles are being populated.

Exercise 10.14 will show you how to set up the basic search service application for People Search. In this exercise, you will specifically select the URLs where search is to start crawling to acquire content specific to People Search.

EXERCISE 10.14

Configuring the Search Service Application for People Search

In this exercise, you will learn how to configure the search service application for People Search.

1. In Central Administration under Service Applications, click Search Service Application.

2. On the Search Service Application page, click the Manage button.

3. Go to Content Sources and select Local SharePoint Sites.

4. On the Edit Content Source page under Start Addresses, type the URLs where you want search to start crawling. The start address looks something like http://sp2010.

5. If necessary, edit the other settings on this page, such as Crawl Settings, Crawl Schedules, and Content Source Priority.

6. If this source has never been crawled before, select the Start Full Crawl Of This Content Source check box.

7. Click OK when finished.

Planning Search Reporting

On the Search Service Application Search Administration page, the final category in the left-hand menu is Reports. By default, two report types are displayed: Administration Reports and Web Analytics Reports.

Administration Reports

Under Reports, when you click on Administration Reports, you can view the different default report types to determine the health and functioning of the search service. The default folder is the Search Administration Reports folder. Clicking that link takes you to a list of the available reports for search:

- CrawlRatePerContentSource: This is the graphic view of recent crawl activity aggregated by content course.

- CrawlRatePerType: This offers you a graphic view of recent crawl activity by items and actions for specific URLs.

- QueryLatency: This is the graphic view of recent query activity displaying latency from the major segments of the query pipeline, as well as the query averages per minute.

- QueryLatencyTrend: This is the graphic view of recent query activity that is trending.

- SharepointBackendQueryLatency: This is the graphic view of recent query activity with latency details for the index and property database portion of the query pipeline as well as query averages per minute.

    Advanced Reports, another folder on that page, contains:

- CrawlProcessingPerActivity: This is the graphic view of where crawl processing happens in the pipeline.

- CrawlProcessingPerComponent: This is the graphic view of where crawl processing happens in the pipeline per minute.

- CrawlQueue: This is the graphic view of the state of the crawl queue.

    You can click to the right of any of these reports to view or modify the report properties or permissions.

Click on the name of a report to open it, such as Crawl Rate Per Content Source. On this page, you can see the report of crawl rate activity for the past 12 hours by default. You can filter the results by application type, individual content sources, and the date and time range, and then click Apply Filters on the right side of the page to view your selections.

On the All Documents page for Search Administration Reports, you can also click to the left of a particular report and select a check box in order to activate the Library Tools Ribbon and perform various actions. You can select either the Documents or Library tabs under Library Tools to access different features.

Web Analytics Reports

Along with reports on search features, you can view reports on usage data for the different SharePoint sites and site collections on the Search Administration page under Reports by clicking Web Analytics Reports. On the Web Analytics Reports page, click the desired web application and then on the Summary page, click the name of the desired report. The following reports are available:

- Summary
- Number of Page Views
- Number of Daily Unique Visitors
- Number of Referrers
- Top Pages
- Top Visitors
- Top Referrers
- Top Destinations
- Top Browsers
- Number of Queries
- Number of Collections
- Top Site Collection Templates
- Customized Reports

You can filter these reports by date range and export them to spreadsheet format.

Summary

In this chapter, you learned how to define the business requirements for Search in SharePoint 2010, as well as how to plan a search topology and how to plan an Enterprise Search strategy. This involved managing indexing, content sources, and search scopes, as well as designing logical and physical Search Server environments.

Exam Essentials

Be able to define search requirements.   You should understand how to define the business requirements for Enterprise Search in SharePoint, which includes being able to identify types of data, understanding how data is to be segregated, and understanding content sources, federation requirements, and search scopes.

Be able to plan a search topology.   Know how to design a search topology taking into account elements such as index partitioning, query components, property databases, and crawler servers.

Be able to plan an Enterprise Search strategy.   Demonstrate the ability to design an information access and search strategy, plan for metadata in the search environment, and incorporate people search and search reporting.

Chapter 11

Planning Business Management Strategies

TOPICS COVERED IN THIS CHAPTER

- ✓ Designing Collaboration Components
- ✓ Designing Content Management
- ✓ Planning for Social Computing
- ✓ Planning for Business Intelligence Strategy

Business Management is at the heart of the purpose and function of SharePoint 2010. This chapter addresses how to take all of the tools and features you've put together and plan your strategy for applying SharePoint to your business needs.

The first part of the chapter will take you through a high-level view of the various collaboration components that make up SharePoint. You will see what you must consider when you begin developing a business management plan designed to provide an interface for your employees, partners, and customers in which they can manage documentation, locate resources, and create teams in order to solve problems and achieve business goals.

Next, you will drill down to content management planning for the enterprise, which takes into consideration the vast scope of what is considered information within SharePoint. The topics reviewed here will include records deployment and management, document and web content management, information rights management, information management policies, and metadata planning.

The "Planning for Social Computing" section will let you design a plan for deployment and use of the User Profile Service, user profiles, organizational profiles, social tags, and audiences—all as they're applied to viewing individuals and groups as resources to be located and accessed via SharePoint. Platforms to be considered are My Sites, personalization sites, and enterprise wikis.

Finally, you will learn to plan a business intelligence strategy. Business intelligence includes using SharePoint applications, processes, and technologies to support business decision making and to plan future business projections. SharePoint features and utilities to be considered during business intelligence planning include PerformancePoint Services dashboards and scorecards, chart web parts, Excel and Visio services, SQL reporting services, and the Report Center.

By the end of the chapter, you should be thoroughly grounded in the skills and techniques required for planning business and collaboration strategies within SharePoint.

The Microsoft SharePoint 2010 Administrator (Exam 70-668) exam tests the skills of candidates to design and deploy SharePoint Server 2010 platforms in a production environment on scales including the enterprise infrastructure. One of the most important features and functions of SharePoint is in the area of business management and business intelligence. This chapter presents a comprehensive treatment of the different aspects of SharePoint functionality for business management, from collaboration components to content management, and to business intelligence implementation.

Planning Collaboration Components

Collaboration component planning should always be associated with a business outcome. When someone is working with a technology platform, there can be a tendency to focus on the technology first and then work backward to the business problems and goals. This is more or less like putting the cart before the horse. SharePoint is designed to provide community and collaboration solutions to business problems, but you still have to identify the problems and goals first.

Here's a brief list of what you should consider in the realm of business collaboration:

- Accessing internal subject-matter experts
- Expanding online communication venues
- Connecting learners with mentors
- Building teams "without walls"
- Allowing teams to manage content at the same "table"

In general, one of the major problems with collaboration in the business place is discovering who should be collaborating. In a real-world environment, you may not always know the people who have the necessary skill set and experience required to develop a team to reach a certain goal. SharePoint has the ability to recognize and locate such human resources within its framework, and it can show you how employees in different departments, divisions, and offices can join together using SharePoint's interface to become a virtual team.

This, in essence, is a "team without walls" or a group that can be developed without regard for geographic location. This also presents the opportunity to develop teacher and learner relationships so that knowledge and experience held by your most seasoned workers can be passed down to more recently acquired employees.

Once you've established a team, SharePoint operates as a "location" where the members can meet, discuss strategies, and create and develop content mutually. Managers can be brought into a workflow to review and approve deliverables and provide feedback. With SharePoint, the business process and goals are served by the technology, not the other way around.

Collaboration Component Overview

SharePoint 2010 provides a combination of established, new, and enhanced collaboration features and components to be used in the service of business management. These components can be divided into three primary areas: enterprise content management, social computing, and business intelligence.

Enterprise Content Management

Enterprise content management (ECM) is a cover-all term for a set of software solutions that let an organization create, manage, secure, store, publish, retire, and destroy any digital content used for business purposes. A number of key components are involved in the implementation of ECM:

- Document management
- Forms management
- Web content management
- Digital asset management
- Records management

Each of these terms will be defined and explored in the "Designing Content Management" section of this chapter.

Social Computing

Social computing is a cover-all term for that portion of computer technology that addresses the interaction between human social activity and networked computing systems. It is ubiquitous not only in the general computing environment, but also in business computing systems. Regarding SharePoint as a social computing solution, the key components include:

- Enterprise wikis
- My Sites
- Social tagging
- Personalization sites
- Search for People

You will learn much more about SharePoint and social computing in the "Planning for Social Computing" section of this chapter.

Business Intelligence

Business intelligence is a collection of tools and techniques that allow key decision makers and stakeholders to view, evaluate, and filter information in real time for the purpose of making present and future decisions regarding the company's business process. Although numerous elements make up business intelligence, just a small set of main components are involved:

- Excel Services
- PerformancePoint Services
- Visio Services
- Chart Web Parts

You'll learn more about each of these services and how they interact with all of the elements involved in business intelligence in the "Planning for Business Intelligence Strategy" section of this chapter.

Collaboration Component Environments

Another aspect to SharePoint collaboration planning is designing the topology that most suits your business goals. This section will offer three sample topologies:

- **Enterprise Intranet Collaboration Environment:** A SharePoint topology designed to provide publishing portals for divisions, groups, and teams in an enterprise business environment

- **Departmental Collaboration Environment:** A SharePoint topology designed to provide sites and portals for multiple teams within a single division in a company

- **Social Collaboration Environment:** A SharePoint topology optimized to provide a central location for personal My Sites and shared documentation

The examples in the following sections are not the only ways to deploy a SharePoint topology for the specified purpose.

Enterprise Intranet Collaboration Environment

This section summarizes the logical topological design for an Enterprise Intranet Collaboration SharePoint server farm designed to serve a large corporation environment comprised of multiple business locations comprised of numerous divisions, each containing groups and teams who plan to collaborate across department and divisional barriers. See Figure 11.1.

FIGURE 11.1   An Enterprise Intranet Collaboration environment

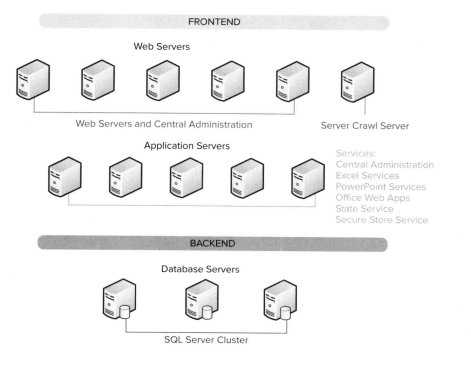

The frontend of the topology contains two levels, the web-server level and application-server level. The backend contains the SQL server cluster providing database services for the farm.

To service an enterprise environment requiring cross-department and divisional barriers, each web server also contains the Central Administration website and one server is dedicated as a search crawl server. Application servers on the second level all contain Excel and PowerPoint services as well as Office web applications, the State Service and the Secure Store Service.

In the backend, SQL Server 2008 database servers are clustered.

Departmental Collaboration Environment

In contrast to an enterprise collaboration environment, the farm topology for departmental collaboration assigns more specific roles to each server in the farm. (See Figure 11.2.) Web Front End (WFE) servers do not always possess identical roles. In the following sample topology, all servers possess the web server role, several also possess the search query server role, and one also functions as a search crawl server.

FIGURE 11.2   A Departmental Collaboration environment

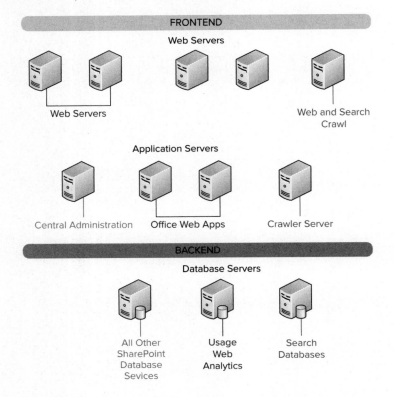

The same is true for the application servers. In this situation, only one also possesses the Central Administration role, while one also works as a crawler server.

In the backend, database servers operate as a SharePoint database server, a database server specifically for usage web analytics, and a database server specifically for searching.

Social Collaboration Environment

A Social Collaboration server farm topology is designed to span an enterprise environment specifically for the purpose of locating and connecting people together as resources. Company employees use My Sites to post relevant information about their positions, locations, and skill sets so anyone else in the company needing to access a particular employee as a resource for a project can easily find that person. Social collaboration environments also allow hosting for personal sites where employees can gather as if for an impromptu meeting and share, edit, and collaborate on documents for a common purpose.

A farm topology optimized for social collaboration requires fewer physical assets in the server farm and can combine roles into one or two servers on each tier in the frontend and backend of the farm. SQL servers are clustered for this specific solution. See Figure 11.3.

FIGURE 11.3 A Social Collaboration environment

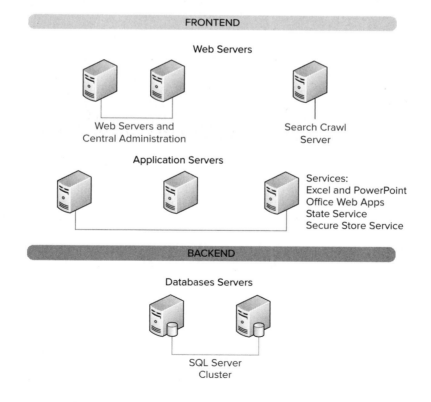

As mentioned at the beginning of the "Collaboration Component Environments" section, these collaboration environments are examples and don't represent the only ways to deploy a SharePoint topology for the specified purpose.

Designing Content Management

SharePoint 2010 is the first version of this platform that operates as a complete Enterprise Content Management system. Previous versions possessed powerful document management components, but often it was necessary to purchase third-party applications and add-ons in order to provide the necessary range of content management services required in an enterprise environment.

ECM, an embedded feature set in SharePoint 2010, allows users to directly access features such as Document Management, Forms Management, Records Management, and Web Content Management as normative elements within the SharePoint interface.

Two important concepts of content management are information rights and metadata.

Information rights in SharePoint entail the ability of authors and other content creators to manage access to their documents using a rights-based document encryption system. This is more than a simple "yes or no" access system, as each user is provided with a license that defines their level of access to documents based on the user's permissions level. For instance, one user may have read-only access, while another may specifically experience a disabling of copy and paste functions for a document, and so on.

The simple definition of metadata is "data about data." In SharePoint, managed metadata is the result of the ability to control and administer managed terms used to define data from a central, hierarchical collection. In other words, SharePoint allows you to create and manage a set of terms that you can use to apply as attributes to various items contained within SharePoint. These items can then be located and manipulated based on their managed attributes.

A great deal of the following information is conceptual, but a detailed understanding of all of the features and elements that make up content management is required to first plan for and then implement a content management system. This is information that is not only "SharePoint-centric" but is focused on the nature and character of what content is in terms of the "big picture." Once you have that picture firmly in place, you can drill back down into the details by performing a number of the exercises included in this section of the chapter to experience the "hands-on" aspects of SharePoint content management.

ECM Component Overview

There are a wide variety of SharePoint ECM components. An overview of some of the key features and components will give you a better handle on resource availability within this realm.

Document Management

This is the method of managing documents throughout their entire lifecycle—from creation, publication, distribution, storage, search, archiving, and destruction. Within the document management process, users are able to check out a document for revision or editing and then check it back into the system. Versioning is also available to track and manage the different iterations of a document, and SharePoint workflow capacities allow for a complex set of collaborative and approval activities. Documents are created and exist as living, evolving entities within SharePoint. Within Document Management, there are a couple of specific features of which you should be aware.

Document Sets

Any collection of documents with common management requirements or a common purpose can be considered a document set. A document set can be made up of a variety of document file types. For instance, you can create a document set as a presentation to your board of directors on your company's product roadmap for the next fiscal year. The documents you create for the presentation can include Word documents for containing a detailed report, a PowerPoint slideshow as the visual component of the main presentation, Visio diagrams containing timeline and workflow information, and an Excel spreadsheet containing revenue forecasts.

Document IDs

This is a site-level feature that lets the system assign each document within a site its own unique identifier, which is then used to access the document using Search, a direct link, or via page navigation. This is an improvement from SharePoint 2007. If you moved a document from one location to another in SharePoint 2007, all of the links and references to the document would be broken, making the document unable to be located within the system. The Document ID feature now makes a document searchable and findable within SharePoint 2010 regardless of how many times it was moved or where it's been relocated within the system.

One caveat is that, because this feature is managed at the Site Collection level, document IDs aren't necessarily unique across site collections within a SharePoint farm.

Records Management

Think of Records Management as the big brother to Document Content Management because documents comprise only a subset of all records maintained within SharePoint.

This ECM component manages the complete life cycle of all records within SharePoint including documents, web pages, forms, and any other container of corporate information that must be maintained in a consistent and stable state. Most often, this refers to legal and policy records that must be retained in an unchanging state pursuant to various local, national, and international laws as they pertain to your business practices and operations.

Forms Management

Businesses continue to make substantial use of forms, both in a paper version and as web forms, to allow the input of data into a standardized format. Forms can be any sort of document, from an employment application, to a customer satisfaction form, to an order form, to an inventory form.

While forms can be treated as documents when completed, forms designed in InfoPath for SharePoint are usually standardized and versioned so that the same order form is used—for instance, for a particular product line or product version release so that the appropriate fields are available for use by a customer and so that fields that are not required or that are required for a separate product aren't displayed.

Web Content Management

In a sense, you might think of all content management within SharePoint as web content management, given that SharePoint's UI is web-based—but in fact, this specifically refers to content that is created for web access by SharePoint users. Web content can be created either using tools directly within SharePoint or from within the Microsoft Office suite. Like other documents, web content can be versioned and workflowed for greater control of the product and the life cycle of the web documents. Also, web content can contain connections to virtually any other type of content available, including forms, documents, and rich media such as video or audio.

Digital Asset Management

All of the other content types we've reviewed so far exist in a generally static state in terms of their presentation. Digital assets by contrast are wholly dynamic methods of communicating data, such as in the form of videos or podcasts. YouTube has become a virtual standard for not only entertainment, but education and information presentation on the Web, thanks to the ubiquitous presence of broadband Internet access.

Within the corporate enterprise network infrastructure, high-speed connections allow the generous use of digital assets by accessing rich media in the business intranet. Rich media, like any other form of content, requires a method of controlling the creation, iteration, storage, and archiving of these data forms. While such media is closely related with web content management, it also exists as its own entity due to the nature of the file types involved.

Document Management Planning

The primary container of documents in SharePoint is the document library. Libraries can contain a wide variety of content types including Word documents, Excel spreadsheets, PowerPoint slides, images, and reports. Documents created in an Office application can be stored and managed within a site collection's document library as the central location for document management operations.

Document Library Planning

A document library is a virtual container for collections of document files within the SharePoint environment. These documents are available for sharing and collaboration, and the library is a fundamental feature in your document management plan. The first step in document library planning is to select the library type that best meets your specific organizational requirements.

Keep in mind that you may need more than one type of document library, depending on your specific corporate goals and needs. You may create numerous different sites within a single site collection or numerous site collections to satisfy those needs. Each site or a site within specific site collections will then contain different document libraries that match up with the site's or the site collection's purpose.

The following list shows you the different document library types available in SharePoint 2010, along with a brief description of each library.

- **Document Center Site Library:** This is an enterprise-level document library typically used for large-scale archiving or as a comprehensive knowledge base containing a deep hierarchy of documents.

- **Internet Site Library:** This library contains web pages as the primary content for Internet and intranet website development and editing and can manage each site's underlying content library. This library type can also be used to manage content that is intended to be downloaded from web pages you manage.

- **Portal Library:** This is a large-scale to enterprise-level library that is similar in structure to a team site library but with a larger scope. This library utilizes a strict review and approval process for document management. A wide variety of documents, including web pages are often generated in an authoring portal site that contains multiple libraries.

- **Records Repository Library:** This is a collection of libraries, with each individual library being used to manage a specific record type such as a contract library or a policy library in order to comply with statutory or policy requirements.

- **Slide Library:** This library is a container for managing PowerPoint slides and slideshows.

- **Team Site Library:** This is a team collaboration library optimized for peer sharing of documents, content control, versioning, and search.

Library Workflow Planning

Authoring portal sites are often large containers for many different library types. Within each of these libraries, different types of content are developed and then published within the originating library, workflowed to a different library, or published to another library specifically for employee, partner, or customer consumption.

Much of the activity within the various libraries is contained within the authoring portal. For instance, the various different libraries serving different team or group projects will generate workflow and edit documents that will either largely stay within their original libraries or be copied to an enterprise content repository within the portal.

The documents can generally be accessed and consumed from the content repository. The enterprise documents repository can also be housed in a site outside the authoring portal, depending on the level of access you want to provide to the material and what level of security you need for the authoring portal. Another destination for various project documents is publication to libraries or web pages on an intranet site for employees or an Internet site for partners or customers. These documents can be white papers, solution briefs, case studies, or similar documents for more general consumption.

The Contracts library in the portal is specialized and typically accessed by legal staff for the creation and versioning of contracts. The most recent iterations of contract documents are published to the enterprise records repository (not the enterprise documents repository) as the official container for the corporation's legal documentation.

Web pages for intranet and Internet sites themselves are also documents that can be created, workflowed, edited, shared, and published. Any changes you make to your employee or customer facing sites should first be generated within a private library within the authoring portal and published to the desired websites only after they have been workflowed and approved.

Develop the libraries within your authoring portal based on your organization's documentation requirements, documentation types, and access requirements.

Managed Metadata Planning

Managed metadata services are used to provide tagging to content in order to centrally control a keyword taxonomy. This taxonomy is used to locate content when executing a search in SharePoint.

The short definition of the metadata is that it's "data about data." That doesn't seem terribly illuminating, though. In slightly more detail, metadata is information about the data to which it refers, and it is used by disciplines such as information management, information science, and information technology to organize content. In an old-fashioned library, it is somewhat similar to what the Dewey Decimal System used to be to the books in the library.

The advantage of using metadata for data management is that a single metadata system can organize and track not only a wide variety of content, but a wide variety of content containers including books, CDs, database tables, DVDs, graphics, web pages, and so on.

Specifically applied to SharePoint, managed metadata is a hierarchical collection of managed items that lets you define data and then structure that information within SharePoint information containers, such as libraries and lists. A division within a company can use a managed metadata service for all of the site collections within a web application the division manages. This allows the division to control how metadata terms are applied as attributes to items and documents within those site collections, since this particular division uses those items for specific business roles not shared with other divisions within the company.

Metadata Term and Term Sets

There are a number of words and phrases associated with metadata management with which you will need to be familiar. A term is any word or collection of words that is associated with a specific item in SharePoint. A term set is a collection of terms that are related in some manner. Terms and term sets, once created, can be specified for use in a column on a SharePoint page. Managed metadata refers to these terms and term sets as existing independently from the presence of these columns.

Term sets can be local, meaning that they apply only within a particular site collection, or they can be global, meaning they exist outside the context of one specific site collection.

One way of understanding this is to think of a term set as a big bucket containing a group of related terms. For instance, you could create a term set called "Classes" to represent a collection of classes being held at a school. Add a term for each class being taught and a content type called "Class Materials." You can add columns to the content type for each of the different types of materials being used and then indicate that any value assigned to your columns must originate from the Classes term set. Finally, you can create a list of class materials.

The terms you created are known as managed terms. You can also create enterprise keywords, which are also added to items in SharePoint. Keywords are all contained in a single term set called a keyword set. Managed terms and Enterprise keywords are collected in a database called the term store.

Managing a Term Store

A term store is a container for terms, which are words or phrases that are associated with a particular item in SharePoint. Terms can be collected in sets of related terms and term sets can then be collected into groups. You can create managed terms or terms you can predefine, and then organize them into a hierarchy. These terms can then be selected by users in a column in a document library. Figure 11.4 shows you the Term Store Management Tool interface.

FIGURE 11.4 The Term Store Management Tool interface

You can also use managed keywords, which are words and phrases you add to SharePoint items, tagging them in whatever manner you choose and developing an appropriate folksonomy.

You can learn more about folksonomies at `http://en.wikipedia.org/wiki/Folksonomy`.

Users can then tag items using whatever keywords they believe fit the items. Unlike managed terms, keywords are not organized into hierarchies, and at least some of the content types in SharePoint probably will have a keyword column available by default, so you as the administrator won't have to add it as you would with a Managed Term column.

While all this may seem rather conceptual, the practical use for managed metadata allows departments and divisions to develop different metadata services with different scopes. For instance, each department can have its own local metadata service for site collections in a web application, another metadata service can be shared among all the departments in a single division that uses multiple web applications within a server farm, and another global metadata service can be used for the entire enterprise-level organization across all server farms.

A term store must exist before you can administer it. Exercise 11.1 starts you off with the creation of a Managed Metadata column in a library, such as a document library, which will allow you to create terms that you can assign to documents in the library. In this example, you'll need to have a document library available and navigate to the library in order to get started.

EXERCISE 11.1

Creating Metadata Terms for a Library

In this exercise, you will learn how to create the library's Managed Metadata column and terms.

1. Navigate to the desired document library.

2. On the Library Tools menu, click the Library tab, and then on the Ribbon, click Create Column.

3. When the Create Column window opens, enter the name you want the column to have in the Column Name field.

4. Under The Type Of Information In This Column Is, select Managed Metadata.

5. Select Customize Your Term Set and give the term set a descriptive name in the Description field.

6. Use the Term Set Manager to create individual terms.

Once a term store exists, you can add an administrator to the store and, if necessary, remove the administrator later. Exercise 11.2 shows you how to add a term store administrator.

EXERCISE 11.2

Adding a Term Store Administrator

In this exercise, you will learn how to add an administrator to the term store.

1. On the Central Administration home page, under Application Management, click Manage Service Applications.

2. On the Manage Service Applications page, click the Service Applications tab if it isn't already selected.

3. Select the managed metadata service you want, and then in the Ribbon, click Manage.

4. When the Term Store Management Tool opens, in the Properties pane, in the Term Store Administrators field, either enter the name of the user or use the address book to add a user.

5. When you are finished, click Save.

If you later need to remove an administrator, repeat the process and in the Term Store Administrators field, select the name you want to remove and delete the name. Click Save to make the process final.

Term store administrators are able to perform a variety of tasks for the term store, including being able to create and delete term groups, assign or remove users from the group manager role, assign or remove users from the contributor role, import a term set, create, edit, or remove term sets, and edit the working languages for a term store.

Information Management Policy Planning

An *information management policy* is a collection of rules that are applied to each type of content in SharePoint. Each of the rules in a policy is called a policy feature, which is an attribute or specification for the content type, such as providing instructions on the proper method of archiving the content type. The overall policy controls who can access and manage information in your company, how they can use the information, and how long the information is retained within SharePoint.

Policies within a company exist to facilitate compliance with legal or statutory requirements in relation to records keeping. For instance, certain types of financial or auditing records are required to be retained by the company for a certain number of years before disposal. Policies also control document auditing to verify compliance and methods of locating and identifying required records.

To plan for information policies in your organization, first determine what legal requirements exist and are applied to your company and then design site collection policies to comply with these requirements. Site collection policies are included in the Site Collection Policy galleries for all of the specified site collections and may require the creation and use of custom policy features.

Policies can be organization-wide or specific to a site collection. An organization-wide policy might describe how auditing practices are to be used for all information within the entire company, while a site collection policy might be created to apply only to management of white papers and information sheets for a particular class of products produced by one division.

Policies can be associated with different levels of containers or items. For instance, policy features can be associated with a site collection policy that's applied to a specific content type contained within a given list or library. You can also associate the policy features directly to a content type first, and then add that content type to one or more lists or libraries within a site collection. Finally, you can choose to associate a collection of policy features directly to a list or library, but only if the list or library isn't expected to contain a number of different types of content.

Web Content Management Planning

Web content is just like any other form of documentation used by your organization. The content and presentation need to be planned for current and future needs, the presentation needs to be designed (usually using multiple CSS style sheets), content needs to be generated and added (often in HTML); and once the web document is workflowed and approved, it is published to the desired intranet or Internet website for consumption by the target audience.

Web content is usually generated in an authoring portal. Specific libraries should be created within the portal for the different types of websites that are to be serviced. You can create libraries based on each of your customer or employee facing websites and, if your sites contain a large number of web pages organized by topic or product, you can create a library for the creation and management of web pages based on those organizational structures.

Web Content Deployment

Content deployment is the process of moving content from one site collection to another, usually across two or more server farms. The most common purpose for content deployment is to move content from an authoring environment to a production environment. The authoring environment is kept separate from your consumer's experience so that information is not prematurely released or released in an erroneous form.

The following sections show how to configure content deployment settings and how to manage deployment paths and jobs.

Content Deployment Management Planning

Content deployment settings must be configured for both the source and destination site collections. Another way of looking at it is that a site collection must be set up for both incoming and outgoing content deployment jobs. This is performed on the Central Administration site for the source and destination site collections in the relevant server farms. Once done, you can use the Content Deployment Settings page to accept or reject incoming content jobs for your entire server farm. You can also delegate the responsibility for receiving incoming jobs and sending outgoing jobs to specific servers in the farm.

There are three typical roles for farms in terms of content deployment.

- **Authoring Farm:** This is the source of the content to be exported and must be configured for outgoing (export) settings.

- **Staging Farm:** This is a management area for incoming and outgoing content and must be configured for incoming (import) and outgoing (export) settings.

- **Production Farm:** This is the destination for content and must be configured for incoming (import) settings.

Any particular piece of content travels in only one direction, from source to destination. A staging area can exist if you have numerous authoring and production platforms so that all content passes through a single launching environment, but once content is deployed from an authoring site, it does not return.

Exercise 11.3 will show you how to configure content deployment settings. You will need to be a member of the Farm Administrators group to perform Exercise 11.3, Exercise 11.4, and Exercise 11.5. Before you begin, be aware that both the export server and the import server must host an instance of the Central Administration website.

EXERCISE 11.3

Configuring Content Deployment Settings

In this exercise, you will learn how to configure content deployment settings.

1. On the Central Administration home page, click General Application Settings.

2. On the General Application Settings page, under Content Deployment, click Configure Content Deployment.

3. To configure the web application for importing content, on the Content Deployment Settings page and under Accept Content Deployment Jobs, select Accept Incoming Content Deployment Jobs, which is the typical setting for a production environment, as shown in the following screenshot.

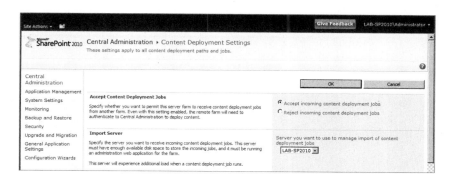

4. To configure the web application for exporting content, select Reject Incoming Content Deployment Jobs, which is the typical setting for an authoring environment.

5. To select a server in your farm to receive incoming content, under Import Server, use the "Server you want to use to manage import content deployment jobs" menu to select the desired server, which is the typical setting for a production environment.

6. To select a server in your farm to send deployment jobs to, under Export Server, use the "Server you want to use to manage export of content deployment jobs" drop-down menu to select the desired server. This is the typical setting for an authoring environment.

7. Under Connection Security, if you require HTTPS for security reasons, select Require Encryption (Recommended); the destination Central Administration website must begin with `https://` for the content deployment path. If you do not require encryption and want to use HTTP, select Do Not Require Encryption.

8. Under Temporary Files, enter the path to the temporary file that both import and/or export servers will use for storage of temporary files, which typically is on the local system drive.

9. Under Reporting, in the Number Of Reports To Retain For Each Job field, enter the number of reports you want to keep for each deployment job originating at your farm.

10. Click OK.

 Although Exercise 11.3 illustrates how to configure content deployment production and authoring in a single set of steps, usually you will create a content deployment job for an authoring environment separately rather than one for a production environment. The steps are virtually identical in each case.

Content Deployment Paths and Job Management

The next step in the process of administering content deployment is to create a path between the source and destination site collections. The connection is used to publish content from the source to destination. These site collections can be in the same server farm or in two different server farms.

To create a destination site collection for content deployment, you must select the Select Template Later option when you create the site. This is not the same thing as using the Blank Site template. Another option is to use Windows PowerShell and create the destination site collection using New-SPSite.

A content deployment job is used to schedule the actual movement of content across the content deployment path from source to destination. You can customize the scheduling and frequency of content deployment to meet your publishing requirements. Once the content is deployed, it should not be changed on the destination site. This may cause content deployment jobs to fail. Content must be changed or added at the source site.

A content deployment job can be set up to copy the entire contents of the source site collection or only a subset of sites within the collection. You can also choose to deploy only new, changed, or deleted content or to deploy all content. You can use Quick Deploy to deploy content outside the usual schedule.

The initial required tasks are to create a new content deployment path and a new content deployment job. Exercise 11.4 covers the steps for creating a deployment path. A prerequisite for this task is that Central Administration on the destination server must have been configured to accept incoming content deployment jobs. You must also be a member of the Farm Administrators group on the Central Administration server.

EXERCISE 11.4

Creating a New Content Deployment Path

In this exercise, you will learn how to create a new content deployment path.

1. On the Central Administration home page, click General Application Settings, and then under Content Deployment, click Configure Content Deployment Paths And Jobs.

2. On the Manage Content Deployment Paths and Jobs page, click New Path.

3. On the Create Content Deployment Path page, enter the name for the new path in the Type The Name Of This Path field.

4. Enter a description for the path in the Type A Description Of The Content Deployment Path field.

5. Under Source Web Application and Site Collection, use the Source Web Application menu to select the desired web application.

6. Use the Source Site Collection menu to select the desired source site collection.

7. After the source location is displayed in the URL, under Destination Central Administration Web Application, enter the URL of the destination Central Administration server in the Type The URL Of The Destination Central Administration Server field, using either `http://` or `https://`.

8. Under Authentication Information, select either "Use Integrated Windows authentication to encrypt credentials sent from the source to destination" or "Use Basic authentication for no encryption of credentials."

9. Enter the username and password for the account to be used to connect to the destination server and then click Connect.

EXERCISE 11.4 *(continued)*

10. Verify that the Connection Succeeded message appears and that the list of relevant destination web applications and site collections appears in the Destination Web Application And Site Collection section, and then select the desired destination web application.

11. Select the desired site collection in the Destination Site Collection list.

12. Under User Names, if you want the usernames associated with the content to be included when the path issued, select the Deploy User Names check box.

13. Under Security Information, in the Security Information In The Content Deployment list, select All, which is the default, to deploy all security information associated with the content when it is deployed. Select Role Definitions Only to send only role definitions when content is deployed, or select None to send no security information during deployment.

14. Click OK.

If you want to deploy content to another site collection within the same web application, you must make sure that the source and destination site collections are in separate content databases.

Creating a new content deployment job lets you schedule the job to run on a specified schedule, from one time only to once every 15 minutes. You can also run a job manually. A job schedule can be created using either Central Administration or Windows PowerShell. Exercise 11.5 will show you the Central Administration method. To successfully complete this task, you must be a member of the Farm Administrators group on the server running Central Administration.

EXERCISE 11.5

Creating a New Content Deployment Job

In this exercise, you will learn how to use the Central Administration method for creating a new content deployment job.

1. On the Central Administration home page, click General Application Settings, and then click Configure Content Deployment Paths And Jobs.

2. On the Manage Content Deployment Paths and Jobs page, click New Job.

3. On the Create Content Deployment Job page, use the Name and Description fields to give the new job a name and description.

4. Under Path, use the Select A Content Deployment Path menu to select the desired deployment path.

5. Under SQL Snapshots, select either Do Not Use SQL Snapshots or Automatically Create And Manage Snapshots For Content Deployment. This option is available only if Microsoft SQL Server 2008 Enterprise edition is being used.

6. Under Scope, select either Entire Site Collection To Deploy The Content Of The Whole Site Collection or select Specific Sites Within The Collection, and then click Select Sites to specify which sites in the collection should be used for the deployment.

7. Under Frequency, to specify a schedule, select the Run This Job On The Following Schedule check box, and then select the desired frequency.

8. Under Notification, to receive an email notification when the job succeeds, select the Send E-Mail When The Content Deployment Job Succeeds check box.

9. To receive an email notification if a job fails, select the Send E-Mail If The Content Deployment Job Fails check box.

10. In the Type E-Mail Addresses field, enter the email address or addresses to which you want the notifications sent.

11. Click OK.

The Specific Sites With The Collection option in step 6 creates a scoped content deployment job, which assumes all content in the site hierarchy above the specified scope has previously been deployed to the destination site collection. Do not select his option for a content deployment job if you have not already deployed the content above the specified level in the content hierarchy.

Records Management Planning

On the surface, you might imagine that *records management* is synonymous with document management, but a record is actually a distinct entity. Think of a record as any document type, either physical or electronic, that acts as evidence of any organizational transaction or act and that by law or policy is required to be retained for a particular period of time.

In developing a records management plan, you must first determine what sort of documents within your company are defined as records and then determine what active documents (of any type) within the company should be retained as records. Planning then determines the length of time each record should be retained, how to retain such records in a cost-effective and efficient manner, and by what process said records, once the retention requirement has expired, should be disposed.

Keep in mind that a record can be taken from a wide variety of active organizational digital media, such as:

- Local computer documents
- File server documents
- Email server documents

Records can also be taken from active physical media, such as:

- CDs/DVDs
- Paper hardcopies
- Audio and video cassettes

Once these documents have been identified, they are collected and retained in a records management container, which must be accessible upon demand by the proper legal or other authorities. The process must also identify which records have reached the end of their retention requirement so that they can be removed from the records management container and be disposed of in a permanent manner.

Records Management Roles

Within your organization, you must assign appropriate personnel to occupy the required roles in the records management process. For instance, content managers are the front line of the records management process. Their responsibility is to identify which documents within the entire business information infrastructure, including but not limited to SharePoint, qualify as records and need to be collected into the records management container.

Once the content managers have identified the appropriate documents, records managers verify that said documents are indeed required by policy or law to be defined as records, to assign each record the necessary length of time for retention, and to collect and include those records into the records repository for the organization.

Specified IT staff must be tasked to create and maintain the necessary records management systems within the server infrastructure and to make sure that this technological system meets the legal, policy, and security requirements to manage the company's records.

Creating a File Plan

The planning process for file identification and retention in the records management process has two broad steps. The first is to identify and categorize at a document level, and the second is to create a detailed organization tracking matrix for all records and records types.

As far as the initial identification goes, you should consider each document in terms of:

- Record type
- Record category
- Record description

For example, a record could be typed as email, categorized as electronic communication, and described as "Any electronic mail message containing information related to the corporation policy and legal responsibilities."

Once the appropriate records have been identified and categorized, they need to be collected—but not as a single, haphazard information dump. Each record needs to be specifically organized by a number of different descriptors. Tag each record as follows:

- Type
- Description

- Media type
- Category
- Retention length
- Disposition plan
- Contact person

The aforementioned email record would be represented here as email by type. You can use the previous description and category. The media type in this case would be the file type for Exchange email files, such as MSG. Look to the necessary legal requirements for your local jurisdiction, as well as state and federal requirements, for the retention length and disposition method. There should always be a contact person who is responsible for managing this records type and who can be contacted in the case of any questions. Someone should also be responsible for retrieving a particular record from this category at the request of the proper authority.

It is beyond the scope of this book to provide resources regarding records management laws for local state jurisdictions. However, you can find information about the laws pertaining to records management of federal documents at http://www.archives.gov/records-mgmt/laws. Wikipedia has general information and links to more information: http://en.wikipedia.org/wiki/Records_management. Also, ictus.com has a PDF of a slideshow that provides a good overview of the laws related to records management (http://www.ictus.com/docs/Compliance_RM_Law_2008 .pdf). There should be a specified person (such as the Chief Operations Officer) or department (Legal Department) within your specific company who is responsible for knowing all of these details.

Planning Records Archiving

In Microsoft Office SharePoint Server (MOSS) 2007 and before, you were required to create a records archive for storing and retaining records. SharePoint 2010 allows you to create a records archive or to manage records in-place (that is, without collecting the records in one container but managing them as records in the various and numerous containers across your enterprise records management system). This includes records within and outside of the SharePoint server infrastructure.

While it is generally easier to manage records in-place (because no collection process is involved), it is harder to locate a specific record (because they are not all in a single repository). With an in-place solution, you have to identify individual records by content type and location and maintain a method of locating those records. In-place records are more difficult to manage in terms of security, because anyone who originally had access to the document and library, depending on how security is configured, still can have access. A records archive is a more secure and manageable location. An in-place solution also requires that various libraries and sites retain both active documents and records, increasing clutter; the records archive solution requires that libraries maintain only active documents. Records audits are also simplified in an archiving solution.

Planning eDiscovery

eDiscovery or electronic discovery is the method of locating and delivering individual records that are specific to a particular audit, investigation, or legal proceeding. There are two broad aspects to eDiscovery:

- Locating the record
- Determining how the record can be treated once located

If your records are being maintained in a records center site, the hold feature is automatically enabled. A hold is the collection of records that have been located and identified as relevant to a specific proceeding. Records within a hold can be managed relative to their necessity in a legal proceeding, audit, or similar event. Records in a hold are copied and routed to a specific location for further use in the necessary proceeding, or they can be locked down in their original location, preventing the locked records in the hold from being modified or deleted.

Within SharePoint, if you use an in-place records management solution, you must enable the hold and eDiscovery features for each site collection in which you have records and then configure the Search Service to crawl the eDiscovery enabled sites and site collections.

You should review the contents of the hold and identify and remove any irrelevant records that may have been collected as the result of the eDiscovery search. You can also manually locate and add any relevant records to the hold that the search may have missed.

Planning Email and Messaging Management

Planning for email and messaging records management and retention is something of a special case because both Exchange Server 2010 and SharePoint Server 2010 have built-in records management features. In the case of this book, you are considering email and messaging records management within the context of SharePoint; therefore, it probably makes more sense to use SharePoint for all your records management needs. However, a brief mention of Exchange's records management features should be mentioned here as they contrast with SharePoint.

The primary advantage of using Exchange Server's records management features is that you can maintain message records separately from all other records within your organization. Keep in mind that this doesn't remove any of the policy and legal requirements relative to emails functioning as records that need to remain available and recoverable for auditing or court purposes; therefore, legal requirements cannot figure into keeping messaging records isolated from records maintained in SharePoint.

While Exchange can apply retention policies widely across messaging types, SharePoint possesses a broader ability to apply detailed retention policies using advanced metadata models not available within Exchange.

For a completely comprehensive records management solution, it probably makes more sense to use SharePoint to manage all record types, including emails, and to use the Exchange records retention solution only when SharePoint is not being utilized as part of its overall IT infrastructure.

> ### 🌐 Real World Scenario
>
> #### Developing a Messaging Records Plan
>
> You are a SharePoint administrator for your company. As a member of the records development team, you are working with the Exchange Server Manager and the Records Manager to develop a records retention strategy that is specific to email communications.
>
> The Exchange Server Manager is reluctant to surrender control of email content to a server infrastructure outside of Exchange and insists that Exchange Server 2010 has sufficient tools to manage email messages as records within the Exchange Server system. She outlines the use of retention tags that are created and used to link messages to a retention policy that is configured to manage messages as records. You object to this method, because it requires email users to tag their messages and folders to use specific records retention policies. The Exchange Manager points out that managed folders could be used instead, which would allow administrators to create folders linked to a managed mail folder policy; however, you mention that users could organize their messages as they wished within the managed folders and apply specific policies as they desired.
>
> After consulting with the CIO, the records development team receives instructions to use SharePoint Server 2010 for all records retention needs, including email messages, because emails can be managed on the same platform as all other related records and can be included and managed under the same records policies. The CIO specifically cites internal policies that require legal holds to apply to all content types within a single records archive. You, the Exchange Manager, and the Records Manager respond by developing a records retention plan that treats emails in the same manner as all other company records and that manages emails under SharePoint.

Digital Asset Management Planning

Digital assets are content types, such as audio, video, images, and other reusable content segments. SharePoint can contain and manage such assets in an asset library. Web parts and web part pages can be used for the storage and playback of digital media, and the Microsoft Silverlight 3 can also be included within the SharePoint environment to enhance media playback for your users.

Digital Asset Management Requirements

Digital asset management within SharePoint allows you to create, collect, store, manage, and dispose of all audio, video, image, and other rich media data files within your organization. SharePoint Server 2010 includes an asset library with such capacities, and this library can be customized for the digital content types you intend to manage.

Digital asset management planning considerations include:

- Developing the required storage space
- Identifying the location or locations for digital asset storage and management
- The process for moving digital assets from storage to locations for consumption
- Policies and other requirements for treating digital assets as records (see the previous section of this chapter)

Digital asset planning requires that you determine a plan for how these assets are to be accessed. If security isn't a concern, you can allow SharePoint users to access these assets within the asset library. You can also require that, in order to be accessed, specific assets must be inserted in a web part and then included on a web part page for consumption. You can also use a video field control on a publishing page within a publishing site.

Digital asset access includes three role types:

- Asset creators
- Asset managers
- Asset consumers

As previously stated, access by consumers can be managed through a number of different methods. The creators role includes video and audio media producers, graphic artists, and training and marketing managers—all of whom may create or be part of a creation team for a specific type or set of digital media.

Asset managers are a group who usually have no creative responsibilities but who must determine and manage the start to finish workflow process for assets, as well as determine and control all storage, retention, publishing, and deletion requirements.

Digital Asset Library Planning

Planning for digital asset libraries starts with determining if a single library is to be used for the entire enterprise or if multiple libraries are to be located in different site collections. This decision is based on access and security requirements. For instance, it may be more convenient for teams in each division of your company to maintain their own digital media assets for collaborative purposes. Conversely, you may decide that all digital media should be centrally maintained for consistency of use and user access.

If your business plan does not require that digital media be available for dynamic editing and development within or across different creative teams, you can maintain your media in fixed asset libraries, where the media is accessible, but only in read-only form.

As with other content types, you will need to plan for the specific types of media files you intend to manage. There is a plethora of different audio, video, and image file types. For support purposes, you can specify that your asset libraries maintain only a limited selection. You can also create different asset libraries for different digital media types in order to isolate different digital file types from each other.

Other reasons for creating different asset media library types are for access and security requirements or to satisfy storage or performance limitations within the server infrastructure.

Planning for Social Computing

Social computing in general is the use of technology solutions to establish and enhance communication and collaboration between two or more people. Most people with Internet access are at least aware of Facebook and Twitter as well as a number of other web-based networking and discussion venues that service the needs of every population from gamers to music enthusiasts. Within SharePoint, social computing describes the tools and processes involved in establishing and enhancing collaboration between SharePoint users.

SharePoint social computing can include familiar solutions such as wikis and RSS, but it also utilizes technologies specific to SharePoint, such as My Site websites. SharePoint social computing allows groups of SharePoint users to work together and collaborate on common projects, and it enables them to locate and contact people within SharePoint who have specific skill sets and experiences in order for those people to act as resources for projects and to help achieve business goals.

The User Profile Service

Central to SharePoint social computing planning is the User Profile Service. This is a service application in SharePoint that provides a resource to be consumed across multiple sites within a site collection or even to be shared across multiple SharePoint server farms. Elements that are specific to the User Profile Service include:

- Audiences
- Profile synchronization settings
- My Sites
- User profile properties

This section teaches you the process for creating and configuring the User Profile Service Application. Before you can continue with this part of the chapter, you must meet the following requirements:

- The version of SharePoint Server 2010 you are using must be either Standard or Enterprise.
- You must have configured at least one site collection that uses the My Site Host template.
- You must have an application pool that can be used by My Sites.
- You must be running an instance of the Managed Metadata Services.
- At least one managed path must exist.

Creating the User Profile Service Application

The first step in administering user profiles is to create a User Profile Service application. This can be done either in Central Administration or with Windows PowerShell.

Exercise 11.6 will show you how to accomplish the task in Central Administration. You must be a member of the Farm Administrator group to successfully complete the exercise.

EXERCISE 11.6

Using Central Administration to Create a User Profile Service Application

In this exercise, you will learn how to create a User Profile Service application in Central Administration.

1. Navigate to Central Administration and under Application Management, click Manage Service Applications.

2. On the Manage Service Applications page, select the Service Applications tab, if it isn't already selected, to activate the Ribbon.

3. Click Create on the Ribbon, and click New in the Create section of the Ribbon, as shown in the following screenshot.

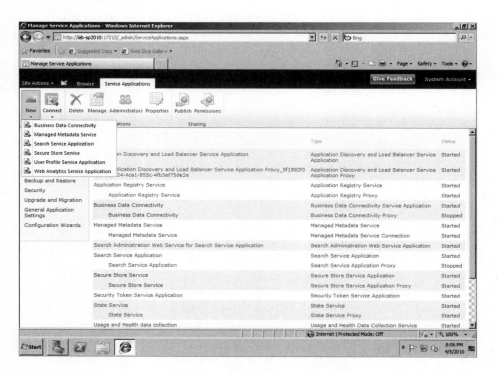

4. When the Create New User Profile Service Application box opens, under Name, enter a unique name for the User Profile Service application.

5. Under Application Pool, select Use Existing Application Pool to choose an existing pool or select Create A New Application Pool to create a new pool.

6. For Select A Security Account For This Application Pool, select Predefined to choose an existing predefined security account, or select Configurable to select an existing managed account.

7. Under Profile Database, enter the name of the database server where the profile database will be located in the Database Server field.

8. In the Database Name field, enter the name of the database.

9. Select either Windows Authentication (Recommended) or SQL Authentication. If you choose the latter, enter the username and password for the SQL authentication method.

10. If you want to use SQL Server database mirroring, enter the name of the database server to be used in the Failover Database Server field and then select an authentication method, as you did for the database server.

11. To use a synchronization database, under Synchronization Database, enter the name of the server in the Database Server field and then the name of the synchronization database in the Database Name field.

12. Select either Windows Authentication (Recommended) or SQL Authentication. If you choose the latter, enter the username and password for the SQL server.

13. If you want to use SQL Server database mirroring for the synchronization server, enter the name of the database server to be used in the Failover Database Server field and then select an authentication method, as you did for the database server.

14. Under Social Tagging, enter the name of the database server and database as well as the authentication method, just as you did for the Failover database server and the Synchronization database server.

15. If you want to use SQL Server database mirroring for the Social Tagging database server, enter the name of the database server to be used in the Failover Database Server field and then select an authentication method, as you did for the database server.

16. Under Profile Synchronization Instance, select a machine in the server farm on which you want to run the Profile Synchronization Service.

17. Under My Site Host URL, enter the URL of the site collection where the My Site host was created.

EXERCISE 11.6 *(continued)*

18. Under My Site Managed Path, enter the managed path where individual My Site websites are to be created, as shown in the following screenshot.

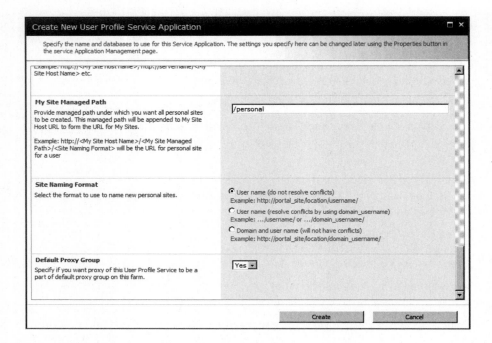

19. Under Site Naming Format, select a format for naming personal sites, such as User Name (Do Not Resolve Conflicts), User Name (Resolve Conflicts By Using domain_username), or Domain And User Name (Will Not Have Conflicts).

20. Under Default Proxy Group, choose if you want to make the proxy of the User Profile Service as part of the default proxy group.

You can enable self-service site creation in a web application hosting My Site websites to allow users the ability to create their own My Site websites. Users must possess the Create Personal Site permission, which is enabled by default for all authenticated users.

One of the prerequisites for creating a User Profile Service application is that at least one managed path must be present. Exercise 11.7 takes you through the steps of defining a managed path using Central Administration. You must be a member of the Farm Administrator group to successfully complete this exercise.

EXERCISE 11.7

Defining a Managed Path

In this exercise, you will learn how to define a managed path using Central Administration.

1. Navigate to Central Administration, and click Application Management.

2. On the Application Management page, under Web Applications, click Manage Web Applications.

3. On the Manage Web Applications page, select the desired web application and then, on the Ribbon, click Managed Paths.

4. When the Define Managed Paths box appears, under Add A New Path, enter the path within the URL namespace in the Path field, such as the top-level site for the web application hosting the desired site collections.

5. Click Check URL to verify that the URL functions and that the site indicated in the Path field opens in a separate browser window.

6. In the Type list, select Wildcard Inclusion to include all paths that are subordinate to the specified path or select Explicit Inclusion to include the site indicated by the specified path and not include subordinate sites.

7. To delete a specific path or paths, under Included Paths, select the check boxes for the undesired paths and then click Delete Selected Paths.

8. When you are finished, click OK.

Once you've created a User Profile Service application, you may want to edit its settings. Exercise 11.8 shows you how this is done. You must be a member of the Farm Administrator group to successfully complete this exercise.

EXERCISE 11.8

Editing a User Profile Application

In this exercise, you will learn how to edit a User Profile Service application.

1. Navigate to Central Administration, and under Application Management, click Manage Service Applications.

2. On the Manage Service Applications page, in the Type column, click User Profile Service Application to select it.

3. On the Ribbon, click Properties from the Operations section and then click Properties.

4. When the Edit User Profile Service Application box opens, edit the desired properties.

5. When you are done, click OK.

The process of deleting a User Profile Service application is almost the same as editing that service application. Once you've selected the User Profile Service application in the Type column and clicked Operations, click Delete in the menu that appears. Then, in the Delete Service Application box, verify you've selected the correct service application and then select Delete Data Associated With The Service Applications. Click OK when you're finished.

Delegating Authority of a User Profile Service Application

Once you have created and configured a User Profile Service application, you can assign managerial authority over the service application to another user, easing the administrative burden on you. This task can be performed using Central Administration or Windows PowerShell.

Exercise 11.9 will illustrate the Central Administration method. You must be a member of the Farm Administrator group to successfully complete this exercise.

EXERCISE 11.9

Using Central Administration to Assign an Administrator to a User Profile Service

In this exercise, you will learn how to use Central Administration to assign an administrator to a User Profile Service application.

1. Navigate to Central Administration, and under Application Management, click Manage Service Applications.

2. On the Manage Service Applications page, select the desired User Profile Service application.

3. On the Ribbon, click Administrators.

4. When the Administrators For User Profile Service Application box opens, enter the user or group account in the available field and then click Add.

5. For Permissions for Administrator, select Full Control.

6. Click OK when you are finished.

The same task can be performed using Windows PowerShell; Exercise 11.10 explains the procedure. To successfully complete this exercise, you need to be a member of the SharePoint_Shell_Access role on the configuration database and a member of the WSS_ADMIN_WPG local group on the computer where SharePoint 2010 Products is present.

EXERCISE 11.10

Using Windows PowerShell to Assign an Administrator to a User Profile Service Application

In this exercise, you will learn how to use PowerShell to assign an administrator to a User Profile Service application.

1. Run Windows PowerShell as an administrator.

2. Enter the following lines of code at the command prompt, each on a separate line, and then click Enter. You don't need to enter the comment lines, which are designated with two slashes (//).

```
// Display a list of all service applications and their GUIDs
Get-SPServiceApplication
// Create a variable that contains the guid for the User Profile Service for
// which you want to delegate Full Control
$serviceapp = Get-SPServiceApplication <guid>
// Create a variable that contains the list of administrators for the service
application
$security = Get-SPServiceApplicationSecurity $serviceapp -Admin
// Create a variable that contains the claims principal for a user account
$principalUser1 = New-SPClaimsPrincipal -Identity "domain\user" -IdentityType
WindowsSamAccountName
// Give Full Control permissions to the claims principal you just created
Grant-SPObjectSecurity $security -Principal $principalUser1 -Rights "Full Control"
// Apply the changes to the User Profile Service application
Set-SPServiceApplicationSecurity $serviceapp -objectSecurity $security -Admin
```

You must change some of the values in the lines of sample code presented in Exercise 11.10. For <guid>, enter the GUID for the User Profile Service for which you want to delegate full control to the new administrator. For <domain\user>, enter the *domain\ username* pair for the user being assigned to administrate the User Profile Service.

There will come a time when you'll need to remove an administrator of a User Profile Service application, as when the user changes job duties or leaves the company. You can also perform this task on the Manage Service Application page under Application Management in Central Administration. Just select the User Profile Service application, click Operations on the Ribbon, and then click Administrators. On the Administrators For User Profile Service Application page, select the desired user or group account, click Remove, and then click OK.

The same task can be performed in Windows PowerShell. Open Windows PowerShell as an administrator, enter the following code—minus the comments (//)—and then press Enter.

```
// Get a list of all service applications and their GUIDs
Get-SPServiceApplication
// Create a variable that contains the guid of the User Profile Service
application
// for which you want to remove an administrator
$serviceapp = Get-SPServiceApplication <guid>
// Create a variable that contains the list of administrators for the User
Profile Service application
$security = Get-SPServiceApplicationSecurity $serviceapp -Admin
// Remove the user from the list of service application administrators
Revoke-SPObjectSecurity $security -Principal <user name> -Rights "Full Control"
// Apply the changes to the User Profile Service application
Set-SPServiceApplicationSecurity $serviceapp -objectSecurity $security -Admin
```

For <guid>, enter the GUID of the User Profile Service for which you want to remove the administrator, and for *<user name>*, substitute the username of the administrator.

Delegating Authority Over User Profile Service Features

In addition to assigning administrative authority over a User Profile Service application, SharePoint administrators with farm administrator rights can assign authority over selected features of the User Profile Service application to specific users. For instance, you could assign a particular user the right to manage audiences in a User Profile Service application, but with no authority over any other features. This person would be known as a feature administrator. The ability to create one or more feature administrators is helpful when you want to delegate some authority over a User Profile Service application but retain authority over other, more key features.

You can delegate authority over any of the following tasks to a feature administrator:

- Manage audiences
- Manage permissions
- Manage profiles
- Manage social data
- Retrieve people data for search crawlers

You can perform this task using either Central Administration or Windows PowerShell; however, the use of the different interfaces isn't interchangeable. You usually perform the task in Central Administration if you are running SharePoint as a standalone deployment. You are more likely to use Windows PowerShell to perform this task in an enterprise-level environment where you want to automate the process.

Exercise 11.11 shows you how to create a feature administrator using Central Administration. To successfully complete this exercise, you must belong to the Farm Administrator group or you must have been delegated permission to administer the User Profile Service application.

EXERCISE 11.11

Using Central Administration to Delegate User Profile Service Feature Administration

In this exercise, you will learn how to create a feature administrator.

1. Navigate to Central Administration, and under Application Management, click Manage Service Applications.

2. In the list of service applications that appears, click User Profile Service Application.

3. On the Ribbon, click Administrators in the Operations section, and then click Administrators.

4. When the Administrators for User Profile Service Application box opens, enter the name of the user or group account you want to delegate to in the available field, and then click Add.

5. Under Permissions for Administrator, select the feature or features you want to delegate to the designated user.

6. Click OK.

As previously mentioned, the steps performed in Exercise 11.11 are usually performed in a standalone SharePoint deployment. In an enterprise-level server farm environment, you are more likely to perform this task using Windows PowerShell.

Open Windows PowerShell as an administrator and enter the following commands, typing them one line at a time without the comments (//), and then press Enter:

```
// Display a list of all service applications and their GUIDs
Get-SPServiceApplication
// Create a variable that contains the guid for the User
// Profile service for which you want to delegate Full Control
$serviceapp = Get-SPServiceApplication <guid>
// Create a variable that contains the list of administrators
// for the service application
$security = Get-SPServiceApplicationSecurity $serviceapp -Admin
// Create a variable that contains the claims principal for a user account
$principalUser1 = New-SPClaimsPrincipal -Identity "domain\user" -IdentityType
WindowsSamAccountName
```

```
// Give "Manage Social Data" permissions to the claims
// principal you just created
Grant-SPObjectSecurity $security -Principal $principalUser1 -Rights "Manage
Social Data"
// Apply the changes to the User Profile Service application
Set-SPServiceApplicationSecurity $serviceapp -objectSecurity $security -Admin
```

For <guid>, enter the GUID of the User Profile Service for which you want to delegate feature authority. For <domain/user>, enter the domain-username pair for the user to whom you want to delegate authority. In the previous sample code, the feature being delegated is the Manage Social Data permission. If you want to delegate authority over a different feature, substitute the name of that feature in the relevant sections of the code.

User and Organization Profile Management

The User Profile Service application comes with a default set of user profile properties. In addition to the defaults, you can add, edit, and delete customized user profile properties in the service application. This allows you to track specific data by associating specific properties of users with important business processes.

In addition to managing user profiles, you can also administer organizational profiles including components such as organization profile properties and organization subtypes. This section of the chapter will show you the various related tasks.

Administering Custom User Profile Properties

The first step in administrating a customized user profile property is to create one. Exercise 11.12 will show you how. To successfully complete the task, you must belong to the Farm Administrator group or be a service application administrator for the User Profile Service application. This task is related to the creation and management of My Sites.

EXERCISE 11.12

Creating a Custom User Profile Property

In this exercise, you will learn how to create a custom user profile property.

1. Navigate to Central Administration, and under Application Management, click Manage Service Applications.

2. On the Manage Service Applications page, in the Type column, select the desired User Profile Service application.

3. On the Manage Profile Service page, under People, click Manage User Properties.

4. On the Manage User Properties page, click New Property.

5. On the Add User Profile Property page, under Property Settings, enter the name of the new user property to be used by the service application in the Name field.

6. In the Display Name field, enter the name of the custom property as you want it displayed to users.

7. Use the Type drop-down menu to select the data type for the property.

8. In the Length field, enter the maximum number of characters you want to allow for values for this property.

9. To associate the profile property with a managed term set, click Configure A Term Set To Be Used For This Property, and then select a term set from the drop-down menu.

10. Under Sub-Type To Profile, select Default User Profile Subtype to associate a default user profile subtype to use with the user profile property.

11. Under User Description, in the Description field, enter any information or instructions you want to impart to users about this user profile property.

12. Under Policy Settings, select the policy setting and default privacy setting you want to give to this property. If desired, select User Can Override to enable users to override this setting.

13. Under Edit Settings, select whether or not users can edit the values of the property.

14. Under Display Settings, determine if or how the property will be viewed by users.

15. To specify the kinds of searches you want associated with the user profile, under Search Settings, select Alias, Indexed, or both.

16. Under Property Mapping For Synchronization, click Remove to delete or change an existing mapping if desired.

17. Under Add New Mapping, specify the source data connection, attribute, and synchronization direction for the mapping, and then click Add.

18. When you are finished, click OK.

WARNING For step 7, if you select String (Multi Value) in the menu, the property will be permanently set as a multivalued property and you will not be able to change it after you click OK. The only way to edit this value will be to delete the property and add it again as a new, single value property.

If you use multiple languages in your SharePoint sites, you can provide different display names and descriptions for each language by clicking Edit Languages. When the dialog box opens, click Add Language, select the desired language from the menu, and then type the display name.

Administering the Organization Profile Property

Like the default user profile properties, the default organization profile properties can be augmented by adding customized profile properties. This is done for the same reason: to associate such properties with key information for tracking purposes. Organization profile components available to be managed include:

- Delegation for organizations
- Organization profile properties
- Organization properties
- Organization subtypes

As with customized user profile properties, the first step in managing a customized organization profile property is to create one. Exercise 11.13 starts you off. To successfully complete the task, you must belong to the Farm Administrator group or you must be a service application administrator for the User Profile Service application. This task is related to the creation and management of My Sites.

EXERCISE 11.13

Creating a Custom Organization Profile Property

In this exercise, you will learn how to create a custom organization profile property.

1. Navigate to Central Administration, and under Application Management, click Manage Service Applications.

2. On the Manage Service Applications page, click the desired User Profile Service application.

3. On the User Profile Service Application page, under Organizations, click Manage Organization Properties.

4. On the View Organization Profile Properties page, click New Property.

5. On the Add Organization Profile Property page, under Property Settings, enter the name of the customized profile property to be used by the User Profile Service application into the Name field.

6. In the Display Name field, enter the name for the customized property you want to be displayed to users.

7. Open the Type drop-down list and select a data type for the property.

8. In the Length field, enter the maximum number of characters allowed for values of the property.

9. Under Sub-Type of Profile, select Default Organization Profile Subtype to associate the organization profile property with the default organization profile subtype.

10. In the Description field under User Description, enter the information or instructions about the property you want users to see.

11. Under Property Settings, select the policy setting and default privacy setting you want for the property.

12. Under Edit Settings, choose whether or not users will be able to change the values of the property.

13. Under Display Settings, choose if or how the property will be viewed by users.

14. Under Search Settings, select Alias, Indexed, or both, depending on the type of searches you want associated with this profile property.

15. Under Add New Mapping, specify the source data connection, attribute, and synchronization direction for the mapping, and then click Add.

16. When you are finished, click OK.

Managing Profile Synchronization

Thus far, we've explored user and organizational profiles that are specific to SharePoint. In fact, profile information can be stored in more than one location. User and group profiles stored in SharePoint's store profile can be synchronized with profile data stored in both directory services and business systems throughout the enterprise. To perform the following tasks related to profile synchronization, you must be a member of the User Profile Service Administrator group. You must also possess at least Replicate Directory Changes permissions on Active Directory Domain Services (AD DS) if this is the directory service to be used.

In order for you to perform profile synchronization tasks, one or more directory services must be available on the same network where you are running SharePoint Server 2010. Directory services that can be synchronized with SharePoint include:

- Active Directory Domain Services (AD DS)
- Business Data Connectivity Services
- Novell eDirectory version 8.7.3 (LDAP)
- SunOne version 5.2 (LDAP)
- IBM Trivoli 6.2 (LDAP)

WARNING   You must use either a Standard or Enterprise version of SharePoint Server 2010 and run in a server farm. You cannot perform profile synchronization using a standalone installation of SharePoint with a built-in database.

Additional requirements include:

- An instance of the User Profile Service application must exist and be started.
- If you are using SQL Server 2008, it specifically must be with Service Pack 1 (SP1) with Cumulative Update 2 (CU2).
- If you are using Windows Server 2008 R2, hotfix KB976462 must be installed.

 As of this writing, hotfix KB976462 can be located at the MSDN Code Gallery at http://code.msdn.microsoft.com/KB976462/Release/ProjectReleases.aspx?ReleaseId=4317.

Profile synchronization can be set to occur when profile data has changed either in SharePoint or in the directory service. You determine how and when the import and export processes occur when you configure profile synchronization. By default, no user profile property is set to export.

Some user profile properties in SharePoint are automatically mapped to their counterparts in the external directory service by default, including first name and last name. If you set synchronization to occur on a recurring schedule, the synchronization is incremental. This means the only information that is synchronized is data that has changed since the last scheduled synchronization. You can also use either a nonrecurring full synchronization or a nonrecurring incremental synchronization.

The tasks for profile configuring and starting profile synchronization must be performed in the order they are presented here.

Starting the User Profile Synchronization Service

The first task to perform is starting the User Profile Synchronization Service, which is not started by default.

To successfully perform this task, you must be a member of the Farm Administrators group on the computer containing Central Administration and be the local administrator on the computer where the User Profile Synchronization Service is deployed, which should be the same computer. The farm administrator account must also be a service administrator for the User Profile Service you are configuring.

When you start the User Profile Synchronization Service, you are asked to associate the service with the desired User Profile Service application. Use the Select the User Profile Service Application drop-down menu to make your selection and then click OK. You must then wait between 5 and 10 minutes before performing the following:

1. On the computer containing Central Administration and the User Profile Synchronization Service, click Start, Control Panel, Administrative Tools, and then Services.

2. Verify that the Forefront Identity Manager Synchronization Service and the Forefront Identity Manager Service are running, as in Figure 7.4, and if not, start the services.

3. Navigate to `%Programfiles%\Microsoft Office Servers \14.0\Synchronization Service\MaData` and verify that the `ILMMA` and `MOSS-<User Profile Service application name>` are present (the folders will be empty).

4. Restart the IIS service using IISReset by opening a command-line window, enter `iisreset/noforce` *computername*, and then press Enter (replace *computername* with the name of the computer on which you are starting the User Profile Synchronization Service).

Creating a Profile Synchronization Connection

Once the service has started, your next task is to create a new profile synchronization connection. To do this, you must know which directory service containers you want to synchronize with SharePoint. It is also important to create only one profile synchronization connection per directory service forest. If you are synchronizing with AD DS, you must have a minimum of Replicate Directory Changes permissions in AD DS. If you plan to export properties such as profile pictures to AD DS, you will also need AD DS Create All Child Objects permissions.

1. In Central Administration, under Application Management, click Manage Service Applications.

2. On the Manage Service Applications page, click the name of the desired User Profile Service application.

3. On the User Profile Service Application page, under Synchronization, click Configure Synchronization Connections.

4. On the Synchronizations Connections page, click Create New Connection.

5. On the Add New Synchronization Connection page, enter the name of the new synchronization connection in the Connection Name field.

6. Use the Type list to select the desired directory service.

7. If you select Business Data Connectivity, you must enter the name for the connection in the Name box, select a business data connectivity application from the Business Data Connectivity Entity box, select either the 1:1 mapping or the 1:many mapping, and then click OK. Otherwise, skip this step and proceed with the subsequent steps.

8. Under Connection Settings, enter the name of the directory service forest to which you want to connect, enter the account credentials for the directory service and the desired port, and then select Auto Discover Domain Controller or enter the name of the domain controller in the Domain Controller name field.

9. Select the Use SSL-Secured Connection check box if you want to use a Secure Socket Layer connection to connect to the directory service.

10. Under Containers, click Populate Containers, and then select the desired containers for which you want to create connections. Otherwise, click Select All to make connections for all containers.

11. When finished, click OK.

Editing Profile Synchronization Connection Filters

When at least one profile synchronization connection has been made, you can edit the connection filters. To begin, follow steps 1 through 3 of the previous task to get to the Synchronization Connections page. Then perform the following steps. You'll need the same permissions as you did in the previous task.

1. On the Synchronization Connections page, click the connection you want to edit and then select Edit Connection Filters.

2. On the Edit connection filters page, under Exclusion Filters For Users, select the user property for which you want to apply a synchronization filter in the Attributes list.

3. Select All Apply (AND) if you want all filters applied, or select Apply Any (OR) if you only want one filter condition to be met.

4. Configure the specific filter parameters you want and then click Add.

5. Under Exclusion Filters For Groups, select the desired group property from the Attributes list and then select either All Apply (AND) or Apply Any (OR).

6. Select and configure the desired filter parameters and then click Add.

7. When you are finished, click OK.

In steps 3 and 5, you can select from a number of different attributes, each of which requires a different set of steps to configure.

Mapping User Profile Properties

To set up user profile mapping, you need to possess the same permissions as in the previous tasks. In Central Administration, you must navigate to the Manage Service Applications page as you did previously, click the desired User Profile Service application, and then, under People, click Manage User Properties and perform the following steps:

1. On the Manage User Properties page, right-click the desired user property and select Edit from the menu that appears.

2. On the Edit User Profile Property page, under Add New Mapping, select the desired profile synchronization connection from the Source Data Connection list.

3. Select the desired directory service attribute from the Attribute list.

4. Select Import if you want to import the property value from the directory service into SharePoint, or select Export if you want to export the property value from SharePoint to the directory service.

5. When you've made your selection, click Add.

6. When you have finished, click OK.

If you want to synchronize user profile pictures between SharePoint, AD DS, and Outlook 2010 using the Outlook social connector, set the data source connection for the Picture property mapping to Export.

Once the mappings are set up, your next step is to configure the profile synchronization settings. You must possess the same permissions you needed for the Mapping User Profile

Properties task and verify that you have Full Control permissions as a service administrator for the User Profile Service you are configuring. You must also be a system administrator on SQL Server. Navigate to the Manage Profile Service page in Central Administration and under Synchronization, click Configure Synchronization Settings, and then perform the following steps.

1. On the Configure Synchronization Settings page, under Synchronization Entities, select Users And Groups to synchronize both types of information, or select only Users to synchronize just user information.

2. Under Synchronize BDC Connections, clear the Include Existing BDC Connections For Synchronization check box if you want to exclude any data imports from the Business Data Connectivity Service.

3. Under External Identity Manager, select Use SharePoint Profile Synchronization to use SharePoint's synchronization engine, or select Enable External Identity Manager if you want to use an external synchronization application such as Microsoft Identity Lifecycle Manager 2007.

4. When you are finished, click OK.

When setting up synchronization settings, you should run a full synchronization for just users, and then run an incremental synchronization of both users and groups. Also, if you choose to use an external synchronization engine, you will disable all of the profile synchronization options in SharePoint.

Configuring a Nonrecurring Profile Synchronization

Once the configuration of profile synchronization is complete, you can set up nonrecurring or recurring profile synchronization. You must possess the same permissions you needed to create a profile synchronization connection.

1. In Central Administration, under Application Management, click Manage Service Applications.

2. On the Manage Service Applications page, click the desired User Profile Service application.

3. On the User Profile Service Application page, under Synchronization, click Start Profile Synchronization.

4. On the Start Profile Synchronization page, select either Start Incremental Synchronization or Start Full Synchronization and then click OK.

When using AD DS, you must run full synchronization first and then again when any new profile property mapping is created. When the synchronization is complete, you will be able to search for a known profile or accounts beginning with a known domain name from within the Manage User Profiles page.

Configuring a Recurring Profile Synchronization

To set up recurring profile synchronization, follow steps 1 through 3 in the Configuring a Nonrecurring Profile Synchronization task to get to the User Profile Service Application page, and under Synchronization, click Configure Synchronization Timer Job. Then on the Edit Timer Job page under Recurring Schedule, use the radio buttons and menus to set the frequency and start times of the Profile Synchronization job. When finished, click OK.

Daily is the recommended scheduling frequency.

Managing User and Group Social Features

By default, any authenticated user can create a personalized My Site in SharePoint and then configure the personal and social features in their My Site. You can modify how a SharePoint user utilizes the social features within their My Site, including altering their permissions, activating or deactivating social tags, and so on. This section of the chapter will address how you can perform such tasks.

The three general features you can enable for users and groups in the User Profile Service are Use Personal Features, Create Personal Site, and Use Social Features. Personal features include the ability to use My Colleagues, My Links, My Personalization links, and user profile properties within a My Site. The Create Personal Site feature allows users to create a My Site website, and Social Features including using social tags, Note Board, and ratings.

The following exercise shows you how to enable users and groups to use personal and social features. Exercise 11.14 gets you started.

EXERCISE 11.14

Enabling Users or Groups to Use Personal and Social Features

In this exercise, you will learn how to enable users to use personal features.

1. In Central Administration, under Application Management, click Manage Service Applications.

2. On the Manage Service Applications page, click the desired User Profile Service application to open it.

3. Under People, click Manage User Permissions.

4. When the Permissions for User Profile Service Application box opens, enter or select the desired user or group account, and then click Add.

5. Under Permissions For, check the feature or features you want to allow the selected account or accounts to access, and then click OK.

By default in SharePoint Server 2010, users have the option to mark documents and items in document libraries and lists with social tags and referencing note boards. For instance, on the Ribbon of a document library, the selections I Like It and Tags & Notes are available. You, as a SharePoint administrator, have the ability to deactivate these features, but you cannot enable or disable social tags and note boards on the level of the individual web application in a server farm. Any changes you make will be server farm-wide. Also, any user data associated with these features may be lost.

Activating and deactivating these features is usually done in Central Administration for a standalone SharePoint deployment and performed using Windows PowerShell in an Enterprise environment.

Because these social features are activated by default, you must deactivate them if you don't want them. To deactivate them in Central Administration, under System Settings, click Manage Farm Features. On the Manage Farm Features page, click the Deactivate button next to Social Tags and Note Board Ribbon controls. If you have previously deactivated this option, click the Activate button.

To deactivate or activate the social features in the server farm using Windows PowerShell, you must be a member of the SharePoint_Shell_Access group on the configuration database and a member of the WSS_ADMIN_WPG local group on the computer where SharePoint 2010 Products is present.

To deactivate the social features in the farm, open Windows PowerShell as an administrator, enter the following at the prompt, and press Enter.

```
Get-SPFeature -Farm
Disable-SPFeature -Identity "SocialRibbonControl"
To enable these social features, perform the same task using the following code.
Get-SPFeature -Farm
Enable-SPFeature -Identity "SocialRibbonControl"
```

Managing Audiences

An audience is a group of users defined by their membership in a Microsoft Exchange distribution list (DL), a SharePoint group, or by rules configured by a SharePoint administrator. The rules applied to an audience can be based on user profile data or membership in an identity management system, such as Active Directory Domain Services (AD DS) or Business Connectivity Services (BCS). Audiences and their definitions are contained in the User Profile Service application; they allow organizations to target content to specific users or groups of users. This allows you, the SharePoint administrator, to specify data deployment to a specific group or groups only and not to all authenticated SharePoint users.

In SharePoint Server 2010, information targeting can be defined down to the list item level. Before an audience can be targeted, the audience must be compiled to identify its membership using data crawling in the identity management system. This process cannot run during user profile synchronization, and audiences are not used in place of configuring permissions for SharePoint users and groups.

The first task you'll need to perform is to add an audience. When you add an audience, you are creating a group of members for which you want to target specific information. When you add an audience, you also add an audience rule by default; you also create an owner for the audience. You'll learn how to add more audience rules later; for now, Exercise 11.15 will show you how to add your first audience. You won't be able to view the audience members until you compile the audience, which you will also do later.

To successfully complete this exercise, you must be a member of the Farm Administrators group, a service application administrator for the User Profile Service application containing the audience, or an administrator for the Audience feature in the User Profile Service application containing the audience.

EXERCISE 11.15

Adding an Audience

In this exercise, you will learn how to create an audience.

1. In Central Administration, under Application Management, click Manage Service Applications.

2. On the Manage Service Applications page, click the desired User Profile Service application.

3. On the Manage Profile Service page, under People, click Manage Audiences.

4. On the View Audiences page, click New Audience.

5. On the Create Audience page, under Properties, enter the name for the new audience in the Name field.

6. Enter a detailed description of the audience in the Description field.

7. Enter the name of the user account you want to own the audience in the Owner field, and then click Check Names.

8. Select Satisfy All Of The Rules or Satisfy Any Of The Rules to determine the members of the audience, and then click OK.

9. On the Add Audience Rule page, to add a rule based on a user, follow steps 10 through 12. To add a rule based on a user profile property, follow steps 13 through 15.

10. To add a rule based on the user, under Operand, select User.

11. Select Reports Under to create a rule based on your organization's hierarchy or select Member Of to create a rule based on group or distribution list.

12. To test the rule, enter or select the username in the Value field, select someone to manage the users you want in your audience to test the Reports Under rule, and select the group or distribution you want to test the Member Of rule.

13. To add a rule based on a user profile property, under Operand, select Property and then select the appropriate property from the available list.

14. Use the Operator list to select an operator for the property.

15. In the Value field, type the value you want to use to evaluate the property against the rule.

16. When you are done, click OK.

To add a rule that contains more complex logic, you must use the SharePoint Server 2010 object model. To find out more about this object model, visit http://msdn.microsoft.com/library/microsoft.office .server.audience.audience%28office.14%29.aspx.

Planning Audience and Audience Rule Organization

SharePoint administrators are often tasked with creating a number of audiences for the purpose of targeting relevant information based on user profile data. Such assignments can expand a large and complicated area. You may be required to authenticate SharePoint users across several cities to receive information based on their locale. You could also be required to create different audiences for managers, sales and marketing, and new employees so that relevant data can be routed appropriately.

User profile data, Active Directory service group membership, and Microsoft Exchange distribution lists can be the basis for creating those audiences. Default SharePoint and other "off-the-shelf" rules may or may not be sufficient. The Microsoft Office Server Audience class can be used to create complex audience rules that offer more flexibility when creating audiences. Information on this topic can be found at msdn.microsoft.com.

After you have studied the audience and the options for creating that audience, the next steps are to develop a targeting plan and get it approved. Once you have created an audience with one default rule, you can add more rules, edit the rules, and delete the rules for the audience. Each audience rule is made up of an operand, an operator, and a value. The operand is used to identify the user or property you want to include in the query for the rule. The operator determines whether users being compared to the value are included or excluded by the rule. The value is the point of comparison used by the query.

When you create multiple rules for an audience, you must apply one of the two available sets of logic: satisfy all of the rules or satisfy any of the rules. If you choose the first option, users must match all of the rules for the audience in order to be members of the audience. If you select the second option, users can match any one of the existing rules to be considered audience members.

To add a rule to an audience, follow the steps in Exercise 11.16. Begin by navigating to the People section of the Manage Profile Service page.

EXERCISE 11.16

Adding an Audience Rule

In this exercise, you will learn how to create audience rules.

1.   Under People, click Manage Audiences.

2.   On the View Audiences page, click next to the name of the desired audience to make the arrow appear and then click View Properties.

3.   On the View Audience Properties page, under Audience Rules, click Add Rule.

4.   Depending on the type of rule you want to add, follow the required activities contained and, when you are done adding the rule, click OK.

Editing an audience rule is virtually the same as adding an audience rule, as you did in Exercise 11.16. In step 3 on the View Audience Properties page under Audience rules, instead of clicking on Add Rule, click on the rule you want to edit and then modify any of the elements present, changing them as you desire on the Edit Audience Rule page. To delete a rule, select the rule on the View Audience Properties page, and then on the bottom of the Edit Audience Rule page, click Delete and then click OK to confirm your action.

So far, all of the tasks you've performed are well and good, but as you recall, an audience cannot be used until it's compiled. Once you have created an audience and added the necessary rules, the next step is to compile it. Exercise 11.17 guides you through this process. The compiling task is very straightforward.

EXERCISE 11.17

Compiling an Audience

In this exercise, you will learn how to compile an audience.

1.   In Central Administration, under Application Management, click Manage Service Applications.

2.   On the Manage Service Applications page, click the User Profile Service application.

3.   On the Manage Profile Service page, under People, click Compile Audiences.

Although that was a very simple task, you may not always want to manually compile your audiences. Fortunately, you can schedule the compilation process to occur at regular intervals. Exercise 11.18 shows you how to do this step-by-step.

EXERCISE 11.18

Scheduling an Audience to Be Compiled

In this exercise, you will learn how to automate the audience compilation process.

1. In Central Administration, under Application Management, click Manage Service Applications.

2. On the Manage Service Applications page, click the User Profile Service application.

3. On the Manage Profile Service page, under People, click Schedule Audience Compilation.

4. On the Specify Compilation Schedule page, select the Enable Scheduling check box.

5. Select the start time using the Start At list.

6. Schedule the frequency of the compiling process by choosing daily, weekly, or monthly.

7. When you are finished, click OK.

The audience will be compiled automatically based on the schedule you have created.

Finding just a few audiences may not be much of a chore. However, if you create a large number of audiences, locating a specific one may not be easy if you are searching manually. You can use the Search feature to locate any particular audience. Just navigate to the Manage Profile Service page and under People, click Manage Audiences. On the View Audiences page, enter the first few letters of the name of the audience in the Find Audiences That Start With field, and then click Find. The desired audience will appear in the search results.

Administering a SharePoint Wiki

While Wikipedia is probably the world's most famous wiki, wiki sites are ubiquitous on the Web and within the realm of business as a means to publish, contain, and organize information in an enterprise environment. A wiki allows collaboration and coauthoring of content in a single location and allows for discussion and management of such data relative to team- and group-level projects. Exercise 11.19 shows you how to create an enterprise wiki in Central Administration.

EXERCISE 11.19

Using Central Administration to Create a Wiki

In this exercise, you will learn how to create an enterprise-level wiki using Central Administration.

1. On the Central Administration home page, under Application Management, click Create Site Collection.

2. On the Create a Site Collection page, under Web Application, use the drop-down list to select the web application with which you want to create the wiki site.

3. Give the new wiki site a name in the Title field and a description in the Description field.

4. Under Web Site Address, select root (/) to create an Enterprise wiki or /sites/ to create the wiki at a specific path and then add a site name after /sites/.

5. Under Template Selection, click the Publishing tab and then click Enterprise Wiki.

6. Under Primary Site Collection Administrator, enter the name of the user you want to make the primary administrator for the wiki and then check the name.

7. Under Secondary Site Collection Administrator, enter the name of the user you want to designate as the secondary administrator for the wiki, and then check the name.

8. If you want to use quotas to manage storage for the wiki site, click the desired template in the Select A Quota Template list under Quota Template.

9. Click OK.

Instead of creating the wiki as a site collection, you can also create it as a subsite to another site. On the site's main page, under Site Actions, click New Site and create the wiki site using the appropriate template and steps.

My Site Management

My Site websites are the personal sites provided to each SharePoint user. They allow users to construct and customize their own website environments. These sites are specifically oriented toward social networking and include a My Networks page for managing each individual's colleagues, interests, and newsfeed settings. The My Content page lets users manage their own documents and photos, and the My Profile page provides an interface with which users can maintain social tags and notes.

A SharePoint Administrator must create the User Profile Service application and designate an administrator for the User Profile Service application. The SharePoint administrator or a User Profile Service application designated administrator can then create the My Site websites, the Trusted My Site host locations, personalization site links, and links to Microsoft Office 2010 client applications.

The exercises presented in this section will walk you through the processes of setting up, configuring, and deleting My Sites. You can get started with Exercise 11.20, which tells you how to set up a My Sites website. You should already have created the User Profile Service and the My Site host location in the desired web application.

To complete this exercise, you must be a member of the Farm Administrators group or be a service application administrator for the User Profile Service application.

EXERCISE 11.20

Setting Up a My Site

In this exercise, you will learn how to set up a My Site.

1. On the Central Administration home page, under Application Management, click Manage Service Applications.

2. On the Manage Service Applications page, click the name of the desired User Profile Service.

3. On the Manage Profile Service page, under My Site Settings, click Setup My Sites.

4. On the My Site Settings page, under Preferred Search Settings, enter the URL that the Search Center users will use in the Preferred Search Center field—for example, http://mysitename/SearchCenter/pages/.

5. Select a search scope for finding people and documents using the available drop-down menu.

6. Under My Site Host, enter the URL for the dedicated site collection hosting personal sites in the My Site Host Location—for example, http://main_portal_site/—or accept the default URL.

7. Under Personal Site Location, enter the URL of the location where you want to create the personal sites—for example, http://main_portal_site/location/personal_sites/.

8. Under Site Naming Format, select the format you want to use to name new personal sites.

9. Under Language Options, select Allow Users To Choose The Language Of Their Personal Site if you want users to be able to determine the language used to their My Site content.

10. Under Read Permission Level, enter the accounts for which you want to grant Read permissions for the personal site.

11. Under My Site E-Mail Notifications, enter the sender's name for all My Site email notifications in the Sender's Name field.

12. Click OK.

In step 6, if you change the default My Site Host location, you will create a link to a new My Site host location but you will not provision, or provide the required services to the My Site host at the new location. Changing the default settings for Personal Site Location and Site Naming Format will not affect any existing personal sites.

To make sure that email notifications sent from a My Site aren't treated as junk mail by your Microsoft Exchange server, add the IP address of the server hosting the My Site to the Save list in Exchange.

You can add links to trusted My Site host locations so that your users can access My Site websites on more than one User Profile Service application. You typically perform this task when you want to target specific users or groups based on specific organizational or business requirements. This task can be performed by SharePoint administrators who are members of the Farm Administrators group and by User Profile Service application administrators. Exercise 11.21 shows you how to add a trusted My Site host location.

EXERCISE 11.21

Adding Trusted My Site Host Locations

In this exercise, you will learn how to add a trusted My Site host location.

1. On the Central Administration home page, under Application Management, click Manage Service Applications.

2. On the Manage Service Applications page, on the Service Applications tab, select the desired User Profile Service.

3. On the Ribbon, click Manage.

4. On the Manage Profile Service page, under My Site Settings, click Configure Trusted Host Locations.

5. On the Trusted My Site Host Locations page, click New Link.

6. On the Add Trusted Host Location page, enter the URL of the trusted personal site location in the URL field.

7. Enter a description for the location in the Description field.

8. If you want to, you can enter usernames or group names for the targeted audiences in the Target Audience field and then verify the names.

9. Click OK.

To delete a trusted host location, follow steps 1 through 4 from Exercise 11.21; then, on the Trusted My Site Host Locations page, select the check box next to the trusted host location you want to delete and click Delete Link.

There is a great deal of interoperability between Office 2010 clients and SharePoint Server 2010. One item in the vast list of connections between the two Microsoft products is the ability to save an Office 2010 document to a My Site website in SharePoint. After a link to Office 2010 client applications has been added, SharePoint users can go into the Favorite Links area of the Save As dialog box and select their SharePoint My Site as a location to which to save an Office document. To successfully complete Exercise 11.22, you must be an administrator on the local server computer hosting the SharePoint Central Administration website.

EXERCISE 11.22

Adding a Link to Office 2010 Client Applications

In this exercise, you will learn how to add a link to an Office 2010 client application.

1. On the Central Administration home page, under Application Management, click Manage Service Applications.

2. On the Manage Service Applications page, click in the Type column next to the desired User Profile Service to select it.

3. On the Ribbon, click Manage.

4. On the Manage Profile Service page, under My Site Settings, click Publish Links to Office Client Applications.

5. On the Published Links to Office Client Applications page, click New Link.

6. On the Add Published Link page, in the URL field, enter the URL of the location where users will be able to publish their links.

7. In the Description field, enter a description of the link; the description will appear in the Favorite Links area when a user employs Save As to save a document.

8. Select the target location that the link represents—for example, a document library.

9. To use the targeted audiences feature, enter the user or group you want to add in the Target Audiences field and then verify the name. (If you enter more than one name, use semicolons between them.)

10. Click OK.

To delete a link, follow steps 1 through 4 in Exercise 11.22; then, on the Published Linked To Office Client Applications page, select the check box next to the link you want to delete and click Delete Link.

Planning for Business Intelligence Strategy

Business intelligence (BI) is the use of a combination of applications and utilities for the purpose of organizing and displaying business-relevant data to be used to create and establish corporate goals, performance, and process requirements. Providing a business intelligence solution is one of the key strengths of SharePoint, and Business intelligence planning always starts with determining the business needs and business data needs of your company. Once those requirements have been identified, you can locate, construct, and configure the Business Intelligence tools within SharePoint that will satisfy those requirements.

SharePoint has a number of tools and features that either individually or in combination with several utilities allow you to configure and display BI information. In the following sections, you will learn how to perform numerous BI-related tasks using three essential services:

- PerformancePoint Services
- Visio Graphics Service
- Excel Services

Administering PerformancePoint

PerformancePoint Services within SharePoint Server 2010 is a performance management service used to monitor and analyze business activities using a variety of tools including dashboards, scorecards, and key performance indicators (KPIs). This service is available as a standalone solution called Microsoft Office PerformancePoint Server 2007, but it is integrated into SharePoint Server 2010, Enterprise edition. Although PerformancePoint is currently under the SharePoint umbrella, so to speak, it retains the features contained in the previous server version while offering additional features.

Configuring PerformancePoint Services

Enabling and configuring PerformancePoint Services in SharePoint 2010 requires that you perform a series of prerequisite steps. In all likelihood, you've already performed at least some of them.

- You must have at least one web application in which you want to create a site collection.
- To be able to open the PerformancePoint Dashboard Designer from a site other than the Business Intelligence Center, you will need to enable the PerformancePoint Services site feature on the desired site.
- When you ran the Farm Configuration Wizard to create service applications and proxies, the PerformancePoint Services application was also created. If you did not run the wizard, you will need to create the PerformancePoint Services application to provide a resource that can be shared across sites in a server farm.
- Once PerformancePoint Services is created, you must start the service.

The Secure Store Service application and proxy must be created and running in order for the PerformancePoint Services service to store the Unattended Service Account password, which is a shared domain account that's used to allow access to PerformancePoint Services data sources.

- PerformancePoint Services and the Secure Store Service must be associated with the same web application.

- The Unattended Service Account must be configured for PerformancePoint Services to connect to data sources.

- The most typical site collection scenario relative to PerformancePoint is to create a site below the top-level site of a site collection using the Business Intelligence Center site template. By default, the template provides a PerformancePoint Services site that allows you to use all of the various PerformancePoint objects, including dashboards.

By this point, one or more web applications should have been created in your SharePoint deployment if you've been following the exercises in this book in a linear fashion.

If you ran the Farm Configuration Wizard after installing SharePoint, you had the option to select PerformancePoint Services as one of the services to run in the farm. If you didn't make that selection, you can run the wizard again and choose PerformancePoint Services. If you don't want to run the wizard, you can create a PerformancePoint Services service application, either in Central Administration or using Windows PowerShell. Exercise 11.23 will show you the Central Administration method.

EXERCISE 11.23

Using Central Administration to Create a PerformancePoint Services Service Application

In this exercise, you will learn how to create a PerformancePoint Services application.

1. Navigate to Central Administration and under Application Management, click Manage Service Applications.

2. On the Manage Service Applications page, on the Ribbon, click New and then select PerformancePoint Services.

3. When the Create a PerformancePoint Services Service Application box appears, enter a name for the new service application in the available field.

4. Either choose an existing application pool or create a new pool.

5. Accept the default managed account that's available, and then click Create.

If in step 5, you had chosen to register a new managed account and use it as the application pool identity, you would have needed to run the following Windows PowerShell script granting you access to the associated database. This will grant you db_owner access to the SharePoint Foundation content databases. If you register a new managed account but do not run the script, PerformancePoint Services will fail to work. Substitute your production values for the sample values in the following code.

```
PS> $w = Get-SPWebApplication -identity <your web application>
PS> $w.GrantAccessToProcessIdentity("<insert service account>")
```

You can also create a PerformancePoint Services service application using Windows PowerShell. Open and run Windows PowerShell as an administrator, enter the following code and then press Enter, substituting your production values for the sample values.

```
New-SPPerformancePointServiceApplication -Name  <PPS ServiceApp Name> -
applicationpool <App Pool Name>
```

Enter the following code and press Enter again, also substituting production values for sample values.

```
New-SPPerformancePointServiceApplicationProxy -ServiceApplication <PPS ServiceApp
Name> -Name  <PPS Service AppProxy> -Default
```

Creating Data Connections for PerformancePoint Services

PerformancePoint Services uses a trusted data connection library in SharePoint Server 2010 to store data sources for the PerformancePoint Dashboard Designer. The trusted data connection library is a document library that has been determined to be secure and safe, and it restricts the data files in the library. By default, this library is created when PerformancePoint Services is provisioned.

You can configure the security settings for the data sources and have users connect using:

- Unattended Service Account
- Unattended User Account and add authenticated user in connection (Analysis services only)
- Per-User Identity (requires Kerberos protocol)

SharePoint administrators can manage data connections on a server by creating more than one data connection library. When a user updates a data source connection in a document library, the data is shared and updated when a workspace file is opened in the Dashboard Designer.

Data source connections are created in the PerformancePoint Dashboard Designer. To open the Dashboard Designer, navigate to the Business Intelligence Center site you created earlier in this chapter. Under Create Scorecards With PerformancePoint Services, click the Start Using PerformancePoint Services link. Then, click the Run Dashboard Designer button. Once Dashboard Designer is installed, you will be ready to develop PerformancePoint dashboards and perform the following set of tasks.

The first data connection type you'll create is for an Analysis Services Data Source. You can create this data source in Dashboard Designer by entering the name of the Analysis Services server, the database name and cube name, or by using a connection string and the cube name. The authentication method for the web application and site collection should already be configured. Exercise 11.24 will show you how to use Dashboard Designer to create an Analysis Services data connection.

Creating an Analysis Services Data Connection

This exercise will show you how to create an analysis services data connection using Dashboard Designer.

1. In Dashboard Designer on the Create tab, click Data Source.

2. When the Select A Data Source Template box opens, in the Category pane, click Multidimensional, click Analysis Services, and then click OK.

3. In the left navigation pane, enter the name for the data source.

4. Under Data Source Settings, select the authentication method for the data source.

5. Use the Formatting Dimension drop-down menu to select the dimension formatting required for the report.

6. In the Cache Lifetime field, enter the refresh rate (in minutes) for the cache.

7. In the center pane, click the Editor tab.

8. Under Connection Settings, select either Use Standard Connection or Use The Following Connection.

   - If you select Use Standard Connection, enter the full path name for the server to which you want to connect, select the database name in the Database box, and optionally enter the name of the role, such as administrator or database, in the Roles field.

   - If you select Use The Following Connection, enter the connection string to the server to which you want to connect, including the cube name, and use the Cube drop-down menu to select the specific cube you want to use as the data source in the data base.

9. Click Test Connection to verify that the connection works.

PerformancePoint Services can use PowerPivot models as data sources, using the data to construct interactive dashboards featuring PerformancePoint Services objects such as KPIs, analytic charts, scorecards, and so on. PowerPivot for SharePoint 2010 must be installed and enabled for you to take advantage of this data source. ADOMD 10 must also be installed on the server on which you are creating the dashboard. Otherwise, you will not have access to the PowerPivot workbook as a data source. The Unattended Service Account And Add Authenticated User Name In Connection String Authentication option is unavailable when you use PowerPivot as a data source. Exercise 11.25 will show you how to create a PowerPivot data connection.

EXERCISE 11.25

Creating a PowerPivot Data Connection

Follow these steps to create a PowerPivot data connection.

1. In Dashboard Designer on the Create tab, click Data Source.

2. When the Select A Data Source Template box opens, in the Category pane, click Multidimensional, click Analysis Services, and then click OK.

3. In the left navigation pane, enter the name for the data source.

4. In the center pane, click the Editor tab; and under Connection Setting, select Use The Following Connection.

5. Enter the connection string to the PowerPivot data source using the format `PROVIDER=MSOLAP;DATA SOURCE=http://testing/Documents/PowerPivot_Example .xlsx`, substituting your production values for the sample values.

6. Select the cube from the drop-down menu, and always use the cube name Sandbox for a PowerPivot model.

7. Under Data Source Settings, select the desired authentication method.

8. Select the desired dimension in the Formatting Dimension list.

9. Enter the refresh rate (in minutes) in Cache Lifetime.

10. Click Test Connection.

A limitation to using Excel Services data as a data source connection is that only the Unattended Service Account and Per-User Identity can be used to authenticate. Also, you cannot use Excel Services as a data source when the site or library containing the workbook allows Anonymous Access. Exercise 11.26 shows you how to create an Excel Services data source connection.

EXERCISE 11.26

Creating an Excel Services Data Source Connection

Follow these steps to create an Excel Services data source connection.

1. In Dashboard Designer on the Create tab, click Data Source.

2. When the Select a Data Source Template box opens, in the Category pane, click Tabular List and then click Excel Services.

3. Click OK.

4. In the left navigation pane, enter the name of the data source.

5. In the center pane, click the Editor tab; and under Data Source Settings, select the desired authentication method.

6. Enter the refresh rate (in minutes) in Refresh Interval.

7. Under Connection Settings, in the available field, enter the URL to the SharePoint site.

8. Use the Document Library drop-down menu to select the document library in SharePoint where the Excel workbook is located.

9. Use the Excel Workbook drop-down menu to select the desired workbook.

10. Use the Item Name drop-down menu to select either Named Range or Table.

11. Click Test Data Source to confirm that the connection works.

Deploying PerformancePoint Objects

Once PerformancePoint is configured, the next step is to create the actual PerformancePoint objects, such as dashboards, charts, grids, maps, and so on. This section of the chapter will show you the related tasks.

As you might guess from its name, the PerformancePoint Dashboard Designer creates the various items used in PerformancePoint dashboards, such as filters, reports, and scorecards. When you create these items, they are saved in a SharePoint list so you can reuse the items and share them with other dashboard authors. Once you have assembled all of your items into a dashboard, deploy it to a document library in SharePoint that you've created specifically for PerformancePoint dashboards.

To successfully perform Exercise 11.27, you must possess at least Design permission at the top-level SharePoint site containing the subsite or folder in which your dashboard content is contained.

EXERCISE 11.27

Deploying a PerformancePoint Dashboard

Follow these steps to deploy a PerformancePoint dashboard.

1. Navigate to the Business Intelligence Site and then to the PerformancePoint Services site.

2. Launch Dashboard Designer.

3. In the Workspace Browser pane, click PerformancePoint Content.

4. On the Ribbon, click the Home tab and then click Refresh.

5. In the center pane of the workspace, double-click the dashboard you want to publish. Wait for the pane to refresh and display the list of dashboard items dashboard authors have saved to SharePoint.

6. If you like, click the Editor tab to verify that each dashboard page contains all of the items you want to include in your dashboard.

7. Make any necessary additions or changes in the dashboard. Then, in the Workspace Browser, right-click the dashboard and click Save.

8. Right-click the dashboard again, and then click Deploy To SharePoint.

9. When you deploy a dashboard to SharePoint for the first time, the Deploy To box opens. There you can select the desired Dashboards library and use the Master Page list to specify the page template for the dashboard. If the dashboard is larger than one page, the Include Page List For Navigation check box will appear so you can check it.

10. When you are finished with these selections, click OK.

11. In the Deploy To SharePoint Site box that opens, review the information available and test the dashboard items. Make a note of the URL of the dashboard; you can send it to interested parties via email when you are ready to share the dashboard.

Although the instructions for deploying a dashboard were presented first in this list of exercises, deployment is really the last step in the process. You will need to add or create a number of items that can be included in a dashboard. Exercise 11.28 shows you how to create analytic reports, which are dynamic visuals representing data. Examples include: bar charts, line charts, pie charts, tables, and grids. These items pull information from SQL Server 2008 Analysis Services or SQL Server 2005 Analysis Services.

The first part of the task is to make sure your data source is available. After that, you'll create and configure the chart for the dashboard. Exercise 11.28 assumes that you have already navigated to the PerformancePoint Services site under the Business Intelligence site.

Creating an Analytic Chart or Grid

Go through this exercise to learn how to create an analytic chart or grid.

1. In the Dashboard Designer, click Home tab and then click Refresh.

2. In the Workspace Browser, click Data Connections.

3. In the center pane of the workspace, review the list of data sources on the Server and Workspace tabs and verify the desired data sources are present.

4. In the Workspace Browser, click PerformancePoint Content.

5. On the Ribbon, click the Create tab.

6. On the Ribbon, under Reports, click Analytic Chart or Analytic Grid, depending on your requirements (this exercise will use Analytic Chart).

7. When the Create An Analytic Chart Report Wizard launches, for Select A Data Source, select the desired SQL Server Analysis Services data source.

8. Click Finish.

9. When the analytic report opens in the center pane of the workspace, click the Properties tab.

10. In the Name field, enter the name you want to use for the report.

11. If you desire, specify a location for the report by clicking the Display Folder button and then selecting or creating a folder.

12. In the Workspace Browser, right-click the report and then click Save.

Now that the basic structure of the report has been constructed, you must configure it to display data. When performing this function, you can choose between the Details and the Query methods.

To use the Details option, in the Designer, click the Design tab and drag items from the Details pane into the preview window of the report. Continue this process until the preview appears as you desire.

To use the Query option, click the Query tab and then specify or edit the custom Multidimensional Expressions (MDX) query used to display data. One problem with using the Query option is that dashboard users might be unable to drill up or down in the data. For this reason, the Design option is recommended. Use the Query option if you are familiar with MDX.

Exercise 11.29 shows you how to use Dashboard Designer to set up a report to display data.

EXERCISE 11.29

Using Dashboard Designer to Configure a Report

In this exercise, you'll see how to configure a report to display data using Dashboard Designer.

1. In Dashboard Designer, in the center pane, click the Design tab.

2. In the Details pane, expand Measures, Dimensions, Or Named Sets to show the desired list of items.

3. Depending on the specific option you expanded in the previous step, drag an item into Series (Or Rows), Bottom Axis (Or Columns), or Background—but make sure you put at least one item in each Series (Or Rows) and Bottom Axis (Or Columns) section so that data will be displayed in the report.

4. For Dimension Members, accept the default selection of All, or right-click a dimension and then click Select Members.

5. If you use the Select Members option, when the Select Members dialog box opens, expand the desired list of members in the dimension hierarchy, select the desired items to be displayed in the report, and then click OK.

6. To add more items, in the Details pane, expand Measures, Dimensions, or Named Sets, drag items into the available sections, and then configure the dimension members as needed.

7. In the Ribbon, on the Edit tab, use the View group to specify the view type and settings for the report.

8. In the Workspace Browser, right-click the report and then click Save.

 Real World Scenario

Setting up PerformancePoint Services

You are a SharePoint administrator for the Acme Development Company. You have been tasked with creating a test Business Intelligence environment for the management team to demonstrate SharePoint's ROI in the area of monitoring and presenting business data for company sales revenue by product and department.

You are provided with several data sources and a list of how the information is to be displayed in a dashboard using KPIs, scorecards, strategy maps, and charts.

With the required information available, you begin by creating a PerformancePoint Services service application in SharePoint's Central Administration and configuring an unattended service account. You then create a web application specifically for the BI task and associate the service application with the web application. Then, you create a site collection in the new web application and enable the site collection for SharePoint Publishing infrastructure as well as the PerformancePoint Services site feature. Now you're able to create a site within the site collection using the Business Intelligence Center Site template.

Using the information provided to you by the management team, you create a number of data source connections on the BI center site using the Dashboard Designer, and then in Designer, you create the specific PerformancePoint objects. Finally, you deploy the requested PerformancePoint dashboard and notify the management team so they can review the results.

Administering Excel Services

Excel Services is a significant source of information for business intelligence, particularly relevant to PerformancePoint Services. This section provides more detail on this classic service in SharePoint.

Managing the Excel Services Custom Application

In general, the main focus of Excel Services in SharePoint is to extend the abilities of Excel Calculation Services and Excel workbooks in SharePoint. As a SharePoint administrator, you will work primarily with user-defined functions (UDFs) to customize applications and workbooks in Excel Services.

For this exercise, you will need to configure Excel Services to support UDFs, enable UDFs on trusted file locations, and register UDF assemblies on the Excel Services user-defined function assembly list. These tasks are performed in Central Administration. Exercise 11.30 gets you started by showing you how to enable user-defined functions on trusted file locations.

EXERCISE 11.30

Enabling User-Defined Functions on a Trusted File Location

In this exercise, you will learn how to enable user-defined functions on trusted file locations.

1. Navigate to Central Administration and under Application Management, click Manage Service Applications.

2. On the Manage Service Applications page, click the desired Excel Services web service application.

3. On the Manage Excel Services page, click Trusted File Locations.

4. On the Trusted File Locations page, click the trusted file for which you want to enable user-defined functions.

5. On the Edit Trusted File Location page, under User-Defined Functions, select the User-Defined Functions Allowed check box.

6. Click OK.

The next task involves managing Excel Services user-defined function assemblies and includes adding, editing, and deleting a user-defined function assembly. Exercise 11.31 walks you through the steps.

EXERCISE 11.31

Managing Excel Services User-Defined Function Assemblies

In this exercise, you will learn how to add, edit, and delete a user-defined function assembly.

1. Navigate to Central Administration and under Application Management, click Manage Service Applications.

2. On the Manage Service Applications page, click the desired Excel Services Web Service Application.

3. On the Manage Excel Services page, click User Defined Function Assemblies.

4. On the Excel Services User Defined Functions page, click Add User-Defined Function Assembly.

5. On the Add User-Defined Function Assembly page, under Assembly, in the Assembly field, enter the name of the assembly or the full path name of an assembly that contains the user-defined functions.

6. For User Assembly location, select Global Assembly Cache, which is a global location from where signed assemblies can be deployed and run with full trust, or select File Path, which is the local or network file location.

7. Under Enable Assembly, select the Assembly Enabled check box to allow Excel Calculation Services to call the assembly.

8. Enter a description in the Description field and then click OK.

To edit a user-defined function assembly, on the Excel Services User Defined Functions page, click next to the desired user-defined function assembly to make the arrow available. In the list that appears, click Edit.

To delete a user-defined function assembly, on the Excel Services User Defined Functions page, click next to the desired user-defined function assembly to make the arrow available. In the list that appears, click Delete. When prompted, click OK.

Managing Excel Services Connections

SharePoint's Excel Services has the ability to connect to external data sources and refresh the available data. To connect to external data sources, Excel Services uses trusted data connection libraries. These are lists in SharePoint that contain the data connection files designed to work with external data connections and enable Excel Services and Excel clients to make such connections.

Both trusted data connection libraries and trusted data providers must be configured in SharePoint before Excel Services can access these sources.

Managing Excel Services Trusted Locations

When you install SharePoint Server 2010 and run the Microsoft SharePoint 2010 Product Wizard, a default trusted file location is created for Excel Services. This trusted location site trusts the entire SharePoint server farm and enables any file to be loaded from the farm or standalone deployment on Excel Services. This makes it easier for Administrators to perform the initial configuration. You can also define other trusted file locations in order to expand Excel workbook abilities and to augment security.

Configuring a Secure Store for Excel Services

The Secure Store Service replaced the single sign-on (SSO) feature you may have known in Microsoft Office SharePoint Server (MOSS) 2007. Excel Services supports Secure Store Services and can use it to store credentials for a database, using the credentials to authenticate to data sources.

The general set of steps you need to perform in order to configure a Secure Store Service for Excel Services are

- Creating the shared Secure Store Service
- Generating a key
- Adding an application ID
- Setting credentials to be associated with the application ID

You'll need to add an application ID to map the credentials of a user, group, or claim to a set of credentials on the external data source Excel Services wants to use.

Managing Visio Services

Like Excel Services, the Visio Graphics Service lets users view and share Visio diagrams in SharePoint. When you data-connect a Visio diagram in SharePoint, the diagram refreshes in SharePoint whenever it is modified at the source.

The following information demonstrates how to enable Visio services in SharePoint if you have not already enabled them using the Farm Configuration Wizard.

Creating and deleting the Visio Graphics Service in Central Administration is virtually identical to performing the same tasks for other services, such as Excel Services; however, you can also create and delete the service using Windows PowerShell. You must be a member of the SharePoint_Shell_Access role on the configuration database and a member of the WSS_ADMIN_WPG local group on the computer containing SharePoint 2010 Products.

Exercise 11.32 introduces you to Visio services management. All of the values provided in the PowerShell code shown in this exercise are sample code. In a production environment, you must substitute actual values in place of the sample values.

EXERCISE 11.32

Using Windows PowerShell to Create and Delete the Visio Service Application

In this exercise, you'll learn how to create and delete the Visio Graphics Service application using the Windows PowerShell interface.

1. Open Windows PowerShell, enter `New-SPVisioServiceApplication <ServiceAppName> -serviceapplicationpool <AppPoolName> -AddToDefaultGroup` at the prompt, and then press Enter.

2. To delete the service application, enter `Remove-SPServiceApplication <ServiceAppName>` at the prompt, and press Enter.

Once you have created one or more Visio Graphics Service applications, you can view them by executing `Get-SPVisioServiceApplication` in Windows PowerShell.

You can also use Windows PowerShell to create and delete a Visio Graphics Service service application proxy. A service application proxy allows other farms to access and use the service application remotely. In Windows PowerShell, you use `New-SPVisioServiceApplicationProxy <ServiceAppName>` to create a trusted provider. The code to delete a provider is `Remove-SPServiceApplicationProxy <ProxyID>`. Substitute the sample values in this code with your own production values.

Trusted data providers are external databases used by Excel Services and Visio Graphics Service that are specifically trusted by these services when processing information. You can create a trusted data provider for Visio Graphics Service in Central Administration or Windows PowerShell. This first example uses Central Administration. Exercise 11.33 shows you this process.

EXERCISE 11.33

Using Central Administration to Create a Trusted Data Provider for Visio Graphics Service

This exercise shows you how to use Central Administration to create a trusted data provider for the Visio Graphics Service.

1. On the Central Administration main page, under Application Management, click Manage Service Applications.

2. Click on the Visio Graphics Service service application where you want to create a trusted data provider.

3. Click Trusted Data Providers.

4. Click Add A New Trusted Data Provider.

5. Enter the provider ID in the Trusted Data Provider ID field.

6. Enter the provider type in the Trusted Data Provider Type field.

7. Enter a description of the trusted data provider in the Trusted Data Provider Type Description field.

8. When you are finished, click OK.

Summary

In this chapter, you learned how to plan and initiate business management strategies in a number of related domains, including enterprise content management, social computing and collaboration, and business intelligence. Planning in each of these areas requires knowledge of a number of different SharePoint features and technologies including using libraries for document, records, and web content management; understanding the User Profile Service and My Sites; and comprehending the management of business intelligence tools such as PerformancePoint, Excel, and Visio.

Exam Essentials

Be able to plan enterprise content management.   You should understand the various tools and SharePoint features related to records management, document management, metadata planning, information management policies, implementation of data taxonomy structure, and web content management, as applied to an enterprise content management plan.

Be able to plan for social computing and collaboration.   Know how to plan for the configuration and use of SharePoint features and services such as User Profile Service, user profiles, organization profiles, audiences, My Sites, social tags, enterprise wikis, and personalization sites.

Be able to plan for business intelligence.   Know how to plan for creating and managing of services related to business intelligence performance such as PerformancePoint Service, Excel Services Service, and Visio Graphics Service.

Chapter

12

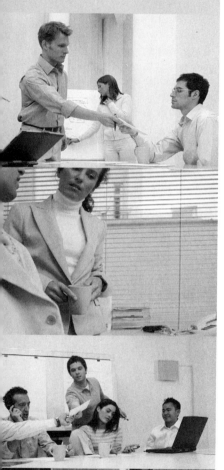

Planning an Upgrade and Migration Strategy

TOPICS COVERED IN THIS CHAPTER

✓ Planning a Strategy for Upgrades

✓ Designing a Migration Strategy

Many organizations will upgrade from a previous version of SharePoint to SharePoint 2010. It is important to understand how to plan for upgrades and migrations. In this chapter, you will first learn planning strategies for upgrades. As you explore upgrades, you will consider the following: the move to 64-bit computing, and how to plan for availability, upgrade the operating systems, and move from earlier versions of SharePoint to SharePoint 2010.

Next, you will explore the design of a migration strategy. This knowledge domain will include the creation of testing and quality assurance plans, database migration options, moving content within and between farms, and migrating custom features.

When you are finished reading this chapter, you will have the knowledge necessary to plan a move from an earlier version of SharePoint to the newest SharePoint 2010 products. You will also understand the upgrade options for the background components such as the Windows servers and database servers.

If you are preparing for the 70-668 MCITP examination, this chapter covers important topics for you. "Planning SharePoint 2010 Deployment" is a major objective of the exam, and this chapter covers both the "Plan an upgrade strategy" and "Design a migration strategy" subobjectives. The section titled "Planning a Strategy for Upgrades" teaches important information for the "Plan an upgrade strategy" objective, including planning for 64-bit computing, planning for availability, and upgrading the operating systems from earlier versions of SharePoint and SQL Server. The section titled "Designing a Migration Strategy" covers important topics including database migrations, content migrations, and custom feature migrations.

Planning a Strategy for Upgrades

SharePoint 2010 includes specific requirements that may demand a *forklift* upgrade, which is an entire infrastructure replacement. This possibility is, in part, due to the 64-bit computing requirements of SharePoint 2010, but it is also a simple factor of performance demands. In this section, you will explore the considerations made to plan for an effective upgrade from either SharePoint Server 2007 or 2003. This planning will include:

- Planning for 64-bit computing
- Planning for availability for the upgrade
- Upgrading operating systems
- Upgrading early SharePoint versions

- Performing MOSS 2007 upgrades
- Performing SQL Server upgrades
- Performing In-place upgrades
- Performing a rollback

Side-by-side upgrades, better called migrations, will be covered in the next section titled "Designing a Migration Strategy."

Planning for 64-Bit Computing

The landscape of computer processors is changing quickly over to 64-bit computing. It is difficult to purchase a new standard laptop or desktop today that does not include a 64-bit processor. Of course, you can still get 32-bit processors in Netbooks and you can build custom PCs and servers with 32-bit processors, but even that will become more difficult in the coming years. SharePoint 2010, as with most recent Microsoft releases, requires a 64-bit system.

Sixty-four-bit computing provides several advantages over 32-bit computing. First, you can use more than 4 GB of RAM in the system. This extended RAM support is a very important feature for database servers that access multigigabyte or even multiterabyte databases. Sixty-four-bit processors can theoretically address hundreds of terabytes of RAM; however, the actual amount varies depending on processor design. Second, the processor can work with larger chunks of data at a time, which can improve performance for applications that are optimized and compiled for 64-bit computing. Third, because of the preceding two benefits, intensive applications perform much better. As an example, the testing of encryption algorithms run on 64-bit systems has shown an increase in performance by three to five times. Of course, the typical user running Microsoft Word is not likely to notice any different in performance.

 While some 32-bit systems can exceed the 4 GB limitation, we will not go into the details here because it is not relevant to SharePoint 2010, which does require 64-bit computing regardless of the RAM you place in the server.

So what does it mean to move from 32-bit computing to 64-bit computing? The good news is that the interface is no different and the applications work just the same. The only people who really have to worry about the differences are the software developers. As an administrator, you only have to ensure you are using 64-bit drivers and 64-bit versions of your applications when they are available. Most 64-bit operating systems can still run 32-bit applications, and Windows Server 2008 or Windows Server 2008 R2 running a 64-bit edition is no different.

Because SharePoint 2010 requires 64-bit computing, you must plan your upgrades with this in mind. If you have servers that could run SharePoint 2010 from a processing speed and memory perspective, but they have 32-bit processors, you will have to perform a forklift upgrade to deploy SharePoint 2010. SharePoint 2010 requires a 64-bit operating system (Windows Vista x64, Windows 7 x64, Windows Server 2008 x64, or Windows Server 2008 R2) and a 64-bit edition of SQL Server 2005 with SP4 or later. If your servers run a 32-bit edition of Windows Server, but have 64-bit capable processors, an operating system upgrade may be all that is required to run SharePoint 2010 and you can leave the forklift in the garage.

I Forget. Did We Do This Already?

If you search the Internet as I (Tom) have done over the years for 64-bit computing articles, you will read a lot about how 64-bit computing breaks the memory constraints of 32-bit computing. This is certainly true. For example, Windows servers running the 32-bit edition typically support a maximum of 4 GB or RAM. Either 2 or 3 GB of that RAM is used for applications and the other 1 or 2 GB of RAM is used for the operating system. This configuration didn't leave a lot of room for memory intensive applications such as database servers.

However, I recall the big move to Windows 95 in August of 1995. People lined up outside of computer stores at midnight to buy this new 32-bit operating system. Of course, it wasn't fully 32-bit, but it was 32-bit enough for most people to get excited. The next year Windows NT 4.0 was released, and a truly 32-bit operating system with the Windows 95 style interface was made available to businesses around the world.

So, what was the big deal about these 32-bit operating systems and computers? They could support up to 4 GB of RAM. This was an amazing amount of RAM in 1995 and 1996. But there was an even more important barrier that was being broken. This barrier was the 640K barrier. Back in these good old days (and, yes, we could go back even further and talk about Commodores and Apple IIs, but we'll stop at 16-bit computing) of 16-bit computing, you had two kinds of memory: conventional memory and extended memory. *Conventional* memory was where you loaded all of your device drivers—much like the operating system section of RAM today. *Extended* memory could be used to run applications; however, even applications needed a footprint in conventional memory and so, when this memory was too low, applications would fail to run.

Sound familiar? Sure it does, but today we're dealing with gigabyte limits in 32-bit operating systems. Now for the big question: Why did I share all of this history? The answer is really simple. If you plan to work in Information Systems or Information Technology for the next 20 years, go ahead and get ready for the transition to 128-bit computing. It will come eventually, and when it does we'll have to deal with the same compatibility issues that we're facing now with Windows 7 and Windows Server 2008 R2 upgrades.

Although 64-bit systems are compatible with 32-bit applications (with rare exceptions), they are not at all compatible with 16-bit applications. You will be amazed at how many of these old 16-bit Windows 3.x applications are still in use in your company. These 16-bit applications may not directly impact SharePoint 2010, but they could become an issue for your Windows Server 2008 R2 machines running Remote Desktop Services for remote application execution. Virtualization is the only real solution we have for this today.

Finally, 64-bit computing will impact your SharePoint application in one key area: customizations. If you have developed custom DLLs that are 32-bit, they should be recompiled as 64-bit DLLs. They may work without recompilation, but the performance will be inferior. Trust me on this; I've already been there and done that.

Planning for Availability for the Upgrade

Over the years, many organizations have placed more and more of their business data and processes into SharePoint servers. Because of this important business function, availability for SharePoint servers has become more important than ever. In this section, you will explore mirroring and clustering for SQL Server databases or farms. You will also investigate the methods used to determine acceptable downtime and plan for storage fault tolerance.

Database Mirroring

SQL Server is the database engine behind SharePoint 2010, and the availability features it offers are, therefore, made available to SharePoint. *Database mirroring* is a process provided by SQL Server 2005 or later that provides a mechanism for duplicating databases across servers. This section will give you the information you need to understand database mirroring.

Database mirroring maintains two copies of one database with each copy stored in a separate instance of SQL Server. At least two server instances are involved in every mirroring configuration, and up to three servers can be used. You can create a warm standby server using just two servers or a hot standby server using a third server. The *warm* standby server is created when a production server is used for the user interactions and another server is receiving the transactions but is not available for user access. You create a *hot* standby server by implementing a third instance of SQL Server that monitors the previously mentioned two servers for failure and automatic failover. The three servers for a hot standby server are the principal server, the mirror server, and the witness server.

The *principal* server instance stores the active database that is accessed by the SharePoint server. This principal instance contains the database that is modified through normal application usage and is treated much like a normal single database server instance. The principal instance is said to be *serving* the database because it allows transactions to be performed against the database.

The *mirror* server instance stores the second copy of the database and is not accessed by SharePoint while in the mirror role. The mirror instance contains a copy of the database that is modified only by the principal instance.

The *witness* server instance is the optional server and, when it is provided, is used to provide automatic failover. This witness instance does not contain a copy of the database being mirrored, but instead it monitors the primary instance and, should it fail, it switches the mirror instance to act as the primary instance and in so doing provides automatic failover. The witness server may run SQL Server Express Edition so that licensing costs may be reduced.

The principal and mirror instances must be running either SQL Server Standard or Enterprise edition. The witness instance, if used, can run any edition of SQL Server except the Mobile edition. This means you could use the free edition—SQL Server Express—to act as the witness instance for an automatic failover configuration of database mirroring. Database mirroring roles defined at the database level include the principal and mirror roles; however, the witness role is configured at the instance level as a copy of the database is not placed on the witness server.

SQL Server database mirroring provides two different operating modes. The operating mode determines how transactions are transferred between the principal and mirror databases and the failover mechanism to be used. The modes are called high safety and high performance.

The *high safety* operating mode requires all three server roles and is called high availability in some Microsoft literature because of the automatic failover. This operating mode provides guaranteed transaction committal on both the principal and the mirror instance. The guaranteed transaction committal is provided through synchronous operations. All committed transactions are committed on both partners (synchronous), which provides the guarantee of committal at both the principal and the mirror instance. When you need to guarantee synchronicity between the principal and the mirror more than you need to provide high performance, you will want to use the high safety operating mode.

High safety mode may also be used without automatic failover. This mode is sometimes called high protection. The data is protected, but availability is not as good because manual failover must be performed by an administrator.

The *high performance* operating mode uses asynchronous transaction committal. When a transaction is submitted to the principal, it is processed in the same way a standalone instance would process the transaction. The mirroring service is also monitoring these transactions and sending them to the mirror instance. There is no verification that the transaction has been written to the mirror database before more transactions are accepted at the principal. This may result in a lag on the mirror instance and a risk of data loss in the event of principal database failure; however, the performance gains can be substantial, and when you are implementing mirroring across WAN links or other slower connections, it may be the only option you have.

To implement database mirroring, you will need to perform a number of tasks and ensure that the databases involved in the mirroring processes are configured to support mirroring. It is very important to remember that a database participating in database mirroring must use the Full recovery model. The first step to implementing mirroring is to back up the database on the principal instance and recover the database to the intended mirror instance. When you recover the database to the intended mirror instance, be sure to use the NORECOVERY option of the RESTORE T-SQL command so that the database is left in the proper state to begin mirroring operations.

In addition to the backup and restore of the database, you should also be sure that any system objects in existence on the principal server are also created on the mirror server. These may include users, roles, custom error messages, Integration Services packages, SQL Server Agent jobs, and linked servers. Remember, you only need to create the system objects on the mirror instance that are actually used by the database being mirrored. The principal instance may have other databases as well, and the system objects that those databases use exclusively will not need to be created on the mirror instance because those databases are not being mirrored to the mirror instance.

After you've performed these initial steps, you'll need to do the following:

- Create endpoints for the mirroring configuration.
- Configure the mirroring partners.
- Configure a witness server, if needed.
- Configure operating modes.

Each instance in the database mirroring partnership requires a mirroring endpoint. You will need to know how to create the endpoints for the principal and the mirror servers. The endpoints can use either Windows authentication or certificate-based authentication. Most implementations will choose to use Windows authentication. In addition, only one mirroring endpoint can exist in each SQL Server instance. Because of this limitation, you will want to ensure that no mirroring endpoints exist on your SQL server before actually creating an endpoint. The following code can be used to test for the existence of a mirroring endpoint:

```
SELECT name, role_desc, state_desc
FROM sys.database_mirroring_endpoints;
```

If you get zero results, you are ready to execute code like that which is shown in Exercise 12.1. You should only run the principal code on the principal instance and the mirror code on the mirror instance.

EXERCISE 12.1

Creating the Mirroring Endpoints

In this exercise, the code needed to create mirroring endpoints is presented. This code may require modification in order to work on your systems. To create mirroring endpoints:

1. Log on to the principle server as an administrator and connect to the SQL server, using SSMS, as an administrator.

2. Execute the following code in a New Query window:

```
--Endpoint for principal server instance.
CREATE ENDPOINT mirroring
  STATE = STARTED
  AS TCP ( LISTENER_PORT = 7575 )
  FOR DATABASE_MIRRORING (ROLE=PARTNER);
GO
```

3. Now, log on to the mirror server as an administrator and connect to the SQL server, using SSMS, as an administrator.

4. Execute the following code in a New Query window:

```
--Endpoint for mirror server instance.
CREATE ENDPOINT mirroring
  STATE = STARTED
  AS TCP ( LISTENER_PORT = 7575 )
  FOR DATABASE_MIRRORING (ROLE=PARTNER);
GO
```

5. Finally, log on to the witness server as an administrator and connect to the SQL server, using SSMS, as an administrator.

6. Execute the following code in a New Query window:

```
--Endpoint for the witness server instance.
CREATE ENDPOINT mirroring
  STATE = STARTED
  AS TCP ( LISTENER_PORT = 7575 )
  FOR DATABASE_MIRRORING (ROLE=WITNESS);
GO
```

Keep in mind the fact that you can use any available TCP port for the listener_port parameter shown in Exercise 12.1, and the name mirroring can be changed to any valid and available name you choose. Notice that there is no authentication setting specified.

This is because Windows authentication is the default and that's exactly what you want to use in most cases as it is more secure.

You can also configure the endpoints in a more automated fashion by using the Mirroring page of the Database Properties dialog box. To access this page, right-click the database you want to mirror and select Properties. From here, click the Mirroring page. You should see something similar to Figure 12.1.

FIGURE 12.1   The Mirroring page in the Database Properties dialog

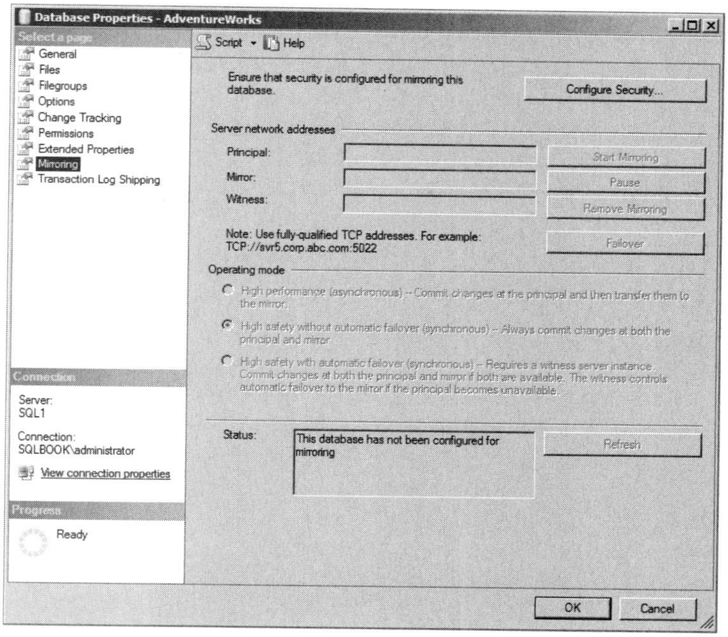

The Configure Security button on the Mirroring page allows you to execute code that will create the appropriate endpoints on the servers involved in the mirroring partnership. After you set up the endpoints, using this feature, you will want to fill in the IP addresses of the participating servers. You could also use the FQDN (fully qualified domain name) if you have a DNS infrastructure, which is likely in modern networks. Finally, you will need to select the operating mode. Notice that the available operating modes change depending on whether you specify a witness server or not. When everything is configured, click Start Mirroring.

Clustering Solutions

Clustering is different from database mirroring. Database mirroring can provide you with high availability for the content and configuration databases used by SharePoint. Clustering can be used for the SQL server and also for the application and web frontend servers. To help you understand clustering, you will explore Windows Failover Clustering, which is the feature of Windows that allows for SQL Server clustering. Then you will learn about SQL

Server's support of failover clustering specifically, and finally you'll review the possibility of creating an entire farm failover cluster.

Windows Failover Clustering

The Windows Failover Clustering service provides server clustering for Windows-based servers. A *cluster* is a collection of servers that work together to provide services to the network. The unique thing about a cluster of servers, as opposed to separate servers performing independent functions, is that the collection of clustered servers is accessed as a single server from the client perspective. You can have two servers in a cluster, but they appear as one to the users and applications. For example, SharePoint will still point to a single SQL Server database server even though you may be using failover clustering for the SQL server.

Clusters share storage. If you have two physical servers that you want to use in a cluster for SQL Server 2008, both servers must have access to shared storage. It is this shared storage that allows the servers to access the same data and the services to failover from one server to another rapidly. The shared storage should be a fault-tolerant storage solution in order to prevent downtime from storage failures. Fault-tolerant storage solutions include RAID cabinets, storage area networks (SANs), and distributed storage. RAID cabinets are storage devices that support various implementations of RAID, such as RAID 0 (striping), RAID 1 (mirroring), and RAID 5 (striping with parity).

> You will learn more about RAID in a later section titled "Storage Fault Tolerance." For now, just know that it provides fault tolerance and high availability for the storage used by the cluster.

It is important that you remember the following rule of high availability:

Your system is only as available as its weakest link.

What does this rule mean? It means that you have to look at the cluster nodes, the network between these nodes, the shared storage, and the stability of hardware components. It is for this reason that Microsoft recommends using the Failover Clustering service only with validated hardware. Validated hardware has been tested by Microsoft or service providers to ensure stability and compatibility with the Failover Clustering service.

The Weakest Link

As an example of the "weakest link" concept, consider the Windows Vista and Windows 7 feature called the Windows Experience Index (WEI). WEI rates various hardware components and uses these ratings to determine the performance expectations of the system. Microsoft knew that a system with a very fast processor but a very slow hard drive would still have performance problems. In the same way, a system with a very fast hard drive and very fast memory but a very slow processor will also have performance problems. For this reason, the WEI is actually based on the weakest link or the lowest performing component.

I (Tom) am typing this paragraph on a machine with a WEI of 5.9 in Windows 7. The 5.9 rating comes from the hard disk. All other evaluated components (graphics, memory, and processor) are rated from 6.0 to 7.3; however, the Windows 7 report is more realistic than the evaluation of a single component.

The same is true for your clusters. If you have expensive and stable servers but faulty storage, the cluster will not live up to your expectations. If the network is slow between the SQL Server cluster and the SharePoint server accessing it, the performance will suffer. All components must be selected, installed, and configured in order to achieve the level of performance and reliability required.

Four key factors impact the availability of your systems. These four factors are security, stability, life expectancy, and redundancy.

Security   Security must be considered as an availability issue because a security incident can indeed make a resource unavailable. For example, a denial of service (DoS) attack against a SQL server can make it unavailable to the SharePoint servers regardless of clustering or other availability technologies utilized.

Stability   Stability is a factor of hardware and software quality. Quality hardware should not overheat and should operate effectively for long periods of uninterrupted time. Poorly designed systems often suffer from heat problems and shut themselves off or damage hardware components resulting in downtime. For this reason, Microsoft recommends using only certified hardware for clustered installations.

Life Expectancy   Hard drives have a value called mean time between failures (MTBF). MTBF indicates the life expectancy of the drive. While it is important to purchase drives that will last a long time, it is more important to know when drives are expected to fail. Many organizations plan for drive replacements just before the MTBF is reached. In RAID systems with dynamic data regeneration, the drives can be replaced one-by-one with no downtime at all. For other hardware, check with the vendor to determine life expectancy.

Redundancy   The key to high availability is redundancy. This is true in every area of life. If you are designing an application and the application is due in thirty days and you are the only programmer working on the application, you carry great risk. If you are sick and unable to work for a week, the deadline is sure to be missed; however, if you have other programmers who can take up the work when you are unavailable, the work of the project continues. In the same way, redundant hardware helps keep systems running and available for user access.

Windows servers also offer a feature called Network Load Balancing (NLB) that should not be confused with failover clustering. NLB is used to distribute workloads across multiple servers on a session-by-session basis.

Clustering Terminology

Several terms are used to describe and define clustering technology. You should understand the following terms:

Node A cluster node is a single server that participates in the cluster. Failover clusters must have at least two nodes (two servers). One node will be the active node and the other will be the passive node. Should the active node fail, the services are provided by the passive node and the passive node automatically becomes the active node.

Shared Storage The nodes in a cluster must have access to centralized and shared storage. Windows Failover Clustering supports Fibre Channel, internet SCSI (iSCSI), or Serial Attached SCSI (SAS) for the shared storage. These storage options fall into the category of storage area networks and are the only shared storage formats supported by Windows Server 2008 and Windows Server 2008 R2 Failover Clustering. The storage area network may implement RAID technologies within its disk management functions.

Clustered Services Clustered services are cluster-aware services. Cluster-aware services can operate on a cluster and communicate with the Failover Clustering service. SQL Server 2008 is such a cluster-aware service. SharePoint itself will not use failover clustering, but it can use network load balancing for similar results.

Quorum The final element is the quorum. The *quorum* is used to decide which node should be active at any time in the cluster. The Oxford American College Dictionary defines a quorum as the "minimum number of members of an assembly that must be present to make a meeting valid." In clustering, the quorum is the minimum number of cluster components (storage, services, nodes) that must be available to offer services. If the quorum is intact, the cluster is available. If it is not intact, the cluster is unavailable.

The concept of the quorum may require further explanation. As an analogy, consider a board of trustees. If the charter for an organization indicates that at least five trustees must exist on the board and at least four must attend a meeting for board activities to occur, the quorum for that board is any four trustees. Decisions can be made even if one trustee is unavailable. However, if two of the five trustees are unavailable, quorum is not met and decisions cannot be made. With Windows clustering, the quorum works in a similar manner. As long as the minimum components are present, the cluster can provide services.

The quorum in Windows Server 2008 and 2008 R2 is based on votes. Nodes, shared disks, and even file shares—depending on the quorum mode—get to vote. If sufficient votes are available, the cluster is active. If the votes are not there, the cluster is not available. The process used to establish quorum is as follows:

1. A cluster node starts and looks for other nodes with which it may communicate.

2. The nodes agree on the cluster configuration and determine whether or not sufficient quorum votes are available to bring the cluster online.

3. If the quorum votes are insufficient (too few voting resources are available), the nodes enter a dormant state and wait for more votes to arrive.

4. If sufficient quorum votes are available, the nodes bring the appropriate resources and applications online (based on active and passive node configurations) and start monitoring the health of the cluster.

5. At this point, quorum is attained and the cluster is online and functioning.

Failover clustering supports four different quorum modes in Windows Server 2008 and 2008 R2. These modes are outlined in Table 12.1.

TABLE 12.1   Failover Clustering Quorum Modes and Functionality

Mode	Functionality
Node Majority	Clustered nodes have the only votes. When half or more of the nodes are online, quorum is achieved.
Node and Disk Majority	Clustered nodes have a vote and a witness disk also has a vote. When more than half the votes are online, quorum is achieved.
Node and File Share Majority	Clustered nodes have a vote and a witness file share has a vote. When more than half the votes are online, quorum is achieved.
No Majority: Disk Only	The shared disk has the only vote. If the shared disk is online, quorum is achieved.

When you think of the votes in the quorum, do not think of them as actions taken by the voting components. Instead, realize that the cluster service looks for these items and if they exist (are online) their votes are counted.

Choosing the quorum mode is an important part of planning a Windows Server cluster. By default, the cluster service will use Node Majority quorum mode when an odd number of nodes exist in the cluster, and it will use Node and Disk Majority quorum mode when an even number of nodes exist in the cluster. The only situation that would demand Node and File Share majority quorum mode is when the clustered nodes are spread over some distance. For example, one server may exist at one WAN location and the other exists at a separate WAN location. In this configuration, a file share is often used to provide quorum because strict shared storage is not used. No Majority: Disk Only is used when you want the cluster to be available as long as one node and the shared storage is online. No Majority: Disk Only is common for small-scale SQL Server 2008 clusters with only two nodes.

In addition to the terms used in relation to clustering, you should understand the networks used. Typically, three networks will exist in a failover clustering solution. The first network is the public network, which is used by clients to access the cluster. The public network is the same as any other network used to connect to a standard single-server installation. The second network is the private network. The private network exists only between the clustered nodes. You will usually use separate network cards for the public and private networks. The third network is the storage network. The storage network is used to connect with the shared storage location. A specialized adapter (known as a host bus adapter) may be required for Fibre Channel or SAS, but iSCSI may be accessed using standard network cards. Special iSCSI adapters also exist that offload the TCP/IP process from the operating system in order to improve performance when accessing iSCSI storage devices.

 Multiple network cards are not required for the public and private networks; however, it is recommended that you use multiple network cards for improved performance.

Once the server cluster is in place, cluster resources must be managed. These resources include shared storage, IP addresses, and network names. SharePoint will connect to the SQL Server cluster using network names, which are resolved to IP addresses. Only one node in the cluster can respond to a request. The node currently configured to respond is the active node. In order for other nodes to respond, the active node must fail—either intentionally or unintentionally—and the resources will then failover to the alternative node.

SQL Server Failover Clustering Strategies

When considering a SQL Server cluster installation, you must be aware of the end goal. The goal of a failover cluster is to provide high availability. The goal of a load-balancing cluster is to provide high availability with performance. SQL Server 2008 supports only failover clustering. The performance must be achieved using separate measures such as increased hardware capacity in each clustered server or distribution of the workload among multiple clusters or servers. The point is that high availability does not automatically equate to high performance. If you have a single server that is not performing well and you add another identical server and configure the two as a failover cluster, you will achieve no better performance than that which the single server provided. In a failover cluster, only one server is working with the applications at a time. The backup server in the cluster only becomes active if the primary server fails. Hence, high availability is not equal to high performance.

You must also differentiate between high availability and disaster recovery. High availability ensures that the resource is available with as little downtime as possible. Disaster recovery ensures that downtime is as short as possible. Do you see the difference? Stated differently, disaster recovery helps you get things back up and running, and high availability helps you keep things running.

Even with high availability solutions, such as the Failover Clustering service, you must plan for disaster recovery. In most cases, the servers in a cluster will be located in the same physical space, such as a server room or network operations center. Because this is true, a fire or flood could easily take out both servers. This is where disaster recovery kicks in. The Windows Failover Clustering service cannot help you when the server room is full of water.

Entire Farm as a Failover Cluster

SharePoint does support clustering from the frontend to the backend database; however, only the database supports failover clustering. The frontend and application servers will use another type of clustering called Network Load Balancing (NLB). Unlike failover clustering, NLB allows all participating nodes to respond to requests. NLB is commonly used for

Internet Information Services (IIS) servers to provide both increased performance and availability. Performance is improved because multiple servers are providing access to the same websites. Availability is improved because if one of the NLB member servers fails, the others will still be available for client access.

Figure 12.2 shows the architecture of an entire farm failover cluster. Notice the different clustering technologies used at each of the levels in the three-tier topology (frontend, applications, and databases). SQL Server failover clusters are used for the database backend, and this clustering depends on the Windows Failover Cluster services.

FIGURE 12.2   Entire farm failover cluster architecture

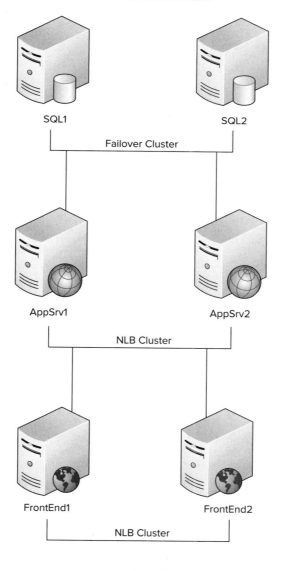

Installing Failover Clustering

Before you can install a Windows failover cluster, you must ensure that your systems meet the requirements of the Failover Clustering service. Don't be alarmed by the long list of requirements because you can typically work with the server vendor to simply purchase an entire solution that meets all requirements, but here is the list:

- The network hardware must be marked with the Certified for Windows Server 2008 logo.

- The server nodes should be connected to multiple networks to provide communication resiliency.

- The network infrastructure must not contain single points of failure (for example, a single router that connects a network segment to the rest of the infrastructure).

- Network adapters must be configured with the same IP version, speed settings, duplex capabilities, and flow control capabilities.

- The cluster storage device controllers must be identical and have the same firmware versions installed on each node.

- You must use separate networks for client access and iSCSI storage, if iSCSI is utilized instead of Fibre Channel or SAS.

- The Microsoft Storport driver model must be used in the development of the storage drivers.

- Basic disks should be configured on the storage.

- Multipath solutions must be based on MPIO (Microsoft Multipath I/O).

- All cluster nodes must use DNS for name resolution and, therefore, a DNS server must be available.

- All cluster nodes must be members of the same Active Directory domain.

- Administrator rights must be granted on all cluster nodes to the user account that creates the cluster, and this account must have Create Computer Object permissions within the Active Directory domain.

- All nodes must run the same edition of Windows Server 2008 and only Enterprise and DataCenter editions support the Failover Clustering service.

- All nodes must run the same processor type (for example, 32-bit, 64-bit, etc.).

- All nodes should be updated to the same level with service packs and updates.

It's important to remember that Microsoft supports failover clustering only on hardware marked with the Certified for Windows Server 2008 logo. Additionally, all tests in the Validate a Configuration Wizard must pass to get support for the cluster form Microsoft.

After you ensure that your hardware and software meet the requirements for the Failover Clustering service and the network connections and shared storage have been installed and configured, you are ready to install the Failover Clustering feature. Exercise 12.2 provides the steps required to install failover clustering.

EXERCISE 12.2

Installing Failover Clustering

In this exercise, you will install the Failover Clustering service on a Windows Server 2008 node. To do this:

1. Log on to the Windows Server 2008 machine as a domain administrator.

2. Click Start ➢ Server Manager to open the Server Manager window.

3. In the left pane, select the Features node.

4. In the Features Summary window, click the Add Features link.

5. In the list of features, choose Failover Clustering, as in the following image, and click Next.

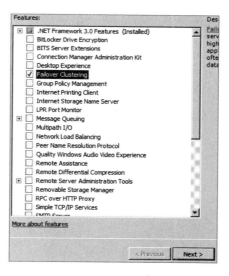

6. Click the Install button to begin the installation.

7. When the installation is complete, you may need to restart your server. If prompted, select to Restart Now. If a prompt does not appear, click Close to complete the installation.

8. You may close the Server Manager window at this point.

As Exercise 12.2 shows, installing Failover Clustering is a very simple process. Now that it is installed, you'll need to validate your configuration. The validation is performed from the Failover Cluster Management tool found in Administrative Tools on the Start menu. From here, you can run the Validate a Configuration Wizard. Keep the following facts about the Validate a Configuration Wizard in mind:

- The wizard verifies that Microsoft will support the configuration.
- The wizard requires the Failover Clustering feature be installed on each node to be tested.
- The wizard should be executed before you actually create the failover cluster.
- Each test will result in one of four outcomes: pass, passed with warnings, fail, or test not run.
- Anytime major cluster changes are made you should run the wizard again.
- The wizard confirms that the cluster hardware and software is compatible with the Failover Clustering service.

When the Validate a Configuration Wizard runs, it performs four primary tests. The first is an inventory test. The inventory test ensures that the required components exist in order for clustering to work. The second is a network test, which is used to make sure the network connections are configured appropriately. The third test is a storage test and it is used to ensure that the nodes can all contact and access the shared storage. The fourth and final test is a system configuration test, which ensures that the nodes are all running the same operating systems, service packs, updates, and components. For more details on the actions taken during each of the four tests, refer to Table 12.2.

TABLE 12.2 Validate a Configuration Wizard Tests and Actions

Test	Actions
Inventory Test	Reports on BIOS information, environment variables, Fibre Channel HBAs, iSCSI HBAs, SAS HBAs, memory, OS information, Plug and Play devices, running processes, services running, software updates, system information, drivers, and unsigned drivers.
Network Test	Network configuration is verified for the cluster network, IP settings, network communications, and Windows firewall settings.
Storage Test	The storage test verifies disk failover, disk access latency, file system selection, MPIO version, SCSI-3 persistent reservation, and simultaneous failover.
System Configuration Test	The system configuration analysis checks that Active Directory is configured, all drivers are signed, operating system versions match, required services are installed, processor types match, service pack levels are consistent, and software update levels are consistent.

Exercise 12.3 provides steps for running the Validate a Configuration Wizard.

EXERCISE 12.3

Running the Validate a Configuration Wizard

In this exercise, you will run the Validate a Configuration Wizard and view the resulting report. In order to perform these steps, you will need two Windows Server 2008 servers with the Failover Clustering feature installed as described in Exercise 12.2. To run the wizard:

1. Log on to one of the intended nodes as a domain administrator.

2. Click Start ➢ All Programs ➢ Administrative Tools ➢ Failover Cluster Management.

3. In the Management pane, choose Validate A Configuration.

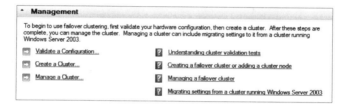

4. Read the information on the Before You Begin page of the wizard and then click Next.

5. On the Select Servers Or A Cluster page, click Browse to choose the servers to be validated as functional for a cluster.

6. In the Select Computers window, click Advanced.

7. Click Find Now to list all servers available in the domain.

8. While holding the Ctrl key, click the servers you want to become part of the cluster and then click OK.

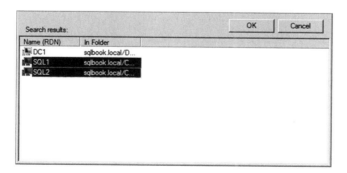

EXERCISE 12.3 *(continued)*

9. Click OK again to add the servers. If you receive an error indicating that Failover Clustering is not installed on one of the nodes, you must log on to that node and install Failover Clustering before proceeding.

10. Click Next to move on in the wizard.

11. On the Testing Options page, accept the default option to Run All Tests and click Next.

12. Click Next on the Confirmation page to begin the actual validation process. As the process runs, you will see a screen similar to the following:

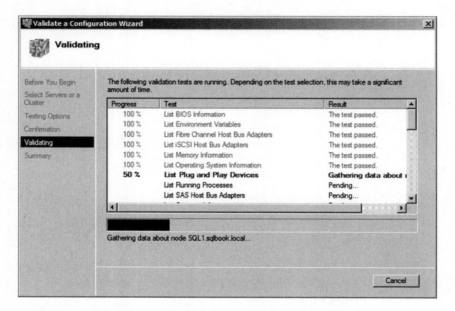

13. When the validation completes and you are taken to the Summary page, click View Report to read the HTML report created by the wizard.

When reading the report generated by the Validate a Configuration Wizard, look for the items with a description of warning. Click the link for any such items to find out what caused the warning. For example, Figure 12.3 shows a report with a warning for the Validate Network Communication item. Figure 12.4 shows the detailed information for this warning.

FIGURE 12.3 Viewing the warnings in a Validate a Configuration Wizard report

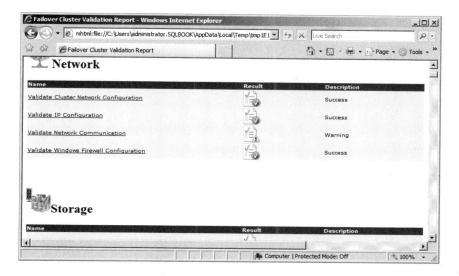

FIGURE 12.4 Viewing the warning details in the report

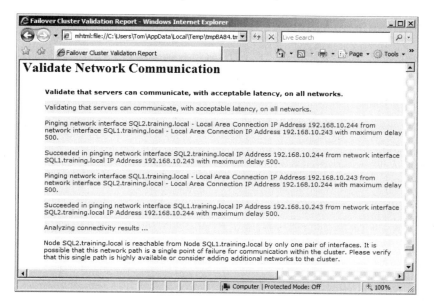

If you find warnings in the report, you should read the warning details and then take any necessary actions to resolve the warning. For example, the warning pictured in Figure 12.4 is related to the fact that the servers are connected to each other using a single network and not multiple networks. Clustering will work with a single network, but it will not provide the higher levels of availability you may require (because the single network is a single point of failure). If the single point of failure in the network is acceptable to you, you can ignore the warning.

With the Validate a Configuration Wizard completed and assuming no significant problems were encountered, you're ready to create the cluster. You create cluster configurations with the Create Cluster Wizard in the Failover Cluster Management tool. Exercise 12.4 provides the steps required to create a cluster.

EXERCISE 12.4

Creating a Failover Cluster

In this exercise you will create a cluster using the Failover Cluster Management tool. To do this:

1. Log on to a cluster node as a domain administrator.

2. Click Start ➢ All Programs ➢ Administrative Tools ➢ Failover Cluster Management.

3. In the Management pane, choose the Create A Cluster option to launch the Create Cluster Wizard.

4. On the Before You Begin page, read the information and then click Next to begin the creation process.

5. Click Browse to select the Windows Server 2008 instances with the Failover Clustering service installed.

6. Click the Advanced button and then click Find Now to list all available Windows servers.

7. Press Ctrl and then click on each of the servers to be included in the cluster. With the servers selected, click OK.

8. Click OK again to add the servers.

9. When you're returned to the Select Servers page, click Next.

10. On the Access Point For Administering The Cluster page, enter the name you want to use for the cluster and the IP address (if only one network adapter exists in each node, the IP address option will not be displayed) and then click Next.

11. Click Next to create the cluster.

12. When the cluster-creation process is complete, you'll see the Summary page. Click Finish to finish the wizard.

After the cluster is created, using the steps in Exercise 12.4, you can begin assigning resources to the cluster. Several resource types can be assigned to the cluster right out-of-the-box. The resources include:

- DHCP Service
- Distributed File System
- Distributed Transaction Coordinator
- File Server
- File Share Quorum Witness
- Generic Application
- Generic Script
- Generic Service
- IP Address
- IPv6 Address
- IPv6 Tunnel Address
- iSNSClusRes
- Network Name
- NFS Share
- Physical Disk
- Print Spooler
- Volume Shadow Copy Service Task
- WINS Service

When you look through this list, it becomes apparent that the resources that can be assigned to the cluster are very similar to resources that are assigned to a standalone server. For example, just as you can have multiple IP addresses assigned to a single network adapter in a server, you can have multiple IP addresses assigned to a cluster as well. As another example, just as you can install and manage printers on standalone servers, you can install the Print Spooler service and share printers through the cluster. This collection of resources is known as a cluster resource group.

Clustering in a Virtual Environment

When you implement a cluster using physical hardware, the process is very straightforward. But what if you want to implement a cluster using virtualization? Well, the short answer is that you can, but the long answer is that it's not quite as easy. To implement clustered virtual machines (VMs) with Windows Server 2008, you'll need four VMs.

The first VM will be the Active Directory domain controller, since the new Failover Clustering service in Windows Server 2008 requires a domain. For this VM, you will need between 756 and 1,024 MB of RAM. You should provide more RAM to this machine if you plan to have virtual or physical clients connecting to the machine.

The second VM will run the iSCSI service software. This software is needed because Windows Server 2008 no longer allows you to configure attached disks as the "shared storage" within a virtual environment. The best solution is, therefore, iSCSI. Two excellent free software-based iSCSI solutions are FreeNAS (www.freenas.org) and Openfiler (www.openfiler.org). I (Tom) prefer Openfiler for such virtual test environments because it can be downloaded as a VMware appliance. This makes the setup much easier.

Finally, the last two VMs will run Windows Server 2008 Enterprise Edition and will act as the Failover Clustering nodes. These nodes will connect through iSCSI with the second VM for shared storage. With a configuration like this, you can build a cluster test environment for certification preparation or lab testing without the expense of a hardware-based SAN.

Storage Fault Tolerance

RAID (redundant array of independent disks) is an internal server or external storage technology that may be hardware or software based. RAID provides either performance improvements or fault tolerance for the storage system. Hardware-based RAID uses hardware drive controllers that have the RAID processing software built-in. Software-based RAID uses standard hard drive controllers and handles the RAID processing as a software layer that is either built into the operating system or is installed as an extra feature.

The RAID levels define the type of RAID that is implemented. The type of RAID dictates the minimum number of drives required and the way in which the drives work together as an array. Many different RAID levels exist, but the most commonly used RAID levels are

- RAID 0
- RAID 1
- RAID 5
- RAID 0+1
- RAID 1+0 or RAID 10

Figure 12.5 shows various RAID levels in a graphical representation. RAID 0 is depicted as three physical drives acting as one virtual drive. Under the hood, data is striped evenly across the three drives. For example, should 99 KB of data be writing to drive D: using RAID 0, one third would be writing to Drive 1, one third to Drive 2, and the final third to Drive 3. There is actually no fault tolerance provided by RAID 0 alone. RAID 0 is used to improve read and write performance only. Most controllers require two drives to create a stripe set without parity or a RAID 0 array. Some will require three drives in the array. The negatives of RAID 0 include the fact that one drive failure makes the entire array unavailable and that the large amount of storage represented by the physical drives now aggregates into one, possibly difficult to manage, storage location. The positives include faster data access and storage as well as no loss of storage space.

FIGURE 12.5 RAID levels 0, 1, and 5 represented

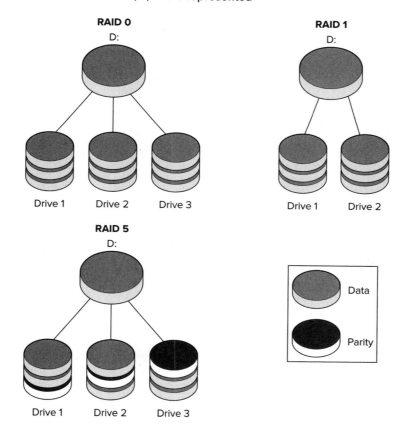

The next level of RAID represented is RAID level 1. At level 1, data is mirrored to two physical drives, but the user sees only one drive at the operating system level—if the RAID is implemented through hardware as opposed to software. Software-based RAID levels 0, 1, and 5 are supported through the Disk Management snap-in in Windows Server. RAID 1 provides fault tolerance through the fact that all data is written twice. The data is written once to the "visible" drive and once to the "invisible" drive. There is no striping of data during writes, but some RAID controllers (hardware drive controllers that support RAID configurations) will read the data from both drives. RAID 1 is used to provide fault tolerance and quick failover. The negatives of RAID 1 include the loss of half of your storage space and the reduced performance of writes. The positive is that RAID 1 provides the highest level of data availability because all the data is completely written to two separate physical devices.

RAID 5 attempts to balance RAID 0 and RAID 1. RAID 5 arrays stripe data across the drives in the array. However, unlike RAID 0, RAID 5 arrays also provide fault tolerance. This is done through the generation of parity bits. Parity bits are used to regenerate the data through advanced mathematical calculations. You do not have to understand the generation of parity bits or how they are used to regenerate data to understand and implement RAID solutions. For example, assume there are three physical drives that make up the logical drive array. When data is written to the array, half the data will be written to one drive, half the data to another, and then parity bits will be written to the third drive. In most implementations, the parity bits are stored evenly across the drives in the array. Now, if any single physical drive fails, the controller or software can regenerate the data that was stored on the failed drive. This regeneration generally occurs on-the-fly with no administrative intervention. Of course, should another drive fail at this time, the entire array will be lost.

To understand how RAID 5 functions, consider this simple analogy. Imagine you have the numbers 5 and 7 that you want to store. If you store 5 in one notebook and 7 in another, when either notebook is lost, you've lost the ability to recover all of your meaningful data. However, imagine you have a third notebook. In this third notebook, you store the number 12 (5+7). Now, if you lose one of the three notebooks, you will always be able to get your data back. For example, if you lose notebook two, you can subtract 5 (the number in notebook 1) from 12 and recover the number 7 that was in the second notebook. While RAID 5 striping and parity algorithms are more complex than this, it should help you to conceptualize how the RAID level functions. It is also important to keep in mind that when you add more drives to your system you increase the likelihood that one of those drives will fail on any given day and actually increase the need for fault tolerance.

RAID 0+1 combines the stripe sets with mirroring. You would configure two stripe sets first and then configure those two stripe sets to show up as one drive that is a RAID 1 implementation. For example, you might have three drives in each stripe set and all six drives will show up as one virtual drive. This gives you a balance between the performance of RAID 0 and the complete fault tolerance of RAID 1.

RAID 1+0, also known as RAID 10, is just the opposite of RAID 0+1. In this case, you will actually implement two or three mirror sets first and then stripe data across those mirror sets. This provides fault tolerance as the foundation and performance as an added layer.

Understanding the various levels of RAID is important, and this knowledge will be used as you make decisions related to the SharePoint server hardware that you purchase. If you determine that you will need fault tolerance at the drive level, you will want to be sure to purchase a server that provides this feature through hardware. Though you can implement RAID through software, the performance is not generally as good and it will take away processing power from the database server software.

Exercise 12.5 provides instructions for using an online RAID calculator that can help you determine the results you will achieve with different RAID configurations.

EXERCISE 12.5

Using an Online Raid Calculator

In this exercise, you will use the online RAID calculator at http://www.ibeast.com/content/tools/RaidCalc/RaidCalc.asp to determine the different results you will achieve with RAID configurations. For this exercise, assume you have four drives to be configured in the RAID array and that each drive is a 250 GB drive.

1. Open your web browser and navigate to http://www.ibeast.com/content/tools/RaidCalc/RaidCalc.asp.

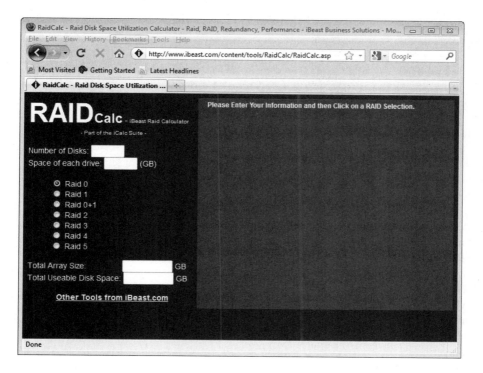

2. Enter the number **4** in the Number Of Disks field.

3. Enter the number **250** in the Space Of Each Drive field.

4. Choose RAID 5 from the list of RAID types.

5. Click in the Total Array Size field to see the results.

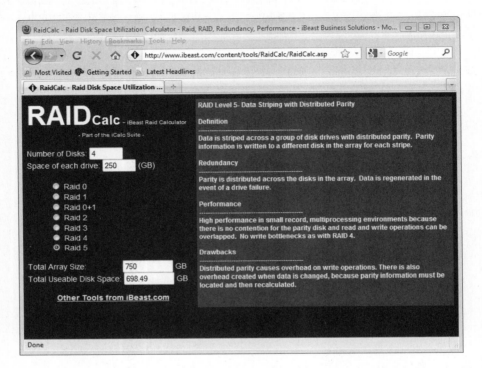

Determining Acceptable Downtime

The final component of availability planning for SharePoint 2010 upgrades is the determination of acceptable downtime. Acceptable downtime is determined by two factors:

Recovery Time Objective (RTO) The RTO is the maximum tolerable amount of time for recovery in a disaster recovery scenario. If you determine that this value is less than one hour, you will need warm standby servers in most cases to achieve it. It is very uncommon to have a backup and restoration engine that can recover a large server with databases and applications in less than one hour. If you determine that this value is not more than four hours, you may be able to tune the recovery process and perform a restoration without a warm standby server.

Recovery Point Objective (RPO) The RPO is the acceptable amount of data loss. Many organizations will not tolerate more than 30 minutes of data loss and a few organizations want less than 1 minute of data loss. The RPO will help you determine the best backup procedure for your environment. For example, if you back up the SQL Server content database transaction logs every 10 minutes, you know that you can recovery all data with the exception of the most recent 5 minutes on average.

Once you've established your RTO and RPO, you can plan your availability solutions to prevent the need to comply with them as much as possible, but you can also implement backup procedures so that you are prepared for a disaster should it occur.

 Remember that, even with high availability features such as mirroring, clustering, and RAID storage, servers still fail. You must determine the acceptable downtime for these worst case scenarios.

Upgrading Operating Systems

SharePoint Server 2010 requires Windows Server 2008 or Windows Server 2008 R2 64-bit editions only. Windows Server 2008 R2 only comes in a 64-bit edition, but you must ensure you install a 64-bit edition if you use Windows Server 2008. The operating system upgrade should be performed according to best practices and your organization's policies and procedures. You have three options for the operating system upgrade depending on how you plan to upgrade SharePoint Server 2007 to SharePoint Server 2010:

In-Place SharePoint and Operating System Upgrade   When you perform an in-place SharePoint and operating system upgrade, you will perform an in-place upgrade of the operating system first. Next, you will perform the in-place upgrade of the SharePoint Server 2007 installation to SharePoint Server 2010. If you choose this option, the current version of Windows Server must be a 64-bit installation. You cannot upgrade from Windows Server 2003 32-bit to Windows Server 2008 64-bit.

In-Place SharePoint Upgrade with Operating System Clean Install   When you perform this upgrade option, you will first back up your SharePoint 2007 installation. Second, you will perform a clean install of the operating system on the server or servers. Third, you will reinstall and restore SharePoint Server 2007. Finally, you will perform the in-place upgrade to SharePoint 2010. This method is a good choice when you want to upgrade SharePoint, but your existing operating system is 32-bit. Existing operating system settings outside of SharePoint will be lost.

Database Attach SharePoint Upgrade with Operating System Clean Install   You can create an entirely new SharePoint 2010 farm and then attach the databases from SharePoint 2007 to upgrade them to the SharePoint 2010 structure. This method is preferred when you want to move one site collection at a time from the existing farm over to the new SharePoint 2010 farm.

Upgrading Early SharePoint Versions

You may still be running SharePoint Portal Server 2003 (or SharePoint Server 2003 for short) in your environment. If this is the case, you have no direct upgrade path to SharePoint Server 2010. Instead, you have to use what is called a double-database attach upgrade. Effectively, you will first perform a database attack upgrade to SharePoint Server 2007 and then take the databases that have been converted to SharePoint Server 2007 and attach them to SharePoint Server 2010. (Attach upgrade procedures are discussed in the preceding section, "Upgrading Operating Systems.")

The double-database upgrade procedure is a large undertaking. You must create three farms. The first farm will already be created as it is the SharePoint Server 2003 farm. The second farm must be created, and it is a temporary SharePoint Server 2007 farm. The third farm is the real target. It is the SharePoint Server 2010 farm.

According to Microsoft, you may use the trial version of SharePoint Server 2007 to build the temporary farm. Paid licenses will not be required. The trial version of SharePoint Server 2007 in the 64-bit edition is available at http://go.microsoft.com/fwlink/?LinkID=120684. The later section of this chapter titled "Database Migration Considerations" provides instructions for detaching and attaching databases in SQL Server 2005. If you are using SQL Server 2000 with SharePoint Server 2003, you will need to perform different actions in the Enterprise Manager, and they are described at http://technet.microsoft.com/en-us/library/cc917621.aspx.

MOSS 2007 Upgrades

Now that the operating system has been upgraded or replaced, you can upgrade the SharePoint Server application itself. When upgrading from SharePoint Server 2007 or Microsoft Office SharePoint Server 2007, you have two basic options:

In-Place Upgrades   SharePoint Server 2010 is installed on the same hardware as SharePoint Server 2007 and all databases are upgraded automatically. During this upgrade, the existing SharePoint server farm will be unavailable and the process can take several hours. Microsoft provides an article with advice on estimating the time required to perform an upgrade at http://technet.microsoft.com/en-us/library/cc262891.aspx.

Database Attach Upgrades   SharePoint Server 2010 is installed on different hardware from the existing SharePoint Server 2007 installation. The cost of this method is greater, but it may be required if you currently use 32-bit hardware to run SharePoint Server 2007. Databases can be upgraded in any order, and the SharePoint farm can go live before all site collections are restored.

SQL Server Upgrades

Before you upgrade to SharePoint Server 2010, you should be sure your database servers are ready for it. This means upgrading them to SQL Server 2008 or later. Upgrading an application on a client computer is a risky business. Upgrading a database server that is accessed by many users is downright scary. However, much of the concern can be removed by following two important best practices. First, always perform a full backup of your databases (including the system databases used by SQL Server) before beginning the upgrade process. Second, you should attempt to discover as many potential problems as you can before you start the upgrade.

2000 to 2008   The upgrade from SQL Server 2000 to 2008 is the upgrade to result in application problems. More SQL Server 2000 features have been removed in SQL Server 2008 than SQL Server 2005 features. For this reason alone, you are likely to experience application problems. It's important to look for the use of deprecated features in the current SQL Server 2000 application and database. Finding the deprecated features that were either dropped when SQL Server 2000 was released or dropped between the 2000 and 2005 release can be a bit difficult. Two sources, however, are helpful. In the SQL Server 2000 Books Online, you can read about features that were in 6.5 and 7.0 that were no longer in SQL Server 2000. In the SQL Server 2005 Books Online, you can read the Installation section and look for the Backwards Compatibility section. Here, the deprecated features are listed. If your application uses any of these features, it will fail in those areas.

You may also use the Upgrade Advisor to see if it can detect any problems in your databases or applications. Remember, however, that the Upgrade Advisor looks at the database and may not have access to analyze all of your application code. You will need to ensure the code is compatible.

2005 to 2008   When you need to find the features that were in SQL Server 2005, but are no longer in SQL Server 2008, your job is much easier. You can run the SQL Server 2005 profile and monitor for deprecated features and specifically for the deprecated features under final notice. These features will no longer exist in SQL Server 2008. The good news is that you can have your users run against the existing SQL Server 2005 database as they normally do. All the while, you're monitoring the access to look for these deprecated features. If you find any, you'll have to either rewrite the code for that section of the application or contact the vendor and request an upgrade or a patch.

SQL Server Migrations

In-place upgrades, performed by installing the new version of SQL Server right on top of the old version, are certainly available; however, many database administrators choose to perform database migrations instead. The migration method of SQL Server upgrades is often chosen because the existing server is getting old and may be losing support or may simply not provide sufficient performance for the new version.

Migrations are usually simpler than upgrades from a pure database access point of view. However, the feature deprecation issue is still a concern. Whether you upgrade the SQL Server 2000 database to 2008 or copy a database from a 2000 instance to a 2008 instance, you still have to deal with application compatibility issues. That said, migrating a database from SQL Server 7.0 (or earlier) is possible, but you can only upgrade to SQL Server 2008 from a SQL Server 2000 or higher installation.

7.0 to 2008   The trick to migrating a SQL Server 7.0 database over to a SQL Server 2008 instance is to migrate it to a SQL Server 2000 instance first. That's right. You simply have to attach the database to a SQL Server 2000 instance and it will be automatically converted to a SQL Server 2000 database. Now, you can detach the database from SQL Server 2000 and attach it directly to SQL Server 2008 in order to migrate it to the new server. However—and this can't be emphasized enough—you must still ensure that the database works with SQL Server 2008. Just because you can attach it doesn't mean that all the stored procedures and application code will function properly.

2000 and 2005 to 2008   As you might have guessed while reading the previous paragraph, you can migrate a 2000 database over to a 2008 server by simply attaching the database to the 2008 server. Yes, you can use the Copy Database Wizard and it may make things simple for a beginning DBA, but eventually, you'll need to learn how to manually detach and attach databases. SQL Server 2005 databases are migrated in the same way.

Performing In-Place Upgrades

In-place upgrades are very popular choices for administrators running SharePoint Server 2007 on 64-bit platforms. Even on a 32-bit platform, it may be preferable to upgrade or reinstall the OS with a 64-bit edition, restore SharePoint 2007 from a backup, and then perform the in-place upgrade instead of performing a database attach upgrade.

An interesting option is available that allows you to perform an in-place upgrade while doing a clean install to a separate server farm. To do this, you would install SharePoint Server 2007 on a 64-bit edition of Windows Server 2008 or later. This new installation will also be a new server farm. You would then restore the backups of your existing SharePoint Server 2007 server farm to the new farm. Of course, this farm would not be on the same network as the existing farm if you want the new farm to have the same domain names and machine names for simplicity when the users access the farm for the first time.

Next, you will upgrade the new farm to SharePoint Server 2010. Keep in mind that the old SharePoint 2007 farm is live online during all this time. The old farm should be placed in read-only mode during the entire process. If you cannot place the existing old farm into a read-only state, you may not be able to use this option; however, this is an excellent option in smaller organizations for fast weekend upgrades. The final step is to take the old farm offline and configure the appropriate IP and DNS settings so that the new farm is accessed at the same URL the old farm was using.

Both methods—the operating system upgrade route and the completely new server farm route—are viable in-place upgrade solutions when dealing with existing 32-bit SharePoint Server 2007 installations. If you run a single-server installation of SharePoint Server 2007, you will probably choose the operating system upgrade route. If you run a multiserver farm, you will probably choose the new server farm route.

In-place upgrades of SharePoint servers that run 64-bit operating systems are much simpler. According to Microsoft, performing an in-place upgrade of a 64-bit SharePoint Server 2007 installation is a seven-step process:

1. Run the pre-upgrade checker.

2. Install prerequisites on all servers in the farm.

3. Disconnect users.

4. Run SETUP on each server in the farm.

5. Install language packs.

6. Run the SharePoint Products Configuration Wizard.

7. Monitor the upgrade process.

Before performing any of these steps, you should make a complete system backup. Back up the entire server and the SharePoint 2007 databases.

 Microsoft provides detailed instructions for each of these steps at their TechNet website at http://technet.microsoft.com/en-us/library/ ff608117.aspx.

Assuming that you have run the pre-upgrade checker and the prerequisites are in place (steps 1 and 2 in Microsoft's seven-step process), you can install SharePoint Server 2010 on a SharePoint 2007 server using the steps in Exercise 12.6. You can install prerequisites using a tool provided on the SharePoint Server 2010 installation media named PrerequisiteInstaller.exe. It is located in the Installation folder. Before performing the steps in Exercise 12.6 on a live SharePoint 2007 server, you should disconnect the users (step 3 in Microsoft's seven-step process). You can easily disconnect the users by stopping the World Wide Web Publishing Service (W3SVC) in the Services console. The steps in Exercise 12.6 represent step 4 of the seven-step process.

EXERCISE 12.6

Installing SharePoint Server 2010 on a SharePoint 2007 Server

In this exercise, you will install SharePoint Server 2010 on an existing SharePoint 2007 server. This will not upgrade the farm, but it will place the binaries on the server so that an upgrade may be performed.

1. Run Setup.exe from the SharePoint Server 2010 media.

2. Enter the product key and click Continue.

3. Accept the terms of the license agreement and click Continue.

4. On the Upgrade Earlier Versions screen, select Install Now.

5. SharePoint Server 2010 is installed and then the completion page is shown. Deselect Run The SharePoint Products Configuration Wizard Now and click Close.

After performing the steps in Exercise 12.6, you will have SharePoint installed on the server, but it will not be configured and the existing SharePoint Server 2007 installation will not have been upgraded.

Before running the SharePoint Products Configuration Wizard, as instructed in Exercise 12.7, you should install any language packs required for your organization, which is step 5 in Microsoft's seven-step process. Once the language packs are installed, you can then run the wizard and monitor the upgrade process. Exercise 12.7 represents steps 6 and 7 for the in-place SharePoint Server upgrade.

EXERCISE 12.7

Running the SharePoint Products Configuration Wizard and Monitoring the Upgrade Process

In this exercise, you will run the wizard that actually performs the upgrade from SharePoint Server 2007 to SharePoint Server 2010. The steps in Exercise 12.6 must be performed before this exercise.

1. Click Start ➤ All Programs ➤ Administrative Tools ➤ SharePoint Products Configuration Wizard.

2. On the Welcome to SharePoint Products page, click Next.

3. A message appears indicating that the IIS, SharePoint Administration Services, and SharePoint Timer Services may be restarted or reset. Click Yes.

4. On the Specify Farm Settings page, enter a passphrase in the Passphrase and Confirm Passphrase boxes and then click Next.

5. On the Visual Upgrade page, select either Change Existing SharePoint Sites To Use The New User Experience or Preserve The Look And Feel Of Existing SharePoint Sites, and Allow End Users To Update Their Sites' User Experience and click Next.

6. On the Completing The SharePoint Products Configuration Wizard page, review the settings and click Next.

7. You may be notified that several farm servers exist and that SETUP must be run on each server if you have run SETUP on the other servers already or are upgrading a single-server farm. Click OK to continue. Otherwise, exit the wizard and run SETUP on all servers before running the wizard again.

8. On the Configuration Successful page, click Finish.

9. The Upgrade Status page opens. Monitor the status of the upgrade in this page.

The upgrade process can take from several minutes to several hours depending on the size of your SharePoint server farm. Do not be alarmed if the process takes more than an hour. If no errors appear as you monitor the upgrade process, you can usually trust that everything is working fine.

Performing a Rollback

It would be nice if all upgrades simply worked the first time with no errors or problems of any kind. That, however, is not how things typically work in the real world. For this reason, it's important to understand your options for recovering after an upgrade fails. Microsoft calls this action performing a *rollback*. Three rollback options are available:

Recovering When You Have Read-Only Databases in a Standby Environment (Database Attach Upgrade)   If the upgrade that failed was a database attach upgrade and you chose to leave your existing environment available as a read-only environment, the original SharePoint environment is still available and you can switch the read-only databases to read/write again in order to resume operations.

Recovering When You Have a Full Environment Backup (In-Place Upgrade)   If you created a full backup of your environment (which is recommended) before beginning the upgrade, you can recover the entire environment, which will include SharePoint and the databases. This option will take longer that the preceding option, but it is faster than the third alternative, which must be used when you have only database backups.

Recovering When You Have Database Backups (In-Place Upgrade)   Because the environment is not backed up and only the databases are backed up, you will have to completely reinstall the environment and then restore from the database backups. This is the longest rollback option and can be avoided by creating an environment backup (back up the entire server including the SharePoint components and databases) before performing the upgrade.

Designing a Migration Strategy

In the preceding section, the database attach method was referenced as an upgrade option. Indeed it is an upgrade option, but it is probably better called a migration option. You are actually migrate databases from the existing SharePoint installation over to the new installation. This can also be referred to as a side-by-site installation.

In this section, you will learn more about the migration processes including creating a test and quality assurance implementation plan. However, before you cover the testing and quality assurance, you'll need to discover database migration options and content migration options. You'll also need to discover how to migrate custom features.

Database Migration Considerations

Database management is an important part of the database administrator's job, but it also falls to many SharePoint administrators—particularly in smaller organizations. In addition to the backups you learned about in Chapter 7, "Designing a Strategy for Business Continuity," you should understand how to move databases from one SharePoint installation to another. This task is called database migration. It may be part of an upgrade process, but it can also be part of normal operations. For example, you may choose to move a content database from one farm to another farm for performance reasons. In this section, you will learn to work with configuration and content databases.

Migrating Configuration Databases

The most common reason for the migration of a configuration database from one server to another is that you are upgrading or replacing the SQL server. The process is not as simple as you may think if you have worked with SQL servers extensively in the past. For a typical SQL Server database, you need only to detach the database, move the database physical files (the *.mdf, *.ndf, and *.ldf files associated with the database) to the new server and then attach the database. This is a very simple process.

The process is complicated by the fact that SharePoint Server 2010 must know where the databases are located and for what they are used. The more complicated process of database migration with SharePoint Server 2010 looks like this:

1. Stop the SharePoint farm. This means closing any open management sessions in PowerShell or using the Stsadm command and then using the Services snap-in, stopping the following services:

   - SharePoint 2010 Administration
   - SharePoint 2010 Timer
   - SharePoint 2010 Tracing
   - SharePoint 2010 User Code Host
   - SharePoint 2010 VSS Writer
   - SharePoint Foundation Search V4
   - World Wide Web Publishing Service
   - SharePoint Server Search 14
   - Web Analytics Data Processing Service
   - Web Analytics Web Service

2. Stop IIS on the Central Administration server using the iisreset /stop command. Central Administration cannot be running while the configuration database is relocated.

3. Detach the databases from SQL Server. The following URLs provide information on detaching databases:

   - http://go.microsoft.com/fwlink/?LinkId=194806
   - http://go.microsoft.com/fwlink/?LinkId=194807
   - http://go.microsoft.com/fwlink/?LinkId=194808

4. Move the database files over to the new SQL server.

5. Attach the databases to the new SQL server. The following URLs provide information on attaching databases:

   - http://go.microsoft.com/fwlink/?LinkId=194809
   - http://go.microsoft.com/fwlink/?LinkId=194810

6. Point the SharePoint WebApp to the new database server through a SQL Server connection alias. This is accomplished in SQL Server Management Studio. Instructions are available at http://technet.microsoft.com/en-us/library/cc512725.aspx.

7. Restart the services in the farm. Begin by restarting IIS with the iisreset /start command. Then use the Sevices snap-in to restart the services that were stopped in step 1.

As you can see from the preceding list, moving configuration databases is a bit more complex than moving content databases. The next section covers the simpler process used when migrating content databases.

Migrating Content Databases

Migrating content databases is much simpler. You simply have to detach the database from the WebApp using either Central Administration or the Windows PowerShell interface. Detach the database from SQL Server. Move the database to the new server. Attach the database to the new SQL server. Attach the database to the new WebApp using either Central Administration or the Windows PowerShell interface.

> In addition to the practice steps required, if the content database is being indexed by search crawls or has timer jobs that run against it, you will have to pause the timer jobs before moving the database. Timer jobs can be paused using the `Get-SPTimerJob` command in Windows PowerShell or using the Monitoring section of Central Administration.

Content databases are removed from WebApps using Central Administration and the Application Management Section. When you select to Manage Content databases, you are provided with a list of databases. From here, you simply click on the database you want to remove and select Remove Content Database and click OK to remove it from the WebApp as shown in Figure 12.6.

FIGURE 12.6   Removing a content database from a WebApp in Central Administration

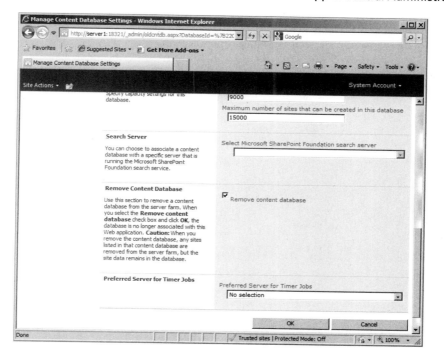

After the content database is removed from the WebApp, it can be detached from the SQL server. This is not a requirement. In many cases, you want to move the content database from a WebApp on one application server to a WebApp on another application server while still using the same SQL server. In such cases, you can skip the detach, move, and attach procedure typically required.

After you have moved the database to the new SQL server, if desired, you can attach the content database to the WebApp using Central Administration. You will use the Application Management section again and choose to Manage Content databases. This time, you will add a content database. You must choose the target WebApp, the database name, and authentication methods, and specify search server and failover server settings, if required. Figure 12.7 shows the Add Content Database screen in Central Administration.

FIGURE 12.7   Adding a content database in Central Administration

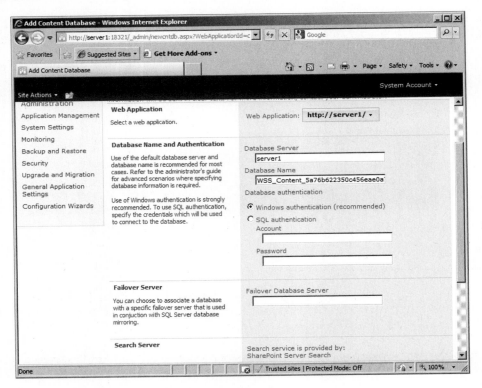

Read Only and Detached Databases

When a farm is placed in read-only mode, users may still access the farm, but they cannot perform tasks that require write operations. Some tasks will properly show up as unavailable, but others will show available and then return an error when the user attempts to use them. For this reason, user training will be required when granting access to a read-only farm.

A farm may be placed into read-only mode for several reasons. One common reason is to have a warm standby farm for disaster recovery. Additionally, you may be in the process of performing a patch or update and you do not want users writing to the farm during this process. Finally, read-only farms are often used during a side-by-side migration. You can set the existing farm to read-only mode and then migrate the databases over to a new farm with assurance that no changes will be made to the farm during the migration.

Before you can configure a site's content databases to work in read-only mode, you have to determine which database the site uses for content storage. Exercise 12.8 provides instructions for determining the content database using a simple command in the SharePoint 2010 Management Shell.

EXERCISE 12.8

Determining the Content Database for a Site

In this exercise, you will use the Get-SpContentDatabase command to retrieve the name of the content database for a SharePoint site. You will retrieve the content database for a site at the URL of http://server1.

1. Click Start ➤ All Programs ➤ Microsoft SharePoint 2010 Products ➤ SharePoint 2010 Management Shell.

2. In the PowerShell window that appears, type **Get-SpContentDatabase -Site http://server1** and press Enter.

3. Note the name of the database. In this case, it is WSS_Content.

After you know the name of the database you want to convert to read-only mode, you can perform the steps in Exercise 12.9 to set the database to read-only mode. This action is performed in the SQL Server Management Studio.

EXERCISE 12.9

Configuring a Database for Read-Only Operations

In this exercise, you will use the SQL Server Management Studio to set the WSS_Content database to read-only.

1. Click Start ➤ All Programs ➤ Microsoft SQL Server 2008 ➤ SQL Server Management Studio.

2. Connect to the SQL Server used by the SharePoint server farm.

EXERCISE 12.9 *(continued)*

3. Expand the Databases container in Object Explorer.

4. Right-click on the WSS_Content database and select Properties.

5. Select the Options page.

6. Scroll down in the list of Other Options to the State category and change the Database Read-Only value to True and click OK.

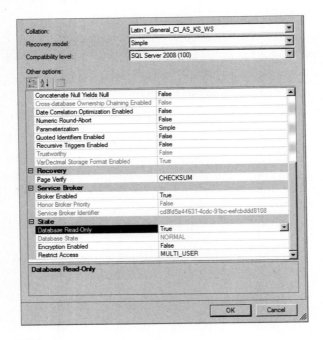

7. Close the SQL Server Management Studio.

After making the changes in Exercise 12.9, you can open the site, in this case, `http://server1`, and try to make a change. You will see a screen similar to the one in Figure 12.8. Notice that you can modify the values in the fields, but the OK button is disabled. To undo this change, simply go back into SQL Server Management Studio and change the Database Read-Only value back to False.

If a content database is detached from the SQL server and you attempt to access the SharePoint site, you will see an error similar to the one in Figure 12.9. The database may have been detached for maintenance and the administrator simply forgot to attach it when the maintenance was complete. It is also possible that the master database on the SQL server was corrupted and you will have to attach the databases again. Simply use the SQL Server Management Studio to attach the database, and you should be able to access the site again.

FIGURE 12.8 Viewing a read-only SharePoint site

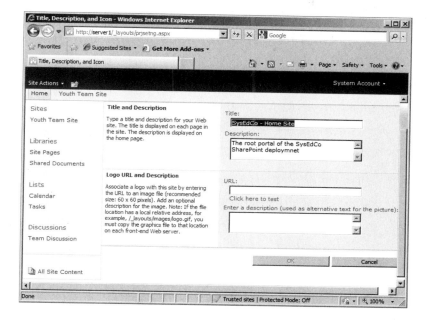

FIGURE 12.9 Accessing a SharePoint site with a detached database generates a 500 server error.

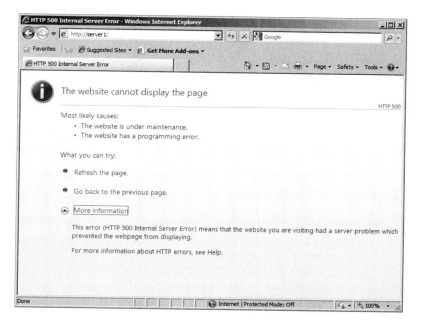

Managing Content

Site collections can be moved from one content database to another within a farm or between farms. You can add content to a farm by attaching a content database as you saw in previous sections. You can remove content from a farm by removing a content database. Whether the site collection is being moved between farms or within a farm is no different from a command perspective. You will use the Move-SPSite command at the Windows PowerShell command prompt with the following syntax:

```
Move-SPSite <http://ServerName/Sites/SiteName>

-DestinationDatabase <DestinationContentDb>
```

For example, if the site is located at http://server1/project35 and the destination content database is named PROJECTS_Content, you would execute the following command at the PowerShell command prompt:

```
Move-SPSite http://server1/project35

-DestinationDatabase PROJECTS_Content
```

Migrating Custom Features

Custom features are those SharePoint features you have developed in-house or purchased as third-party add-ons. Custom features can break when moved to SharePoint Server 2010—particularly if they were originally developed for 32-bit platforms. As a general guideline, keep the following in mind when upgrading SharePoint 2007 to SharePoint 2010 in relation to custom features:

- Custom web parts will usually work without changes in SharePoint 2010. Perform a test in-place upgrade to be sure.

- Third-party add-ons should be handled with care. Contact the vendor to discover any known compatibility issues.

- Custom site templates should be re-created in SharePoint 2010 to make sure they work properly. Create the custom site template as a Solution package in SharePoint 2010 for better future upgrade support.

- Custom site definitions will need a UDF file created for the upgrade. Alternatively, you can use a default SharePoint template and then customize the site definitions again as a Solution package.

- Custom event handlers will usually work without changes in SharePoint 2010, but you should test the in-place upgrade to be sure.

Creating a Test and QA Implementation Plan

Now that you have explored upgrading and migration options, it's time to put it all together into a plan for testing and quality assurance (QA) during the upgrade or migration implementation. The following items should be included in your plan as a baseline for quality assurance:

- The selected upgrade approach. Will you use an in-place upgrade or database attach upgrade?

- The hardware modifications or replacements required to meet the minimum SharePoint 2010 requirements or greater.

- A plan for addressing customizations. This should include customization identification and evaluation. You may choose to discard many customizations during the upgrade.

- A communications plan. Who needs to be informed of what throughout the upgrade process?

- A schedule. When will you be performing the upgrade and what kind of downtime issues can be expected?

These five components will form the core of your plan. In addition, depending on your existing SharePoint installation, you may be required to plan for upgrades to Business Connectivity Services and for upgrades to form templates for InfoPath forms.

The purpose of the plan is simple: to provide a benchmark against which your progress and results can be measured.

 In addition to your own testing and QA implementation plan, consider reviewing Microsoft's best practices for SharePoint Server 2010 upgrades. It is located at http://technet.microsoft.com/en-us/library/cc261992.aspx.

Summary

In this chapter, you learned about the different factors involved in a SharePoint server farm upgrade, and there are many. The SQL Server may require an upgrade before it can support SharePoint Server 2010. SharePoint Server 2010 requires 64-bit components across the board. Only Windows Server 2008 and later versions can be used. Support for Windows Server 2003 has been completely removed from SharePoint Server 2010. You learned that you can perform an in-place or database attach upgrade. You also learned about important migration issues such as database attach, content migration, and custom feature migration. Finally, you explored the parts and pieces that come together to make up an implementation plan.

Exam Essentials

Planning a strategy for upgrades. Know how to plan for availability in the new installation. Know that you can perform in-place or database attach upgrades and understand the difference between the two. Remember that SharePoint Server 2010 requires 64-bit computing across all farm servers.

Designing a migration strategy. Know how to move databases from one SQL server to another and from one SharePoint server farm to another. Understand the different ways to move content around in a SharePoint environment. Know the components that make up a quality testing and QA implementation plan.

Appendix

A

Microsoft's Certification Program

Since the inception of its certification program, Microsoft has certified more than two million people. As the computer network industry continues to increase in both size and complexity, this number is sure to grow—and the need for *proven* ability will also increase. Certifications can help companies verify the skills of prospective employees and contractors.

Microsoft has developed its Microsoft Certified Professional (MCP) program to give you credentials that verify your ability to work with Microsoft products effectively and professionally. Several levels of certification are available based on specific suites of exams. With the release of Windows Vista, Microsoft created a new generation of certification programs:

Microsoft Certified Technology Specialist (MCTS) The MCTS can be considered the entry-level certification for the new generation of Microsoft certifications. The MCTS certification program targets specific technologies instead of specific job roles. You must take and pass one to three exams.

Microsoft Certified IT Professional (MCITP) The MCITP certification is a Professional Series certification that tests network and system administrators on job roles rather than only on a specific technology. The MCITP certification program generally consists of one to three exams in addition to obtaining an MCTS-level certification.

Microsoft Certified Professional Developer (MCPD) The MCPD certification is a Professional Series certification for application developers. Similar to the MCITP, the MCPD is focused on a job role rather than on a single technology. The MCPD certification program generally consists of one to three exams in addition to obtaining an MCTS-level certification.

Microsoft Certified Architect (MCA) The MCA is Microsoft's premier certification series. Obtaining the MCA requires a minimum of 10 years of experience and passing a review board consisting of peer architects.

How Do You Become Certified on SharePoint 2010?

Attaining Microsoft certification has always been a challenge. In the past, students have been able to acquire detailed exam information—even most of the exam questions—from online "brain dumps" and third-party "cram" books or software products. For the new generation of exams, this is simply not the case.

Microsoft has taken strong steps to protect the security and integrity of its new certification tracks. Now prospective candidates should complete a course of study that develops detailed knowledge about a wide range of topics. It should supply them with the true skills needed, derived from working with the technology being tested.

The new generations of Microsoft certification programs are heavily weighted toward hands-on skills and experience. Candidates should have troubleshooting skills acquired through hands-on experience and working knowledge.

The MCITP: SharePoint 2010 Administrator must pass a total of two exams:

- TS: Microsoft SharePoint 2010, Configuring (70-667)
- Pro: Microsoft SharePoint 2010, Administrator (70-668)

This book covers only the objectives for exam 70-668. For study materials for 70-667, read Sybex's *MCTS: MCTS Microsoft SharePoint 2010 Configuration Study Guide* (ISBN: 978-0-470-62701-3). The detailed exam objectives for exam 70-668, and the chapters in which those objectives are discussed, can be found in the section "Certification Objectives Map" later in this appendix.

For a more detailed description of the Microsoft certification programs, including a list of all the exams, visit the Microsoft Learning website at www.microsoft.com/learning.

Tips for Taking a Microsoft Exam

Here are some general tips for achieving success on your certification exam:

- Arrive early at the exam center so that you can relax and review your study materials. During this final review, you can look over tables and lists of exam-related information.

- Read the questions carefully. Don't be tempted to jump to an early conclusion. Make sure you know *exactly* what the question is asking.

- Answer all questions. If you are unsure about a question, mark it for review and come back to it at a later time.

- On simulations, do not change settings that are not directly related to the question. Also, assume default settings if the question does not specify or imply which settings are used.

- For questions you're not sure about, use a process of elimination to get rid of the obviously incorrect answers first. This will improve your odds of selecting the correct answer when you need to make an educated guess.

Exam Registration

You may take the Microsoft exams at any of more than 1,000 Authorized Prometric Testing Centers (APTCs) around the world. For the location of a testing center near you, call Prometric at 800-755-EXAM (755-3926). Outside the United States and Canada, contact your local Prometric registration center.

Find out the number of the exam you want to take, and then register with the Prometric registration center nearest to you. At this point, you will be asked for advance payment for the exam. You must take the exams within one year of payment. You can schedule exams up to six weeks in advance or as late as one working day prior to the date of the exam. You can cancel or reschedule your exam if you contact the center at least two working days prior to the exam. Same-day registration is available in some locations, subject to space availability. Where same-day registration is available, you must register a minimum of two hours before test time.

> You can also register for your exams online at www.prometric.com. As of this writing, VUE no longer offers Microsoft exams. If you have taken Microsoft exams with VUE, continue to watch VUE's website (www.vue.com) to see if it starts offering Microsoft exams again.

When you schedule the exam, you will be provided with instructions regarding appointment and cancellation procedures, ID requirements, and information about the testing center location. In addition, you will receive a registration and payment confirmation letter from Prometric.

Microsoft requires certification candidates to accept the terms of a nondisclosure agreement before taking certification exams.

Certification Objectives Map

Table A.1 provides objective mappings for the 70-668 exam. In addition to the book chapters, you will find coverage of exam objectives in the flashcards, practice exam, and videos on the book's companion CD.

TABLE A.1 Exam 70-668 Objectives Map

Objectives	
Designing a SharePoint 2010 Farm Topology	**Chapters 1, 2, 3, 4, and 7**
Design physical architecture. This objective may include but is not limited to: translating information architecture to physical architecture, determining capacity for a SharePoint farm (storage, number of users, bandwidth utilization, intranet/extranet, hardware), and scaling web farm and services infrastructure	Chapter 2

Objectives

Design SharePoint integration with network infrastructure. This objective may include but is not limited to: planning for internal and external farm communications, establishing network perimeter configuration, networking, Active Directory, DNS, SQL storage, IIS, and analyzing infrastructure services.	Chapter 3
Design logical taxonomy. This objective may include but is not limited to: planning sites and site collections, planning for collaboration sites, planning My Site sites, planning for zones, planning for service applications, web applications, content databases, sites and subsites vs. libraries, libraries vs. folders vs. document sets, security boundaries, site hierarchy, and content deployment path methodology.	Chapter 1
Plan for sandbox solutions. This objective may include but is not limited to: content isolation, feature deployments, and trusted solution.	Chapter 4
Plan for farm deployment. This objective may include but is not limited to: sequential deployment, planning standalone deployment (Microsoft SQL Server Express), planning single-server farm (SQL Server), planning multiserver deployment in an N-tier farm, and designing a SharePoint virtual environment.	Chapter 4
Plan for availability. This objective may include but is not limited to: designing SQL Server failover clustering strategy, types of availability (high-performance, acceptable downtime, Recovery Point Objective, Recovery Time Objective), types of mirroring, high availability, high protection, whole farm as a failover cluster, and designing the web frontend NLB strategy.	Chapter 7

Planning SharePoint 2010 Deployment	**Chapters 5, 8, 9, and 12**
Plan service applications. This objective may include but is not limited to: formulating a Business Connectivity Services (BCS) strategy, planning a Microsoft Excel Services strategy, implementing a BI solution, planning service application server roles, and planning a web server forms strategy (Plan InfoPath Forms Services).	Chapter 8
Plan a SharePoint component strategy. This objective may include but is not limited to: web parts, web applications, Microsoft .NET, Microsoft Silverlight, SharePoint features and solutions, workflow, site templates, site definitions, multilingual deployment, master pages and layout files, and email integration.	Chapter 9

TABLE A.1   Exam 70-668 Objectives Map *(continued)*

Objectives	
Plan an upgrade strategy. This objective may include but is not limited to: supporting hardware upgrades (for example, 32 to 64 bit), Operating System upgrade, in-place upgrade, MOSS upgrade, and SQL Server upgrade.	Chapter 12
Design a migration strategy. This objective may include but is not limited to: database migration, custom features, read-only and detached databases, designing a test and QA implementation plan (for example, development to production), migrating content databases, moving content between farms, moving content to and from the farm, moving content within the farm, and rollback.	Chapter 12
Design security architecture. This objective may include but is not limited to: planning security for WebApp site collection, designing SharePoint users and groups administration, taxonomy of SharePoint security groups, managed accounts, site security (permission levels, list permissions, site permissions, personal permissions, default and custom security groups), and planning for Secure Sockets Layer (SSL).	Chapter 5
Plan and deploy authentication methods. This objective may include but is not limited to: planning for integration of multiple authentication sources/types, planning for NTLM authentication, planning for Kerberos authentication, planning for Forms-Based Authentication (FBA), planning for Claims Authentication (Identity and Access Management), planning for Secure Store Service.	Chapter 5
Defining a SharePoint 2010 Operations Strategy and Business Continuity	**Chapters 6, 7, 9, and 11**
Design a maintenance strategy. This objective may include but is not limited to: preparing test plans for patching and maintenance, SharePoint Maintenance Manager, rebuilding SQL indexes, and search maintenance.	Chapter 6
Recommend provisioning strategies. This objective may include but is not limited to: managing self-service components (My Sites, service architecture administration), delegating site administration, limiting site templates and page layouts, assigning quotas, defining policy for web applications.	Chapters 9 and 11

Objectives

Establish an enterprise monitoring plan. This objective may include but is not limited to: developing monitoring points for performance and availability, utilizing performance monitoring, analyzing search reports, web analytics, diagnostic logging, usage logging, analyzing health and usage data (SharePoint Health Analyzer), and validating farm topology against performance requirements.	Chapter 6
Plan SharePoint backup and restore. This objective may include but is not limited to: developing and testing recovery strategy and implementation plan, server recovery, site recovery, granular backup and recovery strategy, exporting a site or list, recovering data from an unattached content database, and backup and restore of the following: farm, farm configuration, site collection, web applications, Secure Store Service, snapshots, content database, configuration database, custom features, solutions, code, service, site, list, document library, performance site collection, and recycle bin.	Chapter 7

Planning for Search and Business Solutions   **Chapters 10 and 11**

Define search requirements. This objective may include but is not limited to: types of data, types of distribution (Internet, extranet), segregation of data, index file location, index size, federation requirements, content sources, search scopes, search taxonomy, server name mappings, promoting or demoting exclusions, synonyms and compound search processing, and defining facets for search.	Chapter 10
Plan search topology. This objective may include but is not limited to: indexing strategy, index partition, query component, property database, crawler component, separate crawler servers, and administration component.	Chapter 10
Plan an enterprise search strategy. This objective may include but is not limited to: designing information access and enterprise search strategy, planning for metadata and search, people search, search reporting, and planning enterprise search technology.	Chapter 10
Plan enterprise content management. This objective may include but is not limited to: records management, BPM (record deployment), document management, metadata planning, information management policies, implement data taxonomy structure, Web Content Management (WCM), and Information Rights Management (IRM).	Chapter 11

TABLE A.1 Exam 70-668 Objectives Map *(continued)*

Objectives	
Plan for social computing and collaboration. This objective may include but is not limited to: user profile service, user profiles, organization profiles, audiences, My Sites, social tags, and planning enterprise wikis, blogs, and personalization sites.	Chapter 11
Plan for a business intelligence strategy. This objective may include but is not limited to: PerformancePoint service (dashboards and scorecards), Excel Services Service, Visio Graphics Service, SQL Reporting Services, chart web parts, and Report Center.	Chapter 11

Exam objectives are subject to change at any time without prior notice and at Microsoft's sole discretion. Please visit Microsoft's website (www.microsoft.com/learning) for the most current listing of exam objectives.

Appendix

B

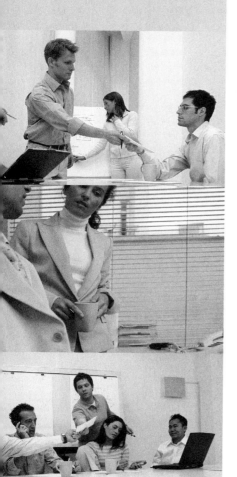

About the Companion CD

IN THIS APPENDIX:

- ✓ What you'll find on the CD
- ✓ System requirements
- ✓ Using the CD
- ✓ Troubleshooting

What You'll Find on the CD

The following sections are arranged by category and summarize the software and other goodies you'll find on the CD. If you need help with installing the items provided on the CD, refer to the installation instructions in the "Using the CD" section of this appendix.

Video Walkthroughs

The CD contains over an hour of video walkthroughs from author Tom Carpenter who shows readers how to perform some of the more difficult tasks they can expect to encounter on the job.

Sybex Test Engine

The CD contains the Sybex test engine, which includes one bonus exam for Exam 70-668.

Electronic Flashcards

These handy electronic flashcards are just what they sound like. One side contains the question and the other side shows the answer.

PDF of the Glossary

We have included an electronic version of the Glossary in .pdf format. You can view the electronic version of the book with Adobe Reader.

Adobe Reader

We've also included a copy of Adobe Reader so you can view PDF files that accompany the book's content. For more information on Adobe Reader or to check for a newer version, visit Adobe's website at www.adobe.com/products/reader/.

System Requirements

Make sure your computer meets the minimum system requirements shown in the following list. If your computer doesn't match up to most of these requirements, you may have problems using the software and files on the companion CD. For the latest and greatest information, please refer to the ReadMe file located at the root of the CD-ROM.

- A PC running Microsoft Windows 98, Windows 2000, Windows NT4 (with SP4 or later), Windows Me, Windows XP, Windows Vista, or Windows 7
- An Internet connection
- A CD-ROM drive

Using the CD

To install the items from the CD to your hard drive, follow these steps:

1. Insert the CD into your computer's CD-ROM drive. The license agreement appears.

Windows users: The interface won't launch if you have autorun disabled. In that case, click Start ➤ Run (for Windows Vista or Windows 7, Start ➤ All Programs ➤ Accessories ➤ Run). In the dialog box that appears, type **D:\Start.exe**. (Replace *D* with the proper letter if your CD drive uses a different letter. If you don't know the letter, see how your CD drive is listed under My Computer.) Click OK.

2. Read the license agreement, and then click the Accept button if you want to use the CD.

   The CD interface appears. The interface allows you to access the content with just one or two clicks.

Troubleshooting

Wiley has attempted to provide programs that work on most computers with the minimum system requirements. Alas, your computer may differ, and some programs may not work properly for some reason.

   The two likeliest problems are that you don't have enough memory (RAM) for the programs you want to use or you have other programs running that are affecting installation or running of a program. If you get an error message such as "Not enough memory" or "Setup cannot continue," try one or more of the following suggestions and then try using the software again:

Turn off any antivirus software running on your computer. Installation programs sometimes mimic virus activity and may make your computer incorrectly believe that it's being infected by a virus.

Close all running programs. The more programs you have running, the less memory is available to other programs. Installation programs typically update files and programs; so if you keep other programs running, installation may not work properly.

Have your local computer store add more RAM to your computer. This is, admittedly, a drastic and somewhat expensive step. However, adding more memory can really help the speed of your computer and allow more programs to run at the same time.

Customer Care

If you have trouble with the book's companion CD-ROM, please call the Wiley Product Technical Support phone number at (800) 762-2974.

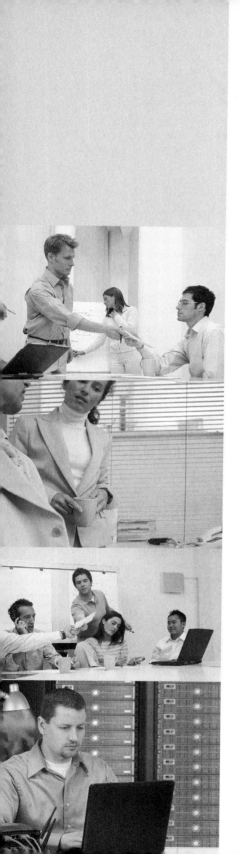

Glossary

64-bit computing   A computing model that uses a 64-bit data size and bus size for communications. The model provides increased memory capacities over 32-bit computing.

A

Access Services   The SharePoint 2010 service application (SA) that allows viewing, editing, and interacting with Access 2010 databases within a web browser.

Active Directory domain   A logical Microsoft network entity used to define the boundary for administration and security in AD DS networks.

Active Directory Domain Services (AD DS)   The Microsoft network directory service used to store users, groups, computers, and other objects in relation to the network.

Active Directory sites   Physical locations on the network defined by IP subnets and site configuration objects in Active Directory.

Anonymous Policy   In a SharePoint Server 2010 web application, the policy that determines the permissions applied to anonymous users who access the sites.

application pool   An Internet Information Services (IIS) term used to reference the process in which websites are executed.

application server   The server that runs the service applications for the server farm.

availability   A measurement of the level of access provided by a resource. Usually measured as having or not having high availability.

B

bit   A single binary unit equal to 1 or 0.

business context   A description or explanation of the current environment into which a new technology, such as SharePoint 2010, will be deployed.

Business Data Connectivity (BDC) Service   The SharePoint 2010 SA that provides access to line-of-business (LOB) applications and other external data.

Business Intelligence (BI)   The use of a combination of applications and utilities for the purpose of organizing and displaying business-relevant data to be used to create and establish corporate goals, performance, and process requirements.

byte   Also called an octet, a byte is a collection of eight bits.

C

capacity planning   The process used to ensure that a system design will meet the demands placed on it for storage, network bandwidth, and processing (CPU and memory consumption).

claim   In CBA, an identity attribute such as the login name, group membership, and so forth.

Claims Based Authentication (CBA)   A new authentication method in SharePoint Server 2010 that supports the same methods offered by Windows integrated authentication and adds forms-based authentication and Secure Assertion Markup Language (SAML) token-based authentication.

clustered index   The way in which the table data is stored in a SQL Server table. The clustered index determines the ordering of the records within the table.

configuration database   In a SharePoint Server installation, the database that contains the configuration settings for the server farm.

content deployment path   A configuration object in SharePoint 2010 that allows content to be synchronized from a source site to a destination site.

context source   Any information repository containing items, such as web pages and Word documents that are crawled for search.

crawl database   This database type is used by a specific search service application to store information about the location of content sources, as well as crawl schedules and other crawl operation-related data.

credentials   Information used to identify and authentication a user, device, or system within an authentication solution.

D

dashboards   In a Business Intelligence (BI) solution, a central location for health and performance monitoring related to business objectives.

data   Meaningful information used for analysis, reporting, and decision making.

database   A storage location for data. Usually managed by a database management system.

database management system   The software that manages the integrity of databases and access to those databases.

database server   The server that contains the configuration and content for the SharePoint sites.

diagnostic logging   The SharePoint Server 2010 feature used to determine what information is written to event logs and trace logs from the SharePoint server farm.

differential backup   A backup of only changed data.

digital assets   Content types such as audio and video as well as images and other reusable content segments.

DNS   The solution for name resolution through a centralized server. The DNS server responds to DNS queries to resolve host names to IP addresses (forward lookups) or IP addresses to host names (reverse lookups). Also called Domain Naming System or Domain Name Service.

DNS zone   The authoritative boundary for a DNS server or set of DNS servers. Usually defines a DNS namespace (or a DNS domain) such as company.local.

document management   The method of managing documents throughout their entire lifecycle, including creation, publication, distribution, storage, search, archiving, and destruction.

E

Enterprise Content Management   A cover-all term for a set of software solutions that lets an organization create, manage, secure, store, publish, retire, and destroy any digital content used for business purposes.

Excel Services   The SharePoint 2010 SA that allows for live interaction with Excel 2010 files within a web browser.

F

features   In a SharePoint environment, solutions or components that are used to manipulate the SharePoint installation in some way.

forest   One or more domain trees sharing a Global Catalog but having different namespace roots such as company.local and company.com.

forms-based authentication   An authentication method that uses ASP.NET connections to databases for authentication credential sources used in the authentication process.

full backup   A complete backup of a system or data.

H

high availability mirroring   An implementation of the high safety SQL Server database mirroring solution that provides automatic failover through the use of a witness server.

high-performance mirroring   A SQL Server database mirroring mode that does not provide automatic failover and does not validate transactions on the mirror instance.

HTTP   HTTP is the Hypertext Transfer Protocol, and it is the primary protocol used for communications with web servers on the Internet and in SharePoint deployments.

I

identity   In Claims Based Authentication (CBA), the security principle used to configure the security policy and the authentication processes.

index   An index is a database object used to provide improved performance for a database when implemented properly.

index partition   This is a group of query components, where each component is used to contain a subset of the full text index and return search results to the submitter of the search query.

information management policy   A collection of rules that are applied to each type of content in SharePoint.

in-place upgrade   An upgrade of SharePoint products that is performed on top of the existing installation.

IT provisioning   Also known as manual provisioning, IT provisioning is a site collection and site provisioning model that requires actions by the IT administrators any time a new site collection or site is required. IT provisioning is the default provisioning model used when self-service provisioning is disabled.

K

key performance indicator (KPI)   A number that indicates success or failure in an instance. The KPI will measure the results in a simple way so that managers can make effective decisions.

M

master pages   The pages that define the look and feel of individual pages in a site.

mirroring   A process used to duplicate data on-the-fly as changes are made to a data store. In SQL Server, mirroring is supported through database mirroring and may be used to provide high availability in SharePoint deployments.

multi-server farm   A SharePoint 2010 deployment model that includes more than one server for the SharePoint components. Also called an N-tier deployment, where N is the number of tiers in the topology.

N

Network Load Balancing (NLB)   A high-availability solution that distributes the workload among multiple hosts or nodes in a NLB cluster.

node   An alternative name for a host. An individual server in a Windows failover cluster or a NLB cluster.

non-clustered index   A separately stored index used to provide faster query results when the non-ID column is queried.

O

OSI model   The Open System Interconnection (OSI) model is a theoretical model used to define and describe networking technologies.

P

patch   An update intended to fix a single problem on a server or within an application.

Performance Monitor   The application most frequently used to track performance statistics and information on Windows servers. The tool used to create Data Collector Sets.

permission levels   In SharePoint Server 2010, collections of permissions used for easier permission management.

permission policy   In a SharePoint Server 2010 web application, the policy that is used to create custom permission levels.

permissions   Rights or capabilities that can be granted or denied to users or groups.

physical design   The design that includes the implementation of hardware components known as servers and the placement of those servers. It includes the specification for services running on the servers as well.

processor affinity   A term used to reference the association of a process to a processor or processor core in multiprocessing and multicore computers.

Q

quorum   In a Windows failover cluster, the element used to decide which node should be active at any time in the cluster.

R

RAID (redundant array of independent disks)   An internal server or external storage technology that provides either performance improvements or fault tolerance for the storage system.

records management   The management of any document type, either physical or electronic, that acts as evidence of any organizational transaction or act and by law or policy, is required to be retained for a particular period of time.

recycling   In reference to application pools, a feature that allows the web server to restart the application pool periodically for stability and performance benefits.

redundancy   A technique used to provide high availability through the implementation of more resources than the minimum requirement.

router   A device used to segment networks into multiple sections or to connect a network to other networks.

RPO (Recovery Point Objective)   The acceptable amount of data loss in a disaster recovery scenario.

RTO (Recovery Time Objective)   The maximum tolerable amount of time for recovery in a disaster recovery scenario.

S

sandbox solutions   Solutions that are installed into a protected environment that limits their capabilities and protects the rest of the SharePoint farm.

scalability   The measurement of a system's ability to grow and expand with the demands of the environment. *Scaling up* refers to an increase in capabilities or power in a single server. *Scaling out* refers to the distribution of services and features across multiple servers.

search index   A collection of data, keywords, and other pointer information from content crawled by Search Crawler servers that are made available for search results in response to a search query.

search scope   A search feature that allows filtering of end-user search queries so that user queries address only a subset of the entire search index.

Secure Store Service   The SharePoint service application that provides single sign-on capabilities in SharePoint Server 2010.

security token   In Claims Based Authentication, a set of claims in a digitally signed package created by the issuing authority.

segmentation   The process of separating groups of network devices with routers in order to improve performance or provide security. Segmentation is synonymous with subnetting in most network topologies.

self-service provisioning   A site and site collection provisioning model that allows selected users to create sites without requiring actions by the IT administrators.

server farm   The top-level container within the SharePoint 2010 logical architecture and the container for site collections and farm-wide configuration settings.

Service Application (SA)   In SharePoint 2010, the architecture used to provide services to SharePoint farms and sites.

service pack   An update for an operating system or an application that repairs multiple problems and may introduce new features.

SharePoint Health Analyzer (SHA)   The SharePoint Server 2010 component used to monitor the configuration of the SharePoint server farm and alert the administrator when configuration and security problems are detected.

SharePoint Maintenance Manager (SMM)   An automated process that runs on a SharePoint server for health analysis and monitoring.

Silverlight   A rich development environment offering interactive capabilities for users to access websites; a solution similar to the popular Adobe Flash add-on for websites.

Simple Mail Transfer Protocol (SMTP)   The Internet standard for email transmission. A service provided by IIS and used by SharePoint for sending and receiving email.

single-server farm   A SharePoint 2010 deployment model that includes all SharePoint components in a single server, while the infrastructure components are installed on separate servers.

site collection   The container of sites that share administration practices, permission sets, and rights sets by default.

site template   In SharePoint 2010, a site definition that determines the content and features available within a site.

sites   The container for the actual content (pages, lists, and libraries) created, managed, and deleted by the SharePoint users. Within Active Directory, physical locations on the network defined by IP subnets and site configuration objects.

social computing   The use of technology solutions to establish and enhance communication and collaboration between two or more people.

standalone deployment   A SharePoint 2010 deployment model that includes all SharePoint components and infrastructure components in a single server.

switch   A device used to provide communication among devices on the same subnet or network while establishing individual broadcast domains with each connected device.

T

taxonomy   The hierarchical organization of the content managed within SharePoint implementations, which consists of server farms, site collections and sites. The formal name for the logical architecture.

TCP/IP   The Transmission Control Protocol/Internet Protocol is the most popular suite of protocols used for network communications today.

transaction log backup   A SQL Server database backup that backs up the actions that resulted in changes to the data taken against a database.

transitive trusts   Trust relationships that pass through trusts above and below them in the domain tree hierarchy.

tree   A hierarchical set of domains sharing a root namespace such as `sales.company.local`, `marketing.company.local`, and `company.local`.

trust relationship   A security relationship between two domains allowing users from one domain to be granted access to resources in the other domain.

U

usage logging   The SharePoint Server 2010 feature used to track user actions. Usage logging may assist with regulatory compliance, troubleshooting, and future planning.

user policy   In a SharePoint Server 2010 Web application, the policy that determines the permissions for users.

W

Web Analytics   The website statistics tracking engine within SharePoint Server 2010. Web Analytics provides page view information as well as information about referrers and visitors.

web frontend (WFE) server   The server that serves up the web pages for users visiting the SharePoint sites.

web part   A component that may be added to a SharePoint page to provide complex functionality without requiring users to learn complicated programming languages.

Web Solution Package (WSP)   The storage container for SharePoint solutions; an archive storage container that uses the CAB file structure.

Windows failover clustering   A clustering solution that provides a backup server of a production server at all times. Should the production server fail, the backup server automatically assumes the production server's roles.

Windows integrated authentication   Also known as Classic Mode Authentication (CMA), an authentication model that uses integration with Windows accounts for access to resources.

Windows Recovery Environment   A recovery environment accessed from the operating system boot disk or by pressing F8 during system boot that allows for bare metal restores and other recovery options.

Windows Server Backup   A graphical tool provided with Windows Server used to perform backups. Also provides a command-line tool called wbadmin for interfacing with the Windows Server Backup functions.

Windows Server Update Services (WSUS)   A Microsoft solution that allows centralized patch management for Microsoft clients, servers, and applications.

Z

zone   In SharePoint, a URL used to access a SharePoint site that is usually implemented to provide a different authentication method. In DNS, the authoritative boundary for a DNS server.

Index

Note to the reader: Throughout this index **boldfaced** page numbers indicate primary discussions of a topic. *Italicized* page numbers indicate illustrations.

The Perfect Companion for all Exchange Server 2010 Administrators !

Contains over an hour of video walkthroughs with author Tom Carpenter:

- Tom walks you through some of the more difficult tasks you can expect to face as a SharePoint 2010 Administrator.

- See firsthand how to upgrade to SharePoint 2010, plan farm deployment, perform a backup, and much, much more.

For Certification candidates, we've included one practice test for:

- MCITP: Microsoft SharePoint 2010, Administrator (70-668)

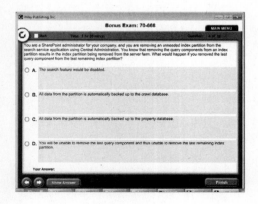

- Reinforce your understanding of key concepts with these hardcore flashcard-style questions.

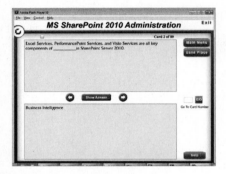

- Access the entire *Microsoft SharePoint 2010 Administration*, complete with figures and tables, in electronic format.

- Search the *Microsoft SharePoint 2010 Administration* chapters to find information on any topic in seconds.